Reuben Sagman

W9-BEZ-714

The developers of Web 3.0...

... may be sitting right in your classroom! Every one of your students has the potential to make a difference. And realizing that potential starts right here, in your course.

When students succeed in your course—when they stay on-task and make the breakthrough that turns confusion into confidence—they are empowered to realize the possibilities for greatness that lie within each of them. We know your goal is to create an environment where students reach their full potential and experience the exhilaration of academic success that will last them a lifetime. *WileyPLUS* can help you reach that goal.

Wiley**PLUS** is an online suite of resources—including the complete text—that will help your students:

- come to class better prepared for your lectures
- get immediate feedback and context-sensitive help on assignments and quizzes
- track their progress throughout the course

"I just wanted to say how much this program helped me in studying... I was able to actually see my mistakes and correct them. ... I really think that other students should have the chance to use *WileyPLUS*."

Ashlee Krisko, *Oakland University*

www.wiley.com/college/wileyplus

80% of students surveyed said it improved their understanding of the material. *

Prepare & Present

Create outstanding class presentations using a wealth of resources, such as PowerPoint™ slides, image galleries, interactive simulations, and more. Plus you can easily upload any materials you have created into your course, and combine them with the resources Wiley provides you with.

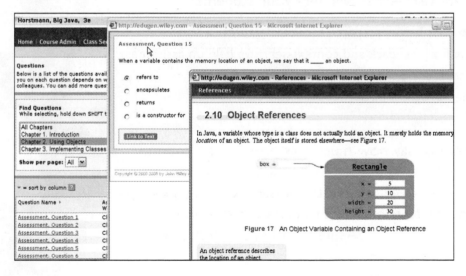

Create Assignments

Automate the assigning and grading of homework or quizzes by using the provided question banks, or by writing your own. Student results will be automatically graded and recorded in your gradebook. *WileyPLUS* also links home-work problems to relevant sections of the online text, hints, or solutions—context-sensitive help where students need it most!

*Based on a spring 2005 survey of 972 student users of *WileyPLUS*

Track Student Progress

Keep track of your students' progress via an instructor's gradebook, which allows you to analyze individual and overall class results. This gives you an accurate and realistic assessment of your students' progress and level of understanding.

Now Available with WebCT and Blackboard!

Now you can seamlessly integrate all of the rich content and resources available with *WileyPLUS* with the power and convenience of your WebCT or BlackBoard course. You and your students get the best of both worlds with single sign-on, an integrated gradebook, list of assignments and roster, and more. If your campus is using another course management system, contact your local Wiley Representative.

"I studied more for this class than I would have without *WileyPLUS*."

Melissa Lawler, *Western Washington Univ.*

For more information on what *WileyPLUS* can do to help your students reach their potential, please visit

www.wiley.com/college/wileyplus

76% of students surveyed said it made them better prepared for tests. *

You have the potential to make a difference!

WileyPLUS is a powerful online system packed with features to help you make the most of your potential, and get the best grade you can!

With Wiley**PLUS** you get:

A complete online version of your text and other study resources

Study more effectively and get instant feedback when you practice on your own. Resources like self-assessment quizzes, tutorials, and animations bring the subject matter to life, and help you master the material.

Problem-solving help, instant grading, and feedback on your homework and quizzes

You can keep all of your assigned work in one location, making it easy for you to stay on task. Plus, many homework problems contain direct links to the relevant portion of your text to help you deal with problem-solving obstacles at the moment they come up.

The ability to track your progress and grades throughout the term.

A personal gradebook allows you to monitor your results from past assignments at any time. You'll always know exactly where you stand.

If your instructor uses *WileyPLUS*, you will receive a URL for your class. If not, your instructor can get more information about *WileyPLUS* by visiting www.wiley.com/college/wileyplus

"It has been a great help, and I believe it has helped me to achieve a better grade."
Michael Morris, *Columbia Basin College*

69% of students surveyed said it helped them get a better grade.*

Java
Concepts
for AP* Computer Science
FIFTH EDITION

THE WILEY BICENTENNIAL—KNOWLEDGE FOR GENERATIONS

Each generation has its unique needs and aspirations. When Charles Wiley first opened his small printing shop in lower Manhattan in 1807, it was a generation of boundless potential searching for an identity. And we were there, helping to define a new American literary tradition. Over half a century later, in the midst of the Second Industrial Revolution, it was a generation focused on building the future. Once again, we were there, supplying the critical scientific, technical, and engineering knowledge that helped frame the world. Throughout the 20th Century, and into the new millennium, nations began to reach out beyond their own borders and a new international community was born. Wiley was there, expanding its operations around the world to enable a global exchange of ideas, opinions, and know-how.

For 200 years, Wiley has been an integral part of each generation's journey, enabling the flow of information and understanding necessary to meet their needs and fulfill their aspirations. Today, bold new technologies are changing the way we live and learn. Wiley will be there, providing you the must-have knowledge you need to imagine new worlds, new possibilities, and new opportunities.

Generations come and go, but you can always count on Wiley to provide you the knowledge you need, when and where you need it!

WILLIAM J. PESCE
PRESIDENT AND CHIEF EXECUTIVE OFFICER

PETER BOOTH WILEY
CHAIRMAN OF THE BOARD

Java
Concepts
for AP* Computer Science
FIFTH EDITION

Cay Horstmann
SAN JOSE STATE UNIVERSITY

BICENTENNIAL
1807
WILEY
2007
BICENTENNIAL

John Wiley & Sons, Inc.

EXECUTIVE PUBLISHER:	Don Fowley
ASSOCIATE PUBLISHER:	Dan Sayre
SENIOR EDITORIAL ASSISTANT:	Lindsay Murdock
MEDIA EDITOR:	Lauren Sapira
WEB PROJECT MANAGER:	Todd Eaton
SENIOR PRODUCTION EDITOR:	Ken Santor
SENIOR DESIGNER:	Madelyn Lesure
TEXT DESIGNER:	Nancy Field
COVER DESIGNER:	Howard Grossman
COVER ILLUSTRATOR:	Susan Cyr
PHOTO EDITOR:	Lisa Gee
ANNIVERSARY LOGO DESIGN:	Richard J. Pacifico
PRODUCTION MANAGEMENT:	Cindy Johnson

This book was set in 10.5/12 Stempel Garamond by Publishing Services and printed and bound by Von Hoffmann, Inc. The cover was printed by Von Hoffmann, Inc.

This book is printed on acid-free paper ∞

Copyright © 2008 John Wiley & Sons, Inc. All rights reserved.

No part of this publication may be reproduced, stored in a retrieval system or transmitted in any form or by any means, electronic, mechanical, photocopying, recording, scanning or otherwise, except as permitted under Sections 107 or 108 of the 1976 United States Copyright Act, without either the prior written permission of the Publisher, or authorization through payment of the appropriate per-copy fee to the Copyright Clearance Center, 222 Rosewood Drive, Danvers, MA 01923, (978) 750-8400, fax (978) 646-8600. Requests to the Publisher for permission should be addressed to the Permissions Department, John Wiley and Sons, Inc., 111 River Street, Hoboken, NJ 07030-5774, (201) 748-6011, fax (201) 748-6008.
To order books, or for customer service, please call 1-800-CALL-Wiley (225-5945).

*AP and Advanced Placement Program are registered trademarks of the College Board, which was not involved in the production of, and does not endorse, this product.

ISBN 978-0-470-18160-7

Printed in the United States of America

10 9 8 7 6 5 4 3 2 1

Preface

This book is an introductory text in computer science, focusing on programming principles and practices. Why should you choose this book for your first course in computer science? Here are the key reasons:

- The book's point of view goes beyond language syntax and focuses on computer science concepts.

- The object-oriented paradigm is emphasized from the outset, exposing you to objects and classes from the first chapters so you won't have to un-learn procedural habits.

- Rather than following a rigid "objects-early" or "objects-late" approach, object-oriented concepts are introduced gradually.

- A focus on test-driven development encourages you to test your programs as you develop them, giving you greater confidence in the correctness of your solutions.

- The book will motivate you to master the practical aspects of programming, with lots of useful tips on good software engineering practices.

- The book teaches the standard Java language—not a specialized "training wheels" environment. The Java language, library, and tools are presented at a depth that is sufficient to solve real-world programming problems.

The Use of Java

This book is based on the Java programming language. Java was chosen for four reasons:

- Object orientation
- Safety
- Simplicity
- Breadth of the standard library

At this point, the object-oriented point of view is the predominant paradigm for software design. Object orientation enables programmers to spend more time on the design of their programs and less time coding and debugging. This book starts out with objects and classes early so that readers do not have to un-learn procedural programming habits later.

Safety is an important feature of the Java language, and highly beneficial for beginning programmers. Common programming errors are reliably diagnosed when a Java program is compiled or executed. Using Java, you will be able to spend more time on completing substantial software projects instead of debugging programs with mysterious and irreproducible behavior.

Another major advantage of Java is its simplicity. It is possible to master the essential language constructs in a semester-long course.

Finally, the standard Java library has sufficient breadth that it can be used for most courses in a computer science curriculum. Graphics, user-interface construction, database access, multithreading, and network programming are all part of the standard library. Thus, the skills learned in a beginning course based on Java will serve you well in subsequent courses.

New in This Edition

Test-Driven Development

The methodology of test-driven development promises to quickly deliver defect-free software by avoiding tedious debugging sessions. The central principle is to develop test cases together with, or even in advance of, implementing desired behavior.

In an industrial setting, test-driven development is aided by a set of libraries and tools that can be challenging for the beginner to master. In this book, we focus on the essential aspect of test-driven development—thinking about the expected results while developing a program. Tester programs are required to do no more than print the expected result together with any program output. This straightforward requirement encourages you to think more deeply about your programs as you develop them.

A testing track is distributed over several chapters, starting with Chapter 2. Topics range from the development of simple tester programs to regression testing and the use of a debugger.

Objects Gradual

There has been much discussion in the computer science community as to whether object-oriented programming should be introduced "early" or "late". Neither approach is ideal. The "objects gradual" approach used in this book has been further refined in this edition. In Chapter 2, you will learn to use objects and classes from the standard library. In Chapter 3, you will learn how to implement classes from a given specification. These two chapters allow you to use objects soundly when studying the core algorithmic topics in Chapters 4 through 7—without learning bad habits that you have to un-learn later. In Chapter 8, you will learn how to design the specification of a class. Finally, in Chapter 12, you will learn how to discover collaborating classes in order to develop object-oriented solutions to complex programming problems.

Updated for Java 6

Java 6, released in December 2006, contains a number of useful library enhancements, principally for user-interface, database, and XML programming. The book has been updated to cover these enhancements. The core material is not affected by Java 6, and the book can be used equally well with Java 5 or Java 6.

Optional Graphics Track

An optional graphics track is provided because many students enjoy writing programs that create drawings, and because graphical shapes are splendid examples of objects. All sections in the graphics track can be skipped if desired.

In this edition, the graphics coverage has been broken up into smaller chunks. Chapter 2 contains material on simple drawings, and Chapter 3 describes how to implement objects that draw themselves. Chapter 9, which introduces the notion of an interface, uses event-driven programming to reinforce the interface concept. Chapter 10 covers inheritance, and its graphics section shows how to use inheritance for customizing frames.

WileyPLUS

The first four pages of this book describe an innovative online tool for teachers and students: WileyPLUS can be adopted by instructors who wish their students to take full advantage of a wide range of online tools for drill and practice, homework and quizzing, animations and lab projects. WileyPLUS can be adopted with the book at no additional cost to the student, or as an alternative to the printed text for about half the cost of print. WileyPLUS integrates all of the instructor and student web resources into an online version of this text. For more information and a demo, please visit the web site listed on pages i-iv, or talk to your Wiley representative.

LabRat: A Programming Assignment Tool

All programming exercises in this edition have been revised to allow for computer-assisted grading. More detailed specifications and starter code for assignments are available in the WileyPLUS course that accompanies this book. An innovative tool within the WileyPLUS course, LabRat, allows instructors to assign code completion and programming exercises online. Students can use LabRat to check that their solutions conform to the program specifications before they submit them online for grading. LabRat gives instructors a report of the students' test results, the students' code, and recommended grades that the instructor can accept or override in the WileyPLUS gradebook.

Student and Instructor Resources in WileyPLUS

The following resources for students and instructors can be found in the Wiley-PLUS course for this text:

• Solutions to all exercises (for instructors only)
• A test bank (for instructors only)
• A laboratory manual
• Additional review and programming exercises
• A list of frequently asked questions
• Help with common compilers
• Lecture presentation slides that summarize each chapter and include code listings and figures from the book
• Source code for all examples (also at www.wiley.com/college/horstmann)
• The programming style guide in electronic form
• A conversion guide for moving from the last edition (for instructors only)

Study Guide for AP Computer Science

The Study Guide, by Frances P. Trees, that accompanies this text connects the study of Java to the topics and competencies tested on the Computer Science A and AB examinations. In addition to supplemental examples and explanations, the Study Guide offers practice questions modeled after those on the AP exam, tips for preparing for the exam, cumulative reviews, and more.

BlueJ Companion

Also available with this text is a BlueJ manual that has been customized specifically for use with this book. The manual is accompanied by all the code examples from this book, formatted as BlueJ projects, and available at www.wiley.com/college/horstmann. For more information, please talk to your Wiley representative.

A Tour of the Book

The book can be naturally grouped into three parts, as illustrated by Figure 1. The organization of chapters offers the same flexibility as the previous edition; dependencies among the chapters are also shown in the figure.

Part A: Fundamentals (Chapters 1-7)

Chapter 1 contains a brief introduction to computer science and Java programming. Chapter 2 shows how to manipulate objects of predefined classes. In Chapter 3, you will build your own simple classes from given specifications.

Fundamental data types, branches, loops, and arrays are covered in Chapters 4–7.

Part B: Object-Oriented Design (Chapters 8-12)

Chapter 8 takes up the subject of class design in a systematic fashion, and it introduces a very simple subset of the UML notation.

The discussion of polymorphism and inheritance is split into two chapters. Chapter 9 covers interfaces and polymorphism, whereas Chapter 10 covers inheritance. Introducing interfaces before inheritance pays off in an important way: Students immediately see polymorphism before getting bogged down with technical details such as superclass construction.

Exception handling and basic file input/output are covered in Chapter 11. The exception hierarchy gives a useful example for inheritance.

Chapter 12 contains an introduction to object-oriented design, including two significant case studies.

Part C: Data Structures and Algorithms (Chapters 13-16)

Chapters 13 through 16 contain an introduction to algorithms and data structures, covering recursion, sorting and searching, linked lists, binary trees, and hash tables. These topics may be outside the scope of a one-semester course, but can be covered as desired after Chapter 7 (see Figure 1).

Recursion is introduced from an object-oriented point of view: An object that solves a problem recursively constructs another object of the same class that solves a simpler problem. The idea of having the other object do the simpler job is more intuitive than having a function call itself.

Each data structure is presented in the context of the standard Java collections library. You will learn the essential abstractions of the standard library (such as iterators, sets, and maps) as well as the performance characteristics of the various collections. However, a detailed discussion of the implementation of advanced data structures is beyond the scope of this book.

Figure 1   Chapter Dependencies

Appendices

Appendix A contains a style guide for use with this book. Many instructors find it highly beneficial to require a consistent style for all assignments. If this style guide conflicts with instructor sentiment or local customs, however, it is available in electronic form so that it can be modified. Appendix B lists the Basic Latin and Latin-1 subsets of Unicode. Appendix C contains an overview of the classes and interfaces in the standard library covered in this book. Additional appendices are available in WileyPLUS or at www.wiley.com/college/horstmann.

The Pedagogical Structure

This edition builds on the pedagogical elements in the last edition and offers additional aids for the reader. Each chapter begins with the customary overview of chapter objectives and motivational introduction. A listing of the chapter contents then provides a quick reference to the special features in the chapter.

Throughout each chapter, margin notes show where new concepts are introduced and provide an outline of key ideas. These notes are summarized at the end of the chapter as a chapter review.

> Margin notes mark and reinforce new concepts and are summarized at chapter end.

Each section concludes with a set of self-check exercises. Use these exercises to check that you have understood the newly introduced topics. The self-check exercises are not trivial—they are purposefully designed to make you think through the new material. Answers to the self-check exercises are at the end of each chapter.

The program listings are carefully designed for easy reading, going well beyond simple color coding. Comments are typeset in a separate font that is easier to read than the monospaced "computer" font. Methods are set off by a subtle color outline. Keywords, strings, and numbers are color coded as they would be in a development environment such as BlueJ. (The code for all program listings in the book (plus any additional files needed for each example) is available in the WileyPLUS course for the book or at www.wiley.com/college/horstmann.)

Throughout the chapters, special features set off topics for added flexibility and easy reference. Syntax boxes highlight new syntactical constructs and their purpose. An alphabetical list of all of these constructs can be found on page xxv.

Six additional features, entitled "Common Error", "How To", "Productivity Hint", "Quality Tip", "Advanced Topic", and "Random Fact", are identified with the icons below and set off so they don't interrupt the flow of the main material. Some of these are quite short; others extend over a page. Each topic is given the space that is needed for a full and convincing explanation—instead of being forced into a one-paragraph "tip". You can use the tables on pages xxvi–xxxi to see the features in each chapter and the page numbers where they can be found.

- **Common Errors** describe the kinds of errors that students often make, with an explanation of why the errors occur, and what to do about them. Most students quickly discover the Common Error sections and read them on their own.

- **How To** sections are inspired by the Linux HOWTO guides. These sections are intended to answer the beginner's question, "Now what do I do?", by giving step-by-step instructions for common tasks.

- **Quality Tips** explain good programming practices. Because most of them require an initial investment of effort, these notes carefully motivate the reason behind the advice, and explain why the effort will be repaid later.

- **Productivity Hints** teach students how to use their tools more effectively. Many beginning students put little thought into their use of computers and software. They are often unfamiliar with tricks of the trade, such as keyboard shortcuts, global search and replace, or automation of common tasks with scripts.

- **Advanced Topics** cover nonessential or more difficult material. Some of these topics introduce alternative syntactical constructions that are not necessarily technically advanced. In many cases, the book uses one particular language construct but explains alternatives as Advanced Topics. You should feel free to use those constructs in your own programs if you prefer them. It has, however, been my experience that many students are grateful for the "keep it simple" approach, because it greatly reduces the number of gratuitous decisions they have to make.

- **Random Facts** provide historical and social information on computing—to fulfill the "historical and social context" requirements of the ACM curriculum guidelines—as well as capsule reviews of advanced computer science topics. Many students will read the Random Facts on their own while pretending to follow the lecture.

Acknowledgments

I am very grateful to my editor, Dan Sayre, for continuing to develop this book and its companion web sites. Many thanks to Lauren Sapira, Todd Eaton, Don Fowley, Lindsay Murdock, Lisa Wojcik, Lisa Gee, and Bud Peters at John Wiley & Sons, and the team at Publishing Services for their help with this project. An especially deep acknowledgment and thanks goes to Cindy Johnson for her hard work, sound judgment, and amazing atttention to detail. Thanks also to Rick Giles for his work on the slides.

I am very grateful to the many individuals who reviewed the manuscript for this and prior editions, made valuable suggestions, and brought an embarrassingly large number of errors and omissions to my attention. They include:

Tim Andersen, *Boise State University*
Ivan Bajic, *San Diego State University*

Ted Bangay, *Sheridan Institute of Technology*
George Basham, *Franklin University*
Sambit Bhattacharya, *Fayetteville State University*
Joseph Bowbeer, *Vizrea Corporation*
Timothy A. Budd, *Oregon State University*
Robert Burton, *Brigham Young University*
Frank Butt, *IBM*
Jerry Cain, *Stanford University*
Adam Cannon, *Columbia University*
Nancy Chase, *Gonzaga University*
Archana Chidanandan, *Rose-Hulman Institute of Technology*
Vincent Cicirello, *The Richard Stockton College of New Jersey*
Deborah Coleman, *Rochester Institute of Technology*
Valentino Crespi, *California State University, Los Angeles*
Jim Cross, *Auburn University*
Russell Deaton, *University of Arkansas*
H. E. Dunsmore, *Purdue University*
Robert Duvall, *Duke University*
Henry A. Etlinger, *Rochester Institute of Technology*
John Fendrich, *Bradley University*
John Fulton, *Franklin University*
David Geary, *Sabreware, Inc.*
Margaret Geroch, *Wheeling Jesuit University*
Rick Giles, *Acadia University*
Stacey Grasso, *College of San Mateo*
Jianchao Han, *California State University, Dominguez Hills*
Lisa Hansen, *Western New England College*
Elliotte Harold
Eileen Head, *Binghamton University*
Cecily Heiner, *University of Utah*
Brian Howard, *Depauw University*
Lubomir Ivanov, *Iona College*
Norman Jacobson, *University of California, Irvine*
Curt Jones, *Bloomsburg University*
Aaron Keen, *California Polytechnic State University, San Luis Obispo*
Elliot Koffman, *Temple University*
Kathy Liszka, *University of Akron*
Hunter Lloyd, *Montana State University*
Youmin Lu, *Bloomsburg University*

John S. Mallozzi, *Iona College*
John Martin, *North Dakota State University*
Scott McElfresh, *Carnegie Mellon University*
Joan McGrory, *Christian Brothers University*
Carolyn Miller, *North Carolina State University*
Teng Moh, *San Jose State University*
John Moore, *The Citadel*
Faye Navabi, *Arizona State University*
Kevin O'Gorman, *California Polytechnic State University, San Luis Obispo*
Michael Olan, *Richard Stockton College*
Kevin Parker, *Idaho State University*
Cornel Pokorny, *California Polytechnic State University, San Luis Obispo*
Roger Priebe, *University of Texas, Austin*
C. Robert Putnam, *California State University, Northridge*
Cyndi Rader, *Colorado School of Mines*
Neil Rankin, *Worcester Polytechnic Institute*
Brad Rippe, *Fullerton College*
Pedro I. Rivera Vega, *University of Puerto Rico, Mayaguez*
Daniel Rogers, *SUNY Brockport*
Carolyn Schauble, *Colorado State University*
Christian Shin, *SUNY Geneseo*
Jeffrey Six, *University of Delaware*
Don Slater, *Carnegie Mellon University*
Ken Slonneger, *University of Iowa*
Peter Stanchev, *Kettering University*
Ron Taylor, *Wright State University*
Joseph Vybihal, *McGill University*
Xiaoming Wei, *Iona College*
Todd Whittaker, *Franklin University*
Robert Willhoft, *Roberts Wesleyan College*
David Womack, *University of Texas at San Antonio*
Catherine Wyman, *DeVry University*
Arthur Yanushka, *Christian Brothers University*
Salih Yurttas, *Texas A&M University*

Contents

Chapter 3 Implementing Classes   81

Chapter 4 Fundamental Data Types   133

Chapter 5 Decisions   181

Alphabetical List of Syntax Boxes

Chapter	Common Errors	How Tos	Quality Tips
1 Introduction	Omitting Semicolons 22 Misspelling Words 24		
2 Using Objects	Trying to Invoke a Constructor Like a Method 46		
3 Implementing Classes	Forgetting to Initialize Object References in a Constructor 106 Trying to Call a Method Without an Implicit Parameter 109	Implementing a Class 99 Drawing Graphical Shapes 117	
4 Fundamental Data Types	Integer Division 151 Unbalanced Parentheses 152 Roundoff Errors 155	Carrying Out Computations 155	Do Not Use Magic Numbers 145 Choose Descriptive Variable Names 145 White Space 152 Factor Out Common Code 153
5 Decisions	Using == to Compare Strings 190 The Dangling else Problem 202 Multiple Relational Operators 207 Confusing && and || Conditions 208		Brace Layout 185 Avoid Conditions with Side Effects 193 Calculate Sample Data Manually 213 Prepare Test Cases Ahead of Time 214
6 Iteration	Infinite Loops 232 Off-by-One Errors 233 Forgetting a Semicolon 242 A Semicolon Too Many 242	Implementing Loops 250 Debugging 273	Use for Loops for Their Intended Purpose 241 Don't Use != to Test the End of a Range 243 Symmetric and Asymmetric Bounds 252 Count Iterations 252

Chapter	🐍 Common Errors	📷 How Tos	🦚 Quality Tips
7 Arrays and Array Lists	Bounds Errors 291 Uninitialized Arrays 292 Length and Size 297 Underestimating the Size of a Data Set 315	Working with Array Lists and Arrays 309	Prefer Parameterized Array Lists 297 Make Parallel Arrays into Arrays of Objects 315
8 Designing Classes	Trying to Modify Primitive Type Parameters 343 Shadowing 361 Confusing Dots 368	Programming with Packages 368	Consistency 340 Minimize Side Effects 345 Don't Change the Contents of Parameter Variables 345
9 Interfaces and Polymorphism	Forgetting to Define Implementing Methods as Public 394 Trying to Instantiate an Interface 396 Modifying the Signature in the Implementing Method 411 Forgetting to Attach a Listener 417 Forgetting to Repaint 421		
10 Inheritance	Confusing Super- and Subclasses 442 Shadowing Instance Fields 449 Failing to Invoke the Superclass Method 450 Accidental Package Access 463 Making Inherited Methods Less Accessible 463 Defining the equals Method with the Wrong Parameter Type 470 Forgetting to Clone 472 By Default, Components Have Zero Width and Height 487	Implementing a Graphical User Interface (GUI) 486	Clone Mutable Instance Fields in Accessor Methods 472

Introduction

CHAPTER GOALS

- To understand the activity of programming
- To learn about the architecture of computers
- To learn about machine code and high-level programming languages
- To become familiar with your computing environment and your compiler
- To compile and run your first Java program
- To recognize syntax and logic errors

The purpose of this chapter is to familiarize you with the concept of programming. It reviews the architecture of a computer and discusses the difference between machine code and high-level programming languages. Finally, you will see how to compile and run your first Java program, and how to diagnose errors that may occur when a program is compiled or executed.

CHAPTER CONTENTS

1.1 What Is Programming?

You have probably used a computer for work or fun. Many people use computers for everyday tasks such as balancing a checkbook or writing a term paper. Computers are good for such tasks. They can handle repetitive chores, such as totaling up numbers or placing words on a page, without getting bored or exhausted. Computers also make good game machines because they can play sequences of sounds and pictures, involving the human user in the process.

The flexibility of a computer is quite an amazing phenomenon. The same machine can balance your checkbook, print your term paper, and play a game. In contrast, other machines carry out a much narrower range of tasks—a car drives and a toaster toasts.

> A computer must be programmed to perform tasks. Different tasks require different programs.

To achieve this flexibility, the computer must be *programmed* to perform each task. A computer itself is a machine that stores data (numbers, words, pictures), interacts with devices (the monitor screen, the sound system, the printer), and executes programs. Programs are sequences of instructions and decisions that the computer carries out to achieve a task. One program balances checkbooks; a different program, perhaps designed and constructed by a different company, processes words; and a third program, probably from yet another company, plays a game.

> A computer program executes a sequence of very basic operations in rapid succession.

Today's computer programs are so sophisticated that it is hard to believe that they are all composed of extremely primitive operations.

A typical operation may be one of the following:

- Put a red dot onto this screen position.
- Send the letter A to the printer.
- Get a number from this location in memory.
- Add up two numbers.
- If this value is negative, continue the program at that instruction.

A computer program contains the instruction sequences for all tasks that it can execute.

A computer program tells a computer, in minute detail, the sequence of steps that are needed to complete a task. A program contains a huge number of simple operations, and the computer executes them at great speed. The computer has no intelligence—it simply executes instruction sequences that have been prepared in advance.

To use a computer, no knowledge of programming is required. When you write a term paper with a word processor, that software package has been programmed by the manufacturer and is ready for you to use. That is only to be expected—you can drive a car without being a mechanic and toast bread without being an electrician.

A primary purpose of this book is to teach you how to design and implement computer programs. You will learn how to formulate instructions for all tasks that your programs need to execute.

Keep in mind that programming a sophisticated computer game or word processor requires a team of many highly skilled programmers, graphic artists, and other professionals. Your first programming efforts will be more mundane. The concepts and skills you learn in this book form an important foundation, but you should not expect to immediately produce professional software. A typical college program in computer science or software engineering takes four years to complete; this book is intended as an introductory course in such a program.

Many students find that there is an immense thrill even in simple programming tasks. It is an amazing experience to see the computer carry out a task precisely and quickly that would take you hours of drudgery.

SELF CHECK

1. What is required to play a music CD on a computer?
2. Why is a CD player less flexible than a computer?
3. Can a computer program develop the initiative to execute tasks in a better way than its programmers envisioned?

1.2 The Anatomy of a Computer

To understand the programming process, you need to have a rudimentary understanding of the building blocks that make up a computer. This section will describe a personal computer. Larger computers have faster, larger, or more powerful components, but they have fundamentally the same design.

Figure 1   Central Processing Unit

At the heart of the computer lies the central processing unit (CPU).

At the heart of the computer lies the *central processing unit* (CPU) (see Figure 1). It consists of a single *chip* (integrated circuit) or a small number of chips. A computer chip is a component with a plastic or metal housing, metal connectors, and inside wiring made principally from silicon. For a CPU chip, the inside wiring is enormously complicated. For example, the Pentium 4 chip (a popular CPU for personal computers at the time of this writing) contains over 50 million structural elements called *transistors*— the elements that enable electrical signals to control other electrical signals, making automatic computing possible. The CPU locates and executes the program instructions; it carries out arithmetic operations such as addition, subtraction, multiplication, and division; and it fetches data from storage and input/output devices and sends data back.

Data and programs are stored in primary storage (memory) and secondary storage (such as a hard disk).

The computer keeps data and programs in *storage.* There are two kinds of storage. *Primary storage,* also called *random-access memory* (RAM) or simply *memory,* is fast but expensive; it is made from memory chips (see Figure 2). Primary storage has two disadvantages. It is comparatively expensive, and it loses all its data when the power is turned off. *Secondary storage,* usually a *hard disk* (see Figure 3), provides less expensive storage that persists without electricity. A hard disk consists of rotating platters, which are coated with a magnetic material, and read/write heads, which can detect and change the patterns of varying magnetic flux on the platters. This is essentially the same recording and playback process that is used in audio or video tapes.

Some computers are self-contained units, whereas others are interconnected through *networks.* Home computers are usually intermittently connected to the Internet via a dialup or broadband connection. The computers in your computer lab are probably permanently connected to a local area network. Through the network cabling, the computer can read programs from central storage locations or

Figure 2
A Memory Module with Memory Chips

send data to other computers. For the user of a networked computer, it may not even be obvious which data reside on the computer itself and which are transmitted through the network.

Most computers have *removable storage* devices that can access data or programs on media such as floppy disks, tapes, or compact discs (CDs).

Figure 3 A Hard Disk

Figure 4   A Motherboard

To interact with a human user, a computer requires other peripheral devices. The computer transmits information to the user through a display screen, loudspeakers, and printers. The user can enter information and directions to the computer by using a keyboard or a pointing device such as a mouse.

The CPU, the RAM, and the electronics controlling the hard disk and other devices are interconnected through a set of electrical lines called a *bus.* Data travel along the bus from the system memory and peripheral devices to the CPU and back. Figure 4 shows a *motherboard,* which contains the CPU, the RAM, and connectors to peripheral devices.

> The CPU reads machine instructions from memory. The instructions direct it to communicate with memory, secondary storage, and peripheral devices.

Figure 5 gives a schematic overview of the architecture of a computer. Program instructions and data (such as text, numbers, audio, or video) are stored on the hard disk, on a CD, or on a network. When a program is started, it is brought into memory where it can be read by the CPU. The CPU reads the program one instruction at a time. As directed by these instructions, the CPU reads data, modifies it, and writes it back to RAM or to secondary storage. Some program instructions will cause the CPU to interact with the devices that control the display screen or the speaker. Because these actions happen many times over and at great speed, the human user will perceive images and sound. Similarly, the CPU can send instructions to a printer to mark the paper with patterns of closely spaced dots, which a human recognizes as text characters and pictures. Some program instructions read user input from the keyboard or mouse. The program analyzes the nature of these inputs and then executes the next appropriate instructions.

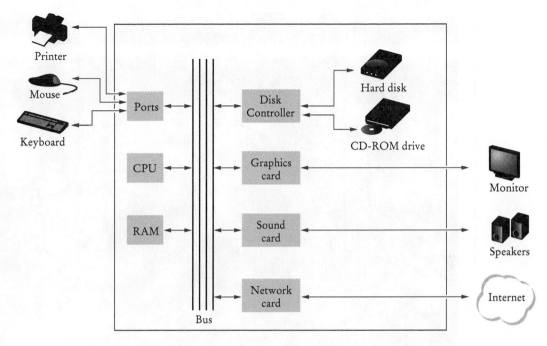

Figure 5 Schematic Diagram of a Computer

4. Where is a program stored when it is not currently running?
5. Which part of the computer carries out arithmetic operations, such as addition and multiplication?

RANDOM FACT 1.1

The ENIAC and the Dawn of Computing

The ENIAC (*electronic numerical integrator and computer*) was the first usable electronic computer. It was designed by J. Presper Eckert and John Mauchly at the University of Pennsylvania and was completed in 1946. Instead of transistors, which were not invented until two years after it was built, the ENIAC contained about 18,000 *vacuum tubes* in many cabinets housed in a large room (see The ENIAC figure). Vacuum tubes burned out at the rate of several tubes per day. An attendant with a shopping cart full of tubes constantly made the rounds and replaced defective ones. The computer was programmed by connecting wires on panels. Each wiring configuration would set up the computer for a particular problem. To have the computer work on a different problem, the wires had to be replugged.

Work on the ENIAC was supported by the U.S. Navy, which was interested in computations of ballistic tables that would give the trajectory of a projectile, depending on the wind resistance, initial velocity, and atmospheric conditions. To compute the trajectories, one must

The ENIAC

find the numerical solutions of certain differential equations; hence the name "numerical integrator". Before machines like ENIAC were developed, humans did this kind of work, and until the 1950s the word "computer" referred to these people. The ENIAC was later used for peaceful purposes, such as the tabulation of U.S. census data.

1.3 Translating Human-Readable Programs to Machine Code

Generally, machine code depends on the CPU type. However, the instruction set of the Java virtual machine (JVM) can be executed on many CPUs.

On the most basic level, computer instructions are extremely primitive. The processor executes *machine instructions*. CPUs from different vendors, such as the Intel Pentium or the Sun SPARC, have different sets of machine instructions. To enable Java applications to run on multiple CPUs without modification, Java programs contain machine instructions for a so-called "Java virtual machine" (JVM), an idealized CPU that is simulated by a program run on the actual CPU. The difference between actual and virtual machine instructions is not important— all you need to know is that machine instructions are very simple, are encoded as numbers and stored in memory, and can be executed very quickly.

A typical sequence of machine instructions is

1. Load the contents of memory location 40.
2. Load the value 100.
3. If the first value is greater than the second value, continue with the instruction that is stored in memory location 240.

Actually, machine instructions are encoded as numbers so that they can be stored in memory. On the Java virtual machine, this sequence of instruction is encoded as the sequence of numbers

```
21 40
16 100
163 240
```

When the virtual machine fetches this sequence of numbers, it decodes them and executes the associated sequence of commands.

> Because machine instructions are encoded as numbers, it is difficult to write programs in machine code.

How can you communicate the command sequence to the computer? The most direct method is to place the actual numbers into the computer memory. This is, in fact, how the very earliest computers worked. However, a long program is composed of thousands of individual commands, and it is tedious and error-prone to look up the numeric codes for all commands and manually place the codes into memory. As we said before, computers are really good at automating tedious and error-prone activities, and it did not take long for computer programmers to realize that computers could be harnessed to help in the programming process.

> High-level languages allow you to describe tasks at a higher conceptual level than machine code.

In the mid-1950s, *high-level* programming languages began to appear. In these languages, the programmer expresses the idea behind the task that needs to be performed, and a special computer program, called a *compiler,* translates the high-level description into machine instructions for a particular processor.

For example, in Java, the high-level programming language that you will use in this book, you might give the following instruction:

```
if (intRate > 100)
    System.out.println("Interest rate error");
```

This means, "If the interest rate is over 100, display an error message". It is then the job of the compiler program to look at the sequence of characters if (intRate > 100) and translate that into

```
21 40 16 100 163 240 . . .
```

> A compiler translates programs written in a high-level language into machine code.

Compilers are quite sophisticated programs. They translate logical statements, such as the if statement, into sequences of computations, tests, and jumps. They assign memory locations for *variables*—items of information identified by symbolic names—like intRate. In this course, we will generally take the existence of a compiler for granted. If you decide to become a professional computer scientist, you may well learn more about compiler-writing techniques later in your studies.

6. What is the code for the Java virtual machine instruction "Load the contents of memory location 100"?

7. Does a person who uses a computer for office work ever run a compiler?

1.4 The Java Programming Language

Java was originally designed for programming consumer devices, but it was first successfully used to write Internet applets.

In 1991, a group led by James Gosling and Patrick Naughton at Sun Microsystems designed a programming language that they code-named "Green" for use in consumer devices, such as intelligent television "set-top" boxes. The language was designed to be simple and architecture neutral, so that it could be executed on a variety of hardware. No customer was ever found for this technology.

Gosling recounts that in 1994 the team realized, "We could write a really cool browser. It was one of the few things in the client/server mainstream that needed some of the weird things we'd done: architecture neutral, real-time, reliable, secure". Java was introduced to an enthusiastic crowd at the SunWorld exhibition in 1995.

Java was designed to be safe and portable, benefiting both Internet users and students.

Since then, Java has grown at a phenomenal rate. Programmers have embraced the language because it is simpler than its closest rival, C++. In addition, Java has a rich *library* that makes it possible to write portable programs that can bypass proprietary operating systems—a feature that was eagerly sought by those who wanted to be independent of those proprietary systems and was bitterly fought by their vendors. A "micro edition" and an "enterprise edition" of the Java library make Java programmers at home on hardware ranging from smart cards and cell phones to the largest Internet servers.

Because Java was designed for the Internet, it has two attributes that make it very suitable for beginners: safety and portability. If you visit a web page that contains Java code (so-called *applets*—see Figure 6 for an example), the code automatically starts running. It is important that you can trust that applets are inherently safe. If an applet could do something evil, such as damaging data or reading personal information on your computer, then you would be in real danger every time you browsed the Web—an unscrupulous designer might put up a web page containing dangerous code that would execute on your machine as soon as you visited the page. The Java language has an assortment of security features that guarantees that no evil applets can run on your computer. As an added benefit, these features also help you to learn the language faster. The Java virtual machine can catch many kinds of beginners' mistakes and report them accurately. (In contrast, many beginners' mistakes in the C++ language merely produce programs that act in random and confusing ways.) The other benefit of Java is portability. The same Java program will run, without change, on Windows, UNIX, Linux, or the Macintosh. This too is a requirement for applets. When you visit a web page, the web server that serves up

Figure 6   An Applet for Visualizing Molecules ([1])

the page contents has no idea what computer you are using to browse the Web. It simply returns you the portable code that was generated by the Java compiler. The virtual machine on your computer executes that portable code. Again, there is a benefit for the student. You do not have to learn how to write programs for different operating systems.

At this time, Java is firmly established as one of the most important languages for general-purpose programming as well as for computer science instruction. However, although Java is a good language for beginners, it is not perfect, for three reasons.

Because Java was not specifically designed for students, no thought was given to making it really simple to write basic programs. A certain amount of technical machinery is necessary in Java to write even the simplest programs. This is not a problem for professional programmers, but it is a drawback for beginning students. As you learn how to program in Java, there will be times when you will be asked to be satisfied with a preliminary explanation and wait for complete details in a later chapter.

Java was revised and extended many times during its life—see Table 1. In this book, we assume that you have Java version 5 or later.

Finally, you cannot hope to learn all of Java in one semester. The Java language itself is relatively simple, but Java contains a vast set of *library packages* that are

Java has a very large library. Focus on learning those parts of the library that you need for your programming projects.

required to write useful programs. There are packages for graphics, user interface design, cryptography, networking, sound, database storage, and many other purposes. Even expert Java programmers cannot hope to know the contents of all of the packages—they just use those that they need for particular projects.

Using this book, you should expect to learn a good deal about the Java language and about the most important packages. Keep in mind that the central goal of this book is not to make you memorize Java minutiae, but to teach you how to think about programming.

Table 1 Java Versions

Version	Year	Important New Features
1.0	1996	
1.1	1997	Inner classes
1.2	1998	Swing, Collections
1.3	2000	Performance enhancements
1.4	2002	Assertions, XML
5	2004	Generic classes, enhanced for loop, auto-boxing, enumerations
6	2006	Library improvements

SELF CHECK

8. What are the two most important benefits of the Java language?
9. How long does it take to learn the entire Java library?

1.5 Becoming Familiar with Your Computer

Set aside some time to become familiar with the computer system and the Java compiler that you will use for your class work.

You may be taking your first programming course as you read this book, and you may well be doing your work on an unfamiliar computer system. Spend some time familiarizing yourself with the computer. Because computer systems vary widely, this book can only give an outline of the steps you need to follow. Using a new and unfamiliar computer system can be frustrating, especially if you are on your own. Look for training courses that your campus offers, or ask a friend to give you a brief tour.

Figure 7
A Shell Window

Step 1. Log In

If you use your home computer, you probably don't need to worry about this step. Computers in a lab, however, are usually not open to everyone. You may need an account name or number and a password to gain access to such a system.

Step 2. Locate the Java Compiler

Computer systems differ greatly in this regard. On some systems you must open a *shell window* (see Figure 7) and type commands to launch the compiler. Other systems have an *integrated development environment* in which you can write and test your programs (see Figure 8). Many university labs have information sheets and

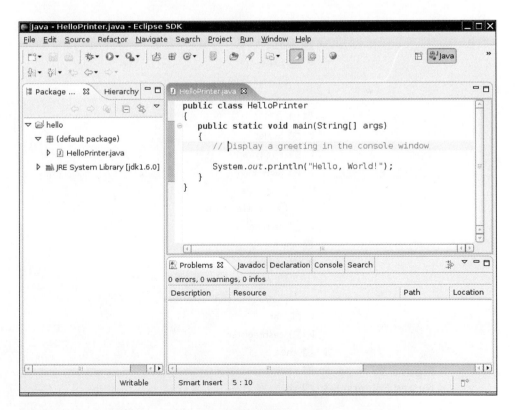

Figure 8   An Integrated Development Environment

tutorials that walk you through the tools that are installed in the lab. Instructions for several popular compilers are available in WileyPLUS.

Step 3. Understand Files and Folders

As a programmer, you will write Java programs, try them out, and improve them. Your programs are kept in *files*. A file is a collection of items of information that are kept together, such as the text of a word-processing document or the instructions of a Java program. Files have names, and the rules for legal names differ from one system to another. Some systems allow spaces in file names; others don't. Some distinguish between upper- and lowercase letters; others don't. Most Java compilers require that Java files end in an *extension* — .java; for example, Test.java. Java file names cannot contain spaces, and the distinction between upper- and lowercase letters is important.

Files are stored in *folders* or *directories*. These file containers can be *nested*. That is, a folder can contain not only files but also other folders, which themselves can contain more files and folders (see Figure 9). This hierarchy can be quite large, especially on networked computers, where some of the files may be on your local disk, others elsewhere on the network. While you need not be concerned with

Figure 9
Nested Folders

every branch of the hierarchy, you should familiarize yourself with your local environment. Different systems have different ways of showing files and directories. Some use a graphical display and let you move around by clicking the mouse on folder icons. In other systems, you must enter commands to visit or inspect different locations.

Step 4. Write a Simple Program

In the next section, we will introduce a very simple program. You will need to learn how to type it in, how to run it, and how to fix mistakes.

Step 5. Save Your Work

Develop a strategy for keeping backup copies of your work before disaster strikes.

You will spend many hours typing Java program code and improving it. The resulting program files have some value, and you should treat them as you would other important property. A conscientious safety strategy is particularly important for computer files. They are more fragile than paper documents or other more tangible objects. It is easy to delete a file accidentally, and occasionally files are lost because of a computer malfunction. Unless you keep a copy, you must then retype the contents. Because you probably won't remember the entire file, you will likely find yourself spending almost as much time as you did to enter and improve it in the first place. This costs time, and it may cause you to miss deadlines. It is therefore crucial that you learn how to safeguard files and that you get in the habit of doing so *before* disaster strikes. You can make safety or *backup* copies of files by saving copies on a floppy or CD, into another folder, to your local area network, or on the Internet.

SELF CHECK

10. How are programming projects stored on a computer?
11. What do you do to protect yourself from data loss when you work on programming projects?

PRODUCTIVITY HINT 1.1

Understand the File System

In recent years, computers have become easier to use for home or office users. Many inessential details are now hidden from casual users. For example, many casual users simply place all their work inside a default folder (such as "Home" or "My Documents") and are blissfully ignorant about details of the file system.

But you need to know how to impose an organization on the data that you create. You also need to be able to locate and inspect files that are required for translating and running Java programs.

If you are not comfortable with files and folders, be sure to set aside some time to learn about these concepts. Enroll in a short course, or take a web tutorial. Many free tutorials are available on the Internet, but unfortunately their locations change frequently. Search the Web for "files and folders tutorial" and pick a tutorial that goes beyond the basics.

PRODUCTIVITY HINT 1.2

Have a Backup Strategy

Come up with a strategy for your backups *now*, before you lose any data. Here are a few pointers to keep in mind.

- *Select a backup medium.* Floppy disks are the traditional choice, but they can be unreliable. CD media are more reliable and hold far more information, but they are more expensive. An increasingly popular form of backup is Internet file storage. Many people use two levels of backup: a folder on the hard disk for quick and dirty backups, and a CD-ROM for higher security. (After all, a hard disk can crash—a particularly common problem with laptop computers.)

- *Back up often.* Backing up a file takes only a few seconds, and you will hate yourself if you have to spend many hours recreating work that you easily could have saved.

- *Rotate backups.* Use more than one set of disks or folders for backups, and rotate them. That is, first back up onto the first backup destination, then to the second and third, and then go back to the first. That way you always have three recent backups. Even if one of the floppy disks has a defect, or you messed up one of the backup directories, you can use one of the others.

- *Back up source files only.* The compiler translates the files that you write into files consisting of machine code. There is no need to back up the machine code files, because you can recreate them easily by running the compiler again. Focus your backup activity on those files that represent your effort. That way your backups won't fill up with files that you don't need.

- *Pay attention to the backup direction.* Backing up involves copying files from one place to another. It is important that you do this right—that is, copy from your work location to the backup location. If you do it the wrong way, you will overwrite a newer file with an older version.

- *Check your backups once in a while.* Double-check that your backups are where you think they are. There is nothing more frustrating than finding out that the backups are not there when you need them. This is particularly true if you use a backup program that stores files on an unfamiliar device (such as data tape) or in a compressed format.

- *Relax before restoring.* When you lose a file and need to restore it from backup, you are likely to be in an unhappy, nervous state. Take a deep breath and think through the recovery process before you start. It is not uncommon for an agitated computer user to wipe out the last backup when trying to restore a damaged file.

1.6 Compiling a Simple Program

You are now ready to write and run your first Java program. The traditional choice for the very first program in a new programming language is a program that displays a simple greeting: "Hello, World!". Let us follow that tradition. Here is the "Hello, World!" program in Java.

ch01/hello/HelloPrinter.java

```
1  public class HelloPrinter
2  {
3     public static void main(String[] args)
4     {
5        // Display a greeting in the console window
6
7        System.out.println("Hello, World!");
8     }
9  }
```

Output

```
Hello, World!
```

We will examine this program in a minute. For now, you should make a new program file and call it `HelloPrinter.java`. Enter the program instructions and compile and run the program, following the procedure that is appropriate for your compiler.

> Java is case sensitive. You must be careful about distinguishing between upper- and lowercase letters.

Java is *case sensitive*. You must enter upper- and lowercase letters exactly as they appear in the program listing. You cannot type `MAIN` or `PrintLn`. If you are not careful, you will run into problems—see Common Error 1.2.

On the other hand, Java has *free-form layout*. You can use any number of spaces and line breaks to separate words. You can cram as many words as possible into each line,

```
public class HelloPrinter{public static void main(String[]
args){// Display a greeting in the console window
System.out.println("Hello, World!");}}
```

You can even write every word and symbol on a separate line,

```
public
class
HelloPrinter
{
public
static
void
main
(
. . .
```

Lay out your programs so that they are easy to read.

However, good taste dictates that you lay out your programs in a readable fashion. We will give you recommendations for good layout throughout this book. Appendix A contains a summary of our recommendations.

When you run the test program, the message

```
Hello, World!
```

will appear somewhere on the screen (see Figures 10 and 11). The exact location depends on your programming environment.

Now that you have seen the program working, it is time to understand its makeup. The first line,

```
public class HelloPrinter
```

Classes are the fundamental building blocks of Java programs.

starts a new *class*. Classes are a fundamental concept in Java, and you will begin to study them in Chapter 2. In Java, every program consists of one or more classes.

The keyword `public` denotes that the class is usable by the "public". You will later encounter `private` features. At this point, you should simply regard the

```
public class ClassName
{
    . . .
}
```

as a necessary part of the "plumbing" that is required to write any Java program. In Java, every source file can contain at most one public class, and the name of the public class must match the name of the file containing the class. For example, the class `HelloPrinter` *must* be contained in a file `HelloPrinter.java`. It is very important that the names *and the capitalization* match exactly. You can get strange error messages if you call the class `HELLOPrinter` or the file `helloprinter.java`.

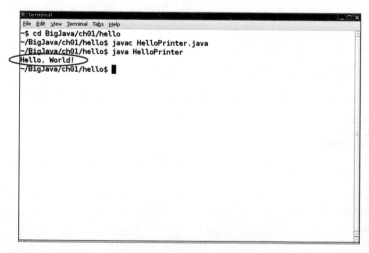

Figure 10   Running the `HelloPrinter` Program in a Console Window

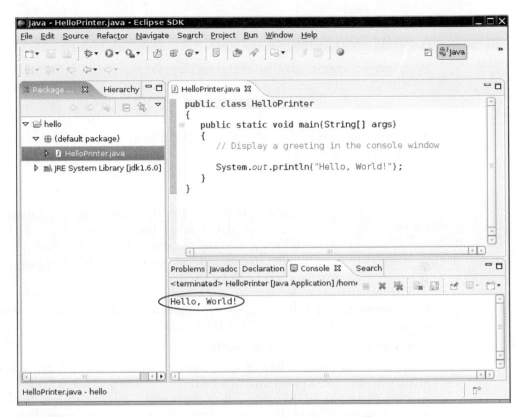

Figure 11
Running the HelloPrinter Program in an Integrated Development Environment

> Every Java application contains a class with a main method. When the application starts, the instructions in the main method are executed.

> Each class contains definitions of methods. Each method contains a sequence of instructions.

The construction

```
public static void main(String[] args)
{
}
```

defines a *method* called main. A method contains a collection of programming instructions that describe how to carry out a particular task. Every Java application must have a main method. Most Java programs contain other methods besides main, and you will see in Chapter 3 how to write other methods.

The *parameter* String[] args is a required part of the main method. (It contains *command line arguments*, which we will not discuss until Chapter 11.) The keyword static indicates that the main method does not operate on an *object*. (As you will see in Chapter 2, most methods in Java do operate on objects, and static methods are not common in large Java programs. Nevertheless, main must always be static, because it starts running before the program can create objects.)

At this time, simply consider

```
public class ClassName
{
    public static void main(String[] args)
    {
        . . .
    }
}
```

as yet another part of the "plumbing". Our first program has all instructions inside the main method of a class.

The first line inside the main method is a *comment*

```
// Display a greeting in the console window
```

> Use comments to help human readers understand your program.

This comment is purely for the benefit of the human reader, to explain in more detail what the next statement does. Any text enclosed between // and the end of the line is completely ignored by the compiler. Comments are used to explain the program to other programmers or to yourself.

The instructions or *statements* in the *body* of the main method—that is, the statements inside the curly braces ({})—are executed one by one. Each statement ends in a semicolon (;). Our method has a single statement:

```
System.out.println("Hello, World!");
```

This statement prints a line of text, namely "Hello, World!". However, there are many places where a program can send that string: to a window, to a file, or to a networked computer on the other side of the world. You need to specify that the destination for the string is the *system output*—that is, a console window. The console window is represented in Java by an object called out. Just as you needed to place the main method in a HelloPrinter class, the designers of the Java library needed to place the out object into a class. They placed it in the System class, which contains useful objects and methods to access system resources. To use the out object in the System class, you must refer to it as System.out.

To use an object, such as System.out, you specify what you want to do to it. In this case, you want to print a line of text. The println method carries out this task.

You do not have to implement this method—the programmers who wrote the Java library already did that for us—but you do need to *call* the method.

> A method is called by specifying an object, the method name, and the method parameters.

Whenever you call a method in Java, you need to specify three items (see Figure 12):

1. The object that you want to use (in this case, System.out)
2. The name of the method you want to use (in this case, println)
3. A pair of parentheses, containing any other information the method needs (in this case, "Hello, World!"). The technical term for this information is a *parameter* for the method. Note that the two periods in System.out.println have different meanings. The first period means "locate the out object in the System class". The second period means "apply the println method to that object".

Figure 12
Calling a Method

Object   Method   Parameters

`System.out.println("Hello, World!")`

A sequence of characters enclosed in quotation marks

`"Hello, World!"`

> A string is a sequence of characters enclosed in quotation marks.

is called a *string*. You must enclose the contents of the string inside quotation marks so that the compiler knows you literally mean `"Hello, World!"`. There is a reason for this requirement. Suppose you need to print the word *main*. By enclosing it in quotation marks, `"main"`, the compiler knows you mean the sequence of characters m a i n, not the method named `main`. The rule is simply that you must enclose all text strings in quotation marks, so that the compiler considers them plain text and does not try to interpret them as program instructions.

You can also print numerical values. For example, the statement

`System.out.println(3 + 4);`

displays the number 7.

The `println` method prints a string or a number and then starts a new line. For example, the sequence of statements

```
System.out.println("Hello");
System.out.println("World!");
```

prints two lines of text:

```
Hello
World!
```

There is a second method, called `print`, that you can use to print an item without starting a new line. For example, the output of the two statements

```
System.out.print("00");
System.out.println(3 + 4);
```

is the single line

```
007
```

Syntax 1.1 Method Call

object.methodName(parameters)

Example:

`System.out.println("Hello, Dave!")`

Purpose:

To invoke a method on an object and supply any additional parameters

12. How would you modify the `HelloPrinter` program to print the words "Hello," and "World!" on two lines?

13. Would the program continue to work if you omitted the line starting with `//`?

14. What does the following set of statements print?

```
System.out.print("My lucky number is");
System.out.println(3 + 4 + 5);
```

COMMON ERROR 1.1

Omitting Semicolons

In Java every statement must end in a semicolon. Forgetting to type a semicolon is a common error. It confuses the compiler, because the compiler uses the semicolon to find where one statement ends and the next one starts. The compiler does not use line breaks or closing braces to recognize the end of statements. For example, the compiler considers

```
System.out.println("Hello")
System.out.println("World!");
```

a single statement, as if you had written

```
System.out.println("Hello") System.out.println("World!");
```

Then it doesn't understand that statement, because it does not expect the word `System` following the closing parenthesis after `"Hello"`. The remedy is simple. Scan every statement for a terminating semicolon, just as you would check that every English sentence ends in a period.

ADVANCED TOPIC 1.1

Alternative Comment Syntax

In Java there are two methods for writing comments. You already learned that the compiler ignores anything that you type between `//` and the end of the current line. The compiler also ignores any text between a `/*` and `*/`.

```
/* A simple Java program */
```

The `//` comment is easier to type if the comment is only a single line long. If you have a comment that is longer than a line, then the `/* . . . */` comment is simpler:

```
/*
   This is a simple Java program that you can use to try out
   your compiler and virtual machine.
*/
```

It would be somewhat tedious to add the `//` at the beginning of each line and to move them around whenever the text of the comment changes.

> In this book, we use // for comments that will never grow beyond a line, and /* . . . */
> for longer comments. If you prefer, you can always use the // style. The readers of your code
> will be grateful for *any* comments, no matter which style you use.

1.7 Errors

Experiment a little with the HelloPrinter program. What happens if you make a typing error such as

```
System.ouch.println("Hello, World!");
System.out.println("Hello, World!);
System.out.println("Hello, Word!");
```

A syntax error is a violation of the rules of the programming language. The compiler detects syntax errors.

In the first case, the compiler will complain. It will say that it has no clue what you mean by ouch. The exact wording of the error message is dependent on the compiler, but it might be something like "Undefined symbol ouch". This is a *compile-time error* or *syntax error*. Something is wrong according to the language rules and the compiler finds it. When the compiler finds one or more errors, it refuses to translate the program to Java virtual machine instructions, and as a consequence you have no program that you can run. You must fix the error and compile again. In fact, the compiler is quite picky, and it is common to go through several rounds of fixing compile-time errors before compilation succeeds for the first time.

If the compiler finds an error, it will not simply stop and give up. It will try to report as many errors as it can find, so you can fix them all at once. Sometimes, however, one error throws it off track. This is likely to happen with the error in the second line. Because the closing quotation mark is missing, the compiler will think that the); characters are still part of the string. In such cases, it is common for the compiler to emit bogus error reports for neighboring lines. You should fix only those error messages that make sense to you and then recompile.

The error in the third line is of a different kind. The program will compile and run, but its output will be wrong. It will print

```
Hello, Word!
```

A logic error causes a program to take an action that the programmer did not intend. You must test your programs to find logic errors.

This is a *run-time error* or *logic error*. The program is syntactically correct and does something, but it doesn't do what it is supposed to do. The compiler cannot find the error. You, the programmer, must flush out this type of error. Run the program, and carefully look at its output.

During program development, errors are unavoidable. Once a program is longer than a few lines, it requires superhuman concentration to enter it correctly without slipping up once. You will find yourself omitting semicolons or quotes more often than you would like, but the compiler will track down these problems for you.

Logic errors are more troublesome. The compiler will not find them—in fact, the compiler will cheerfully translate any program as long as its syntax is correct—but the resulting program will do something wrong. It is the responsibility of the program author to test the program and find any logic errors. Testing programs is an important topic that you will encounter many times in this book. Another important aspect of good craftsmanship is *defensive programming:* structuring programs and development processes in such a way that an error in one part of a program does not trigger a disastrous response.

The error examples that you saw so far were not difficult to diagnose or fix, but as you learn more sophisticated programming techniques, there will also be much more room for error. It is an uncomfortable fact that locating all errors in a program is very difficult. Even if you can observe that a program exhibits faulty behavior, it may not at all be obvious what part of the program caused it and how you can fix it. Special software tools (so-called *debuggers*) let you trace through a program to find *bugs*—that is, logic errors. In Chapter 6 you will learn how to use a debugger effectively.

Note that these errors are different from the types of errors that you are likely to make in calculations. If you total up a column of numbers, you may miss a minus sign or accidentally drop a carry, perhaps because you are bored or tired. Computers do not make these kinds of errors.

This book uses a three-part error management strategy. First, you will learn about common errors and how to avoid them. Then you will learn defensive programming strategies to minimize the likelihood and impact of errors. Finally, you will learn debugging strategies to flush out those errors that remain.

SELF CHECK

15. Suppose you omit the `//` characters from the `HelloPrinter.java` program but not the remainder of the comment. Will you get a compile-time error or a run-time error?

16. How can you find logic errors in a program?

COMMON ERROR 1.2

Misspelling Words

If you accidentally misspell a word, then strange things may happen, and it may not always be completely obvious from the error messages what went wrong. Here is a good example of how simple spelling errors can cause trouble:

```
public class HelloPrinter
{
    public static void Main(String[] args)
    {
        System.out.println("Hello, World!");
    }
}
```

This class defines a method called Main. The compiler will not consider this to be the same as the main method, because Main starts with an uppercase letter and the Java language is case sensitive. Upper- and lowercase letters are considered to be completely different from each other, and to the compiler Main is no better match for main than rain. The compiler will cheerfully compile your Main method, but when the Java virtual machine reads the compiled file, it will complain about the missing main method and refuse to run the program. Of course, the message "missing main method" should give you a clue where to look for the error.

If you get an error message that seems to indicate that the compiler is on the wrong track, it is a good idea to check for spelling and capitalization. All Java keywords use only lowercase letters. Names of classes usually start with an uppercase letter, names of methods and variables with a lowercase letter. If you misspell the name of a symbol (for example, ouch instead of out), the compiler will complain about an "undefined symbol". That error message is usually a good clue that you made a spelling error.

1.8 The Compilation Process

Some Java development environments are very convenient to use. Enter the code in one window, click on a button to compile, and click on another button to execute your program. Error messages show up in a second window, and the program runs in a third window. With such an environment you are completely shielded from the details of the compilation process. On other systems you must carry out every step manually, by typing commands into a shell window.

An editor is a program for entering and modifying text, such as a Java program.

No matter which compilation environment you use, you begin your activity by typing in the program statements. The program that you use for entering and modifying the program text is called an *editor*. Remember to *save* your work to disk frequently, because otherwise the text editor stores the text only in the computer's memory. If something goes wrong with the computer and you need to restart it, the contents of the primary memory (including your program text) are lost, but anything stored on the hard disk is permanent even if you need to restart the computer.

The Java compiler translates source code into class files that contain instructions for the Java virtual machine.

When you compile your program, the compiler translates the Java *source code* (that is, the statements that you wrote) into *class files*, which consist of virtual machine instructions and other information that is required for execution. The class files have the extension .class. For example, the virtual machine instructions for the Hello-Printer program are stored in a file HelloPrinter.class. As already mentioned, the compiler produces a class file only after you have corrected all syntax errors.

The class file contains the translation of only the instructions that you wrote. That is not enough to actually run the program. To display a string in a window, quite a bit of low-level activity is necessary. The authors of the System and Print-Stream classes (which define the out object and the println method) have implemented all necessary actions and placed the required class files into a *library*. A

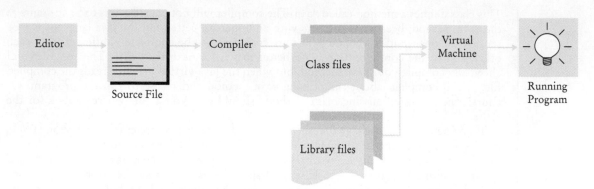

Figure 13   From Source Code to Running Program

library is a collection of code that has been programmed and translated by someone else, ready for you to use in your program.

The Java virtual machine loads the instructions for the program that you wrote, starts your program, and loads the necessary library files as they are required.

The steps of compiling and running your program are outlined in Figure 13.

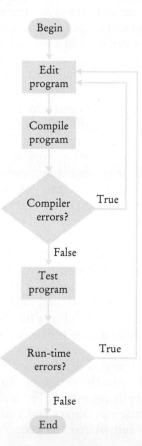

Figure 14
The Edit–Compile–Test Loop

The Java virtual machine loads program instructions from class files and library files.

Programming activity centers around these steps. Start in the editor, writing the source file. Compile the program and look at the error messages. Go back to the editor and fix the syntax errors. When the compiler succeeds, run the program. If you find a run-time error, you must look at the source code in the editor to try to determine the reason. Once you find the cause of the error, fix it in the editor. Compile and run again to see whether the error has gone away. If not, go back to the editor. This is called the *edit–compile–test loop* (see Figure 14). You will spend a substantial amount of time in this loop when working on programming assignments.

SELF CHECK

17. What do you expect to see when you load a class file into your text editor?

18. Why can't you test a program for run-time errors when it has compiler errors?

CHAPTER SUMMARY

1. A computer must be programmed to perform tasks. Different tasks require different programs.

2. A computer program executes a sequence of very basic operations in rapid succession.

3. A computer program contains the instruction sequences for all tasks that it can execute.

4. At the heart of the computer lies the central processing unit (CPU).

5. Data and programs are stored in primary storage (memory) and secondary storage (such as a hard disk).

6. The CPU reads machine instructions from memory. The instructions direct it to communicate with memory, secondary storage, and peripheral devices.

7. Generally, machine code depends on the CPU type. However, the instruction set of the Java virtual machine (JVM) can be executed on many CPUs.

8. Because machine instructions are encoded as numbers, it is difficult to write programs in machine code.

9. High-level languages allow you to describe tasks at a higher conceptual level than machine code.

10. A compiler translates programs written in a high-level language into machine code.

11. Java was originally designed for programming consumer devices, but it was first successfully used to write Internet applets.

12. Java was designed to be safe and portable, benefiting both Internet users and students.

13. Java has a very large library. Focus on learning those parts of the library that you need for your programming projects.

14. Set aside some time to become familiar with the computer system and the Java compiler that you will use for your class work.

15. Develop a strategy for keeping backup copies of your work before disaster strikes.

16. Java is case sensitive. You must be careful about distinguishing between upper- and lowercase letters.

17. Lay out your programs so that they are easy to read.

18. Classes are the fundamental building blocks of Java programs.

19. Every Java application contains a class with a `main` method. When the application starts, the instructions in the `main` method are executed.

20. Each class contains definitions of methods. Each method contains a sequence of instructions.

21. Use comments to help human readers understand your program.

22. A method is called by specifying an object, the method name, and the method parameters.

23. A string is a sequence of characters enclosed in quotation marks.

24. A syntax error is a violation of the rules of the programming language. The compiler detects syntax errors.

25. A logic error causes a program to take an action that the programmer did not intend. You must test your programs to find logic errors.

26. An editor is a program for entering and modifying text, such as a Java program.

27. The Java compiler translates source code into class files that contain instructions for the Java virtual machine.

28. The Java virtual machine loads program instructions from class files and library files.

FURTHER READING

1. `http://jmol.sourceforge.net/applet/`   The web site for the jmol applet for visualizing molecules.

CLASSES, OBJECTS, AND METHODS INTRODUCED IN THIS CHAPTER

Here is a list of all classes, methods, static variables, and constants introduced in this chapter. Turn to the documentation in Appendix C for more information.

```
java.io.PrintStream
    print
    println
java.lang.System
    out
```

REVIEW EXERCISES

★ **Exercise R1.1.** Explain the difference between using a computer program and programming a computer.

★ **Exercise R1.2.** What distinguishes a computer from a typical household appliance?

★ **Exercise R1.3.** Rank the storage devices that can be part of a computer system by
   a. Speed
   b. Cost
   c. Storage capacity

★★ **Exercise R1.4.** What is the Java virtual machine?

★ **Exercise R1.5.** What is an applet?

★ **Exercise R1.6.** What is an integrated programming environment?

★ **Exercise R1.7.** What is a console window?

★★ **Exercise R1.8.** Describe *exactly* what steps you would take to back up your work after you have typed in the HelloPrinter.java program.

★★ **Exercise R1.9.** On your own computer or on a lab computer, find the exact location (folder or directory name) of
   a. The sample file HelloPrinter.java, which you wrote with the editor
   b. The Java program launcher java.exe or java
   c. The library file rt.jar that contains the run-time library

★ **Exercise R1.10.** How do you discover syntax errors? How do you discover logic errors?

★★ **Exercise R1.11.** Write three versions of the HelloPrinter.java program that have different syntax errors. Write a version that has a logic error.

★★★   **Exercise R1.12.** What do the following statements print? Don't guess; write programs to find out.

    a. `System.out.println("3 + 4");`

    b. `System.out.println(3 + 4);`

    c. `System.out.println(3 + "4");`

Additional review exercises are available in WileyPLUS.

PROGRAMMING EXERCISES

★   **Exercise P1.1.** Write a program `NamePrinter` that displays your name inside a box on the console screen, like this:

Do your best to approximate lines with characters, such as |, -, and +.

★   **Exercise P1.2.** Write a program `FacePrinter` that prints a face, using text characters, hopefully better looking than this one:

Use *comments* to indicate the statements that print the hair, ears, mouth, and so on.

★   **Exercise P1.3.** Write a program `TicTacToeBoardPrinter` that prints a tic-tac-toe board:

```
+---+---+---+
|   |   |   |
+---+---+---+
|   |   |   |
+---+---+---+
|   |   |   |
+---+---+---+
```

★   **Exercise P1.4.** Write a program `StaircasePrinter` that prints a staircase:

```
            +---+
            |   |
        +---+---+
        |   |   |
    +---+---+---+
    |   |   |   |
+---+---+---+---+
|   |   |   |   |
+---+---+---+---+
```

★★   **Exercise P1.5.** Write a program that computes the sum of the first ten positive integers, $1 + 2 + \cdots + 10$. *Hint:* Write a program of the form

```
public class Sum10
{
    public static void main(String[] args)
    {
```

```
        System.out.println(              );
    }
}
```

★★ **Exercise P1.6.** Write a program Sum10Reciprocals that computes the sum of the reciprocals $1/1 + 1/2 + \cdots + 1/10$. This is harder than it sounds. Try writing the program,
and check the result. The program's result isn't likely to be correct. Then write the
denominators as *floating-point numbers*, $1.0, 2.0, \ldots, 10.0$, and run the program
again. Can you explain the difference in the results? We will explore this phenomenon
in Chapter 4.

★★ **Exercise P1.7.** Type in and run the following program:

```
import javax.swing.JOptionPane;

public class DialogViewer
{
    public static void main(String[] args)
    {
        JOptionPane.showMessageDialog(null, "Hello, World!");
        System.exit(0);
    }
}
```

Then modify the program to show the message "Hello, *your name!*".

★★ **Exercise P1.8.** Type in and run the following program:

```
import javax.swing.JOptionPane;

public class DialogViewer
{
    public static void main(String[] args)
    {
        String name = JOptionPane.showInputDialog("What is your name?");
        System.out.println(name);
        System.exit(0);
    }
}
```

Then modify the program to print "Hello, *name!*", displaying the name that the
user typed in.

Additional programming exercises are available in WileyPLUS.

PROGRAMMING PROJECTS

★★★ **Project 1.1.** This project builds on Exercises P1.7 and P1.8. Your program should
read the user's name, then show a sequence of two dialog boxes:

- First, an input dialog box that asks: "What would you like me to do?"
- Then a message dialog box that says: "I'm sorry, (*your name*). I'm afraid I
  can't do that."

ANSWERS TO SELF-CHECK QUESTIONS

1. A program that reads the data on the CD and sends output to the speakers and the screen.
2. A CD player can do one thing—play music CDs. It cannot execute programs.
3. No—the program simply executes the instruction sequences that the programmers have prepared in advance.
4. In secondary storage, typically a hard disk.
5. The central processing unit.
6. 21 100
7. No—a compiler is intended for programmers, to translate high-level programming instructions into machine code.
8. Safety and portability.
9. No one person can learn the entire library—it is too large.
10. Programs are stored in files, and files are stored in folders or directories.
11. You back up your files and folders.
12. `System.out.println("Hello,"); System.out.println("World!");`
13. Yes—the line starting with `//` is a comment, intended for human readers. The compiler ignores comments.
14. The printout is `My lucky number is12`. It would be a good idea to add a space after the `is`.
15. A compile-time error. The compiler will not know what to do with the word `Display`.
16. You need to run the program and observe its behavior.
17. A sequence of random characters, some funny-looking. Class files contain virtual machine instructions that are encoded as binary numbers.
18. When a program has compiler errors, no class file is produced, and there is nothing to run.

Chapter

2

Using Objects

CHAPTER GOALS

- To learn about variables
- To understand the concepts of classes and objects
- To be able to call methods
- To learn about parameters and return values

T To implement test programs

- To be able to browse the API documentation
- To realize the difference between objects and object references

G To write programs that display simple shapes

Most useful programs don't just manipulate numbers and strings. Instead, they deal with data items that are more complex and that more closely represent entities in the real world. Examples of these data items include bank accounts, employee records, and graphical shapes.

The Java language is ideally suited for designing and manipulating such data items, or *objects*. In Java, you define *classes* that describe the behavior of these objects. In this chapter, you will learn how to manipulate objects that belong to predefined classes. This knowledge will prepare you for the next chapter in which you will learn how to implement your own classes.

CHAPTER CONTENTS

2.1 Types and Variables

> In Java, every value has a type.

In Java, every value has a *type*. For example, "Hello, World" has the type String, the object System.out has the type PrintStream, and the number 13 has the type int (an abbreviation for "integer"). The type tells you what you can do with the values. You can call println on any object of type PrintStream. You can compute the sum or product of any two integers.

You often want to store values so that you can use them at a later time. To remember an object, you need to hold it in a *variable*. A variable is a storage location in the computer's memory that has a *type*, a *name*, and a contents. For example, here we declare three variables:

```
String greeting = "Hello, World!";
PrintStream printer = System.out;
int luckyNumber = 13;
```

> You use variables to store values that you want to use at a later time.

The first variable is called greeting. It can be used to store String values, and it is set to the value "Hello, World!". The second variable stores a PrintStream value, and the third stores an integer.

Variables can be used in place of the objects that they store:

```
printer.println(greeting); // Same as System.out.println("Hello, World!")
printer.println(luckyNumber); // Same as System.out.println(13)
```

SYNTAX 2.1 Variable Definition

typeName variableName = *value*;
or
typeName variableName;

Example:
```
String greeting = "Hello, Dave!";
```

Purpose:
To define a new variable of a particular type and optionally supply an initial value

When you declare your own variables, you need to make two decisions.

- What type should you use for the variable?
- What name should you give the variable?

The type depends on the intended use. If you need to store a string, use the `String` type for your variable.

It is an error to store a value whose class does not match the type of the variable. For example, the following is an error:

```
String greeting = 13; // ERROR: Types don't match
```

You cannot use a `String` variable to store an integer. The compiler checks type mismatches to protect you from errors.

> Identifiers for variables, methods, and classes are composed of letters, digits, and underscore characters.

When deciding on a name for a variable, you should make a choice that describes the purpose of the variable. For example, the variable name `greeting` is a better choice than the name `g`.

An *identifier* is the name of a variable, method, or class. Java imposes the following rules for identifiers:

- Identifiers can be made up of letters, digits, and the underscore (_) and dollar sign ($) characters. They cannot start with a digit, though. For example, `greeting1` is legal but `1greeting` is not.

- You cannot use other symbols such as ? or %. For example, `hello!` is not a legal identifier.

- Spaces are not permitted inside identifiers. Therefore, `lucky number` is not legal.

- Furthermore, you cannot use *reserved words*, such as `public`, as names; these words are reserved exclusively for their special Java meanings.

- Identifiers are also *case sensitive*; that is, `greeting` and `Greeting` are *different*.

> By convention, variable names should start with a lowercase letter.

These are firm rules of the Java language. If you violate one of them, the compiler will report an error. Moreover, there are a couple of *conventions* that you should follow so that other programmers will find your programs easy to read:

- Variable and method names should start with a lowercase letter. It is OK to use an occasional uppercase letter, such as `luckyNumber`. This mixture of lowercase and uppercase letters is sometimes called "camel case" because the uppercase letters stick out like the humps of a camel.
- Class names should start with an uppercase letter. For example, `Greeting` would be an appropriate name for a class, but not for a variable.

If you violate these conventions, the compiler won't complain, but you will confuse other programmers who read your code.

SELF CHECK

1. What is the type of the values `0` and `"0"`?

2. Which of the following are legal identifiers?

```
Greeting1
g
void
101dalmatians
Hello, World
<greeting>
```

3. Define a variable to hold your name. Use camel case in the variable name.

2.2 The Assignment Operator

> Use the assignment operator (=) to change the value of a variable.

You can change the value of an existing variable with the assignment operator (=). For example, consider the variable definition

```
int luckyNumber = 13;  ❶
```

If you want to change the value of the variable, simply assign the new value:

```
luckyNumber = 12;  ❷
```

The assignment replaces the original value of the variable (see Figure 1).

In the Java programming language, the = operator denotes an *action*, to replace the value of a variable. This usage differs from the traditional usage of the = symbol, as a statement about equality.

Figure 1
Assigning a New Value to a Variable

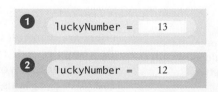

Figure 2
An Uninitialized Object Variable   `luckyNumber =` ⬜

It is an error to use a variable that has never had a value assigned to it. For example, the sequence of statements

```
int luckyNumber;
System.out.println(luckyNumber);    // ERROR—uninitialized variable
```

is an error. The compiler will complain about an "uninitialized variable" when you use a variable that has never been assigned a value. (See Figure 2.)

> All variables must be initialized before you access them.

The remedy is to assign a value to the variable before you use it:

```
int luckyNumber;
luckyNumber = 13;
System.out.println(luckyNumber); // OK
```

Or, even better, initialize the variable when you define it.

```
int luckyNumber = 13;
System.out.println(luckyNumber); // OK
```

SYNTAX 2.2 Assignment

variableName = *value*;

Example:

`luckyNumber = 12;`

Purpose:

To assign a new value to a previously defined variable

SELF CHECK

4. Is `12 = 12` a valid expression in the Java language?
5. How do you change the value of the `greeting` variable to `"Hello, Nina!"`?

2.3 Objects, Classes, and Methods

> Objects are entities in your program that you manipulate by calling methods.

An *object* is an entity that you can manipulate in your program. You don't usually know how the object is organized internally. However, the object has well-defined behavior, and that is what matters to us when we use it.

You manipulate an object by calling one or more of its *methods*. A method consists of a sequence of instructions that accesses the internal

Figure 3
Representation of the System.out Object

A method is a sequence of instructions that accesses the data of an object.

data. When you call the method, you do not know exactly what those instructions are, but you do know the purpose of the method.

For example, you saw in Chapter 1 that System.out refers to an object. You manipulate it by calling the println method. When the println method is called, some activities occur inside the object, and the ultimate effect is that text appears in the console window. You don't know how that happens, and that's OK. What matters is that the method carries out the work that you requested.

Figure 3 shows a representation of the System.out object. The internal data is symbolized by a sequence of zeroes and ones. Think of each method (symbolized by the gears) as a piece of machinery that carries out its assigned task.

In Chapter 1, you encountered two objects:

- System.out
- "Hello, World!"

These objects belong to different *classes*. The System.out object belongs to the class PrintStream. The "Hello, World!" object belongs to the class String. A class specifies the methods that you can apply to its objects.

A class defines the methods that you can apply to its objects.

You can use the println method with any object that belongs to the PrintStream class. System.out is one such object. It is possible to obtain other objects of the PrintStream class. For example, you can construct a PrintStream object to send output to a file. However, we won't discuss files until Chapter 11.

Just as the PrintStream class provides methods such as println and print for its objects, the String class provides methods that you can apply to String objects. One of them is the length method. The length method counts the number of characters in a string. You can apply that method to any object of type String. For example, the sequence of statements

```
String greeting = "Hello, World!";
int n = greeting.length();
```

sets n to the number of characters in the String object "Hello, World!". After the instructions in the length method are executed, n is set to 13. (The quotation marks are not part of the string, and the length method does not count them.)

The length method—unlike the println method—requires no input inside the parentheses. However, the length method yields an output, namely the character count.

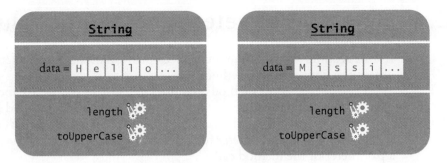

Figure 4 A Representation of Two String Objects

In the next section, you will see in greater detail how to supply method inputs and obtain method outputs.

Let us look at another method of the String class. When you apply the toUpperCase method to a String object, the method creates another String object that contains the characters of the original string, with lowercase letters converted to uppercase. For example, the sequence of statements

```
String river = "Mississippi";
String bigRiver = river.toUpperCase();
```

sets bigRiver to the String object "MISSISSIPPI".

When you apply a method to an object, you must make sure that the method is defined in the appropriate class. For example, it is an error to call

```
System.out.length(); // This method call is an error
```

The PrintStream class (to which System.out belongs) has no length method.

> The public interface of a class specifies what you can do with its objects. The hidden implementation describes how these actions are carried out.

Let us summarize. In Java, *every object belongs to a class. The class defines the methods for the objects.* For example, the String class defines the length and toUpperCase methods (as well as other methods—you will learn about most of them in Chapter 4). The methods form the *public interface* of the class, telling you what you can do with the objects of the class. A class also defines a *private implementation*, describing the data inside its objects and the instructions for its methods. Those details are hidden from the programmers who use objects and call methods.

Figure 4 shows two objects of the String class. Each object stores its own data (drawn as boxes that contain characters). Both objects support the same set of methods—the interface that is specified by the String class.

SELF CHECK

6. How can you compute the length of the string "Mississippi"?

7. How can you print out the uppercase version of "Hello, World!"?

8. Is it legal to call river.println()? Why or why not?

2.4 Method Parameters and Return Values

In this section, we will examine how to provide inputs into a method, and how to obtain the output of the method.

A parameter is an input to a method.

Some methods require inputs that give details about the work that they need to do. For example, the println method has an input: the string that should be printed. Computer scientists use the technical term *parameter* for method inputs. We say that the string greeting is a parameter of the method call

```
System.out.println(greeting)
```

Figure 5 illustrates passing of the parameter to the method.

The implicit parameter of a method call is the object on which the method is invoked.

Technically speaking, the greeting parameter is an *explicit parameter* of the println method. The object on which you invoke the method is also considered a parameter of the method call, called the *implicit parameter*. For example, System.out is the implicit parameter of the method call

```
System.out.println(greeting)
```

Some methods require multiple explicit parameters, others don't require any explicit parameters at all. An example of the latter is the length method of the String class (see Figure 6). All the information that the length method requires to do its job—namely, the character sequence of the string—is stored in the implicit parameter object.

The return value of a method is a result that the method has computed for use by the code that called it.

The length method differs from the println method in another way: it has an output. We say that the method *returns a value*, namely the number of characters in the string. You can store the return value in a variable:

```
int n = greeting.length();
```

You can also use the return value as a parameter of another method:

```
System.out.println(greeting.length());
```

Figure 5   Passing a Parameter to the println Method

Figure 6 Invoking the `length` Method on a `String` Object

The method call `greeting.length()` returns a value—the integer 13. The return value becomes a parameter of the `println` method. Figure 7 shows the process.

Not all methods return values. One example is the `println` method. The `println` method interacts with the operating system, causing characters to appear in a window. But it does not return a value to the code that calls it.

Let us analyze a more complex method call. Here, we will call the `replace` method of the `String` class. The `replace` method carries out a search-and-replace operation, similar to that of a word processor. For example, the call

```
river.replace("issipp", "our")
```

constructs a new string that is obtained by replacing all occurrences of `"issipp"` in `"Mississippi"` with `"our"`. (In this situation, there was only one replacement.) The method returns the `String` object `"Missouri"` (which you can save in a variable or pass to another method).

As Figure 8 shows, this method call has

- one implicit parameter: the string `"Mississippi"`
- two explicit parameters: the strings `"issipp"` and `"our"`
- a return value: the string `"Missouri"`

Figure 7 Passing the Result of a Method Call to Another Method

Figure 8   Calling the `replace` Method

When a method is defined in a class, the definition specifies the types of the explicit parameters and the return value. For example, the `String` class defines the `length` method as

```
public int length()
```

That is, there are no explicit parameters, and the return value has the type `int`. (For now, all the methods that we consider will be "public" methods—see Chapter 10 for more restricted methods.)

The type of the implicit parameter is the class that defines the method—`String` in our case. It is not mentioned in the method definition—hence the term "implicit".

The `replace` method is defined as

```
public String replace(String target, String replacement)
```

To call the `replace` method, you supply two explicit parameters, `target` and `replacement`, which both have type `String`. The returned value is another string.

When a method returns no value, the return type is declared with the reserved word `void`. For example, the `PrintStream` class defines the `println` method as

```
public void println(String output)
```

> A method name is overloaded if a class has more than one method with the same name (but different parameter types).

Occasionally, a class defines two methods with the same name and different explicit parameter types. For example, the `PrintStream` class defines a second method, also called `println`, as

```
public void println(int output)
```

That method is used to print an integer value. We say that the `println` name is *overloaded* because it refers to more than one method.

SELF CHECK

9. What are the implicit parameters, explicit parameters, and return values in the method call `river.length()`?
10. What is the result of the call `river.replace("p", "s")`?

11. What is the result of the call `greeting.replace("World", "Dave").length()`?

12. How is the `toUpperCase` method defined in the `String` class?

2.5 Number Types

The double type denotes floating-point numbers that can have fractional parts.

Java has separate types for *integers* and *floating-point numbers*. Integers are whole numbers; floating-point numbers can have fractional parts. For example, 13 is an integer and 1.3 is a floating-point number.

The name "floating-point" describes the representation of the number in the computer as a sequence of the significant digits and an indication of the position of the decimal point. For example, the numbers 13000, 1.3, 0.00013 all have the same decimal digits: 13. When a floating-point number is multiplied or divided by 10, only the position of the decimal point changes; it "floats". This representation is related to the "scientific" notation 1.3×10^{-4}. (Actually, the computer represents numbers in base 2, not base 10, but the principle is the same.)

If you need to process numbers with a fractional part, you should use the type called `double`, which stands for "double precision floating-point number". Think of a number in `double` format as any number that can appear in the display panel of a calculator, such as 1.3 or –0.333333333.

Do not use commas when you write numbers in Java. For example, 13,000 must be written as 13000. To write numbers in exponential notation in Java, use the notation E*n* instead of "$\times 10^n$". For example, 1.3×10^{-4} is written as `1.3E-4`.

You may wonder why Java has separate integer and floating-point number types. Pocket calculators don't need a separate integer type; they use floating-point numbers for all calculations. However, integers have several advantages over floating-point numbers. They take less storage space, are processed faster, and don't cause rounding errors. You will want to use the `int` type for quantities that can never have fractional parts, such as the length of a string. Use the `double` type for quantities that can have fractional parts, such as a grade point average.

There are several other number types in Java that are not as commonly used. We will discuss these types in Chapter 4. For most practical purposes, however, the `int` and `double` types are all you need for processing numbers.

In Java, numbers are not objects and number types are not classes.

In Java, the number types (`int`, `double`, and the less commonly used types) are *primitive types*, not classes. Numbers are not objects. The number types have no methods.

However, you can combine numbers with operators such as + and -, as in 10 + n or n - 1. To multiply two numbers, use the * operator. For example, $10 \times n$ is written as 10 * n.

Numbers can be combined by arithmetic operators such as +, –, and *.

As in mathematics, the * operator binds more strongly than the + operator. That is, x + y * 2 means the sum of x and y * 2. If you want to multiply the sum of x and y with 2, use parentheses:

    (x + y) * 2

13. Which number type would you use for storing the area of a circle?

14. Why is the expression 13.println() an error?

15. Write an expression to compute the average of the values x and y.

2.6 Constructing Objects

Most Java programs will want to work on a variety of objects. In this section, you will see how to *construct* new objects. This allows you to go beyond String objects and the predefined System.out object.

To learn about object construction, let us turn to another class: the Rectangle class in the Java class library. Objects of type Rectangle describe rectangular shapes—see Figure 9. These objects are useful for a variety of purposes. You can assemble rectangles into bar charts, and you can program simple games by moving rectangles inside a window.

Note that a Rectangle object isn't a rectangular shape—it is an object that contains a set of numbers. The numbers *describe* the rectangle (see Figure 10). Each rectangle is described by the *x*- and *y*-coordinates of its top-left corner, its width, and its height.

Figure 9
Rectangular Shapes

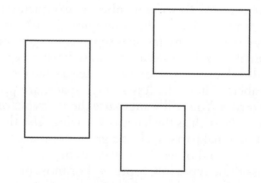

Figure 10
Rectangle Objects

It is very important that you understand this distinction. In the computer, a Rectangle object is a block of memory that holds four numbers, for example $x = 5$, $y = 10$, *width* = 20, *height* = 30. In the imagination of the programmer who uses a Rectangle object, the object describes a geometric figure.

> Use the new operator, followed by a class name and parameters, to construct new objects.

To make a new rectangle, you need to specify the *x*, *y*, *width*, and *height* values. Then *invoke the* new *operator*, specifying the name of the class and the parameters that are required for constructing a new object. For example, you can make a new rectangle with its top-left corner at (5, 10), width 20, and height 30 as follows:

```
new Rectangle(5, 10, 20, 30)
```

Here is what happens in detail.

1. The new operator makes a Rectangle object.
2. It uses the parameters (in this case, 5, 10, 20, and 30) to initialize the data of the object.
3. It returns the object.

Usually the output of the new operator is stored in a variable. For example,

```
Rectangle box = new Rectangle(5, 10, 20, 30);
```

The process of creating a new object is called *construction*. The four values 5, 10, 20, and 30 are called the *construction parameters*. Note that the new expression is *not* a complete statement. You use the value of a new expression just like a method return value: Assign it to a variable or pass it to another method.

Some classes let you construct objects in multiple ways. For example, you can also obtain a Rectangle object by supplying no construction parameters at all (but you must still supply the parentheses):

```
new Rectangle()
```

This expression constructs a (rather useless) rectangle with its top-left corner at the origin (0, 0), width 0, and height 0.

SYNTAX 2.3 Object Construction

new *ClassName(parameters)*

Example:

```
new Rectangle(5, 10, 20, 30)
new Rectangle()
```

Purpose:

To construct a new object, initialize it with the construction parameters, and return a reference to the constructed object

SELF CHECK

16. How do you construct a square with center (100, 100) and side length 20?

17. What does the following statement print?

```
System.out.println(new Rectangle().getWidth());
```

COMMON ERROR 2.1

Trying to Invoke a Constructor Like a Method

Constructors are not methods. You can only use a constructor with the new operator, not to reinitialize an existing object:

```
box.Rectangle(20, 35, 20, 30); // Error—can't reinitialize object
```

The remedy is simple: Make a new object and overwrite the current one.

```
box = new Rectangle(20, 35, 20, 30); // OK
```

2.7 Accessor and Mutator Methods

An accessor method does not change the state of its implicit parameter. A mutator method changes the state.

In this section we introduce a useful terminology for the methods of a class. A method that accesses an object and returns some information about it, without changing the object, is called an *accessor* method. In contrast, a method whose purpose is to modify the state of an object is called a *mutator* method.

For example, the length method of the String class is an accessor method. It returns information about a string, namely its length. But it doesn't modify the string at all when counting the characters.

The Rectangle class has a number of accessor methods. The getX, getY, getWidth, and getHeight methods return the *x*- and *y*-coordinates of the top-left corner, the width, and the height values. For example,

```
double width = box.getWidth();
```

Now let us consider a mutator method. Programs that manipulate rectangles frequently need to move them around, for example, to display animations. The Rectangle class has a method for that purpose, called translate. (Mathematicians use the term "translation" for a rigid motion of the plane.) This method moves a rectangle by a certain distance in the *x*- and *y*-directions. The method call,

```
box.translate(15, 25);
```

moves the rectangle by 15 units in the *x*-direction and 25 units in the *y*-direction (see Figure 11). Moving a rectangle doesn't change its width or height, but it changes the top-left corner. Afterwards, the top-left corner is at (20, 35).

This method is a mutator because it modifies the implicit parameter object.

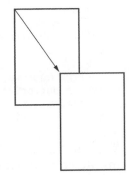

Figure 11
Using the `translate` Method to Move a Rectangle

18. Is the `toUpperCase` method of the `String` class an accessor or a mutator?
19. Which call to `translate` is needed to move the box rectangle so that its top-left corner is the origin (0, 0)?

2.8 Implementing a Test Program

In this section, we discuss the steps that are necessary to implement a test program. The purpose of a test program is to verify that one or more methods have been implemented correctly. A test program calls methods and checks that they return the expected results. Writing test programs is a very important activity. When you implement your own methods, you should always supply programs to test them.

In this book, we use a very simple format for test programs. You will now see such a test program that tests a method in the `Rectangle` class. The program performs the following steps:

1. Provide a tester class.
2. Supply a `main` method.
3. Inside the `main` method, construct one or more objects.
4. Apply methods to the objects.
5. Display the results of the method calls.
6. Display the values that you expect to get.

Whenever you write a program to test your own classes, you need to follow these steps as well.

Our sample test program tests the behavior of the `translate` method. Here are the key steps (which have been placed inside the `main` method of the `Rectangle-Tester` class).

```
Rectangle box = new Rectangle(5, 10, 20, 30);

// Move the rectangle
box.translate(15, 25);

// Print information about the moved rectangle
System.out.print("x: ");
System.out.println(box.getX());
System.out.println("Expected: 20");
```

We print the value that is returned by the getX method, and then we print a message that describes what value we expect to see.

> Determining the expected result in advance is an important part of testing.

This is a very important step. You want to spend some time thinking what the expected result is before you run a test program. This thought process will help you understand how your program should behave, and it can help you track down errors at an early stage.

In our case, the rectangle has been constructed with the top left corner at (5, 10). The *x*-direction is moved by 15 pixels, so we expect an *x*-value of 5 + 15 = 20 after the move.

Here is a complete program that tests the moving of a rectangle.

ch02/rectangle/MoveTester.java

```
1   import java.awt.Rectangle;
2
3   public class MoveTester
4   {
5      public static void main(String[] args)
6      {
7         Rectangle box = new Rectangle(5, 10, 20, 30);
8
9         // Move the rectangle
10        box.translate(15, 25);
11
12        // Print information about the moved rectangle
13        System.out.print("x: ");
14        System.out.println(box.getX());
15        System.out.println("Expected: 20");
16
17        System.out.print("y: ");
18        System.out.println(box.getY());
19        System.out.println("Expected: 35");
20     }
21  }
```

Output

```
x: 20
Expected: 20
y: 35
Expected: 35
```

Java classes are grouped into packages. Use the import statement to use classes that are defined in other packages.

For this program, we needed to carry out another step: We needed to *import* the Rectangle class from a *package*. A package is a collection of classes with a related purpose. All classes in the standard library are contained in packages. The Rectangle class belongs to the package java.awt (where awt is an abbreviation for "Abstract Windowing Toolkit"), which contains many classes for drawing windows and graphical shapes.

To use the Rectangle class from the java.awt package, simply place the following line at the top of your program:

```
import java.awt.Rectangle;
```

Why don't you have to import the System and String classes? Because the System and String classes are in the java.lang package, and all classes from this package are automatically imported, so you never need to import them yourself.

SYNTAX 2.4 Importing a Class from a Package

```
import packageName.ClassName;
```

Example:

```
import java.awt.Rectangle;
```

Purpose:

To import a class from a package for use in a program

SELF CHECK

20. Suppose we had called box.translate(25, 15) instead of box.translate(15, 25). What are the expected outputs?
21. Why doesn't the MoveTester program need to print the width and height of the rectangle?
22. The Random class is defined in the java.util package. What do you need to do in order to use that class in your program?

ADVANCED TOPIC 2.1

Testing Classes in an Interactive Environment

Some development environments are specifically designed to help students explore objects without having to provide tester classes. These environments can be very helpful for gaining insight into the behavior of objects, and for promoting object-oriented thinking. The BlueJ environment (shown in Testing a Method Call in BlueJ) displays objects as blobs on a workbench. You can construct new objects, put them on the workbench, invoke methods, and see the return values, all without writing a line of code. You can download BlueJ at no charge from [1]. Another excellent environment for interactively exploring objects is Dr. Java [2].

Testing a Method Call in BlueJ

2.9 The API Documentation

The classes and methods of the Java library are listed in the *API documentation*. The API is the "application programming interface". A programmer who uses the Java classes to put together a computer program (or *application*) is an *application programmer*. That's you. In contrast, the programmers who designed and implemented the library classes such as PrintStream and Rectangle are *system programmers*.

> The API (Application Programming Interface) documentation lists the classes and methods of the Java library.

You can find the API documentation on the Web [3]. Point your web browser to http://java.sun.com/javase/6/docs/api/index.html. Alternatively, you can download and install the API documentation onto your own computer—see Productivity Hint 2.1.

The API documentation documents all classes in the Java library—there are thousands of them (see Figure 12). Most of the classes are rather specialized, and only a few are of interest to the beginning programmer.

Locate the Rectangle link in the left pane, preferably by using the search function of your browser. Click on the link, and the right pane shows all the features of the Rectangle class (see Figure 13).

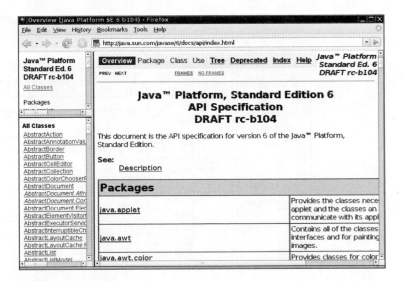

Figure 12   The API Documentation of the Standard Java Library

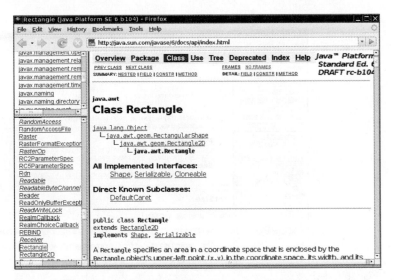

Figure 13   The API Documentation for the Rectangle Class

The API documentation for each class starts out with a section that describes the purpose of the class. Then come summary tables for the constructors and methods (see Figure 14). Click on the link of a method to get a detailed description (see Figure 15).

As you can see, the Rectangle class has quite a few methods. While occasionally intimidating for the beginning programmer, this is a strength of the standard library. If you ever need to do a computation involving rectangles, chances are that there is a method that does all the work for you.

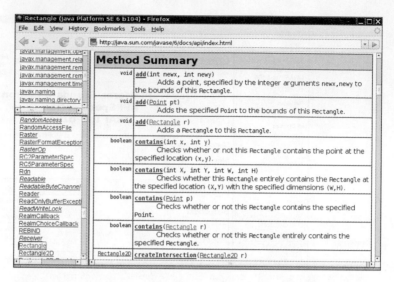

Figure 14   The Method Summary for the Rectangle Class

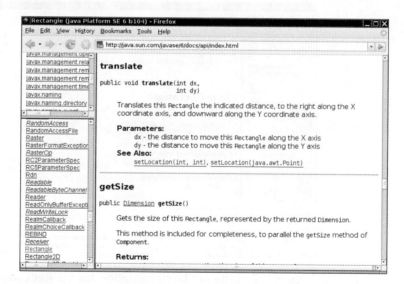

Figure 15   The API Documentation of the translate Method

Appendix C contains an abbreviated version of the API documentation. You may find the abbreviated documentation easier to use than the full documentation. It is fine if you rely on the abbreviated documentation for your first programs, but you should eventually move on to the real thing.

SELF CHECK

23. Look at the API documentation of the String class. Which method would you use to obtain the string "hello, world!" from the string "Hello, World!"?

24. In the API documentation of the String class, look at the description of the trim method. What is the result of applying trim to the string " Hello, Space ! "? (Note the spaces in the string.)

PRODUCTIVITY HINT 2.1

Don't Memorize—Use Online Help

The Java library has thousands of classes and methods. It is neither necessary nor useful trying to memorize them. Instead, you should become familiar with using the API documentation. Since you will need to use the API documentation all the time, it is best to download and install it onto your computer, particularly if your computer is not always connected to the Internet. You can download the documentation from http://java.sun.com/javase/downloads/index.html.

2.10 Object References

In Java, a variable whose type is a class does not actually hold an object. It merely holds the memory *location* of an object. The object itself is stored elsewhere—see Figure 16.

> An object reference describes the location of an object.

We use the technical term *object reference* to denote the memory location of an object. When a variable contains the memory location of an object, we say that it *refers* to an object. For example, after the statement

```
Rectangle box = new Rectangle(5, 10, 20, 30);
```

Figure 16 An Object Variable Containing an Object Reference

Figure 17   Two Object Variables Referring to the Same Object

Figure 18   A Number Variable Stores a Number

the variable box refers to the Rectangle object that the new operator constructed. Technically speaking, the new operator returned a reference to the new object, and that reference is stored in the box variable.

It is very important that you remember that the box variable *does not contain* the object. It *refers* to the object. You can have two object variables refer to the same object:

```
Rectangle box2 = box;
```

> Multiple object variables can contain references to the same object.

Now you can access the same Rectangle object both as box and as box2, as shown in Figure 17.

However, number variables actually store numbers. When you define

```
int luckyNumber = 13;
```

then the luckyNumber variable holds the number 13, not a reference to the number (see Figure 18).

> Number variables store numbers. Object variables store references.

You can see the difference between number variables and object variables when you make a copy of a variable. When you copy a primitive type value, the original and the copy of the number are independent values. But when you copy an object reference, both the original and the copy are references to the same object.

Consider the following code, which copies a number and then changes the copy (see Figure 19):

```
int luckyNumber = 13;        ❶
int luckyNumber2 = luckyNumber;  ❷
luckyNumber2 = 12;           ❸
```

Now the variable luckyNumber contains the value 13, and luckyNumber2 contains 12. Now consider the seemingly analogous code with Rectangle objects.

```
Rectangle box = new Rectangle(5, 10, 20, 30);  ❶
Rectangle box2 = box; // See Figure 20    ❷
box2.translate(15, 25);      ❸
```

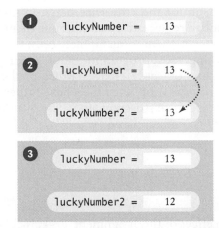

Figure 19
Copying Numbers

Since box and box2 refer to the same rectangle after step ②, both variables refer to the moved rectangle after the call to the translate method.

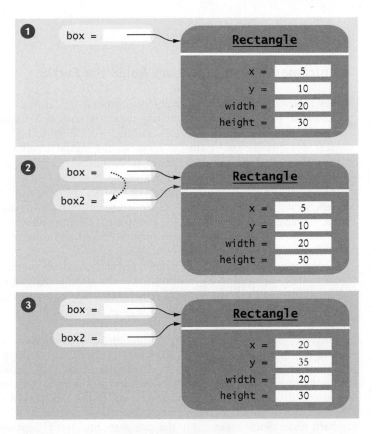

Figure 20   Copying Object References

There is a reason for the difference between numbers and objects. In the computer, each number requires a small amount of memory. But objects can be very large. It is far more efficient to manipulate only the memory location.

Frankly speaking, most programmers don't worry too much about the difference between objects and object references. Much of the time, you will have the correct intuition when you think of "the object box" rather than the technically more accurate "the object reference stored in box". The difference between objects and object references only becomes apparent when you have multiple variables that refer to the same object.

SELF CHECK

25. What is the effect of the assignment greeting2 = greeting?
26. After calling greeting2.toUpperCase(), what are the contents of greeting and greeting2?

RANDOM FACT 2.1

Mainframes—When Dinosaurs Ruled the Earth

When International Business Machines Corporation (IBM), a successful manufacturer of punched-card equipment for tabulating data, first turned its attention to designing computers in the early 1950s, its planners assumed that there was a market for perhaps 50 such devices, for installation by the government, the military, and a few of the country's largest corporations. Instead, they sold about 1,500 machines of their System 650 model and went on to build and sell more powerful computers.

The so-called mainframe computers of the 1950s, 1960s, and 1970s were huge. They filled rooms, which had to be climate-controlled to protect the delicate equipment (see A Mainframe Computer). Today, because of miniaturization technology, even mainframes are getting smaller, but they are still very expensive. (At the time of this writing, the cost for a typical mainframe is several million dollars.)

These huge and expensive systems were an immediate success when they first appeared, because they replaced many roomfuls of even more expensive employees, who had previously performed the tasks by hand. Few of these computers do any exciting computations. They keep mundane information, such as billing records or airline reservations; they just keep lots of them.

IBM was not the first company to build mainframe computers; that honor belongs to the Univac Corporation. However, IBM soon became the major player, partially because of technical excellence and attention to customer needs and partially because it exploited its strengths and structured its products and services in a way that made it difficult for customers to mix them with those of other vendors. In the 1960s, IBM's competitors, the so-called "Seven Dwarfs"—GE, RCA, Univac, Honeywell, Burroughs, Control Data, and NCR—fell on hard times. Some went out of the computer business altogether, while others tried unsuccessfully to combine their strengths by merging their computer operations. It was generally

A Mainframe Computer

predicted that they would eventually all fail. It was in this atmosphere that the U.S. government brought an antitrust suit against IBM in 1969. The suit went to trial in 1975 and dragged on until 1982, when the Reagan Administration abandoned it, declaring it "without merit".

Of course, by then the computing landscape had changed completely. Just as the dinosaurs gave way to smaller, nimbler creatures, three new waves of computers had appeared: the minicomputers, workstations, and microcomputers, all engineered by new companies, not the Seven Dwarfs. Today, the importance of mainframes in the marketplace has diminished, and IBM, while still a large and resourceful company, no longer dominates the computer market.

Mainframes are still in use today for two reasons. They still excel at handling large data volumes. More importantly, the programs that control the business data have been refined over the last 30 or more years, fixing one problem at a time. Moving these programs to less expensive computers, with different languages and operating systems, is difficult and error-prone. In the 1990s, Sun Microsystems, a leading manufacturer of workstations and servers—and the inventor of Java—was eager to prove that its mainframe system could be "downsized" and replaced by its own equipment. Sun eventually succeeded, but it took over five years—far longer than it expected.

2.11 Graphical Applications and Frame Windows

This is the first of several sections that teach you how to write *graphical applications*: applications that display drawings inside a window. Graphical applications look more attractive than the console applications that show plain text in a console window.

The material in this section, as well as the sections labeled "Graphics Track" in other chapters, are entirely optional. Feel free to skip them if you are not interested in drawing graphics.

> To show a frame, construct a JFrame object, set its size, and make it visible.

A graphical application shows information inside a frame window: a window with a title bar, as shown in Figure 21. In this section, you will learn how to display a frame window. In Section 3.9, you will learn how to create a drawing inside the frame.

To show a frame, carry out the following steps:

1. Construct an object of the JFrame class:

   ```
   JFrame frame = new JFrame();
   ```

2. Set the size of the frame

   ```
   frame.setSize(300, 400);
   ```

   This frame will be 300 pixels wide and 400 pixels tall. If you omit this step the frame will be 0 by 0 pixels, and you won't be able to see it.

3. If you'd like, set the title of the frame.

   ```
   frame.setTitle("An Empty Frame");
   ```

   If you omit this step, the title bar is simply left blank.

4. Set the "default close operation":

   ```
   frame.setDefaultCloseOperation(JFrame.EXIT_ON_CLOSE);
   ```

Figure 21   A Frame Window

When the user closes the frame, the program automatically exits. Don't omit this step. If you do, the program continues running even after the frame is closed.

5. Make the frame visible.

```
frame.setVisible(true);
```

The simple program below shows all of these steps. It produces the empty frame shown in Figure 21.

The JFrame class is a part of the javax.swing package. Swing is the nickname for the graphical user interface library in Java. The "x" in javax denotes the fact that Swing started out as a Java *extension* before it was added to the standard library.

We will go into much greater detail about Swing programming in Chapters 3, 9, 10, and 18. For now, consider this program to be the essential plumbing that is required to show a frame.

ch02/emptyframe/EmptyFrameViewer.java

```
1  import javax.swing.JFrame;
2
3  public class EmptyFrameViewer
4  {
5     public static void main(String[] args)
6     {
7        JFrame frame = new JFrame();
8
9        frame.setSize(300, 400);
10       frame.setTitle("An Empty Frame");
11       frame.setDefaultCloseOperation(JFrame.EXIT_ON_CLOSE);
12
13       frame.setVisible(true);
14    }
15 }
```

SELF CHECK

27. How do you display a square frame with a title bar that reads "Hello, World!"?
28. How can a program display two frames at once?

2.12 Drawing on a Component

This section continues the optional graphics track. You will learn how to make shapes appear inside a frame window. The first drawing will be exceedingly modest: just two rectangles (see Figure 22). You'll soon see how to produce more interesting drawings. The purpose of this example is to show you the basic outline of a program that creates a drawing. You cannot draw directly onto a frame. Whenever you want to show anything inside a frame, be it a button or a drawing, you have to

Figure 22
Drawing Rectangles

construct a *component* object and add it to the frame. In the Swing toolkit, the JComponent class represents a blank component.

Since we don't want to add a blank component, we have to modify the JComponent class and specify how the component should be painted. The solution is to define a new class that extends the JComponent class. You will learn about the process of extending classes in Chapter 10. For now, simply use the following code as a template.

> In order to display a drawing in a frame, define a class that extends the JComponent class.

```
public class RectangleComponent extends JComponent
{
    public void paintComponent(Graphics g)
    {
        Drawing instructions go here
    }
}
```

The extends keyword indicates that our component class, RectangleComponent, inherits the methods of JComponent. However, the RectangleComponent is different from the plain JComponent in one respect: The paintComponent method will contain instructions to draw the rectangles.

> Place drawing instructions inside the paintComponent method. That method is called whenever the component needs to be repainted.

When the window is shown for the first time, the paintComponent method is called automatically. The method is also called when the window is resized, or when it is shown again after it was hidden.

The paintComponent method receives an object of type Graphics. The Graphics object stores the graphics state—the current color, font, and so on, that are used for drawing operations.

> The Graphics class lets you manipulate the graphics state (such as the current color).

However, the Graphics class is primitive. When programmers clamored for a more object-oriented approach for drawing graphics, the designers of Java created the Graphics2D class, which extends the

The Graphics2D class has methods to draw shape objects.

Use a cast to recover the Graphics2D object from the Graphics parameter of the paintComponent method.

Graphics class. Whenever the Swing toolkit calls the paintComponent method, it actually passes a parameter of type Graphics2D. Programs with simple graphics do not need this feature. Because we want to use the more sophisticated methods to draw two-dimensional graphics objects, we need to recover the Graphics2D. This is accomplished by using a *cast*:

```java
public class RectangleComponent extends JComponent
{
   public void paintComponent(Graphics g)
   {
      // Recover Graphics2D
      Graphics2D g2 = (Graphics2D) g;
      . . .
   }
}
```

Now you are ready to draw shapes. The draw method of the Graphics2D class can draw shapes, such as rectangles, ellipses, line segments, polygons, and arcs. Here we draw a rectangle:

```java
public class RectangleComponent extends JComponent
{
   public void paintComponent(Graphics g)
   {
      . . .
      Rectangle box = new Rectangle(5, 10, 20, 30);
      g2.draw(box);
      . . .
   }
}
```

Following is the source code for the RectangleComponent class. Note that the paintComponent method of the RectangleComponent class draws two rectangles.

As you can see from the import statements, the Graphics and Graphics2D classes are part of the java.awt package.

ch02/rectangles/RectangleComponent.java

```java
1  import java.awt.Graphics;
2  import java.awt.Graphics2D;
3  import java.awt.Rectangle;
4  import javax.swing.JComponent;
5
6  /**
7     A component that draws two rectangles.
8  */
9  public class RectangleComponent extends JComponent
10 {
11    public void paintComponent(Graphics g)
12    {
13       // Recover Graphics2D
14       Graphics2D g2 = (Graphics2D) g;
15
```

```
16          // Construct a rectangle and draw it
17          Rectangle box = new Rectangle(5, 10, 20, 30);
18          g2.draw(box);
19
20          // Move rectangle 15 units to the right and 25 units down
21          box.translate(15, 25);
22
23          // Draw moved rectangle
24          g2.draw(box);
25       }
26   }
```

In order to see the drawing, one task remains. You need to display the frame into which you added a component object. Follow these steps:

1. Construct a frame as described in the preceding section.

2. Construct an object of your component class:

   ```
   RectangleComponent component = new RectangleComponent();
   ```

3. Add the component to the frame:

   ```
   frame.add(component);
   ```

4. Make the frame visible, as described in the preceding section.

The following listing shows the complete process.

ch02/rectangles/RectangleViewer.java

```
1   import javax.swing.JFrame;
2
3   public class RectangleViewer
4   {
5      public static void main(String[] args)
6      {
7         JFrame frame = new JFrame();
8         frame.setSize(300, 400);
9         frame.setTitle("Two rectangles");
10        frame.setDefaultCloseOperation(JFrame.EXIT_ON_CLOSE);
11
12        RectangleComponent component = new RectangleComponent();
13        frame.add(component);
14
15        frame.setVisible(true);
16     }
17   }
```

Note that the rectangle drawing program consists of two classes:

- The RectangleComponent class, whose paintComponent method produces the drawing

- The RectangleViewer class, whose main method constructs a frame and a RectangleComponent, adds the component to the frame, and makes the frame visible

SELF CHECK

29. How do you modify the program to draw two squares?
30. How do you modify the program to draw one rectangle and one square?
31. What happens if you call g.draw(box) instead of g2.draw(box)?

ADVANCED TOPIC 2.2

Applets

> Applets are programs that run inside a web browser.

In the preceding section, you learned how to write a program that displays graphical shapes. Some people prefer to use applets for learning about graphics programming. Applets have two advantages. They don't need separate component and viewer classes; you only implement a single class. And, more importantly, applets run inside a web browser, allowing you to place your creations on a web page for all the world to admire.

To implement an applet, use this code outline:

```
public class MyApplet extends JApplet
{
    public void paint(Graphics g)
    {
        // Recover Graphics2D
        Graphics2D g2 = (Graphics2D) g;

        // Drawing instructions go here
        . . .
    }
}
```

This is almost the same outline as for a component, with two minor differences:

1. You extend JApplet, not JComponent.
2. You place the drawing code inside the paint method, not inside paintComponent.

The following applet draws two rectangles:

ch02/applet/RectangleApplet.java

```
1  import java.awt.Graphics;
2  import java.awt.Graphics2D;
3  import java.awt.Rectangle;
4  import javax.swing.JApplet;
5
6  /**
7      An applet that draws two rectangles.
8  */
9  public class RectangleApplet extends JApplet
10 {
11     public void paint(Graphics g)
12     {
```

```
13        // Prepare for extended graphics
14        Graphics2D g2 = (Graphics2D) g;
15
16        // Construct a rectangle and draw it
17        Rectangle box = new Rectangle(5, 10, 20, 30);
18        g2.draw(box);
19
20        // Move rectangle 15 units to the right and 25 units down
21        box.translate(15, 25);
22
23        // Draw moved rectangle
24        g2.draw(box);
25     }
26  }
```

> To run an applet, you need an HTML file with the applet tag.

To run this applet, you need an HTML file with an `applet` tag. HTML, the hypertext markup language, is the language used to describe web pages. (See Appendix H for more information on HTML.) Here is the simplest possible file to display the rectangle applet:

ch02/applet/RectangleApplet.html

```
1  <applet code="RectangleApplet.class" width="300" height="400">
2  </applet>
```

If you know HTML, you can proudly explain your creation, by adding text and more HTML tags:

ch02/applet/RectangleAppletExplained.html

```
1  <html>
2     <head>
3        <title>Two rectangles</title>
4     </head>
5     <body>
6        <p>Here is my <i>first applet</i>:</p>
7        <applet code="RectangleApplet.class" width="300" height="400">
8        </applet>
9     </body>
10  </html>
```

An HTML file can have multiple applets. Simply add a separate `applet` tag for each applet.

You can give the HTML file any name you like. It is easiest to give the HTML file the same name as the applet. But some development environments already generate an HTML file with the same name as your project to hold your project notes; then you must give the HTML file containing your applet a different name.

To run the applet, you have two choices. You can use the applet viewer, a program that is included with the Java Software Development Kit from Sun Microsystems. You simply start the applet viewer, giving it the name of the HTML file that contains your applets:

```
appletviewer RectangleApplet.html
```

An Applet in the Applet Viewer   An Applet in a Web Browser

> You view applets with the applet viewer or a Java-enabled browser.

The applet viewer only shows the applet, not the HTML text (see An Applet in the Applet Viewer).

You can also show the applet inside any Java 2–enabled web browser, such as Netscape or Mozilla. (If you use Internet Explorer, you probably need to configure it. By default, Microsoft supplies either an outdated version of Java or no Java at all. Go to the web site [4] and install the Java plugin.) An Applet in a Web Browser shows the applet running in a browser. As you can see, both the text and the applet are displayed.

2.13 Ellipses, Lines, Text, and Color

In Section 2.12 you learned how to write a program that draws rectangles. In this section you will learn how to draw other shapes: ellipses and lines. With these graphical elements, you can draw quite a few interesting pictures.

To draw an ellipse, you specify its bounding box (see Figure 23) in the same way that you would specify a rectangle, namely by the x- and y-coordinates of the top-left corner and the width and height of the box.

However, there is no simple Ellipse class that you can use. Instead, you must use one of the two classes Ellipse2D.Float and Ellipse2D.Double, depending on whether you want to store the ellipse coordinates as single- or double-precision

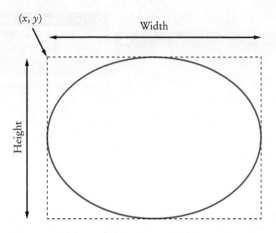

Figure 23   An Ellipse and Its Bounding Box

floating-point values. Because the latter are more convenient to use in Java, we will always use the `Ellipse2D.Double` class. Here is how you construct an ellipse:

```
Ellipse2D.Double ellipse = new Ellipse2D.Double(x, y, width, height);
```

> Ellipse2D.Double and Line2D.Double are classes that describe graphical shapes.

The class name `Ellipse2D.Double` looks different from the class names that you have encountered up to now. It consists of two class names `Ellipse2D` and `Double` separated by a period (.). This indicates that `Ellipse2D.Double` is a so-called *inner class* inside `Ellipse2D`. When constructing and using ellipses, you don't actually need to worry about the fact that `Ellipse2D.Double` is an inner class—just think of it as a class with a long name. However, in the `import` statement at the top of your program, you must be careful that you import only the outer class:

```
import java.awt.geom.Ellipse2D;
```

Drawing an ellipse is easy: Use exactly the same `draw` method of the `Graphics2D` class that you used for drawing rectangles.

```
g2.draw(ellipse);
```

To draw a circle, simply set the width and height to the same values:

```
Ellipse2D.Double circle = new Ellipse2D.Double(x, y, diameter, diameter);
g2.draw(circle);
```

Figure 24   Basepoint and Baseline

Notice that (x, y) is the top-left corner of the bounding box, not the center of the circle.

To draw a line, use an object of the `Line2D.Double` class. A line is constructed by specifying its two end points. You can do this in two ways. Simply give the *x*- and *y*-coordinates of both end points:

```
Line2D.Double segment = new Line2D.Double(x1, y1, x2, y2);
```

Or specify each end point as an object of the `Point2D.Double` class:

```
Point2D.Double from = new Point2D.Double(x1, y1);
Point2D.Double to = new Point2D.Double(x2, y2);

Line2D.Double segment = new Line2D.Double(from, to);
```

The second option is more object-oriented and is often more useful, particularly if the point objects can be reused elsewhere in the same drawing.

> The drawString method draws a string, starting at its basepoint.

You often want to put text inside a drawing, for example, to label some of the parts. Use the `drawString` method of the `Graphics2D` class to draw a string anywhere in a window. You must specify the string and the *x*- and *y*-coordinates of the basepoint of the first character in the string (see Figure 24). For example,

```
g2.drawString("Message", 50, 100);
```

2.13.1 Colors

When you first start drawing, all shapes and strings are drawn with a black pen. To change the color, you need to supply an object of type `Color`. Java uses the RGB color model. That is, you specify a color by the amounts of the primary colors—red, green, and blue—that make up the color. The amounts are given as integers between 0 (primary color not present) and 255 (maximum amount present). For example,

```
Color magenta = new Color(255, 0, 255);
```

constructs a `Color` object with maximum red, no green, and maximum blue, yielding a bright purple color called magenta.

> When you set a new color in the graphics context, it is used for subsequent drawing operations.

For your convenience, a variety of colors have been predefined in the `Color` class. Table 1 shows those predefined colors and their RGB values. For example, `Color.PINK` has been predefined to be the same color as new `Color(255, 175, 175)`.

To draw a rectangle in a different color, first set the color of the `Graphics2D` object, then call the `draw` method:

```
g2.setColor(Color.RED);
g2.draw(circle); // draws the shape in red
```

If you want to color the inside of the shape, use the `fill` method instead of the `draw` method. For example,

```
g2.fill(circle);
```

fills the inside of the circle with the current color.

Table 1 Predefined Colors and Their RGB Values	
Color	**RGB Value**
Color.BLACK	0, 0, 0
Color.BLUE	0, 0, 255
Color.CYAN	0, 255, 255
Color.GRAY	128, 128, 128
Color.DARKGRAY	64, 64, 64
Color.LIGHTGRAY	192, 192, 192
Color.GREEN	0, 255, 0
Color.MAGENTA	255, 0, 255
Color.ORANGE	255, 200, 0
Color.PINK	255, 175, 175
Color.RED	255, 0, 0
Color.WHITE	255, 255, 255
Color.YELLOW	255, 255, 0

The following program puts all these shapes to work, creating a simple drawing (see Figure 25).

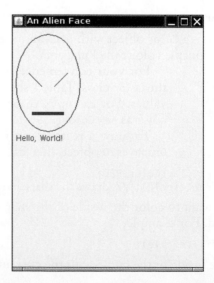

Figure 25   An Alien Face

ch02/faceviewer/FaceComponent.java

```java
1  import java.awt.Color;
2  import java.awt.Graphics;
3  import java.awt.Graphics2D;
4  import java.awt.Rectangle;
5  import java.awt.geom.Ellipse2D;
6  import java.awt.geom.Line2D;
7  import javax.swing.JPanel;
8  import javax.swing.JComponent;
9
10 /**
11    A component that draws an alien face.
12 */
13 public class FaceComponent extends JComponent
14 {
15    public void paintComponent(Graphics g)
16    {
17       // Recover Graphics2D
18       Graphics2D g2 = (Graphics2D) g;
19
20       // Draw the head
21       Ellipse2D.Double head = new Ellipse2D.Double(5, 10, 100, 150);
22       g2.draw(head);
23
24       // Draw the eyes
25       Line2D.Double eye1 = new Line2D.Double(25, 70, 45, 90);
26       g2.draw(eye1);
27
28       Line2D.Double eye2 = new Line2D.Double(85, 70, 65, 90);
29       g2.draw(eye2);
30
31       // Draw the mouth
32       Rectangle mouth = new Rectangle(30, 130, 50, 5);
33       g2.setColor(Color.RED);
34       g2.fill(mouth);
35
36       // Draw the greeting
37       g2.setColor(Color.BLUE);
38       g2.drawString("Hello, World!", 5, 175);
39    }
40 }
```

ch02/faceviewer/FaceViewer.java

```java
1  import javax.swing.JFrame;
2
3  public class FaceViewer
4  {
5     public static void main(String[] args)
6     {
7        JFrame frame = new JFrame();
8        frame.setSize(300, 400);
9        frame.setTitle("An Alien Face");
10       frame.setDefaultCloseOperation(JFrame.EXIT_ON_CLOSE);
```

```
11
12          FaceComponent component = new FaceComponent();
13          frame.add(component);
14
15          frame.setVisible(true);
16       }
17  }
```

SELF CHECK

32. Give instructions to draw a circle with center (100, 100) and radius 25.

33. Give instructions to draw a letter "V" by drawing two line segments.

34. Give instructions to draw a string consisting of the letter "V".

35. What are the RGB color values of Color.BLUE?

36. How do you draw a yellow square on a red background?

RANDOM FACT 2.2

The Evolution of the Internet

In 1962, J.C.R. Licklider was head of the first computer research program at DARPA, the Defense Advanced Research Projects Agency. He wrote a series of papers describing a "galactic network" through which computer users could access data and programs from other sites. This was well before computer networks were invented. By 1969, four computers—three in California and one in Utah—were connected to the ARPANET, the precursor of the Internet. The network grew quickly, linking computers at many universities and research organizations. It was originally thought that most network users wanted to run programs on remote computers. Using remote execution, a researcher at one institution would be able to access an underutilized computer at a different site. It quickly became apparent that remote execution was not what the network was actually used for. Instead, the "killer application" was electronic mail: the transfer of messages between computer users at different locations.

In 1972, Bob Kahn proposed to extend ARPANET into the *Internet:* a collection of interoperable networks. All networks on the Internet share common *protocols* for data transmission. Kahn and Vinton Cerf developed protocols, now called TCP/IP (Transmission Control Protocol/Internet Protocol). On January 1, 1983, all hosts on the Internet simultaneously switched to the TCP/IP protocol (which is used to this day).

Over time, researchers, computer scientists, and hobbyists published increasing amounts of information on the Internet. For example, the GNU (GNU's Not UNIX) project is producing a free set of high-quality operating system utilities and program development tools [5]. Project Gutenberg makes available the text of important classical books, whose copyright has expired, in computer-readable form [6]. In 1989, Tim Berners-Lee started work on hyperlinked documents, allowing users to browse by following links to related documents. This infrastructure is now known as the World Wide Web (WWW).

The first interfaces to retrieve this information were, by today's standards, unbelievably clumsy and hard to use. In March 1993, WWW traffic was 0.1% of all Internet traffic. All that changed when Marc Andreesen, then a graduate student working for NCSA (the National Center for Supercomputing Applications), released Mosaic. Mosaic displayed web pages in graphical form, using images, fonts, and colors (see The NCSA Mosaic Browser figure). Andreesen went on to fame and fortune at Netscape, and Microsoft licensed the Mosaic code to create Internet Explorer. By 1996, WWW traffic accounted for more than half of the data transported on the Internet.

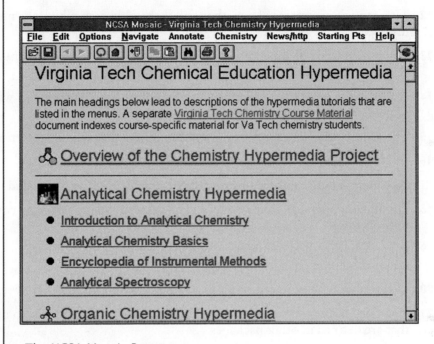

The NCSA Mosaic Browser

CHAPTER SUMMARY

1. In Java, every value has a type.

2. You use variables to store values that you want to use at a later time.

3. Identifiers for variables, methods, and classes are composed of letters, digits, and underscore characters.

4. By convention, variable names should start with a lowercase letter.

5. Use the assignment operator (=) to change the value of a variable.

6. All variables must be initialized before you access them.

7. Objects are entities in your program that you manipulate by calling methods.

8. A method is a sequence of instructions that accesses the data of an object.

9. A class defines the methods that you can apply to its objects.

10. The public interface of a class specifies what you can do with its objects. The hidden implementation describes how these actions are carried out.

11. A parameter is an input to a method.

12. The implicit parameter of a method call is the object on which the method is invoked.

13. The return value of a method is a result that the method has computed for use by the code that called it.

14. A method name is overloaded if a class has more than one method with the same name (but different parameter types).

15. The double type denotes floating-point numbers that can have fractional parts.

16. In Java, numbers are not objects and number types are not classes.

17. Numbers can be combined by arithmetic operators such as +, -, and *.

18. Use the new operator, followed by a class name and parameters, to construct new objects.

19. An accessor method does not change the state of its implicit parameter. A mutator method changes the state.

20. Determining the expected result in advance is an important part of testing.

21. Java classes are grouped into packages. Use the import statement to use classes that are defined in other packages.

22. The API (Application Programming Interface) documentation lists the classes and methods of the Java library.

23. An object reference describes the location of an object.

24. Multiple object variables can contain references to the same object.

25. Number variables store numbers. Object variables store references.

26. To show a frame, construct a JFrame object, set its size, and make it visible.

27. In order to display a drawing in a frame, define a class that extends the JComponent class.

28. Place drawing instructions inside the paintComponent method. That method is called whenever the component needs to be repainted.

29. The Graphics class lets you manipulate the graphics state (such as the current color).

30. The Graphics2D class has methods to draw shape objects.

31. Use a cast to recover the `Graphics2D` object from the `Graphics` parameter of the `paintComponent` method.

32. Applets are programs that run inside a web browser.

33. To run an applet, you need an HTML file with the applet tag.

34. You view applets with the applet viewer or a Java-enabled browser.

35. `Ellipse2D.Double` and `Line2D.Double` are classes that describe graphical shapes.

36. The `drawString` method draws a string, starting at its basepoint.

37. When you set a new color in the graphics context, it is used for subsequent drawing operations.

FURTHER READING

1. `http://www.bluej.org`   The BlueJ development environment.

2. `http://drjava.sourceforge.net`   The Dr. Java development environment.

3. `http://java.sun.com/javase/6/docs/api/index.html`   The documentation of the Java API.

4. `http://java.com`   The consumer-oriented web site for Java technology. Download the Java plugin from this site.

5. `http://www.gnu.org`   The web site of the GNU project.

6. `http://www.gutenberg.org`   The web site of Project Gutenberg, offering the text of classical books.

CLASSES, OBJECTS, AND METHODS INTRODUCED IN THIS CHAPTER

```
java.awt.Color                  java.awt.Graphics2D         java.lang.String
java.awt.Component                 draw                        length
   getHeight                       drawString                  replace
   getWidth                        fill                        toLowerCase
   setSize                      java.awt.Rectangle             toUpperCase
   setVisible                      translate                javax.swing.JComponent
java.awt.Frame                     getX                        paintComponent
   setTitle                        getY                     javax.swing.JFrame
java.awt.geom.Ellipse2D.Double     getHeight                   setDefaultCloseOperation
java.awt.geom.Line2D.Double        getWidth
java.awt.geom.Point2D.Double
java.awt.Graphics
   setColor
```

REVIEW EXERCISES

★   **Exercise R2.1.** Explain the difference between an object and an object reference.

★   **Exercise R2.2.** Explain the difference between an object and an object variable.

★   **Exercise R2.3.** Explain the difference between an object and a class.

★★ **Exercise R2.4.** Give the Java code for constructing an *object* of class Rectangle, and for declaring an *object variable* of class Rectangle.

★★ **Exercise R2.5.** Explain the difference between the = symbol in Java and in mathematics.

★★★ **Exercise R2.6.** Uninitialized variables can be a serious problem. Should you always initialize every int or double variable with zero? Explain the advantages and disadvantages of such a strategy.

★★ **Exercise R2.7.** Give Java code to construct the following objects:
   a. A rectangle with center (100, 100) and all side lengths equal to 50
   b. A string "Hello, Dave!"
Create objects, not object variables.

★★ **Exercise R2.8.** Repeat Exercise R2.7, but now define object variables that are initialized with the required objects.

★★ **Exercise R2.9.** Find the errors in the following statements:
   a. Rectangle r = (5, 10, 15, 20);
   b. double width = Rectangle(5, 10, 15, 20).getWidth();
   c. Rectangle r;
       r.translate(15, 25);
   d. r = new Rectangle();
       r.translate("far, far away!");

★   **Exercise R2.10.** Name two accessor methods and two mutator methods of the Rectangle class.

★★ **Exercise R2.11.** Look into the API documentation of the Rectangle class and locate the method

```
void add(int newx, int newy)
```

Read through the method documentation. Then determine the result of the following statements:

```
Rectangle box = new Rectangle(5, 10, 20, 30);
box.add(0, 0);
```

If you are not sure, write a small test program or use BlueJ.

★ **Exercise R2.12.** Find an overloaded method of the String class.

★ **Exercise R2.13.** Find an overloaded method of the Rectangle class.

★G **Exercise R2.14.** What is the difference between a console application and a graphical application?

★★G **Exercise R2.15.** Who calls the paintComponent method of a component? When does the call to the paintComponent method occur?

★★G **Exercise R2.16.** Why does the parameter of the paintComponent method have type Graphics and not Graphics2D?

★★G **Exercise R2.17.** What is the purpose of a graphics context?

★★G **Exercise R2.18.** Why are separate viewer and component classes used for graphical programs?

★G **Exercise R2.19.** How do you specify a text color?

Additional review exercises are available in WileyPLUS.

PROGRAMMING EXERCISES

★T **Exercise P2.1.** Write an AreaTester program that constructs a Rectangle object and then computes and prints its area. Use the getWidth and getHeight methods. Also print the expected answer.

★T **Exercise P2.2.** Write a PerimeterTester program that constructs a Rectangle object and then computes and prints its perimeter. Use the getWidth and getHeight methods. Also print the expected answer.

★★ **Exercise P2.3.** Write a program called FourRectanglePrinter that constructs a Rectangle object, prints its location by calling System.out.println(box), and then translates and prints it three more times, so that, if the rectangles were drawn, they would form one large rectangle:

★★★   **Exercise P2.4.** The `intersection` method computes the *intersection* of two rectangles—that is, the rectangle that is formed by two overlapping rectangles:

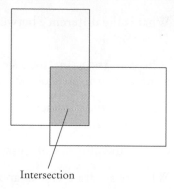

Intersection

You call this method as follows:

```
Rectangle r3 = r1.intersection(r2);
```

Write a program `IntersectionPrinter` that constructs two rectangle objects, prints them, and then prints the rectangle object that describes the intersection. Then the program should print the result of the `intersection` method when the rectangles do not overlap. Add a comment to your program that explains how you can tell whether the resulting rectangle is empty.

★★   **Exercise P2.5.** In the Java library, a color is specified by its red, green, and blue components between 0 and 255. Write a program `BrighterDemo` that constructs a `Color` object with red, green, and blue values of 50, 100, and 150. Then apply the `brighter` method and print the red, green, and blue values of the resulting color. (You won't actually see the color—see Section 2.13 on how to display the color.)

★★   **Exercise P2.6.** Repeat Exercise P2.5, but apply the `darker` method twice to the predefined object `Color.RED`. Call your class `DarkerDemo`.

★★   **Exercise P2.7.** The `Random` class implements a *random number generator*, which produces sequences of numbers that appear to be random. To generate random integers, you construct an object of the `Random` class, and then apply the `nextInt` method. For example, the call `generator.nextInt(6)` gives you a random number between 0 and 5.

Write a program `DieSimulator` that uses the `Random` class to simulate the cast of a die, printing a random number between 1 and 6 every time that the program is run.

★★★   **Exercise P2.8.** Write a program `LotteryPrinter` that picks a combination in a lottery. In this lottery, players can choose 6 numbers (possibly repeated) between 1 and 49. (In a real lottery, repetitions aren't allowed, but we haven't yet discussed the programming constructs that would be required to deal with that problem.) Your program should print out a sentence such as "Play this combination—it'll make you rich!", followed by a lottery combination.

★★T **Exercise P2.9.** Write a program `ReplaceTester` that encodes a string by replacing all letters "i" with "!" and all letters "s" with "$". Use the `replace` method. Demonstrate that you can correctly encode the string "Mississippi". Print both the actual and expected result.

★★★ **Exercise P2.10.** Write a program `HollePrinter` that switches the letters "e" and "o" in a string. Use the `replace` method repeatedly. Demonstrate that the string "Hello, World!" turns into "Holle, Werld!"

★★G **Exercise P2.11.** Write a graphics program that draws your name in red, contained inside a blue rectangle. Provide a class `NameViewer` and a class `NameComponent`.

★★G **Exercise P2.12.** Write a graphics program that draws 12 strings, one each for the 12 standard colors, besides `Color.WHITE`, each in its own color. Provide a class `ColorNameViewer` and a class `ColorNameComponent`.

★★G **Exercise P2.13.** Write a program that draws two solid squares: one in pink and one in purple. Use a standard color for one of them and a custom color for the other. Provide a class `TwoSquareViewer` and a class `TwoSquareComponent`.

★★★G **Exercise P2.14.** Write a program that fills the window with a large ellipse, with a black outline and filled with your favorite color. The ellipse should touch the window boundaries, even if the window is resized.

★★G **Exercise P2.15.** Write a program to plot the following face.

Provide a class `FaceViewer` and a class `FaceComponent`.

Additional programming exercises are available in WileyPLUS.

PROGRAMMING PROJECTS

★★★ **Project 2.1.** The `GregorianCalendar` class describes a point in time, as measured by the Gregorian calendar, the standard calendar that is commonly used throughout the world today. You construct a `GregorianCalendar` object from a year, month, and day of the month, like this:

```
GregorianCalendar cal = new GregorianCalendar(); // Today's date
GregorianCalendar eckertsBirthday = new GregorianCalendar(1919,
    Calendar.APRIL, 9);
```

Use constants `Calendar.JANUARY` . . . `Calendar.DECEMBER` to specify the month.

The add method can be used to add a number of days to a `GregorianCalendar` object:

```
cal.add(Calendar.DAY_OF_MONTH, 10); // Now cal is ten days from today
```

This is a mutator method—it changes the cal object.

The get method can be used to query a given GregorianCalendar object:

```
int dayOfMonth = cal.get(Calendar.DAY_OF_MONTH);
int month = cal.get(Calendar.MONTH);
int year = cal.get(Calendar.YEAR);
int weekday = cal.get(Calendar.DAY_OF_WEEK);
    // 1 is Sunday, 2 is Monday, ... , 7 is Saturday
```

Your task is to write a program that prints the following information:

- The date and weekday that is 100 days from today
- The weekday of your birthday
- The date that is 10,000 days from your birthday

Use the birthday of a computer scientist if you don't want to reveal your own birthday.

★★★G   **Project 2.2.** Run the following program:

```
import java.awt.Color;
import javax.swing.JFrame;
import javax.swing.JTextField;

public class FrameTester
{
    public static void main(String[] args)
    {
        JFrame frame = new JFrame();
        frame.setSize(200, 200);
        JTextField text = new JTextField("Hello, World!");
        text.setBackground(Color.PINK);
        frame.add(text);
        frame.setDefaultCloseOperation(JFrame.EXIT_ON_CLOSE);
        frame.setVisible(true);
    }
}
```

Modify the program as follows:

- Double the frame size
- Change the greeting to "Hello, *your name*!"
- Change the background color to pale green (see Exercise P2.5)

ANSWERS TO SELF-CHECK QUESTIONS

1. `int` and `String`
2. Only the first two are legal identifiers.
3. `String myName = "John Q. Public";`
4. No, the left-hand side of the = operator must be a variable.
5. `greeting = "Hello, Nina!";`
   Note that
   `String greeting = "Hello, Nina!";`
   is not the right answer—that statement defines a new variable.
6. `river.length()` or `"Mississippi".length()`
7. `System.out.println(greeting.toUpperCase());`
8. It is not legal. The variable `river` has type `String`. The `println` method is not a method of the `String` class.
9. The implicit parameter is `river`. There is no explicit parameter. The return value is 11.
10. `"Missississi"`
11. 12
12. As `public String toUpperCase()`, with no explicit parameter and return type `String`.
13. `double`
14. An `int` is not an object, and you cannot call a method on it.
15. `(x + y) * 0.5`
16. `new Rectangle(90, 90, 20, 20)`
17. 0
18. An accessor—it doesn't modify the original string but returns a new string with uppercase letters.
19. `box.translate(-5, -10)`, provided the method is called immediately after storing the new rectangle into box.
20. `x: 30, y: 25`
21. Because the `translate` method doesn't modify the shape of the rectangle.
22. Add the statement `import java.util.Random;` at the top of your program.
23. `toLowerCase`
24. `"Hello, Space !"`—only the leading and trailing spaces are trimmed.
25. Now `greeting` and `greeting2` both refer to the same `String` object.
26. Both variables still refer to the same string, and the string has not been modified. Recall that the `toUpperCase` method constructs a new string that contains uppercase characters, leaving the original string unchanged.

27. Modify the EmptyFrameViewer program as follows:

```
frame.setSize(300, 300);
frame.setTitle("Hello, World!");
```

28. Construct two JFrame objects, set each of their sizes, and call setVisible(true) on each of them.

29. Rectangle box = new Rectangle(5, 10, 20, 20);

30. Replace the call to box.translate(15, 25) with

```
box = new Rectangle(20, 35, 20, 20);
```

31. The compiler complains that g doesn't have a draw method.

32. g2.draw(new Ellipse2D.Double(75, 75, 50, 50));

33. Line2D.Double segment1 = new Line2D.Double(0, 0, 10, 30);
g2.draw(segment1);
Line2D.Double segment2 = new Line2D.Double(10, 30, 20, 0);
g2.draw(segment2);

34. g2.drawString("V", 0, 30);

35. 0, 0, 255

36. First fill a big red square, then fill a small yellow square inside:

```
g2.setColor(Color.RED);
g2.fill(new Rectangle(0, 0, 200, 200));
g2.setColor(Color.YELLOW);
g2.fill(new Rectangle(50, 50, 100, 100));
```

3

Implementing Classes

CHAPTER GOALS

- To become familiar with the process of implementing classes
- To be able to implement simple methods
- To understand the purpose and use of constructors
- To understand how to access instance fields and local variables
- To appreciate the importance of documentation comments
- **G** To implement classes for drawing graphical shapes

In this chapter, you will learn how to implement your own classes. You will start with a given design that specifies the public interface of the class—that is, the methods through which programmers can manipulate the objects of the class. You then need to implement the methods. This step requires that you find a data representation for the objects, and supply the instructions for each method. You then provide a tester to validate that your class works correctly. You also document your efforts so that other programmers can understand and use your creation.

CHAPTER CONTENTS

3.1 Levels of Abstraction

3.1.1 Black Boxes

When you lift the hood of a car, you will find a bewildering collection of mechanical components. You will probably recognize the motor and the tank for the windshield washer fluid. Your car mechanic will be able to identify many other components, such as the transmission and the electronic control module—the device that controls the timing of the spark plugs and the flow of gasoline into the motor. But ask your mechanic what is inside the electronic control module, and you will likely get a shrug.

It is a *black box*, something that magically does its thing. A car mechanic would never open the box—it contains electronic parts that can only be serviced at the factory. Of course, the device may have a color other than black, and it may not even be box-shaped. But engineers use the term "black box" to describe any device whose inner workings are hidden. Note that a black box is not totally mysterious. Its interaction with the outside world is well-defined. For example, the car mechanic can test that the engine control module sends the right firing signals to the spark plugs.

Why do car manufacturers put black boxes into cars? The black box greatly simplifies the work of the car mechanic, leading to lower repair costs. If the box fails, it is simply replaced with a new one. Before engine control modules were invented, gasoline flow into the engine was regulated by a mechanical device called a carburetor, a notoriously fussy mess of springs and latches that was expensive to adjust and repair.

Of course, for many drivers, the *entire car* is a "black box". Most drivers know nothing about its internal workings and never want to open the hood in the first place. The car has pedals, buttons, and a gas tank door. If you give it the right inputs, it does its thing, transporting you from here to there.

And for the engine control module manufacturer, the transistors and capacitors that go inside are black boxes, magically produced by an electronics component manufacturer.

In technical terms, a black box provides *encapsulation*, the hiding of unimportant details. Encapsulation is very important for human problem solving. A car mechanic is more efficient when the only decision is to test the electronic control module and to replace it when it fails, without having to think about the sensors and transistors inside. A driver is more efficient when the only worry is putting gas in the tank, not thinking about the motor or electronic control module inside.

However, there is another aspect to encapsulation. Somebody had to come up with the right *concept* for each particular black box. Why do the car parts manufacturers build electronic control modules and not another device? Why do the transportation device manufacturers build cars and not personal helicopters?

Concepts are discovered through the process of *abstraction*, taking away inessential features, until only the essence of the concept remains. For example, "car" is an abstraction, describing devices that transport small groups of people, traveling on the ground, and consuming gasoline. Is that the right abstraction? Or is a vehicle with an electric engine a "car"? We won't answer that question and instead move on to the significance of encapsulation and abstraction in computer science.

3.1.2 Object-Oriented Design

In old times, computer programs manipulated *primitive types* such as numbers and characters. As programs became more complex, they manipulated more and more of these primitive quantities, until programmers could no longer keep up. It was just too confusing to keep all that detail in one's head. As a result, programmers gave wrong instructions to their computers, and the computers faithfully executed them, yielding wrong answers.

Of course, the answer to this problem was obvious. Software developers soon learned to manage complexity. They encapsulated routine computations, forming software "black boxes" that can be put to work without worrying about the internals. They used the process of abstraction to invent data types that are at a higher level than numbers and characters.

At the time that this book is written, the most common approach for structuring computer programming is the *object-oriented* approach. The black boxes from

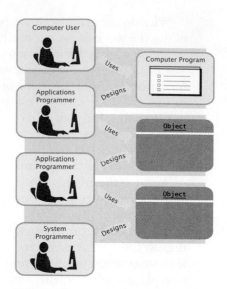

Figure 1
Levels of Abstraction in Automotive Design

Figure 2
Levels of Abstraction in Software Design

which a program is manufactured are called objects. An object has an internal structure—perhaps just some numbers, perhaps other objects—and a well-defined behavior. Of course, the internal structure is hidden from the programmer who uses it. That programmer only learns about the object's behavior and then puts it to work in order to achieve a higher-level goal.

Who designs these objects? Other programmers! What do they contain? Other objects! This is where things get confusing for beginning students. In real life, the users of black boxes are quite different from their designers, and it is easy to understand the levels of abstraction (see Figure 1). With computer programs, there are also levels of abstraction (see Figure 2), but they are not as intuitive to the uninitiated. To make matters potentially more confusing, you will often need to switch roles, being the designer of objects in the morning and the user of the same objects in the afternoon. In that regard, you will be like the builders of the first automobiles, who singlehandedly produced steering wheels and axles and then assembled their own creations into a car.

There is another challenging aspect of designing objects. Software is infinitely more flexible than hardware because it is unconstrained from physical limitations. Designers of electronic parts can exploit a limited number of physical effects to create transistors, capacitors, and the like. Transportation device manufacturers can't easily produce personal helicopters because of a whole host of physical limitations, such as fuel consumption and safety. But in software, anything goes. With few constraints from the outside world, you can design good and bad abstractions with equal facility. Understanding what makes good design is an important part of the education of a software engineer.

3.1.3 Crawl, Walk, Run

In Chapter 2, you learned to be an object user. You saw how to obtain objects, how to manipulate them, and how to assemble them into a program. In that chapter, your role was analogous to the automotive engineer who learns how to use an engine control module, and how to take advantage of its behavior in order to build a car.

In this chapter, you will move on to implementing classes. A design will be handed to you that describes the behavior of the objects of a class. You will learn the necessary Java programming techniques that enable your objects to carry out the desired behavior. In these sections, your role is analogous to the car parts manufacturer who puts together an engine control module from transistors, capacitors, and other electronic parts.

In Chapters 8 and 12, you will learn more about designing your own classes. You will learn rules of good design, and how to discover the appropriate behavior of objects. In those chapters, your job is analogous to the car parts engineer who specifies how an engine control module should function.

SELF CHECK

1. In Chapters 1 and 2, you used System.out as a black box to cause output to appear on the screen. Who designed and implemented System.out?

2. Suppose you are working in a company that produces personal finance software. You are asked to design and implement a class for representing bank accounts. Who will be the users of your class?

3.2 Specifying the Public Interface of a Class

In this section, we will discuss the process of specifying the behavior of a class. Imagine that you are a member of a team that works on banking software. A fundamental concept in banking is a *bank account*. Your task is to understand the design of a BankAccount class so that you can implement it, which in turn allows other programmers on the team to use it.

> In order to implement a class, you first need to know which methods are required.

You need to know exactly what features of a bank account need to be implemented. Some features are essential (such as deposits), whereas others are not important (such as the gift that a customer may receive for opening a bank account). Deciding which features are essential is not always an easy task. We will revisit that issue in Chapters 8 and 12. For now, we will assume that a competent designer has decided that the following are considered the essential operations of a bank account:

- Deposit money
- Withdraw money
- Get the current balance

In Java, operations are expressed as method calls. To figure out the exact specification of the method calls, imagine how a programmer would carry out the bank account operations. We'll assume that the variable harrysChecking contains a reference to an object of type BankAccount. We want to support method calls such as the following:

```
harrysChecking.deposit(2000);
harrysChecking.withdraw(500);
System.out.println(harrysChecking.getBalance());
```

Note that the first two methods are mutators. They modify the balance of the bank account and don't return a value. The third method is an accessor. It returns a value that you can print or store in a variable.

As you can see from the sample calls, the BankAccount class should define three methods:

- `public void deposit(double amount)`
- `public void withdraw(double amount)`
- `public double getBalance()`

Recall from Chapter 2 that double denotes the double-precision floating-point type, and void indicates that a method does not return a value.

When you define a method, you also need to provide the method *body*, consisting of statements that are executed when the method is called.

```
public void deposit(double amount)
{
    body—filled in later
}
```

You will see in Section 3.5 how to fill in the method body.

Every method definition contains the following parts:

- An *access specifier* (usually public)
- The *return type* (such as void or double)
- The name of the method (such as deposit)
- A list of the *parameters* of the method (if any), enclosed in parentheses (such as double amount)
- The *body* of the method: statements enclosed in braces

> A method definition contains an access specifier (usually public), a return type, a method name, parameters, and the method body.

The access specifier controls which other methods can call this method. Most methods should be declared as public. That way, all other methods in a program can call them. (Occasionally, it can be useful to have private methods. They can only be called from other methods of the same class.)

The return type is the type of the output value. The deposit method does not return a value, whereas the getBalance method returns a value of type double.

SYNTAX 3.1 Method Definition

accessSpecifier returnType methodName(parameterType parameterName, . . .)
{
   method body
}

Example:

```
public void deposit(double amount)
{
   . . .
}
```

Purpose:

To define the behavior of a method

Each parameter (or input) to the method has both a type and a name. For example, the deposit method has a single parameter named amount of type double. For each parameter, choose a name that is both a legal variable name and a good description of the purpose of the input.

Next, you need to supply constructors. We will want to construct bank accounts that initially have a zero balance, by using the default constructor:

```
BankAccount harrysChecking = new BankAccount();
```

What if a programmer who uses our class wants to start out with another balance? A second constructor that sets the balance to an initial value will be useful:

```
BankAccount momsSavings = new BankAccount(5000);
```

To summarize, it is specified that two constructors will be provided:

- public BankAccount()
- public BankAccount(double initialBalance)

A constructor is very similar to a method, with two important differences.

- The name of the constructor is always the same as the name of the class (e.g., BankAccount)
- Constructors have no return type (not even void)

Constructors contain instructions to initialize objects. The constructor name is always the same as the class name.

Just like a method, a constructor also has a body—a sequence of statements that is executed when a new object is constructed.

```
public BankAccount()
{
   body—filled in later
}
```

The statements in the constructor body will set the internal data of the object that is being constructed—see Section 3.5.

Don't worry about the fact that there are two constructors with the same name—*all* constructors of a class have the same name, that is, the name of the class. The compiler can tell them apart because they take different parameters.

When defining a class, you place all constructor and method definitions inside, like this:

```
public class BankAccount
{
   // Constructors
   public BankAccount()
   {
      body—filled in later
   }

   public BankAccount(double initialBalance)
   {
      body—filled in later
   }

   // Methods
   public void deposit(double amount)
   {
      body—filled in later
   }

   public void withdraw(double amount)
   {
      body—filled in later
   }

   public double getBalance()
   {
      body—filled in later
   }

   private fields—filled in later
}
```

You will see how to supply the missing pieces in the following sections.

The public constructors and methods of a class form the *public interface* of the class. These are the operations that any programmer can use to create and manipulate BankAccount objects. Our BankAccount class is simple, but it allows programmers to carry out all of the important operations that commonly occur with bank accounts. For example, consider this program segment, authored by a programmer who uses the BankAccount class. These statements transfer an amount of money from one bank account to another:

```
// Transfer from one account to another
double transferAmount = 500;
momsSavings.withdraw(transferAmount);
harrysChecking.deposit(transferAmount);
```

SYNTAX 3.2 Constructor Definition

accessSpecifier ClassName (*parameterType parameterName* , . . .)
{
    constructor body
}

Example:

```
public BankAccount(double initialBalance)
{
    . . .
}
```

Purpose:

To define the behavior of a constructor

SYNTAX 3.3 Class Definition

accessSpecifier class *ClassName*
{
    constructors
    methods
    fields
}

Example:

```
public class BankAccount
{
    public BankAccount(double initialBalance) { . . . }
    public void deposit(double amount) { . . . }
    . . .
}
```

Purpose:

To define a class, its public interface, and its implementation details

And here is a program segment that adds interest to a savings account:

```
double interestRate = 5; // 5% interest
double interestAmount
    = momsSavings.getBalance() * interestRate / 100;
momsSavings.deposit(interestAmount);
```

As you can see, programmers can use objects of the BankAccount class to carry out meaningful tasks, without knowing how the BankAccount objects store their data or how the BankAccount methods do their work.

Of course, as implementors of the BankAccount class, we will need to supply the internal details. We will do so in Section 3.5. First, however, an important step remains: *documenting* the public interface. That is the topic of the next section.

SELF CHECK

3. How can you use the methods of the public interface to *empty* the harrys-Checking bank account?

4. Suppose you want a more powerful bank account abstraction that keeps track of an *account number* in addition to the balance. How would you change the public interface to accommodate this enhancement?

3.3 Commenting the Public Interface

When you implement classes and methods, you should get into the habit of thoroughly *commenting* their behaviors. In Java there is a very useful standard form for *documentation comments*. If you use this form in your classes, a program called javadoc can automatically generate a neat set of HTML pages that describe them. (See Productivity Hint 3.1 for a description of this utility.)

> Use documentation comments to describe the classes and public methods of your programs.

A documentation comment is placed before the class or method definition that is being documented. It starts with a /**, a special comment delimiter used by the javadoc utility. Then you describe the method's *purpose*. Then, for each method parameter, you supply a line that starts with @param, followed by the parameter name and a short explanation. Finally, you supply a line that starts with @return, describing the return value. You omit the @param tag for methods that have no parameters, and you omit the @return tag for methods whose return type is void.

The javadoc utility copies the *first* sentence of each comment to a summary table in the HTML documentation. Therefore, it is best to write that first sentence with some care. It should start with an uppercase letter and end with a period. It does not have to be a grammatically complete sentence, but it should be meaningful when it is pulled out of the comment and displayed in a summary.

Here are two typical examples.

```
/**
    Withdraws money from the bank account.
    @param amount the amount to withdraw
*/
public void withdraw(double amount)
{
    implementation—filled in later
```

```
    }

    /**
        Gets the current balance of the bank account.
        @return the current balance
    */
    public double getBalance()
    {
```
implementation—filled in later
```
    }
```

The comments you have just seen explain individual *methods*. Supply a brief comment for each *class*, explaining its purpose. The comment syntax for class comments is very simple: Just place the documentation comment above the class.

```
    /**
        A bank account has a balance that can be changed by
        deposits and withdrawals.
    */
    public class BankAccount
    {
        . . .
    }
```

Your first reaction may well be "Whoa! Am I supposed to write all this stuff?" These comments do seem pretty repetitive. But you should take the time to write them, even if it feels silly.

It is always a good idea to write the method comment *first*, before writing the code in the method body. This is an excellent test to see that you firmly understand what you need to program. If you can't explain what a class or method does, you aren't ready to implement it.

> Provide documentation comments for every class, every method, every parameter, and every return value.

What about very simple methods? You can easily spend more time pondering whether a comment is too trivial to write than it takes to write it. In practical programming, very simple methods are rare. It is harmless to have a trivial method overcommented, whereas a complicated method without any comment can cause real grief to future maintenance programmers. According to the standard Java documentation style, *every* class, *every* method, *every* parameter, and *every* return value should have a comment.

The javadoc utility formats your comments into a neat set of documents that you can view in a web browser. It makes good use of the seemingly repetitive phrases. The first sentence of the comment is used for a *summary table* of all methods of your class (see Figure 3). The @param and @return comments are neatly formatted in the detail description of each method (see Figure 4). If you omit any of the comments, then javadoc generates documents that look strangely empty.

This documentation format should look familiar. The programmers who implement the Java library use javadoc themselves. They too document every class, every method, every parameter, and every return value, and then use javadoc to extract the documentation in HTML format.

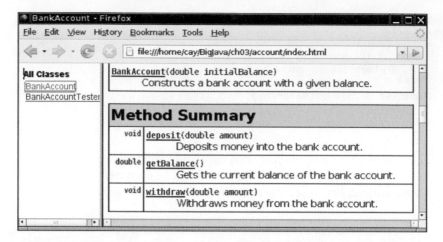

Figure 3   A Method Summary Generated by javadoc

Figure 4   Method Detail Generated by javadoc

SELF CHECK

5. Suppose we enhance the BankAccount class so that each account has an account number. Supply a documentation comment for the constructor

   ```
   public BankAccount(int accountNumber, double initialBalance)
   ```

6. Why is the following documentation comment questionable?

   ```
   /**
       Each account has an account number.
       @return  the account number of this account
   */
   public int getAccountNumber()
   ```

PRODUCTIVITY HINT 3.1

The javadoc Utility

Always insert documentation comments in your code, whether or not you use javadoc to produce HTML documentation. Most people find the HTML documentation convenient, so it is worth learning how to run javadoc. Some programming environments (such as BlueJ) can execute javadoc for you. Alternatively, you can invoke the javadoc utility from a command shell, by issuing the command

```
javadoc MyClass.java
```

or , if you want to document multiple Java files,

```
javadoc *.java
```

The javadoc utility produces files such as MyClass.html in HTML format, which you can inspect in a browser. If you know HTML (see Appendix H), you can embed HTML tags into the comments to specify fonts or add images. Perhaps most importantly, javadoc automatically provides *hyperlinks* to other classes and methods.

You can run javadoc before implementing any methods. Just leave all the method bodies empty. Don't run the compiler—it would complain about missing return values. Simply run javadoc on your file to generate the documentation for the public interface that you are about to implement.

The javadoc tool is wonderful because it does one thing right: It allows you to put the documentation *together with your code*. That way, when you update your programs, you can see right away which documentation needs to be updated. Hopefully, you will update it right then and there. Afterward, run javadoc again and get updated information that is timely and nicely formatted.

3.4 Instance Fields

Now that you understand the specification of the public interface of the BankAccount class, let's provide the implementation.

First, we need to determine the data that each bank account object contains. In the case of our simple bank account class, each object needs to store a single value, the current balance. (A more complex bank account class might store additional data—perhaps an account number, the interest rate paid, the date for mailing out the next statement, and so on.)

> An object uses instance fields to store its state— the data that it needs to execute its methods.

An object stores its data in *instance fields*. A *field* is a technical term for a storage location inside a block of memory. An *instance* of a class is an object of the class. Thus, an instance field is a storage location that is present in each object of the class.

The class declaration specifies the instance fields:

```
public class BankAccount
{
    . . .
    private double balance;
}
```

Figure 5   Instance Fields

An instance field declaration consists of the following parts:

- An *access specifier* (usually `private`)
- The *type* of the instance field (such as `double`)
- The name of the instance field (such as `balance`)

> Each object of a class has its own set of instance fields.

Each object of a class has its own set of instance fields. For example, if `harrysChecking` and `momsSavings` are two objects of the `BankAccount` class, then each object has its own `balance` field, called `harrys-Checking.balance` and `momsSavings.balance` (see Figure 5).

> You should declare all instance fields as private.

Instance fields are generally declared with the access specifier `private`. That specifier means that they can be accessed only by the methods of the *same class*, not by any other method. For example, the `balance` variable can be accessed by the `deposit` method of the BankAccount class but not the `main` method of another class.

```
public class BankRobber
{
    public static void main(String[] args)
    {
        BankAccount momsSavings = new BankAccount(1000);
        . . .
        momsSavings.balance = -1000;  // Error
    }
}
```

> Encapsulation is the process of hiding object data and providing methods for data access.

In other words, if the instance fields are declared as private, then all data access must occur through the public methods. Thus, the instance fields of an object are effectively hidden from the programmer who uses a class. They are of concern only to the programmer who implements the class. The process of hiding the data and providing methods

---

SYNTAX 3.4 Instance Field Declaration

```
accessSpecifier class ClassName
{
    . . .
    accessSpecifier fieldType fieldName;
    . . .
}
```

Example:

```
public class BankAccount
{
    . . .
    private double balance;
    . . .
}
```

Purpose:

To define a field that is present in every object of a class

---

for data access is called *encapsulation*. Although it is theoretically possible in Java to leave instance fields public, that is a very uncommon practice. We will always make instance fields private in this book.

SELF CHECK

7. Suppose we modify the BankAccount class so that each bank account has an account number. How does this change affect the instance fields?
8. What are the instance fields of the Rectangle class?

3.5 Implementing Constructors and Methods

Constructors contain instructions to initialize the instance fields of an object.

Now that we have determined the instance fields, let us complete the BankAccount class by supplying the bodies of the constructors and methods. Each body contains a sequence of statements. We'll start with the constructors because they are very straightforward. A constructor has a simple job: to initialize the instance fields of an object.

Recall that we designed the BankAccount class to have two constructors. The first constructor simply sets the balance to zero:

```
public BankAccount()
{
    balance = 0;
}
```

The second constructor sets the balance to the value supplied as the construction parameter:

```
public BankAccount(double initialBalance)
{
   balance = initialBalance;
}
```

To see how these constructors work, let us trace the statement

```
BankAccount harrysChecking = new BankAccount(1000);
```

one step at a time. Here are the steps that are carried out when the statement executes.

- Create a new object of type BankAccount.
- Call the second constructor (since a construction parameter is supplied).
- Set the parameter variable initialBalance to 1000.
- Set the balance instance field of the newly created object to initialBalance.
- Return an object reference, that is, the memory location of the object, as the value of the new expression.
- Store that object reference in the harrysChecking variable.

Let's move on to implementing the BankAccount methods. Here is the deposit method:

```
public void deposit(double amount)
{
   double newBalance = balance + amount;
   balance = newBalance;
}
```

To understand exactly what the method does, consider this statement:

```
harrysChecking.deposit(500);
```

This statement carries out the following steps:

- Set the parameter variable amount to 500.
- Fetch the balance field of the object whose location is stored in harrysChecking.
- Add the value of amount to balance and store the result in the variable newBalance.
- Store the value of newBalance in the balance instance field, overwriting the old value.

The withdraw method is very similar to the deposit method:

```
public void withdraw(double amount)
{
   double newBalance = balance - amount;
   balance = newBalance;
}
```

SYNTAX 3.5 **The return Statement**

```
return expression;
or
return;
```

Example:

```
return balance;
```

Purpose:

To specify the value that a method returns, and exit the method immediately. The return value becomes the value of the method call expression.

There is only one method left, getBalance. Unlike the deposit and withdraw methods, which modify the instance fields of the object on which they are invoked, the getBalance method returns an output value:

```
public double getBalance()
{
    return balance;
}
```

Use the return statement to specify the value that a method returns to its caller.

The return statement is a special statement that instructs the method to terminate and return an output to the statement that called the method. In our case, we simply return the value of the balance instance field. You will later see other methods that compute and return more complex expressions.

We have now completed the implementation of the BankAccount class—see the code listing below. There is only one step remaining: testing that the class works correctly. That is the topic of the next section.

ch03/account/BankAccount.java

```
 1  /**
 2      A bank account has a balance that can be changed by
 3      deposits and withdrawals.
 4  */
 5  public class BankAccount
 6  {
 7      /**
 8          Constructs a bank account with a zero balance.
 9      */
10      public BankAccount()
11      {
12          balance = 0;
13      }
14
```

```
15      /**
16          Constructs a bank account with a given balance.
17          @param initialBalance the initial balance
18      */
19      public BankAccount(double initialBalance)
20      {
21          balance = initialBalance;
22      }
23
24      /**
25          Deposits money into the bank account.
26          @param amount the amount to deposit
27      */
28      public void deposit(double amount)
29      {
30          double newBalance = balance + amount;
31          balance = newBalance;
32      }
33
34      /**
35          Withdraws money from the bank account.
36          @param amount the amount to withdraw
37      */
38      public void withdraw(double amount)
39      {
40          double newBalance = balance - amount;
41          balance = newBalance;
42      }
43
44      /**
45          Gets the current balance of the bank account.
46          @return the current balance
47      */
48      public double getBalance()
49      {
50          return balance;
51      }
52
53      private double balance;
54  }
```

SELF CHECK

9. The Rectangle class has four instance fields: x, y, width, and height. Give a possible implementation of the getWidth method.

10. Give a possible implementation of the translate method of the Rectangle class.

How To 3.1

Implementing a Class

This is the first of several "How To" sections in this book. Users of the Linux operating system have how to guides that give answers to the common questions "How do I get started?" and "What do I do next?". Similarly, the How To sections in this book give you step-by-step procedures for carrying out specific tasks.

You will often be asked to implement a class. For example, a homework assignment might ask you to implement a CashRegister class.

Step 1 Find out which methods you are asked to supply.

In the cash register example, you won't have to provide every feature of a real cash register—there are too many. The assignment should tell you *which aspects* of a cash register your class should simulate. You should have received a description, in plain English, of the operations that an object of your class should carry out, such as this one:

- Ring up the sales price for a purchased item.
- Enter the amount of payment.
- Calculate the amount of change due to the customer.

For simplicity, we are looking at a very simple cash register here. A more sophisticated model would be able to compute sales tax, daily sales totals, and so on.

Step 2 Specify the public interface.

Turn the list in Step 1 into a set of methods, with specific types for the parameters and the return values. Many programmers find this step simpler if they write out method calls that are applied to a sample object, like this:

```
CashRegister register = new CashRegister();
register.recordPurchase(29.95);
register.recordPurchase(9.95);
register.enterPayment(50);
double change = register.giveChange();
```

Now we have a specific list of methods.

- `public void recordPurchase(double amount)`
- `public void enterPayment(double amount)`
- `public double giveChange()`

To complete the public interface, you need to specify the constructors. Ask yourself what information you need in order to construct an object of your class. Sometimes you will want two constructors: one that sets all fields to a default and one that sets them to user-supplied values.

In the case of the cash register example, we can get by with a single constructor that creates an empty register. A more realistic cash register would start out with some coins and bills so that we can give exact change, but that is beyond the scope of our assignment.

Thus, we add a single constructor:

- `public CashRegister()`

Step 3 Document the public interface.

Here is the documentation, with comments, that describes the class and its methods:

```java
/**
    A cash register totals up sales and computes change due.
*/
public class CashRegister
{
    /**
        Constructs a cash register with no money in it.
    */
    public CashRegister()
    {
    }

    /**
        Records the sale of an item.
        @param amount the price of the item
    */
    public void recordPurchase(double amount)
    {
    }

    /**
        Enters the payment received from the customer.
        @param amount the amount of the payment
    */
    public void enterPayment(double amount)
    {
    }

    /**
        Computes the change due and resets the machine for the next customer.
        @return the change due to the customer
    */
    public double giveChange()
    {
    }
}
```

Step 4 Determine instance fields.

Ask yourself what information an object needs to store to do its job. Remember, the methods can be called in any order! The object needs to have enough internal memory to be able to process every method using just its instance fields and the method parameters. Go through each method, perhaps starting with a simple one or an interesting one, and ask yourself what you need to carry out the method's task. Make instance fields to store the information that the method needs.

In the cash register example, you would want to keep track of the total purchase amount and the payment. You can compute the change due from these two amounts.

```java
public class CashRegister
{
    . . .
    private double purchase;
    private double payment;
}
```

Step 5 Implement constructors and methods.

Implement the constructors and methods in your class, one at a time, starting with the easiest ones. For example, here is the implementation of the recordPurchase method:

```
public void recordPurchase(double amount)
{
   double newTotal = purchase + amount;
   purchase = newTotal;
}
```

Here is the giveChange method. Note that this method is a bit more sophisticated—it computes the change due, and it also resets the cash register for the next sale.

```
public double giveChange()
{
   double change = payment - purchase;
   purchase = 0;
   payment = 0;
   return change;
}
```

If you find that you have trouble with the implementation, you may need to rethink your choice of instance fields. It is common for a beginner to start out with a set of fields that cannot accurately reflect the state of an object. Don't hesitate to go back and add or modify fields.

Once you have completed the implementation, compile your class and fix any compiler errors.

Step 6 Test your class.

Write a short tester program and execute it. The tester program can carry out the method calls that you found in Step 2.

```
public class CashRegisterTester
{
   public static void main(String[] args)
   {
      CashRegister register = new CashRegister();

      register.recordPurchase(29.50);
      register.recordPurchase(9.25);
      register.enterPayment(50);

      double change = register.giveChange();

      System.out.println(change);
      System.out.println("Expected: 11.25");
   }
}
```

The output of this test program is:

```
11.25
Expected: 11.25
```

Alternatively, if you use a program that lets you test objects interactively, such as BlueJ, construct an object and apply the method calls.

3.6 Unit Testing

In the preceding section, we completed the implementation of the BankAccount class. What can you do with it? Of course, you can compile the file BankAccount.java. However, you can't *execute* the resulting BankAccount.class file. It doesn't contain a main method. That is normal—most classes don't contain a main method.

> A unit test verifies that a class works correctly in isolation, outside a complete program.

In the long run, your class may become a part of a larger program that interacts with users, stores data in files, and so on. However, before integrating a class into a program, it is always a good idea to test it in isolation. Testing in isolation, outside a complete program, is called *unit testing*.

To test your class, you have two choices. Some interactive development environments have commands for constructing objects and invoking methods (see Advanced Topic 2.1). Then you can test a class simply by constructing an object, calling methods, and verifying that you get the expected return values. Figure 6 shows the result of calling the getBalance method on a BankAccount object in BlueJ.

> To test a class, use an environment for interactive testing, or write a tester class to execute test instructions.

Alternatively, you can write a *tester class*. A tester class is a class with a main method that contains statements to run methods of another class. A tester class typically carries out the following steps:

1. Construct one or more objects of the class that is being tested.
2. Invoke one or more methods.
3. Print out one or more results.
4. Print the expected results.

Figure 6
The Return Value of the
getBalance Method in BlueJ

The MoveTester class in Section 2.8 is a good example of a tester class. That class runs methods of the Rectangle class—a class in the Java library.

Here is a class to run methods of the BankAccount class. The main method constructs an object of type BankAccount, invokes the deposit and withdraw methods, and then displays the remaining balance on the console.

We also print the value that we expect to see. In our sample program, we deposit $2,000 and withdraw $500. We therefore expect a balance of $1500.

ch03/account/BankAccountTester.java

```java
1   /**
2        A class to test the BankAccount class.
3   */
4   public class BankAccountTester
5   {
6      /**
7          Tests the methods of the BankAccount class.
8          @param args not used
9      */
10     public static void main(String[] args)
11     {
12        BankAccount harrysChecking = new BankAccount();
13        harrysChecking.deposit(2000);
14        harrysChecking.withdraw(500);
15        System.out.println(harrysChecking.getBalance());
16        System.out.println("Expected: 1500");
17     }
18  }
```

Output

```
1500
Expected: 1500
```

To produce a program, you need to combine the BankAccount and the BankAccountTester classes. The details for building the program depend on your compiler and development environment. In most environments, you need to carry out these steps:

1. Make a new subfolder for your program.
2. Make two files, one for each class.
3. Compile both files.
4. Run the test program.

Many students are surprised that such a simple program contains two classes. However, this is normal. The two classes have entirely different purposes. The BankAccount class describes objects that compute bank balances. The BankAccountTester class runs a test that puts a BankAccount object through its paces.

SELF CHECK

11. When you run the BankAccountTester program, how many objects of class BankAccount are constructed? How many objects of type BankAccountTester?

12. Why is the BankAccountTester class unnecessary in development environments that allow interactive testing, such as BlueJ?

PRODUCTIVITY HINT 3.2

Using the Command Line Effectively

If your programming environment allows you to accomplish all routine tasks using menus and dialog boxes, you can skip this note. However, if you must invoke the editor, the compiler, the linker, and the program to test manually, then it is well worth learning about *command line editing*.

Most operating systems (including Linux, Mac OS X, UNIX, and Windows) have a *command line interface* to interact with the computer. (In Windows XP, you can get a command line window by selecting "Run . . . " from the Start menu and typing cmd.) You launch commands at a *prompt*. The command is executed, and on completion you get another prompt.

When you develop a program, you find yourself executing the same commands over and over. Wouldn't it be nice if you didn't have to type commands, such as

```
javac MyProg.java
```

more than once? Or if you could fix a mistake rather than having to retype the command in its entirety? Many command line interfaces have an option to do just that, by using the up and down arrow keys to recall old commands and the left and right arrow keys to edit lines. You can also perform *file completion*. For example, to select the file BankAccount.java, you only need to type the first couple of letters and then hit the "Tab" key.

The details depend on your operating system and its configuration—experiment on your own, or ask a "power user" for help.

3.7 Categories of Variables

We close this chapter with two sections of a more technical nature, examining variables and parameters in some detail.

You have seen three different categories of variables in this chapter:

1. *Instance fields* (sometimes called *instance variables*), such as the balance variable of the BankAccount class

2. *Local variables*, such as the newBalance variable of the deposit method

3. *Parameter variables*, such as the amount variable of the deposit method

Instance fields belong to an object. Parameter variables and local variables belong to a method—they die when the method exits.

These variables are similar in one respect—they all hold values that belong to specific types. But they have a couple of important differences. The first difference is their *lifetime*.

An instance field belongs to an object. Each object has its own copy of each instance field. For example, if you have two BankAccount objects (say, harrysChecking and momsSavings), then each of them has its own balance field. When an object is constructed, its instance fields are created. The fields stay alive until no method uses the object any longer. (The Java virtual machine contains an agent called a *garbage collector* that periodically reclaims objects when they are no longer used.)

Local and parameter variables belong to a method. When the method runs, these variables come to life. When the method exits, they die immediately (see Figure 7).

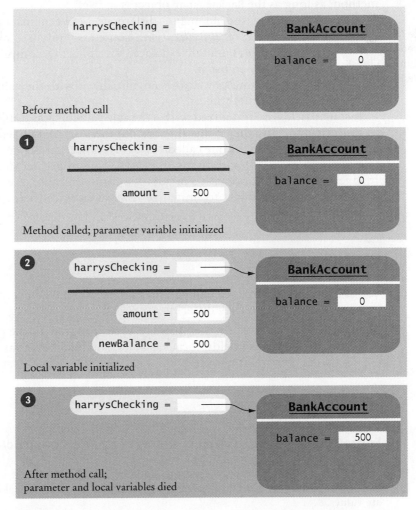

Figure 7 Lifetime of Variables

For example, if you call

`harrysChecking.deposit(500);` ❶

then a parameter variable called `amount` is created and initialized with the parameter value, 500. When the method returns, the `amount` variable dies. The same holds for the local variable `newBalance`. When the `deposit` method reaches the line

`double newBalance = balance + amount;` ❷

the variable comes to life and is initialized with the sum of the object's balance and the deposit amount. The lifetime of that variable extends to the end of the method.

However, the `deposit` method has a lasting effect. Its next line,

`balance = newBalance;` ❸

sets the `balance` instance field, and that field lives beyond the end of the `deposit` method, as long as the `BankAccount` object is in use.

> Instance fields are initialized to a default value, but you must initialize local variables.

The second major difference between instance fields and local variables is *initialization*. You must initialize all local variables. If you don't initialize a local variable, the compiler complains when you try to use it.

Parameter variables are initialized with the values that are supplied in the method call.

Instance fields are initialized with a default value if you don't explicitly set them in a constructor. Instance fields that are numbers are initialized to 0. Object references are set to a special value called `null`. If an object reference is `null`, then it refers to no object at all. We will discuss the `null` value in greater detail in Section 5.2.5. Inadvertent initialization with 0 or `null` is a common cause of errors. Therefore, it is a matter of good style to initialize *every* instance field explicitly in every constructor.

SELF CHECK

13. What do local variables and parameter variables have in common? In which essential aspect do they differ?

14. During execution of the `BankAccountTester` program in the preceding section, how many instance fields, local variables, and parameter variables were created, and what were their names?

COMMON ERROR 3.1

Forgetting to Initialize Object References in a Constructor

Just as it is a common error to forget to initialize a local variable, it is easy to forget about instance fields. Every constructor needs to ensure that all instance fields are set to appropriate values.

If you do not initialize an instance field, the Java compiler will initialize it for you. Numbers are initialized with 0, but object references—such as string variables—are set to the null reference.

Of course, 0 is often a convenient default for numbers. However, null is hardly ever a convenient default for objects. Consider this "lazy" constructor for a modified version of the BankAccount class:

```java
public class BankAccount
{
    public BankAccount() {} // No statements
    . . .
    private double balance;
    private String owner;
}
```

The balance is set to 0, and the owner field is set to a null reference. This is a problem—it is illegal to call methods on the null reference.

If you forget to initialize a *local* variable in a *method*, the compiler flags this as an error, and you must fix it before the program runs. If you make the same mistake with an *instance* field in a class, the compiler provides a default initialization, and the error becomes apparent only when the program runs.

To avoid this problem, make it a habit to initialize every instance field in every constructor.

3.8 Implicit and Explicit Method Parameters

In Section 2.4, you learned that a method has an implicit parameter—the object on which the method is invoked—and explicit parameters, which are enclosed in parentheses. In this section, we will examine these parameters in greater detail.

Have a look at a particular invocation of the deposit method:

```java
momsSavings.deposit(500);
```

Now look again at the code of the deposit method:

```java
public void deposit(double amount)
{
    double newBalance = balance + amount;
    balance = newBalance;
}
```

The parameter variable amount is set to 500 when the deposit method starts. But what does balance mean exactly? After all, our program may have multiple BankAccount objects, and *each of them* has its own balance.

Of course, since we deposit the money into momsSavings, balance must mean momsSavings.balance. In general, when you refer to an instance field inside a method, it means the instance field of the object on which the method was called.

The implicit parameter of a method is the object on which the method is invoked. The this reference denotes the implicit parameter.

Thus, the call to the deposit method depends on two values: the object to which momsSavings refers, and the value 500. The amount parameter inside the parentheses is called an *explicit* parameter, because it is explicitly named in the method definition. However, the reference to the bank account object is not explicit in the method definition—it is called the *implicit parameter* of the method.

If you need to, you can access the implicit parameter—the object on which the method is called—with the keyword this. For example, in the preceding method invocation, this was set to momsSavings and amount was set to 500 (see Figure 8).

Every method has one implicit parameter. You don't give the implicit parameter a name. It is always called this. (There is one exception to the rule that every method has an implicit parameter: static methods do not. We will discuss them in Chapter 8.) In contrast, methods can have any number of explicit parameters—which you can name any way you like—or no explicit parameter at all.

Next, look closely at the implementation of the deposit method. The statement

```
double newBalance = balance + amount;
```

actually means

```
double newBalance = this.balance + amount;
```

Use of an instance field name in a method denotes the instance field of the implicit parameter.

When you refer to an instance field in a method, the compiler automatically applies it to the this parameter. Some programmers actually prefer to manually insert the this parameter before every instance field because they find it makes the code clearer. Here is an example:

```
public void deposit(double amount)
{
    double newBalance = this.balance + amount;
    this.balance = newBalance;
}
```

You may want to try it out and see if you like that style.

You have now seen how to use objects and implement classes, and you have learned some important technical details about variables and method parameters. In the next chapter, you will learn more about the most fundamental data types of the Java language.

Figure 8   The Implicit Parameter of a Method Call

SELF CHECK

15. How many implicit and explicit parameters does the `withdraw` method of the BankAccount class have, and what are their names and types?

16. In the `deposit` method, what is the meaning of `this.amount`? Or, if the expression has no meaning, why not?

17. How many implicit and explicit parameters does the `main` method of the BankAccountTester class have, and what are they called?

COMMON ERROR 3.2

Trying to Call a Method Without an Implicit Parameter

Suppose your `main` method contains the instruction

```
withdraw(30); // Error
```

The compiler will not know which account to access to withdraw the money. You need to supply an object reference of type BankAccount:

```
BankAccount harrysChecking = new BankAccount();
harrysChecking.withdraw(30);
```

However, there is one situation in which it is legitimate to invoke a method without, seemingly, an implicit parameter. Consider the following modification to the BankAccount class. Add a method to apply the monthly account fee:

```
public class BankAccount
{  . . .
    public void monthlyFee()
    {
        withdraw(10); // Withdraw $10 from this account
    }
}
```

That means to withdraw from the same bank account object that is carrying out the monthlyFee operation. In other words, the implicit parameter of the `withdraw` method is the (invisible) implicit parameter of the monthlyFee method.

If you find it confusing to have an invisible parameter, you can always use the `this` parameter to make the method easier to read:

```
public class BankAccount
{  . . .
    public void monthlyFee()
    {
        this.withdraw(10); // Withdraw $10 from this account
    }
}
```

ADVANCED TOPIC 3.1

Calling One Constructor from Another

Consider the BankAccount class. It has two constructors: a constructor without parameters to initialize the balance with zero, and another constructor to supply an initial balance. Rather than explicitly setting the balance to zero, one constructor can call another constructor of the same class instead. There is a shorthand notation to achieve this result:

```java
public class BankAccount
{
    public BankAccount (double initialBalance)
    {
        balance = initialBalance;
    }

    public BankAccount()
    {
        this(0);
    }
    . . .
}
```

The command this(0); means "Call another constructor of this class and supply the value 0". Such a constructor call can occur only as the *first. line in another constructor.*

This syntax is a minor convenience. We will not use it in this book. Actually, the use of the keyword this is a little confusing. Normally, this denotes a reference to the implicit parameter, but if this is followed by parentheses, it denotes a call to another constructor of this class.

RANDOM FACT 3.1

Electronic Voting Machines

In the 2000 presidential elections in the United States, votes were tallied by a variety of machines. Some machines processed cardboard ballots into which voters punched holes to indicate their choices (see Punch Card Ballot figure). When voters were not careful, remains of paper—the now infamous "chads"—were partially stuck in the punch cards, causing votes to be miscounted. A manual recount was necessary, but it was not carried out everywhere due to time constraints and procedural wrangling. The election was very close, and there remain doubts in the minds of many people whether the election outcome would have been different if the voting machines had accurately counted the intent of the voters.

Subsequently, voting machine manufacturers have argued that electronic voting machines would avoid the problems caused by punch cards or optically scanned forms. In an electronic voting machine, voters indicate their preferences by pressing buttons or touching icons on a computer screen. Typically, each voter is presented with a summary screen for review before casting the ballot. The process is very similar to using an automatic bank teller machine (see Touch Screen Voting Machine figure).

It seems plausible that these machines make it more likely that a vote is counted in the same way that the voter intends. However, there has been significant controversy

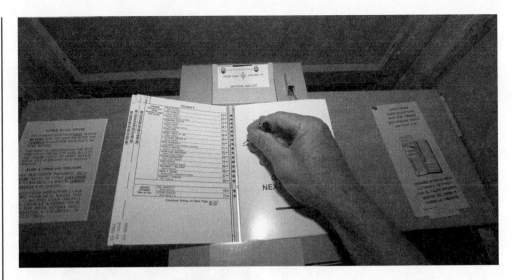

Punch Card Ballot

surrounding some types of electronic voting machines. If a machine simply records the votes and prints out the totals after the election has been completed, then how do you know that the machine worked correctly? Inside the machine is a computer that executes a program, and, as you may know from your own experience, programs can have bugs.

In fact, some electronic voting machines do have bugs. There have been isolated cases where machines reported tallies that were impossible. When a machine reports far more or far fewer votes than voters, then it is clear that it malfunctioned. Unfortunately, it is then impossible to find out the actual votes. Over time, one would expect these bugs to be fixed in the software. More insidiously, if the results are plausible, nobody may ever investigate.

Many computer scientists have spoken out on this issue and confirmed that it is impossible, with today's technology, to tell that software is error free and has not been tampered with. Many of them recommend that electronic voting machines should be complemented by a *voter verifiable audit trail*. (A good source of information is [1].) Typically, a voter-verifiable machine prints out the choices that are being tallied. Each voter has a chance to review the printout, and then deposits it in an old-fashioned ballot box. If there is a problem with the electronic equipment, the printouts can be counted by hand.

As this book is written, this concept is strongly resisted both by manufacturers of electronic voting machines and by their customers, the cities and counties that run elections. Manufacturers are reluctant to increase the cost of the machines because they may not be able to pass the cost increase on to their customers, who tend to have tight budgets. Election officials fear problems with malfunctioning printers, and some of them have publicly stated that they actually prefer equipment that eliminates bothersome recounts.

What do you think? You probably use an automatic bank teller machine to get cash from your bank account. Do you review the paper record that the machine issues? Do you check your bank statement? Even if you don't, do you put your faith in other people who double-check their balances, so that the bank won't get away with widespread cheating?

At any rate, is the integrity of banking equipment more important or less important than that of voting machines? Won't every voting process have some room for error and fraud anyway? Is the added cost for equipment, paper, and staff time reasonable to combat a potentially slight risk of malfunction and fraud? Computer scientists cannot answer these

Touch Screen Voting Machine

questions—an informed society must make these tradeoffs. But, like all professionals, they have an obligation to speak out and give accurate testimony about the capabilities and limitations of computing equipment.

3.9 Shape Classes

We continue the optional graphics track by discussing how to organize complex drawings in a more object-oriented fashion. Feel free to skip this section if you are not interested in graphical applications.

> It is a good idea to make a class for any part of a drawing that that can occur more than once.

When you produce a drawing that is composed of complex parts, such as the one in Figure 9, it is a good idea to make a separate class for each part. Provide a draw method that draws the shape, and provide a constructor to set the position of the shape. For example, here is the outline of the Car class.

```
public class Car
{
    public Car(int x, int y)
    {
        // Remember position
        . . .
    }
    public void draw(Graphics2D g2)
    {
        // Drawing instructions
        . . .
    }
}
```

Figure 9
The Car Component Draws Two Car Shapes

> To figure out how to draw a complex shape, make a sketch on graph paper.

You will find the complete class definition at the end of this section. The draw method contains a rather long sequence of instructions for drawing the body, roof, and tires.

The coordinates of the car parts seem a bit arbitrary. To come up with suitable values, draw the image on graph paper and read off the coordinates (Figure 10).

The program that produces Figure 9 is composed of three classes.

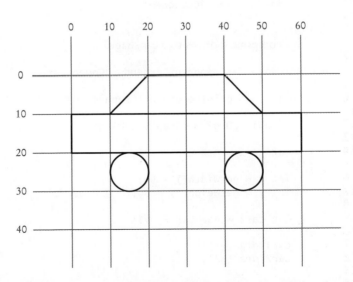

Figure 10   Using Graph Paper to Find Shape Coordinates

- The Car class is responsible for drawing a single car. Two objects of this class are constructed, one for each car.
- The CarComponent class displays the drawing.
- The CarViewer class shows a frame that contains a CarComponent.

Let us look more closely at the CarComponent class. The paintComponent method draws two cars. We place one car in the top-left corner of the window, and the other car in the bottom right. To compute the bottom right position, we call the getWidth and getHeight methods of the JComponent class. These methods return the dimensions of the component. We subtract the dimensions of the car:

```
Car car1 = new Car(0, 0);

int x = getWidth() - 60;
int y = getHeight() - 30;
Car car2 = new Car(x, y);
```

Pay close attention to the call to getWidth inside the paintComponent method of CarComponent. The method call has no implicit parameter, which means that the method is applied to the same object that executes the paintComponent method. The component simply obtains *its own* width.

Run the program and resize the window. Note that the second car always ends up at the bottom-right corner of the window. Whenever the window is resized, the paintComponent method is called and the car position is recomputed, taking the current component dimensions into account.

ch03/car/CarComponent.java

```java
1  import java.awt.Graphics;
2  import java.awt.Graphics2D;
3  import javax.swing.JComponent;
4
5  /**
6      This component draws two car shapes.
7  */
8  public class CarComponent extends JComponent
9  {
10     public void paintComponent(Graphics g)
11     {
12        Graphics2D g2 = (Graphics2D) g;
13
14        Car car1 = new Car(0, 0);
15
16        int x = getWidth() - 60;
17        int y = getHeight() - 30;
18
19        Car car2 = new Car(x, y);
20
21        car1.draw(g2);
22        car2.draw(g2);
23     }
24  }
```

ch03/car/Car.java

```
1  import java.awt.Graphics2D;
2  import java.awt.Rectangle;
3  import java.awt.geom.Ellipse2D;
4  import java.awt.geom.Line2D;
5  import java.awt.geom.Point2D;
6
7  /**
8     A car shape that can be positioned anywhere on the screen.
9  */
10 public class Car
11 {
12    /**
13       Constructs a car with a given top-left corner.
14       @param x the x-coordinate of the top-left corner
15       @param y the y-coordinate of the top-left corner
16    */
17    public Car(int x, int y)
18    {
19       xLeft = x;
20       yTop = y;
21    }
22
23    /**
24       Draws the car.
25       @param g2 the graphics context
26    */
27    public void draw(Graphics2D g2)
28    {
29       Rectangle body
30             = new Rectangle(xLeft, yTop + 10, 60, 10);
31       Ellipse2D.Double frontTire
32             = new Ellipse2D.Double(xLeft + 10, yTop + 20, 10, 10);
33       Ellipse2D.Double rearTire
34             = new Ellipse2D.Double(xLeft + 40, yTop + 20, 10, 10);
35
36       // The bottom of the front windshield
37       Point2D.Double r1
38             = new Point2D.Double(xLeft + 10, yTop + 10);
39       // The front of the roof
40       Point2D.Double r2
41             = new Point2D.Double(xLeft + 20, yTop);
42       // The rear of the roof
43       Point2D.Double r3
44             = new Point2D.Double(xLeft + 40, yTop);
45       // The bottom of the rear windshield
46       Point2D.Double r4
47             = new Point2D.Double(xLeft + 50, yTop + 10);
48
49       Line2D.Double frontWindshield
50             = new Line2D.Double(r1, r2);
51       Line2D.Double roofTop
52             = new Line2D.Double(r2, r3);
```

```
53          Line2D.Double rearWindshield
54                = new Line2D.Double(r3, r4);
55
56          g2.draw(body);
57          g2.draw(frontTire);
58          g2.draw(rearTire);
59          g2.draw(frontWindshield);
60          g2.draw(roofTop);
61          g2.draw(rearWindshield);
62       }
63
64       private int xLeft;
65       private int yTop;
66    }
```

ch03/car/CarViewer.java

```
1   import javax.swing.JFrame;
2
3   public class CarViewer
4   {
5      public static void main(String[] args)
6      {
7         JFrame frame = new JFrame();
8
9         frame.setSize(300, 400);
10        frame.setTitle("Two cars");
11        frame.setDefaultCloseOperation(JFrame.EXIT_ON_CLOSE);
12
13        CarComponent component = new CarComponent();
14        frame.add(component);
15
16        frame.setVisible(true);
17     }
18  }
```

SELF CHECK

18. Which class needs to be modified to have the two cars positioned next to each other?

19. Which class needs to be modified to have the car tires painted in black, and what modification do you need to make?

20. How do you make the cars twice as big?

How To 3.2

Drawing Graphical Shapes

You can write programs that display a wide variety of graphical shapes. These instructions give you a step-by-step procedure for decomposing a drawing into parts and implementing a program that produces the drawing.

Step 1   Determine the shapes that you need for the drawing.

You can use the following shapes:

- Squares and rectangles
- Circles and ellipses
- Lines

The outlines of these shapes can be drawn in any color, and you can fill the insides of these shapes with any color. You can also use text to label parts of your drawing.

Some national flag designs consist of three equally wide sections of different colors, side by side:

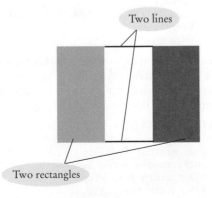

You could draw such a flag using three rectangles. But if the middle rectangle is white, as it is, for example, in the flag of Italy (green, white, red), it is easier and looks better to draw a line on the top and bottom of the middle portion:

Step 2   Find the coordinates for the shapes.

You now need to find the exact positions for the geometric shapes.

- For rectangles, you need the x- and y-position of the top-left corner, the width, and the height.
- For ellipses, you need the top-left corner, width, and height of the bounding rectangle.
- For lines, you need the x- and y-positions of the starting point and the end point.
- For text, you need the x- and y-positions of the basepoint.

A commonly-used size for a window is 300 by 300 pixels. You may not want the flag crammed all the way to the top, so perhaps the upper-left corner of the flag should be at point (100, 100).

Many flags, such as the flag of Italy, have a width : height ratio of 3 : 2. (You can often find exact proportions for a particular flag by doing a bit of Internet research on one of several Flags of the World sites.) For example, if you make the flag 90 pixels wide, then it should be 60 pixels tall. (Why not make it 100 pixels wide? Then the height would be 100 · 2 / 3 ≈ 67, which seems more awkward.)

Now you can compute the coordinates of all the important points of the shape:

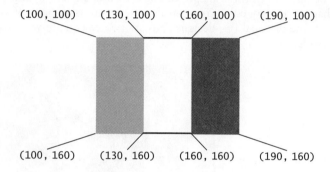

Step 3   Write Java statements to draw the shapes.

In our example, there are two rectangles and two lines:

```
Rectangle leftRectangle
    = new Rectangle(100, 100, 30, 60);
Rectangle rightRectangle
    = new Rectangle(160, 100, 30, 60);
Line2D.Double topLine
    = new Line2D.Double(130, 100, 160, 100);
Line2D.Double bottomLine
    = new Line2D.Double(130, 160, 160, 160);
```

If you are more ambitious, then you can express the coordinates in terms of a few variables. In the case of the flag, we have arbitrarily chosen the top-left corner and the width. All other coordinates follow from those choices. If you decide to follow the ambitious approach, then the rectangles and lines are determined as follows:

```
Rectangle leftRectangle = new Rectangle(
    xLeft, yTop,
    width / 3, width * 2 / 3);
Rectangle rightRectangle = new Rectangle(
    xLeft + 2 * width / 3, yTop,
    width / 3, width * 2 / 3);
Line2D.Double topLine = new Line2D.Double(
    xLeft + width / 3, yTop,
    xLeft + width * 2 / 3, yTop);
```

```
Line2D.Double bottomLine = new Line2D.Double(
      xLeft + width / 3, yTop + width * 2 / 3,
      xLeft + width * 2 / 3, yTop + width * 2 / 3);
```

Now you need to fill the rectangles and draw the lines. For the flag of Italy, the left rectangle is green and the right rectangle is red. Remember to switch colors before the filling and drawing operations:

```
g2.setColor(Color.GREEN);
g2.fill(leftRectangle);
g2.setColor(Color.RED);
g2.fill(rightRectangle);
g2.setColor(Color.BLACK);
g2.draw(topLine);
g2.draw(bottomLine);
```

Step 4   Combine the drawing statements with the component "plumbing".

```
public class MyComponent extends JComponent
{
    public void paintComponent(Graphics g)
    {
        Graphics2D g2 = (Graphics2D) g;
        // Your drawing code goes here
        . . .
    }
}
```

In our example, you can simply add all shapes and drawing instructions inside the paint-Component method:

```
public class ItalianFlagComponent extends JComponent
{
    public void paintComponent(Graphics g)
    {
        Graphics2D g2 = (Graphics2D) g;
        Rectangle leftRectangle
            = new Rectangle(100, 100, 30, 60);
        . . .
        g2.setColor(Color.GREEN);
        g2.fill(leftRectangle);
        . . .
    }
}
```

That approach is acceptable for simple drawings, but it is not very object-oriented. After all, a flag is an object. It is better to make a separate class for the flag. Then you can draw different flags at different positions and sizes. Specify the sizes in a constructor and supply a draw method:

```
public class ItalianFlag
{
    public ItalianFlag(double x, double y, double aWidth)
    {
        xLeft = x;
        yTop = y;
        width = aWidth;
```

```
      }

      public void draw(Graphics2D g2)
      {
         Rectangle leftRectangle = new Rectangle(
               xLeft, yTop,
               width / 3, width * 2 / 3);
         . . .
         g2.setColor(Color.GREEN);
         g2.fill(leftRectangle);
         . . .
      }

      private int xLeft;
      private int yTop;
      private double width;
   }
```

You still need a separate class for the component, but it is very simple:

```
public class ItalianFlagComponent extends JComponent
{
   public void paintComponent(Graphics g)
   {
      Graphics2D g2 = (Graphics2D) g;
      ItalianFlag flag = new ItalianFlag(100, 100, 90);
      flag.draw(g2);
   }
}
```

Step 5 Write the viewer class.

Provide a viewer class, with a main method in which you construct a frame, add your component, and make your frame visible. The viewer class is completely routine; you only need to change a single line to show a different component.

```
import javax.swing.*;

public class ItalianFlagViewer
{
   public static void main(String[] args)
   {
      JFrame frame = new JFrame();

      frame.setSize(300, 400);
      frame.setDefaultCloseOperation(JFrame.EXIT_ON_CLOSE);

      ItalianFlagComponent component = new ItalianFlagComponent();
      frame.add(component);

      frame.setVisible(true);
   }
}
```

RANDOM FACT 3.2

Computer Graphics

Generating and manipulating visual images is one of the most exciting applications of the computer. We distinguish different kinds of graphics.

Diagrams, such as numeric charts or maps, are artifacts that convey information to the viewer (see Diagrams figure). They do not directly depict anything that occurs in the natural world, but are a tool for visualizing information.

Scenes are computer-generated images that attempt to depict images of the real or an imagined world (see Scene figure). It turns out to be quite challenging to render light and shadows accurately. Special effort must be taken so that the images do not look too neat and simple; clouds, rocks, leaves, and dust in the real world have a complex and somewhat random appearance. The degree of realism in these images is constantly improving.

Manipulated images are photographs or film footage of actual events that have been converted to digital form and edited by the computer (see Manipulated Image figure). For example, film sequences in the movie *Apollo 13* were produced by starting from actual images and changing the perspective, showing the launch of the rocket from a more dramatic viewpoint.

Computer graphics is one of the most challenging fields in computer science. It requires processing of massive amounts of information at very high speed. New algorithms are constantly invented for this purpose. Displaying an overlapping set of three-dimensional objects

Diagrams

Scene

Manipulated Image

with curved boundaries requires advanced mathematical tools. Realistic modeling of textures and biological entities requires extensive knowledge of mathematics, physics, and biology.

CHAPTER SUMMARY

1. In order to implement a class, you first need to know which methods are required.

2. A method definition contains an access specifier (usually `public`), a return type, a method name, parameters, and the method body.

3. Constructors contain instructions to initialize objects. The constructor name is always the same as the class name.

4. Use documentation comments to describe the classes and public methods of your programs.

5. Provide documentation comments for every class, every method, every parameter, and every return value.

6. An object uses instance fields to store its state—the data that it needs to execute its methods.

7. Each object of a class has its own set of instance fields.

8. You should declare all instance fields as private.

9. Encapsulation is the process of hiding object data and providing methods for data access.

10. Constructors contain instructions to initialize the instance fields of an object.

11. Use the `return` statement to specify the value that a method returns to its caller.

12. A unit test verifies that a class works correctly in isolation, outside a complete program.

13. To test a class, use an environment for interactive testing, or write a tester class to execute test instructions.

14. Instance fields belong to an object. Parameter variables and local variables belong to a method—they die when the method exits.

15. Instance fields are initialized to a default value, but you must initialize local variables.

16. The implicit parameter of a method is the object on which the method is invoked. The `this` reference denotes the implicit parameter.

17. Use of an instance field name in a method denotes the instance field of the implicit parameter.

18. It is a good idea to make a class for any part of a drawing that that can occur more than once.

19. To figure out how to draw a complex shape, make a sketch on graph paper.

FURTHER READING

1. http://verifiedvoting.org A site with information on voter-verifiable voting machines, founded by Stanford computer science professor David Dill.

REVIEW EXERCISES

★ **Exercise R3.1.** Why is the BankAccount(double initialBalance) constructor not strictly necessary?

★ **Exercise R3.2.** Explain the difference between

```
BankAccount b;
```

and

```
BankAccount b = new BankAccount(5000);
```

★ **Exercise R3.3.** Explain the difference between

```
new BankAccount(5000);
```

and

```
BankAccount b = new BankAccount(5000);
```

★ **Exercise R3.4.** What happens in our implementation of the BankAccount class when more money is withdrawn from the account than the current balance?

★ **Exercise R3.5.** What is the value returned from the method call b.getBalance() after the following operations?

```
BankAccount b = new BankAccount(10);
b.deposit(5000);
b.withdraw(b.getBalance() / 2);
```

★★ **Exercise R3.6.** If b1 and b2 refer to objects of class BankAccount, consider the following instructions.

```
b1.deposit(b2.getBalance());
b2.deposit(b1.getBalance());
```

Are the balances of b1 and b2 now identical? Explain.

★★ **Exercise R3.7.** What is the this reference? Why would you use it?

★★ **Exercise R3.8.** What does the following method do? Give an example of how you can call the method.

```
public class BankAccount
{
   public void mystery(BankAccount that, double amount)
   {
      this.balance = this.balance - amount;
      that.balance = that.balance + amount;
```

```
        }
    . . . // Other bank account methods
}
```

★★ **Exercise R3.9.** Suppose you want to implement a class `TimeDepositAccount`. A time deposit account has a fixed interest rate that should be set in the constructor, together with the initial balance. Provide a method to get the current balance. Provide a method to add the earned interest to the account. This method should have no parameters because the interest rate is already known. It should have no return value because you already provided a method for obtaining the current balance. It is not possible to deposit additional funds into this account. Provide a `withdraw` method that removes the entire balance. Partial withdrawals are not allowed.

★★ **Exercise R3.10.** What are the accessors and mutators of the `CashRegister` class?

★ **Exercise R3.11.** Explain the difference between a local variable and a parameter variable.

★ **Exercise R3.12.** Explain the difference between an instance field and a local variable.

★★G **Exercise R3.13.** Suppose you want to extend the car viewer program in Section 3.9 to show a suburban scene, with several cars and houses. Which classes do you need?

★★★G **Exercise R3.14.** Explain why the calls to the `getWidth` and `getHeight` methods in the `CarComponent` class have no explicit parameter.

★★G **Exercise R3.15.** How would you modify the `Car` class in order to show cars of varying sizes?

 Additional review exercises are available in WileyPLUS.

PROGRAMMING EXERCISES

★ **Exercise P3.1.** Write a `BankAccountTester` class whose `main` method constructs a bank account, deposits $1,000, withdraws $500, withdraws another $400, and then prints the remaining balance. Also print the expected result.

★ **Exercise P3.2.** Add a method

```
public void addInterest(double rate)
```

to the `BankAccount` class that adds interest at the given rate. For example, after the statements

```
BankAccount momsSavings = new BankAccount(1000);
momsSavings.addInterest(10); // 10% interest
```

the balance in `momsSavings` is $1,100. Also supply a `BankAccountTester` class that prints the actual and expected balance.

★★ **Exercise P3.3.** Write a class SavingsAccount that is similar to the BankAccount class, except that it has an added instance field interest. Supply a constructor that sets both the initial balance and the interest rate. Supply a method addInterest (with no explicit parameter) that adds interest to the account. Write a SavingsAccountTester class that constructs a savings account with an initial balance of $1,000 and an interest rate of 10%. Then apply the addInterest method and print the resulting balance. Also compute the expected result by hand and print it.

★★ **Exercise P3.4.** Implement a class Employee. An employee has a name (a string) and a salary (a double). Provide a constructor with two parameters

```
public Employee(String employeeName, double currentSalary)
```

and methods

```
public String getName()
public double getSalary()
public void raiseSalary(double byPercent)
```

These methods return the name and salary, and raise the employee's salary by a certain percentage. Sample usage:

```
Employee harry = new Employee("Hacker, Harry", 50000);
harry.raiseSalary(10); // Harry gets a 10% raise
```

Supply an EmployeeTester class that tests all methods.

★★ **Exercise P3.5.** Implement a class Car with the following properties. A car has a certain fuel efficiency (measured in miles/gallon or liters/km—pick one) and a certain amount of fuel in the gas tank. The efficiency is specified in the constructor, and the initial fuel level is 0. Supply a method drive that simulates driving the car for a certain distance, reducing the amount of gasoline in the fuel tank. Also supply methods getGasInTank, returning the current amount of gasoline in the fuel tank, and addGas, to add gasoline to the fuel tank. Sample usage:

```
Car myHybrid = new Car(50); // 50 miles per gallon
myHybrid.addGas(20); // Tank 20 gallons
myHybrid.drive(100); // Drive 100 miles
double gasLeft = myHybrid.getGasInTank(); // Get gas remaining in tank
```

You may assume that the drive method is never called with a distance that consumes more than the available gas. Supply a CarTester class that tests all methods.

★★ **Exercise P3.6.** Implement a class Student. For the purpose of this exercise, a student has a name and a total quiz score. Supply an appropriate constructor and methods getName(), addQuiz(int score), getTotalScore(), and getAverageScore(). To compute the latter, you also need to store the *number of quizzes* that the student took. Supply a StudentTester class that tests all methods.

★ **Exercise P3.7.** Implement a class Product. A product has a name and a price, for example new Product("Toaster", 29.95). Supply methods getName, getPrice, and reducePrice. Supply a program ProductPrinter that makes two products, prints the name and price, reduces their prices by $5.00, and then prints the prices again.

★★   **Exercise P3.8.** Provide a class for authoring a simple letter. In the constructor, supply the names of the sender and the recipient:

```
public Letter(String from, String to)
```

Supply a method

```
public void addLine(String line)
```

to add a line of text to the body of the letter.

Supply a method

```
public String getText()
```

that returns the entire text of the letter. The text has the form:

> *Dear recipient name :*
> *blank line*
> *first line of the body*
> *second line of the body*
> *. . .*
> *last line of the body*
> *blank line*
> *Sincerely,*
> *blank line*
> *sender name*

Also supply a program `LetterPrinter` that prints this letter.

```
Dear John:

I am sorry we must part.
I wish you all the best.

Sincerely,

Mary
```

Construct an object of the `Letter` class and call `addLine` twice.

Hints: (1) Use the `concat` method to form a longer string from two shorter strings. (2) The special string `"\n"` represents a new line. For example, the statement

```
body = body.concat("Sincerely,").concat("\n");
```

adds a line containing the string `"Sincerely,"` to the body.

★★   **Exercise P3.9.** Write a class `Bug` that models a bug moving along a horizontal line. The bug moves either to the right or left. Initially, the bug moves to the right, but it can turn to change its direction. In each move, its position changes by one unit in the current direction. Provide a constructor

```
public Bug(int initialPosition)
```

and methods

```
public void turn()
public void move()
public int getPosition()
```

Sample usage:

```
Bug bugsy = new Bug(10);
bugsy.move(); // now the position is 11
bugsy.turn();
bugsy.move(); // now the position is 10
```

Your `BugTester` should construct a bug, make it move and turn a few times, and print the actual and expected position.

★★ **Exercise P3.10.** Implement a class `Moth` that models a moth flying across a straight line. The moth has a position, the distance from a fixed origin. When the moth moves toward a point of light, its new position is halfway between its old position and the position of the light source. Supply a constructor

```
public Moth(double initialPosition)
```

and methods

```
public void moveToLight(double lightPosition)
public void getPosition()
```

Your `MothTester` should construct a moth, move it toward a couple of light sources, and check that the moth's position is as expected.

★★ **Exercise P3.11.** Implement a class `RoachPopulation` that simulates the growth of a roach population. The constructor takes the size of the initial roach population. The `breed` method simulates a period in which the roaches breed, which doubles their population. The `spray` method simulates spraying with insecticide, which reduces the population by 10%. The `getRoaches` method returns the current number of roaches. A program called `RoachSimulation` simulates a population that starts out with 10 roaches. Breed, spray, and print the roach count. Repeat three more times.

★★ **Exercise P3.12.** Implement a `VotingMachine` class that can be used for a simple election. Have methods to clear the machine state, to vote for a Democrat, to vote for a Republican, and to get the tallies for both parties. Extra credit if your program gives the nod to your favored party if the votes are tallied after 8 p.m. on the first Tuesday in November, but acts normally on all other dates. (*Hint:* Use the `Gregorian-Calendar` class—see Programming Project 2.1.)

★★G **Exercise P3.13.** Draw a "bull's eye"—a set of concentric rings in alternating black and white colors. *Hint:* Fill a black circle, then fill a smaller white circle on top, and so on.

Your program should be composed of classes `BullsEye`, `BullsEyeComponent`, and `BullsEyeViewer`.

★★G **Exercise P3.14.** Write a program that draws a picture of a house. It could be as simple as the accompanying figure, or if you like, make it more elaborate (3-D, skyscraper, marble columns in the entryway, whatever).

Implement a class House and supply a method draw(Graphics2D g2) that draws the house.

★★G **Exercise P3.15.** Extend Exercise P3.14 by supplying a House constructor for specifying the position and size. Then populate your screen with a few houses of different sizes.

★★G **Exercise P3.16.** Change the car viewer program in Section 3.9 to make the cars appear in different colors. Each Car object should store its own color. Supply modified Car and CarComponent classes.

★★G **Exercise P3.17.** Change the Car class so that the size of a car can be specified in the constructor. Change the CarComponent class to make one of the cars appear twice the size of the original example.

★★G **Exercise P3.18.** Write a program to plot the string "HELLO", using only lines and circles. Do not call drawString, and do not use System.out. Make classes LetterH, LetterE, LetterL, and LetterO.

★★G **Exercise P3.19.** Write a program that displays the Olympic rings. Color the rings in the Olympic colors.

Provide a class OlympicRingViewer and a class OlympicRingComponent.

★★G **Exercise P3.20.** Make a bar chart to plot the following data set. Label each bar. Make the bars horizontal for easier labeling. Provide a class BarChartViewer and a class BarChartComponent.

Bridge Name	Longest Span (ft)
Golden Gate	4,200
Brooklyn	1,595
Delaware Memorial	2,150
Mackinac	3,800

Additional programming exercises are available in WileyPLUS.

PROGRAMMING PROJECTS

★★★ **Project 3.1.** In this project, you will enhance the BankAccount class and see how abstraction and encapsulation enable evolutionary changes to software.

Begin with a simple enhancement: charging a fee for every deposit and withdrawal. Supply a mechanism for setting the fee and modify the deposit and withdraw methods so that the fee is levied. Test your resulting class and check that the fee is computed correctly.

Now make a more complex change. The bank will allow a fixed number of free transactions (deposits or withdrawals) every month, and charge for transactions exceeding the free allotment. The charge is not levied immediately but at the end of the month.

Supply a new method deductMonthlyCharge to the BankAccount class that deducts the monthly charge and resets the transaction count. Produce a test program that verifies that the fees are calculated correctly over several months.

★★★ **Project 3.2.** In this project, you will explore an object-oriented alternative to the "Hello, World" program in Chapter 1.

Begin with a simple Greeter class that has a single method, sayHello. That method should *return* a string, not print it. Use BlueJ to create two objects of this class and invoke their sayHello methods.

That is boring—of course, both objects return the same answer.

Enhance the Greeter class so that each object produces a customized greeting. For example, the object constructed as new Greeter("Dave") should say "Hello, Dave". (Use the concat method to combine strings to form a longer string, or peek ahead at Section 4.6 to see how you can use the + operator for the same purpose.)

Add a method sayGoodbye to the Greeter class.

Finally, add a method refuseHelp to the Greeter class. It should return a string such as "I am sorry, Dave. I am afraid I can't do that."

Test your class in BlueJ. Make objects that greet the world and Dave, and invoke methods on them.

ANSWERS TO SELF-CHECK QUESTIONS

1. The programmers who designed and implemented the Java library.

2. Other programmers who work on the personal finance application.

3. `harrysChecking.withdraw(harrysChecking.getBalance())`

4. Add an `accountNumber` parameter to the constructors, and add a `getAccount-Number` method. There is no need for a `setAccountNumber` method—the account number never changes after construction.

5. ```
   /**
       Constructs a new bank account with a given initial balance.
       @param accountNumber the account number for this account
       @param initialBalance the initial balance for this account
   */
   ```

6. The first sentence of the method description should describe the method—it is displayed in isolation in the summary table.

7. An instance field

   `private int accountNumber;`

   needs to be added to the class.

8. There are four fields: `x`, `y`, `width`, `height`. All four fields have type `int`.

9. ```
   public int getWidth()
   {
       return width;
   }
   ```

10. There is more than one correct answer. One possible implementation is as follows:
    ```
    public void translate(int dx, int dy)
    {
        int newx = x + dx;
        x = newx;
        int newy = y + dy;
        y = newy;
    }
    ```

11. One `BankAccount` object, no `BankAccountTester` object. The purpose of the `BankAccountTester` class is merely to hold the `main` method.

12. In those environments, you can issue interactive commands to construct `BankAccount` objects, invoke methods, and display their return values.

13. Variables of both categories belong to methods—they come alive when the method is called, and they die when the method exits. They differ in their initialization. Parameter variables are initialized with the call values; local variables must be explicitly initialized.

14. One instance field, named `balance`. Three local variables, one named `harrysChecking` and two named `newBalance` (in the `deposit` and `withdraw` methods); two parameter variables, both named `amount` (in the `deposit` and `withdraw` methods).

15. One implicit parameter, called `this`, of type `BankAccount`, and one explicit parameter, called `amount`, of type `double`.

16. It is not a legal expression. `this` is of type `BankAccount` and the `BankAccount` class has no field named `amount`.

17. No implicit parameter—the method is static—and one explicit parameter, called `args`.

18. `CarComponent`

19. In the `draw` method of the `Car` class, call

```
g2.fill(frontTire);
g2.fill(rearTire);
```

20. Double all measurements in the `draw` method of the `Car` class.

Fundamental Data Types

CHAPTER GOALS

- To understand integer and floating-point numbers

- To recognize the limitations of the numeric types

- To become aware of causes for overflow and roundoff errors

- To understand the proper use of constants

- To write arithmetic expressions in Java

- To use the String type to define and manipulate character strings

- To learn how to read program input and produce formatted output

This chapter teaches how to manipulate numbers and character strings in Java. The goal of this chapter is to gain a firm understanding of the fundamental Java data types.

You will learn about the properties and limitations of the number types in Java. You will see how to manipulate numbers and strings in your programs. Finally, we cover the important topic of input and output, which enables you to implement interactive programs.

CHAPTER CONTENTS

4.1 Number Types

> Java has eight primitive types, including four integer types and two floating-point types.

In Java, every value is either a reference to an object, or it belongs to one of the eight *primitive types* shown in Table 1.

Six of the primitive types are number types, four of them for integers and two for floating-point numbers.

Each of the integer types has a different range—Advanced Topic 4.2 explains why the range limits are related to powers of two. Generally, you will use the int type for integer quantities. However, occasionally, calculations involving integers can *overflow*. This happens if the result of a computation exceeds the range for the number type. For example:

> A numeric computation overflows if the result falls outside the range for the number type.

```
int n = 1000000;
System.out.println(n * n);   // Prints –727379968
```

The product n * n is 10^{12}, which is larger than the largest integer (about $2 \cdot 10^9$). The result is truncated to fit into an int, yielding a value that is completely wrong. Unfortunately, there is no warning when an integer overflow occurs.

Table 1 Primitive Types		
Type	**Description**	**Size**
int	The integer type, with range –2,147,483,648 . . . 2,147,483,647 (about 2 billion)	4 bytes
byte	The type describing a single byte, with range –128 . . . 127	1 byte
short	The short integer type, with range –32768 . . . 32767	2 bytes
long	The long integer type, with range –9,223,372,036,854,775,808 . . . 9,223,372,036,854,775,807	8 bytes
double	The double-precision floating-point type, with a range of about $\pm 10^{308}$ and about 15 significant decimal digits	8 bytes
float	The single-precision floating-point type, with a range of about $\pm 10^{38}$ and about 7 significant decimal digits	4 bytes
char	The character type, representing code units in the Unicode encoding scheme (see Advanced Topic 4.5)	2 bytes
boolean	The type with the two truth values false and true (see Chapter 5)	1 bit

If you run into this problem, the simplest remedy is to use the long type. Advanced Topic 4.1 shows you how to use the arbitary-precision BigInteger type in the unlikely event that even the long type overflows.

Overflow is not usually a problem for double-precision floating-point numbers. The double type has a range of about $\pm 10^{308}$ and about 15 significant digits. However, you want to avoid the float type—it has less than 7 significant digits. (Some programmers use float to save on memory if they need to store a huge set of numbers that do not require much precision.)

> Rounding errors occur when an exact conversion between numbers is not possible.

Rounding errors are a more serious issue with floating-point values. Rounding errors can occur when you convert between binary and decimal numbers, or between integers and floating-point numbers. When a value cannot be converted exactly, it is rounded to the nearest match. Consider this example:

```
double f = 4.35;
System.out.println(100 * f); // Prints 434.99999999999994
```

This problem is caused because computers represent numbers in the binary number system. In the binary number system, there is no exact representation of the fraction 1/10, just as there is no exact representation of the fraction 1/3 = 0.33333 in the decimal number system. (See Advanced Topic 4.2 for more information.)

For this reason, the double type is not appropriate for financial calculations. In this book, we will continue to use double values for bank balances and other financial quantities so that we keep our programs as simple as possible. However, professional programs need to use the `BigDecimal` type for this purpose—see Advanced Topic 4.1.

In Java, it is legal to assign an integer value to a floating-point variable:

```
int dollars = 100;
double balance = dollars; // OK
```

But the opposite assignment is an error: You cannot assign a floating-point expression to an integer variable.

```
double balance = 13.75;
int dollars = balance; // Error
```

To overcome this problem, you can convert the floating-point value to an integer with a cast:

```
int dollars = (int) balance;
```

> You use a cast (*typeName*) to convert a value to a different type.

The cast `(int)` converts the floating-point value `balance` to an integer by discarding the fractional part. For example, if `balance` is 13.75, then `dollars` is set to 13.

The cast tells the compiler that you agree to *information loss,* in this case, to the loss of the fractional part. You can also cast to other types, such as `(float)` or `(byte)`.

> Use the `Math.round` method to round a floating-point number to the nearest integer.

If you want to round a floating-point number to the nearest whole number, use the `Math.round` method. This method returns a `long` integer, because large floating-point numbers cannot be stored in an `int`.

```
long rounded = Math.round(balance);
```

If `balance` is 13.75, then `rounded` is set to 14.

SYNTAX 4.1 Cast

(*typeName*) *expression*

Example:

(int) (balance * 100)

Purpose:

To convert an expression to a different type

SELF CHECK

1. Which are the most commonly used number types in Java?
2. When does the cast `(long)` x yield a different result from the call `Math.round(x)`?
3. How do you round the `double` value x to the nearest `int` value, assuming that you know that it is less than $2 \cdot 10^9$?

ADVANCED TOPIC 4.1

Big Numbers

If you want to compute with really large numbers, you can use big number objects. Big number objects are objects of the `BigInteger` and `BigDecimal` classes in the `java.math` package. Unlike the number types such as `int` or `double`, big number objects have essentially no limits on their size and precision. However, computations with big number objects are much slower than those that involve number types. Perhaps more importantly, you can't use the familiar arithmetic operators such as (+ - *) with them. Instead, you have to use methods called `add`, `subtract`, and `multiply`. Here is an example of how to create two big integers and how to multiply them.

```
BigInteger a = new BigInteger("1234567890");
BigInteger b = new BigInteger("9876543210");
BigInteger c = a.multiply(b);
System.out.println(c); // Prints 12193263111263526900
```

The `BigDecimal` type carries out floating-point computation without roundoff errors. For example,

```
BigDecimal d = new BigDecimal("4.35");
BigDecimal e = new BigDecimal("100");
BigDecimal f = d.multiply(e);
System.out.println(f); // Prints 435.00
```

ADVANCED TOPIC 4.2

Binary Numbers

You are familiar with decimal numbers, which use the digits 0, 1, 2, ..., 9. Each digit has a place value of 1, 10, $100 = 10^2$, $1000 = 10^3$, and so on. For example,

$$435 = 4 \cdot 10^2 + 3 \cdot 10^1 + 5 \cdot 10^0$$

Fractional digits have place values with negative powers of ten: $0.1 = 10^{-1}$, $0.01 = 10^{-2}$, and so on. For example,

$$4.35 = 4 \cdot 10^0 + 3 \cdot 10^{-1} + 5 \cdot 10^{-2}$$

Computers use binary numbers instead, which have just two digits (0 and 1) and place values that are powers of 2. Binary numbers are easier for computers to manipulate, because it is easier to build logic circuits that differentiate between "off" and "on" than it is to build circuits that can accurately tell ten different voltage levels apart.

It is easy to transform a binary number into a decimal number. Just compute the powers of two that correspond to ones in the binary number. For example,

$$1101 \text{ binary} = 1 \cdot 2^3 + 1 \cdot 2^2 + 0 \cdot 2^1 + 1 \cdot 2^0 = 8 + 4 + 1 = 13$$

Fractional binary numbers use negative powers of two. For example,

$$1.101 \text{ binary} = 1 \cdot 2^0 + 1 \cdot 2^{-1} + 0 \cdot 2^{-2} + 1 \cdot 2^{-3} = 1 + 0.5 + 0.125 = 1.625$$

Converting decimal numbers to binary numbers is a little trickier. Here is an algorithm that converts a decimal integer into its binary equivalent: Keep dividing the integer by 2, keeping track of the remainders. Stop when the number is 0. Then write the remainders as a binary number, starting with the last one. For example,

$$100 \div 2 = 50 \text{ remainder } 0$$

$$50 \div 2 = 25 \text{ remainder } 0$$

$$25 \div 2 = 12 \text{ remainder } 1$$

$$12 \div 2 = 6 \text{ remainder } 0$$

$$6 \div 2 = 3 \text{ remainder } 0$$

$$3 \div 2 = 1 \text{ remainder } 1$$

$$1 \div 2 = 0 \text{ remainder } 1$$

Therefore, 100 in decimal is 1100100 in binary.

To convert a fractional number <1 to its binary format, keep multiplying by 2. If the result is >1, subtract 1. Stop when the number is 0. Then use the digits before the decimal points as the binary digits of the fractional part, starting with the first one. For example,

$$0.35 \cdot 2 = 0.7$$

$$0.7 \cdot 2 = 1.4$$

$$0.4 \cdot 2 = 0.8$$

$$0.8 \cdot 2 = 1.6$$

$$0.6 \cdot 2 = 1.2$$

$$0.2 \cdot 2 = 0.4$$

Here the pattern repeats. That is, the binary representation of 0.35 is 0.01 0110 0110 0110 . . .

To convert any floating-point number into binary, convert the whole part and the fractional part separately. For example, 4.35 is 100.01 0110 0110 0110 . . . in binary.

You don't actually need to know about binary numbers to program in Java, but at times it can be helpful to understand a little about them. For example, knowing that an int is represented as a 32-bit binary number explains why the largest integer that you can represent in Java is 0111 1111 1111 1111 1111 1111 1111 1111 binary = 2,147,483,647 decimal. (The first bit is the sign bit. It is off for positive values.)

To convert an integer into its binary representation, you can use the static toString method of the Integer class. The call Integer.toString(n, 2) returns a string with the binary digits of the integer n. Conversely, you can convert a string containing binary digits into an integer with the call Integer.parseInt(digitString, 2). In both of these method calls, the second parameter denotes the base of the number system. It can be any number between 0 and 36. You can use these two methods to convert between decimal and binary integers. However, the Java library has no convenient method to do the same for floating-point numbers.

Now you can see why we had to fight with a roundoff error when computing 100 times 4.35. If you actually carry out the long multiplication, you get:

```
1 1 0 0 1 0 0 * 1 0 0.0 1|0 1 1 0|0 1 1 0|0 1 1 0 . . .

1 0 0.0 1|0 1 1 0|0 1 1 0|0 1 1 0 . . .
  1 0 0.0 1|0 1 1 0|0 1 1 0|0 1 1 . . .
     0
        0
            1 0 0.0 1|0 1 1 0|0 1 1 0 . . .
               0
                  0
_____
1 1 0 1 1 0 0 1 0.1 1 1 1 1 1 1 1 . . .
```

That is, the result is 434, followed by an infinite number of 1s. The fractional part of the product is the binary equivalent of an infinite decimal fraction 0.999999 . . . , which is equal to 1. But the CPU can store only a finite number of 1s, and it discards some of them when converting the result to a decimal number.

RANDOM FACT 4.1

The Pentium Floating-Point Bug

In 1994, Intel Corporation released what was then its most powerful processor, the first of the Pentium series. Unlike previous generations of Intel's processors, the Pentium had a very fast floating-point unit. Intel's goal was to compete aggressively with the makers of higher-end processors for engineering workstations. The Pentium was an immediate success.

In the summer of 1994, Dr. Thomas Nicely of Lynchburg College in Virginia ran an extensive set of computations to analyze the sums of reciprocals of certain sequences of prime numbers. The results were not always what his theory predicted, even after he took into account the inevitable roundoff errors. Then Dr. Nicely noted that the same program did produce the correct results when run on the slower 486 processor, which preceded the Pentium in Intel's lineup. This should not have happened. The optimal roundoff behavior of floating-point calculations had been standardized by the Institute of Electrical and Electronics Engineers (IEEE), and Intel claimed to adhere to the IEEE standard in both the 486 and the Pentium processors. Upon further checking, Dr. Nicely discovered that indeed there was a very small set of numbers for which the product of two numbers was computed differently on the two processors. For example,

$$4{,}195{,}835 = ((4{,}195{,}835 / 3{,}145{,}727) \times 3{,}145{,}727)$$

is mathematically equal to 0, and it did compute as 0 on a 486 processor. On a Pentium processor, however, the result was 256.

As it turned out, Intel had independently discovered the bug in its testing and had started to produce chips that fixed it. (Subsequent versions of the Pentium, such as the Pentium III and IV, are free of the problem.) The bug was caused by an error in a table that was used to speed up the floating-point multiplication algorithm of the processor. Intel determined that the problem was exceedingly rare. They claimed that under normal use a typical consumer would only notice the problem once every 27,000 years. Unfortunately for Intel, Dr. Nicely had not been a normal user.

Now Intel had a real problem on its hands. It figured that replacing all the Pentium processors that it had already sold would cost it a great deal of money. Intel already had more orders for the chip than it could produce, and it would be particularly galling to have to give out the scarce chips as free replacements instead of selling them. Intel's management decided to punt on the issue and initially offered to replace the processors only for those customers who could prove that their work required absolute precision in mathematical calculations. Naturally, that did not go over well with the hundreds of thousands of customers who had paid retail prices of $700 and more for a Pentium chip and did not want to live with the nagging feeling that perhaps, one day, their income tax program would produce a faulty return.

Ultimately, Intel had to cave in to public demand and replaced all defective chips, at a cost of about 475 million dollars.

What do you think? Intel claims that the probability of the bug occurring in any calculation is extremely small—smaller than many chances you take every day, such as driving to work in an automobile. Indeed, many users had used their Pentium computers for many months without reporting any ill effects, and the computations that Professor Nicely was doing are hardly examples of typical user needs. As a result of its public relations blunder, Intel ended up paying a large amount of money. Undoubtedly, some of that money was added to chip prices and thus actually paid by Intel's customers. Also, a large number of processors, whose manufacture consumed energy and caused some environmental impact, were destroyed without benefiting anyone. Could Intel have been justified in wanting to replace only the processors of those users who could reasonably be expected to suffer an impact from the problem?

Suppose that, instead of stonewalling, Intel had offered you the choice of a free replacement processor or a $200 rebate. What would you have done? Would you have replaced your faulty chip, or would you have taken your chances and pocketed the money?

4.2 Constants

In many programs, you need to use numerical *constants*—values that do not change and that have a special significance for a computation.

A typical example for the use of constants is a computation that involves coin values, such as the following:

```
payment = dollars + quarters * 0.25 + dimes * 0.1
    + nickels * 0.05 + pennies * 0.01;
```

Most of the code is self-documenting. However, the four numeric quantities, 0.25, 0.1, 0.05, and 0.01 are included in the arithmetic expression without any explanation. Of course, in this case, you know that the value of a nickel is five cents, which explains the 0.05, and so on. However, the next person who needs to maintain this code may live in another country and may not know that a nickel is worth five cents.

Thus, it is a good idea to use symbolic names for all values, even those that appear obvious. Here is a clearer version of the computation of the total:

```
double quarterValue = 0.25;
double dimeValue = 0.1;
double nickelValue = 0.05;
double pennyValue = 0.01;
payment = dollars + quarters * quarterValue + dimes * dimeValue
        + nickels * nickelValue + pennies * pennyValue;
```

A final variable is a constant. Once its value has been set, it cannot be changed.

There is another improvement we can make. There is a difference between the nickels and nickelValue variables. The nickels variable can truly vary over the life of the program, as we calculate different payments. But nickelValue is always 0.05.

In Java, constants are identified with the keyword final. A variable tagged as final can never change after it has been set. If you try to change the value of a final variable, the compiler will report an error and your program will not compile.

Use named constants to make your programs easier to read and maintain.

Many programmers use all-uppercase names for constants (final variables), such as NICKEL_VALUE. That way, it is easy to distinguish between variables (with mostly lowercase letters) and constants. We will follow this convention in this book. However, this rule is a matter of good style, not a requirement of the Java language. The compiler will not complain if you give a final variable a name with lowercase letters.

Here is an improved version of the code that computes the value of a payment.

```
final double QUARTER_VALUE = 0.25;
final double DIME_VALUE = 0.1;
final double NICKEL_VALUE = 0.05;
final double PENNY_VALUE = 0.01;
payment = dollars + quarters * QUARTER_VALUE + dimes * DIME_VALUE
        + nickels * NICKEL_VALUE + pennies * PENNY_VALUE;
```

Frequently, constant values are needed in several methods. Then you should declare them together with the instance fields of a class and tag them as static and final. As before, final indicates that the value is a constant. The static keyword means that the constant belongs to the class—this is explained in greater detail in Chapter 8.)

```
public class CashRegister
{
   // Methods
   . . .

   // Constants
   public static final double QUARTER_VALUE = 0.25;
   public static final double DIME_VALUE = 0.1;
   public static final double NICKEL_VALUE = 0.05;
   public static final double PENNY_VALUE = 0.01;

   // Instance fields
   private double purchase;
   private double payment;
}
```

We declared the constants as `public`. There is no danger in doing this because constants cannot be modified. Methods of other classes can access a public constant by first specifying the name of the class in which it is defined, then a period, then the name of the constant, such as `CashRegister.NICKEL_VALUE`.

The `Math` class from the standard library defines a couple of useful constants:

```
public class Math
{
   . . .
   public static final double E = 2.7182818284590452354;
   public static final double PI = 3.14159265358979323846;
}
```

You can refer to these constants as `Math.PI` and `Math.E` in any of your methods. For example,

```
double circumference = Math.PI * diameter;
```

The sample program at the end of this section puts constants to work. The program shows a refinement of the `CashRegister` class of How To 3.1. The public interface of that class has been modified in order to solve a common business problem.

Busy cashiers sometimes make mistakes totaling up coin values. Our `CashRegister` class features a method whose inputs are the *coin counts*. For example, the call

```
register.enterPayment(1, 2, 1, 1, 4);
```

enters a payment consisting of one dollar, two quarters, one dime, one nickel, and four pennies. The `enterPayment` method figures out the total value of the payment, $1.69. As you can see from the code listing, the method uses named constants for the coin values.

Syntax 4.2 Constant Definition

In a method:
final *typeName* *variableName* = *expression*;

In a class:
accessSpecifier static final *typeName* *variableName* = *expression*;

Example:

```
final double NICKEL_VALUE = 0.05;
public static final double LITERS_PER_GALLON = 3.785;
```

Purpose:

To define a constant in a method or a class

ch04/cashregister/CashRegister.java

```java
1  /**
2     A cash register totals up sales and computes change due.
3  */
4  public class CashRegister
5  {
6     /**
7        Constructs a cash register with no money in it.
8     */
9     public CashRegister()
10    {
11       purchase = 0;
12       payment = 0;
13    }
14
15    /**
16       Records the purchase price of an item.
17       @param amount the price of the purchased item
18    */
19    public void recordPurchase(double amount)
20    {
21       purchase = purchase + amount;
22    }
23
24    /**
25       Enters the payment received from the customer.
26       @param dollars the number of dollars in the payment
27       @param quarters the number of quarters in the payment
28       @param dimes the number of dimes in the payment
29       @param nickels the number of nickels in the payment
30       @param pennies the number of pennies in the payment
31    */
32    public void enterPayment(int dollars, int quarters,
33          int dimes, int nickels, int pennies)
34    {
35       payment = dollars + quarters * QUARTER_VALUE + dimes * DIME_VALUE
36             + nickels * NICKEL_VALUE + pennies * PENNY_VALUE;
37    }
38
39    /**
40       Computes the change due and resets the machine for the next customer.
41       @return the change due to the customer
42    */
43    public double giveChange()
44    {
45       double change = payment - purchase;
46       purchase = 0;
47       payment = 0;
48       return change;
49    }
50
51    public static final double QUARTER_VALUE = 0.25;
52    public static final double DIME_VALUE = 0.1;
```

```
53      public static final double NICKEL_VALUE = 0.05;
54      public static final double PENNY_VALUE = 0.01;
55
56      private double purchase;
57      private double payment;
58  }
```

ch04/cashregister/CashRegisterTester.java

```
1   /**
2       This class tests the CashRegister class.
3   */
4   public class CashRegisterTester
5   {
6      public static void main(String[] args)
7      {
8         CashRegister register = new CashRegister();
9
10        register.recordPurchase(0.75);
11        register.recordPurchase(1.50);
12        register.enterPayment(2, 0, 5, 0, 0);
13        System.out.print("Change: ");
14        System.out.println(register.giveChange());
15        System.out.println("Expected: 0.25");
16
17        register.recordPurchase(2.25);
18        register.recordPurchase(19.25);
19        register.enterPayment(23, 2, 0, 0, 0);
20        System.out.print("Change: ");
21        System.out.println(register.giveChange());
22        System.out.println("Expected: 2.0");
23     }
24  }
```

Output

```
Change: 0.25
Expected: 0.25
Change: 2.0
Expected: 2.0
```

SELF CHECK

4. What is the difference between the following two statements?

    ```
    final double CM_PER_INCH = 2.54;
    ```

    and

    ```
    public static final double CM_PER_INCH = 2.54;
    ```

5. What is wrong with the following statement?

    ```
    double circumference = 3.14 * diameter;
    ```

QUALITY TIP 4.1

Do Not Use Magic Numbers

A magic number is a numeric constant that appears in your code without explanation. For example, consider the following scary example that actually occurs in the Java library source:

```
h = 31 * h + ch;
```

Why 31? The number of days in January? One less than the number of bits in an integer? Actually, this code computes a "hash code" from a string—a number that is derived from the characters in such a way that different strings are likely to yield different hash codes. The value 31 turns out to scramble the character values nicely.

A better solution is to use a named constant:

```
final int HASH_MULTIPLIER = 31;
h = HASH_MULTIPLIER * h + ch;
```

You should never use magic numbers in your code. Any number that is not completely self-explanatory should be declared as a named constant. Even the most reasonable cosmic constant is going to change one day. You think there are 365 days in a year? Your customers on Mars are going to be pretty unhappy about your silly prejudice. Make a constant

```
final int DAYS_PER_YEAR = 365;
```

By the way, the device

```
final int THREE_HUNDRED_AND_SIXTY_FIVE = 365;
```

is counterproductive and frowned upon.

QUALITY TIP 4.2

Choose Descriptive Variable Names

In algebra, variable names are usually just one letter long, such as p or A, maybe with a subscript such as p_1. You might be tempted to save yourself a lot of typing by using short variable names in your Java programs:

```
payment = d + q * QV + di * DIV + n * NV + p * PV;
```

Compare this with the following statement:

```
payment = dollars + quarters * QUARTER_VALUE + dimes * DIME_VALUE
    + nickels * NICKEL_VALUE + pennies * PENNY_VALUE;
```

The advantage is obvious. Reading `dollars` is a lot less trouble than reading `d` and then figuring out that it must mean "dollars".

In practical programming, descriptive variable names are particularly important when programs are written by more than one person. It may be obvious to you that `d` stands for dollars, but is it obvious to the person who needs to update your code years later, long after you were promoted (or laid off)? For that matter, will you remember yourself what `d` means when you look at the code six months from now?

4.3 Assignment, Increment, and Decrement

The = operator is called the assignment operator. On the left, you need a variable name. The right-hand side can be a single value or an expression. The assignment operator sets the variable to the given value. So far, that's straightforward. But now let's look at a more interesting use of the assignment operator. Consider the statement

```
items = items + 1;
```

It means, "Compute the value of the expression items + 1, and place the result again into the variable items." (See Figure 1.) The net effect of executing this statement is to increment items by 1. For example, if items was 3 before execution of the statement, it is set to 4 afterwards. (This statement would be useful if the cash register kept track of the number of purchased items.)

The = sign does *not* mean that the left-hand side is equal to the right-hand side. Instead, it is an instruction to copy the right-hand-side value into the left-hand-side variable. You should not confuse this assignment operation with the = relation used in algebra to denote equality. The assignment operator is an instruction to do something, namely place a value into a variable. The mathematical equality states the fact that two values are equal. Of course, in mathematics it would make no sense to write that $i = i + 1$; no integer can equal itself plus 1.

> Assignment to a variable is not the same as mathematical equality.

The concepts of assignment and equality have no relationship with each other, and it is a bit unfortunate that the Java language (following C and C++) uses = to denote assignment. Other programming languages use a symbol such as <- or :=, which avoids the confusion.

> The ++ and -- operators increment and decrement a variable.

The increment operation is so common when writing programs that there is a special shorthand for it, namely

```
items++;
```

This statement also adds 1 to items. However, it is easier to type and read than the explicit assignment statement. As you might have guessed, there is also a decrement operator --. The statement

```
items--;
```

subtracts 1 from items.

Figure 1
Incrementing a Variable

SELF CHECK

6. What is the meaning of the following statement?

```
balance = balance + amount;
```

7. What is the value of n after the following sequence of statements?

```
n--;
n++;
n--;
```

PRODUCTIVITY HINT 4.1

Avoid Unstable Layout

Arrange program code and comments so that the program is easy to read. For example, do not cram all statements on a single line, and make sure that braces { } line up.

However, be careful when you embark on beautification efforts. Some programmers like to line up the = signs in a series of assignments, like this:

```
nickels  = 0;
dimes    = 0;
quarters = 0;
```

This looks very neat, but the layout is not stable. Suppose you add a line like the one at the bottom of this:

```
nickels  = 0;
dimes    = 0;
quarters = 0;
halfDollars = 0;
```

Oops, now the = signs no longer line up, and you have the extra work of lining them up again.

Here is another example. Some programmers like to put a column of asterisks (*) in documentation comments, like this:

```
/**
 * Computes the change due and resets the cash register for the
 * next customer.
 * @return the change due to the customer
 */
```

It looks pretty, but it is tedious to rearrange the asterisks when editing comments.

You may not care about these issues. Perhaps you plan to beautify your program just before it is finished, when you are about to turn in your homework. That is not a particularly useful approach. In practice, programs are never finished. They are continuously improved and updated. It is better to develop the habit of laying out your programs well from the start and keeping them legible at all times. Therefore, it is a good idea to avoid layout schemes that are hard to maintain.

ADVANCED TOPIC 4.3

Combining Assignment and Arithmetic

In Java you can combine arithmetic and assignment. For example, the instruction

```
balance += amount;
```

is a shortcut for

```
balance = balance + amount;
```

Similarly,

```
items *= 2;
```

is another way of writing

```
items = items * 2;
```

Many programmers find this a convenient shortcut. If you like it, go ahead and use it in your own code. For simplicity, we won't use it in this book.

4.4 Arithmetic Operations and Mathematical Functions

You already saw how to add, subtract, and multiply values. Division is indicated with a /, not a fraction bar. For example,

$$\frac{a + b}{2}$$

becomes

```
(a + b) / 2
```

Parentheses are used just as in algebra: to indicate in which order the subexpressions should be computed. For example, in the expression (a + b) / 2, the sum a + b is computed first, and then the sum is divided by 2. In contrast, in the expression

```
a + b / 2
```

only b is divided by 2, and then the sum of a and b / 2 is formed. Just as in regular algebraic notation, multiplication and division bind more strongly than addition and subtraction. For example, in the expression a + b / 2, the / is carried out first, even though the + operation occurs farther to the left.

Division works as you would expect, as long as at least one of the numbers involved is a floating-point number. That is,

> If both arguments of the / operator are integers, the result is an integer and the remainder is discarded.

```
7.0 / 4.0
7 / 4.0
7.0 / 4
```

all yield 1.75. However, if both numbers are integers, then the result of the division is always an integer, with the remainder discarded. That is,

```
7 / 4
```

evaluates to 1, because 7 divided by 4 is 1 with a remainder of 3 (which is discarded). This can be a source of subtle programming errors—see Common Error 4.1.

If you are interested only in the remainder of an integer division, use the % operator:

> The % operator computes the remainder of a division.

```
7 % 4
```

is 3, the remainder of the integer division of 7 by 4. The % symbol has no analog in algebra. It was chosen because it looks similar to /, and the remainder operation is related to division.

Here is a typical use for the integer / and % operations. Suppose you want to know how much change a cash register should give, using separate values for dollars and cents. You can compute the value as an integer, denominated in cents, and then compute the whole dollar amount and the remaining change:

```
final int PENNIES_PER_NICKEL = 5;
final int PENNIES_PER_DIME = 10;
final int PENNIES_PER_QUARTER = 25;
final int PENNIES_PER_DOLLAR = 100;

// Compute total value in pennies
int total = dollars * PENNIES_PER_DOLLAR + quarters * PENNIES_PER_QUARTER
      + nickels * PENNIES_PER_NICKEL + dimes * PENNIES_PER_DIME + pennies;

// Use integer division to convert to dollars, cents
int dollars - total / PENNIES_PER_DOLLAR;
int cents = total % PENNIES_PER_DOLLAR;
```

For example, if total is 243, then dollars is set to 2 and cents to 43.

To compute x^n, you write Math.pow(x, n). However, to compute x^2 it is significantly more efficient simply to compute x * x.

> The Math class contains methods sqrt and pow to compute square roots and powers.

To take the square root of a number, you use the Math.sqrt method. For example, $\sqrt{x}$ is written as Math.sqrt(x).

In algebra, you use fractions, superscripts for exponents, and radical signs for roots to arrange expressions in a compact two-dimensional form. In Java, you have to write all expressions in a linear arrangement. For example, the subexpression

$$\frac{-b + \sqrt{b^2 - 4ac}}{2a}$$

of the quadratic formula becomes

```
(-b + Math.sqrt(b * b - 4 * a * c)) / (2 * a)
```

Figure 2 shows how to analyze such an expression. With complicated expressions like these, it is not always easy to keep the parentheses ( ) matched—see Common Error 4.2.

Table 2 shows additional methods of the Math class. Inputs and outputs are floating-point numbers.

Table 2   Mathematical Methods

Function	Returns
Math.sqrt(x)	Square root of x (≥ 0)
Math.pow(x, y)	x^y ($x > 0$, or $x = 0$ and $y > 0$, or $x < 0$ and y is an integer)
Math.sin(x)	Sine of x (x in radians)
Math.cos(x)	Cosine of x
Math.tan(x)	Tangent of x
Math.asin(x)	Arc sine ($\sin^{-1}x \in [-\pi/2, \pi/2]$, $x \in [-1, 1]$)
Math.acos(x)	Arc cosine ($\cos^{-1}x \in [0, \pi]$, $x \in [-1, 1]$)
Math.atan(x)	Arc tangent ($\tan^{-1}x \in [-\pi/2, \pi/2]$)
Math.atan2(y, x)	Arc tangent ($\tan^{-1}y/x \in [-\pi, \pi]$), x may be 0
Math.toRadians(x)	Convert x degrees to radians (i.e., returns $x \cdot \pi/180$)
Math.toDegrees(x)	Convert x radians to degrees (i.e., returns $x \cdot 180/\pi$)
Math.exp(x)	e^x
Math.log(x)	Natural log ($\ln(x)$, $x > 0$)
Math.round(x)	Closest integer to x (as a long)
Math.ceil(x)	Smallest integer $\geq x$ (as a double)
Math.floor(x)	Largest integer $\leq x$ (as a double)
Math.abs(x)	Absolute value $|x|$
Math.max(x, y)	The larger of x and y
Math.min(x, y)	The smaller of x and y

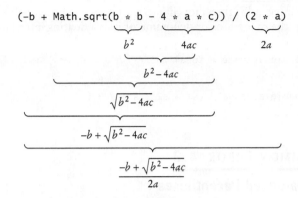

Figure 2 Analyzing an Expression

SELF CHECK

8. What is the value of 1729 / 100? Of 1729 % 100?

9. Why doesn't the following statement compute the average of s1, s2, and s3?

   ```
   double average = s1 + s2 + s3 / 3; // Error
   ```

10. What is the value of Math.sqrt(Math.pow(x, 2) + Math.pow(y, 2)) in mathematical notation?

COMMON ERROR 4.1

Integer Division

It is unfortunate that Java uses the same symbol, namely /, for both integer and floating-point division. These are really quite different operations. It is a common error to use integer division by accident. Consider this program segment that computes the average of three integers.

```
int s1 = 5; // Score of test 1
int s2 = 6; // Score of test 2
int s3 = 3; // Score of test 3
double average = (s1 + s2 + s3) / 3;  // Error
System.out.print("Your average score is ");
System.out.println(average);
```

What could be wrong with that? Of course, the average of s1, s2, and s3 is

$$\frac{s_1 + s_2 + s_3}{3}$$

Here, however, the / does not mean division in the mathematical sense. It denotes integer division, because the values s1 + s2 + s3 and 3 are both integers. For example, if the scores add up to 14, the average is computed to be 4, the result of the integer division of 14 by 3.

That integer 4 is then moved into the floating-point variable average. The remedy is to make either the numerator or denominator into a floating-point number:

```
double total = s1 + s2 + s3;
double average = total / 3;
```

or

```
double average = (s1 + s2 + s3) / 3.0;
```

COMMON ERROR 4.2

Unbalanced Parentheses

Consider the expression

```
1.5 * ((-(b - Math.sqrt(b * b - 4 * a * c)) / (2 * a))
```

What is wrong with it? Count the parentheses. There are five opening parentheses (and four closing parentheses). The parentheses are unbalanced. This kind of typing error is very common with complicated expressions. Now consider this expression.

```
1.5 * (Math.sqrt(b * b - 4 * a * c))) - ((b / (2 * a))
```

This expression has five opening parentheses (and five closing parentheses), but it is still not correct. In the middle of the expression,

```
1.5 * (Math.sqrt(b * b - 4 * a * c))) - ((b / (2 * a))
```

there are only two opening parentheses (but three closing parentheses), which is an error. In the middle of an expression, the count of opening parentheses must be greater than or equal to the count of closing parentheses, and at the end of the expression the two counts must be the same.

Here is a simple trick to make the counting easier without using pencil and paper. It is difficult for the brain to keep two counts simultaneously, so keep only one count when scanning the expression. Start with 1 at the first opening parenthesis; add 1 whenever you see an opening parenthesis; subtract 1 whenever you see a closing parenthesis. Say the numbers aloud as you scan the expression. If the count ever drops below zero, or if it is not zero at the end, the parentheses are unbalanced. For example, when scanning the previous expression, you would mutter

```
1.5 * (Math.sqrt(b * b - 4 * a * c) )  ) - ((b / (2 * a))
        1         2                 1 0 -1
```

and you would find the error.

QUALITY TIP 4.3

White Space

The compiler does not care whether you write your entire program onto a single line or place every symbol onto a separate line. The human reader, though, cares very much. You should use blank lines to group your code visually into sections. For example, you can signal to the reader that an output prompt and the corresponding input statement belong together by inserting a blank line before and after the group. You will find many examples in the source code listings in this book.

White space inside expressions is also important. It is easier to read

```
x1 = (-b + Math.sqrt(b * b - 4 * a * c)) / (2 * a);
```

than

```
x1=(-b+Math.sqrt(b*b-4*a*c))/(2*a);
```

Simply put spaces around all operators + - * / % =. However, don't put a space after a unary minus: a - used to negate a single quantity, as in -b. That way, it can be easily distinguished from a binary minus, as in a - b. Don't put spaces between a method name and the parentheses, but do put a space after every Java keyword. That makes it easy to see that the sqrt in Math.sqrt(x) is a method name, whereas the if in if (x > 0) . . . is a keyword.

QUALITY TIP 4.4

Factor Out Common Code

Suppose you want to find both solutions of the quadratic equation $ax^2 + bx + c = 0$. The quadratic formula tells us that the solutions are

$$x_{1,2} = \frac{-b \pm \sqrt{b^2 - 4ac}}{2a}$$

In Java, there is no analog to the $\pm$ operation, which indicates how to obtain two solutions simultaneously. Both solutions must be computed separately:

```
x1 = (-b + Math.sqrt(b * b - 4 * a * c)) / (2 * a);
x2 = (-b - Math.sqrt(b * b - 4 * a * c)) / (2 * a);
```

This approach has two problems. First, the computation of Math.sqrt(b * b - 4 * a * c) is carried out twice, which wastes time. Second, whenever the same code is replicated, the possibility of a typing error increases. The remedy is to factor out the common code:

```
double root = Math.sqrt(b * b - 4 * a * c);
x1 = (-b + root) / (2 * a);
x2 = (-b - root) / (2 * a);
```

You could go even further and factor out the computation of 2 * a, but the gain from factoring out very simple computations is too small to warrant the effort.

4.5 Calling Static Methods

In the preceding section, you encountered the Math class, which contains a collection of helpful methods for carrying out mathematical computations. These methods have a special form: they are static methods that do not operate on an object.

That is, you don't call

```
double x = 4;
double root = x.sqrt(); // Error
```

because, in Java, numbers are not objects, so you can never invoke a method on a number. Instead, you pass a number as an explicit parameter to a method, enclosing the number in parentheses after the method name. For example, the number value x can be a parameter of the Math.sqrt method: Math.sqrt(x).

> A static method does not operate on an object.

This call makes it appear as if the sqrt method is applied to an object called Math, because Math precedes sqrt just as harrysChecking precedes getBalance in a method call harrysChecking.getBalance(). However, Math is a class, not an object. A method such as Math.round that does not operate on any object is called a *static* method. (The term "static" is a historical holdover from the C and C++ programming languages. It has nothing to do with the usual meaning of the word.) Static methods do not operate on objects, but they are still defined inside classes. You must specify the class to which the sqrt method belongs—hence the call is Math.sqrt(x).

How can you tell whether Math is a class or an object? All classes in the Java library start with an uppercase letter (such as System). Objects and methods start with a lowercase letter (such as out and println). (You can tell objects and methods apart because method calls are followed by parentheses.) Therefore, System.out.println() denotes a call of the println method on the out object inside the System class. On the other hand, Math.sqrt(x) denotes a call to the sqrt method inside the Math class. This use of upper- and lowercase letters is merely a convention, not a rule of the Java language. It is, however, a convention that the authors of the Java class libraries follow consistently. You should do the same in your programs. If you give names to objects or methods that start with uppercase letters, you will likely confuse your fellow programmers. Therefore, we strongly recommend that you follow the standard naming convention.

SYNTAX 4.3 Static Method Call

ClassName.*methodName*(*parameters*)

Example:

Math.sqrt(4)

Purpose:

To invoke a static method (a method that does not operate on an object) and supply its parameters

SELF CHECK

11. Why can't you call x.pow(y) to compute x^y?

12. Is the call System.out.println(4) a static method call?

COMMON ERROR 4.3

Roundoff Errors

Roundoff errors are a fact of life when calculating with floating-point numbers. You probably have encountered this phenomenon yourself with manual calculations. If you calculate 1/3 to two decimal places, you get 0.33. Multiplying again by 3, you obtain 0.99, not 1.00.

In the processor hardware, numbers are represented in the binary number system, not in decimal. You still get roundoff errors when binary digits are lost. They just may crop up at different places than you might expect. Here is an example:

```
double f = 4.35;
int n = (int) (100 * f);
System.out.println(n); // Prints 434!
```

Of course, one hundred times 4.35 is 435, but the program prints 434.

Computers represent numbers in the binary system (see Advanced Topic 4.2). In the binary system, there is no exact representation for 4.35, just as there is no exact representation for 1/3 in the decimal system. The representation used by the computer is just a little less than 4.35, so 100 times that value is just a little less than 435. When a floating-point value is converted to an integer, the entire fractional part is discarded, even if it is almost 1. As a result, the integer 434 is stored in n. Remedy: Use Math.round to convert floating-point numbers to integers. The round method returns the *closest* integer.

```
int n = (int) Math.round(100 * f);   // OK, n is 435
```

HOW TO 4.1

Carrying Out Computations

Many programming problems require that you use mathematical formulas to compute values. It is not always obvious how to turn a problem statement into a sequence of mathematical formulas and, ultimately, statements in the Java programming language.

Step 1   Understand the problem: What are the inputs? What are the desired outputs?

For example, suppose you are asked to simulate a postage stamp vending machine. A customer inserts money into the vending machine. Then the customer pushes a "First class stamps" button. The vending machine gives out as many first-class stamps as the customer paid for. (A first-class stamp cost 39 cents at the time this book was written.) Finally, the customer pushes a "Penny stamps" button. The machine gives the change in penny (1-cent) stamps.

In this problem, there is one input:

• The amount of money the customer inserts

There are two desired outputs:

• The number of first-class stamps the machine returns
• The number of penny stamps the machine returns

Step 2   Work out examples by hand.

This is a very important step. If you can't compute a couple of solutions by hand, it's unlikely that you'll be able to write a program that automates the computation.

Let's assume that a first-class stamp costs 39 cents and the customer inserts $1.00. That's enough for two stamps (78 cents) but not enough for three stamps ($1.17). Therefore, the machine returns two first-class stamps and 22 penny stamps.

Step 3 Find mathematical equations that compute the answers.

Given an amount of money and the price of a first-class stamp, how can you compute how many first-class stamps can be purchased with the money? Clearly, the answer is related to the quotient

$$\frac{\text{amount of money}}{\text{price of first-class stamp}}$$

For example, suppose the customer paid $1.00. Use a pocket calculator to compute the quotient: $1.00/$0.39 ≈ 2.5641.

How do you get "2 stamps" out of 2.5641? It's the integer part. By discarding the fractional part, you get the number of whole stamps the customer has purchased.

In mathematical notation,

$$\text{number of first-class stamps} = \left\lfloor \frac{\text{money}}{\text{price of first-class stamp}} \right\rfloor$$

where $\lfloor x \rfloor$ denotes the largest integer $\leq x$. That function is sometimes called the "floor function".

You now know how to compute the number of stamps that are given out when the customer pushes the "First-class stamps" button. When the customer gets the stamps, the amount of money is reduced by the value of the stamps purchased. For example, if the customer gets two stamps, the remaining money is $0.22—the difference between $1.00 and 2 · $0.39. Here is the general formula:

remaining money = money – number of first-class stamps · price of first-class stamp

How many penny stamps does the remaining money buy? That's easy. If $0.22 is left, the customer gets 22 stamps. In general, the number of penny stamps is

number of penny stamps = 100 · remaining money

Step 4 Turn the mathematical equations into Java statements.

In Java, you can compute the integer part of a nonnegative floating-point value by applying an (int) cast. Therefore, you can compute the number of first-class stamps with the following statement:

```
firstClassStamps = (int) (money / FIRST_CLASS_STAMP_PRICE);
money = money - firstClassStamps * FIRST_CLASS_STAMP_PRICE;
```

Finally, the number of penny stamps is

```
pennyStamps = 100 * money;
```

That's not quite right, though. The value of pennyStamps should be an integer, but the right-hand side is a floating-point number. Therefore, the correct statement is

```
pennyStamps = (int) Math.round(100 * money);
```

Step 5 Build a class that carries out your computations.

How To 3.1 explains how to develop a class by finding methods and instance variables. In our case, we can find three methods:

- void insert(double amount)
- int giveFirstClassStamps()
- int givePennyStamps()

The state of a vending machine can be described by the amount of money that the customer has available for purchases. Therefore, we supply one instance variable, money.

Here is the implementation:

```
public class StampMachine
{
    public StampMachine()
    {
        money = 0;
    }

    public void insert(double amount)
    {
        money = money + amount;
    }

    public int giveFirstClassStamps()
    {
        int firstClassStamps = (int) (money / FIRST_CLASS_STAMP_PRICE);
        money = money - firstClassStamps * FIRST_CLASS_STAMP_PRICE;
        return firstClassStamps;
    }

    public int givePennyStamps()
    {
        int pennyStamps = (int) Math.round(100 * money);
        money = 0;
        return pennyStamps;
    }

    public static final double FIRST_CLASS_STAMP_PRICE = 0.39;
    private double money;
}
```

Step 6 Test your class.

Run a test program (or use an integrated environment such as BlueJ) to verify that the values that your class computes are the same values that you computed by hand. In our example, try the statements

```
StampMachine machine = new StampMachine();
machine.insert(1);
System.out.print("First class stamps: ");
System.out.println(machine.giveFirstClassStamps());
System.out.println("Expected: 2");
System.out.print("Penny stamps: ");
System.out.println(machine.givePennyStamps());
System.out.println("Expected: 22");
```

Check that the result is

```
First class stamps: 2
Expected: 2
Penny stamps: 22
Expected: 22
```

4.6 Strings

Next to numbers, strings are the most important data type that most programs use. A string is a sequence of characters, such as "Hello, World!". In Java, strings are enclosed in quotation marks, which are not themselves part of the string. Note that, unlike numbers, strings are objects. (You can tell that String is a class name because it starts with an uppercase letter. The primitive types int and double start with lowercase letters.)

> A string is a sequence of characters. Strings are objects of the String class.

The number of characters in a string is called the length of the string. For example, the length of "Hello, World!" is 13. You can compute the length of a string with the length method.

```
int n = message.length();
```

A string of length zero, containing no characters, is called the empty string and is written as "".

Use the + operator to put strings together to form a longer string.

```
String name = "Dave";
String message = "Hello, " + name;
```

> Strings can be concatenated, that is, put end to end to yield a new longer string. String concatenation is denoted by the + operator.

The + operator concatenates two strings, provided one of the expressions, either to the left or the right of a + operator, is a string. The other one is automatically forced to become a string as well, and both strings are concatenated.

For example, consider this code:

```
String a = "Agent";
int n = 7;
String bond = a + n;
```

> Whenever one of the arguments of the + operator is a string, the other argument is converted to a string.

Because a is a string, n is converted from the integer 7 to the string "7". Then the two strings "Agent" and "7" are concatenated to form the string "Agent7".

This concatenation is very useful to reduce the number of System.out.print instructions. For example, you can combine

```
System.out.print("The total is ");
System.out.println(total);
```

to the single call

```
System.out.println("The total is " + total);
```

The concatenation "The total is " + total computes a single string that consists of the string "The total is ", followed by the string equivalent of the number total.

Sometimes you have a string that contains a number, usually from user input. For example, suppose that the string variable input has the value "19". To get the integer value 19, you use the static parseInt method of the Integer class.

```
int count = Integer.parseInt(input);
    // count is the integer 19
```

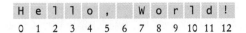

Figure 3 String Positions

If a string contains the digits of a number, you use the Integer.parseInt or Double.parseDouble method to obtain the number value.

To convert a string containing floating-point digits to its floating-point value, use the static parseDouble method of the Double class. For example, suppose input is the string "3.95".

```
double price = Double.parseDouble(input);
   // price is the floating-point number 3.95
```

However, if the string contains spaces or other characters that cannot occur inside numbers, an error occurs. For now, we will always assume that user input does not contain invalid characters.

Use the substring method to extract a part of a string.

The substring method computes substrings of a string. The call

```
s.substring(start, pastEnd)
```

returns a string that is made up of the characters in the string s, starting at position start, and containing all characters up to, but not including, the position pastEnd. Here is an example:

```
String greeting = "Hello, World!";
String sub = greeting.substring(0, 5); // sub is "Hello"
```

String positions are counted starting with 0.

The substring operation makes a string that consists of five characters taken from the string greeting. A curious aspect of the substring operation is the numbering of the starting and ending positions. The first string position is labeled 0, the second one 1, and so on. For example, Figure 3 shows the position numbers in the greeting string.

The position number of the last character (12 for the string "Hello, World!") is always 1 less than the length of the string.

Let us figure out how to extract the substring "World". Count characters starting at 0, not 1. You find that W, the eighth character, has position number 7. The first character that you don't want, !, is the character at position 12 (see Figure 4). Therefore, the appropriate substring command is

```
String sub2 = greeting.substring(7, 12);
```

It is curious that you must specify the position of the first character that you do want and then the first character that you don't want. There is one advantage to this

Figure 4 Extracting a Substring

setup. You can easily compute the length of the substring: It is pastEnd - start. For example, the string "World" has length 12 – 7 = 5.

If you omit the second parameter of the substring method, then all characters from the starting position to the end of the string are copied. For example,

```
String tail = greeting.substring(7); // Copies all characters from position 7 on
```

sets tail to the string "World!".

If you supply an illegal string position (a negative number, or a value that is larger than the length of the string), then your program terminates with an error message.

In this section, we have made the assumption that each character in a string occupies a single position. Unfortunately, that assumption is not quite correct. If you process strings that contain characters from international alphabets or special symbols, some characters may occupy two positions—see Advanced Topic 4.5.

SELF CHECK

13. Assuming the String variable s holds the value "Agent", what is the effect of the assignment s = s + s.length()?

14. Assuming the String variable river holds the value "Mississippi", what is the value of river.substring(1, 2)? Of river.substring(2, river.length() - 3)?

PRODUCTIVITY HINT 4.2

Reading Exception Reports

You will often have programs that terminate and display an error message, such as

```
Exception in thread "main" java.lang.StringIndexOutOfBoundsException:
        String index out of range: -4
    at java.lang.String.substring(String.java:1444)
    at Homework1.main(Homework1.java:16)
```

An amazing number of students simply give up at that point, saying "it didn't work", or "my program died", without ever reading the error message. Admittedly, the format of the exception report is not very friendly. But it is actually easy to decipher it.

When you have a close look at the error message, you will notice two pieces of useful information:

1. The name of the exception, such as StringIndexOutOfBoundsException
2. The line number of the code that contained the statement that caused the exception, such as Homework1.java:16

The name of the exception is always in the first line of the report, and it ends in Exception. If you get a StringIndexOutOfBoundsException, then there was a problem with accessing an invalid position in a string. That is useful information.

The line number of the offending code is a little harder to determine. The exception report contains the entire stack trace—that is, the names of all methods that were pending when the exception hit. The first line of the stack trace is the method that actually generated the exception. The last line of the stack trace is a line in `main`. Often, the exception was thrown by a method that is in the standard library. Look for the first line in your code that appears in the exception report. For example, skip the line that refers to

```
java.lang.String.substring(String.java:1444)
```

The next line in our example mentions a line number in your code, `Homework1.java`. Once you have the line number in your code, open up the file, go to that line, and look at it! In the great majority of cases, knowing the name of the exception and the line that caused it make it completely obvious what went wrong, and you can easily fix your error.

ADVANCED TOPIC 4.4

Escape Sequences

Suppose you want to display a string containing quotation marks, such as

```
Hello, "World"!
```

You can't use

```
System.out.println("Hello, "World"!");
```

As soon as the compiler reads `"Hello, "`, it thinks the string is finished, and then it gets all confused about `World` followed by two quotation marks. A human would probably realize that the second and third quotation marks were supposed to be part of the string, but a compiler has a one-track mind. If a simple analysis of the input doesn't make sense to it, it just refuses to go on, and reports an error. Well, how do you then display quotation marks on the screen? You precede the quotation marks inside the string with a *backslash* character. Inside a string, the sequence `\"` denotes a literal quote, not the end of a string. The correct display statement is, therefore

```
System.out.println("Hello, \"World\"!");
```

The backslash character is used as an *escape* character; the character sequence `\"` is called an escape sequence. The backslash does not denote itself; instead, it is used to encode other characters that would otherwise be difficult to include in a string.

Now, what do you do if you actually want to print a backslash (for example, to specify a Windows file name)? You must enter two `\\` in a row, like this:

```
System.out.println("The secret message is in C:\\Temp\\Secret.txt");
```

This statement prints

```
The secret message is in C:\Temp\Secret.txt
```

Another escape sequence occasionally used is `\n`, which denotes a *newline* or line feed character. Printing a newline character causes the start of a new line on the display. For example, the statement

```
System.out.print("*\n**\n***\n");
```

prints the characters

```
*
**
***
```

on three separate lines. Of course, you could have achieved the same effect with three separate calls to println.

Finally, escape sequences are useful for including international characters in a string. For example, suppose you want to print "All the way to San José!", with an accented letter (é). If you use a U.S. keyboard, you may not have a key to generate that letter. Java uses the *Unicode* encoding scheme to denote international characters. For example, the é character has Unicode encoding 00E9. You can include that character inside a string by writing \u, followed by its Unicode encoding:

```
System.out.println("All the way to San Jos\u00E9!");
```

You can look up the codes for the U.S. English and Western European characters in Appendix B, and codes for thousands of characters in reference [1].

ADVANCED TOPIC 4.5

Strings and the char Type

Strings are sequences of Unicode characters (see Random Fact 4.2). Character constants look like string constants, except that character constants are delimited by single quotes: 'H' is a character, "H" is a string containing a single character. You can use escape sequences (see Advanced Topic 4.4) inside character constants. For example, '\n' is the newline character, and '\u00E9' is the character é. You can find the values of the character constants that are used in Western European languages in Appendix B.

Characters have numeric values. For example, if you look at Appendix B, you can see that the character 'H' is actually encoded as the number 72.

When Java was first designed, each Unicode character was encoded as a two-byte quantity. The char type was intended to hold the code of a Unicode character. However, as of 2003, Unicode had grown so large that some characters needed to be encoded as pairs of char values. Thus, you can no longer think of a char value as a character. Technically speaking, a char value is a *code unit* in the UTF-16 encoding of Unicode. That encoding represents the most common characters as a single char value, and less common or *supplementary* characters as a pair of char values.

The charAt method of the String class returns a code unit from a string. As with the substring method, the positions in the string are counted starting at 0. For example, the statement

```
String greeting = "Hello";
char ch = greeting.charAt(0);
```

sets ch to the value 'H'.

However, if you use char variables, your programs may fail with some strings that contain international or symbolic characters. For example, the single character $\mathbb{Z}$ (the mathematical symbol for the set of integers) is encoded by the two code units '\uD835' and '\uDD6B'.

If you call charAt(0) on the string containing the single character $\mathbb{Z}$ (that is, the string "\uD835\uDD6B"), you only get the first half of a supplementary character.

Therefore, you should only use char values if you are absolutely sure that you won't need to encode supplementary characters.

Random Fact 4.2

International Alphabets

The English alphabet is pretty simple: upper- and lowercase a to z. Other European languages have accent marks and special characters. For example, German has three umlaut characters (ä, ö, ü) and a double-s character (ß). These are not optional frills; you couldn't write a page of German text without using these characters. German computer keyboards have keys for these characters (see A German Keyboard).

This poses a problem for computer users and designers. The American standard character encoding (called ASCII, for American Standard Code for Information Interchange) specifies 128 codes: 52 upper- and lowercase characters, 10 digits, 32 typographical symbols, and 34 control characters (such as space, newline, and 32 others for controlling printers and other devices). The umlaut and double-s are not among them. Some German data processing systems replace seldom-used ASCII characters with German letters: [\ ] { | } ~ are replaced with Ä Ö Ü ä ö ü ß. Most people can live without those ASCII characters, but programmers using Java definitely cannot. Other encoding schemes take advantage of the fact that one byte can encode 256 different characters, but only 128 are standardized by ASCII. Unfortunately, there are multiple incompatible standards for using the remaining 128 characters, resulting in a certain amount of aggravation among e-mail correspondents in different European countries.

Many countries don't use the Roman script at all. Russian, Greek, Hebrew, Arabic, and Thai letters, to name just a few, have completely different shapes (see The Thai Alphabet). To complicate matters, scripts like Hebrew and Arabic are written from right to left instead of from left to right, and many of these scripts have characters that stack above or below other characters, as those marked with a dotted circle in The Thai Alphabet do in Thai. Each of these alphabets has between 30 and 100 letters, and the countries using them have established encoding standards for them.

The situation is much more dramatic in languages that use Chinese script: the Chinese dialects, Japanese, and Korean. The Chinese script is not alphabetic but ideographic—a character represents an idea or thing rather than a single sound. (See A Menu with Chinese Characters; can you identify the characters for soup, chicken, and wonton?) Most words are made up of one, two, or three of these ideographic characters. Tens of thousands of ideographs are in active use, and China, Taiwan, Hong Kong, Japan, and Korea developed incompatible encoding standards for them.

A German Keyboard

จ	ฐ	ธ	ฦ	ศ	ะ	ิ	เ	่	๐	๘	๒
ก	ฒ	ท	น	ม	ษ	◌	◌	แ	◌	๑	๙	๒
ข	ช	ฑ	บ	ย	ส	า	◌	โ	◌	๒	ๆ	ๅ
ข	ซ	ฌ	ป	ร	ห	๎	◌	ใ	◌	๓	๛	ๅ
ค	ฌ	ด	ผ	ฤ	ฬ	◌	ไ	◌	๔	ๅ
ฅ	ญ	ต	ฝ	ล	อ	◌	ฦ	◌	๕
ฆ	ฎ	ถ	พ	ฦ	ฮ	◌	ๅ	ε	๖
ง	ฏ	ท	ฟ	ว	ๆ	◌	◌	๗

The Thai Alphabet

The inconsistencies among character encodings have been a major nuisance for international electronic communication and for software manufacturers vying for a global market. Between 1988 and 1991 a consortium of hardware and software manufacturers developed a uniform encoding scheme called Unicode that is expressly designed to encode text in all written languages of the world (see reference [1]). In the first version of Unicode, about 39,000 characters were given codes, including 21,000 Chinese ideographs. A 2-byte code (which can encode over 65,000 characters) was chosen. It was thought to leave ample space for expansion for esoteric scripts, such as Egyptian hieroglyphs and the ancient script used on the island of Java.

Java was one of the first programming languages to embrace Unicode. The primitive type char denotes a 2-byte Unicode character. (All Unicode characters can be stored in Java strings, but which ones can actually be displayed depends on your computer system.)

CLASSIC SOUPS

		Sm.	Lg.
清燉雞湯 57.	House Chicken Soup (Chicken, Celery, Potato, Onion, Carrot)	1.50	2.75
雞飯湯 58.	Chicken Rice Soup	1.85	3.25
雞麵湯 59.	Chicken Noodle Soup	1.85	3.25
廣東雲吞 60.	Cantonese Wonton Soup	1.50	2.75
蕃茄蛋湯 61.	Tomato Clear Egg Drop Soup	1.65	2.95
雲吞湯 62.	Regular Wonton Soup	1.10	2.10
酸辣湯 63. ❧	Hot & Sour Soup	1.10	2.10
蛋花湯 64.	Egg Drop Soup	1.10	2.10
雲蛋湯 65.	Egg Drop Wonton Mix	1.10	2.10
豆腐菜湯 66.	Tofu Vegetable Soup	NA	3.50
雞玉米湯 67.	Chicken Corn Cream Soup	NA	3.50
蟹肉玉米湯 68.	Crab Meat Corn Cream Soup	NA	3.50
海鮮湯 69.	Seafood Soup	NA	3.50

A Menu with Chinese Characters

> Unfortunately, in 2003, the inevitable happened. Another large batch of Chinese ideo-graphs had to be added to Unicode, pushing it beyond the 16-bit limit. Now, some characters need to be encoded with a pair of char values.

4.7 Reading Input

Use the Scanner class to read keyboard input in a console window.

The Java programs that you have made so far have constructed objects, called methods, printed results, and exited. They were not interactive and took no user input. In this section, you will learn one method for reading user input.

Because output is sent to System.out, you might think that you use System.in for input. Unfortunately, it isn't quite that simple. When Java was first designed, not much attention was given to reading keyboard input. It was assumed that all programmers would produce graphical user interfaces with text fields and menus. System.in was given a minimal set of features—it can only read one byte at a time. Finally, in Java version 5, a Scanner class was added that lets you read keyboard input in a convenient manner.

To construct a Scanner object, simply pass the System.in object to the Scanner constructor:

```
Scanner in = new Scanner(System.in);
```

You can create a scanner out of any input stream (such as a file), but you will usually want to use a scanner to read keyboard input from System.in.

Once you have a scanner, you use the nextInt or nextDouble methods to read the next integer or floating-point number.

```
System.out.print("Enter quantity: ");
int quantity = in.nextInt();

System.out.print("Enter price: ");
double price = in.nextDouble();
```

When the nextInt or nextDouble method is called, the program waits until the user types a number and hits the Enter key. You should always provide instructions for the user (such as "Enter quantity:") before calling a Scanner method. Such an instruction is called a *prompt*.

The nextLine method returns the next line of input (until the user hits the Enter key) as a String object. The next method returns the next *word*, terminated by any *white space*, that is, a space, the end of a line, or a tab.

```
System.out.print("Enter city: ");
String city = in.nextLine();

System.out.print("Enter state code: ");
String state = in.next();
```

Here, we use the nextLine method to read a city name that may consist of multiple words, such as San Francisco. We use the next method to read the state code (such as CA), which consists of a single word.

Here is an example of a class that takes user input. This class uses the CashRegister class and simulates a transaction in which a user purchases an item, pays for it, and receives change.

We call this class CashRegisterSimulator, not CashRegisterTester. We reserve the Tester suffix for classes whose sole purpose is to test other classes.

ch04/cashregister/CashRegisterSimulator.java

```java
1   import java.util.Scanner;
2
3   /**
4      This program simulates a transaction in which a user pays for an item
5      and receives change.
6   */
7   public class CashRegisterSimulator
8   {
9      public static void main(String[] args)
10     {
11        Scanner in = new Scanner(System.in);
12
13        CashRegister register = new CashRegister();
14
15        System.out.print("Enter price: ");
16        double price = in.nextDouble();
17        register.recordPurchase(price);
18
19        System.out.print("Enter dollars: ");
20        int dollars = in.nextInt();
21        System.out.print("Enter quarters: ");
22        int quarters = in.nextInt();
23        System.out.print("Enter dimes: ");
24        int dimes = in.nextInt();
25        System.out.print("Enter nickels: ");
26        int nickels = in.nextInt();
27        System.out.print("Enter pennies: ");
28        int pennies = in.nextInt();
29        register.enterPayment(dollars, quarters, dimes, nickels, pennies);
30
31        System.out.print("Your change: ");
32        System.out.println(register.giveChange());
33     }
34  }
```

Output

```
Enter price: 7.55
Enter dollars: 10
Enter quarters: 2
Enter dimes: 1
Enter nickels: 0
Enter pennies: 0
Your change: 3.05
```

15. Why can't input be read directly from `System.in`?

16. Suppose `in` is a `Scanner` object that reads from `System.in`, and your program calls

    ```
    String name = in.next();
    ```

    What is the value of `name` if the user enters `John Q. Public`?

ADVANCED TOPIC 4.6

Formatting Numbers

The default format for printing numbers is not always what you would like. For example, consider the following code segment:

```
double total = 3.50;
final double TAX_RATE = 8.5; // Tax rate in percent
double tax = total * TAX_RATE / 100; // tax is 0.2975
System.out.println("Total: " + total);
System.out.println("Tax:   " + tax);
```

The output is

```
Total: 3.5
Tax:   0.2975
```

You may prefer the numbers to be printed with two digits after the decimal point, like this:

```
Total: 3.50
Tax:   0.30
```

You can achieve this with the `printf` method of the `PrintStream` class. (Recall that `System.out` is an instance of `PrintStream`.) The first parameter of the `printf` method is a *format string* that shows how the output should be formatted. The format string contains characters that are simply printed, and *format specifiers:* codes that start with a % character and end with a letter that indicates the format type. There are quite a few formats—Table 3 shows the most important ones. The remaining parameters of `printf` are the values to be formatted. For example,

```
System.out.printf("Total:%5.2f", total);
```

prints the string `Total:`, followed by a floating-point number with a *width* of 5 and a *precision* of 2. The width is the total number of characters to be printed: in our case, a space, the digit 3, a period, and two digits. If you increase the width, more spaces are added. The precision is the number of digits after the decimal point.

This simple use of `printf` is sufficient for most formatting needs. Once in a while, you may see a more complex example, such as this one:

```
System.out.printf("%-6s%5.2f%n", "Tax:", total);
```

Here, we have three format specifiers. The first one is `%-6s`. The s indicates a string. The hyphen is a *flag*, modifying the format. (See Table 4 for the most common format flags. The flags immediately follow the % character.) The hyphen indicates left alignment. If the string

Table 3   Format Types

Code	Type	Example
d	Decimal integer	123
x	Hexadecimal integer	7B
o	Octal integer	173
f	Fixed floating-point	12.30
e	Exponential floating-point	1.23e+1
g	General floating-point (exponential notation used for very large or very small values)	12.3
s	String	Tax:
n	Platform-independent line end	

to be formatted is shorter than the width, it is placed to the left, and spaces are added to the right. (The default is right alignment, with spaces added to the left.) Thus, `%-6s` denotes a left-aligned string of width 6.

You have already seen `%5.2f`: a floating-point number of width 5 and precision 2. The final specifier is `%n`, indicating a platform-independent line end. In Windows, lines need to be terminated by *two* characters: a carriage return `'\r'` and a newline `'\n'`. In other operating systems, a `'\n'` suffices. The `%n` format emits the appropriate line terminators.

Moreover, this call to `printf` has two parameters. You can supply any number of parameter values to the `printf` method. Of course, they must match the format specifiers in the format string.

Table 4   Format Flags

Flag	Meaning	Example
-	Left alignment	1.23 followed by spaces
0	Show leading zeroes	001.23
+	Show a plus sign for positive numbers	+1.23
(	Enclose negative numbers in parentheses	(1.23)
,	Show decimal separators	12,300
^	Convert letters to uppercase	1.23E+1

The format method of the String class is similar to the printf method. However, it returns a string instead of producing output. For example, the call

```
String message = String.format("Total:%5.2f", total);
```

sets the message variable to the string "Total: 3.50".

ADVANCED TOPIC 4.7

Using Dialog Boxes for Input and Output

Most program users find the console window rather old-fashioned. The easiest alternative is to create a separate pop-up window for each input (see An Input Dialog Box).

Call the static showInputDialog method of the JOptionPane class, and supply the string that prompts the input from the user. For example,

```
String input = JOptionPane.showInputDialog("Enter price:");
```

That method returns a String object. Of course, often you need the input as a number. Use the Integer.parseInt and Double.parseDouble methods to convert the string to a number:

```
double price = Double.parseDouble(input);
```

You can also display output in a dialog box:

```
JOptionPane.showMessageDialog(null, "Price: " + price);
```

Finally, whenever you call the showInputDialog or showMessageDialog method in a program that does not show any other frame windows, you need to add a line

```
System.exit(0);
```

to the end of your main method. The showInputDialog method starts a user interface thread to handle user input. When the main method reaches the end, that thread is still running, and your program won't exit automatically. To force the program to exit, you need to call the exit method of the System class. The parameter of the exit method is the status code of the program. A code of 0 denotes successful completion; you can use nonzero status codes to denote various error conditions.

An Input Dialog Box

CHAPTER SUMMARY

1. Java has eight primitive types, including four integer types and two floating-point types.

2. A numeric computation overflows if the result falls outside the range for the number type.

3. Rounding errors occur when an exact conversion between numbers is not possible.

4. You use a cast (*typeName*) to convert a value to a different type.

5. Use the `Math.round` method to round a floating-point number to the nearest integer.

6. A `final` variable is a constant. Once its value has been set, it cannot be changed.

7. Use named constants to make your programs easier to read and maintain.

8. Assignment to a variable is not the same as mathematical equality.

9. The `++` and `--` operators increment and decrement a variable.

10. If both arguments of the `/` operator are integers, the result is an integer and the remainder is discarded.

11. The `%` operator computes the remainder of a division.

12. The `Math` class contains methods `sqrt` and `pow` to compute square roots and powers.

13. A static method does not operate on an object.

14. A string is a sequence of characters. Strings are objects of the `String` class.

15. Strings can be concatenated, that is, put end to end to yield a new longer string. String concatenation is denoted by the + operator.

16. Whenever one of the arguments of the + operator is a string, the other argument is converted to a string.

17. If a string contains the digits of a number, you use the `Integer.parseInt` or `Double.parseDouble` method to obtain the number value.

18. Use the `substring` method to extract a part of a string.

19. String positions are counted starting with 0.

20. Use the `Scanner` class to read keyboard input in a console window.

FURTHER READING

1. `http://www.unicode.org/` The web site of the Unicode consortium. It contains character tables that show the Unicode values of characters from many scripts.

CLASSES, OBJECTS, AND METHODS INTRODUCED IN THIS CHAPTER

```
java.io.PrintStream            java.lang.String
    printf                         format
java.lang.Double                   substring
    parseDouble                java.lang.System
java.lang.Integer                  in
    parseInt                   java.math.BigDecimal
    toString                       add
    MAX_VALUE                      multiply
    MIN_VALUE                      subtract
java.lang.Math                 java.math.BigInteger
    E                              add
    PI                             multiply
    abs                            subtract
    acos                       java.util.Scanner
    asin                           next
    atan                           nextDouble
    atan2                          nextInt
    ceil                           nextLine
    cos                        javax.swing.JOptionPane
    exp                            showInputDialog
    floor                          showMessageDialog
    log
    max
    min
    pow
    round
    sin
    sqrt
    tan
    toDegrees
    toRadians
```

REVIEW EXERCISES

★★ **Exercise R4.1.** Write the following mathematical expressions in Java.

$$s = s_0 + v_0 t + \tfrac{1}{2} g t^2$$

$$G = 4\pi^2 \frac{a^3}{P^2(m_1 + m_2)}$$

$$FV = PV \cdot \left(1 + \frac{INT}{100}\right)^{YRS}$$

$$c = \sqrt{a^2 + b^2 - 2ab\cos\gamma}$$

★★ **Exercise R4.2.** Write the following Java expressions in mathematical notation.

    a. `dm = m * (Math.sqrt(1 + v / c) / (Math.sqrt(1 - v / c) - 1));`

    b. `volume = Math.PI * r * r * h;`

    c. `volume = 4 * Math.PI * Math.pow(r, 3) / 3;`

    d. `p = Math.atan2(z, Math.sqrt(x * x + y * y));`

★★★ **Exercise R4.3.** What is wrong with this version of the quadratic formula?

```
x1 = (-b - Math.sqrt(b * b - 4 * a * c)) / 2 * a;
x2 = (-b + Math.sqrt(b * b - 4 * a * c)) / 2 * a;
```

★★ **Exercise R4.4.** Give an example of integer overflow. Would the same example work correctly if you used floating-point?

★★ **Exercise R4.5.** Give an example of a floating-point roundoff error. Would the same example work correctly if you used integers and switched to a sufficiently small unit, such as cents instead of dollars, so that the values don't have a fractional part?

★★ **Exercise R4.6.** Consider the following code:

```
CashRegister register = new CashRegister();
register.recordPurchase(19.93);
register.enterPayment(20, 0, 0, 0, 0);
System.out.print("Change: ");
System.out.println(register.giveChange());
```

The code segment prints the total as 0.07000000000000028. Explain why. Give a recommendation to improve the code so that users will not be confused.

★ **Exercise R4.7.** Let n be an integer and x a floating-point number. Explain the difference between

```
n = (int) x;
```

and

```
n = (int) Math.round(x);
```

★★★ **Exercise R4.8.** Let n be an integer and x a floating-point number. Explain the difference between

```
n = (int) (x + 0.5);
```

and

```
n = (int) Math.round(x);
```

For what values of x do they give the same result? For what values of x do they give different results?

★ **Exercise R4.9.** Explain the differences between 2, 2.0, '2', "2", and "2.0".

★ **Exercise R4.10.** Explain what each of the following two program segments computes:

```
int x = 2;
int y = x + x;
```

and

```
String s = "2";
String t = s + s;
```

★★ **Exercise R4.11.** True or false? (x is an int and s is a String)

    a. `Integer.parseInt("" + x)` is the same as x

    b. `"" + Integer.parseInt(s)` is the same as s

    c. `s.substring(0, s.length())` is the same as s

★★ **Exercise R4.12.** How do you get the first character of a string? The last character? How do you remove the first character? The last character?

★★★ **Exercise R4.13.** How do you get the last digit of an integer? The first digit? That is, if n is 23456, how do you find out that the first digit is 2 and the last digit is 6? Do not convert the number to a string. *Hint:* `%`, `Math.log`.

★★ **Exercise R4.14.** This chapter contains several recommendations regarding variables and constants that make programs easier to read and maintain. Summarize these recommendations.

★★★ **Exercise R4.15.** What is a `final` variable? Can you define a `final` variable without supplying its value? (Try it out.)

★ **Exercise R4.16.** What are the values of the following expressions? In each line, assume that

```
double x = 2.5;
double y = -1.5;
int m = 18;
int n = 4;
String s = "Hello";
String t = "World";
```

    a. `x + n * y - (x + n) * y`

    b. `m / n + m % n`

    c. `5 * x - n / 5`

    d. `Math.sqrt(Math.sqrt(n))`

    e. `(int) Math.round(x)`

    f. `(int) Math.round(x) + (int) Math.round(y)`

    g. `s + t`

    h. `s + n`

    i. `1 - (1 - (1 - (1 - (1 - n))))`

    j. `s.substring(1, 3)`

    k. `s.length() + t.length()`

Additional review exercises are available in WileyPLUS.

PROGRAMMING EXERCISES

★ **Exercise P4.1.** Enhance the CashRegister class by adding separate methods enterDollars, enterQuarters, enterDimes, enterNickels, and enterPennies. Use this tester class:

```
public class CashRegisterTester
{
    public static void main (String[] args)
    {
        CashRegister register = new CashRegister();
        register.recordPurchase(20.37);
        register.enterDollars(20);
        register.enterQuarters(2);
        System.out.println("Change: " + register.giveChange());
        System.out.println("Expected: 0.13");
    }
}
```

★ **Exercise P4.2.** Enhance the CashRegister class so that it keeps track of the total number of items in a sale. Count all recorded purchases and supply a method

```
int getItemCount()
```

that returns the number of items of the current purchase. Remember to reset the count at the end of the purchase.

★★ **Exercise P4.3.** Implement a class IceCreamCone with methods getSurfaceArea() and getVolume(). In the constructor, supply the height and radius of the cone. Be careful when looking up the formula for the surface area—you should only include the outside area along the side of the cone since the cone has an opening on the top to hold the ice cream.

★★ **Exercise P4.4.** Write a program that prompts the user for two numbers, then prints

- The sum
- The difference
- The product
- The average
- The distance (absolute value of the difference)
- The maximum (the larger of the two)
- The minimum (the smaller of the two)

To do so, implement a class

```
public class Pair
{
    /**
        Constructs a pair.
        @param aFirst the first value of the pair
        @param aSecond the second value of the pair
    */
    public Pair(double aFirst, double aSecond) { . . . }
```

```
/**
    Computes the sum of the values of this pair.
    @return the sum of the first and second values
*/
public double getSum() { . . . }
    . . .
}
```

Then implement a class `PairTester` that constructs a `Pair` object, invokes its methods, and prints the results.

★ **Exercise P4.5.** Define a class `DataSet` that computes the sum and average of a sequence of integers. Supply methods

- `void addValue(int x)`
- `int getSum()`
- `double getAverage()`

Hint: Keep track of the sum and the count of the values.

Then write a test program `DataSetTester` that calls `addValue` four times and prints the expected and actual results.

★★ **Exercise P4.6.** Write a class `DataSet` that computes the largest and smallest values in a sequence of numbers. Supply methods

- `void addValue(int x)`
- `int getLargest()`
- `int getSmallest()`

Keep track of the smallest and largest values that you've seen so far. Then use the `Math.min` and `Math.max` methods to update them in the `addValue` method. What should you use as initial values? *Hint:* `Integer.MIN_VALUE`, `Integer.MAX_VALUE`.

Write a test program `DataSetTester` that calls `addValue` four times and prints the expected and actual results.

★ **Exercise P4.7.** Write a program that prompts the user for a measurement in meters and then converts it into miles, feet, and inches. Use a class

```
public class Converter
{
    /**
        Constructs a converter that can convert between two units.
        @param aConversionFactor the factor by which to multiply
        to convert to the target unit
    */
    public Converter(double aConversionFactor) { . . . }

    /**
        Converts from a source measurement to a target measurement.
        @param fromMeasurement the measurement
        @return the input value converted to the target unit
    */
    public double convertTo(double fromMeasurement) { . . . }
```

```
/**
    Converts from a target measurement to a source measurement.
    @param toMeasurement  the target measurement
    @return  the value whose conversion is the target measurement
*/
public double convertFrom(double toMeasurement) { . . . }
}
```

In your `ConverterTester` class, construct and test the following `Converter` object:

```
final double MILE_TO_KM = 1.609;
Converter milesToMeters = new Converter(1000 * MILE_TO_KM);
```

★ **Exercise P4.8.** Write a class `Square` whose constructor receives the length of the sides. Then supply methods to compute

- The area and perimeter of the square
- The length of the diagonal (use the Pythagorean theorem)

★★ **Exercise P4.9.** Implement a class `SodaCan` whose constructor receives the height and diameter of the soda can. Supply methods `getVolume` and `getSurfaceArea`. Supply a `SodaCanTester` class that tests your class.

★★★ **Exercise P4.10.** Implement a class `Balloon` that models a spherical balloon that is being filled with air. The constructor constructs an empty balloon. Supply these methods:

- `void addAir(double amount)` adds the given amount of air
- `double getVolume()` gets the current volume
- `double getSurfaceArea()` gets the current surface area
- `double getRadius()` gets the current radius

Supply a `BalloonTester` class that constructs a balloon, adds 100 cm^3 of air, tests the three accessor methods, adds another 100 cm^3 of air, and tests the accessor methods again.

★★ **Exercise P4.11.** *Giving change.* Enhance the `CashRegister` class so that it directs a cashier how to give change. The cash register computes the amount to be returned to the customer, in pennies.

Add the following methods to the `CashRegister` class:

- `int giveDollars()`   - `int giveNickels()`
- `int giveQuarters()`   - `int givePennies()`
- `int giveDimes()`

Each method computes the number of dollar bills or coins to return to the customer, and reduces the change due by the returned amount. You may assume that the methods are called in this order. Here is a test class:

```
public class CashRegisterTester
{
    public static void main(String[] args)
    {
```

```
        CashRegister register = new CashRegister();

        register.recordPurchase(8.37);
        register.enterPayment(10, 0, 0, 0, 0);
        System.out.println("Dollars: " + register.giveDollars());
        System.out.println("Expected: 1");
        System.out.println("Quarters: " + register.giveQuarters());
        System.out.println("Expected: 2");
        System.out.println("Dimes: " + register.giveDimes());
        System.out.println("Expected: 1");
        System.out.println("Nickels: " + register.giveNickels());
        System.out.println("Expected: 0");
        System.out.println("Pennies: " + register.givePennies());
        System.out.println("Expected: 3");
    }
}
```

★★★ **Exercise P4.12.** Write a program that reads in an integer and breaks it into a sequence of individual digits in reverse order. For example, the input 16384 is displayed as

```
4
8
3
6
1
```

You may assume that the input has no more than five digits and is not negative.

Define a class `DigitExtractor`:

```
public class DigitExtractor
{
    /**
        Constructs a digit extractor that gets the digits
        of an integer in reverse order.
        @param anInteger the integer to break up into digits
    */
    public DigitExtractor(int anInteger) { . . . }

    /**
        Returns the next digit to be extracted.
        @return the next digit
    */
    public int nextDigit() { . . . }
}
```

In your main class `DigitPrinter`, call `System.out.println(myExtractor.nextDigit())` five times.

★★ **Exercise P4.13.** Implement a class `QuadraticEquation` whose constructor receives the coefficients a, b, c of the quadratic equation $ax^2 + bx + c = 0$. Supply methods `getSolution1` and `getSolution2` that get the solutions, using the quadratic formula. Write a test class `QuadraticEquationTester` that constructs a `QuadraticEquation` object, and prints the two solutions.

★★★   **Exercise P4.14.** Write a program that reads two times in military format (0900, 1730) and prints the number of hours and minutes between the two times. Here is a sample run. User input is in color.

```
Please enter the first time: 0900
Please enter the second time: 1730
8 hours 30 minutes
```

Extra credit if you can deal with the case where the first time is later than the second time:

```
Please enter the first time: 1730
Please enter the second time: 0900
15 hours 30 minutes
```

Implement a class TimeInterval whose constructor takes two military times. The class should have two methods getHours and getMinutes.

★   **Exercise P4.15.** *Writing large letters.* A large letter H can be produced like this:

```
*   *
*   *
*****
*   *
*   *
```

Use the class

```
public class LetterH
{
   public String toString()
   {
      return "*   *\n*   *\n*****\n*   *\n*   *\n";
   }
}
```

Define similar classes for the letters E, L, and O. Then write the message

```
H
E
L
L
O
```

in large letters.

★★   **Exercise P4.16.** Write a class ChristmasTree whose toString method yields a string depicting a Christmas tree:

Remember to use escape sequences.

★★ **Exercise P4.17.** Your job is to transform numbers 1, 2, 3, . . ., 12 into the corresponding month names January, February, March, . . ., December. Implement a class Month whose constructor parameter is the month number and whose getName method returns the month name. *Hint:* Make a very long string "January February March . . . ", in which you add spaces such that each month name has the same length. Then use substring to extract the month you want.

★★ **Exercise P4.18.** Write a class to compute the date of Easter Sunday. Easter Sunday is the first Sunday after the first full moon of spring. Use this algorithm, invented by the mathematician Carl Friedrich Gauss in 1800:

1. Let y be the year (such as 1800 or 2001).
2. Divide y by 19 and call the remainder a. Ignore the quotient.
3. Divide y by 100 to get a quotient b and a remainder c.
4. Divide b by 4 to get a quotient d and a remainder e.
5. Divide 8 * b + 13 by 25 to get a quotient g. Ignore the remainder.
6. Divide 19 * a + b - d - g + 15 by 30 to get a remainder h. Ignore the quotient.
7. Divide c by 4 to get a quotient j and a remainder k.
8. Divide a + 11 * h by 319 to get a quotient m. Ignore the remainder.
9. Divide 2 * e + 2 * j - k - h + m + 32 by 7 to get a remainder r. Ignore the quotient.
10. Divide h - m + r + 90 by 25 to get a quotient n. Ignore the remainder.
11. Divide h - m + r + n + 19 by 32 to get a remainder p. Ignore the quotient.

Then Easter falls on day p of month n. For example, if y is 2001:

```
a = 6            g = 6            r = 6
b = 20           h = 18           n = 4
c = 1            j = 0, k = 1     p = 15
d = 5, e = 0     m = 0
```

Therefore, in 2001, Easter Sunday fell on April 15. Write a class Easter with methods getEasterSundayMonth and getEasterSundayDay.

Additional programming exercises are available in WileyPLUS.

PROGRAMMING PROJECTS

★★★ **Project 4.1.** In this project, you will perform calculations with triangles. A triangle is defined by the *x*- and *y*-coordinates of its three corner points.

Your job is to compute the following properties of a given triangle:

- the lengths of all sides   - the perimeter
- the angles at all corners   - the area

Of course, you should implement a `Triangle` class with appropriate methods. Supply a program that prompts a user for the corner point coordinates and produces a nicely formatted table of the triangle properties.

This is a good team project for two students. Both students should agree on the `Triangle` interface. One student implements the `Triangle` class, the other simultaneously implements the user interaction and formatting.

★★★   **Project 4.2.** The `CashRegister` class has an unfortunate limitation: It is closely tied to the coin system in the United States and Canada. Research the system used in most of Europe. Your goal is to produce a cash register that works with euros and cents. Rather than designing another limited `CashRegister` implementation for the European market, you should design a separate `Coin` class and a cash register that can work with coins of all types.

ANSWERS TO SELF-CHECK QUESTIONS

1. `int` and `double`.
2. When the fractional part of x is ≥0.5.
3. By using a cast: `(int) Math.round(x)`.
4. The first definition is used inside a method, the second inside a class.
5. (1) You should use a named constant, not the "magic number" 3.14.
   (2) 3.14 is not an accurate representation of π.
6. The statement adds the `amount` value to the `balance` variable.
7. One less than it was before.
8. 17 and 29.
9. Only s3 is divided by 3. To get the correct result, use parentheses. Moreover, if s1, s2, and s3 are integers, you must divide by 3.0 to avoid integer division:
   `(s1 + s2 + s3) / 3.0`
10. $\sqrt{x^2 + y^2}$
11. x is a number, not an object, and you cannot invoke methods on numbers.
12. No—the `println` method is called on the object `System.out`.
13. s is set to the string `Agent5`.
14. The strings `"i"` and `"ssissi"`.
15. The class only has a method to read a single byte. It would be very tedious to form characters, strings, and numbers from those bytes.
16. The value is `"John"`. The `next` method reads the next *word*.

Chapter 5

Decisions

CHAPTER GOALS

- To be able to implement decisions using `if` statements
- To understand how to group statements into blocks
- To learn how to compare integers, floating-point numbers, strings, and objects
- To recognize the correct ordering of decisions in multiple branches
- To program conditions using Boolean operators and variables
- **T** To understand the importance of test coverage

The programs we have seen so far were able to do fast computations and render graphs, but they were very inflexible. Except for variations in the input, they worked the same way with every program run. One of the essential features of nontrivial computer programs is their ability to make decisions and to carry out different actions, depending on the nature of the inputs. The goal of this chapter is to learn how to program simple and complex decisions.

CHAPTER CONTENTS

5.1 The if Statement

Computer programs often need to make *decisions*, taking different actions depending on a condition.

Consider the bank account class of Chapter 3. The withdraw method allows you to withdraw as much money from the account as you like. The balance just moves ever further into the negatives. That is not a realistic model for a bank account. Let's implement the withdraw method so that you cannot withdraw more money than you have in the account. That is, the withdraw method must make a *decision*: whether to allow the withdrawal or not.

> The if statement lets a program carry out different actions depending on a condition.

The if statement is used to implement a decision. The if statement has two parts: a condition and a body. If the *condition* is true, the *body* of the statement is executed. The body of the if statement consists of a statement:

```
if (amount <= balance)
    balance = balance - amount;
```

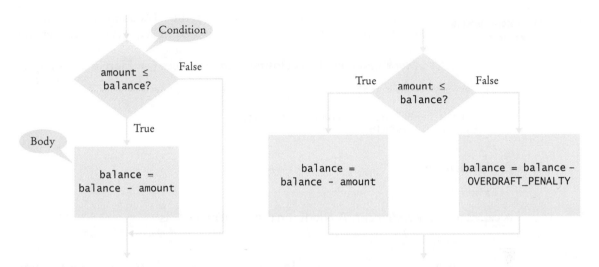

Figure 1
Flowchart for an if Statement

Figure 2
Flowchart for an if/else Statement

The assignment statement is carried out only when the amount to be withdrawn is less than or equal to the balance (see Figure 1).

Let us make the withdraw method of the BankAccount class even more realistic. Most banks not only disallow withdrawals that exceed your account balance; they also charge you a penalty for every attempt to do so.

This operation can't be programmed simply by providing two complementary if statements, such as:

```
if (amount <= balance)
    balance = balance - amount;
if (amount > balance) // NO
    balance = balance - OVERDRAFT_PENALTY;
```

There are two problems with this approach. First, if you need to modify the condition amount <= balance for some reason, you must remember to update the condition amount > balance as well. If you do not, the logic of the program will no longer be correct. More importantly, if you modify the value of balance in the body of the first if statement (as in this example), then the second condition uses the new value.

To implement a choice between alternatives, use the if/else statement:

```
if (amount <= balance)
    balance = balance - amount;
else
    balance = balance - OVERDRAFT_PENALTY;
```

Now there is only one condition. If it is satisfied, the first statement is executed. Otherwise, the second is executed. The flowchart in Figure 2 gives a graphical representation of the branching behavior.

A block statement groups several statements together.

Quite often, however, the body of the if statement consists of multiple statements that must be executed in sequence whenever the condition is true. These statements must be grouped together to form a *block statement* by enclosing them in braces { }. Here is an example.

```
if (amount <= balance)
{
   double newBalance = balance - amount;
   balance = newBalance;
}
```

A statement such as

```
balance = balance - amount;
```

is called a *simple statement*. A conditional statement such as

```
if (x >= 0) y = x;
```

is called a *compound statement*. In Chapter 6, you will encounter loop statements; they too are compound statements.

The body of an if statement or the else alternative must be a statement—that is, a simple statement, a compound statement (such as another if statement), or a block statement.

SYNTAX 5.1 **The if Statement**

```
if (condition)
   statement
```

```
if (condition)
   statement₁
else
   statement₂
```

Example:

```
if (amount <= balance)
   balance = balance - amount;
```

```
if (amount <= balance)
   balance = balance - amount;
else
   balance = balance - OVERDRAFT_PENALTY;
```

Purpose:

To execute a statement when a condition is true or false

SYNTAX 5.2 Block Statement

```
{
    statement₁
    statement₂
    . . .
}
```

Example:

```
{
    double newBalance = balance - amount;
    balance = newBalance;
}
```

Purpose:

To group several statements together to form a single statement

---

SELF CHECK

1. Why did we use the condition `amount <= balance` and not `amount < balance` in the example for the `if/else` statement?

2. What is logically wrong with the statement

   ```
   if (amount <= balance)
       newBalance = balance - amount; balance = newBalance;
   ```

   and how do you fix it?

QUALITY TIP 5.1

Brace Layout

The compiler doesn't care where you place braces, but we strongly recommend that you follow a simple rule: *Line up* { and }.

```
if (amount <= balance)
{
    double newBalance = balance - amount;
    balance = newBalance;
}
```

This scheme makes it easy to spot matching braces.

Some programmers put the opening brace on the same line as the `if`:

```
if (amount <= balance) {
    double newBalance = balance - amount;
    balance = newBalance;
}
```

This saves a line of code, but it makes it harder to match the braces.

It is important that you pick a layout scheme and stick with it. Which scheme you choose may depend on your personal preference or a coding style guide that you must follow.

PRODUCTIVITY HINT 5.1

Indentation and Tabs

When writing Java programs, use indentation to indicate nesting levels:

```
public class BankAccount
{
|   . . .
|   public void withdraw(double amount)
|   {
|   |   if (amount <= balance)
|   |   {
|   |   |   double newBalance = balance - amount;
|   |   |   balance = newBalance;
|   |   }
|   }
|   . . .
}
0   1   2   3
Indentation level
```

How many spaces should you use per indentation level? Some programmers use eight spaces per level, but that isn't a good choice:

```
public class BankAccount
{
        . . .
        public void withdraw(double amount)
        {
                if (amount <= balance)
                {
                        double newBalance =
                                balance - amount;
                        balance = newBalance;
                }
        }
        . . .
}
```

It crowds the code too much to the right side of the screen. As a consequence, long expressions frequently must be broken into separate lines. More common values are two, three, or four spaces per indentation level.

How do you move the cursor from the leftmost column to the appropriate indentation level? A perfectly reasonable strategy is to hit the space bar a sufficient number of times. However, many programmers use the Tab key instead. A tab moves the cursor to the next tab stop. By default, there are tab stops every eight columns, but most editors let you change that value; you should find out how to set your editor's tab stops to, say, every three columns.

Some editors help you out with an *autoindent* feature. They automatically insert as many tabs or spaces as the preceding line because the new line is quite likely to belong to the same logical indentation level. If it isn't, you must add or remove a tab, but that is still faster than tabbing all the way from the left margin.

As nice as tabs are for data entry, they have one disadvantage: They can mess up printouts. If you send a file with tabs to a printer, the printer may either ignore the tabs altogether or set tab stops every eight columns. It is therefore best to save and print your files with spaces instead of tabs. Most editors have settings that convert tabs to spaces before you save or print a file.

ADVANCED TOPIC 5.1

The Selection Operator

Java has a selection operator of the form

condition ? *value*$_1$: *value*$_2$

The value of that expression is either *value*$_1$ if the condition is true or *value*$_2$ if it is false. For example, we can compute the absolute value as

```
y = x >= 0 ? x : -x;
```

which is a convenient shorthand for

```
if (x >= 0)
    y = x;
else
    y = -x;
```

The selection operator is similar to the if/else statement, but it works on a different syntactical level. The selection operator combines *values* and yields another value. The if/else statement combines *statements* and yields another statement.

For example, it would be an error to write

```
y = if (x > 0) x; else -x; // Error
```

The if/else construct is a statement, not a value, and you cannot assign it to a variable.

We don't use the selection operator in this book, but it is a convenient and legitimate construct that you will find in many Java programs.

5.2 Comparing Values

5.2.1 Relational Operators

> Relational operators compare values. The == operator tests for equality.

A *relational operator* tests the relationship between two values. An example is the <= operator that we used in the test

```
if (amount <= balance)
```

Java has six relational operators:

Java	Math Notation	Description
>	>	Greater than
>=	≥	Greater than or equal
<	<	Less than
<=	≤	Less than or equal
==	=	Equal
!=	≠	Not equal

As you can see, only two relational operators (> and <) look as you would expect from the mathematical notation. Computer keyboards do not have keys for ≥, ≤, or ≠, but the >=, <=, and != operators are easy to remember because they look similar.

The == operator is initially confusing to most newcomers to Java. In Java, the = symbol already has a meaning, namely assignment. The == operator denotes equality testing:

```
a = 5; // Assign 5 to a
if (a == 5) . . . // Test whether a equals 5
```

You will have to remember to use == for equality testing, and to use = for assignment.

5.2.2 Comparing Floating-Point Numbers

You have to be careful when comparing floating-point numbers, in order to cope with roundoff errors. For example, the following code multiplies the square root of 2 by itself and then subtracts 2.

```
double r = Math.sqrt(2);
double d = r * r - 2;
if (d == 0)
    System.out.println("sqrt(2) squared minus 2 is 0");
```

```
else
    System.out.println(
        "sqrt(2) squared minus 2 is not 0 but " + d);
```

Even though the laws of mathematics tell us that $\left(\sqrt{2}\right)^2 - 2$ equals 0, this program fragment prints

```
sqrt(2) squared minus 2 is not 0 but 4.440892098500626E-16
```

Unfortunately, such roundoff errors are unavoidable. It plainly does not make sense in most circumstances to compare floating-point numbers exactly. Instead, test whether they are *close enough*.

> When comparing floating-point numbers, don't test for equality. Instead, check whether they are close enough.

To test whether a number x is close to zero, you can test whether the absolute value $|x|$ (that is, the number with its sign removed) is less than a very small threshold number. That threshold value is often called ε (the Greek letter epsilon). It is common to set ε to 10^{-14} when testing $double$ numbers.

Similarly, you can test whether two numbers are approximately equal by checking whether their difference is close to 0.

$$|x - y| \leq \varepsilon$$

In Java, we program the test as follows:

```
final double EPSILON = 1E-14;
if (Math.abs(x - y) <= EPSILON)
    // x is approximately equal to y
```

5.2.3 Comparing Strings

To test whether two strings are equal to each other, you must use the method called `equals`:

```
if (string1.equals(string2)) . . .
```

> Do not use the == operator to compare strings. Use the equals method instead.

Do not use the `==` operator to compare strings. The expression

```
if (string1 == string2) // Not useful
```

has an unrelated meaning. It tests whether the two string variables refer to the identical string object. You can have strings with identical contents stored in different objects, so this test never makes sense in actual programming; see Common Error 5.1.

In Java, letter case matters. For example, `"Harry"` and `"HARRY"` are not the same string. To ignore the letter case, use the `equalsIgnoreCase` method:

```
if (string1.equalsIgnoreCase(string2)) . . .
```

> The compareTo method compares strings in dictionary order.

If two strings are not identical to each other, you still may want to know the relationship between them. The `compareTo` method compares strings in dictionary order. If

```
string1.compareTo(string2) < 0
```

Figure 3
Lexicographic Comparison

Letters   r comes
match   before t

then the string `string1` comes before the string `string2` in the dictionary. For example, this is the case if `string1` is `"Harry"`, and `string2` is `"Hello"`. If

```
string1.compareTo(string2) > 0
```

then `string1` comes after `string2` in dictionary order. Finally, if

```
string1.compareTo(string2) == 0
```

then `string1` and `string2` are equal.

Actually, the "dictionary" ordering used by Java is slightly different from that of a normal dictionary. Java is case sensitive and sorts characters by putting numbers first, then uppercase characters, then lowercase characters. For example, 1 comes before B, which comes before a. The space character comes before all other characters.

Let us investigate the comparison process closely. When Java compares two strings, corresponding letters are compared until one of the strings ends or the first difference is encountered. If one of the strings ends, the longer string is considered the later one. If a character mismatch is found, the characters are compared to determine which string comes later in the dictionary sequence. This process is called lexicographic comparison. For example, let's compare `"car"` with `"cargo"`. The first three letters match, and we reach the end of the first string. Therefore `"car"` comes before `"cargo"` in the lexicographic ordering. Now compare `"cathode"` with `"cargo"`. The first two letters match. In the third character position, t comes after r, so the string `"cathode"` comes after `"cargo"` in lexicographic ordering. (See Figure 3.)

COMMON ERROR 5.1

Using == to Compare Strings

It is an extremely common error in Java to write `==` when `equals` is intended. This is particularly true for strings. If you write

```
if (nickname == "Rob")
```

then the test succeeds only if the variable `nickname` refers to the exact same string object as the string constant `"Rob"`. For efficiency, Java makes only one string object for every string constant. Therefore, the following test will pass:

```
String nickname = "Rob";
. . .
if (nickname == "Rob") // Test is true
```

However, if the string with the letters R o b has been assembled in some other way, then the test will fail:

```
String name = "Robert";
String nickname = name.substring(0, 3);
. . .
if (nickname == "Rob") // Test is false
```

This is a particularly distressing situation: The wrong code will sometimes do the right thing, sometimes the wrong thing. Because string objects are always constructed by the compiler, you never have an interest in whether two string objects are shared. You must remember never to use == to compare strings. Always use equals or compareTo to compare strings.

5.2.4 Comparing Objects

If you compare two object references with the == operator, you test whether the references refer to the same object. Here is an example:

```
Rectangle box1 = new Rectangle(5, 10, 20, 30);
Rectangle box2 = box1;
Rectangle box3 = new Rectangle(5, 10, 20, 30);
```

The comparison

```
box1 == box2
```

is true. Both object variables refer to the same object. But the comparison

```
box1 == box3
```

is false. The two object variables refer to different objects (see Figure 4). It does not matter that the objects have identical contents.

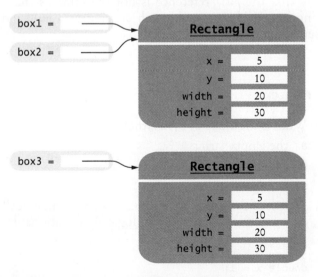

Figure 4 Comparing Object References

> The == operator tests whether two object references are identical. To compare the contents of objects, you need to use the equals method.

You can use the equals method to test whether two rectangles have the same contents, that is, whether they have the same upper-left corner and the same width and height. For example, the test

```
box1.equals(box3)
```

is true.

However, you must be careful when using the equals method. It works correctly only if the implementors of the class have defined it. The Rectangle class has an equals method that is suitable for comparing rectangles.

For your own classes, you need to supply an appropriate equals method. You will learn how to do that in Chapter 10. Until that point, you should not use the equals method to compare objects of your own classes.

5.2.5 Testing for null

> The null reference refers to no object.

An object reference can have the special value null if it refers to no object at all. It is common to use the null value to indicate that a value has never been set. For example,

```
String middleInitial = null; // Not set
if ( . . . )
   middleInitial = middleName.substring(0, 1);
```

You use the == operator (and not equals) to test whether an object reference is a null reference:

```
if (middleInitial == null)
   System.out.println(firstName + " " + lastName);
else
   System.out.println(firstName + " " + middleInitial + ". " + lastName);
```

Note that the null reference is not the same as the empty string "". The empty string is a valid string of length 0, whereas a null indicates that a string variable refers to no string at all.

SELF CHECK

3. What is the value of s.length() if s is

    a. the empty string ""?

    b. the string " " containing a space?

    c. null?

4. Which of the following comparisons are syntactically incorrect? Which of them are syntactically correct, but logically questionable?

```
String a = "1";
String b = "one";
double x = 1;
double y = 3 * (1.0 / 3);
```

a. `a == "1"`

b. `a == null`

c. `a.equals("")`

d. `a == b`

e. `a == x`

f. `x == y`

g. `x - y == null`

h. `x.equals(y)`

QUALITY TIP 5.2

Avoid Conditions with Side Effects

In Java, it is legal to nest assignments inside test conditions:

```
if ((d = b * b - 4 * a * c) >= 0) r = Math.sqrt(d);
```

It is legal to use the decrement operator inside other expressions:

```
if (n-- > 0) . . .
```

These are bad programming practices, because they mix a test with another activity. The other activity (setting the variable d, decrementing n) is called a *side effect* of the test.

As you will see in Advanced Topic 6.2, conditions with side effects can occasionally be helpful to simplify loops; for if statements they should always be avoided.

5.3 Multiple Alternatives

5.3.1 Sequences of Comparisons

Many computations require more than a single if/else decision. Sometimes, you need to make a series of related comparisons.

> Multiple conditions can be combined to evaluate complex decisions. The correct arrangement depends on the logic of the problem to be solved.

The following program asks for a value describing the magnitude of an earthquake on the Richter scale and prints a description of the likely impact of the quake. The Richter scale is a measurement for the strength of an earthquake. Every step in the scale, for example from 6.0 to 7.0, signifies a tenfold increase in the strength of the quake. The 1989 Loma Prieta earthquake that damaged the Bay Bridge in San Francisco and destroyed many buildings in several Bay area cities registered 7.1 on the Richter scale.

ch05/quake/Earthquake.java

```
1  /**
2     A class that describes the effects of an earthquake.
3  */
4  public class Earthquake
5  {
```

```
 6      /**
 7          Constructs an Earthquake object.
 8          @param magnitude the magnitude on the Richter scale
 9      */
10      public Earthquake(double magnitude)
11      {
12          richter = magnitude;
13      }
14
15      /**
16          Gets a description of the effect of the earthquake.
17          @return the description of the effect
18      */
19      public String getDescription()
20      {
21          String r;
22          if (richter >= 8.0)
23              r = "Most structures fall";
24          else if (richter >= 7.0)
25              r = "Many buildings destroyed";
26          else if (richter >= 6.0)
27              r = "Many buildings considerably damaged, some collapse";
28          else if (richter >= 4.5)
29              r = "Damage to poorly constructed buildings";
30          else if (richter >= 3.5)
31              r = "Felt by many people, no destruction";
32          else if (richter >= 0)
33              r = "Generally not felt by people";
34          else
35              r = "Negative numbers are not valid";
36          return r;
37      }
38
39      private double richter;
40  }
```

ch05/quake/EarthquakeRunner.java

```
 1  import java.util.Scanner;
 2
 3  /**
 4      This program prints a description of an earthquake of a given magnitude.
 5  */
 6  public class EarthquakeRunner
 7  {
 8      public static void main(String[] args)
 9      {
10          Scanner in = new Scanner(System.in);
11
12          System.out.print("Enter a magnitude on the Richter scale: ");
13          double magnitude = in.nextDouble();
14          Earthquake quake = new Earthquake(magnitude);
15          System.out.println(quake.getDescription());
16      }
17  }
```

Output

```
Enter a magnitude on the Richter scale: 7.1
Many buildings destroyed
```

Here we must sort the conditions and test against the largest cutoff first. Suppose we reverse the order of tests:

```
if (richter >= 0) // Tests in wrong order
    r = "Generally not felt by people";
else if (richter >= 3.5)
    r = "Felt by many people, no destruction";
else if (richter >= 4.5)
    r = "Damage to poorly constructed buildings";
else if (richter >= 6.0)
    r = "Many buildings considerably damaged, some collapse";
else if (richter >= 7.0)
    r = "Many buildings destroyed";
else if (richter >= 8.0)
    r = "Most structures fall";
```

This does not work. All nonnegative values of `richter` fall into the first case, and the other tests will never be attempted.

In this example, it is also important that we use an `if/else/else` test, not just multiple independent `if` statements. Consider this sequence of independent tests:

```
if (richter >= 8.0) // Didn't use else
    r = "Most structures fall";
if (richter >= 7.0)
    r = "Many buildings destroyed";
if (richter >= 6.0)
    r = "Many buildings considerably damaged, some collapse";
if (richter >= 4.5)
    r = "Damage to poorly constructed buildings";
if (richter >= 3.5)
    r = "Felt by many people, no destruction";
if (richter >= 0)
    r = "Generally not felt by people";
```

Now the alternatives are no longer exclusive. If `richter` is 6.0, then the last four tests all match, and r is set four times.

PRODUCTIVITY HINT 5.2

Keyboard Shortcuts for Mouse Operations

Programmers spend a lot of time with the keyboard. Programs and documentation are many pages long and require a lot of typing. This makes you different from the average computer user who uses the mouse more often than the keyboard.

Unfortunately for you, modern user interfaces are optimized for the mouse. The mouse is the most obvious tool for switching between windows, and for selecting commands. The constant switching between the keyboard and the mouse slows you down. You need to move a hand off the keyboard, locate the mouse, move the mouse, click the mouse, and move the hand back onto the keyboard. For that reason, most user interfaces have keyboard shortcuts: combinations of keystrokes that allow you to achieve the same tasks without having to switch to the mouse at all.

All Microsoft Windows applications use the following conventions:

- The Alt key plus the underlined letter in a menu name (such as the F in "File") pulls down that menu. Inside a menu, just type the underlined character in the name of a submenu to activate it. For example, Alt+F followed by O selects "File" "Open". Once your fingers know about this combination, you can open files faster than the fastest mouse artist.

- Inside dialog boxes, the Tab key is important; it moves from one option to the next. The arrow keys move within an option. The Enter key accepts the entire dialog box, and Esc cancels it.

- In a program with multiple windows, Ctrl+Tab usually toggles through the windows managed by that program, for example between the source and error windows.

- Alt+Tab toggles between applications, allowing you to toggle quickly between, for example, the text editor and a command shell window.

- Hold down the Shift key and press the arrow keys to highlight text. Then use Ctrl+X to cut the text, Ctrl+C to copy it, and Ctrl+V to paste it. These keys are easy to remember. The V looks like an insertion mark that an editor would use to insert text. The X should remind you of crossing out text. The C is just the first letter in "Copy". (OK, so it is also the first letter in "Cut"—no mnemonic rule is perfect.) You find these reminders in the Edit menu of most text editors.

Take a little bit of time to learn about the keyboard shortcuts that the program designers provided for you, and the time investment will be repaid many times during your programming career. When you blaze through your work in the computer lab with keyboard shortcuts, you may find yourself surrounded by amazed onlookers who whisper, "I didn't know you could do *that*."

Productivity Hint 5.3

Copy and Paste in the Editor

When you see code like

```
if (richter >= 8.0)
   r = "Most structures fall";
else if (richter >= 7.0)
   r = "Many buildings destroyed";
else if (richter >= 6.0)
   r = "Many buildings considerably damaged, some collapse";
else if (richter >= 4.5)
   r = "Damage to poorly constructed buildings";
else if (richter >= 3.5)
   r = "Felt by many people, no destruction";
```

you should think "copy and paste".

Make a template:

```
else if (richter >= )
    r = "";
```

and copy it. This is usually done by highlighting with the mouse and then selecting Edit and then Copy from the menu bar. If you follow Productivity Hint 5.2, you are smart and use the keyboard. Hit Shift+End to highlight the entire line, then Ctrl+C to copy it. Then paste it (Ctrl+V) multiple times and fill the text into the copies. Of course, your editor may use different commands, but the concept is the same.

The ability to copy and paste is always useful when you have code from an example or another project that is similar to your current needs. To copy, paste, and modify is faster than to type everything from scratch. You are also less likely to make typing errors.

ADVANCED TOPIC 5.2

The switch Statement

A sequence of if/else/else that compares a single value against several constant alternatives can be implemented as a switch statement. For example,

```
int digit;
. . .
switch (digit)
{
    case 1: System.out.print("one"); break;
    case 2: System.out.print("two"); break;
    case 3: System.out.print("three"); break;
    case 4: System.out.print("four"); break;
    case 5: System.out.print("five"); break;
    case 6: System.out.print("six"); break;
    case 7: System.out.print("seven"); break;
    case 8: System.out.print("eight"); break;
    case 9: System.out.print("nine"); break;
    default: System.out.print("error"); break;
}
```

This is a shortcut for

```
int digit;
. . .
if (digit == 1) System.out.print("one");
else if (digit == 2) System.out.print("two");
else if (digit == 3) System.out.print("three");
else if (digit == 4) System.out.print("four");
else if (digit == 5) System.out.print("five");
else if (digit == 6) System.out.print("six");
else if (digit == 7) System.out.print("seven");
else if (digit == 8) System.out.print("eight");
else if (digit == 9) System.out.print("nine");
else System.out.print("error");
```

Using the switch statement has one advantage. It is obvious that all branches test the same value, namely digit.

The switch statement can be applied only in narrow circumstances. The test cases must be constants, and they must be integers, characters, or enumerated constants. You cannot use a switch to branch on floating-point or string values. For example, the following is an error:

```
switch (name)
{
   case "one": . . . break; // Error
   . . .
}
```

Note how every branch of the switch was terminated by a break instruction. If the break is missing, execution falls through to the next branch, and so on, until finally a break or the end of the switch is reached. For example, consider the following switch statement:

```
switch (digit)
{
   case 1: System.out.print("one"); // Oops—no break
   case 2: System.out.print("two"); break;
   . . .
}
```

If digit has the value 1, then the statement after the case 1: label is executed. Because there is no break, the statement after the case 2: label is executed as well. The program prints "onetwo".

There are a few cases in which this fall-through behavior is actually useful, but they are very rare. Peter van der Linden [1, p. 38] describes an analysis of the switch statements in the Sun C compiler front end. Of the 244 switch statements, each of which had an average of 7 cases, only 3 percent used the fall-through behavior. That is, the default—falling through to the next case unless stopped by a break—was wrong 97 percent of the time. Forgetting to type the break is an exceedingly common error, yielding incorrect code.

We leave it to you to decide whether or not to use the switch statement. At any rate, you need to have a reading knowledge of switch in case you find it in the code of other programmers.

5.3.2 Nested Branches

Some computations have multiple *levels* of decision making. You first make one decision, and each of the outcomes leads to another decision. Here is a typical example.

In the United States, taxpayers pay federal income tax at different rates depending on their incomes and marital status. There are two main tax schedules: one for single taxpayers and one for married taxpayers "filing jointly", meaning that the married taxpayers add their incomes together and pay taxes on the total. (In fact, there are two other schedules, "head of household" and "married filing separately", which we will ignore for simplicity.) Table 1 gives the tax rate computations for each of the filing categories, using the values for the 1992 federal tax return. (We're using the 1992 tax rate schedule in this illustration because of its simplicity. Legislation in 1993 increased the number of rates in each status and added more complicated rules. By the time that you read this, the tax laws may well have become even more complex.)

Table 1 Federal Tax Rate Schedule (1992)			
If your filing status is Single:		If your filing status is Married:	
Tax Bracket	Percentage	Tax Bracket	Percentage
$0 . . . $21,450	15%	$0 . . . $35,800	15%
Amount over $21,450, up to $51,900	28%	Amount over $35,800, up to $86,500	28%
Amount over $51,900	31%	Amount over $86,500	31%

Now let us compute the taxes due, given a filing status and an income figure. First, we must branch on the filing status. Then, for each filing status, we must have another branch on income level.

The two-level decision process is reflected in two levels of if statements. We say that the income test is *nested* inside the test for filing status. (See Figure 5 for a flowchart.)

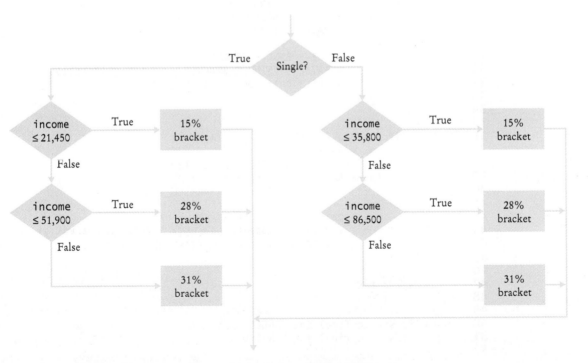

Figure 5 Income Tax Computation Using 1992 Schedule

ch05/tax/TaxReturn.java

```
1   /**
2          A tax return of a taxpayer in 1992.
3   */
4   public class TaxReturn
5   {
6       /**
7           Constructs a TaxReturn object for a given income and
8           marital status.
9           @param anIncome the taxpayer income
10          @param aStatus either SINGLE or MARRIED
11      */
12      public TaxReturn(double anIncome, int aStatus)
13      {
14          income = anIncome;
15          status = aStatus;
16      }
17
18      public double getTax()
19      {
20          double tax = 0;
21
22          if (status == SINGLE)
23          {
24              if (income <= SINGLE_BRACKET1)
25                  tax = RATE1 * income;
26              else if (income <= SINGLE_BRACKET2)
27                  tax = RATE1 * SINGLE_BRACKET1
28                      + RATE2 * (income - SINGLE_BRACKET1);
29              else
30                  tax = RATE1 * SINGLE_BRACKET1
31                      + RATE2 * (SINGLE_BRACKET2 - SINGLE_BRACKET1);
32                      + RATE3 * (income - SINGLE_BRACKET2);
33          }
34          else
35          {
36              if (income <= MARRIED_BRACKET1)
37                  tax = RATE1 * income;
38              else if (income <= MARRIED_BRACKET2)
39                  tax = RATE1 * MARRIED_BRACKET1
40                      + RATE2 * (income - MARRIED_BRACKET1);
41              else
42                  tax = RATE1 * MARRIED_BRACKET1
43                      + RATE2 * (MARRIED_BRACKET2 - MARRIED_BRACKET1);
44                      + RATE3 * (income - MARRIED_BRACKET2);
45          }
46
47          return tax;
48      }
49
50      public static final int SINGLE = 1;
51      public static final int MARRIED = 2;
52
```

```
53      private static final double RATE1 = 0.15;
54      private static final double RATE2 = 0.28;
55      private static final double RATE3 = 0.31;
56
57      private static final double SINGLE_BRACKET1 = 21450;
58      private static final double SINGLE_BRACKET2 = 51900;
59
60      private static final double MARRIED_BRACKET1 = 35800;
61      private static final double MARRIED_BRACKET2 = 86500;
62
63      private double income;
64      private int status;
65   }
```

ch05/tax/TaxCalculator.java

```
1  import java.util.Scanner;
2
3  /**
4      This program calculates a simple tax return.
5  */
6  public class TaxCalculator
7  {
8     public static void main(String[] args)
9     {
10        Scanner in = new Scanner(System.in);
11
12        System.out.print("Please enter your income: ");
13        double income = in.nextDouble();
14
15        System.out.print("Are you married? (Y/N) ");
16        String input = in.next();
17        int status;
18        if (input.equalsIgnoreCase("Y"))
19           status = TaxReturn.MARRIED;
20        else
21           status = TaxReturn.SINGLE;
22        TaxReturn aTaxReturn = new TaxReturn(income, status);
23
24        System.out.println("Tax: "
25              + aTaxReturn.getTax());
26     }
27  }
```

Output

```
Please enter your income: 50000
Are you married? (Y/N) N
Tax: 11211.5
```

SELF CHECK

5. The if/else/else statement for the earthquake strength first tested for higher values, then descended to lower values. Can you reverse that order?

6. Some people object to higher tax rates for higher incomes, claiming that you might end up with *less* money after taxes when you get a raise for working hard. What is the flaw in this argument?

COMMON ERROR 5.2

The Dangling else Problem

When an if statement is nested inside another if statement, the following error may occur.

```
if (richter >= 0)
   if (richter <= 4)
      System.out.println("The earthquake is harmless");
else    // Pitfall!
   System.out.println("Negative value not allowed");
```

The indentation level seems to suggest that the else is grouped with the test richter >= 0. Unfortunately, that is not the case. The compiler ignores all indentation and follows the rule that an else always belongs to the closest if, like this:

```
if (richter >= 0)
   if (richter <= 4)
      System.out.println("The earthquake is harmless");
   else    // Pitfall!
      System.out.println("Negative value not allowed");
```

That isn't what we want. We want to group the else with the first if. For that, we must use braces.

```
if (richter >= 0)
{
   if (richter <= 4)
      System.out.println("The earthquake is harmless");
}
else
   System.out.println("Negative value not allowed");
```

To avoid having to think about the pairing of the else, we recommend that you *always* use a set of braces when the body of an if contains another if. In the following example, the braces are not strictly necessary, but they help clarify the code:

```
if (richter >= 0)
{
   if (richter <= 4)
      System.out.println("The earthquake is harmless");
   else
      System.out.println("Damage may occur");
}
```

The ambiguous else is called a *dangling* else, and it is enough of a syntactical blemish that some programming language designers developed an improved syntax that avoids it altogether. For example, Algol 68 uses the construction

if *condition* then *statement* else *statement* fi;

The else part is optional, but since the end of the if statement is clearly marked, the grouping is unambiguous if there are two ifs and only one else. Here are the two possible cases:

if c_1 then if c_2 then s_1 else s_2 fi fi;
if c_1 then if c_2 then s_1 fi else s_2 fi;

By the way, fi is just if backwards. Other languages use endif, which has the same purpose but is less fun.

PRODUCTIVITY HINT 5.4

Make a Schedule and Make Time for Unexpected Problems

Commercial software is notorious for being delivered later than promised. For example, Microsoft originally promised that the successor to its Windows XP operating system would be available in 2004, then early in 2005, then late in 2005. Some of the early promises might not have been realistic. It is in Microsoft's interest to let prospective customers expect the imminent availability of the product, so that they do not switch to a different product in the meantime. Undeniably, though, Microsoft had not anticipated the full complexity of the tasks it had set itself to solve.

Microsoft can delay the delivery of its product, but it is likely that you cannot. As a student or a programmer, you are expected to manage your time wisely and to finish your assignments on time. You can probably do simple programming exercises the night before the due date, but an assignment that looks twice as hard may well take four times as long, because more things can go wrong. You should therefore make a schedule whenever you start a programming project.

First, estimate realistically how much time it will take you to

- Design the program logic
- Develop test cases
- Type the program in and fix syntax errors
- Test and debug the program

For example, for the income tax program I might estimate 30 minutes for the design, because it is mostly done; 30 minutes for developing test cases; one hour for data entry and fixing syntax errors; and 2 hours for testing and debugging. That is a total of 4 hours. If I work 2 hours a day on this project, it will take me two days.

Then think of things that can go wrong. Your computer might break down. The lab might be crowded. You might be stumped by a problem with the computer system. (That is a particularly important concern for beginners. It is *very* common to lose a day over a trivial problem just because it takes time to track down a person who knows the "magic" command to overcome it.) As a rule of thumb, *double* the time of your estimate. That is, you should start four days, not two days, before the due date. If nothing goes wrong, great; you have the program done two days early. When the inevitable problem occurs, you have a cushion of time that protects you from embarrassment and failure.

ADVANCED TOPIC 5.3

Enumerated Types

In many programs, you use variables that can hold one of a finite number of values. For example, in the tax return class, the status field holds one of the values SINGLE or MARRIED. We arbitrarily defined SINGLE as the number 1 and MARRIED as 2. If, due to some programming error, the status field is set to another integer value (such as –1, 0, or 3), then the programming logic may produce invalid results.

In a simple program, this is not really a problem. But as programs grow over time, and more cases are added (such as the "married filing separately" and "head of household" categories), errors can slip in. Java version 5.0 introduces a remedy: *enumerated types*. An enumerated type has a finite set of values, for example

```
public enum FilingStatus { SINGLE, MARRIED }
```

You can have any number of values, but you must include them all in the enum declaration.

You can declare variables of the enumerated type:

```
FilingStatus status = FilingStatus.SINGLE;
```

If you try to assign a value that isn't a FilingStatus, such as 2 or "S", then the compiler reports an error.

Use the == operator to compare enumerated values, for example:

```
if (status == FilingStatus.SINGLE) . . .
```

It is common to nest an enum declaration inside a class, such as

```
public class TaxReturn
{
   public TaxReturn(double anIncome, FilingStatus aStatus) { . . . }
   . . .
   public enum FilingStatus { SINGLE, MARRIED }
   private FilingStatus status;
}
```

To access the enumeration outside the class in which it is defined, use the class name as a prefix:

```
TaxReturn return = new TaxReturn(income, TaxReturn.FilingStatus.SINGLE);
```

An enumerated type variable can be null. For example, the status field in the previous example can actually have three values: SINGLE, MARRIED, and null. This can be useful, for example to identify an uninitialized variable, or a potential pitfall.

SYNTAX 5.3 Defining an Enumerated Type

accessSpecifier enum *TypeName* { *value*$_1$, *value*$_2$, . . . }

Example:

```
public enum FilingStatus { SINGLE, MARRIED }
```

Purpose:

To define a type with a fixed number of values

5.4 Using Boolean Expressions

5.4.1 The boolean Type

In Java, an expression such as amount < 1000 has a value, just as the expression amount + 1000 has a value. The value of a relational expression is either true or false. For example, if amount is 500, then the value of amount < 1000 is true. Try it out: The program fragment

```
double amount = 0;
System.out.println(amount < 1000);
```

The boolean type has two values: true and false.

prints true. The values true and false are not numbers, nor are they objects of a class. They belong to a separate type, called boolean. The Boolean type is named after the mathematician George Boole (1815–1864), a pioneer in the study of logic.

5.4.2 Predicate Methods

A *predicate method* is a method that returns a boolean value. Here is an example of a predicate method:

A predicate method returns a boolean value.

```
public class BankAccount
{
    public boolean isOverdrawn()
    {
        return balance < 0;
    }
}
```

You can use the return value of the method as the condition of an if statement:

```
if (harrysChecking.isOverdrawn()) . . .
```

There are several useful static predicate methods in the Character class:

```
isDigit
isLetter
isUpperCase
isLowerCase
```

that let you test whether a character is a digit, a letter, an uppercase letter, or a lower-case letter:

```
if (Character.isUpperCase(ch)) . . .
```

It is a common convention to give the prefix "is" or "has" to the name of a predicate method.

The Scanner class has useful predicate methods for testing whether the next input will succeed. The hasNextInt method returns true if the next character sequence denotes an integer. It is a good idea to call that method before calling nextInt:

```
if (in.hasNextInt()) n = in.nextInt();
```

Similarly, the hasNextDouble method tests whether a call to nextDouble will succeed.

5.4.3 The Boolean Operators

Suppose you want to find whether amount is between 0 and 1000. Then two conditions have to be true: amount must be greater than 0, *and* it must be less than 1000. In Java you use the && operator to represent the *and* to combine test conditions. That is, you can write the test as follows:

```
if (0 < amount && amount < 1000) . . .
```

> You can form complex tests with the Boolean operators && (and), || (or), and ! (not).

The && operator combines several tests into a new test that passes only when all conditions are true. An operator that combines test conditions is called a *logical operator*.

The || (*or*) logical operator also combines two or more conditions. The resulting test succeeds if at least one of the conditions is true. For example, here is a test to check whether the string input is an "S" or "M":

```
if (input.equals("S") || input.equals("M")) . . .
```

Figure 6 shows flowcharts for these examples.

Sometimes you need to *invert* a condition with the ! (*not*) logical operator. For example, we may want to carry out a certain action only if two strings are *not* equal:

```
if (!input.equals("S")) . . .
```

The ! operator takes a single condition and evaluates to true if that condition is false and to false if the condition is true.

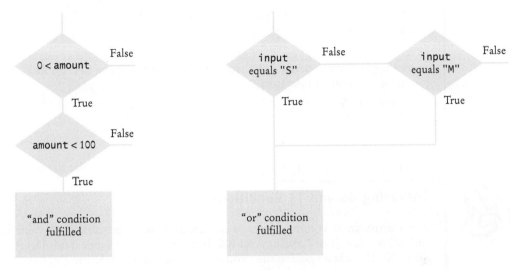

Figure 6 Flowcharts for && and || Combinations

Here is a summary of the three logical operations:

A	B	A && B
true	true	true
true	false	false
false	*Any*	false

A	B	A || B
true	*Any*	true
false	true	true
false	false	false

A	!A
true	false
false	true

COMMON ERROR 5.3

Multiple Relational Operators

Consider the expression

```
if (0 < amount < 1000) . . . // Error
```

This looks just like the mathematical notation for "amount is between 0 and 1000". But in Java, it is a syntax error.

Let us dissect the condition. The first half, `0 < amount`, is a test with outcome `true` or `false`. The outcome of that test (true or false) is then compared against 1000. This seems to make no sense. Is `true` larger than 1000 or not? Can one compare truth values and numbers? In Java, you cannot. The Java compiler rejects this statement.

Instead, use && to combine two separate tests:

```
if (0 < amount && amount < 1000) . . .
```

Another common error, along the same lines, is to write

```
if (ch == 'S' || 'M') . . . // Error
```

to test whether ch is 'S' or 'M'. Again, the Java compiler flags this construct as an error. You cannot apply the || operator to characters. You need to write two Boolean expressions and join them with the || operator:

```
if (ch == 'S' || ch == 'M') . . .
```

COMMON ERROR 5.4

Confusing && and || Conditions

It is a surprisingly common error to confuse *and* and *or* conditions. A value lies between 0 and 100 if it is at least 0 *and* at most 100. It lies outside that range if it is less than 0 *or* greater than 100. There is no golden rule; you just have to think carefully.

Often the *and* or *or* is clearly stated, and then it isn't too hard to implement it. Sometimes, though, the wording isn't as explicit. It is quite common that the individual conditions are nicely set apart in a bulleted list, but with little indication of how they should be combined. The instructions for the 1992 tax return say that you can claim single filing status if any one of the following is true:

- You were never married.
- You were legally separated or divorced on December 31, 1992.
- You were widowed before January 1, 1992, and did not remarry in 1992.

Because the test passes if *any one* of the conditions is true, you must combine the conditions with *or*. Elsewhere, the same instructions state that you may use the more advantageous status of married filing jointly if all five of the following conditions are true:

- Your spouse died in 1990 or 1991 and you did not remarry in 1992.
- You have a child whom you can claim as dependent.
- That child lived in your home for all of 1992.
- You paid over half the cost of keeping up your home for this child.
- You filed (or could have filed) a joint return with your spouse the year he or she died.

Because *all* of the conditions must be true for the test to pass, you must combine them with an *and*.

ADVANCED TOPIC 5.4

Lazy Evaluation of Boolean Operators

The && and || operators in Java are computed using *lazy* (or *short circuit*) evaluation. In other words, logical expressions are evaluated from left to right, and evaluation stops as soon as the truth value is determined. When an *and* is evaluated and the first condition is false, then the second condition is skipped—no matter what it is, the combined condition must be false.

When an *or* is evaluated and the first condition is true, the second condition is not evaluated, because it does not matter what the outcome of the second test is. Here is an example:

```
if (input != null && Integer.parseInt(input) > 0) . . .
```

If `input` is `null`, then the first condition is false, and thus the combined statement is false, no matter what the outcome of the second test. The second test is never evaluated if `input` is `null`, and there is no danger of parsing a `null` string (which would cause an exception).

If you do need to evaluate both conditions, then use the `&` and `|` operators (see Appendix E). When used with Boolean arguments, these operators always evaluate both arguments.

ADVANCED TOPIC 5.5

De Morgan's Law

> De Morgan's law shows how to simplify expressions in which the not operator (!) is applied to terms joined by the && or || operators.

In the preceding section, we programmed a test to see whether amount was between 0 and 1000. Let's find out whether the opposite is true:

```
if (!(0 < amount && amount < 1000)) . . .
```

This test is a little bit complicated, and you have to think carefully through the logic. "When it is *not* true that `0 < amount` and `amount < 1000` . . . " Huh? It is not true that some people won't be confused by this code.

The computer doesn't care, but humans generally have a hard time comprehending logical conditions with *not* operators applied to *and/or* expressions. De Morgan's law, named after the mathematician Augustus de Morgan (1806–1871), can be used to simplify these Boolean expressions. De Morgan's law has two forms: one for the negation of an *and* expression and one for the negation of an *or* expression:

$$!(A \ \&\& \ B) \text{ is the same as } !A \ || \ !B$$

$$!(A \ || \ B) \text{ is the same as } !A \ \&\& \ !B$$

Pay particular attention to the fact that the *and* and *or* operators are *reversed* by moving the *not* inwards. For example, the negation of "the input is S or the input is M",

```
!(input.equals("S") || input.equals("M"))
```

is "the input is not S *and* the input is not M"

```
!input.equals("S") && !input.equals("M")
```

Let us apply the law to the negation of "the amount is between 0 and 1000":

```
!(0 < amount && amount < 1000)
```

is equivalent to

```
!(0 < amount) || !(amount < 1000)
```

which can be further simplified to

```
0 >= amount || amount >= 1000
```

Note that the opposite of `<` is `>=`, not `>`!

5.4.4 Using Boolean Variables

You can use a Boolean variable if you know that there are only two possible values. Have another look at the tax program in Section 5.3.2. The marital status is either single or married. Instead of using an integer, you can use a variable of type `boolean`:

> You can store the outcome of a condition in a Boolean variable.

```
private boolean married;
```

The advantage is that you can't accidentally store a third value in the variable.

Then you can use the Boolean variable in a test:

```
if (married)
    . . .
else
    . . .
```

Sometimes Boolean variables are called *flags* because they can have only two states: "up" and "down".

It pays to think carefully about the naming of Boolean variables. In our example, it would not be a good idea to give the name `maritalStatus` to the Boolean variable. What does it mean that the marital status is `true`? With a name like `married` there is no ambiguity; if `married` is `true`, the taxpayer is married.

By the way, it is considered gauche to write a test such as

```
if (married == true) . . . // Don't
```

Just use the simpler test

```
if (married) . . .
```

In Chapter 6 we will use Boolean variables to control complex loops.

SELF CHECK

7. When does the statement

```
System.out.println(x > 0 || x < 0);
```

print `false`?

8. Rewrite the following expression, avoiding the comparison with `false`:

```
if (Character.isDigit(ch) == false) . . .
```

RANDOM FACT 5.1

Artificial Intelligence

When one uses a sophisticated computer program, such as a tax preparation package, one is bound to attribute some intelligence to the computer. The computer asks sensible questions and makes computations that we find a mental challenge. After all, if doing our taxes were easy, we wouldn't need a computer to do it for us.

As programmers, however, we know that all this apparent intelligence is an illusion. Human programmers have carefully "coached" the software in all possible scenarios, and it simply replays the actions and decisions that were programmed into it.

Would it be possible to write computer programs that are genuinely intelligent in some sense? From the earliest days of computing, there was a sense that the human brain might be nothing but an immense computer, and that it might well be feasible to program computers to imitate some processes of human thought. Serious research into *artificial intelligence* (AI) began in the mid-1950s, and the first twenty years brought some impressive successes. Programs that play chess—surely an activity that appears to require remarkable intellectual powers—have become so good that they now routinely beat all but the best human players. In 1975 an *expert-system* program called Mycin gained fame for being better in diagnosing meningitis in patients than the average physician. *Theorem-proving* programs produced logically correct mathematical proofs. *Optical character recognition* software can read pages from a scanner, recognize the character shapes (including those that are blurred or smudged), and reconstruct the original document text, even restoring fonts and layout.

However, there were serious setbacks as well. From the very outset, one of the stated goals of the AI community was to produce software that could translate text from one language to another, for example from English to Russian. That undertaking proved to be enormously complicated. Human language appears to be much more subtle and interwoven with the human experience than had originally been thought. Even the grammar-checking programs that come with many word processors today are more a gimmick than a useful tool, and analyzing grammar is just the first step in translating sentences.

From 1982 to 1992, the Japanese government embarked on a massive research project, funded at over 50 billion Japanese yen. It was known as the *Fifth-Generation Project*. Its goal was to develop new hard- and software to greatly improve the performance of expert systems. At its outset, the project created great fear in other countries that the Japanese computer industry was about to become the undisputed leader in the field. However, the end results were disappointing and did little to bring artificial intelligence applications to market.

One reason that artificial intelligence programs have not performed as well as it was hoped seems to be that they simply don't know as much as humans do. In the early 1990s, Douglas Lenat and his colleagues decided to do something about it and initiated the CYC project (from enCYClopedia), an effort to codify the implicit assumptions that underlie human speech and writing. The team members started out analyzing news articles and asked themselves what unmentioned facts are necessary to actually understand the sentences. For example, consider the sentence "Last fall she enrolled in Michigan State." The reader automatically realizes that "fall" is not related to falling down in this context, but refers to the season. While there is a State of Michigan, here Michigan State denotes the university. A priori, a computer program has none of this knowledge. The goal of the CYC project was to extract and store the requisite facts—that is, (1) people enroll in universities; (2) Michigan is a state; (3) a state X is likely to have a university named X State University, often abbreviated as X *State*; (4) most people enroll in a university in the fall. In 1995, the project had codified about 100,000 common-sense concepts and about a million facts relating them. Even this massive amount of data has not proven sufficient for useful applications.

Successful artificial intelligence programs, such as chess-playing programs, do not actually imitate human thinking. They are just very fast in exploring many scenarios and have been tuned to recognize those cases that do not warrant further investigation. *Neural networks* are interesting exceptions: coarse simulations of the neuron cells in animal and human brains. Suitably interconnected cells appear to be able to "learn". For example, if a network of cells is presented with letter shapes, it can be trained to identify them. After a lengthy training period, the network can recognize letters, even if they are slanted, distorted, or smudged.

When artificial intelligence programs are successful, they can raise serious ethical issues. There are now programs that can scan résumés, select those that look promising, and show only those to a human for further analysis. How would you feel if you knew that your résumé had been rejected by a computer, perhaps on a technicality, and that you never had a chance to be interviewed? When computers are used for credit analysis, and the analysis software has been designed to deny credit systematically to certain groups of people (say, all applicants with certain ZIP codes), is that illegal discrimination? What if the software has not been designed in this fashion, but a neural network has "discovered" a pattern from historical data? These are troubling questions, especially because those that are harmed by such processes have little recourse.

5.5 Test Coverage

> Black-box testing describes a testing method that does not take the structure of the implementation into account.

Testing the functionality of a program without consideration of its internal structure is called *black-box testing*. This is an important part of testing, because, after all, the users of a program do not know its internal structure. If a program works perfectly on all inputs, then it surely does its job.

> White-box testing uses information about the structure of a program.

However, it is impossible to ensure absolutely that a program will work correctly on all inputs just by supplying a finite number of test cases. As the famous computer scientist Edsger Dijkstra pointed out, testing can show only the presence of bugs—not their absence. To gain more confidence in the correctness of a program, it is useful to consider its internal structure. Testing strategies that look inside a program are called *white-box testing*. Performing unit tests of each method is a part of white-box testing.

> Test coverage is a measure of how many parts of a program have been tested.

You want to make sure that each part of your program is exercised at least once by one of your test cases. This is called *test coverage*. If some code is never executed by any of your test cases, you have no way of knowing whether that code would perform correctly if it ever were executed by user input. That means that you need to look at every if/else branch to see that each of them is reached by some test case. Many conditional branches are in the code only to take care of strange and abnormal inputs, but they still do something. It is a common phenomenon that they end up doing something incorrectly, but those faults are never discovered during testing, because nobody supplied the strange and abnormal inputs. Of course, these flaws become immediately apparent when the program is released and the first user types in an unusual input and is incensed when the program misbehaves. The remedy is to ensure that each part of the code is covered by some test case.

For example, in testing the getTax method of the TaxReturn class, you want to make sure that every if statement is entered for at least one test case. You should test both single and married taxpayers, with incomes in each of the three tax brackets.

When you select test cases, you should make it a habit to include *boundary test cases*: legal values that lie at the boundary of the set of acceptable inputs.

> Boundary test cases are test cases that are at the boundary of acceptable inputs.

For example, what happens when you compute the taxes for an income of 0 or if a bank account has an interest rate of 0%? Boundary cases are still legitimate inputs, and you expect that the program will handle them correctly—often in some trivial way or through special cases. Testing boundary cases is important, because programmers often make mistakes dealing with boundary conditions. Division by zero, extracting characters from empty strings, and accessing null pointers are common symptoms of boundary errors.

SELF CHECK

9. How many test cases do you need to cover all branches of the getDescription method of the Earthquake class?
10. Give a boundary test case for the EarthquakeRunner program. What output do you expect?

QUALITY TIP 5.3

Calculate Sample Data Manually

> You should calculate test cases by hand to double-check that your application computes the correct answer.

It is usually difficult or impossible to prove that a given program functions correctly in all cases. For gaining confidence in the correctness of a program, or for understanding why it does not function as it should, manually calculated sample data are invaluable. If the program arrives at the same results as the manual calculation, our confidence in it is strengthened. If the manual results differ from the program results, we have a starting point for the debugging process.

Surprisingly, many programmers are reluctant to perform any manual calculations as soon as a program carries out the slightest bit of algebra. Their math phobia kicks in, and they irrationally hope that they can avoid the algebra and beat the program into submission by random tinkering, such as rearranging the + and - signs. Random tinkering is always a great time sink, but it rarely leads to useful results.

Let's have another look at the TaxReturn class. Suppose a single taxpayer earns $50,000. The rules in Table 1 state that the first $21,450 are taxed at 15%. Expect to take out your calculator—real world numbers are usually nasty. Compute 21,450 x 0.15 = 3,217.50. Next, since $50,000 is less than the upper limit of the second bracket, the entire amount above $21,450, is taxed at 28%. That is (50,000-21,450) x 0.28 = 7,994. The total tax is the sum, 3,217.50 + 7,994 = 11,211.50. Now, that wasn't so hard.

Run the program and compare the results. Because the results match, we have an increased confidence in the correctness of the program.

It is even better to make manual calculations before writing the program. Doing so helps you understand the task at hand, and you will be able to implement your solution more quickly.

QUALITY TIP 5.4

Prepare Test Cases Ahead of Time

Let us consider how we can test the tax computation program. Of course, we cannot try out all possible inputs of filing status and income level. Even if we could, there would be no point in trying them all. If the program correctly computes one or two tax amounts in a given bracket, then we have a good reason to believe that all amounts within that bracket will be correct. We want to aim for complete *coverage* of all cases.

There are two possibilities for the filing status and three tax brackets for each status. That makes six test cases. Then we want to test *error conditions,* such as a negative income. That makes seven test cases. For the first six, we need to compute manually what answer we expect. For the remaining one, we need to know what error reports we expect. We write down the test cases and then start coding.

Should you really test seven inputs for this simple program? You certainly should. Furthermore, if you find an error in the program that wasn't covered by one of the test cases, make another test case and add it to your collection. After you fix the known mistakes, *run all test cases again.* Experience has shown that the cases that you just tried to fix are probably working now, but that errors that you fixed two or three iterations ago have a good chance of coming back! If you find that an error keeps coming back, that is usually a reliable sign that you did not fully understand some subtle interaction between features of your program.

It is always a good idea to design test cases *before* starting to code. There are two reasons for this. Working through the test cases gives you a better understanding of the algorithm that you are about to program. Furthermore, it has been noted that programmers instinctively shy away from testing fragile parts of their code. That seems hard to believe, but you will often make that observation about your own work. Watch someone else test your program. There will be times when that person enters input that makes you very nervous because you are not sure that your program can handle it, and you never dared to test it yourself. This is a well-known phenomenon, and making the test plan before writing the code offers some protection.

ADVANCED TOPIC 5.6

Logging

Sometimes you run a program and you are not sure where it spends its time. To get a printout of the program flow, you can insert trace messages into the program, such as this one:

```
public double getTax()
{
   . . .
   if (status == SINGLE)
   {
      System.out.println("status is SINGLE");
      . . .
   }
   . . .
}
```

However, there is a problem with using `System.out.println` for trace messages. When you are done testing the program, you need to remove all print statements that produce trace messages. If you find another error, however, you need to stick the print statements back in.

To overcome this problem, you should use the `Logger` class, which allows you to turn off the trace messages without removing them from the program.

Instead of printing directly to `System.out`, use the global logger object `Logger.global` and call

```
Logger.global.info("status is SINGLE");
```

By default, the message is printed. But if you call

```
Logger.global.setLevel(Level.OFF);
```

> Logging messages can be deactivated when testing is complete.

at the beginning of the `main` method of your program, all log message printing is suppressed. Thus, you can turn off the log messages when your program works fine, and you can turn them back on if you find another error. In other words, using `Logger.global.info` is just like `System.out.println`, except that you can easily activate and deactivate the logging.

A common trick for tracing execution flow is to produce log messages when a method is called, and when it returns. At the beginning of a method, print out the parameters:

```
public TaxReturn(double anIncome, int aStatus)
{
   Logger.global.info("Parameters: anIncome = " + anIncome
         + " aStatus = " + aStatus);
   . . .
}
```

At the end of a method, print out the return value:

```
public double getTax()
{
   . . .
   Logger.global.info("Return value = " + tax);
   return tax;
}
```

The `Logger` class has many other options for industrial-strength logging. Check out the API documentation if you want to have more control over logging.

CHAPTER SUMMARY

1. The `if` statement lets a program carry out different actions depending on a condition.

2. A block statement groups several statements together.

3. Relational operators compare values. The `==` operator tests for equality.

4. When comparing floating-point numbers, don't test for equality. Instead, check whether they are close enough.

5. Do not use the `==` operator to compare strings. Use the `equals` method instead.

6. The `compareTo` method compares strings in dictionary order.

7. The `==` operator tests whether two object references are identical. To compare the contents of objects, you need to use the `equals` method.

8. The `null` reference refers to no object.

9. Multiple conditions can be combined to evaluate complex decisions. The correct arrangement depends on the logic of the problem to be solved.

10. The `boolean` type has two values: `true` and `false`.

11. A predicate method returns a `boolean` value.

12. You can form complex tests with the Boolean operators `&&` (and), `||` (or), and `!` (not).

13. De Morgan's law shows how to simplify expressions in which the not operator (`!`) is applied to terms joined by the `&&` or `||` operators.

14. You can store the outcome of a condition in a Boolean variable.

15. Black-box testing describes a testing method that does not take the structure of the implementation into account.

16. White-box testing uses information about the structure of a program.

17. Test coverage is a measure of how many parts of a program have been tested.

18. Boundary test cases are test cases that are at the boundary of acceptable inputs.

19. You should calculate test cases by hand to double-check that your application computes the correct answer.

20. Logging messages can be deactivated when testing is complete.

FURTHER READING

1. Peter van der Linden, *Expert C Programming*, Prentice-Hall, 1994.

2. http://www.irs.ustreas.gov   The web site of the Internal Revenue Service.

CLASSES, OBJECTS, AND METHODS INTRODUCED IN THIS CHAPTER

```
java.lang.Character            java.lang.String              java.util.logging.Logger
  isDigit                        equalsIgnoreCase              getLogger
  isLetter                       compareTo                     info
  isLowerCase                  java.util.logging.Level         setLevel
  isUpperCase                    ALL                         java.util.Scanner
java.lang.Object                 INFO                          hasNextDouble
  equals                         NONE                          hasNextInt
```

REVIEW EXERCISES

★★ **Exercise R5.1.** Find the errors in the following if statements.

a. if quarters > 0 then System.out.println(quarters + " quarters");

b. if (1 + x > Math.pow(x, Math.sqrt(2)) y = y + x;

c. if (x = 1) y++; else if (x = 2) y = y + 2;

d. if (x && y == 0) { x = 1; y = 1; }

e. if (1 <= x <= 10)
    System.out.println(x);

f. if (!s.equals("nickels") || !s.equals("pennies")
        || !s.equals("dimes") || !s.equals("quarters"))
    System.out.print("Input error!");

g. if (input.equalsIgnoreCase("N") || "NO")
    return;

h. int x = Integer.parseInt(input);
   if (x != null) y = y + x;

i. language = "English";
   if (country.equals("US"))
      if (state.equals("PR")) language = "Spanish";
   else if (country.equals("China"))
      language = "Chinese";

★ **Exercise R5.2.** Explain the following terms, and give an example for each construct:

  a. Expression
  b. Condition
  c. Statement
  d. Simple statement
  e. Compound statement
  f. Block

★ **Exercise R5.3.** Explain the difference between an `if/else if/else` statement and nested `if` statements. Give an example for each.

★ **Exercise R5.4.** Give an example for an `if/else if/else` statement where the order of the tests does not matter. Give an example where the order of the tests matters.

★ **Exercise R5.5.** Of the following pairs of strings, which comes first in lexicographic order?

  a. `"Tom"`, `"Dick"`
  b. `"Tom"`, `"Tomato"`
  c. `"church"`, `"Churchill"`
  d. `"car manufacturer"`, `"carburetor"`
  e. `"Harry"`, `"hairy"`
  f. `"C++"`, `" Car"`
  g. `"Tom"`, `"Tom"`
  h. `"Car"`, `"Carl"`
  i. `"car"`, `"bar"`
  j. `"101"`, `"11"`
  k. `"1.01"`, `"10.1"`

★ **Exercise R5.6.** Complete the following truth table by finding the truth values of the Boolean expressions for all combinations of the Boolean inputs p, q, and r.

p	q	r	(p && q) || !r	!(p && (q || !r))
false	false	false		
false	false	true		
false	true	false		
. . .				
5 more combinations				
. . .				

★ **Exercise R5.7.** Before you implement any complex algorithm, it is a good idea to understand and analyze it. The purpose of this exercise is to gain a better understanding of the tax computation algorithm of Section 5.3.2.

One feature of the tax code is the *marriage penalty.* Under certain circumstances, a married couple pays higher taxes than the sum of what the two partners would pay if they both were single. Find examples for such income levels.

★★★ **Exercise R5.8.** True or false? *A && B* is the same as *B && A* for any Boolean conditions *A* and *B*.

★ **Exercise R5.9.** Explain the difference between

```
s = 0;
if (x > 0) s++;
if (y > 0) s++;
```

and

```
s = 0;
if (x > 0) s++;
else if (y > 0) s++;
```

★★ **Exercise R5.10.** Use de Morgan's law to simplify the following Boolean expressions.

a. !(x > 0 && y > 0)

b. !(x != 0 || y != 0)

c. !(country.equals("US") && !state.equals("HI")
&& !state.equals("AK"))

d. !(x % 4 != 0 || !(x % 100 == 0 && x % 400 == 0))

★★ **Exercise R5.11.** Make up another Java code example that shows the dangling else problem, using the following statement: A student with a GPA of at least 1.5, but less than 2, is on probation; with less than 1.5, the student is failing.

★ **Exercise R5.12.** Explain the difference between the == operator and the equals method when comparing strings.

★★ **Exercise R5.13.** Explain the difference between the tests

```
r == s
```

and

```
r.equals(s)
```

where both r and s are of type Rectangle.

★★★ **Exercise R5.14.** What is wrong with this test to see whether r is null? What happens when this code runs?

```
Rectangle r;
. . .
if (r.equals(null))
    r = new Rectangle(5, 10, 20, 30);
```

220 CHAPTER 5 ■ **Decisions**

★ **Exercise R5.15.** Explain how the lexicographic ordering of strings differs from the ordering of words in a dictionary or telephone book. *Hint:* Consider strings, such as IBM, `wiley.com`, `Century 21`, `While-U-Wait`, and 7-11.

★★★ **Exercise R5.16.** Write Java code to test whether two objects of type `Line2D.Double` represent the same line when displayed on the graphics screen. *Do not* use `a.equals(b)`.

```
Line2D.Double a;
Line2D.Double b;

if (your condition goes here)
   g2.drawString("They look the same!", x, y);
```

Hint: If p and q are points, then `Line2D.Double(p, q)` and `Line2D.Double(q, p)` look the same.

★ **Exercise R5.17.** Explain why it is more difficult to compare floating-point numbers than integers. Write Java code to test whether an integer n equals 10 and whether a floating-point number x equals 10.

★★ **Exercise R5.18.** Consider the following test to see whether a point falls inside a rectangle.

```
Point2D.Double p = . . .
Rectangle r = . . .
boolean xInside = false;
if (r.getX() <= p.getX() && p.getX() <= r.getX() + r.getWidth())
   xInside = true;
boolean yInside = false;
if (r.getY() <= p.getY() && p.getY() <= r.getY() + r.getHeight())
   yInside = true;
if (xInside && yInside)
   g2.drawString("p is inside the rectangle.",
         p.getX(), p.getY());
```

Rewrite this code to eliminate the explicit `true` and `false` values, by setting `xInside` and `yInside` to the values of Boolean expressions.

★T **Exercise R5.19.** Give a set of test cases for the earthquake program in Section 5.3.1. Ensure coverage of all branches.

★★T **Exercise R5.20.** Give a set of test cases for the tax program in Section 5.3.2. Compute the expected results manually.

★T **Exercise R5.21.** Give an example of a boundary test case for the tax program in Section 5.3.2. What result do you expect?

Additional review exercises are available in WileyPLUS.

PROGRAMMING EXERCISES

★★ **Exercise P5.1.** Write a program that prints all real solutions to the quadratic equation $ax^2 + bx + c = 0$. Read in a, b, c and use the quadratic formula. If the *discriminant* $b^2 - 4ac$ is negative, display a message stating that there are no real solutions.

Implement a class `QuadraticEquation` whose constructor receives the coefficients a, b, c of the quadratic equation. Supply methods `getSolution1` and `getSolution2` that get the solutions, using the quadratic formula, or 0 if no solution exists. The `getSolution1` method should return the smaller of the two solutions.

Supply a method

```
boolean hasSolutions()
```

that returns `false` if the discriminant is negative.

★★ **Exercise P5.2.** Write a program that takes user input describing a playing card in the following shorthand notation:

Notation	Meaning
A	Ace
2 . . . 10	Card values
J	Jack
Q	Queen
K	King
D	Diamonds
H	Hearts
S	Spades
C	Clubs

Your program should print the full description of the card. For example,

```
Enter the card notation:
4S
Four of spades
```

Implement a class `Card` whose constructor takes the card notation string and whose `getDescription` method returns a description of the card. If the notation string is not in the correct format, the `getDescription` method should return the string `"Unknown"`.

★★ **Exercise P5.3.** Write a program that reads in three floating-point numbers and prints the three inputs in sorted order. For example:

```
Please enter three numbers:
4
9
2.5
The inputs in sorted order are:
2.5
4
9
```

★ **Exercise P5.4.** Write a program that prints the question "Do you want to continue?" and reads a user input. If the user input is "Y", "Yes", "OK", "Sure", or "Why not?", print out "OK". If the user input is "N" or "No", then print out "Terminating". Otherwise, print "Bad input". The case of the user input should not matter. For example, "y" or "yes" are also valid inputs. Write a class YesNoChecker for this purpose.

★ **Exercise P5.5.** Write a program that translates a letter grade into a number grade. Letter grades are A B C D F, possibly followed by + or -. Their numeric values are 4, 3, 2, 1, and 0. There is no F+ or F-. A + increases the numeric value by 0.3, a - decreases it by 0.3. However, an A+ has the value 4.0.

```
Enter a letter grade:
B-
Numeric value: 2.7.
```

Use a class Grade with a method getNumericGrade.

★ **Exercise P5.6.** Write a program that translates a number into the closest letter grade. For example, the number 2.8 (which might have been the average of several grades) would be converted to B-. Break ties in favor of the better grade; for example, 2.85 should be a B.

Use a class Grade with a method getLetterGrade.

★ **Exercise P5.7.** Write a program that reads in three strings and prints the lexicographically smallest and largest one:

```
Please enter three strings:
Tom
Dick
Harry
The inputs in sorted order are:
Dick
Harry
Tom
```

★★ **Exercise P5.8.** Change the implementation of the getTax method in the TaxReturn class, by setting variables bracket1 and bracket2, depending on the marital status. Then have a single formula that computes the tax, depending on the income and the brackets. Verify that your results are identical to that of the TaxReturn class in this chapter.

★ **Exercise P5.9.** A year with 366 days is called a *leap year*. A year is a leap year if it is divisible by 4 (for example, 1980). However, since the introduction of the Gregorian calendar on October 15, 1582, a year is not a leap year if it is divisible by 100 (for example, 1900); however, it is a leap year if it is divisible by 400 (for example, 2000). Write a program that asks the user for a year and computes whether that year is a leap year. Implement a class Year with a predicate method boolean isLeapYear().

★ **Exercise P5.10.** Write a program that asks the user to enter a month (1 = January, 2 = February, and so on) and then prints the number of days of the month. For February, print "28 days".

```
Enter a month (1-12):
5
31 days
```

Implement a class Month with a method int getDays().

★★★ **Exercise P5.11.** Write a program that reads in two floating-point numbers and tests (a) whether they are the same when rounded to two decimal places and (b) whether they differ by less than 0.01. Here are two sample runs.

```
Enter two floating-point numbers:
2.0
1.99998
They are the same when rounded to two decimal places.
They differ by less than 0.01.

Enter two floating-point numbers:
0.999
0.991
They are different when rounded to two decimal places.
They differ by less than 0.01.
```

★ **Exercise P5.12.** Enhance the BankAccount class of Chapter 3 by
- Rejecting negative amounts in the deposit and withdraw methods
- Rejecting withdrawals that would result in a negative balance

★ **Exercise P5.13.** Write a program that reads in the hourly wage of an employee. Then ask how many hours the employee worked in the past week. Be sure to accept fractional hours. Compute the pay. Any overtime work (over 40 hours per week) is paid at 150 percent of the regular wage. Solve this problem by implementing a class Paycheck.

★★ **Exercise P5.14.** Write a unit conversion program that asks users to identify the unit from which they want to convert and the unit to which they want to convert. Legal units are *in*, *ft*, *mi*, *mm*, *cm*, *m*, and *km*. Define two objects of a class UnitConverter that convert between meters and a given unit.

```
Convert from:
in
Convert to:
mm
```

```
Value:
10
10 in = 254 mm
```

★★★   **Exercise P5.15.** A line in the plane can be specified in various ways:

- by giving a point (x, y) and a slope m
- by giving two points $(x_1, y_1), (x_2, y_2)$
- as an equation in slope-intercept form $y = mx + b$
- as an equation $x = a$ if the line is vertical

Implement a class Line with four constructors, corresponding to the four cases above. Implement methods

```
boolean intersects(Line other)
boolean equals(Line other)
boolean isParallel(Line other)
```

★★G   **Exercise P5.16.** Write a program that draws a circle with radius 100 and center (200, 200). Ask the user to specify the x- and y-coordinates of a point. Draw the point as a small circle. If the point lies inside the circle, color the small circle green. Otherwise, color it red. In your exercise, define a class Circle and a method boolean isInside(Point2D.Double p).

★★★G   **Exercise P5.17.** Write a graphics program that asks the user to specify the radii of two circles. The first circle has center (100, 200), and the second circle has center (200, 100). Draw the circles. If they intersect, then color both circles green. Otherwise, color them red. *Hint:* Compute the distance between the centers and compare it to the radii. Your program should draw nothing if the user enters a negative radius. In your exercise, define a class Circle and a method boolean intersects(Circle other).

Additional programming exercises are available in WileyPLUS.

PROGRAMMING PROJECTS

★★★   **Project 5.1.** Implement a *combination lock* class. A combination lock has a dial with 26 positions labeled A . . . Z. The dial needs to be set three times. If it is set to the correct combination, the lock can be opened. When the lock is closed again, the combination can be entered again. If a user sets the dial more than three times, the last three settings determine whether the lock can be opened. An important part of this exercise is to implement a suitable interface for the CombinationLock class.

★★★   **Project 5.2.** Get the instructions for last year's form 1040 from http://www.irs.ustreas.gov [2]. Find the tax brackets that were used last year for all categories of taxpayers (single, married filing jointly, married filing separately, and head of household). Write a program that computes taxes following that schedule. Ignore deductions, exemptions, and credits. Simply apply the tax rate to the income.

ANSWERS TO SELF-CHECK QUESTIONS

1. If the withdrawal amount equals the balance, the result should be a zero balance and no penalty.
2. Only the first assignment statement is part of the `if` statement. Use braces to group both assignment statements into a block statement.
3. (a) 0; (b) 1; (c) an exception is thrown
4. Syntactically incorrect: e, g, h. Logically questionable: a, d, f
5. Yes, if you also reverse the comparisons:

```
if (richter < 3.5)
   r = "Generally not felt by people";
else if (richter < 4.5)
   r = "Felt by many people, no destruction";
else if (richter < 6.0)
   r = "Damage to poorly constructed buildings";
. . .
```

6. The higher tax rate is only applied on the income in the higher bracket. Suppose you are single and make $51,800. Should you try to get a $200 raise? Absolutely—you get to keep 72% of the first $100 and 69% of the next $100.
7. When x is zero.
8. `if (!Character.isDigit(ch)) . . .`
9. 7
10. An input of 0 should yield an output of `"Generally not felt by people"`. (If the output is `"Negative numbers are not allowed"`, there is an error in the program.

6

Iteration

CHAPTER GOALS

- To be able to program loops with the while and for statements
- To avoid infinite loops and off-by-one errors
- To understand nested loops
- To learn how to process input
- To implement simulations
- T To learn about the debugger

This chapter presents the various iteration constructs of the Java language. These constructs execute one or more statements repeatedly until a goal is reached. You will see how the techniques that you learn in this chapter can be applied to the processing of input data and the programming of simulations.

CHAPTER CONTENTS

6.1 while Loops

In this chapter you will learn how to write programs that repeatedly execute one or more statements. We will illustrate these concepts by looking at typical investment situations. Consider a bank account with an initial balance of $10,000 that earns 5% interest. The interest is computed at the end of every year on the current balance and then deposited into the bank account. For example, after the first year, the account has earned $500 (5% of $10,000) of interest. The interest gets added to the bank account. Next year, the interest is $525 (5% of $10,500), and the balance is $11,025. Table 1 shows how the balance grows in the first five years.

How many years does it take for the balance to reach $20,000? Of course, it won't take longer than 20 years, because at least $500 is added to the bank account each year. But it will take less than 20 years, because interest is computed on increasingly larger balances. To know the exact answer, we will write a program that repeatedly adds interest until the balance is reached.

> A while statement executes a block of code repeatedly. A condition controls how often the loop is executed.

In Java, the while statement implements such a repetition. The construct

    while (*condition*)
       statement

keeps executing the statement while the condition is true.

Table 1 Growth of an Investment	
Year	**Balance**
0	$10,000.00
1	$10,500.00
2	$11,025.00
3	$11,576.25
4	$12,155.06
5	$12,762.82

Most commonly, the statement is a block statement, that is, a set of statements delimited by { }.

In our case, we want to know when the bank account has reached a particular balance. While the balance is less, we keep adding interest and incrementing the year counter:

```
while (balance < targetBalance)
{
   years++;
   double interest = balance * rate / 100;
   balance = balance + interest;
}
```

Here is the program that solves our investment problem:

ch06/invest1/Investment.java

```
1  /**
2      A class to monitor the growth of an investment that
3      accumulates interest at a fixed annual rate.
4  */
5  public class Investment
6  {
7      /**
8          Constructs an Investment object from a starting balance and
9          interest rate.
10         @param aBalance the starting balance
11         @param aRate  the interest rate in percent
12     */
13     public Investment(double aBalance, double aRate)
14     {
15         balance = aBalance;
16         rate = aRate;
17         years = 0;
18     }
19
```

```
20      /**
21          Keeps accumulating interest until a target balance has
22          been reached.
23          @param targetBalance the desired balance
24      */
25      public void waitForBalance(double targetBalance)
26      {
27          while (balance < targetBalance)
28          {
29              years++;
30              double interest = balance * rate / 100;
31              balance = balance + interest;
32          }
33      }
34
35      /**
36          Gets the current investment balance.
37          @return the current balance
38      */
39      public double getBalance()
40      {
41          return balance;
42      }
43
44      /**
45          Gets the number of years this investment has accumulated
46          interest.
47          @return the number of years since the start of the investment
48      */
49      public int getYears()
50      {
51          return years;
52      }
53
54      private double balance;
55      private double rate;
56      private int years;
57  }
```

ch06/invest1/InvestmentRunner.java

```
1   /**
2       This program computes how long it takes for an investment
3       to double.
4   */
5   public class InvestmentRunner
6   {
7       public static void main(String[] args)
8       {
9           final double INITIAL_BALANCE = 10000;
10          final double RATE = 5;
11          Investment invest = new Investment(INITIAL_BALANCE, RATE);
12          invest.waitForBalance(2 * INITIAL_BALANCE);
13          int years = invest.getYears();
```

```
14        System.out.println("The investment doubled after "
15            + years + " years");
16    }
17 }
```

Output

```
The investment doubled after 15 years
```

A while statement is often called a *loop.* If you draw a flowchart, you will see that the control loops backwards to the test after every iteration (see Figure 1).

The following loop,

```
while (true)
    statement
```

executes the statement over and over, without terminating. Whoa! Why would you want that? The program would never stop. There are two reasons. Some programs indeed never stop; the software controlling an automated teller machine, a telephone switch, or a microwave oven doesn't ever stop (at least not until the device is turned off). Our programs aren't usually of that kind, but even if you can't terminate the loop, you can exit from the method that contains it. This can be helpful when the termination test naturally falls in the middle of the loop (see Advanced Topic 6.3).

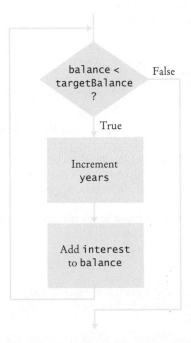

Figure 1   Flowchart of a while Loop

SYNTAX 6.1 The while Statement

```
while (condition)
   statement
```

Example:

```
while (balance < targetBalance)
{
   years++;
   double interest = balance * rate / 100;
   balance = balance + interest;
}
```

Purpose:

To repeatedly execute a statement as long as a condition is true

SELF CHECK

1. How often is the following statement in the loop executed?

   ```
   while (false) statement;
   ```

2. What would happen if RATE was set to 0 in the main method of the InvestmentRunner program?

COMMON ERROR 6.1

Infinite Loops

The most annoying loop error is an infinite loop: a loop that runs forever and can be stopped only by killing the program or restarting the computer. If there are output statements in the loop, then reams and reams of output flash by on the screen. Otherwise, the program just sits there and hangs, seeming to do nothing. On some systems you can kill a hanging program by hitting Ctrl+Break or Ctrl+C. On others, you can close the window in which the program runs.

A common reason for infinite loops is forgetting to advance the variable that controls the loop:

```
int years = 0;
while (years < 20)
{
   double interest = balance * rate / 100;
   balance = balance + interest;
}
```

Here the programmer forgot to add a statement for incrementing years in the loop. As a result, the value of years always stays 0, and the loop never comes to an end.

Another common reason for an infinite loop is accidentally incrementing a counter that should be decremented (or vice versa). Consider this example:

```
int years = 20;
while (years > 0)
{
    years++; // Oops, should have been years--
    double interest = balance * rate / 100;
    balance = balance + interest;
}
```

The years variable really should have been decremented, not incremented. This is a common error, because incrementing counters is so much more common than decrementing that your fingers may type the ++ on autopilot. As a consequence, years is always larger than 0, and the loop never terminates. (Actually, years eventually will exceed the largest representable positive integer and wrap around to a negative number. Then the loop exits—of course, that takes a long time, and the result is completely wrong.)

COMMON ERROR 6.2

Off-by-One Errors

Consider our computation of the number of years that are required to double an investment:

```
int years = 0;
while (balance < 2 * initialBalance)
{
    years++;
    double interest = balance * rate / 100;
    balance = balance + interest;
}
System.out.println(
    "The investment reached the target after "
    + years + " years.");
```

Should years start at 0 or at 1? Should you test for balance < 2 * initialBalance or for balance <= 2 * initialBalance? It is easy to be *off by one* in these expressions.

Some people try to solve off-by-one errors by randomly inserting +1 or -1 until the program seems to work. That is, of course, a terrible strategy. It can take a long time to compile and test all the various possibilities. Expending a small amount of mental effort is a real time saver.

> An off-by-one error is a common error when programming loops. Think through simple test cases to avoid this type of error.

Fortunately, off-by-one errors are easy to avoid, simply by thinking through a couple of test cases and using the information from the test cases to come up with a rationale for the correct loop condition.

Should years start at 0 or at 1? Look at a scenario with simple values: an initial balance of $100 and an interest rate of 50%. After year 1, the balance is $150, and after year 2 it is $225, or over $200. So the investment doubled after 2 years. The loop executed two times, incrementing years each time. Hence years must start at 0, not at 1.

In other words, the balance variable denotes the balance *after* the end of the year. At the outset, the balance variable contains the balance after year 0 and not after year 1.

Next, should you use a < or <= comparison in the test? That is harder to figure out, because it is rare for the balance to be exactly twice the initial balance. Of course, there is one case when this happens, namely when the interest is 100%. The loop executes once. Now years is 1, and `balance` is exactly equal to 2 * `initialBalance`. Has the investment doubled after one year? It has. Therefore, the loop should *not* execute again. If the test condition is `balance < 2 * initialBalance`, the loop stops, as it should. If the test condition had been `balance <= 2 * initialBalance`, the loop would have executed once more.

In other words, you keep adding interest while the balance *has not yet doubled*.

ADVANCED TOPIC 6.1

do Loops

Sometimes you want to execute the body of a loop at least once and perform the loop test after the body was executed. The do loop serves that purpose:

```
do
    statement
while (condition);
```

The *statement* is executed while the *condition* is true. The condition is tested after the statement is executed, so the statement is executed at least once.

For example, suppose you want to make sure that a user enters a positive number. As long as the user enters a negative number or zero, just keep prompting for a correct input. In this situation, a do loop makes sense, because you need to get a user input before you can test it.

```
double value;
do
{
    System.out.print("Please enter a positive number: ");
    value = in.nextDouble();
}
while (value <= 0);
```

The figure shows a flowchart of this loop.

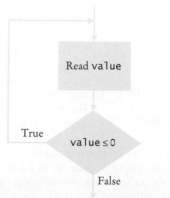

Flowchart of a do Loop

In practice, this situation is not very common. You can always replace a do loop with a while loop, by introducing a boolean control variable.

```java
boolean done = false;
while (!done)
{
    System.out.print("Please enter a positive number: ");
    value = in.nextDouble();
    if (value > 0) done = true;
}
```

RANDOM FACT 6.1

Spaghetti Code

In this chapter we are using flowcharts to illustrate the behavior of the loop statements. It used to be common to draw flowcharts for every method, on the theory that flowcharts were easier to read and write than the actual code (especially in the days of machine-language and assembler programming). Flowcharts are no longer routinely used for program development and documentation.

Flowcharts have one fatal flaw. Although it is possible to express the while and do loops with flowcharts, it is also possible to draw flowcharts that cannot be programmed with loops. Consider the chart in the Spaghetti Code figure. The top of the flowchart is simply a statement

```java
years = 1;
```

The lower part is a do loop:

```java
do
{
    years++;
    double interest - balance * rate / 100;
    balance = balance + interest;
}
while (balance < targetBalance);
```

But how can you join these two parts? According to the flowchart, you are supposed to jump from the first statement into the middle of the loop, skipping the first statement.

```java
years = 1;
goto a; // Not an actual Java statement
do
{
    years++;
    a:
    double interest = balance * rate / 100;
    balance = balance + interest;
}
while (balance < targetBalance);
```

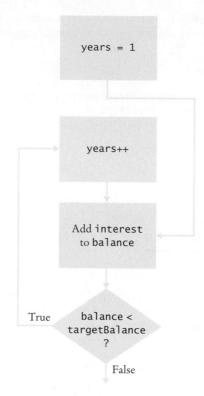

years = 1

years++

Add interest
to balance

True

balance <
targetBalance
?

False

Spaghetti Code

In fact, why even bother with the do loop? Here is a faithful interpretation of the flowchart:

```
years = 1;
goto a;  // Not an actual Java statement
b:
years++;
a:
double interest = balance * rate / 100;
balance = balance + interest;
if (balance < targetBalance) goto b;
```

This nonlinear control flow turns out to be extremely hard to read and understand if you have more than one or two goto statements. Because the lines denoting the goto statements weave back and forth in complex flowcharts, the resulting code is named *spaghetti code*.

In 1968 the influential computer scientist Edsger Dijkstra wrote a famous note, entitled "Goto Statements Considered Harmful" [1], in which he argued for the use of loops instead of unstructured jumps. Initially, many programmers who had been using goto for years were mortally insulted and promptly dug out examples in which the use of goto led to clearer or faster code. Some languages offer weaker forms of goto that are less harmful, such as the break statement in Java, discussed in Advanced Topic 6.4. Nowadays, most computer scientists accept Dijkstra's argument and fight bigger battles than optimal loop design.

6.2 for Loops

One of the most common loop types has the form

```
i = start;
while (i <= end)
{
    . . .
    i++;
}
```

Because this loop is so common, there is a special form for it that emphasizes the pattern:

```
for (i = start; i <= end; i++)
{
    . . .
}
```

You can also declare the loop counter variable inside the for loop header. That convenient shorthand restricts the use of the variable to the body of the loop (as will be discussed further in Advanced Topic 6.2).

```
for (int i = start; i <= end; i++)
{
    . . .
}
```

Let us use this loop to find out the size of our $10,000 investment if 5% interest is compounded for 20 years. Of course, the balance will be larger than $20,000, because at least $500 is added every year. You may be surprised to find out just how much larger the balance is.

SYNTAX 6.2 The for Statement

```
for (initialization; condition; update)
    statement
```

Example:

```
for (i = 1; i <= n; i++)
{
    double interest = balance * rate / 100;
    balance = balance + interest;
}
```

Purpose:

To execute an initialization, then keep executing a statement and updating an expression while a condition is true

You use a for loop when a variable runs from a starting to an ending value with a constant increment or decrement.

In our loop, we let i go from 1 to n, the number of years for which we want to compound interest.

```
for (int i = 1; i <= n; i++)
{
    double interest = balance * rate / 100;
    balance = balance + interest;
}
```

Figure 2 shows the corresponding flowchart.

The three slots in the for header can contain any three expressions. You can count down instead of up:

```
for (years = n; years > 0; years--)
```

The increment or decrement need not be in steps of 1:

```
for (x = -10; x <= 10; x = x + 0.5) . . .
```

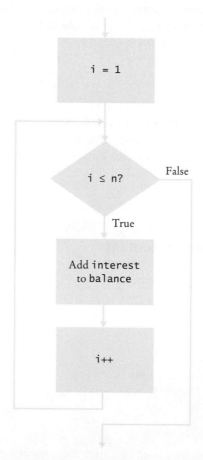

Figure 2 Flowchart of a for Loop

It is possible—but a sign of unbelievably bad taste—to put unrelated conditions into the loop header:

```
for (rate = 5; years-- > 0; System.out.println(balance))
    . . . // Bad taste
```

We won't even begin to decipher what that might mean. You should stick with for loops that initialize, test, and update a single variable.

ch06/invest2/Investment.java

```
 1   /**
 2       A class to monitor the growth of an investment that
 3       accumulates interest at a fixed annual rate.
 4   */
 5   public class Investment
 6   {
 7       /**
 8           Constructs an Investment object from a starting balance and
 9           interest rate.
10           @param aBalance the starting balance
11           @param aRate the interest rate in percent
12       */
13       public Investment(double aBalance, double aRate)
14       {
15           balance = aBalance;
16           rate = aRate;
17           years = 0;
18       }
19
20       /**
21           Keeps accumulating interest until a target balance has
22           been reached.
23           @param targetBalance the desired balance
24       */
25       public void waitForBalance(double targetBalance)
26       {
27           while (balance < targetBalance)
28           {
29               years++;
30               double interest = balance * rate / 100;
31               balance = balance + interest;
32           }
33       }
34
35       /**
36           Keeps accumulating interest for a given number of years.
37           @param n the number of years
38       */
39       public void waitYears(int n)
40       {
41           for (int i = 1; i <= n; i++)
42           {
43               double interest = balance * rate / 100;
44               balance = balance + interest;
```

```
45          }
46          years = years + n;
47       }
48
49       /**
50          Gets the current investment balance.
51          @return  the current balance
52       */
53       public double getBalance()
54       {
55          return balance;
56       }
57
58       /**
59          Gets the number of years this investment has accumulated
60          interest.
61          @return  the number of years since the start of the investment
62       */
63       public int getYears()
64       {
65          return years;
66       }
67
68       private double balance;
69       private double rate;
70       private int years;
71    }
```

ch06/invest2/InvestmentRunner.java

```
1    /**
2       This program computes how much an investment grows in
3       a given number of years.
4    */
5    public class InvestmentRunner
6    {
7       public static void main(String[] args)
8       {
9          final double INITIAL_BALANCE = 10000;
10         final double RATE = 5;
11         final int YEARS = 20;
12         Investment invest = new Investment(INITIAL_BALANCE, RATE);
13         invest.waitYears(YEARS);
14         double balance = invest.getBalance();
15         System.out.printf("The balance after %d years is %.2f\n",
16                 YEARS, balance);
17      }
18   }
```

Output

```
The balance after 20 years is 26532.98
```

SELF CHECK

3. Rewrite the for loop in the waitYears method as a while loop.

4. How many times does the following for loop execute?

```
for (i = 0; i <= 10; i++)
   System.out.println(i * i);
```

QUALITY TIP 6.1

Use for Loops for Their Intended Purpose

A for loop is an *idiom* for a while loop of a particular form. A counter runs from the start to the end, with a constant increment:

```
for (set counter to start; test whether counter at end;
        update counter by increment)
{  . . .
    // counter, start, end, increment not changed here
}
```

If your loop doesn't match this pattern, don't use the for construction. The compiler won't prevent you from writing idiotic for loops:

```
// Bad style—unrelated header expressions
for (System.out.println("Inputs:");
        (x = in.nextDouble()) > 0;
        sum = sum + x)
    count++;

for (int i = 1; i <= years; i++)
{
    // Bad style—modifies counter
    if (balance >= targetBalance)
        i = years + 1;
    else
    {
        double interest = balance * rate / 100;
        balance = balance + interest;
    }
}
```

These loops will work, but they are plainly bad style. Use a while loop for iterations that do not fit the for pattern.

COMMON ERROR 6.3

Forgetting a Semicolon

Occasionally all the work of a loop is already done in the loop header. Suppose you ignored Quality Tip 6.1; then you could write an investment doubling loop as follows:

```
for (years = 1;
        (balance = balance + balance * rate / 100) < targetBalance;
        years++)
    ;
System.out.println(years);
```

The body of the for loop is completely empty, containing just one empty statement terminated by a semicolon.

If you do run into a loop without a body, it is important that you make sure the semicolon is not forgotten. If the semicolon is accidentally omitted, then the next line becomes part of the loop statement!

```
for (years = 1;
        (balance = balance + balance * rate / 100) < targetBalance;
        years++)
System.out.println(years);
```

You can avoid this error by using an empty block { } instead of an empty statement.

COMMON ERROR 6.4

A Semicolon Too Many

What does the following loop print?

```
sum = 0;
for (i = 1; i <= 10; i++);
    sum = sum + i;
System.out.println(sum);
```

Of course, this loop is supposed to compute $1 + 2 + \cdots + 10 = 55$. But actually, the print statement prints 11!

Why 11? Have another look. Did you spot the semicolon at the end of the for loop header? This loop is actually a loop with an empty body.

```
for (i = 1; i <= 10; i++)
    ;
```

The loop does nothing 10 times, and when it is finished, sum is still 0 and i is 11. Then the statement

```
sum = sum + i;
```

is executed, and sum is 11. The statement was indented, which fools the human reader. But the compiler pays no attention to indentation.

Of course, the semicolon at the end of the statement was a typing error. Someone's fingers were so used to typing a semicolon at the end of every line that a semicolon was added to the for loop by accident. The result was a loop with an empty body.

QUALITY TIP 6.2

Don't Use != to Test the End of a Range

Here is a loop with a hidden danger:

```
for (i = 1; i != n; i++)
```

The test i != n is a poor idea. How does the loop behave if n happens to be zero or negative? The test i != n is never false, because i starts at 1 and increases with every step.

The remedy is simple. Use <= rather than != in the condition:

```
for (i = 1; i <= n; i++)
```

ADVANCED TOPIC 6.2

Variables Defined in a for Loop Header

As mentioned, it is legal in Java to declare a variable in the header of a for loop. Here is the most common form of this syntax:

```
for (int i = 1; i <= n; i++)
{
   . . .
}

// i no longer defined here
```

The scope of the variable extends to the end of the for loop. Therefore, i is no longer defined after the loop ends. If you need to use the value of the variable beyond the end of the loop, then you need to define it outside the loop. In this loop, you don't need the value of i—you know it is n + 1 when the loop is finished. (Actually, that is not quite true—it is possible to break out of a loop before its end; see Advanced Topic 6.4.) When you have two or more exit conditions, though, you may still need the variable. For example, consider the loop

```
for (i = 1; balance < targetBalance && i <= n; i++)
{
   . . .
}
```

You want the balance to reach the target, but you are willing to wait only a certain number of years. If the balance doubles sooner, you may want to know the value of i. Therefore, in this case, it is not appropriate to define the variable in the loop header.

Note that the variables named i in the following pair of for loops are independent:

```
for (int i = 1; i <= 10; i++)
   System.out.println(i * i);
for (int i = 1; i <= 10; i++) // Declares a new variable i
   System.out.println(i * i * i);
```

In the loop header, you can declare multiple variables, as long as they are of the same type, and you can include multiple update expressions, separated by commas:

```
for (int i = 0, j = 10; i <= 10; i++, j--)
{
    . . .
}
```

However, many people find it confusing if a for loop controls more than one variable. I recommend that you not use this form of the for statement (see Quality Tip 6.1). Instead, make the for loop control a single counter, and update the other variable explicitly:

```
int j - 10;
for (int i = 0; i <= 10; i++)
{
    . . .
    j--;
}
```

6.3 Nested Loops

Loops can be nested. A typical example of nested loops is printing a table with rows and columns.

Sometimes, the body of a loop is again a loop. We say that the inner loop is *nested* inside an outer loop. This happens often when you process two-dimensional structures, such as tables.

Let's look at an example that looks a bit more interesting than a table of numbers. We want to generate the following triangular shape:

```
[]
[][]
[][][]
[][][][]
[][][][][]
[][][][][][]
[][][][][][][]
```

The basic idea is simple. We generate a sequence of rows:

```
for (int i = 1; i <= width; i++)
{
    // Make triangle row
    . . .
}
```

How do you make a triangle row? Use another loop to concatenate the squares [] for that row. Then add a newline character at the end of the row. The ith row has i symbols, so the loop counter goes from 1 to i.

```
for (int j = 1; j <= i; j++)
    r = r + "[]";
r = r + "\n";
```

Putting both loops together yields two *nested loops:*

```
String r = "";
for (int i = 1; i <= width; i++)
{
   // Make triangle row
   for (int j = 1; j <= i; j++)
      r = r + "[]";
   r = r + "\n";
}
return r;
```

Here is the complete program:

ch06/triangle1/Triangle.java

```
1  /**
2      This class describes triangle objects that can be displayed
3      as shapes like this:
4      []
5      [][]
6      [][][].
7  */
8  public class Triangle
9  {
10     /**
11         Constructs a triangle.
12         @param aWidth the number of [] in the last row of the triangle
13     */
14     public Triangle(int aWidth)
15     {
16        width = aWidth;
17     }
18
19     /**
20         Computes a string representing the triangle.
21         @return a string consisting of [] and newline characters
22     */
23     public String toString()
24     {
25        String r = "";
26        for (int i = 1; i <= width; i++)
27        {
28           // Make triangle row
29           for (int j = 1; j <= i; j++)
30              r = r + "[]";
31           r = r + "\n";
32        }
33        return r;
34     }
35
36     private int width;
37  }
```

ch06/triangle1/TriangleRunner.java

```
1  /**
2      This program prints two triangles.
3  */
4  public class TriangleRunner
5  {
6     public static void main(String[] args)
7     {
8        Triangle small = new Triangle(3);
9        System.out.println(small.toString());
10
11       Triangle large = new Triangle(15);
12       System.out.println(large.toString());
13    }
14 }
```

Output

```
[]
[][]
[][][]

[]
[][]
[][][]
[][][][]
[][][][][]
[][][][][][]
[][][][][][][]
[][][][][][][][]
[][][][][][][][][]
[][][][][][][][][][]
[][][][][][][][][][][]
[][][][][][][][][][][][]
[][][][][][][][][][][][][]
[][][][][][][][][][][][][][]
[][][][][][][][][][][][][][][]
```

SELF CHECK

5. How would you modify the nested loops so that you print a square instead of a triangle?

6. What is the value of n after the following nested loops?

```
int n = 0;
for (int i = 1; i <= 5; i++)
   for (int j = 0; j < i; j++)
      n = n + j;
```

6.4 Processing Sentinel Values

Suppose you want to process a set of values, for example a set of measurements. Your goal is to analyze the data and display properties of the data set, such as the average or the maximum value. You prompt the user for the first value, then the second value, then the third, and so on. When does the input end?

One common method for indicating the end of a data set is a *sentinel value*, a value that is not part of the data. Instead, the sentinel value indicates that the data has come to an end.

Some programmers choose numbers such as 0 or –1 as sentinel values. But that is not a good idea. These values may well be valid inputs. A better idea is to use an input that is not a number, such as the letter Q. Here is a typical program run:

```
Enter value, Q to quit: 1
Enter value, Q to quit: 2
Enter value, Q to quit: 3
Enter value, Q to quit: 4
Enter value, Q to quit: Q
Average = 2.5
Maximum = 4.0
```

Of course, we need to read each input as a string, not a number. Once we have tested that the input is not the letter Q, we convert the string into a number.

```
System.out.print("Enter value, Q to quit: ");
String input = in.next();
if (input.equalsIgnoreCase("Q"))
    We are done
else
{
    double x = Double.parseDouble(input);
    . . .
}
```

Sometimes, the termination condition of a loop can only be evaluated in the middle of a loop. You can introduce a Boolean variable to control such a loop.

Now we have another problem. The test for loop termination occurs in the *middle* of the loop, not at the top or the bottom. You must first try to read input before you can test whether you have reached the end of input. In Java, there isn't a ready-made control structure for the pattern "do work, then test, then do more work". Therefore, we use a combination of a while loop and a boolean variable.

```
boolean done = false;
while (!done)
{
    Print prompt
    String input = read input;
    if (end of input indicated)
        done = true;
    else
    {
        Process input
    }
}
```

This pattern is sometimes called "loop and a half". Some programmers find it clumsy to introduce a control variable for such a loop. Advanced Topic 6.3 shows several alternatives.

Let's put together the data analysis program. To decouple the input handling from the computation of the average and the maximum, we'll introduce a class DataSet. You add values to a DataSet object with the add method. The getAverage method returns the average of all added data and the getMaximum method returns the largest.

ch06/dataset/DataAnalyzer.java

```java
1  import java.util.Scanner;
2
3  /**
4      This program computes the average and maximum of a set
5      of input values.
6  */
7  public class DataAnalyzer
8  {
9     public static void main(String[] args)
10    {
11       Scanner in = new Scanner(System.in);
12       DataSet data = new DataSet();
13
14       boolean done = false;
15       while (!done)
16       {
17          System.out.print("Enter value, Q to quit: ");
18          String input = in.next();
19          if (input.equalsIgnoreCase("Q"))
20             done = true;
21          else
22          {
23             double x = Double.parseDouble(input);
24             data.add(x);
25          }
26       }
27
28       System.out.println("Average = " + data.getAverage());
29       System.out.println("Maximum = " + data.getMaximum());
30    }
31 }
```

ch06/dataset/DataSet.java

```java
1  /**
2      Computes information about a set of data values.
3  */
4  public class DataSet
5  {
```

```
 6      /**
 7          Constructs an empty data set.
 8      */
 9      public DataSet()
10      {
11          sum = 0;
12          count = 0;
13          maximum = 0;
14      }
15
16      /**
17          Adds a data value to the data set.
18          @param x a data value
19      */
20      public void add(double x)
21      {
22          sum = sum + x;
23          if (count == 0 || maximum < x) maximum = x;
24          count++;
25      }
26
27      /**
28          Gets the average of the added data.
29          @return the average or 0 if no data has been added
30      */
31      public double getAverage()
32      {
33          if (count == 0) return 0;
34          else return sum / count;
35      }
36
37      /**
38          Gets the largest of the added data.
39          @return the maximum or 0 if no data has been added
40      */
41      public double getMaximum()
42      {
43          return maximum;
44      }
45
46      private double sum;
47      private double maximum;
48      private int count;
49  }
```

Output

```
Enter value, Q to quit: 10
Enter value, Q to quit: 0
Enter value, Q to quit: -1
Enter value, Q to quit: Q
Average = 3.0
Maximum = 10.0
```

7. Why does the DataAnalyzer class call in.next and not in.nextDouble?

8. Would the DataSet class still compute the correct maximum if you simplified the update of the maximum field in the add method to the following statement?

```
if (maximum < x) maximum = x;
```

HOW TO 6.1

Implementing Loops

You write a loop because your program needs to repeat an action multiple times. As you have seen in this chapter, there are several loop types, and it isn't always obvious how to structure loop statements. This How To walks you through the thought process that is involved when programming a loop.

Step 1   List the work that needs to be done in every step of the loop body.

For example, suppose you need to read in input values in gallons and convert them to liters until the end of input is reached. Then the operations are:

• Read input.
• Convert the input to liters.
• Print out the response.

Suppose you need to scan through the characters of a string and count the vowels. Then the operations are:

• Get the next character.
• If it's a vowel, increase a counter.

Step 2   Find out how often the loop is repeated.

Typical answers might be:

• Ten times
• Once for each character in the string
• Until the end of input is reached
• While the balance is less than the target balance

If a loop is executed for a definite number of times, a for loop is usually appropriate. The first two answers above lead to for loops, such as

```
for (int i = 1; i <= 10; i++) . . .
for (int i = 0; i < str.length(); i++) . . .
```

The next two need to be implemented as while loops—you don't know how many times the loop body is going to be repeated.

Step 3 With a `while` loop, find out where you can determine that the loop is finished.

There are three possibilities:

- Before entering the loop
- In the middle of the loop
- At the end of the loop

For example, if you execute a loop while the balance is less than the target balance, you can check for that condition at the beginning of the loop. If the balance is less than the target balance, you enter the loop. If not, you are done. In such a case, your loop has the form

```
while (condition)
{
    Do work
}
```

However, checking for input requires that you first *read* the input. That means, you'll need to enter the loop, read the input, and then decide whether you want to go any further. Then your loop has the form

```
boolean done = false;
while (!done)
{
    Do the work needed to check the condition
    if (condition)
        done = true;
    else
    {
        Do more work
    }
}
```

This loop structure is sometimes called a *"loop and a half"*.

Finally, if you know whether you need to go on after you have gone through the loop once, then you use a `do/while` loop:

```
do
{
    Do work
}
while (condition)
```

However, these loops are very rare in practice.

Step 4 Implement the loop by putting the operations from Step 1 into the loop body.

When you write a `for` loop, you usually use the loop index inside the loop body. For example, "get the next character" is implemented as the statement

```
char ch = str.charAt(i);
```

Step 5 Double-check your variable initializations.

If you use a Boolean variable `done`, make sure it is initialized to `false`. If you accumulate a result in a `sum` or `count` variable, make sure that you set it to 0 before entering the loop for the first time.

Step 6   Check for off-by-one errors.

Consider the simplest possible scenarios:

- If you read input, what happens if there is no input at all? Exactly one input?
- If you look through the characters of a string, what happens if the string is empty? If it has one character in it?
- If you accumulate values until some target has been reached, what happens if the target is 0? A negative value?

Manually walk through every instruction in the loop, including all initializations. Carefully check all conditions, paying attention to the difference between comparisons such as < and <=. Check that the loop is not traversed at all, or only once, and that the final result is what you expect.

If you write a for loop, check to see whether your bounds should be symmetric or asymmetric (see Quality Tip 6.3), and count the number of iterations (see Quality Tip 6.4).

QUALITY TIP 6.3

Symmetric and Asymmetric Bounds

It is easy to write a loop with i going from 1 to n:

```
for (i = 1; i <= n; i++) . . .
```

The values for i are bounded by the relation $1 \le i \le n$. Because there are $\le$ comparisons on both bounds, the bounds are called *symmetric*.

When traversing the characters in a string, the bounds are *asymmetric*.

```
for (i = 0; i < str.length(); i++) . . .
```

> Make a choice between symmetric and asymmetric loop bounds.

The values for i are bounded by $0 \le i < $ str.length(), with a $\le$ comparison to the left and a < comparison to the right. That is appropriate, because str.length() is not a valid position. It is not a good idea to force symmetry artificially:

```
for (i = 0; i <= str.length() - 1; i++) . . .
```

That is more difficult to read and understand.

For every loop, consider which form is most natural for the problem, and use that.

QUALITY TIP 6.4

Count Iterations

Finding the correct lower and upper bounds for an iteration can be confusing. Should I start at 0? Should I use <= b or < b as a termination condition?

> Count the number of iterations to check that your for loop is correct.

Counting the number of iterations is a very useful device for better understanding a loop. Counting is easier for loops with asymmetric bounds. The loop

```
for (i = a; i < b; i++) . . .
```

is executed b - a times. For example, the loop traversing the characters in a string,

```
for (i = 0; i < str.length(); i++) . . .
```

runs str.length() times. That makes perfect sense, because there are str.length() characters in a string.

The loop with symmetric bounds,

```
for (i = a; i <= b; i++)
```

is executed b - a + 1 times. That "+ 1" is the source of many programming errors. For example,

```
for (n = 0; n <= 10; n++)
```

runs 11 times. Maybe that is what you want; if not, start at 1 or use < 10.

One way to visualize this "+ 1" error is to think of the posts and sections of a fence. Suppose the fence has ten sections (=). How many posts (|) does it have?

```
|=|=|=|=|=|=|=|=|=|=|
```

A fence with ten sections has *eleven* posts. Each section has one post to the left, *and* there is one more post after the last section. Forgetting to count the last iteration of a "<=" loop is often called a "fence post error".

If the increment is a value c other than 1, and c divides b - a, then the counts are

$$(b - a) / c \qquad \text{for the asymmetric loop}$$

$$(b - a) / c + 1 \quad \text{for the symmetric loop}$$

For example, the loop for (i = 10; i <= 40; i += 5) executes $(40 - 10)/5 + 1 = 7$ times.

ADVANCED TOPIC 6.3

The "Loop and a Half" Problem

Reading input data sometimes requires a loop such as the following, which is somewhat unsightly:

```
boolean done = false;
while (!done)
{
   String input = in.next();
   if (input.equalsIgnoreCase("Q"))
      done = true;
   else
   {
      Process data
   }
}
```

The true test for loop termination is in the middle of the loop, not at the top. This is called a "loop and a half", because one must go halfway into the loop before knowing whether one needs to terminate.

Some programmers dislike the introduction of an additional Boolean variable for loop control. Two Java language features can be used to alleviate the "loop and a half" problem. I don't think either is a superior solution, but both approaches are fairly common, so it is worth knowing about them when reading other people's code.

You can combine an assignment and a test in the loop condition:

```java
while (!(input = in.next()).equalsIgnoreCase("Q"))
{
    Process data
}
```

The expression

```java
(input = in.next()).equalsIgnoreCase("Q")
```

means, "First call in.next(), then assign the result to input, then test whether it equals "Q"". This is an expression with a side effect. The primary purpose of the expression is to serve as a test for the while loop, but it also does some work—namely, reading the input and storing it in the variable input. In general, it is a bad idea to use side effects, because they make a program hard to read and maintain. In this case, however, that practice is somewhat seductive, because it eliminates the control variable done, which also makes the code hard to read and maintain.

The other solution is to exit the loop from the middle, either by a return statement or by a break statement (see Advanced Topic 6.4).

```java
public void processInput(Scanner in)
{
    while (true)
    {
        String input = in.next();
        if (input.equalsIgnoreCase("Q"))
            return;
        Process data
    }
}
```

ADVANCED TOPIC 6.4

The break and continue Statements

You already encountered the break statement in Advanced Topic 5.2, where it was used to exit a switch statement. In addition to breaking out of a switch statement, a break statement can also be used to exit a while, for, or do loop. For example, the break statement in the following loop terminates the loop when the end of input is reached.

```java
while (true)
{
    String input = in.next();
    if (input.equalsIgnoreCase("Q"))
        break;
    double x = Double.parseDouble(input);
    data.add(x);
}
```

In general, a break is a very poor way of exiting a loop. In 1990, a misused break caused an AT&T 4ESS telephone switch to fail, and the failure propagated through the entire U.S. network, rendering it nearly unusable for about nine hours. A programmer had used a break to terminate an if statement. Unfortunately, break cannot be used with if, so the program execution broke out of the enclosing switch statement, skipping some variable initializations and running into chaos [2, p. 38]. Using break statements also makes it difficult to use *correctness proof* techniques (see Advanced Topic 6.5).

However, when faced with the bother of introducing a separate loop control variable, some programmers find that break statements are beneficial in the "loop and a half" case. This issue is often the topic of heated (and quite unproductive) debate. In this book, we won't use the break statement, and we leave it to you to decide whether you like to use it in your own programs.

In Java, there is a second form of the break statement that is used to break out of a nested statement. The statement break *label*; immediately jumps to the *end* of the statement that is tagged with a label. Any statement (including if and block statements) can be tagged with a label—the syntax is

label: *statement*

The labeled break statement was invented to break out of a set of nested loops.

```
outerloop:
while (outer loop condition)
{  . . .
   while (inner loop condition)
   {  . . .
      if (something really bad happened)
         break outerloop;
   }
}
Jumps here if something really bad happened
```

Naturally, this situation is quite rare. We recommend that you try to introduce additional methods instead of using complicated nested loops.

Finally, there is another goto-like statement, the continue statement, which jumps to the end of the *current iteration* of the loop. Here is a possible use for this statement:

```
while (!done)
{
   String input = in.next();
   if (input.equalsIgnoreCase("Q"))
   {
      done = true;
      continue; // Jump to the end of the loop body
   }
   double x = Double.parseDouble(input);
   data.add(x);
   // continue statement jumps here
}
```

By using the continue statement, you don't need to place the remainder of the loop code inside an else clause. This is a minor benefit. Few programmers use this statement.

6.5 Random Numbers and Simulations

> In a simulation, you repeatedly generate random numbers and use them to simulate an activity.

In a simulation you generate random events and evaluate their outcomes. Here is a typical problem that can be decided by running a simulation: the *Buffon needle experiment*, devised by Comte Georges-Louis Leclerc de Buffon (1707–1788), a French naturalist. On each *try*, a one-inch long needle is dropped onto paper that is ruled with lines 2 inches apart. If the needle drops onto a line, count it as a hit. (See Figure 3.) Buffon conjectured that the quotient *tries/hits* approximates π.

Now, how can you run this experiment in the computer? You don't actually want to build a robot that drops needles on paper. The Random class of the Java library implements a *random number generator*, which produces numbers that appear to be completely random. To generate random numbers, you construct an object of the Random class, and then apply one of the following methods:

Method	Returns
nextInt(n)	A random integer between the integers 0 (inclusive) and n (exclusive)
nextDouble()	A random floating-point number between 0 (inclusive) and 1 (exclusive)

For example, you can simulate the cast of a die as follows:

```
Random generator = new Random();
int d = 1 + generator.nextInt(6);
```

The call generator.nextInt(6) gives you a random number between 0 and 5 (inclusive). Add 1 to obtain a number between 1 and 6.

To give you a feeling for the random numbers, run the following program a few times.

Figure 3   The Buffon Needle Experiment

ch06/random1/Die.java

```java
1  import java.util.Random;
2
3  /**
4     This class models a die that, when cast, lands on a random
5     face.
6  */
7  public class Die
8  {
9     /**
10        Constructs a die with a given number of sides.
11        @param s the number of sides, e.g., 6 for a normal die
12     */
13     public Die(int s)
14     {
15        sides = s;
16        generator = new Random();
17     }
18
19     /**
20        Simulates a throw of the die.
21        @return the face of the die
22     */
23     public int cast()
24     {
25        return 1 + generator.nextInt(sides);
26     }
27
28     private Random generator;
29     private int sides;
30  }
```

ch06/random1/DieSimulator.java

```java
1  /**
2     This program simulates casting a die ten times.
3  */
4  public class DieSimulator
5  {
6     public static void main(String[] args)
7     {
8        Die d = new Die(6);
9        final int TRIES = 10;
10       for (int i = 1; i <= TRIES; i++)
11       {
12          int n = d.cast();
13          System.out.print(n + " ");
14       }
15       System.out.println();
16    }
17 }
```

Typical Output

```
6 5 6 3 2 6 3 4 4 1
```

Typical Output (Second Run)

```
3 2 2 1 6 5 3 4 1 2
```

As you can see, this program produces a different stream of simulated die casts every time it is run.

Actually, the numbers are not completely random. They are drawn from very long sequences of numbers that don't repeat for a long time. These sequences are computed from fairly simple formulas; they just behave like random numbers. For that reason, they are often called *pseudorandom* numbers. Generating good sequences of numbers that behave like truly random sequences is an important and well-studied problem in computer science. We won't investigate this issue further, though; we'll just use the random numbers produced by the Random class.

To run the Buffon needle experiment, we have to work a little harder. When you throw a die, it has to come up with one of six faces. When throwing a needle, however, there are many possible outcomes. You must generate *two* random numbers: one to describe the starting position and one to describe the angle of the needle with the x-axis. Then you need to test whether the needle touches a grid line. Stop after 10,000 tries.

Let us agree to generate the *lower* point of the needle. Its x-coordinate is irrelevant, and you may assume its y-coordinate y_{low} to be any random number between 0 and 2. However, because it can be a random *floating-point* number, we use the nextDouble method of the Random class. It returns a random floating-point number between 0 and 1. Multiply by 2 to get a random number between 0 and 2.

The angle α between the needle and the x-axis can be any value between 0 degrees and 180 degrees. The upper end of the needle has y-coordinate

$$y_{high} = y_{low} + \sin(\alpha)$$

The needle is a hit if y_{high} is at least 2. See Figure 4.

Figure 4
When Does the Needle Fall on a Line?

Here is the program to carry out the simulation of the needle experiment.

ch06/random2/Needle.java

```java
1   import java.util.Random;
2
3   /**
4       This class simulates a needle in the Buffon needle experiment.
5   */
6   public class Needle
7   {
8       /**
9           Constructs a needle.
10      */
11      public Needle()
12      {
13          hits = 0;
14          tries = 0;
15          generator = new Random();
16      }
17
18      /**
19          Drops the needle on the grid of lines and
20          remembers whether the needle hit a line.
21      */
22      public void drop()
23      {
24          double ylow = 2 * generator.nextDouble();
25          double angle = 180 * generator.nextDouble();
26
27          // Computes high point of needle
28
29          double yhigh = ylow + Math.sin(Math.toRadians(angle));
30          if (yhigh >= 2) hits++;
31          tries++;
32      }
33
34      /**
35          Gets the number of times the needle hit a line.
36          @return the hit count
37      */
38      public int getHits()
39      {
40          return hits;
41      }
42
43      /**
44          Gets the total number of times the needle was dropped.
45          @return the try count
46      */
47      public int getTries()
48      {
49          return tries;
50      }
51
```

```
52        private Random generator;
53        private int hits;
54        private int tries;
55    }
```

ch06/random2/NeedleSimulator.java

```
1    /**
2        This program simulates the Buffon needle experiment
3        and prints the resulting approximations of pi.
4    */
5    public class NeedleSimulator
6    {
7        public static void main(String[] args)
8        {
9            Needle n = new Needle();
10           final int TRIES1 = 10000;
11           final int TRIES2 = 1000000;
12
13           for (int i = 1; i <= TRIES1; i++)
14               n.drop();
15           System.out.printf("Tries = %d, Tries / Hits = %8.5f\n",
16                   TRIES1, (double) n.getTries() / n.getHits());
17
18           for (int i = TRIES1 + 1; i <= TRIES2; i++)
19               n.drop();
20           System.out.printf("Tries = %d, Tries / Hits = %8.5f\n",
21                   TRIES2, (double) n.getTries() / n.getHits());
22       }
23   }
```

Output

```
Tries = 10000, Tries / Hits =  3.08928
Tries = 1000000, Tries / Hits =  3.14204
```

The point of this program is not to compute π—there are far more efficient ways to do that. Rather, the point is to show how a physical experiment can be simulated on the computer. Buffon had to physically drop the needle thousands of times and record the results, which must have been a rather dull activity. The computer can execute the experiment quickly and accurately.

Simulations are very common computer applications. Many simulations use essentially the same pattern as the code of this example: In a loop, a large number of sample values are generated, and the values of certain observations are recorded for each sample. When the simulation is completed, the averages, or other statistics of interest from the observed values are printed out.

A typical example of a simulation is the modeling of customer queues at a bank or a supermarket. Rather than observing real customers, one simulates their arrival and their transactions at the teller window or checkout stand in the computer. One can try different staffing or building layout patterns in the computer simply by making changes in the program. In the real world, making many such changes and measuring their effects would be impossible, or at least, very expensive.

SELF CHECK

9. How do you use a random number generator to simulate the toss of a coin?

10. Why is the NeedleSimulator program not an efficient method for computing π?

ADVANCED TOPIC 6.5

Loop Invariants

Consider the task of computing a^n, where a is a floating-point number and n is a positive integer. Of course, you can multiply $a \cdot a \cdot \ldots \cdot a$, n times, but if n is large, you'll end up doing a lot of multiplication. The following loop computes a^n in far fewer steps:

```
double a = . . .;
int n = . . .;
double r = 1;
double b = a;
int i = n;
while (i > 0)
{
   if (i % 2 == 0) // n is even
   {
      b = b * b;
      i = i / 2;
   }
   else
   {
      r = r * b;
      i--;
   }
}
// Now r equals a to the nth power
```

Consider the case n = 100. The method performs the steps shown in the table below.

Amazingly enough, the algorithm yields exactly a^{100}. Do you understand why? Are you convinced it will work for all values of n? Here is a clever argument to show that the method always computes the correct result. It demonstrates that whenever the program reaches the top of the while loop, it is true that

$$r \cdot b^i = a^n \tag{I}$$

Certainly, it is true the first time around, because b = a and i = n. Suppose that (I) holds at the beginning of the loop. Label the values of r, b, and i as "old" when entering the loop, and as "new" when exiting the loop. Assume that upon entry

$$r_{old} \cdot b_{old}^{\ i_{old}} = a^n$$

Computing a^{100}		
b	i	r
a	100	1
a^2	50	
a^4	25	
	24	a^4
a^8	12	
a^{16}	6	
a^{32}	3	
	2	a^{36}
a^{64}	1	
	0	a^{100}

In the loop you must distinguish two cases: i_{old} even and i_{old} odd. If i_{old} is even, the loop performs the following transformations:

$$r_{new} = r_{old}$$
$$b_{new} = b_{old}^2$$
$$i_{new} = i_{old}/2$$

Therefore,

$$r_{new} \cdot b_{new}^{i_{new}} = r_{old} \cdot \left(b_{old}\right)^{2 \cdot i_{old}/2}$$
$$= r_{old} \cdot b_{old}^{i_{old}}$$
$$= a^n$$

On the other hand, if i_{old} is odd, then

$$r_{new} = r_{old} \cdot b_{old}$$
$$b_{new} = b_{old}$$
$$i_{new} = i_{old} - 1$$

Therefore,

$$r_{new} \cdot b_{new}^{i_{new}} = r_{old} \cdot b_{old} \cdot b_{old}^{i_{old}-1}$$
$$= r_{old} \cdot b_{old}^{i_{old}}$$
$$= a^n$$

In either case, the new values for r, b, and i fulfill the *loop invariant* (I). So what? When the loop finally exits, (I) holds again:

$$r \cdot b^i = a^n$$

Furthermore, we know that i = 0, because the loop is terminating. But because i = 0, $r \cdot b^i = r \cdot b^0 = r$. Hence $r = a^n$, and the method really does compute the nth power of a.

This technique is quite useful, because it can explain an algorithm that is not at all obvious. The condition (I) is called a loop invariant because it is true when the loop is entered, at the top of each pass, and when the loop is exited. If a loop invariant is chosen skillfully, you may be able to deduce correctness of a computation. See [3] for another nice example.

RANDOM FACT 6.2

Correctness Proofs

In Advanced Topic 6.5 we introduced the technique of loop invariants. If you skipped that topic, have a glance at it now. That technique can be used to rigorously prove that a loop computes exactly the value that it is supposed to compute. Such a proof is far more valuable than any testing. No matter how many test cases you try, you always worry whether another case that you haven't tried yet might show a bug. A proof settles the correctness for *all possible inputs.*

For some time, programmers were very hopeful that proof techniques such as loop invariants would greatly reduce the need of testing. You would prove that each simple method is correct, and then put the proven components together and prove that they work together as they should. Once it is proved that main works correctly, no testing is required. Some researchers were so excited about these techniques that they tried to omit the programming step altogether. The designer would write down the program requirements, using the notation of formal logic. An automatic prover would prove that such a program could be written and generate the program as part of its proof.

Unfortunately, in practice these methods never worked very well. The logical notation to describe program behavior is complex. Even simple scenarios require many formulas. It is easy enough to express the idea that a method is supposed to compute a^n, but the logical formulas describing all methods in a program that controls an airplane, for instance, would fill many pages. These formulas are created by humans, and humans make errors when they deal with difficult and tedious tasks. Experiments showed that instead of buggy programs, programmers wrote buggy logic specifications and buggy program proofs.

Van der Linden [2, p. 287], gives some examples of complicated proofs that are much harder to verify than the programs they are trying to prove.

Program proof techniques are valuable for proving the correctness of individual methods that make computations in nonobvious ways. At this time, though, there is no hope to prove any but the most trivial programs correct in such a way that the specification and the proof can be trusted more than the program. There is hope that correctness proofs will become more applicable to real-life programming situations in the future. However, engineering and management are at least as important as mathematics and logic for the successful completion of large software projects.

6.6 Using a Debugger

As you have undoubtedly realized by now, computer programs rarely run perfectly the first time. At times, it can be quite frustrating to find the bugs. Of course, you can insert print commands, run the program, and try to analyze the printout. If the printout does not clearly point to the problem, you may need to add and remove print commands and run the program again. That can be a time-consuming process.

> A debugger is a program that you can use to execute another program and analyze its run-time behavior.

Modern development environments contain special programs, called debuggers, that help you locate bugs by letting you follow the execution of a program. You can stop and restart your program and see the contents of variables whenever your program is temporarily stopped. At each stop, you have the choice of what variables to inspect and how many program steps to run until the next stop.

Some people feel that debuggers are just a tool to make programmers lazy. Admittedly some people write sloppy programs and then fix them up with a debugger, but the majority of programmers make an honest effort to write the best program they can before trying to run it through a debugger. These programmers realize that a debugger, while more convenient than print commands, is not cost-free. It does take time to set up and carry out an effective debugging session.

In actual practice, you cannot avoid using a debugger. The larger your programs get, the harder it is to debug them simply by inserting print commands. You will find that the time investment to learn about a debugger is amply repaid in your programming career.

Like compilers, debuggers vary widely from one system to another. On some systems they are quite primitive and require you to memorize a small set of arcane commands; on others they have an intuitive window interface. The screen shots in this chapter show the debugger in the Eclipse development environment, downloadable for free from the Eclipse Foundation web site [4]. Other integrated environments, such as BlueJ, also include debuggers. A free standalone debugger called JSwat is available from the JSwat Graphical Java Debugger web page [5].

You will have to find out how to prepare a program for debugging and how to start a debugger on your system. If you use an integrated development environment, which contains an editor, compiler, and debugger, this step is usually very easy. You just build the program in the usual way and pick a menu command to start debugging. On some systems, you must manually build a debug version of your program and invoke the debugger.

> You can make effective use of a debugger by mastering just three concepts: breakpoints, single-stepping, and inspecting variables.

Once you have started the debugger, you can go a long way with just three debugging commands: "set breakpoint", "single step", and "inspect variable". The names and keystrokes or mouse clicks for these commands differ widely between debuggers, but all debuggers support these basic commands. You can find out how, either from the documentation or a lab manual, or by asking someone who has used the debugger before.

When a debugger executes a program, the execution is suspended whenever a breakpoint is reached.

When you start the debugger, it runs at full speed until it reaches a *breakpoint*. Then execution stops, and the breakpoint that causes the stop is displayed (see Figure 5). You can now inspect variables and step through the program a line at a time, or continue running the program at full speed until it reaches the next breakpoint. When the program terminates, the debugger stops as well.

Breakpoints stay active until you remove them, so you should periodically clear the breakpoints that you no longer need.

Once the program has stopped, you can look at the current values of variables. Again, the method for selecting the variables differs among debuggers. Some debuggers always show you a window with the current local variables. On other debuggers you issue a command such as "inspect variable" and type in or click on the variable. The debugger then displays the contents of the variable. If all variables

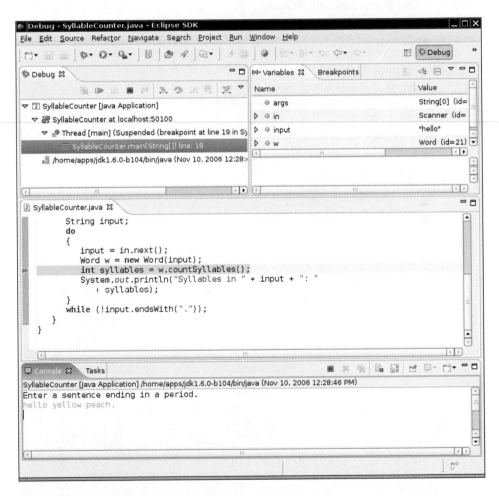

Figure 5   Stopping at a Breakpoint

contain what you expected, you can run the program until the next point where you want to stop.

When inspecting objects, you often need to give a command to "open up" the object, for example by clicking on a tree node. Once the object is opened up, you see its instance variables (see Figure 6).

> The single-step command executes the program one line at a time.

Running to a breakpoint gets you there speedily, but you don't know how the program got there. You can also step through the program a line at a time. Then you know how the program flows, but it can take a long time to step through it. The *single-step command* executes the current line and stops at the next program line. Most debuggers have two single-step commands, one called *step into*, which steps inside method calls, and one called *step over*, which skips over method calls.

For example, suppose the current line is

```
String input = in.next();
Word w = new Word(input);
int syllables = w.countSyllables();
System.out.println("Syllables in " + input + ": " + syllables);
```

When you step over method calls, you get to the next line:

```
String input = in.next();
Word w = new Word(input);
int syllables = w.countSyllables();
System.out.println("Syllables in " + input + ": " + syllables);
```

However, if you step into method calls, you enter the first line of the countSyllables method.

```
public int countSyllables()
{
    int count = 0;
    int end = text.length() - 1;
    . . .
}
```

Figure 6
Inspecting Variables

You should step *into* a method to check whether it carries out its job correctly. You should step *over* a method if you know it works correctly.

Finally, when the program has finished running, the debug session is also finished. To run the program again, you may be able to reset the debugger, or you may need to exit the debugging program and start over. Details depend on the particular debugger.

SELF CHECK

11. In the debugger, you are reaching a call to System.out.println. Should you step into the method or step over it?

12. In the debugger, you are reaching the beginning of a method with a couple of loops inside. You want to find out the return value that is computed at the end of the method. Should you set a breakpoint, or should you step through the method?

6.7 A Sample Debugging Session

To have a realistic example for running a debugger, we will study a Word class whose primary purpose is to count the number of syllables in a word. The class uses this rule for counting syllables:

Each group of adjacent vowels (a, e, i, o, u, y) counts as one syllable (for example, the "ea" in "peach" contributes one syllable, but the "e . . . o" in "yellow" counts as two syllables). However, an "e" at the end of a word doesn't count as a syllable. Each word has at least one syllable, even if the previous rules give a count of 0.

Also, when you construct a word from a string, any characters at the beginning or end of the string that aren't letters are stripped off. That is useful when you read the input using the next method of the Scanner class. Input strings can still contain quotation marks and punctuation marks, and we don't want them as part of the word.

Here is the source code. There are a couple of bugs in this class.

ch06/debugger/Word.java

```
1  public class Word
2  {
3     /**
4        Constructs a word by removing leading and trailing non-
5        letter characters, such as punctuation marks.
6        @param s the input string
7     */
8     public Word(String s)
```

```
 9       {
10          int i = 0;
11          while (i < s.length() && !Character.isLetter(s.charAt(i)))
12             i++;
13          int j = s.length() - 1;
14          while (j > i && !Character.isLetter(s.charAt(j)))
15             j--;
16          text = s.substring(i, j);
17       }
18
19       /**
20          Returns the text of the word, after removal of the
21          leading and trailing nonletter characters.
22          @return the text of the word
23       */
24       public String getText()
25       {
26          return text;
27       }
28
29       /**
30          Counts the syllables in the word.
31          @return the syllable count
32       */
33       public int countSyllables()
34       {
35          int count = 0;
36          int end = text.length() - 1;
37          if (end < 0) return 0; // The empty string has no syllables
38
39          // An e at the end of the word doesn't count as a vowel
40          char ch = Character.toLowerCase(text.charAt(end));
41          if (ch == 'e') end--;
42
43          boolean insideVowelGroup = false;
44          for (int i = 0; i <= end; i++)
45          {
46             ch = Character.toLowerCase(text.charAt(i));
47             if ("aeiouy".indexOf(ch) >= 0)
48             {
49                // ch is a vowel
50                if (!insideVowelGroup)
51                {
52                   // Start of new vowel group
53                   count++;
54                   insideVowelGroup = true;
55                }
56             }
57          }
58
59          // Every word has at least one syllable
60          if (count == 0)
61             count = 1;
62
```

```
63          return count;
64      }
65
66      private String text;
67  }
```

Here is a simple test class. Type in a sentence, and the syllable counts of all words are displayed.

ch06/debugger/SyllableCounter.java

```
1   import java.util.Scanner;
2
3   /**
4       This program counts the syllables of all words in a sentence.
5   */
6   public class SyllableCounter
7   {
8       public static void main(String[] args)
9       {
10          Scanner in = new Scanner(System.in);
11
12          System.out.println("Enter a sentence ending in a period.");
13
14          String input;
15          do
16          {
17              input = in.next();
18              Word w = new Word(input);
19              int syllables = w.countSyllables();
20              System.out.println("Syllables in " + input + ": "
21                      + syllables);
22          }
23          while (!input.endsWith("."));
24      }
25  }
```

Supply this input:

```
hello yellow peach.
```

Then the output is

```
Syllables in hello: 1
Syllables in yellow: 1
Syllables in peach.: 1
```

That is not very promising.

First, set a breakpoint in the first line of the countSyllables method of the Word class, in line 33 of Word.java. Then start the program. The program will prompt you for the input. The program will stop at the breakpoint you just set.

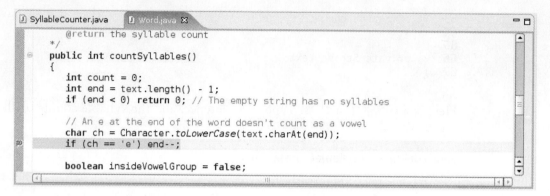

Figure 7   Debugging the countSyllables Method

First, the countSyllables method checks the last character of the word to see if it is a letter 'e'. Let's just verify that this works correctly. Run the program to line 41 (see Figure 7).

Now inspect the variable ch. This particular debugger has a handy display of all current local and instance variables—see Figure 8. If yours doesn't, you may need to inspect ch manually. You can see that ch contains the value 'l'. That is strange. Look at the source code. The end variable was set to text.length() - 1, the last position in the text string, and ch is the character at that position.

Looking further, you will find that end is set to 3, not 4, as you would expect. And text contains the string "hell", not "hello". Thus, it is no wonder that count-Syllables returns the answer 1. We'll need to look elsewhere for the culprit. Apparently, the Word constructor contains an error.

Unfortunately, a debugger cannot go back in time. Thus, you must stop the debugger, set a breakpoint in the Word constructor, and restart the debugger. Supply the input once again. The debugger will stop at the beginning of the Word constructor. The constructor sets two variables i and j, skipping past any nonletters at the beginning and the end of the input string. Set a breakpoint past the end of the second loop (see Figure 9) so that you can inspect the values of i and j.

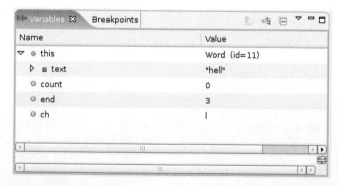

Figure 8   The Current Values of the Local and Instance Variables

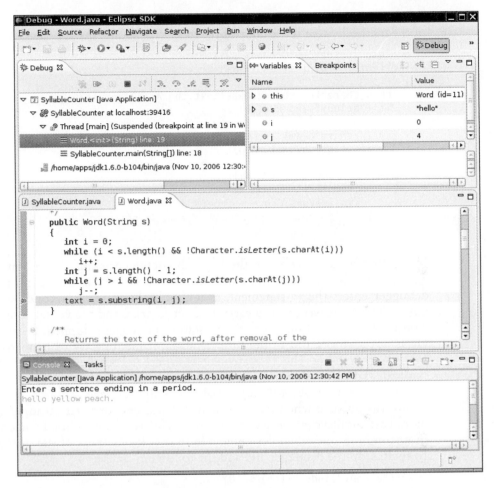

Figure 9   Debugging the Word Constructor

At this point, inspecting i and j shows that i is 0 and j is 4. That makes sense—there were no punctuation marks to skip. So why is text being set to "hell"? Recall that the substring method counts positions up to, but not including, the second parameter. Thus, the correct call should be

```
text = s.substring(i, j + 1);
```

This is a very typical off-by-one error.

Fix this error, recompile the program, and try the three test cases again. You will now get the output

```
Syllables in hello: 1
Syllables in yellow: 1
Syllables in peach.: 1
```

As you can see, there still is a problem. Erase all breakpoints and set a breakpoint in the countSyllables method. Start the debugger and supply the input "hello.".

When the debugger stops at the breakpoint, start single stepping through the lines of the method. Here is the code of the loop that counts the syllables:

```
boolean insideVowelGroup = false;
for (int i = 0; i <= end; i++)
{
    ch = Character.toLowerCase(text.charAt(i));
    if ("aeiouy".indexOf(ch) >= 0)
    {
        // ch is a vowel
        if (!insideVowelGroup)
        {
            // Start of new vowel group
            count++;
            insideVowelGroup = true;
        }
    }
}
```

In the first iteration through the loop, the debugger skips the if statement. That makes sense, because the first letter, 'h', isn't a vowel. In the second iteration, the debugger enters the if statement, as it should, because the second letter, 'e', is a vowel. The insideVowelGroup variable is set to true, and the vowel counter is incremented. In the third iteration, the if statement is again skipped, because the letter 'l' is not a vowel. But in the fifth iteration, something weird happens. The letter 'o' is a vowel, and the if statement is entered. But the second if statement is skipped, and count is not incremented again.

Why? The insideVowelGroup variable is still true, even though the first vowel group was finished when the consonant 'l' was encountered. Reading a consonant should set insideVowelGroup back to false. This is a more subtle logic error, but not an uncommon one when designing a loop that keeps track of the processing state. To fix it, stop the debugger and add the following clause:

```
if ("aeiouy".indexOf(ch) >= 0)
{
    . . .
}
else insideVowelGroup = false;
```

Now recompile and run the test once again. The output is:

```
Syllables in hello: 2
Syllables in yellow: 2
Syllables in peach.: 1
```

> A debugger can be used only to analyze the presence of bugs, not to show that a program is bug-free.

Is the program now free from bugs? That is not a question the debugger can answer. Remember: Testing can show only the presence of bugs, not their absence.

SELF CHECK

13. What caused the first error that was found in this debugging session?

14. What caused the second error? How was it detected?

HOW TO 6.2

Debugging

Now you know about the mechanics of debugging, but all that knowledge may still leave you helpless when you fire up a debugger to look at a sick program. There are a number of strategies that you can use to recognize bugs and their causes.

Step 1   Reproduce the error.

As you test your program, you notice that your program sometimes does something wrong. It gives the wrong output, it seems to print something completely random, it goes in an infinite loop, or it crashes. Find out exactly how to reproduce that behavior. What numbers did you enter? Where did you click with the mouse?

Run the program again; type in exactly the same answers, and click with the mouse on the same spots (or as close as you can get). Does the program exhibit the same behavior? If so, then it makes sense to fire up a debugger to study this particular problem. Debuggers are good for analyzing particular failures. They aren't terribly useful for studying a program in general.

Step 2   Simplify the error.

Before you fire up a debugger, it makes sense to spend a few minutes trying to come up with a simpler input that also produces an error. Can you use shorter words or simpler numbers and still have the program misbehave? If so, use those values during your debugging session.

Step 3   Divide and conquer.

> Use the divide-and-conquer technique to locate the point of failure of a program.

Now that you have a particular failure, you want to get as close to the failure as possible. The key point of debugging is to locate the code that produces the failure. Just as with real insect pests, finding the bug can be hard, but once you find it, squashing it is usually the easy part. Suppose your program dies with a division by 0. Because there are many division operations in a typical program, it is often not feasible to set breakpoints to all of them. Instead, use a technique of divide and conquer. Step over the methods in `main`, but don't step inside them. Eventually, the failure will happen again. Now you know which method contains the bug: It is the last method that was called from `main` before the program died. Restart the debugger and go back to that line in `main`, then step inside that method. Repeat the process.

Eventually, you will have pinpointed the line that contains the bad division. Maybe it is completely obvious from the code why the denominator is not correct. If not, you need to find the location where it is computed. Unfortunately, you can't go back in the debugger. You need to restart the program and move to the point where the denominator computation happens.

Step 4   Know what your program should do.

> During debugging, compare the actual contents of variables against the values you know they should have.

A debugger shows you what the program does. You must know what the program *should* do, or you will not be able to find bugs. Before you trace through a loop, ask yourself how many iterations you expect the program to make. Before you inspect a variable, ask yourself what you expect to see. If you have no clue, set aside some time and think first. Have a calculator handy to make independent computations. When you know what the value should be, inspect the variable. This is the moment of truth. If the program is still on the right track, then that value is what you expected, and you must look further for the bug. If the value is different, you may be on to something. Double-check your computation. If you are sure your value is correct, find out why your program comes up with a different value.

In many cases, program bugs are the result of simple errors such as loop termination conditions that are off by one. Quite often, however, programs make computational errors. Maybe they are supposed to add two numbers, but by accident the code was written to subtract them. Unlike your calculus instructor, programs don't make a special effort to ensure that everything is a simple integer (and neither do real-world problems). You will need to make some calculations with large integers or nasty floating-point numbers. Sometimes these calculations can be avoided if you just ask yourself, "Should this quantity be positive? Should it be larger than that value?" Then inspect variables to verify those theories.

Step 5 Look at all details.

When you debug a program, you often have a theory about what the problem is. Nevertheless, keep an open mind and look around at all details. What strange messages are displayed? Why does the program take another unexpected action? These details count. When you run a debugging session, you really are a detective who needs to look at every clue available.

If you notice another failure on the way to the problem that you are about to pin down, don't just say, "I'll come back to it later". That very failure may be the original cause for your current problem. It is better to make a note of the current problem, fix what you just found, and then return to the original mission.

Step 6 Make sure you understand each bug before you fix it.

Once you find that a loop makes too many iterations, it is very tempting to apply a "Band-Aid" solution and subtract 1 from a variable so that the particular problem doesn't appear again. Such a quick fix has an overwhelming probability of creating trouble elsewhere. You really need to have a thorough understanding of how the program should be written before you apply a fix.

It does occasionally happen that you find bug after bug and apply fix after fix, and the problem just moves around. That usually is a symptom of a larger problem with the program logic. There is little you can do with the debugger. You must rethink the program design and reorganize it.

RANDOM FACT 6.3

The First Bug

According to legend, the first bug was one found in 1947 in the Mark II, a huge electro-mechanical computer at Harvard University. It really was caused by a bug—a moth was trapped in a relay switch. Actually, from the note that the operator left in the log book next to the moth (see The First Bug figure), it appears as if the term "bug" had already been in active use at the time.

The pioneering computer scientist Maurice Wilkes wrote: "Somehow, at the Moore School and afterwards, one had always assumed there would be no particular difficulty in

The First Bug

getting programs right. I can remember the exact instant in time at which it dawned on me that a great part of my future life would be spent finding mistakes in my own programs."

CHAPTER SUMMARY

1. A `while` statement executes a block of code repeatedly. A condition controls how often the loop is executed.

2. An off-by-one error is a common error when programming loops. Think through simple test cases to avoid this type of error.

3. You use a `for` loop when a variable runs from a starting to an ending value with a constant increment or decrement.

4. Loops can be nested. A typical example of nested loops is printing a table with rows and columns.

5. Sometimes, the termination condition of a loop can only be evaluated in the middle of a loop. You can introduce a Boolean variable to control such a loop.

6. Make a choice between symmetric and asymmetric loop bounds.

7. Count the number of iterations to check that your `for` loop is correct.

8. In a simulation, you repeatedly generate random numbers and use them to simulate an activity.

9. A debugger is a program that you can use to execute another program and analyze its run-time behavior.

10. You can make effective use of a debugger by mastering just three concepts: breakpoints, single-stepping, and inspecting variables.

11. When a debugger executes a program, the execution is suspended whenever a breakpoint is reached.

12. The single-step command executes the program one line at a time.

13. A debugger can be used only to analyze the presence of bugs, not to show that a program is bug-free.

14. Use the divide-and-conquer technique to locate the point of failure of a program.

15. During debugging, compare the actual contents of variables against the values you know they should have.

FURTHER READING

1. E. W. Dijkstra, "Goto Statements Considered Harmful", *Communications of the ACM*, vol. 11, no. 3 (March 1968), pp. 147–148.

2. Peter van der Linden, *Expert C Programming*, Prentice-Hall, 1994.

3. Jon Bentley, *Programming Pearls*, Chapter 4, "Writing Correct Programs", Addison-Wesley, 1986.

4. http://eclipse.org   The Eclipse Foundation web site.

5. http://www.bluemarsh.com/java/jswat   The JSwat Graphical Java Debugger web page.

6. Kai Lai Chung, *Elementary Probability Theory with Stochastic Processes*, Undergraduate Texts in Mathematics, Springer-Verlag, 1974.

7. Rudolf Flesch, *How to Write Plain English*, Barnes & Noble Books, 1979.

CLASSES, OBJECTS, AND METHODS INTRODUCED IN THIS CHAPTER

```
java.util.Random
    nextDouble
    nextInt
```

REVIEW EXERCISES

★★   **Exercise R6.1.** Which loop statements does Java support? Give simple rules when to use each loop type.

★★   **Exercise R6.2.** What does the following code print?

```
for (int i = 0; i < 10; i++)
{
    for (int j = 0; j < 10; j++)
        System.out.print(i * j % 10);
    System.out.println();
}
```

★★ **Exercise R6.3.** How often do the following loops execute? Assume that i is an integer variable that is not changed in the loop body.

    a. for (i = 1; i <= 10; i++) . . .

    b. for (i = 0; i < 10; i++) . . .

    c. for (i = 10; i > 0; i--) . . .

    d. for (i = -10; i <= 10; i++) . . .

    e. for (i = 10; i >= 0; i++) . . .

    f. for (i = -10; i <= 10; i = i + 2) . . .

    g. for (i = -10; i <= 10; i = i + 3) . . .

★ **Exercise R6.4.** Rewrite the following for loop into a while loop.

```
int s = 0;
for (int i = 1; i <= 10; i++) s = s + i;
```

★★ **Exercise R6.5.** Rewrite the following do loop into a while loop.

```
int n = 1;
double x = 0;
double s;
do
{
    s = 1.0 / (n * n);
    x = x + s;
    n++;
}
while (s > 0.01);
```

★ **Exercise R6.6.** What is an infinite loop? On your computer, how can you terminate a program that executes an infinite loop?

★★★ **Exercise R6.7.** Give three strategies to implement the following "loop and a half":

```
loop
{
```
    Read name of bridge
    If not OK, exit loop
    Read length of bridge in feet
    If not OK, exit loop
    Convert length to meters
    Print bridge data
```
}
```

Use a Boolean variable, a break statement, and a method with multiple return statements. Which of these three approaches do you find clearest?

★ **Exercise R6.8.** Implement a loop that prompts a user to enter a number between 1 and 10, giving three tries to get it right.

★ **Exercise R6.9.** Sometimes students write programs with instructions such as "Enter data, 0 to quit" and that exit the data entry loop when the user enters the number 0. Explain why that is usually a poor idea.

★ **Exercise R6.10.** How would you use a random number generator to simulate the drawing of a playing card?

★ **Exercise R6.11.** What is an "off-by-one error"? Give an example from your own programming experience.

★★ **Exercise R6.12.** Give an example of a for loop in which symmetric bounds are more natural. Give an example of a for loop in which asymmetric bounds are more natural.

★ **Exercise R6.13.** What are nested loops? Give an example where a nested loop is typically used.

★T **Exercise R6.14.** Explain the differences between these debugger operations:
- Stepping into a method
- Stepping over a method

★★T **Exercise R6.15.** Explain in detail how to inspect the string stored in a String object in your debugger.

★★T **Exercise R6.16.** Explain in detail how to inspect the information stored in a Rectangle object in your debugger.

★★T **Exercise R6.17.** Explain in detail how to use your debugger to inspect the balance stored in a BankAccount object.

★★T **Exercise R6.18.** Explain the divide-and-conquer strategy to get close to a bug in a debugger.

Additional review exercises are available in WileyPLUS.

PROGRAMMING EXERCISES

★ **Exercise P6.1.** *Currency conversion.* Write a program CurrencyConverter that asks the user to enter today's exchange rate between U.S. dollars and the euro. Then the program reads U.S. dollar values and converts each to euro values. Stop when the user enters Q.

★★★ **Exercise P6.2.** *Projectile flight.* Suppose a cannonball is propelled vertically into the air with a starting velocity v_0. Any calculus book will tell us that the position of the ball after t seconds is $s(t) = -0.5 \cdot g \cdot t^2 + v_0 \cdot t$, where $g = 9.81$ m/sec^2 is the gravitational force of the earth. No calculus book ever mentions why someone would want to carry out such an obviously dangerous experiment, so we will do it in the safety of the computer.

In fact, we will confirm the theorem from calculus by a simulation. In our simulation, we will consider how the ball moves in very short time intervals Δt. In a short time interval the velocity v is nearly constant, and we can compute the distance the ball moves as $\Delta s = v \cdot \Delta t$. In our program, we will simply set

```
double deltaT = 0.01;
```

and update the position by

```
s = s + v * deltaT;
```

The velocity changes constantly—in fact, it is reduced by the gravitational force of the earth. In a short time interval, v decreases by $g \cdot \Delta t$, and we must keep the velocity updated as

```
v = v - g * deltaT;
```

In the next iteration the new velocity is used to update the distance.

Now run the simulation until the cannonball falls back to the earth. Get the initial velocity as an input (100 m/sec is a good value). Update the position and velocity 100 times per second, but only print out the position every full second. Also print out the values from the exact formula $s(t) = -0.5 \cdot g \cdot t^2 + v_0 \cdot t$ for comparison. Use a class Cannonball.

What is the benefit of this kind of simulation when an exact formula is available? Well, the formula from the calculus book is *not* exact. Actually, the gravitational force diminishes the farther the cannonball is away from the surface of the earth. This complicates the algebra sufficiently that it is not possible to give an exact formula for the actual motion, but the computer simulation can simply be extended to apply a variable gravitational force. For cannonballs, the calculus-book formula is actually good enough, but computers are necessary to compute accurate trajectories for higher-flying objects such as ballistic missiles.

★★ **Exercise P6.3.** Write a program that prints the powers of ten

```
1.0
10.0
100.0
1000.0
10000.0
100000.0
1000000.0
1.0E7
1.0E8
1.0E9
1.0E10
1.0E11
```

Implement a class

```
public class PowerGenerator
{
    /**
        Constructs a power generator.
        @param aFactor the number that will be multiplied by itself
    */
    public PowerGenerator(double aFactor) { . . . }
```

```
/**
    Computes the next power.
*/
public double nextPower() { . . . }
    . . .
}
```

Then supply a test class `PowerGeneratorRunner` that calls `System.out.println(myGenerator.nextPower())` twelve times.

★★   **Exercise P6.4.** The *Fibonacci sequence* is defined by the following rule. The first two values in the sequence are 1 and 1. Every subsequent value is the sum of the two values preceding it. For example, the third value is $1 + 1 = 2$, the fourth value is $1 + 2 = 3$, and the fifth is $2 + 3 = 5$. If f_n denotes the nth value in the Fibonacci sequence, then

$$f_1 = 1$$
$$f_2 = 1$$
$$f_n = f_{n-1} + f_{n-2} \quad \text{if } n > 2$$

Write a program that prompts the user for n and prints the first n values in the Fibonacci sequence. Use a class `FibonacciGenerator` with a method `nextNumber`.

Hint: There is no need to store all values for f_n. You only need the last two values to compute the next one in the series:

```
fold1 = 1;
fold2 = 1;
fnew = fold1 + fold2;
```

After that, discard `fold2`, which is no longer needed, and set `fold2` to `fold1` and `fold1` to `fnew`.

Your generator class will be tested with this runner program:

```
public class FibonacciRunner
{
    public static void main(String[] args)
    {
        Scanner in = new Scanner(System.in);

        System.out.println("Enter n:");
        int n = in.nextInt();

        FibonacciGenerator fg = new FibonacciGenerator();

        for (int i = 1; i <= n; i++)
            System.out.println(fg.nextNumber());
    }
}
```

★★   **Exercise P6.5.** *Mean and standard deviation.* Write a program that reads a set of floating-point data values from the input. When the user indicates the end of input, print out the count of the values, the average, and the standard deviation. The average of a data set $x_1, \ldots, x_n$ is

$$\bar{x} = \frac{\sum x_i}{n}$$

where $\sum x_i = x_1 + \cdots + x_n$ is the sum of the input values. The standard deviation is

$$s = \sqrt{\frac{\sum (x_i - \bar{x})^2}{n - 1}}$$

However, that formula is not suitable for our task. By the time you have computed the mean, the individual x_i are long gone. Until you know how to save these values, use the numerically less stable formula

$$s = \sqrt{\frac{\sum x_i^2 - \frac{1}{n}\left(\sum x_i\right)^2}{n - 1}}$$

You can compute this quantity by keeping track of the count, the sum, and the sum of squares in the DataSet class as you process the input values.

★★ **Exercise P6.6.** *Factoring of integers.* Write a program that asks the user for an integer and then prints out all its factors in increasing order. For example, when the user enters 150, the program should print

```
2
3
5
5
```

Use a class FactorGenerator with a constructor FactorGenerator(int numberToFactor) and methods nextFactor and hasMoreFactors. Supply a class FactorPrinter whose main method reads a user input, constructs a FactorGenerator object, and prints the factors.

★★ **Exercise P6.7.** *Prime numbers.* Write a program that prompts the user for an integer and then prints out all prime numbers up to that integer. For example, when the user enters 20, the program should print

```
2
3
5
7
11
13
17
19
```

Recall that a number is a prime number if it is not divisible by any number except 1 and itself.

Supply a class PrimeGenerator with a method nextPrime.

★★ **Exercise P6.8.** The *Heron method* is a method for computing square roots that was known to the ancient Greeks. If x is a guess for the value $\sqrt{a}$, then the average of x and a/x is a better guess.

Implement a class RootApproximator that starts with an initial guess of 1 and whose nextGuess method produces a sequence of increasingly better guesses. Supply a method hasMoreGuesses that returns false if two successive guesses are sufficiently close to each other (that is, they differ by no more than a small value ε). Then test your class like this:

```
RootApproximator approx = new RootApproximator(a, EPSILON);
while (approx.hasMoreGuesses())
    System.out.println(approx.nextGuess());
```

★★ **Exercise P6.9.** The best known iterative method for computing the roots of a function f (that is, the x-values for which $f(x)$ is 0) is Newton–Raphson approximation. To find the zero of a function whose derivative is also known, compute

$$x_{\text{new}} = x_{\text{old}} - f\!\left(x_{\text{old}}\right)/f'\!\left(x_{\text{old}}\right).$$

For this exercise, write a program to compute nth roots of floating-point numbers. Prompt the user for a and n, then obtain $\sqrt[n]{a}$ by computing a zero of the function $f(x) = x^n - a$. Follow the approach of Exercise P6.8.

★★ **Exercise P6.10.** The value of e^x can be computed as the power series

$$e^x = \sum_{n=0}^{\infty} \frac{x^n}{n!}$$

where $n! = 1 \cdot 2 \cdot 3 \cdot \ldots \cdot n$.

Write a program that computes e^x using this formula. Of course, you can't compute an infinite sum. Just keep adding values until an individual summand (term) is less than a certain threshold. At each step, you need to compute the new term and add it to the total. Update these terms as follows:

```
term = term * x / n;
```

Follow the approach of the preceding two exercises, by implementing a class ExpApproximator. Its first guess should be 1.

★ **Exercise P6.11.** Write a program RandomDataAnalyzer that generates 100 random numbers between 0 and 1000 and adds them to a DataSet. Print out the average and the maximum.

★★ **Exercise P6.12.** Program the following simulation: Darts are thrown at random points onto the square with corners (1,1) and (−1,−1). If the dart lands inside the unit circle (that is, the circle with center (0,0) and radius 1), it is a hit. Otherwise it is a miss. Run this simulation and use it to determine an approximate value for π. Extra credit if you explain why this is a better method for estimating π than the Buffon needle program.

★★★G **Exercise P6.13.** *Random walk.* Simulate the wandering of an intoxicated person in a square street grid. Draw a grid of 20 streets horizontally and 20 streets vertically. Represent the simulated drunkard by a dot, placed in the middle of the grid to start. For 100 times, have the simulated drunkard randomly pick a direction (east, west, north, south), move one block in the chosen direction, and draw the dot. (One might expect that on average the person might not get anywhere because the moves to different directions cancel one another out in the long run, but in fact it can be shown with probability 1 that the person eventually moves outside any finite region. See, for example, [6, Chapter 8] for more details.) Use classes for the grid and the drunkard.

★★★G **Exercise P6.14.** This exercise is a continuation of Exercise P6.2. Most cannonballs are not shot upright but at an angle. If the starting velocity has magnitude v and the starting angle is α, then the velocity is a vector with components $v_x = v \cdot \cos(\alpha)$, $v_y = v \cdot \sin(\alpha)$. In the x-direction the velocity does not change. In the y-direction the gravitational force takes its toll. Repeat the simulation from the previous exercise, but update the x and y components of the location and the velocity separately. In every iteration, plot the location of the cannonball on the graphics display as a tiny circle. Repeat until the cannonball has reached the earth again.

This kind of problem is of historical interest. The first computers were designed to carry out just such ballistic calculations, taking into account the diminishing gravity for high-flying projectiles and wind speeds.

★G **Exercise P6.15.** Write a graphical application that displays a checkerboard with 64 squares, alternating white and black.

★★G **Exercise P6.16.** Write a graphical application that prompts a user to enter a number n and that draws n circles with random diameter and random location. The circles should be completely contained inside the window.

★★★G **Exercise P6.17.** Write a graphical application that draws a spiral, such as the following:

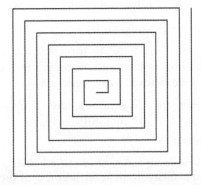

★★G   Exercise P6.18. It is easy and fun to draw graphs of curves with the Java graphics library. Simply draw 100 line segments joining the points $(x, f(x))$ and $(x + d, f(x + d))$, where x ranges from x_{min} to x_{max} and $d = (x_{max} - x_{min})/100$. Draw the curve $f(x) = 0.00005x^3 - 0.03x^2 + 4x + 200$, where x ranges from 0 to 400 in this fashion.

★★★G   Exercise P6.19. Draw a picture of the "four-leaved rose" whose equation in polar coordinates is $r = \cos(2\theta)$. Let θ go from 0 to 2π in 100 steps. Each time, compute r and then compute the (x, y) coordinates from the polar coordinates by using the formula

$$x = r\cos\theta, y = r\sin\theta$$

Additional programming exercises are available in WileyPLUS.

PROGRAMMING PROJECTS

★★★   Project 6.1. *Flesch Readability Index.* The following index [7] was invented by Flesch as a tool to gauge the legibility of a document without linguistic analysis.

- Count all words in the file. A *word* is any sequence of characters delimited by white space, whether or not it is an actual English word.
- Count all syllables in each word. To make this simple, use the following rules: Each *group* of adjacent vowels (a, e, i, o, u, y) counts as one syllable (for example, the "ea" in "real" contributes one syllable, but the "e . . . a" in "regal" count as two syllables). However, an "e" at the end of a word doesn't count as a syllable. Also, each word has at least one syllable, even if the previous rules give a count of 0.
- Count all sentences. A sentence is ended by a period, colon, semicolon, question mark, or exclamation mark.
- The index is computed by

$$\text{Index} = 206.835$$
$$- 84.6 \times \left(\text{Number of syllables/Number of words}\right)$$
$$- 1.015 \times \left(\text{Number of words/Number of sentences}\right)$$

rounded to the nearest integer.

The purpose of the index is to force authors to rewrite their text until the index is high enough. This is achieved by reducing the length of sentences and by removing long words. For example, the sentence

> The following index was invented by Flesch as a simple tool to estimate the legibility of a document without linguistic analysis.

can be rewritten as

> Flesch invented an index to check whether a text is easy to read. To compute the index, you need not look at the meaning of the words.

Flesch's book [7] contains delightful examples of translating government regulations into "plain English".

This index is a number, usually between 0 and 100, indicating how difficult the text is to read. Some example indices for random material from various publications are:

Comics	95
Consumer ads	82
Sports Illustrated	65
Time	57
New York Times	39
Auto insurance policy	10
Internal Revenue Code	−6

Translated into educational levels, the indices are:

91–100	5th grader
81–90	6th grader
71–80	7th grader
66–70	8th grader
61–65	9th grader
51–60	High school student
31–50	College student
0–30	College graduate
Less than 0	Law school graduate

Your program should read a text file in, compute the legibility index, and print out the equivalent educational level. Use classes Word and Document.

★★★ **Project 6.2.** *The game of Nim.* This is a well-known game with a number of variants. We will consider the following variant, which has an interesting winning strategy. Two players alternately take marbles from a pile. In each move, a player chooses how many marbles to take. The player must take at least one but at most half of the marbles. Then the other player takes a turn. The player who takes the last marble loses.

Write a program in which the computer plays against a human opponent. Generate a random integer between 10 and 100 to denote the initial size of the pile. Generate a random integer between 0 and 1 to decide whether the computer or the human takes the first turn. Generate a random integer between 0 and 1 to decide whether the computer plays *smart* or *stupid*. In stupid mode, the computer simply takes a random legal value (between 1 and $n/2$) from the pile whenever it has a turn. In smart mode the computer takes off enough marbles to make the size of the pile a power of two minus 1—that is, 3, 7, 15, 31, or 63. That is always a legal move, except if the size of the pile is currently one less than a power of 2. In that case, the computer makes a random legal move.

Note that the computer cannot be beaten in smart mode when it has the first move, unless the pile size happens to be 15, 31, or 63. Of course, a human player who has the first turn and knows the winning strategy can win against the computer.

Be sure to use classes `Pile`, `Player`, and `Game` in your implementation. A player can be either stupid, smart, or human. (Human `Player` objects prompt for input.)

ANSWERS TO SELF-CHECK QUESTIONS

1. Never.
2. The `waitForBalance` method would never return due to an infinite loop.
3.
```
int i = 1;
while (i <= n)
{
    double interest = balance * rate / 100;
    balance = balance + interest;
    i++;
}
```
4. 11 times.
5. Change the inner loop to `for (int j = 1; j <= width; j++)`.
6. 20.
7. Because we don't know whether the next input is a number or the letter Q.
8. No. If *all* input values are negative, the maximum is also negative. However, the `maximum` field is initialized with 0. With this simplification, the maximum would be falsely computed as 0.
9. `int n = generator.nextInt(2); // 0 = heads, 1 = tails`
10. The program repeatedly calls `Math.toRadians(angle)`. You could simply call `Math.toRadians(180)` to compute π.
11. You should step over it because you are not interested in debugging the internals of the `println` method.
12. You should set a breakpoint. Stepping through loops can be tedious.
13. The programmer misunderstood the second parameter of the substring method—it is the index of the first character not to be included in the substring.
14. The second error was caused by failing to reset `insideVowelGroup` to false at the end of a vowel group. It was detected by tracing through the loop and noticing that the loop didn't enter the conditional statement that increments the vowel count.

Arrays and Array Lists

CHAPTER GOALS

- To become familiar with using arrays and array lists
- To learn about wrapper classes, auto-boxing, and the enhanced for loop
- To study common array algorithms
- To learn how to use two-dimensional arrays
- To understand when to choose array lists and arrays in your programs
- To implement partially filled arrays
- T To understand the concept of regression testing

In order to process large quantities of data, you need to collect values in a data structure. The most commonly used data structures in Java are arrays and array lists. In this chapter, you will learn how to construct arrays and array lists, fill them with values, and access the stored values. We introduce the enhanced for loop, a convenient statement for processing all elements of a collection. You will see how to use the enhanced for loop, as well as ordinary loops, to implement common array algorithms. The chapter concludes with a technical section on copying array values.

Chapter Contents

7.1 Arrays

In many programs, you need to manipulate collections of related values. It would be impractical to use a sequence of variables such as data1, data2, data3, . . . , and so on. The array construct provides a better way of storing a collection of values.

> An array is a sequence of values of the same type.

An *array* is a sequence of values of the same type. For example, here is how you construct an array of 10 floating-point numbers:

```
new double[10]
```

The number of elements (here, 10) is called the length of the array.

The new operator merely constructs the array. You will want to store a reference to the array in a variable so that you can access it later.

The type of an array variable is the element type, followed by []. In this example, the type is double[], because the element type is double. Here is the declaration of an array variable:

```
double[] data = new double[10];
```

That is, data is a reference to an array of floating-point numbers. It is initialized with an array of 10 numbers (see Figure 1).

You can also form arrays of objects, for example

```
BankAccount[] accounts = new BankAccount[10];
```

Figure 1 An Array Reference and an Array

When an array is first created, all values are initialized with 0 (for an array of numbers such as `int[]` or `double[]`), `false` (for a `boolean[]` array), or `null` (for an array of object references).

Each element in the array is specified by an integer index that is placed inside square brackets (`[]`). For example, the expression

```
data[4]
```

denotes the element of the data array with index 4.

You can store a value at a location with an assignment statement, such as the following.

```
data[2] = 29.95;
```

> You access array elements with an integer index, using the notation a[i].

Now the position with index 2 of data is filled with the value 29.95 (see Figure 2).

To read out the data value at index 2, simply use the expression `data[2]` as you would any variable of type `double`:

```
System.out.println("The value of this data item is "
        + data[2]);
```

Figure 2 Storing a Value in an Array

If you look closely at Figure 2, you will notice that the index values start at 0. That is,

> data[0] is the first element
>
> data[1] is the second element
>
> data[2] is the third element

and so on. This convention can be a source of grief for the newcomer, so you should pay close attention to the index values. In particular, the *last* element in the array has an index *one less than* the array length. For example, data refers to an array with length 10. The last element is data[9].

> **Index values of an array range from 0 to length - 1. Accessing a nonexistent element results in a bounds error.**

If you try to access an element that does not exist, then an exception is thrown. For example, the statement

> data[10] = 29.95; // ERROR

is a bounds error.

To avoid bounds errors, you will want to know how many elements are in an array. The length field returns the number of elements: data.length is the length of the data array. Note that there are no parentheses following length—it is an instance variable of the array object, not a method. However, you cannot assign a new value to this instance variable. In other words, length is a final public instance variable. This is quite an anomaly. Normally, Java programmers use a method to inquire about the properties of an object. You just have to remember to omit the parentheses in this case.

> **Use the length field to find the number of elements in an array.**

The following code ensures that you only access the array when the index variable i is within the legal bounds:

> if (0 <= i && i < data.length) data[i] = value;

Arrays suffer from a significant limitation: *their length is fixed*. If you start out with an array of 10 elements and later decide that you need to add additional elements, then you need to make a new array and copy all values of the existing array into the new array. We will discuss this process in detail in Section 7.7.

Syntax 7.1 Array Construction

new *typeName*[*length*]

Example:

new double[10]

Purpose:

To construct an array with a given number of elements

SYNTAX 7.2 Array Element Access

arrayReference[*index*]

Example:

```
data[2]
```

Purpose:

To access an element in an array

SELF CHECK

1. What elements does the data array contain after the following statements?

```
double[] data = new double[10];
for (int i = 0; i < data.length; i++) data[i] = i * i;
```

2. What do the following program segments print? Or, if there is an error, describe the error and specify whether it is detected at compile-time or at run-time.

   a.
   ```
   double[] a = new double[10];
   System.out.println(a[0]);
   ```

   b.
   ```
   double[] b = new double[10];
   System.out.println(b[10]);
   ```

   c.
   ```
   double[] c;
   System.out.println(c[0]);
   ```

COMMON ERROR 7.1

Bounds Errors

The most common array error is attempting to access a nonexistent position.

```
double[] data = new double[10];
data[10] = 29.95;
// Error—only have elements with index values 0 . . . 9
```

When the program runs, an out-of-bounds index generates an exception and terminates the program.

This is a great improvement over languages such as C and C++. With those languages there is no error message; instead, the program will quietly (or not so quietly) corrupt the memory location that is 10 elements away from the start of the array. Sometimes that corruption goes unnoticed, but at other times, the program will act flaky or die a horrible death many instructions later. These are serious problems that make C and C++ programs difficult to debug.

COMMON ERROR 7.2

Uninitialized Arrays

A common error is to allocate an array reference, but not an actual array.

```
double[] data;
data[0] = 29.95; // Error—data not initialized
```

Array variables work exactly like object variables—they are only references to the actual array. To construct the actual array, you must use the new operator:

```
double[] data = new double[10];
```

ADVANCED TOPIC 7.1

Array Initialization

You can initialize an array by allocating it and then filling each entry:

```
int[] primes = new int[5];
primes[0] = 2;
primes[1] = 3;
primes[2] = 5;
primes[3] = 7;
primes[4] = 11;
```

However, if you already know all the elements that you want to place in the array, there is an easier way. List all elements that you want to include in the array, enclosed in braces and separated by commas:

```
int[] primes = { 2, 3, 5, 7, 11 };
```

The Java compiler counts how many elements you want to place in the array, allocates an array of the correct size, and fills it with the elements that you specify.

If you want to construct an array and pass it on to a method that expects an array parameter, you can initialize an anonymous array as follows:

```
new int[] { 2, 3, 5, 7, 11 }
```

7.2 Array Lists

> The ArrayList class manages a sequence of objects.

Arrays are a rather primitive construct. In this section, we introduce the ArrayList class that lets you collect objects, just like an array does. Array lists offer two significant conveniences:

- Array lists can grow and shrink as needed

- The ArrayList class supplies methods for many common tasks, such as inserting and removing elements

Let us define an array list of bank accounts and fill it with objects. (The BankAccount class has been enhanced from the version in Chapter 3. Each bank account has an account number.)

```
ArrayList<BankAccount> accounts = new ArrayList<BankAccount>();
accounts.add(new BankAccount(1001));
accounts.add(new BankAccount(1015));
accounts.add(new BankAccount(1022));
```

> The ArrayList class is a generic class: ArrayList<T> collects objects of type T.

The type ArrayList<BankAccount> denotes an array list of bank accounts. The angle brackets around the BankAccount type tell you that BankAccount is a *type parameter*. You can replace BankAccount with any other class and get a different array list type. For that reason, ArrayList is called a *generic class*. You will learn more about generic classes in Chapter 17. For now, simply use an ArrayList<T> whenever you want to collect objects of type T. However, keep in mind that you cannot use primitive types as type parameters—there is no ArrayList<int> or ArrayList<double>.

When you construct an ArrayList object, it has size 0. You use the add method to add an object to the end of the array list. The size increases after each call to add. The size method yields the current size of the array list.

To get objects out of the array list, use the get method, not the [ ] operator. As with arrays, index values start at 0. For example, accounts.get(2) retrieves the account with index 2, the third element in the array list:

```
BankAccount anAccount = accounts.get(2);
```

As with arrays, it is an error to access a nonexistent element. The most common bounds error is to use the following:

```
int i = accounts.size();
anAccount = accounts.get(i);  // Error
```

The last valid index is accounts.size() - 1.

To set an array list element to a new value, use the set method.

```
BankAccount anAccount = new BankAccount(1729);
accounts.set(2, anAccount);
```

This call sets position 2 of the accounts array list to anAccount, overwriting whatever value was there before.

The set method can only overwrite existing values. It is different from the add method, which adds a new object to the end of the array list.

You can also insert an object in the middle of an array list. The call accounts.add(i, a) adds the object a at position i and moves all elements by one position, from the current element at position i to the last element in the array list.

Before   After

Figure 3   Adding an Element in the Middle of an Array List

Before   After

Figure 4   Removing an Element from the Middle of an Array List

After each call to the add method, the size of the array list increases by 1 (see Figure 3).

Conversely, the call accounts.remove(i) removes the element at position i, moves all elements after the removed element down by one position, and reduces the size of the array list by 1 (see Figure 4).

The following program demonstrates the methods of the ArrayList class. Note that you import the generic class java.util.ArrayList, without the type parameter.

ch07/arraylist/ArrayListTester.java

```
1   import java.util.ArrayList;
2
3   /**
4       This program tests the ArrayList class.
5   */
6   public class ArrayListTester
7   {
```

```
 8      public static void main(String[] args)
 9      {
10         ArrayList<BankAccount> accounts
11                 = new ArrayList<BankAccount>();
12         accounts.add(new BankAccount(1001));
13         accounts.add(new BankAccount(1015));
14         accounts.add(new BankAccount(1729));
15         accounts.add(1, new BankAccount(1008));
16         accounts.remove(0);
17
18         System.out.println("Size: " + accounts.size());
19         System.out.println("Expected: 3");
20         BankAccount first = accounts.get(0);
21         System.out.println("First account number: "
22                 + first.getAccountNumber());
23         System.out.println("Expected: 1008");
24         BankAccount last = accounts.get(accounts.size() - 1);
25         System.out.println("Last account number: "
26                 + last.getAccountNumber());
27         System.out.println("Expected: 1729");
28      }
29  }
```

ch07/arraylist/BankAccount.java

```
 1  /**
 2      A bank account has a balance that can be changed by
 3      deposits and withdrawals.
 4  */
 5  public class BankAccount
 6  {
 7      /**
 8          Constructs a bank account with a zero balance.
 9          @param anAccountNumber the account number for this account
10      */
11      public BankAccount(int anAccountNumber)
12      {
13          accountNumber = anAccountNumber;
14          balance = 0;
15      }
16
17      /**
18          Constructs a bank account with a given balance.
19          @param anAccountNumber the account number for this account
20          @param initialBalance the initial balance
21      */
22      public BankAccount(int anAccountNumber, double initialBalance)
23      {
24          accountNumber = anAccountNumber;
25          balance = initialBalance;
26      }
27
```

```
28      /**
29          Gets the account number of this bank account.
30          @return the account number
31      */
32      public int getAccountNumber()
33      {
34          return accountNumber;
35      }
36
37      /**
38          Deposits money into the bank account.
39          @param amount the amount to deposit
40      */
41      public void deposit(double amount)
42      {
43          double newBalance = balance + amount;
44          balance = newBalance;
45      }
46
47      /**
48          Withdraws money from the bank account.
49          @param amount the amount to withdraw
50      */
51      public void withdraw(double amount)
52      {
53          double newBalance = balance - amount;
54          balance = newBalance;
55      }
56
57      /**
58          Gets the current balance of the bank account.
59          @return the current balance
60      */
61      public double getBalance()
62      {
63          return balance;
64      }
65
66      private int accountNumber;
67      private double balance;
68  }
```

Output

```
Size: 3
Expected: 3
First account number: 1008
Expected: 1008
Last account number: 1729
Expected: 1729
```

3. How do you construct an array of 10 strings? An array list of strings?
4. What is the content of names after the following statements?

```
ArrayList<String> names = new ArrayList<String>();
names.add("A");
names.add(0, "B");
names.add("C");
names.remove(1);
```

COMMON ERROR 7.3

Length and Size

Unfortunately, the Java syntax for determining the number of elements in an array, an array list, and a string is not at all consistent. It is a common error to confuse these. You just have to remember the correct syntax for every data type.

Data Type	Number of Elements
Array	`a.length`
Array list	`a.size()`
String	`a.length()`

QUALITY TIP 7.1

Prefer Parameterized Array Lists

Parameterized array lists, such as `ArrayList<BankAccount>`, were introduced to the Java language in 2004. Versions of Java prior to version 5.0 had only an untyped class `ArrayList`. The untyped array list can hold elements of any class. (Technically, it holds elements of type `Object`, the "lowest common denominator" of all Java classes.) Whenever you retrieve an element from an untyped array list, the compiler requires you to use a cast:

```
ArrayList accounts = new ArrayList();      // Untyped ArrayList
accounts.add(new BankAccount(1729));       // OK—can add any object
BankAccount a = (BankAccount) a.get(0);    // Need cast
```

The cast is needed because the compiler does not keep track of the objects that were inserted into the array list, and the array list `get` method has return type `Object`.

Untyped array lists are still a part of the Java language—after all, we want to continue to use programs that were written before 2004. But you should not use them for new code. The casts are tedious and also a bit error-prone. If you apply the wrong cast, the compiler cannot detect your mistake. Instead, your program will throw an exception.

7.3 Wrappers and Auto-boxing

To treat primitive type values as objects, you must use wrapper classes.

Because numbers are not objects in Java, you cannot directly insert them into array lists. For example, you cannot form an ArrayList<double>. To store sequences of numbers in an array list, you must turn them into objects by using wrapper classes.

There are wrapper classes for all eight primitive types:

Primitive Type	Wrapper Class
byte	Byte
boolean	Boolean
char	Character
double	Double
float	Float
int	Integer
long	Long
short	Short

Note that the wrapper class names start with uppercase letters, and that two of them differ from the names of the corresponding primitive type: Integer and Character.

Each wrapper class object contains a value of the corresponding primitive type. For example, an object of the class Double contains a value of type double (see Figure 5).

Wrapper objects can be used anywhere that objects are required instead of primitive type values. For example, you can collect a sequence of floating-point numbers in an ArrayList<Double>.

Figure 5   An Object of a Wrapper Class

Starting with Java version 5.0, conversion between primitive types and the corresponding wrapper classes is automatic. This process is called *auto-boxing* (even though *auto-wrapping* would have been more consistent).

For example, if you assign a number to a `Double` object, the number is automatically "put into a box", namely a wrapper object.

```
Double d = 29.95; // auto-boxing; same as Double d = new Double(29.95);
```

If you use an older version of Java, you need to provide the constructor yourself.

Conversely, starting with Java version 5.0, wrapper objects are automatically "unboxed" to primitive types.

```
double x = d; // auto-unboxing; same as double x = d.doubleValue();
```

With older versions, you need to call a method such as `doubleValue`, `intValue`, or `booleanValue` for unboxing.

Auto-boxing even works inside arithmetic expressions. For example, the statement

```
Double e = d + 1;
```

is perfectly legal. It means:

- Auto-unbox `d` into a `double`
- Add 1
- Auto-box the result into a new `Double`
- Store a reference to the newly created wrapper object in `e`

If you use Java version 5.0 or higher, array lists of numbers are straightforward. Simply remember to use the wrapper type when you declare the array list, and then rely on auto-boxing.

```
ArrayList<Double> data = new ArrayList<Double>();
data.add(29.95);
double x = data.get(0);
```

With older versions of Java, using wrapper classes to store numbers in an array list is a considerable hassle because you must manually box and unbox the numbers.

No matter which Java version you use, you should know that storing wrapped numbers is quite inefficient. The use of wrappers is acceptable for short array lists, but you should use arrays for long sequences of numbers or characters.

SELF CHECK

5. What is the difference between the types `double` and `Double`?
6. Suppose data is an `ArrayList<Double>` of size > 0. How do you increment the element with index 0?

7.4 The Enhanced for Loop

Java version 5.0 introduces a very convenient shortcut for a common loop type. Often, you need to iterate through a sequence of elements—such as the elements of an array or array list. The enhanced for loop makes this process particularly easy to program.

> The enhanced for loop traverses all elements of a collection.

Suppose you want to total up all data values in an array data. Here is how you use the enhanced for loop to carry out that task.

```
double[] data = . . .;
double sum = 0;
for (double e : data)
{
    sum = sum + e;
}
```

The loop body is executed for each element in the array data. At the beginning of each loop iteration, the next element is assigned to the variable e. Then the loop body is executed. You should read this loop as "for each e in data".

You may wonder why Java doesn't let you write "for each (e in data)". Unquestionably, this would have been neater, and the Java language designers seriously considered this. However, the "for each" construct was added to Java several years after its initial release. Had new keywords each and in been added to the language, then older programs that happened to use those identifiers as variable or method names (such as System.in) would no longer have compiled correctly.

You don't have to use the "for each" construct to loop through all elements in an array. You can implement the same loop with a straightforward for loop and an explicit index variable:

```
double[] data = . . .;
double sum = 0;
for (int i = 0; i < data.length; i++)
{
    double e = data[i];
    sum = sum + e;
}
```

Note an important difference between the "for each" loop and the ordinary for loop. In the "for each" loop, the *element variable* e is assigned values data[0], data[1], and so on. In the ordinary for loop, the *index variable* i is assigned values 0, 1, and so on.

You can also use the enhanced for loop to visit all elements of an array list. For example, the following loop computes the total value of all accounts:

```
ArrayList<BankAccount> accounts = . . . ;
double sum = 0;
for (BankAccount a : accounts)
{
    sum = sum + a.getBalance();
}
```

This loop is equivalent to the following ordinary for loop:

```
double sum = 0;
for (int i = 0; i < accounts.size(); i++)
{
   BankAccount a = accounts.get(i);
   sum = sum + a.getBalance();
}
```

The "for each" loop has a very specific purpose: traversing the elements of a collection, from the beginning to the end. Sometimes you don't want to start at the beginning, or you may need to traverse the collection backwards. In those situations, do not hesitate to use an ordinary for loop.

SYNTAX 7.3 The "for each" Loop

for (*Type variable* : *collection*)
   statement

Example:

for (double e : data)
   sum = sum + e;

Purpose:

To execute a loop for each element in the collection. In each iteration, the variable is assigned the next element of the collection. Then the statement is executed.

SELF CHECK

7. Write a "for each" loop that prints all elements in the array data.
8. Why is the "for each" loop not an appropriate shortcut for the following ordinary for loop?

   for (int i = 0; i < data.length; i++) data[i] = i * i;

7.5 Simple Array Algorithms

7.5.1 Counting Matches

To count values in an array list, check all elements and count the matches until you reach the end of the array list.

Suppose you want to find how many accounts of a certain type you have. Then you must go through the entire collection and increment a counter each time you find a match. Here we count the number of accounts whose balance is at least as much as a given threshold:

```
public class Bank
{
```

```
public int count(double atLeast)
{
    int matches = 0;
    for (BankAccount a : accounts)
    {
        if (a.getBalance() >= atLeast) matches++;
            // Found a match
    }
    return matches;
}
. . .
private ArrayList<BankAccount> accounts;
}
```

7.5.2 Finding a Value

To find a value in an array list, check all elements until you have found a match.

Suppose you want to know whether there is a bank account with a particular account number in your bank. Simply inspect each element until you find a match or reach the end of the array list. Note that the loop might fail to find an answer, namely if none of the accounts match. This search process is called a linear search through the array list.

```
public class Bank
{
    public BankAccount find(int accountNumber)
    {
        for (BankAccount a : accounts)
        {
            if (a.getAccountNumber() == accountNumber) // Found a match
                return a;
        }
        return null; // No match in the entire array list
    }
    . . .
}
```

Note that the method returns null if no match is found.

7.5.3 Finding the Maximum or Minimum

To compute the maximum or minimum value of an array list, initialize a candidate with the starting element. Then compare the candidate with the remaining elements and update it if you find a larger or smaller value.

Suppose you want to find the account with the largest balance in the bank. Keep a candidate for the maximum. If you find an element with a larger value, then replace the candidate with that value. When you have reached the end of the array list, you have found the maximum.

There is just one problem. When you visit the beginning of the array, you don't yet have a candidate for the maximum. One way to overcome that is to set the candidate to the starting element of the array and start the comparison with the next element.

```
    BankAccount largestYet = accounts.get(0);
    for (int i = 1; i < accounts.size(); i++)
    {
        BankAccount a = accounts.get(i);
        if (a.getBalance() > largestYet.getBalance())
            largestYet = a;
    }
    return largestYet;
```

Now we use an explicit for loop because the loop no longer visits all elements—it skips the starting element.

Of course, this approach works only if there is at least one element in the array list. It doesn't make a lot of sense to ask for the largest element of an empty collection. We can return null in that case:

```
    if (accounts.size() == 0) return null;
    BankAccount largestYet = accounts.get(0);
    . . .
```

See Exercises R7.5 and R7.6 for slight modifications to this algorithm.

To compute the minimum of a data set, keep a candidate for the minimum and replace it whenever you encounter a *smaller* value. At the end of the array list, you have found the minimum.

The following sample program implements a Bank class that stores an array list of bank accounts. The methods of the Bank class use the algorithms that we have discussed in this section.

ch07/bank/Bank.java

```java
1   import java.util.ArrayList;
2
3   /**
4       This bank contains a collection of bank accounts.
5   */
6   public class Bank
7   {
8       /**
9           Constructs a bank with no bank accounts.
10      */
11      public Bank()
12      {
13          accounts = new ArrayList<BankAccount>();
14      }
15
16      /**
17          Adds an account to this bank.
18          @param a the account to add
19      */
20      public void addAccount(BankAccount a)
21      {
22          accounts.add(a);
23      }
24
```

```
25    /**
26        Gets the sum of the balances of all accounts in this bank.
27        @return the sum of the balances
28    */
29    public double getTotalBalance()
30    {
31        double total = 0;
32        for (BankAccount a : accounts)
33        {
34            total = total + a.getBalance();
35        }
36        return total;
37    }
38
39    /**
40        Counts the number of bank accounts whose balance is at
41        least a given value.
42        @param atLeast the balance required to count an account
43        @return the number of accounts having at least the given balance
44    */
45    public int count(double atLeast)
46    {
47        int matches = 0;
48        for (BankAccount a : accounts)
49        {
50            if (a.getBalance() >= atLeast) matches++; // Found a match
51        }
52        return matches;
53    }
54
55    /**
56        Finds a bank account with a given number.
57        @param accountNumber the number to find
58        @return the account with the given number, or null if there
59        is no such account
60    */
61    public BankAccount find(int accountNumber)
62    {
63        for (BankAccount a : accounts)
64        {
65            if (a.getAccountNumber() == accountNumber) // Found a match
66                return a;
67        }
68        return null; // No match in the entire array list
69    }
70
71    /**
72        Gets the bank account with the largest balance.
73        @return the account with the largest balance, or null if the
74        bank has no accounts
75    */
76    public BankAccount getMaximum()
77    {
```

```
78          if (accounts.size() == 0) return null;
79          BankAccount largestYet = accounts.get(0);
80          for (int i = 1; i < accounts.size(); i++)
81          {
82             BankAccount a = accounts.get(i);
83             if (a.getBalance() > largestYet.getBalance())
84                largestYet = a;
85          }
86          return largestYet;
87       }
88
89       private ArrayList<BankAccount> accounts;
90    }
```

ch07/bank/BankTester.java

```
1    /**
2       This program tests the Bank class.
3    */
4    public class BankTester
5    {
6       public static void main(String[] args)
7       {
8          Bank firstBankOfJava = new Bank();
9          firstBankOfJava.addAccount(new BankAccount(1001, 20000));
10         firstBankOfJava.addAccount(new BankAccount(1015, 10000));
11         firstBankOfJava.addAccount(new BankAccount(1729, 15000));
12
13         double threshold = 15000;
14         int c = firstBankOfJava.count(threshold);
15         System.out.println("Count: " + c);
16         System.out.println("Expected: 2");
17
18         int accountNumber = 1015;
19         BankAccount a = firstBankOfJava.find(accountNumber);
20         if (a == null)
21            System.out.println("No matching account");
22         else
23            System.out.println("Balance of matching account: "
24                   + a.getBalance());
25         System.out.println("Expected: 10000");
26
27         BankAccount max = firstBankOfJava.getMaximum();
28         System.out.println("Account with largest balance: "
29                + max.getAccountNumber());
30         System.out.println("Expected: 1001");
31      }
32   }
```

Output

```
Count: 2
Expected: 2
Balance of matching account: 10000.0
Expected: 10000
Account with largest balance: 1001
Expected: 1001
```

9. What does the find method do if there are two bank accounts with a matching account number?
10. Would it be possible to use a "for each" loop in the getMaximum method?

7.6 Two-Dimensional Arrays

Arrays and array lists can store linear sequences. Occasionally you want to store collections that have a two-dimensional layout. The traditional example is the tic-tac-toe board (see Figure 6).

> Two-dimensional arrays form a tabular, two-dimensional arrangement. You access elements with an index pair a[i][j].

Such an arrangement, consisting of rows and columns of values, is called a two-dimensional array or matrix. When constructing a two-dimensional array, you specify how many rows and columns you need. In this case, ask for 3 rows and 3 columns:

```
final int ROWS = 3;
final int COLUMNS = 3;
String[][] board = new String[ROWS][COLUMNS];
```

This yields a two-dimensional array with 9 elements

```
board[0][0]    board[0][1]    board[0][2]
board[1][0]    board[1][1]    board[1][2]
board[2][0]    board[2][1]    board[2][2]
```

To access a particular element, specify two subscripts in separate brackets:

```
board[i][j] = "x";
```

When filling or searching a two-dimensional array, it is common to use two nested loops. For example, this pair of loops sets all elements in the array to spaces.

```
for (int i = 0; i < ROWS; i++)
   for (int j = 0; j < COLUMNS; j++)
      board[i][j] = " ";
```

Figure 6
A Tic-Tac-Toe Board

Here is a class and a test program for playing tic-tac-toe. This class does not check whether a player has won the game. That is left as the proverbial "exercise for the reader"—see Exercise P7.10.

ch07/twodim/TicTacToe.java

```java
1   /**
2       A 3 x 3 tic-tac-toe board.
3   */
4   public class TicTacToe
5   {
6       /**
7           Constructs an empty board.
8       */
9       public TicTacToe()
10      {
11          board = new String[ROWS][COLUMNS];
12          // Fill with spaces
13          for (int i = 0; i < ROWS; i++)
14              for (int j = 0; j < COLUMNS; j++)
15                  board[i][j] = " ";
16      }
17
18      /**
19          Sets a field in the board. The field must be unoccupied.
20          @param i the row index
21          @param j the column index
22          @param player the player ("x" or "o")
23      */
24      public void set(int i, int j, String player)
25      {
26          if (board[i][j].equals(" "))
27              board[i][j] = player;
28      }
29
30      /**
31          Creates a string representation of the board, such as
32          |x o|
33          | x |
34          |  o|.
35          @return the string representation
36      */
37      public String toString()
38      {
39          String r = "";
40          for (int i = 0; i < ROWS; i++)
41          {
42              r = r + "|";
43              for (int j = 0; j < COLUMNS; j++)
44                  r = r + board[i][j];
45              r = r + "|\n";
46          }
47          return r;
48      }
```

```
49
50      private String[][] board;
51      private static final int ROWS = 3;
52      private static final int COLUMNS = 3;
53  }
```

ch07/twodim/TicTacToeRunner.java

```
 1  import java.util.Scanner;
 2
 3  /**
 4      This program runs a TicTacToe game. It prompts the
 5      user to set positions on the board and prints out the
 6      result.
 7  */
 8  public class TicTacToeRunner
 9  {
10      public static void main(String[] args)
11      {
12          Scanner in = new Scanner(System.in);
13          String player = "x";
14          TicTacToe game = new TicTacToe();
15          boolean done = false;
16          while (!done)
17          {
18              System.out.print(game.toString());
19              System.out.print(
20                  "Row for " + player + " (-1 to exit): ");
21              int row = in.nextInt();
22              if (row < 0) done = true;
23              else
24              {
25                  System.out.print("Column for " + player + ": ");
26                  int column = in.nextInt();
27                  game.set(row, column, player);
28                  if (player.equals("x"))
29                      player = "o";
30                  else
31                      player = "x";
32              }
33          }
34      }
35  }
```

Output

```
 |  |
 |  |
 |  |
Row for x (-1 to exit): 1
Column for x: 2
 |  |
 | x|
 |  |
```

```
Row for o (-1 to exit): 0
Column for o: 0
|o  |
|  x|
|   |
Row for x (-1 to exit): -1
```

SELF CHECK

11. How do you declare and initialize a 4-by-4 array of integers?

12. How do you count the number of spaces in the tic-tac-toe board?

HOW TO 7.1

Working with Array Lists and Arrays

Step 1   Pick the appropriate data structure.

As a rule of thumb, your first choice should be an array list. Use an array if you collect numbers (or other primitive type values) and efficiency is an issue, or if you need a two-dimensional array.

Step 2   Construct the array list or array and save a reference in a variable.

For both array lists and arrays, you need to specify the element type. For an array, you also need to specify the length.

```
ArrayList<BankAccount> accounts = new ArrayList<BankAccount>();
double[] balances = new double[n];
```

Step 3   Add elements.

For an array list, simply call the add method. Each call adds an element at the end.

```
accounts.add(new BankAccount(1008));
accounts.add(new BankAccount(1729));
```

For an array, you use index values to access the elements.

```
balance[0] = 29.95;
balance[1] = 1000;
```

Step 4   Process elements.

The most common processing pattern involves visiting all elements in the collection. Use the "for each" loop for this purpose:

```
for (BankAccount a : accounts)
    Do something with a
```

If you don't need to look at all of the elements, use an ordinary loop instead. For example, to skip the initial element, you can use this loop.

```
for (int i = 1; i < accounts.size(); i++)
{
    BankAccount a = accounts.get(i);
        Do something with a
```

```
   }
```

For arrays, you use .length instead of .size() and [i] instead of .get(i).

ADVANCED TOPIC 7.2

Two-Dimensional Arrays with Variable Row Lengths

When you declare a two-dimensional array with the command

```
int[][] a = new int[5][5];
```

then you get a 5-by-5 matrix that can store 25 elements:

```
a[0][0] a[0][1] a[0][2] a[0][3] a[0][4]
a[1][0] a[1][1] a[1][2] a[1][3] a[1][4]
a[2][0] a[2][1] a[2][2] a[2][3] a[2][4]
a[3][0] a[3][1] a[3][2] a[3][3] a[3][4]
a[4][0] a[4][1] a[4][2] a[4][3] a[4][4]
```

In this matrix, all rows have the same length. In Java it is possible to declare arrays in which the row length varies. For example, you can store an array that has a triangular shape, such as:

```
b[0][0]
b[1][0] b[1][1]
b[2][0] b[2][1] b[2][2]
b[3][0] b[3][1] b[3][2] b[3][3]
b[4][0] b[4][1] b[4][2] b[4][3] b[4][4]
```

To allocate such an array, you must work harder. First, you allocate space to hold five rows. Indicate that you will manually set each row by leaving the second array index empty:

```
int[][] b = new int[5][];
```

Then allocate each row separately.

```
for (int i = 0; i < b.length; i++)
   b[i] = new int[i + 1];
```

You can access each array element as b[i][j], but be careful that j is less than b[i].length.
Naturally, such "ragged" arrays are not very common.

ADVANCED TOPIC 7.3

Multidimensional Arrays

You can declare arrays with more than two dimensions. For example, here is a three-dimensional array:

```
int[][][] rubiksCube = new int[3][3][3];
```

Each array element is specified by three index values,

```
rubiksCube[i][j][k]
```

However, these arrays are quite rare, particularly in object-oriented programs, and we will not consider them further.

7.7 Copying Arrays

An array variable stores a reference to the array. Copying the variable yields a second reference to the same array.

Array variables work just like object variables—they hold a reference to the actual array. If you copy the reference, you get another reference to the same array (see Figure 7):

```
double[] data = new double[10];
. . .  // Fill array
double[] prices = data;
```

Use the clone method to copy the elements of an array.

If you want to make a true copy of an array, call the clone method (see Figure 8).

```
double[] prices = (double[]) data.clone();
```

The clone method (which we will more closely study in Chapter 10) has the return type Object. You need to cast the return value of the clone method to the appropriate array type such as double[].

Figure 7   Two References to the Same Array

Figure 8   Cloning an Array

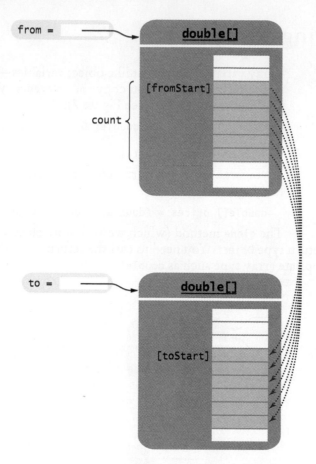

Figure 9   The System.arraycopy Method

Use the System.arraycopy method to copy elements from one array to another.

Occasionally, you need to copy elements from one array into another array. You can use the static System.arraycopy method for that purpose (see Figure 9):

```
System.arraycopy(from, fromStart, to, toStart, count);
```

One use for the System.arraycopy method is to add or remove elements in the middle of an array. To add a new element at position i into data, first move all elements from i onward one position up. Then insert the new value.

```
System.arraycopy(data, i, data, i + 1, data.length - i - 1);
data[i] = x;
```

Note that the last element in the array is lost (see Figure 10).

To remove the element at position i, copy the elements above the position downward (see Figure 11).

```
System.arraycopy(data, i + 1, data, i, data.length - i - 1);
```

Figure 10 Inserting a New Element into an Array

Figure 11 Removing an Element from an Array

Another use for System.arraycopy is to grow an array that has run out of space. Follow these steps:

- Create a new, larger array.

  ```
  double[] newData = new double[2 * data.length]; ①
  ```

- Copy all elements into the new array

  ```
  System.arraycopy(data, 0, newData, 0, data.length); ②
  ```

- Store the reference to the new array in the array variable.

  ```
  data = newData; ③
  ```

Figure 12 shows the process.

Figure 12   Growing an Array

13. How do you add or remove elements in the middle of an array list?

14. Why do we double the length of the array when it has run out of space rather than increasing it by one element?

Common Error 7.4

Underestimating the Size of a Data Set

Programmers commonly underestimate the amount of input data that a user will pour into an unsuspecting program. The most common problem caused by underestimating the amount of input data results from the use of fixed-sized arrays. Suppose you write a program to search for text in a file. You store each line in a string, and keep an array of strings. How big do you make the array? Surely nobody is going to challenge your program with an input that is more than 100 lines. Really? A smart grader can easily feed in the entire text of *Alice in Wonderland* or *War and Peace* (which are available on the Internet). All of a sudden, your program has to deal with tens or hundreds of thousands of lines. What will it do? Will it handle the input? Will it politely reject the excess input? Will it crash and burn?

A famous article [1] analyzed how several UNIX programs reacted when they were fed large or random data sets. Sadly, about a quarter didn't do well at all, crashing or hanging without a reasonable error message. For example, in some versions of UNIX the tape backup program tar cannot handle file names that are longer than 100 characters, which is a pretty unreasonable limitation. Many of these shortcomings are caused by features of the C language that, unlike Java, make it difficult to store strings of arbitrary size.

Quality Tip 7.2

Make Parallel Arrays into Arrays of Objects

Programmers who are familiar with arrays, but unfamiliar with object-oriented programming, sometimes distribute information across separate arrays. Here is a typical example. A program needs to manage bank data, consisting of account numbers and balances. Don't store the account numbers and balances in separate arrays.

```
// Don't do this
int[] accountNumbers;
double[] balances;
```

Arrays such as these are called parallel arrays (see Avoid Parallel Arrays). The ith slice (accountNumbers[i] and balances[i]) contains data that need to be processed together.

Avoid Parallel Arrays

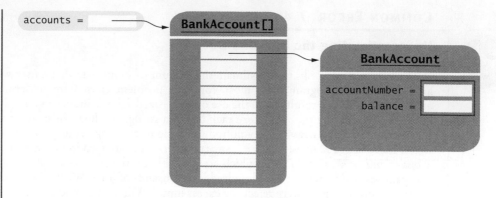

Reorganizing Parallel Arrays into an Array of Objects

> Avoid parallel arrays by changing them into arrays of objects.

If you find yourself using two arrays that have the same length, ask yourself whether you couldn't replace them with a single array of a class type. Look at a slice and find the concept that it represents. Then make the concept into a class. In our example each slice contains an account number and a balance, describing a bank account. Therefore, it is an easy matter to use a single array of objects

```
BankAccount[] accounts;
```

(See figure above.) Or, even better, use an `ArrayList<BankAccount>`.

Why is this beneficial? Think ahead. Maybe your program will change and you will need to store the owner of the bank account as well. It is a simple matter to update the BankAccount class. It may well be quite complicated to add a new array and make sure that all methods that accessed the original two arrays now also correctly access the third one.

ADVANCED TOPIC 7.4

Partially Filled Arrays

Suppose you write a program that reads a sequence of numbers into an array. How many numbers will the user enter? You can't very well ask the user to count the items before entering them—that is just the kind of work that the user expects the computer to do. Unfortunately, you now run into a problem. You need to set the size of the array before you know how many elements you need. Once the array size is set, it cannot be changed.

To solve this problem, make an array that is guaranteed to be larger than the largest possible number of entries, and partially fill it. For example, you can decide that the user will never enter more than 100 data values. Then allocate an array of size 100:

```
final int DATA_LENGTH = 100;
double[] data = new double[DATA_LENGTH];
```

Then keep a companion variable that tells how many elements in the array are actually used. It is an excellent idea always to name this companion variable by adding the suffix Size to the name of the array.

```
int dataSize = 0;
```

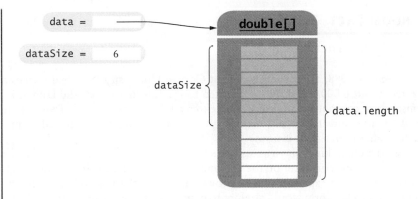

A Partially Filled Array

Now data.length is the capacity of the array data, and dataSize is the current size of the array (see A Partially Filled Array). Keep adding elements into the array, incrementing the dataSize variable each time.

```
data[dataSize] = x;
dataSize++;
```

This way, dataSize always contains the correct element count. When you run out of space, make a new array and copy the elements into it, as described in the preceding section.

Array lists use this technique behind the scenes. An array list contains an array of objects. When the array runs out of space, the array list allocates a larger array and copies the data. However, all of this happens inside the array list methods, so you never need to think about it.

ADVANCED TOPIC 7.5

Methods with a Variable Number of Parameters

Starting with Java version 5.0, it is possible to declare methods that receive a variable number of parameters. For example, we can modify the add method of the DataSet class of Chapter 6 so that one can add any number of values:

```
data.add(1, 3, 7);
data.add(4);
data.add(); // OK but not useful
```

The modified add method must be declared as

```
public void add(double... xs)
```

The ... symbol indicates that the method can receive any number of double values. The xs parameter is actually a double[] array that contains all values that were passed to the method. The method implementation traverses the parameter array and processes the values:

```
for (x : xs)
{
    sum = sum + x;
}
```

RANDOM FACT 7.1

An Early Internet Worm

In November 1988, a graduate student at Cornell University launched a virus program that infected about 6,000 computers connected to the Internet across the United States. Tens of thousands of computer users were unable to read their e-mail or otherwise use their computers. All major universities and many high-tech companies were affected. (The Internet was much smaller then than it is now.)

The particular kind of virus used in this attack is called a worm. The virus program crawled from one computer on the Internet to the next. The entire program is quite complex; its major parts are explained in [2]. However, one of the methods used in the attack is of interest here. The worm would attempt to connect to finger, a program in the UNIX operating system for finding information on a user who has an account on a particular computer on the network. Like many programs in UNIX, finger was written in the C language. C does not have array lists, only arrays, and when you construct an array in C, as in Java, you have to make up your mind how many elements you need. To store the user name to be looked up (say, walters@cs.sjsu.edu), the finger program allocated an array of 512 characters, under the assumption that nobody would ever provide such a long input. Unfortunately, C, unlike Java, does not check that an array index is less than the length of the array. If you write into an array, using an index that is too large, you simply overwrite memory locations that belong to some other objects. In some versions of the finger program, the programmer had been lazy and had not checked whether the array holding the input characters was large enough to hold the input. So the worm program purposefully filled the 512-character array with 536 bytes. The excess 24 bytes would overwrite a return address, which the attacker knew was stored just after the line buffer. When that function was finished, it didn't return to its caller but to code supplied by the worm (see A "Buffer Overrun" Attack). That code ran under the same super-user privileges as finger, allowing the worm to gain entry into the remote system.

Had the programmer who wrote finger been more conscientious, this particular attack would not be possible. In C++ and C, all programmers must be especially careful not to overrun array boundaries.

One may well wonder what would possess a skilled programmer to spend many weeks or months to plan the antisocial act of breaking into thousands of computers and disabling them. It appears that the break-in was fully intended by the author, but the disabling of the computers was a side effect of continuous reinfection and efforts by the worm to avoid being

A "Buffer Overrun" Attack

killed. It is not clear whether the author was aware that these moves would cripple the attacked machines.

In recent years, the novelty of vandalizing other people's computers has worn off somewhat, and there are fewer jerks with programming skills who write new viruses. Other attacks by individuals with more criminal energy, whose intent has been to steal information or money, have surfaced. See [3] for a very readable account of the discovery and apprehension of one such person.

7.8 Regression Testing

> A test suite is a set of tests for repeated testing.

It is a common and useful practice to make a new test whenever you find a program bug. You can use that test to verify that your bug fix really works. Don't throw the test away; feed it to the next version after that and all subsequent versions. Such a collection of test cases is called a *test suite*.

> Regression testing involves repeating previously run tests to ensure that known failures of prior versions do not appear in new versions of the software.

You will be surprised how often a bug that you fixed will reappear in a future version. This is a phenomenon known as *cycling*. Sometimes you don't quite understand the reason for a bug and apply a quick fix that appears to work. Later, you apply a different quick fix that solves a second problem but makes the first problem appear again. Of course, it is always best to think through what really causes a bug and fix the root cause instead of doing a sequence of "Band-Aid" solutions. If you don't succeed in doing that, however, you at least want to have an honest appraisal of how well the program works. By keeping all old test cases around and testing them against every new version, you get that feedback. The process of testing against a set of past failures is called *regression testing*.

How do you organize a suite of tests? An easy technique is to produce multiple tester classes, such as BankTester1, BankTester2, and so on.

Another useful approach is to provide a generic tester, and feed it inputs from multiple files. Consider this tester for the Bank class of Section 7.5:

ch07/regression/BankTester.java

```
1   /**
2       This program tests the Bank class.
3   */
4   public class BankTester
5   {
6       public static void main(String[] args)
7       {
8           Bank firstBankOfJava = new Bank();
9           firstBankOfJava.addAccount(new BankAccount(1001, 20000));
10          firstBankOfJava.addAccount(new BankAccount(1015, 10000));
11          firstBankOfJava.addAccount(new BankAccount(1729, 15000));
12
13          Scanner in = new Scanner(System.in);
14
```

```
15          double threshold = in.nextDouble();
16          int c = firstBankOfJava.count(threshold);
17          System.out.println("Count: " + c);
18          int expectedCount = in.nextInt();
19          System.out.println("Expected: " + expectedCount);
20
21          int accountNumber = in.nextInt;
22          BankAccount a = firstBankOfJava.find(accountNumber);
23          if (a == null)
24             System.out.println("No matching account");
25          else
26          {
27             System.out.println("Balance of matching account: "
28                   + a.getBalance());
29             int matchingBalance = in.nextLine();
30             System.out.println("Expected: " + matchingBalance);
31          }
32       }
33 }
```

Rather than using fixed values for the threshold and the account number to be found, the program reads these values, and the expected responses. By running the program with different inputs, we can test different scenarios, such as the ones for diagnosing off-by-one errors discussed in Common Error 6.2.

Of course, it would be tedious to type in the input values by hand every time the test is executed. It is much better to save the inputs in a file, such as the following:

ch07/regression/input1.txt

```
15000
2
1015
10000
```

The command line interfaces of most operating systems provide a way to link a file to the input of a program, as if all the characters in the file had actually been typed by a user. Type the following command into a shell window:

```
java BankTester < input1.txt
```

The program is executed, but it no longer reads input from the keyboard. Instead, the System.in object (and the Scanner that reads from System.in) gets the input from the file input1.txt. This process is called *input redirection*.

The output is still displayed in the console window:

Output

```
Count: 2
Expected: 2
Balance of matching account: 10000
Expected: 10000
```

You can also redirect output. To capture the output of a program in a file, use the command

```
java BankTester < input1.txt > output1.txt
```

This is useful for archiving test cases.

SELF CHECK

15. Suppose you modified the code for a method. Why do you want to repeat tests that already passed with the previous version of the code?

16. Suppose a customer of your program finds an error. What action should you take beyond fixing the error?

17. Why doesn't the BankTester program contain prompts for the inputs?

PRODUCTIVITY HINT 7.1

Batch Files and Shell Scripts

If you need to perform the same tasks repeatedly on the command line, then it is worth learning about the automation features offered by your operating system.

Under Windows, you use batch files to execute a number of commands automatically. For example, suppose you need to test a program by running three testers:

```
java BankTester1
java BankTester2
java BankTester3 < input1.txt
```

Then you find a bug, fix it, and run the tests again. Now you need to type the three commands once more. There has to be a better way. Under Windows, put the commands in a text file and call it test.bat:

File test.bat

```
1   java BankTester1
2   java BankTester2
3   java BankTester3 < input1.txt
```

Then you just type

```
test.bat
```

and the three commands in the batch file execute automatically.

Batch files are a feature of the operating system, not of Java. On Linux, Mac OS, and UNIX, shell scripts are used for the same purpose. In this simple example, you can execute the commands by typing

```
sh test.bat
```

There are many uses for batch files and shell scripts, and it is well worth it to learn more about advanced features such as parameters and loops.

RANDOM FACT 7.2

The Therac-25 Incidents

The Therac-25 is a computerized device to deliver radiation treatment to cancer patients (see Typical Therac-25 Facility). Between June 1985 and January 1987, several of these machines delivered serious overdoses to at least six patients, killing some of them and seriously maiming the others.

The machines were controlled by a computer program. Bugs in the program were directly responsible for the overdoses. According to Leveson and Turner [4], the program was written by a single programmer, who had since left the manufacturing company producing the device and could not be located. None of the company employees interviewed could say anything about the educational level or qualifications of the programmer.

The investigation by the federal Food and Drug Administration (FDA) found that the program was poorly documented and that there was neither a specification document nor a formal test plan. (This should make you think. Do you have a formal test plan for your programs?)

The overdoses were caused by an amateurish design of the software that had to control different devices concurrently, namely the keyboard, the display, the printer, and of course the radiation device itself. Synchronization and data sharing between the tasks were done in an ad hoc way, even though safe multitasking techniques were known at the time. Had the programmer enjoyed a formal education that involved these techniques, or taken the effort to study the literature, a safer machine could have been built. Such a machine would have probably involved a commercial multitasking system, which might have required a more expensive computer.

The same flaws were present in the software controlling the predecessor model, the Therac-20, but that machine had hardware interlocks that mechanically prevented overdoses.

Typical Therac-25 Facility

The hardware safety devices were removed in the Therac-25 and replaced by checks in the software, presumably to save cost.

Frank Houston of the FDA wrote in 1985: "A significant amount of software for life-critical systems comes from small firms, especially in the medical device industry; firms that fit the profile of those resistant to or uninformed of the principles of either system safety or software engineering" [4].

Who is to blame? The programmer? The manager who not only failed to ensure that the programmer was up to the task but also didn't insist on comprehensive testing? The hospitals that installed the device, or the FDA, for not reviewing the design process? Unfortunately, even today there are no firm standards of what constitutes a safe software design process.

CHAPTER SUMMARY

1. An array is a sequence of values of the same type.

2. You access array elements with an integer index, using the notation a[i].

3. Index values of an array range from 0 to length - 1. Accessing a nonexistent element results in a bounds error.

4. Use the length field to find the number of elements in an array.

5. The ArrayList class manages a sequence of objects.

6. The ArrayList class is a generic class: ArrayList<T> collects objects of type T.

7. To treat primitive type values as objects, you must use wrapper classes.

8. The enhanced for loop traverses all elements of a collection.

9. To count values in an array list, check all elements and count the matches until you reach the end of the array list.

10. To find a value in an array list, check all elements until you have found a match.

11. To compute the maximum or minimum value of an array list, initialize a candidate with the starting element. Then compare the candidate with the remaining elements and update it if you find a larger or smaller value.

12. Two-dimensional arrays form a tabular, two-dimensional arrangement. You access elements with an index pair a[i][j].

13. An array variable stores a reference to the array. Copying the variable yields a second reference to the same array.

14. Use the clone method to copy the elements of an array.

15. Use the System.arraycopy method to copy elements from one array to another.

16. Avoid parallel arrays by changing them into arrays of objects.

17. A test suite is a set of tests for repeated testing.

18. Regression testing involves repeating previously run tests to ensure that known failures of prior versions do not appear in new versions of the software.

FURTHER READING

1. Barton P. Miller, Louis Fericksen, and Bryan So, "An Empirical Study of the Reliability of Unix Utilities", *Communications of the ACM*, vol. 33, no. 12 (December 1990), pp. 32–44.

2. Peter J. Denning, *Computers under Attack*, Addison-Wesley, 1990.

3. Cliff Stoll, *The Cuckoo's Egg*, Doubleday, 1989.

4. Nancy G. Leveson and Clark S. Turner, "An Investigation of the Therac-25 Accidents," *IEEE Computer*, July 1993, pp. 18–41.

CLASSES, OBJECTS, AND METHODS INTRODUCED IN THIS CHAPTER

```
java.lang.Boolean          java.util.ArrayList<E>
   booleanValue               add
java.lang.Double              get
   doubleValue                remove
java.lang.Integer             set
   intValue                   size
java.lang.System
   arraycopy
```


REVIEW EXERCISES

★ **Exercise R7.1.** What is an index? What are the bounds of an array or array list? What is a bounds error?

★ **Exercise R7.2.** Write a program that contains a bounds error. Run the program. What happens on your computer? How does the error message help you locate the error?

★★ **Exercise R7.3.** Write Java code for a loop that simultaneously computes the maximum and minimum values of an array list. Use an array list of accounts as an example.

★ **Exercise R7.4.** Write a loop that reads 10 strings and inserts them into an array list. Write a second loop that prints out the strings in the opposite order from which they were entered.

★★ **Exercise R7.5.** Consider the algorithm that we used for determining the maximum value in an array list. We set largestYet to the starting element, which meant that we were no longer able to use the "for each" loop. An alternate approach is to initialize largestYet with null, then loop through all elements. Of course, inside the loop you need to test whether largestYet is still null. Modify the loop that finds the bank account with the largest balance, using this technique. Is this approach more or less efficient than the one used in the text?

★★★ **Exercise R7.6.** Consider another variation of the algorithm for determining the maximum value. Here, we compute the maximum value of an array of numbers.

```
double max = 0; // Contains an error!
for (x : values)
{
    if (x > max) max = x;
}
```

However, this approach contains a subtle error. What is the error, and how can you fix it?

★ **Exercise R7.7.** For each of the following sets of values, write code that fills an array a with the values.

a. 1 2 3 4 5 6 7 8 9 10

b. 0 2 4 6 8 10 12 14 16 18 20

c. 1 4 9 16 25 36 49 64 81 100

d. 0 0 0 0 0 0 0 0 0 0

e. 1 4 9 16 9 7 4 9 11

Use a loop when appropriate.

★★ **Exercise R7.8.** Write a loop that fills an array a with 10 random numbers between 1 and 100. Write code (using one or more loops) to fill a with 10 different random numbers between 1 and 100.

★ **Exercise R7.9.** What is wrong with the following loop?

```
double[] data = new double[10];
for (int i = 1; i <= 10; i++) data[i] = i * i;
```

Explain two ways of fixing the error.

★★★T **Exercise R7.10.** Write a program that constructs an array of 20 integers and fills the first ten elements with the numbers 1, 4, 9, . . . , 100. Compile it and launch the debugger. After the array has been filled with three numbers, inspect it. What are the contents of the elements in the array beyond those that you filled?

★★   **Exercise R7.11.** Rewrite the following loops without using the "for each" construct. Here, data is an array of double values.

   a. for (x : data) sum = sum + x;

   b. for (x : data) if (x == target) return true;

   c. int i = 0;
      for (x : data) { data [i] = 2 * x; i++; }

★★   **Exercise R7.12.** Rewrite the following loops, using the "for each" construct. Here, data is an array of double values.

   a. for (int i = 0; i < data.length; i++) sum = sum + data[i];

   b. for (int i = 1; i < data.length; i++) sum = sum + data[i];

   c. for (int i = 0; i < data.length; i++)
       if (data[i] == target) return i;

★★★   **Exercise R7.13.** Give an example of

   a. A useful method that has an array of integers as a parameter that is not modified.

   b. A useful method that has an array of integers as a parameter that is modified.

   c. A useful method that has an array of integers as a return value.

Describe each method; don't implement the methods.

★★★   **Exercise R7.14.** A method that has an array list as a parameter can change the contents in two ways. It can change the contents of individual array elements, or it can rearrange the elements. Describe two useful methods with ArrayList<BankAccount> parameters that change an array list of BankAccount objects in each of the two ways just described.

★   **Exercise R7.15.** What are parallel arrays? Why are parallel arrays indications of poor programming? How can they be avoided?

★★   **Exercise R7.16.** How do you perform the following tasks with arrays in Java?

   a. Test that two arrays contain the same elements in the same order

   b. Copy one array to another

   c. Fill an array with zeroes, overwriting all elements in it

   d. Remove all elements from an array list

★   **Exercise R7.17.** True or false?

   a. All elements of an array are of the same type.

   b. Array subscripts must be integers.

   c. Arrays cannot contain string references as elements.

   d. Arrays cannot use strings as subscripts.

   e. Parallel arrays must have equal length.

   f. Two-dimensional arrays always have the same numbers of rows and columns.

     g. Two parallel arrays can be replaced by a two-dimensional array.

     h. Elements of different columns in a two-dimensional array can have different types.

★★ **Exercise R7.18.** True or false?

     a. A method cannot return a two-dimensional array.

     b. A method can change the length of an array parameter.

     c. A method can change the length of an array list that is passed as a parameter.

     d. An array list can hold values of any type.

★T **Exercise R7.19.** Define the terms *regression testing* and *test suite*.

★T **Exercise R7.20.** What is the debugging phenomenon known as *cycling*? What can you do to avoid it?

Additional review exercises are available in WileyPLUS.

PROGRAMMING EXERCISES

★ **Exercise P7.1.** Add the following methods to the Bank class:

```
public void addAccount(int accountNumber, double initialBalance)
public void deposit(int accountNumber, double amount)
public void withdraw(int accountNumber, double amount)
public double getBalance(int accountNumber)
```

★ **Exercise P7.2.** Implement a class Purse. A purse contains a collection of coins. For simplicity, we will only store the coin names in an ArrayList<String>. (We will discuss a better representation in Chapter 8.) Supply a method

```
void addCoin(String coinName)
```

Add a method toString to the Purse class that prints the coins in the purse in the format

```
Purse[Quarter,Dime,Nickel,Dime]
```

★ **Exercise P7.3.** Write a method reverse that reverses the sequence of coins in a purse. Use the toString method of the preceding assignment to test your code. For example, if reverse is called with a purse

```
Purse[Quarter,Dime,Nickel,Dime]
```

then the purse is changed to

```
Purse[Dime,Nickel,Dime,Quarter]
```

★ **Exercise P7.4.** Add a method to the Purse class

```
public void transfer(Purse other)
```

that transfers the contents of one purse to another. For example, if a is

```
Purse[Quarter,Dime,Nickel,Dime]
```

and b is

```
Purse[Dime,Nickel]
```

then after the call a.transfer(b), a is

```
Purse[Quarter,Dime,Nickel,Dime,Dime,Nickel]
```

and b is empty.

★　**Exercise P7.5.** Write a method for the Purse class

```
public boolean sameContents(Purse other)
```

that checks whether the other purse has the same coins in the same order.

★★　**Exercise P7.6.** Write a method for the Purse class

```
public boolean sameCoins(Purse other)
```

that checks whether the other purse has the same coins, perhaps in a different order. For example, the purses

```
Purse[Quarter,Dime,Nickel,Dime]
```

and

```
Purse[Nickel,Dime,Dime,Quarter]
```

should be considered equal.

You will probably need one or more helper methods.

★★　**Exercise P7.7.** A Polygon is a closed curve made up from line segments that join the polygon's corner points. Implement a class Polygon with methods

```
public double perimeter()
```

and

```
public double area()
```

that compute the circumference and area of a polygon. To compute the perimeter, compute the distance between adjacent points, and total up the distances. The area of a polygon with corners $(x_0, y_0), \ldots, (x_{n-1}, y_{n-1})$ is

$$\frac{1}{2}\left(x_0 y_1 + x_1 y_2 + \cdots + x_{n-1} y_0 - y_0 x_1 - y_1 x_2 - \cdots - y_{n-1} x_0\right)$$

As test cases, compute the perimeter and area of a rectangle and of a regular hexagon. *Note:* You need not draw the polygon—that is done in Exercise P7.15.

★　**Exercise P7.8.** Write a program that reads a sequence of integers into an array and that computes the alternating sum of all elements in the array. For example, if the program is executed with the input data

1　4　9　16　9　7　4　9　11

then it computes

$$1 - 4 + 9 - 16 + 9 - 7 + 4 - 9 + 11 = -2$$

★★ **Exercise P7.9.** Write a program that produces random permutations of the numbers 1 to 10. To generate a random permutation, you need to fill an array with the numbers 1 to 10 so that no two entries of the array have the same contents. You could do it by brute force, by calling `Random.nextInt` until it produces a value that is not yet in the array. Instead, you should implement a smart method. Make a second array and fill it with the numbers 1 to 10. Then pick one of those at random, remove it, and append it to the permutation array. Repeat 10 times. Implement a class `PermutationGenerator` with a method

```
int[] nextPermutation
```

★★ **Exercise P7.10.** Add a method `getWinner` to the `TicTacToe` class of Section 7.6. It should return "x" or "o" to indicate a winner, or " " if there is no winner yet. Recall that a winning position has three matching marks in a row, column, or diagonal.

★★★ **Exercise P7.11.** Write an application that plays tic-tac-toe. Your program should draw the game board, change players after every successful move, and pronounce the winner.

★★ **Exercise P7.12.** *Magic squares.* An $n \times n$ matrix that is filled with the numbers 1, 2, 3, ..., n^2 is a magic square if the sum of the elements in each row, in each column, and in the two diagonals is the same value. For example,

16	3	2	13
5	10	11	8
9	6	7	12
4	15	14	1

Write a program that reads in n^2 values from the keyboard and tests whether they form a magic square when arranged as a square matrix. You need to test three features:

- Did the user enter n^2 numbers for some n?
- Do each of the numbers 1, 2, ..., n^2 occur exactly once in the user input?
- When the numbers are put into a square, are the sums of the rows, columns, and diagonals equal to each other?

If the size of the input is a square, test whether all numbers between 1 and n^2 are present. Then compute the row, column, and diagonal sums. Implement a class `Square` with methods

```
public void add(int i)
public boolean isMagic()
```

★★ **Exercise P7.13.** Implement the following algorithm to construct magic n-by-n^2 squares; it works only if n is odd. Place a 1 in the middle of the bottom row. After k has been placed in the (i, j) square, place $k + 1$ into the square to the right and down, wrapping around the borders. However, if the square to the right and down has already been filled, or if you are in the lower-right corner, then you must move to the square straight up instead. Here is the 5 × 5 square that you get if you follow this method:

11	18	25	2	9
10	12	19	21	3
4	6	13	20	22
23	5	7	14	16
17	24	1	8	15

Write a program whose input is the number n and whose output is the magic square of order n if n is odd. Implement a class MagicSquare with a constructor that constructs the square and a toString method that returns a representation of the square.

★G Exercise P7.14. Implement a class Cloud that contains an array list of Point2D.Double objects. Support methods

```
public void add(Point2D.Double aPoint)
public void draw(Graphics2D g2)
```

Draw each point as a tiny circle.

Write a graphical application that draws a cloud of 100 random points.

★★G Exercise P7.15. Implement a class Polygon that contains an array list of Point2D.Double objects. Support methods

```
public void add(Point2D.Double aPoint)
public void draw(Graphics2D g2)
```

Draw the polygon by joining adjacent points with a line, and then closing it up by joining the end and start points.

Write a graphical application that draws a square and a pentagon using two Polygon objects.

★G Exercise P7.16. Write a class Chart with methods

```
public void add(int value)
public void draw(Graphics2D g2)
```

that displays a stick chart of the added values, like this:

You may assume that the values are pixel positions.

★★**G**   **Exercise P7.17.** Write a class `BarChart` with methods

```
public void add(double value)
public void draw(Graphics2D g2)
```

that displays a chart of the added values. You may assume that all values in data are positive. Stretch the bars so that they fill the entire area of the screen. You must figure out the maximum of the values, and then scale each bar.

★★★**G**   **Exercise P7.18.** Improve the `BarChart` class of Exercise P7.17 to work correctly when the data contains negative values.

★★**G**   **Exercise P7.19.** Write a class `PieChart` with methods

```
public void add(double value)
public void draw(Graphics2D g2)
```

that displays a pie chart of the values in data. You may assume that all data values are positive.

Additional programming exercises are available in WileyPLUS.

PROGRAMMING PROJECTS

★★★   **Project 7.1.** *Poker Simulator.* In this assignment, you will implement a simulation of a popular casino game usually called video poker. The card deck contains 52 cards, 13 of each suit. At the beginning of the game, the deck is shuffled. You need to devise a fair method for shuffling. (It does not have to be efficient.) Then the top five cards of the deck are presented to the player. The player can reject none, some, or all of the cards. The rejected cards are replaced from the top of the deck. Now the hand is scored. Your program should pronounce it to be one of the following:

- No pair—The lowest hand, containing five separate cards that do not match up to create any of the hands below.
- One pair—Two cards of the same value, for example two queens.
- Two pairs—Two pairs, for example two queens and two 5's.
- Three of a kind—Three cards of the same value, for example three queens.
- Straight—Five cards with consecutive values, not necessarily of the same suit, such as 4, 5, 6, 7, and 8. The ace can either precede a 2 or follow a king.
- Flush—Five cards, not necessarily in order, of the same suit.
- Full House—Three of a kind and a pair, for example three queens and two 5's
- Four of a Kind—Four cards of the same value, such as four queens.
- Straight Flush—A straight and a flush: Five cards with consecutive values of the same suit.
- Royal Flush—The best possible hand in poker. A 10, jack, queen, king, and ace, all of the same suit.

If you are so inclined, you can implement a wager. The player pays a JavaDollar for each game, and wins according to the following payout chart:

Hand	Payout	Hand	Payout
Royal Flush	250	Straight	4
Straight Flush	50	Three of a Kind	3
Four of a Kind	25	Two Pair	2
Full House	6	Pair of Jacks or Better	1
Flush	5		

★★★ **Project 7.2.** *The Game of Life* is a well-known mathematical game that gives rise to amazingly complex behavior, although it can be specified by a few simple rules. (It is not actually a game in the traditional sense, with players competing for a win.) Here are the rules. The game is played on a rectangular board. Each square can be either empty or occupied. At the beginning, you can specify empty and occupied cells in some way; then the game runs automatically. In each *generation*, the next generation is computed. A new cell is born on an empty square if it is surrounded by exactly three occupied neighbor cells. A cell dies of overcrowding if it is surrounded by four or more neighbors, and it dies of loneliness if it is surrounded by zero or one neighbor. A neighbor is an occupant of an adjacent square to the left, right, top, or bottom or in a diagonal direction. Figure 13 shows a cell and its neighbor cells.

Many configurations show interesting behavior when subjected to these rules. Figure 14 shows a *glider*, observed over five generations. Note how it moves. After four generations, it is transformed into the identical shape, but located one square to the right and below.

One of the more amazing configurations is the glider gun: a complex collection of cells that, after 30 moves, turns back into itself and a glider (see Figure 15).

Cell

Neighbors

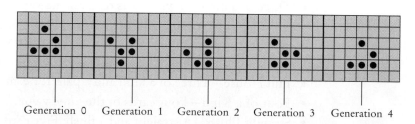

Generation 0   Generation 1   Generation 2   Generation 3   Generation 4

Figure 13
Neighborhood of a Cell in the Game of Life

Figure 14
Glider

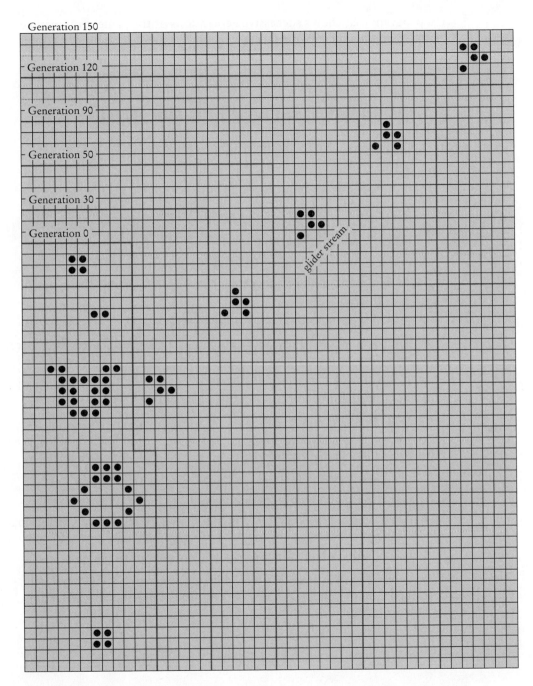

Figure 15   Glider Gun

Program the game to eliminate the drudgery of computing successive generations by hand. Use a two-dimensional array to store the rectangular configuration. Write a program that shows successive generations of the game. You may get extra credit if you implement a graphical application that allows the user to add or remove cells by clicking with the mouse.

ANSWERS TO SELF-CHECK QUESTIONS

1. 0, 1, 4, 9, 16, 25, 36, 49, 64, 81, but *not* 100.

2. **a.** 0

   b. a run-time error: array index out of bounds

   c. a compile-time error: c is not initialized

3. ```
   new String[10];
   new ArrayList<String>();
   ```

4. names contains the strings "B" and "C" at positions 0 and 1.

5. double is one of the eight primitive types. Double is a class type.

6. ```
   data.set(0, data.get(0) + 1);
   ```

7. ```
   for (double x : data) System.out.println(x);
   ```

8. The loop writes a value into data[i]. The "for each" loop does not have the index variable i.

9. It returns the first match that it finds.

10. Yes, but the first comparison would always fail.

11. ```
    int[][] array = new int[4][4];
    ```

12. ```
    int count = 0;
    for (int i = 0; i < ROWS; i++)
       for (int j = 0; j < COLUMNS; j++)
          if (board[i][j].equals(" ")) count++;
    ```

13. Use the add and remove methods.

14. Allocating a new array and copying the elements is time-consuming. You wouldn't want to go through the process every time you add an element.

15. It is possible to introduce errors when modifying code.

16. Add a test case to the test suite that verifies that the error is fixed.

17. There is no human user who would see the prompts because input is provided from a file.
    ```

8

Designing Classes

CHAPTER GOALS

- To learn how to choose appropriate classes to implement
- To understand the concepts of cohesion and coupling
- To minimize the use of side effects
- To document the responsibilities of methods and their callers with preconditions and postconditions
- To understand the difference between instance methods and static methods
- To introduce the concept of static fields
- To understand the scope rules for local variables and instance fields
- To learn about packages
- T To learn about unit testing frameworks

In this chapter you will learn more about designing classes. First, we will discuss the process of discovering classes and defining methods. Next, we will discuss how the concepts of pre- and postconditions enable you to specify, implement, and invoke methods correctly. You will also learn about several more technical issues, such as static methods and variables. Finally, you will see how to use packages to organize your classes.

CHAPTER CONTENTS

8.1 Choosing Classes

You have used a good number of classes in the preceding chapters and probably designed a few classes yourself as part of your programming assignments. Designing a class can be a challenge—it is not always easy to tell how to start or whether the result is of good quality.

Students who have prior experience with programming in another programming language are used to programming *functions*. A function carries out an action. In object-oriented programming, the actions appear as methods. Each method, however, belongs to a class. Classes are collections of objects, and objects are not actions—they are entities. So you have to start the programming activity by identifying objects and the classes to which they belong.

Remember the rule of thumb from Chapter 2: Class names should be nouns, and method names should be verbs.

> A class should represent a single concept from the problem domain, such as business, science, or mathematics.

What makes a good class? Most importantly, a class should *represent a single concept*. Some of the classes that you have seen represent concepts from mathematics:

- Point
- Rectangle
- Ellipse

Other classes are abstractions of real-life entities.

- `BankAccount`
- `CashRegister`

For these classes, the properties of a typical object are easy to understand. A `Rectangle` object has a width and height. Given a `BankAccount` object, you can deposit and withdraw money. Generally, concepts from the part of the universe that a program concerns, such as science, business, or a game, make good classes. The name for such a class should be a noun that describes the concept. Some of the standard Java class names are a bit strange, such as `Ellipse2D.Double`, but you can choose better names for your own classes.

Another useful category of classes can be described as *actors*. Objects of an actor class do some kinds of work for you. Examples of actors are the `Scanner` class of Chapter 4 and the `Random` class in Chapter 6. A `Scanner` object scans a stream for numbers and strings. A `Random` object generates random numbers. It is a good idea to choose class names for actors that end in "-er" or "-or". (A better name for the `Random` class might be `RandomNumberGenerator`.)

Very occasionally, a class has no objects, but it contains a collection of related static methods and constants. The `Math` class is a typical example. Such a class is called a *utility class*.

Finally, you have seen classes with only a `main` method. Their sole purpose is to start a program. From a design perspective, these are somewhat degenerate examples of classes.

What might not be a good class? If you can't tell from the class name what an object of the class is supposed to do, then you are probably not on the right track. For example, your homework assignment might ask you to write a program that prints paychecks. Suppose you start by trying to design a class `PaycheckProgram`. What would an object of this class do? An object of this class would have to do everything that the homework needs to do. That doesn't simplify anything. A better class would be `Paycheck`. Then your program can manipulate one or more `Paycheck` objects.

Another common mistake, particularly by students who are used to writing programs that consist of functions, is to turn an action into a class. For example, if your homework assignment is to compute a paycheck, you may consider writing a class `ComputePaycheck`. But can you visualize a "ComputePaycheck" object? The fact that "ComputePaycheck" isn't a noun tips you off that you are on the wrong track. On the other hand, a `Paycheck` class makes intuitive sense. The word "paycheck" is a noun. You can visualize a paycheck object. You can then think about useful methods of the `Paycheck` class, such as `computeTaxes`, that help you solve the assignment.

SELF CHECK

1. What is the rule of thumb for finding classes?
2. Your job is to write a program that plays chess. Might `ChessBoard` be an appropriate class? How about `MovePiece`?

8.2 Cohesion and Coupling

In this section you will learn two useful criteria for analyzing the quality of the public interface of a class.

> The public interface of a class is cohesive if all of its features are related to the concept that the class represents.

A class should represent a single concept. The public methods and constants that the public interface exposes should be *cohesive*. That is, all interface features should be closely related to the single concept that the class represents.

If you find that the public interface of a class refers to multiple concepts, then that is a good sign that it may be time to use separate classes instead. Consider, for example, the public interface of the CashRegister class in Chapter 4:

```
public class CashRegister
{
    public void enterPayment(int dollars, int quarters,
        int dimes, int nickels, int pennies)
    . . .
    public static final double NICKEL_VALUE = 0.05;
    public static final double DIME_VALUE = 0.1;
    public static final double QUARTER_VALUE = 0.25;
    . . .
}
```

There are really two concepts here: a cash register that holds coins and computes their total, and the values of individual coins. (For simplicity, we assume that the cash register only holds coins, not bills. Exercise P8.1 discusses a more general solution.)

It makes sense to have a separate Coin class and have coins responsible for knowing their values.

```
public class Coin
{
    public Coin(double aValue, String aName) { . . . }
    public double getValue() { . . . }
    . . .
}
```

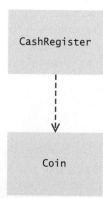

Figure 1
Dependency Relationship Between the CashRegister and Coin Classes

Then the CashRegister class can be simplified:

```
public class CashRegister
{
    public void enterPayment(int coinCount, Coin coinType) { . . . }
    . . .
}
```

Now the CashRegister class no longer needs to know anything about coin values. The same class can equally well handle euros or zorkmids!

This is clearly a better solution, because it separates the responsibilities of the cash register and the coins. The only reason we didn't follow this approach in Chapter 4 was to keep the CashRegister example simple.

> A class depends on another class if it uses objects of that class.

Many classes need other classes in order to do their jobs. For example, the restructured CashRegister class now depends on the Coin class to determine the value of the payment.

To visualize relationships, such as dependence between classes, programmers draw class diagrams. In this book, we use the UML ("Unified Modeling Language") notation for objects and classes. UML is a notation for object-oriented analysis and design invented by Grady Booch, Ivar Jacobson, and James Rumbaugh, three leading researchers in object-oriented software development. The UML notation distinguishes between *object diagrams* and class diagrams. In an object diagram the class names are underlined; in a class diagram the class names are not underlined. In a class diagram, you denote dependency by a dashed line with a   -shaped open arrow tip that points to the dependent class. Figure 1 shows a class diagram indicating that the CashRegister class depends on the Coin class.

Note that the Coin class does *not* depend on the CashRegister class. Coins have no idea that they are being collected in cash registers, and they can carry out their work without ever calling any method in the CashRegister class.

If many classes of a program depend on each other, then we say that the *coupling* between classes is high. Conversely, if there are few dependencies between classes, then we say that the coupling is low (see Figure 2).

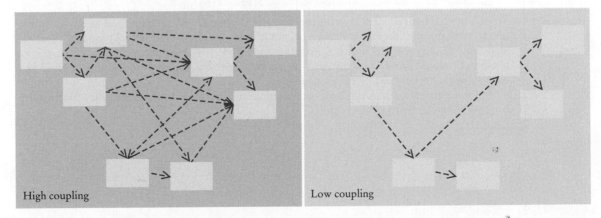

High coupling

Low coupling

Figure 2   High and Low Coupling Between Classes

It is a good practice to minimize the coupling (i.e., dependency) between classes.

Why does coupling matter? If the Coin class changes in the next release of the program, all the classes that depend on it may be affected. If the change is drastic, the coupled classes must all be updated. Furthermore, if we would like to use a class in another program, we have to take with it all the classes on which it depends. Thus, we want to remove unnecessary coupling between classes.

SELF CHECK

3. Why is the CashRegister class from Chapter 4 not cohesive?
4. Why does the Coin class not depend on the CashRegister class?
5. Why should coupling be minimized between classes?

QUALITY TIP 8.1

Consistency

In this section you learned of two criteria to analyze the quality of the public interface of a class. You should maximize cohesion and remove unnecessary coupling. There is another criterion that we would like you to pay attention to—*consistency*. When you have a set of methods, follow a consistent scheme for their names and parameters. This is simply a sign of good craftsmanship.

Sadly, you can find any number of inconsistencies in the standard library. Here is an example. To show an input dialog box, you call

```
JOptionPane.showInputDialog(promptString)
```

To show a message dialog box, you call

```
JOptionPane.showMessageDialog(null, messageString)
```

What's the null parameter? It turns out that the showMessageDialog method needs a parameter to specify the parent window, or null if no parent window is required. But the showInputDialog method requires no parent window. Why the inconsistency? There is no reason. It would have been an easy matter to supply a showMessageDialog method that exactly mirrors the showInputDialog method.

Inconsistencies such as these are not a fatal flaw, but they are an annoyance, particularly because they can be so easily avoided.

8.3 Accessors, Mutators, and Immutable Classes

Recall that a *mutator method* modifies the object on which it is invoked, whereas an *accessor method* merely accesses information without making any modifications. For example, in the `BankAccount` class, the `deposit` and `withdraw` methods are mutator methods. Calling

```
account.deposit(1000);
```

modifies the state of the account object, but calling

```
double balance = account.getBalance();
```

does not modify the state of account.

> An immutable class has no mutator methods.

You can call an accessor method as many times as you like—you always get the same answer, and it does not change the state of your object. That is clearly a desirable property, because it makes the behavior of such a method very predictable. Some classes have been designed to have only accessor methods and no mutator methods at all. Such classes are called *immutable*. An example is the `String` class. Once a string has been constructed, its contents never change. No method in the `String` class can modify the contents of a string. For example, the `toUpperCase` method does not change characters from the original string. Instead, it constructs a *new* string that contains the uppercase characters:

```
String name = "John Q. Public";
String uppercased = name.toUpperCase(); // name is not changed
```

An immutable class has a major advantage: It is safe to give out references to its objects freely. If no method can change the object's value, then no code can modify the object at an unexpected time. In contrast, if you give out a `BankAccount` reference to any other method, you have to be aware that the state of your object may change—the other method can call the `deposit` and `withdraw` methods on the reference that you gave it.

SELF CHECK

6. Is the `substring` method of the `String` class an accessor or a mutator?
7. Is the `Rectangle` class immutable?

8.4 Side Effects

A mutator method modifies the object on which it is invoked, whereas an accessor method leaves it unchanged. This classification relates only to the object on which the method is invoked.

> A side effect of a method is any externally observable data modification.

A *side effect* of a method is any kind of modification of data that is observable outside the method. Mutator methods have a side effect, namely the modification of the implicit parameter.

Here is an example of a method with another kind of side effect, the updating of an explicit parameter:

```java
public class BankAccount
{
   /**
      Transfers money from this account to another account.
      @param amount the amount of money to transfer
      @param other the account into which to transfer the money
   */
   public void transfer(double amount, BankAccount other)
   {
      balance = balance - amount;
      other.balance = other.balance + amount;
   }
   . . .
}
```

> You should minimize side effects that go beyond modification of the implicit parameter.

As a rule of thumb, updating an explicit parameter can be surprising to programmers, and it is best to avoid it whenever possible.

Another example of a side effect is output. Consider how we have always printed a bank balance:

```java
System.out.println("The balance is now $"
      + momsSavings.getBalance());
```

Why don't we simply have a printBalance method?

```java
public void printBalance() // Not recommended
{
   System.out.println("The balance is now $" + balance);
}
```

That would be more convenient when you actually want to print the value. But, of course, there are cases when you want the value for some other purpose. Thus, you can't simply drop the getBalance method in favor of printBalance.

More importantly, the printBalance method forces strong assumptions on the BankAccount class.

- The message is in English—you assume that the user of your software reads English. The majority of people on the planet don't.

- You rely on System.out. A method that relies on System.out won't work in an embedded system, such as the computer inside an automatic teller machine.

In other words, this design violates the rule of minimizing the coupling of the classes. The printBalance method couples the BankAccount class with the System and PrintStream classes. It is best to decouple input/output from the actual work of your classes.

8. If a refers to a bank account, then the call a.deposit(100) modifies the bank account object. Is that a side effect?

9. Consider the DataSet class of Chapter 6. Suppose we add a method

```
void read(Scanner in)
{
   while (in.hasNextDouble())
      add(in.nextDouble());
}
```

Does this method have a side effect other than mutating the data set?

COMMON ERROR 8.1

Trying to Modify Primitive Type Parameters

Methods can't update parameters of primitive type (numbers, char, and boolean). To illustrate this point, let us try to write a method that updates a number parameter:

```
public class BankAccount
{
   /**
      Transfers money from this account and tries to add it to a balance.
      @param amount the amount of money to transfer
      @param otherBalance balance to add the amount to
   */
   void transfer(double amount, double otherBalance)   ❷
   {
      balance = balance - amount;
      otherBalance = otherBalance + amount;
         // Won't work
   }  ❸
   . . .
}
```

This doesn't work. Let's consider a method call.

```
double savingsBalance = 1000;
harrysChecking.transfer(500, savingsBalance);   ❶
System.out.println(savingsBalance);   ❹
```

> In Java, a method can never change parameters of primitive type.

As the method starts, the parameter variable otherBalance is set to the same value as savingsBalance. Then the value of the otherBalance value is modified, but that modification has no effect on savingsBalance, because otherBalance is a separate variable (see Figure 3). When the method terminates, the otherBalance variable dies, and savingsBalance isn't increased.

Why did the example at the beginning of Section 8.4 work, where the second explicit parameter was a BankAccount reference? Then the parameter variable contained a copy of the object reference. Through that reference, the method is able to modify the object.

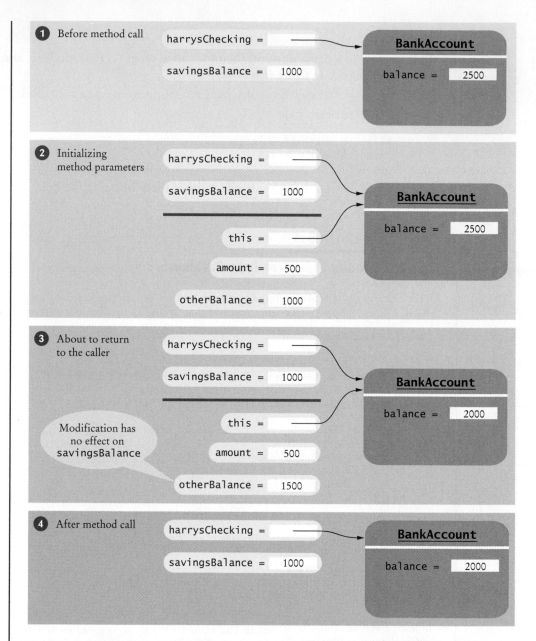

Figure 3   Modifying a Numeric Parameter Has No Effect on Caller

You already saw this difference between objects and primitive types in Chapter 2. As a consequence, a Java method can *never* modify numbers that are passed to it.

QUALITY TIP 8.2

Minimize Side Effects

In an ideal world, all methods would be accessors that simply return an answer without changing any value at all. (In fact, programs that are written in so-called *functional* programming languages, such as Scheme and ML, come close to this ideal.) Of course, in an object-oriented programming language, we use objects to remember state changes. Therefore, a method that just changes the state of its implicit parameter is certainly acceptable. Although side effects cannot be completely eliminated, they can be the cause of surprises and problems and should be minimized. Here is a classification of method behavior.

- Accessor methods with no changes to any explicit parameters—no side effects. Example: `getBalance`.
- Mutator methods with no changes to any explicit parameters—an acceptable side effect. Example: `withdraw`.
- Methods that change an explicit parameter—a side effect that should be avoided when possible. Example: `transfer`.
- Methods that change another object (such as `System.out`)—a side effect that should be avoided. Example: `printBalance`.

QUALITY TIP 8.3

Don't Change the Contents of Parameter Variables

As explained in Common Error 8.1 and Advanced Topic 8.1, a method can treat its parameter variables like any other local variables and change their contents. However, that change affects only the parameter variable within the method itself—not any values supplied in the method call. Some programmers take "advantage" of the temporary nature of the parameter variables and use them as "convenient" holders for intermediate results, as in this example:

```java
public void deposit(double amount)
{
    // Using the parameter variable to hold an intermediate value
    amount = balance + amount;    // Poor style
    . . .
}
```

That code would produce errors if another statement in the method referred to `amount` expecting it to be the value of the parameter, and it will confuse later programmers maintaining this method. You should always treat the parameter variables as if they were constants. Don't assign new values to them. Instead, introduce a new local variable.

```java
public void deposit(double amount)
{
    double newBalance = balance + amount;
    . . .
}
```

ADVANCED TOPIC 8.1

Call by Value and Call by Reference

In Java, method parameters are *copied* into the parameter variables when a method starts. Computer scientists call this call mechanism "call by value". There are some limitations to the "call by value" mechanism. As you saw in Common Error 8.1, it is not possible to implement methods that modify the contents of number variables. Other programming languages such as C++ support an alternate mechanism, called "call by reference". For example, in C++ it would be an easy matter to write a method that modifies a number, by using a so-called *reference parameter*. Here is the C++ code, for those of you who know C++:

```cpp
// This is C++
class BankAccount
{
public:
   void transfer(double amount, double& otherBalance)
      // otherBalance is a double&, a reference to a double
   {
      balance = balance - amount;
      otherBalance = otherBalance + amount; // Works in C++
   }
   . . .
};
```

You will sometimes read in Java books that "numbers are passed by value, objects are passed by reference". That is technically not quite correct. In Java, objects themselves are never passed as parameters; instead, both numbers and *object references* are copied by value. To see this clearly, let us consider another scenario. This method tries to set the otherAccount parameter to a new object:

```java
public class BankAccount
{
   public void transfer(double amount, BankAccount otherAccount)
   {
      balance = balance - amount;
      double newBalance = otherAccount.balance + amount;
      otherAccount = new BankAccount(newBalance); // Won't work
   }
}
```

> In Java, a method can change the state of an object reference parameter, but it cannot replace the object reference with another.

In this situation, we are not trying to change the state of the object to which the parameter variable otherAccount refers; instead, we are trying to replace the object with a different one (see Modifying an Object Reference Parameter Has No Effect on the Caller). Now the parameter variable otherAccount is replaced with a reference to a new account. But if you call the method with

```java
harrysChecking.transfer(500, savingsAccount);
```

then that change does not affect the savingsAccount variable that is supplied in the call.

As you can see, a Java method can update an object's state, but it cannot *replace* the contents of an object reference. This shows that object references are passed by value in Java.

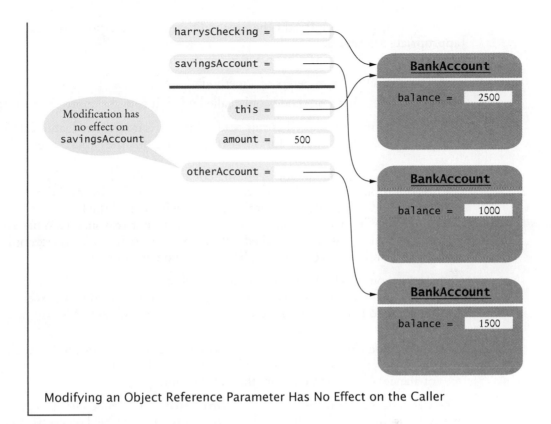

Modifying an Object Reference Parameter Has No Effect on the Caller

8.5 Preconditions and Postconditions

A *precondition* is a requirement that the caller of a method must obey. For example, the deposit method of the BankAccount class has a precondition that the amount to be deposited should not be negative. It is the responsibility of the caller never to call a method if one of its preconditions is violated. If the method is called anyway, it is not responsible for producing a correct result.

> A precondition is a requirement that the caller of a method must meet. If a method is called in violation of a precondition, the method is not responsible for computing the correct result.

Therefore, a precondition is an important part of the method, and you must document it. Here we document the precondition that the amount parameter must not be negative.

```
/**
    Deposits money into this account.
    @param amount the amount of money to deposit
    (Precondition: amount >= 0)
*/
```

Some javadoc extensions support a @precondition or @requires tag, but it is not a part of the standard javadoc program. Because the standard javadoc tool skips all unknown tags, we simply add the precondition to the method explanation or the appropriate @param tag.

Preconditions are typically provided for one of two reasons:

1. To restrict the parameters of a method
2. To require that a method is only called when it is in the appropriate *state*

For example, once a Scanner has run out of input, it is no longer legal to call the next method. Thus, a precondition for the next method is that the hasNext method returns true.

A method is responsible for operating correctly only when its caller has fulfilled all preconditions. The method is free to do *anything* if a precondition is not fulfilled. It would be perfectly legal if the method reformatted the hard disk every time it was called with a wrong input. Naturally, that isn't reasonable. What should a method actually do when it is called with inappropriate inputs? For example, what should account.deposit(-1000) do? There are two choices.

1. A method can check for the violation and *throw an exception*. Then the method does not return to its caller; instead, control is transferred to an exception handler. If no handler is present, then the program terminates. We will discuss exceptions in Chapter 11.

2. A method can skip the check and work under the assumption that the preconditions are fulfilled. If they aren't, then any data corruption (such as a negative balance) or other failures are the caller's fault.

The first approach can be inefficient, particularly if the same check is carried out many times by several methods. The second approach can be dangerous. The *assertion* mechanism was invented to give you the best of both approaches.

> An assertion is a logical condition in a program that you believe to be true.

An *assertion* is a condition that you believe to be true at all times in a particular program location. An assertion check tests whether an assertion is true. Here is a typical assertion check that tests a precondition:

```
public double deposit (double amount)
{
    assert amount >= 0;
    balance = balance + amount;
}
```

In this method, the programmer expects that the quantity amount can never be negative. When the assertion is correct, no harm is done, and the program works in the normal way. If, for some reason, the assertion fails, *and assertion checking is enabled*, then the program terminates with an AssertionError.

However, if assertion checking is disabled, then the assertion is never checked, and the program runs at full speed. By default, assertion checking is disabled when you execute a program. To execute a program with assertion checking turned on, use this command:

```
java -enableassertions MyProg
```

SYNTAX 8.1 Assertion

```
assert condition;
```

Example:

```
assert amount >= 0;
```

Purpose:

To assert that a condition is fulfilled. If assertion checking is enabled and the condition is false, an assertion error is thrown.

You can also use the shortcut -ea instead of -enableassertions. You definitely want to turn assertion checking on during program development and testing.

You don't have to use assertions for checking preconditions—throwing an exception is another reasonable option. But assertions have one advantage: You can turn them off after you have tested your program, so that it runs at maximum speed. That way, you never have to feel bad about putting lots of assertions into your code. You can also use assertions for checking conditions other than preconditions.

Many beginning programmers think that it isn't "nice" to abort the program when a precondition is violated. Why not simply return to the caller instead?

```
public void deposit(double amount)
{
   if (amount < 0)
      return; // Not recommended
   balance = balance + amount;
}
```

That is legal—after all, a method can do anything if its preconditions are violated. But it is not as good as an assertion check. If the program calling the deposit method has a few bugs that cause it to pass a negative amount as an input value, then the version that generates an assertion failure will make the bugs very obvious during testing—it is hard to ignore when the program aborts. The quiet version, on the other hand, will not alert you, and you may not notice that it performs some wrong calculations as a consequence. Think of assertions as the "tough love" approach to precondition checking.

> If a method has been called in accordance with its preconditions, then it must ensure that its postconditions are valid.

When a method is called in accordance with its preconditions, then the method promises to do its job correctly. A different kind of promise that the method makes is called a *postcondition*. There are two kinds of postconditions:

1. The return value is computed correctly.
2. The object is in a certain state after the method call is completed.

Here is a postcondition that makes a statement about the object state after the deposit method is called.

```
/**
    Deposits money into this account.
    (Postcondition: getBalance() >= 0)
    @param amount the amount of money to deposit
    (Precondition: amount >= 0)
*/
```

As long as the precondition is fulfilled, this method guarantees that the balance after the deposit is not negative.

Some javadoc extensions support a @postcondition or @ensures tag. However, just as with preconditions, we simply add postconditions to the method explanation or the @return tag, because the standard javadoc program skips all tags that it doesn't know.

Some programmers feel that they must specify a postcondition for every method. When you use javadoc, however, you already specify a part of the postcondition in the @return tag, and you shouldn't repeat it in a postcondition.

```
// This postcondition statement is overly repetitive.
/**
    Returns the current balance of this account.
    @return the account balance
    (Postcondition: The return value equals the account balance.)
*/
```

Note that we formulate pre- and postconditions only in terms of the *interface* of the class. Thus, we state the precondition of the withdraw method as amount <= getBalance(), not amount <= balance. After all, the caller, which needs to check the precondition, has access only to the public interface, not the private implementation.

Bertrand Meyer [1] compares preconditions and postconditions to contracts. In real life, contracts spell out the obligations of the contracting parties. For example, your mechanic may promise to fix the brakes of your car, and you promise in turn to pay a certain amount of money. If either party breaks the promise, then the other is not bound by the terms of the contract. In the same fashion, pre- and postconditions are contractual terms between a method and its caller. The method promises to fulfill the postcondition for all inputs that fulfill the precondition. The caller promises never to call the method with illegal inputs. If the caller fulfills its promise and gets a wrong answer, it can take the method to "programmer's court". If the caller doesn't fulfill its promise and something terrible happens as a consequence, it has no recourse.

SELF CHECK

10. Why might you want to add a precondition to a method that you provide for other programmers?

11. When you implement a method with a precondition and you notice that the caller did not fulfill the precondition, do you have to notify the caller?

ADVANCED TOPIC 8.2

Class Invariants

Advanced Topic 6.5 introduced the concept of *loop invariants*. A loop invariant is established when the loop is first entered, and it is preserved by all loop iterations. We then know that the loop invariant must be true when the loop exits, and we can use that information to reason about the correctness of a loop.

Class invariants fulfill a similar purpose. A class invariant is a statement about an object that is true after every constructor and that is preserved by every mutator (provided that the caller respects all preconditions). We then know that the class invariant must always be true, and we can use that information to reason about the correctness of our program.

Here is a simple example. Consider a `BankAccount` class with the following preconditions for the constructor and the mutators:

```java
public class BankAccount
{
    /**
        Constructs a bank account with a given balance.
        @param initialBalance the initial balance
        (Precondition: initialBalance >= 0)
    */
    public BankAccount(double initialBalance) { . . . }
    {
        balance = initialBalance;
    }

    /**
        Deposits money into the bank account.
        @param amount the amount to deposit
        (Precondition: amount >= 0)
    */
    public void deposit(double amount) { . . . }

    /**
        Withdraws money from the bank account.
        @param amount the amount to withdraw
        (Precondition: amount <= getBalance())
    */
    public void withdraw(double amount) { . . . }

    . . .
}
```

Now we can formulate the following invariant:

```java
getBalance() >= 0
```

To see why this invariant is true, first check the constructor; because the precondition of the constructor is

```java
initialBalance >= 0
```

we can prove that the invariant is true after the constructor has set `balance` to `initialBalance`.

Next, check the mutators. The precondition of the `deposit` method is

```
amount >= 0
```

We can assume that the invariant condition holds before calling the method. Thus, we know that `balance >= 0` before the method executes. The laws of mathematics tell us that the sum of two nonnegative numbers is again nonnegative, so we can conclude that `balance >= 0` after the completion of the `deposit`. Thus, the `deposit` method preserves the invariant.

A similar argument shows that the `withdraw` method preserves the invariant.

Because the invariant is a property of the class, you document it with the class description:

```
/**
    A bank account has a balance that can be changed by
    deposits and withdrawals.
    (Invariant: getBalance() >= 0)
*/
public class BankAccount
{
    . . .
}
```

8.6 Static Methods

A static method is not invoked on an object.

Sometimes you need a method that is not invoked on an object. Such a method is called a *static method* or a *class method.* In contrast, the methods that you wrote up to now are often called *instance methods* because they operate on a particular instance of an object.

A typical example of a static method is the `sqrt` method in the `Math` class. When you call `Math.sqrt(x)`, you don't supply any implicit parameter. (Recall that `Math` is the name of a class, not an object.)

Why would you want to write a method that does not operate on an object? The most common reason is that you want to encapsulate some computation that involves only numbers. Because numbers aren't objects, you can't invoke methods on them. For example, the call `x.sqrt()` can never be legal in Java.

Here is a typical example of a static method that carries out some simple algebra: to compute p percent of the amount a. Because the parameters are numbers, the method doesn't operate on any objects at all, so we make it into a static method:

```
/**
    Computes a percentage of an amount.
    @param p  the percentage to apply
    @param a  the amount to which the percentage is applied
    @return p percent of a
*/
public static double percentOf(double p, double a)
{
    return (p / 100) * a;
}
```

You need to find a home for this method. Let us come up with a new class (similar to the Math class of the standard Java library). Because the percentOf method has to do with financial calculations, we'll design a class Financial to hold it. Here is the class:

```
public class Financial
{
   public static double percentOf(double p, double a)
   {
      return (p / 100) * a;
   }
   // More financial methods can be added here.
}
```

When calling a static method, you supply the name of the class containing the method so that the compiler can find it. For example,

```
double tax = Financial.percentOf(taxRate, total);
```

Note that you do not supply an object of type Financial when you call the method.

Now we can tell you why the main method is static. When the program starts, there aren't any objects. Therefore, the *first* method in the program must be a static method.

You may well wonder why these methods are called static. The normal meaning of the word *static* ("staying fixed at one place") does not seem to have anything to do with what static methods do. Indeed, it's used by accident. Java uses the static keyword because C++ uses it in the same context. C++ uses static to denote class methods because the inventors of C++ did not want to invent another keyword. Someone noted that there was a relatively rarely used keyword, static, that denotes certain variables that stay in a fixed location for multiple method calls. (Java does not have this feature, nor does it need it.) It turned out that the keyword could be reused to denote class methods without confusing the compiler. The fact that it can confuse humans was apparently not a big concern. You'll just have to live with the fact that "static method" means "class method": a method that does not operate on an object and that has only explicit parameters.

SELF CHECK

12. Suppose Java had no static methods. Then all methods of the Math class would be instance methods. How would you compute the square root of x?

13. Harry turns in his homework assignment, a program that plays tic-tac-toe. His solution consists of a single class with many static methods. Why is this not an object-oriented solution?

8.7 Static Fields

Sometimes, you need to store values outside any particular object. You use *static fields* for this purpose. Here is a typical example. We will use a version of our BankAccount class in which each bank account object has both a balance and an account number:

```
public class BankAccount
{
   . . .
   private double balance;
   private int accountNumber;
}
```

We want to assign account numbers sequentially. That is, we want the bank account constructor to construct the first account with number 1001, the next with number 1002, and so on. Therefore, we must store the last assigned account number somewhere.

It makes no sense, though, to make this value into an instance field:

```
public class BankAccount
{
   . . .
   private double balance;
   private int accountNumber;
   private int lastAssignedNumber = 1000; // NO—won't work
}
```

In that case each *instance* of the BankAccount class would have its own value of lastAssignedNumber.

Instead, we need to have a single value of lastAssignedNumber that is the same for the entire *class*. Such a field is called a static field, because you declare it using the static keyword.

> A static field belongs to the class, not to any object of the class.

```
public class BankAccount
{
   . . .
   private double balance;
   private int accountNumber;
   private static int lastAssignedNumber = 1000;
}
```

Every BankAccount object has its own balance and accountNumber instance fields, but there is only a single copy of the lastAssignedNumber variable (see Figure 4). That field is stored in a separate location, outside any BankAccount objects.

A static field is sometimes called a *class field* because there is a single field for the entire class.

Every method of a class can access its static fields. Here is the constructor of the BankAccount class, which increments the last assigned number and then uses it to initialize the account number of the object to be constructed:

```
public class BankAccount
{
```

```
public BankAccount()
{
    // Generates next account number to be assigned
    lastAssignedNumber++; // Updates the static field

    // Assigns field to account number of this bank account
    accountNumber = lastAssignedNumber; // Sets the instance field
}
. . .
}
```

How do you initialize a static field? You can't set it in the class constructor:

```
public BankAccount()
{
    lastAssignedNumber = 1000; // NO—would reset to 1000 for each new object
    . . .
}
```

Then the initialization would occur each time a new instance is constructed.

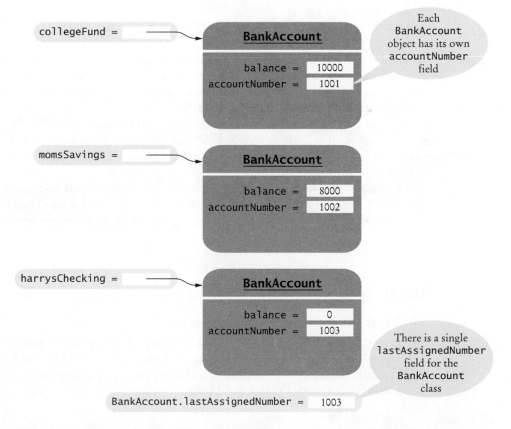

Figure 4 A Static Field and Instance Fields

There are three ways to initialize a static field:

1. Do nothing. The static field is then initialized with 0 (for numbers), false (for boolean values), or null (for objects).

2. Use an explicit initializer, such as

```
public class BankAccount
{
   . . .
    private static int lastAssignedNumber = 1000;
}
```

The initialization is executed once when the class is loaded.

3. Use a static initialization block (see Advanced Topic 8.3).

Like instance fields, static fields should always be declared as private to ensure that methods of other classes do not change their values. The exception to this rule are static *constants*, which may be either private or public. For example, the BankAccount class may want to define a public constant value, such as

```
public class BankAccount
{
   . . .
    public static final double OVERDRAFT_FEE = 5;
}
```

Methods from any class refer to such a constant as BankAccount.OVERDRAFT_FEE.

It makes sense to declare constants as static—you wouldn't want every object of the BankAccount class to have its own set of variables with these constant values. It is sufficient to have one set of them for the class.

Why are class variables called static? As with static methods, the static keyword itself is just a meaningless holdover from C++. But static fields and static methods have much in common: They apply to the entire *class*, not to specific instances of the class.

In general, you want to minimize the use of static methods and fields. If you find yourself using lots of static methods, then that's an indication that you may not have found the right classes to solve your problem in an object-oriented way.

SELF CHECK

14. Name two static fields of the System class.

15. Harry tells you that he has found a great way to avoid those pesky objects: Put all code into a single class and declare all methods and fields static. Then main can call the other static methods, and all of them can access the static fields. Will Harry's plan work? Is it a good idea?

ADVANCED TOPIC 8.3

Alternative Forms of Field Initialization

As you have seen, instance fields are initialized with a default value (0, `false`, or `null`, depending on their type). You can then set them to any desired value in a constructor, and that is the style that we prefer in this book.

However, there are two other mechanisms to specify an initial value for a field. Just as with local variables, you can specify initialization values for fields. For example,

```java
public class Coin
{
    . . .
    private double value = 1;
    private String name = "Dollar";
}
```

These default values are used for *every* object that is being constructed.

There is also another, much less common, syntax. You can place one or more *initialization blocks* inside the class definition. All statements in that block are executed whenever an object is being constructed. Here is an example:

```java
public class Coin
{
    . . .
    {
        value = 1;
        name = "Dollar";
    }
    private double value;
    private String name;
}
```

For static fields, you use a static initialization block:

```java
public class BankAccount
{
    . . .
    private static int lastAssignedNumber;

    static
    {
        lastAssignedNumber = 1000;
    }
}
```

All statements in the static initialization block are executed once when the class is loaded. Initialization blocks are rarely used in practice.

When an object is constructed, the initializers and initialization blocks are executed in the order in which they appear. Then the code in the constructor is executed. Because the rules for the alternative initialization mechanisms are somewhat complex, we recommend that you simply use constructors to do the job of construction.

8.8 Scope

8.8.1 Scope of Local Variables

> The scope of a variable is the region of a program in which the variable can be accessed.

When you have multiple variables or fields with the same name, there is the possibility of conflict. In order to understand the potential problems, you need to know about the *scope* of each variable: the part of the program in which the variable can be accessed.

The scope of a local variable extends from the point of its declaration to the end of the block that encloses it.

It sometimes happens that the same variable name is used in two methods. Consider the variables r in the following example:

```java
public class RectangleTester
{
    public static double area(Rectangle rect)
    {
        double r = rect.getWidth() * rect.getHeight();
        return r;
    }

    public static void main(String[] args)
    {
        Rectangle r = new Rectangle(5, 10, 20, 30);
        double a = area(r);
        System.out.println(r);
    }
}
```

These variables are independent from each other, or, in other words, their scopes are disjoint. You can have local variables with the same name r in different methods, just as you can have different motels with the same name "Bates Motel" in different cities.

> The scope of a local variable cannot contain the definition of another variable with the same name.

In Java, the scope of a local variable can never contain the definition of another local variable with the same name. For example, the following is an error:

```java
Rectangle r = new Rectangle(5, 10, 20, 30);
if (x >= 0)
{
    double r = Math.sqrt(x);
    // Error—can't declare another variable called r here
    . . .
}
```

However, you can have local variables with identical names if their scopes do not overlap, such as

```java
if (x >= 0)
{
    double r = Math.sqrt(x);
    . . .
```

```
    } // Scope of r ends here
    else
    {
        Rectangle r = new Rectangle(5, 10, 20, 30);
        // OK—it is legal to declare another r here
        . . .
    }
```

8.8.2 Scope of Class Members

A qualified name is prefixed by its class name or by an object reference, such as Math.sqrt or other.balance.

An unqualified instance field or method name refers to the this parameter.

In this section, we consider the scope of fields and methods of a class. (These are collectively called the *members* of the class.) Private members have *class scope*: You can access all members in any of the methods of the class.

If you want to use a public field or method outside its class, you must *qualify* the name. You qualify a static field or method by specifying the class name, such as Math.sqrt or Math.PI. You qualify an instance field or method by specifying the object to which the field or method should be applied, such as harrysChecking.getBalance().

Inside a method, you don't need to qualify fields or methods that belong to the same class. Instance fields automatically refer to the implicit parameter of the method, that is, the object on which the method is invoked. For example, consider the transfer method:

```
public class BankAccount
{
    public void transfer(double amount, BankAccount other)
    {
        balance = balance - amount; // i.e., this.balance
        other.balance = other.balance + amount;
    }
    . . .
}
```

Here, the unqualified name balance means this.balance. (Recall from Chapter 3 that this is a reference to the implicit parameter of any method.)

The same rule applies to methods. Thus, another implementation of the transfer method is

```
public class BankAccount
{
    public void transfer(double amount, BankAccount other)
    {
        withdraw(amount); // i.e., this.withdraw(amount);
        other.deposit(amount);
    }
    . . .
}
```

Whenever you see an instance method call without an implicit parameter, then the method is called on the this parameter. Such a method call is called a "self-call".

Similarly, you can use a static field or method of the same class without a qualifier. For example, consider the following version of the withdraw method:

```java
public class BankAccount
{
   public void withdraw(double amount)
   {
      if (balance < amount) balance = balance - OVERDRAFT_FEE;
      else . . .
   }
   . . .
   private static double OVERDRAFT_FEE = 5;
}
```

Here, the unqualified name OVERDRAFT_FEE refers to BankAccount.OVERDRAFT_FEE.

8.8.3 Overlapping Scope

Problems arise if you have two identical variable names with overlapping scope. This can never occur with local variables, but the scopes of identically named local variables and instance fields can overlap. Here is a purposefully bad example.

```java
public class Coin
{
   . . .
   public double getExchangeValue(double exchangeRate)
   {
      double value; // Local variable
      . . .
      return value;
   }

   private String name;
   private double value; // Field with the same name
}
```

> A local variable can shadow a field with the same name. You can access the shadowed field name by qualifying it with the this reference.

Inside the getExchangeValue method, the variable name value could potentially have two meanings: the local variable or the instance field. The Java language specifies that in this situation the *local* variable wins out. It *shadows* the instance field. This sounds pretty arbitrary, but there is actually a good reason: You can still refer to the instance field as this.value.

```java
value = this.value * exchangeRate;
```

It isn't necessary to write code like this. You can easily change the name of the local variable to something else, such as result.

However, you should be aware of one common use of the this reference. When implementing constructors, many programmers find it tiresome to come up with different names for instance fields and parameters. Using the this reference solves that problem. Here is a typical example.

```java
public Coin(double value, String name)
{
```

```
    this.value = value;
    this.name = name;
}
```

The expression this.value refers to the instance field, but value is the parameter. Of course, you can always rename the construction parameters to aValue and aName, as we have done in this book.

SELF CHECK

16. Consider the deposit method of the BankAccount class. What is the scope of the variables amount and newBalance?
17. What is the scope of the balance field of the BankAccount class?

COMMON ERROR 8.2

Shadowing

Accidentally using the same name for a local variable and an instance field is a surprisingly common error. As you saw in the preceding section, the local variable then *shadows* the instance field. Even though you may have meant to access the instance field, the local variable is quietly accessed. For some reason, this problem is most common in constructors. Look at this example of an incorrect constructor:

```
public class Coin
{
    public Coin(double aValue, String aName)
    {
        value = aValue;
        String name = aName; // Oops . . .
    }

    . . .

    private double value;
    private String name;
}
```

The programmer declared a local variable name in the constructor. In all likelihood, that was just a typo—the programmer's fingers were on autopilot and typed the keyword String, even though the programmer all the time intended to access the instance field. Unfortunately, the compiler gives no warning in this situation and quietly sets the local variable to the value of aName. The instance field of the object that is being constructed is never touched, and remains null. Some programmers give all instance field names a special prefix to distinguish them from other variables. A common convention is to prefix all instance field names with the prefix my, such as myValue or myName.

PRODUCTIVITY HINT 8.1

Global Search and Replace

Suppose you chose an unfortunate name for a method—say perc instead of percentOf—and you regret your choice. Of course, you can locate all occurrences of perc in your code and replace them manually. However, most programming editors have a command to search for the perc's automatically and replace them with percentOf.

You need to specify some details about the search:

- Do you want it to ignore case? That is, should Perc be a match? In Java you usually don't want that.

- Do you want it to match whole words only? If not, the perc in superconductor is also a match. In Java you usually want to match whole words.

- Is this a regular-expression search? No, but regular expressions can make searches even more powerful—see Productivity Hint 8.2.

- Do you want to confirm each replace, or simply go ahead and replace all matches? I usually confirm the first three or four, and when I see that it works as expected, I give the go-ahead to replace the rest. (By the way, a *global* replace means to replace all occurrences in the document.) Good text editors can undo a global replace that has gone awry. Find out whether yours will.

- Do you want the search to go from the point where the cursor is in the file through to the rest of the file, or should it search the currently selected text? Restricting replacement to a portion of the file can be very useful, but in this example you would want to move the cursor to the top of the file and then replace until the end of the file.

Not every editor has all these options. You should investigate what your editor offers.

PRODUCTIVITY HINT 8.2

Regular Expressions

Regular expressions describe character patterns. For example, numbers have a simple form. They contain one or more digits. The regular expression describing numbers is [0-9]+. The set [0-9] denotes any digit between 0 and 9, and the + means "one or more".

What good is it? Several utility programs use regular expressions to locate matching text. Also, the search commands of some programming editors understand regular expressions. The most popular program that uses regular expressions is *grep* (which stands for "global regular expression print"). You can run grep from a command prompt or from inside some compilation environments. Grep is part of the UNIX operating system, but versions are available for Windows and MacOS. It needs a regular expression and one or more files to search. When grep runs, it displays a set of lines that match the regular expression.

Suppose you want to look for all magic numbers (see Quality Tip 4.1) in a file. The command

```
grep [0-9]+ Homework.java
```

lists all lines in the file Homework.java that contain sequences of digits. That isn't terribly useful; lines with variable names x1 will be listed. OK, you want sequences of digits that do *not* immediately follow letters:

```
grep [^A-Za-z][0-9]+ Homework.java
```

The set [^A-Za-z] denotes any characters that are *not* in the ranges A to Z and a to z. This works much better, and it shows only lines that contain actual numbers.

For more information on regular expressions, consult one of the many tutorials on the Internet (such as [2]).

ADVANCED TOPIC 8.4

Static Imports

Starting with Java version 5.0, there is a variant of the import directive that lets you use static methods and fields without class prefixes. For example,

```java
import static java.lang.System.*;
import static java.lang.Math.*;

public class RootTester
{
   public static void main(String[] args)
   {
      double r = sqrt(PI)  // Instead of Math.sqrt(Math.PI)
      out.println(r);      // Instead of System.out
   }
}
```

Static imports can make programs easier to read, particularly if they use many mathematical functions.

8.9 Packages

8.9.1 Organizing Related Classes into Packages

A package is a set of related classes.

A Java program consists of a collection of classes. So far, most of your programs have consisted of a small number of classes. As programs get larger, however, simply distributing the classes over multiple files isn't enough. An additional structuring mechanism is needed. In Java, packages provide this structuring mechanism. A Java *package* is a set of related classes. For example, the Java library consists of dozens of packages, some of which are listed in Table 1.

Table 1 Important Packages in the Java Library

Package	Purpose	Sample Class
java.lang	Language support	Math
java.util	Utilities	Random
java.io	Input and output	PrintStream
java.awt	Abstract Windowing Toolkit	Color
java.applet	Applets	Applet
java.net	Networking	Socket
java.sql	Database access through Structured Query Language	ResultSet
javax.swing	Swing user interface	JButton
omg.org.CORBA	Common Object Request Broker Architecture for distributed objects	IntHolder

To put classes in a package, you must place a line

```
package packageName;
```

as the first instruction in the source file containing the classes. A package name consists of one or more identifiers separated by periods. (See Section 8.9.3 for tips on constructing package names.)

For example, let's put the Financial class introduced in this chapter into a package named com.horstmann.bigjava. The Financial.java file must start as follows:

```
package com.horstmann.bigjava;

public class Financial
{
   . . .
}
```

SYNTAX 8.2 Package Specification

```
package packageName;
```

Example:

```
package com.horstmann.bigjava;
```

Purpose:

To declare that all classes in this file belong to a particular package

In addition to the named packages (such as java.util or com.horstmann.bigjava), there is a special package, called the *default package*, which has no name. If you did not include any package statement at the top of your source file, its classes are placed in the default package.

8.9.2 Importing Packages

If you want to use a class from a package, you can refer to it by its full name (package name plus class name). For example, java.util.Scanner refers to the Scanner class in the java.util package:

```
java.util.Scanner in = new java.util.Scanner(System.in);
```

> The import directive lets you refer to a class of a package by its class name, without the package prefix.

Naturally, that is somewhat inconvenient. You can instead *import* a name with an import statement:

```
import java.util.Scanner;
```

Then you can refer to the class as Scanner without the package prefix.

You can import *all classes* of a package with an import statement that ends in .*. For example, you can use the statement

```
import java.util.*;
```

to import all classes from the java.util package. That statement lets you refer to classes like Scanner or Random without a java.util prefix.

However, you never need to import the classes in the java.lang package explicitly. That is the package containing the most basic Java classes, such as Math and Object. These classes are always available to you. In effect, an automatic import java.lang.*; statement has been placed into every source file.

Finally, you don't need to import other classes in the same package. For example, when you implement the class homework1.Tester, you don't need to import the class homework1.Bank. The compiler will find the Bank class without an import statement because it is located in the same package, homework1.

8.9.3 Package Names

Placing related classes into a package is clearly a convenient mechanism to organize classes. However, there is a more important reason for packages: to avoid *name clashes*. In a large project, it is inevitable that two people will come up with the same name for the same concept. This even happens in the standard Java class library (which has now grown to thousands of classes). There is a class Timer in the java.util package and another class called Timer in the javax.swing package. You can still tell the Java compiler exactly which Timer class you need, simply by referring to them as java.util.Timer and javax.swing.Timer.

Of course, for the package-naming convention to work, there must be some way to ensure that package names are unique. It wouldn't be good if the car maker BMW placed all its Java code into the package bmw, and some other programmer (perhaps Bertha M. Walters) had the same bright idea. To avoid this problem, the inventors of Java recommend that you use a package-naming scheme that takes advantage of the uniqueness of Internet domain names.

> Use a domain name in reverse to construct unambiguous package names.

For example, I have a domain name horstmann.com, and there is nobody else on the planet with the same domain name. (I was lucky that the domain name horstmann.com had not been taken by anyone else when I applied. If your name is Walters, you will sadly find that someone else beat you to walters.com.) To get a package name, turn the domain name around to produce a package name prefix, such as com.horstmann.

If you don't have your own domain name, you can still create a package name that has a high probability of being unique by writing your e-mail address backwards. For example, if Bertha Walters has an e-mail address walters@cs.sjsu.edu, then she can use a package name edu.sjsu.cs.walters for her own classes.

Some instructors will want you to place each of your assignments into a separate package, such as homework1, homework2, and so on. The reason is again to avoid name collision. You can have two classes, homework1.Bank and homework2.Bank, with slightly different properties.

8.9.4 How Classes Are Located

If the Java compiler is properly set up on your system, and you use only the standard classes, you ordinarily need not worry about the location of class files and can safely skip this section. If you want to add your own packages, however, or if the compiler cannot locate a particular class or package, you need to understand the mechanism.

> The path of a class file must match its package name.

A package is located in a subdirectory that matches the package name. The parts of the name between periods represent successively nested directories. For example, the package com.horstmann.bigjava would be placed in a subdirectory com/horstmann/bigjava. If the package is to be used only in conjunction with a single program, then you can place the subdirectory inside the directory holding that program's files. For example, if you do your homework assignments in a *base directory* /home/walters, then you can place the class files for the com.horstmann.bigjava package into the directory /home/walters/com/horstmann/bigjava, as shown in Figure 5. (Here, we are using UNIX-style file names. Under Windows, you might use c:\home\walters\com\horstmann\bigjava.)

However, if you want to place your programs into many different directories, such as /home/walters/hw1, /home/walters/hw2, . . . , then you probably don't want to have lots of identical subdirectories /home/walters/hw1/com/horstmann/bigjava, /home/walters/hw2/com/horstmann/bigjava, and so on. In that case, you want to make a single directory with a name such as /home/walters/lib/com/horstmann/bigjava, place all class files for the package in that directory, and tell the Java compiler once and for all how to locate the class files.

You need to add the directories that might contain packages to the *class path*. In the preceding example, you add the /home/walters/lib directory to that class path. The details for doing this depend on your compilation environment; consult the

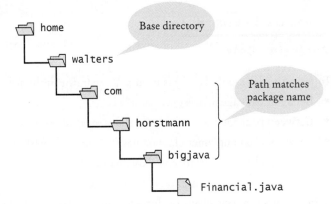

Figure 5
Base Directories and
Subdirectories for Packages

documentation for your compiler, or your instructor. If you use the Sun Java SDK, you need to set the class path. The exact command depends on the operating system. In UNIX, the command might be

```
export CLASSPATH=/home/walters/lib:.
```

This setting places both the /home/walters/lib directory and the current directory onto the class path. (The period denotes the current directory.)

A typical example for Windows would be

```
set CLASSPATH=c:\home\walters\lib;.
```

Note that the class path contains the *base directories* that may contain package directories. It is a common error to place the complete package address in the class path. If the class path mistakenly contains /home/walters/lib/com/horstmann /bigjava, then the compiler will attempt to locate the com.horstmann.bigjava package in /home/walters/lib/com/horstmann/bigjava/com/horstmann/bigjava and won't find the files.

SELF CHECK

18. Which of the following are packages?

   a. java
   b. java.lang
   c. java.util
   d. java.lang.Math

19. Is a Java program without import statements limited to using the default and java.lang packages?

20. Suppose your homework assignments are located in the directory /home/me/ cs101 (c:\me\cs101 on Windows). Your instructor tells you to place your homework into packages. In which directory do you place the class hw1.problem1.TicTacToeTester?

COMMON ERROR 8.3

Confusing Dots

In Java, the dot symbol (.) is used as a separator in the following situations:

- Between package names (`java.util`)
- Between package and class names (`homework1.Bank`)
- Between class and inner class names (`Ellipse2D.Double`)
- Between class and instance variable names (`Math.PI`)
- Between objects and methods (`account.getBalance()`)

When you see a long chain of dot-separated names, it can be a challenge to find out which part is the package name, which part is the class name, which part is an instance variable name, and which part is a method name. Consider

```
java.lang.System.out.println(x);
```

Because `println` is followed by an opening parenthesis, it must be a method name. Therefore, `out` must be either an object or a class with a static `println` method. (Of course, we know that `out` is an object reference of type `PrintStream`.) Again, it is not at all clear, without context, whether `System` is another object, with a public variable `out`, or a class with a `static` variable. Judging from the number of pages that the Java language specification [3] devotes to this issue, even the compiler has trouble interpreting these dot-separated sequences of strings.

To avoid problems, it is helpful to adopt a strict coding style. If class names always start with an uppercase letter, and variable, method, and package names always start with a lower-case letter, then confusion can be avoided.

HOW TO 8.1

Programming with Packages

This How To explains in detail how to place your programs into packages. For example, your instructor may ask you to place each homework assignment into a separate package. That way, you can have classes with the same name but different implementations in separate packages (such as `homework1.Bank` and `homework2.Bank`).

Step 1   Come up with a package name.

Your instructor may give you a package name to use, such as `homework1`. Or, perhaps you want to use a package name that is unique to you. Start with your e-mail address, written backwards. For example, `walters@cs.sjsu.edu` becomes `edu.sjsu.cs.walters`. Then add a sub-package that describes your project or homework, such as `edu.sjsu.cs.walters.homework1`.

Step 2   Pick a *base directory*.

The base directory is the directory that contains the directories for your various packages, for example, `/home/walters` or `c:\cs1`.

Step 3 Make a subdirectory from the base directory that matches your package name.

The subdirectory must be contained in your base directory. Each segment must match a segment of the package name. For example,

```
mkdir /home/walters/homework1
```

If you have multiple segments, build them up one by one:

```
mkdir c:\cs1\edu
mkdir c:\cs1\edu\sjsu
mkdir c:\cs1\edu\sjsu\cs
mkdir c:\cs1\edu\sjsu\cs\walters
mkdir c:\cs1\edu\sjsu\cs\walters\homework1
```

Step 4 Place your source files into the package subdirectory.

For example, if your homework consists of the files Tester.java and Bank.java, then you place them into

```
/home/walters/homework1/Tester.java
/home/walters/homework1/Bank.java
```

or

```
c:\cs1\edu\sjsu\cs\walters\homework1\Tester.java
c:\cs1\edu\sjsu\cs\walters\homework1\Bank.java
```

Step 5 Use the package statement in each source file.

The first noncomment line of each file must be a package statement that lists the name of the package, such as

```
package homework1;
```

or

```
package edu.sjsu.cs.walters.homework1;
```

Step 6 Compile your source files from the *base directory*.

Change to the base directory (from Step 2) to compile your files. For example,

```
cd /home/walters
javac homework1/Tester.java
```

or

```
cd \cs1
javac edu\sjsu\cs\walters\homework1\Tester.java
```

Note that the Java compiler needs the *source file name and not the class name. That is, you need to supply file separators* (/ on UNIX, \ on Windows) *and a file extension* (.java).

Step 7 Run your program from the *base directory*.

Unlike the Java compiler, the Java interpreter needs the *class name (and not a file name) of the class containing the* main *method*. That is, use periods as package separators, and don't use a file extension. For example,

```
cd /home/walters
java homework1.Tester
```

or

```
cd \cs1
java edu.sjsu.cs.walters.homework1.Tester
```

RANDOM FACT 8.1

The Explosive Growth of Personal Computers

In 1971, Marcian E. "Ted" Hoff, an engineer at Intel Corporation, was working on a chip for a manufacturer of electronic calculators. He realized that it would be a better idea to develop a *general-purpose* chip that could be *programmed* to interface with the keys and display of a calculator, rather than to do yet another custom design. Thus, the *microprocessor* was born. At the time, its primary application was as a controller for calculators, washing machines, and the like. It took years for the computer industry to notice that a genuine central processing unit was now available as a single chip.

Hobbyists were the first to catch on. In 1974 the first computer *kit*, the Altair 8800, was available from MITS Electronics for about $350. The kit consisted of the microprocessor, a circuit board, a very small amount of memory, toggle switches, and a row of display lights. Purchasers had to solder and assemble it, then program it in machine language through the toggle switches. It was not a big hit.

The first big hit was the Apple II. It was a real computer with a keyboard, a monitor, and a floppy disk drive. When it was first released, users had a $3000 machine that could play Space Invaders, run a primitive bookkeeping program, or let users program it in BASIC. The original Apple II did not even support lowercase letters, making it worthless for word processing. The breakthrough came in 1979 with a new spreadsheet program, VisiCalc. In a spreadsheet, you enter financial data and their relationships into a grid of rows and columns (see The VisiCalc Spreadsheet Running on an Apple II). Then you modify some of the data and watch in real time how the others change. For example, you can see how changing the mix of widgets in a manufacturing plant might affect estimated costs and profits. Middle managers in companies, who understood computers and were fed up with having to wait for hours or days to get their data runs back from the computing center, snapped up VisiCalc and the computer that was needed to run it. For them, the computer was a spreadsheet machine.

The next big hit was the IBM Personal Computer, ever after known as the PC. It was the first widely available personal computer that used Intel's 16-bit processor, the 8086, whose successors are still being used in personal computers today. The success of the PC was based not on any engineering breakthroughs but on the fact that it was easy to *clone*. IBM published specifications for plug-in cards, and it went one step further. It published the exact source code of the so-called BIOS (Basic Input/Output System), which controls the keyboard, monitor, ports, and disk drives and must be installed in ROM form in every PC. This allowed third-party vendors of plug-in cards to ensure that the BIOS code, and third-party extensions of it, interacted correctly with the equipment. Of course, the code itself was the property of IBM and could not be copied legally. Perhaps IBM did not foresee that functionally equivalent versions of the BIOS nevertheless could be recreated by others. Compaq, one of the first clone vendors, had fifteen engineers, who certified that they had never seen the original IBM code, write a new version that conformed precisely to the IBM specifications. Other companies did the same, and soon a variety of vendors were selling computers that ran the same software as IBM's PC but distinguished themselves by a lower price, increased portability, or better performance. In time, IBM lost its dominant position in the PC market. It is now one of many companies producing IBM PC-compatible computers.

IBM never produced an *operating system* for its PCs—that is, the software that organizes the interaction between the user and the computer, starts application programs, and manages disk storage and other resources. Instead, IBM offered customers the option of three separate operating systems. Most customers couldn't care less about the operating system. They

The VisiCalc Spreadsheet Running on an Apple II

chose the system that was able to launch most of the few applications that existed at the time. It happened to be DOS (Disk Operating System) by Microsoft. Microsoft cheerfully licensed the same operating system to other hardware vendors and encouraged software companies to write DOS applications. A huge number of useful application programs for PC-compatible machines was the result.

PC applications were certainly useful, but they were not easy to learn. Every vendor developed a different *user interface:* the collection of keystrokes, menu options, and settings that a user needed to master to use a software package effectively. Data exchange between applications was difficult, because each program used a different data format. The Apple Macintosh changed all that in 1984. The designers of the Macintosh had the vision to supply an intuitive user interface with the computer and to force software developers to adhere to it. It took Microsoft and PC-compatible manufacturers years to catch up.

Accidental Empires [4] is highly recommended for an amusing and irreverent account of the emergence of personal computers.

At the time of this writing, it is estimated that two in three U.S. households own a personal computer. Most personal computers are used for accessing information from online sources, entertainment, word processing, and home finance (banking, budgeting, taxes). Some analysts predict that the personal computer will merge with the television set and cable network into an entertainment and information appliance.

8.10 Unit Test Frameworks

Up to now, we have used a very simple approach to testing. We provided tester classes whose main method computes values and prints actual and expected values. However, that approach has two limitations. It takes some time to inspect the output and decide whether a test has passed. More importantly, the main method gets messy if it contains many tests.

> Unit test frameworks simplify the task of writing classes that contain many test cases.

Unit testing frameworks were designed to quickly execute and evaluate test suites, and to make it easy to incrementally add test cases. One of the most popular testing frameworks is JUnit. It is freely available at http://junit.org, and it is also built into a number of development environments, including BlueJ and Eclipse.

When you use JUnit, you design a companion test class for each class that you develop. Two versions of JUnit are currently in common use, 3 and 4. We describe both versions. In JUnit 3, your test class has two essential properties:

- The test class must extend the class TestCase from the junit.framework package.
- For each test case, you must define a method whose name starts with test, such as testSimpleCase.

Figure 6   Unit Testing with JUnit

In each test case, you make some computations and then compute some condition that you believe to be true. You then pass the result to a method that communicates a test result to the framework, most commonly the assertEquals method. The assertEquals method takes as parameters the expected and actual values and, for floating-point numbers, a tolerance value.

It is also customary (but not required) that the name of the test class ends in Test, such as CashRegisterTest. Consider this example:

```java
import junit.framework.TestCase;

public class CashRegisterTest extends TestCase
{
    public void testSimpleCase()
    {
        CashRegister register = new CashRegister();
        register.recordPurchase(0.75);
        register.recordPurchase(1.50);
        register.enterPayment(2, 0, 5, 0, 0);
        double expected = 0.25;
        assertEquals(expected, register.giveChange(), EPSILON);
    }

    public void testZeroBalance()
    {
        CashRegister register = new CashRegister();
        register.recordPurchase(2.25);
        register.recordPurchase(19.25);
        register.enterPayment(21, 2, 0, 0, 0);
        assertEquals(0, register.giveChange(), EPSILON);
    }
    // More test cases
    . . .

    private static final double EPSILON = 1E-12;
}
```

If all test cases pass, the JUnit tool shows a green bar (see Figure 6). If any of the test cases fail, the JUnit tool shows a red bar and an error message.

Your test class can also have other methods (whose names should not start with test). These methods typically carry out steps that you want to share among test methods.

JUnit 4 is even simpler. Your test class need not extend any class and you can freely choose names for your test methods. You use "annotations" to mark the test methods. An annotation is an advanced Java feature that places a marker into the code that is interpreted by another tool. In the case of JUnit, the @Test annotation is used to mark test methods.

```java
import org.junit.Test
import org.junit.Assert;

public class CashRegisterTest
{
    @Test public void simpleCase()
    {
```

```
register.recordPurchase(0.75);
register.recordPurchase(1.50);
register.enterPayment(2, 0, 5, 0, 0);
double expected = 0.25;
Assert.assertEquals(expected, register.giveChange(), EPSILON);
}
// More test cases
    . . .
}
```

> The JUnit philosophy is to run all tests whenever you change your code.

The JUnit philosophy is simple. Whenever you implement a class, also make a companion test class. You design the tests as you design the program, one test method at a time. The test cases just keep accumulating in the test class. Whenever you have detected an actual failure, add a test case that flushes it out, so that you can be sure that you won't introduce that particular bug again. Whenever you modify your class, simply run the tests again.

If all tests pass, the user interface shows a green bar and you can relax. Otherwise, there is a red bar, but that's also good. It is much easier to fix a bug in isolation than inside a complex program.

SELF CHECK

21. Provide a JUnit test class with one test case for the Earthquake class in Chapter 5.
22. What is the significance of the EPSILON parameter in the assertEquals method?

CHAPTER SUMMARY

1. A class should represent a single concept from the problem domain, such as business, science, or mathematics.

2. The public interface of a class is cohesive if all of its features are related to the concept that the class represents.

3. A class depends on another class if it uses objects of that class.

4. It is a good practice to minimize the coupling (i.e., dependency) between classes.

5. An immutable class has no mutator methods.

6. A side effect of a method is any externally observable data modification.

7. You should minimize side effects that go beyond modification of the implicit parameter.

8. In Java, a method can never change parameters of primitive type.

9. In Java, a method can change the state of an object reference parameter, but it cannot replace the object reference with another.

10. A precondition is a requirement that the caller of a method must meet. If a method is called in violation of a precondition, the method is not responsible for computing the correct result.

11. An assertion is a logical condition in a program that you believe to be true.

12. If a method has been called in accordance with its preconditions, then it must ensure that its postconditions are valid.

13. A static method is not invoked on an object.

14. A static field belongs to the class, not to any object of the class.

15. The scope of a variable is the region of a program in which the variable can be accessed.

16. The scope of a local variable cannot contain the definition of another variable with the same name.

17. A qualified name is prefixed by its class name or by an object reference, such as `Math.sqrt` or `other.balance`.

18. An unqualified instance field or method name refers to the `this` parameter.

19. A local variable can shadow a field with the same name. You can access the shadowed field name by qualifying it with the `this` reference.

20. A package is a set of related classes.

21. The `import` directive lets you refer to a class of a package by its class name, without the package prefix.

22. Use a domain name in reverse to construct unambiguous package names.

23. The path of a class file must match its package name.

24. Unit test frameworks simplify the task of writing classes that contain many test cases.

25. The JUnit philosophy is to run all tests whenever you change your code.

FURTHER READING

1. Bertrand Meyer, *Object-Oriented Software Construction*, Prentice-Hall, 1989, Chapter 7.
2. http://www.zvon.org/other/PerlTutorial/Output   A dynamic tutorial for regular expressions.
3. http://java.sun.com/docs/books/jls   The Java language specification.
4. Robert X. Cringely, *Accidental Empires*, Addison-Wesley, 1992.

REVIEW EXERCISES

★★ **Exercise R8.1.** Consider the following problem description:

> Users place coins in a vending machine and select a product by pushing a button. If the inserted coins are sufficient to cover the purchase price of the product, the product is dispensed and change is given. Otherwise, the inserted coins are returned to the user.

What classes should you use to implement it?

★★ **Exercise R8.2.** Consider the following problem description:

> Employees receive their biweekly paychecks. They are paid their hourly rates for each hour worked; however, if they worked more than 40 hours per week, they are paid overtime at 150% of their regular wage.

What classes should you use to implement it?

★★ **Exercise R8.3.** Consider the following problem description:

> Customers order products from a store. Invoices are generated to list the items and quantities ordered, payments received, and amounts still due. Products are shipped to the shipping address of the customer, and invoices are sent to the billing address.

What classes should you use to implement it?

★★★ **Exercise R8.4.** Look at the public interface of the java.lang.System class and discuss whether or not it is cohesive.

★★ **Exercise R8.5.** Suppose an Invoice object contains descriptions of the products ordered, and the billing and shipping address of the customer. Draw a UML diagram showing the dependencies between the classes Invoice, Address, Customer, and Product.

★★ **Exercise R8.6.** Suppose a vending machine contains products, and users insert coins into the vending machine to purchase products. Draw a UML diagram showing the dependencies between the classes VendingMachine, Coin, and Product.

★★ **Exercise R8.7.** On which classes does the class Integer in the standard library depend?

★★ **Exercise R8.8.** On which classes does the class Rectangle in the standard library depend?

★ **Exercise R8.9.** Classify the methods of the class Scanner that are used in this book as accessors and mutators.

★ **Exercise R8.10.** Classify the methods of the class Rectangle as accessors and mutators.

★ **Exercise R8.11.** Which of the following classes are immutable?

    a. Rectangle

    b. String

    c. Random

★ **Exercise R8.12.** Which of the following classes are immutable?

    a. PrintStream

    b. Date

    c. Integer

★★ **Exercise R8.13.** What side effect, if any, do the following three methods have:

```java
public class Coin
{
    public void print()
    {
        System.out.println(name + " " + value);
    }

    public void print(PrintStream stream)
    {
        stream.println(name + " " + value);
    }

    public String toString()
    {
        return name + " " + value;
    }
    . . .
}
```

★★★ **Exercise R8.14.** Ideally, a method should have no side effects. Can you write a program in which no method has a side effect? Would such a program be useful?

★★ **Exercise R8.15.** Write preconditions for the following methods. Do not implement the methods.

    a. public static double sqrt(double x)

    b. public static String romanNumeral(int n)

    c. public static double slope(Line2D.Double a)

    d. public static String weekday(int day)

★★ **Exercise R8.16.** What preconditions do the following methods from the standard Java library have?

    a. Math.sqrt

    b. Math.tan

    c. Math.log

    d. Math.exp

    e. Math.pow

    f. Math.abs

★★   **Exercise R8.17.** What preconditions do the following methods from the standard Java library have?

　　a. `Integer.parseInt(String s)`

　　b. `StringTokenizer.nextToken()`

　　c. `Random.nextInt(int n)`

　　d. `String.substring(int m, int n)`

★★★   **Exercise R8.18.** When a method is called with parameters that violate its precondition(s), it can terminate (by throwing an exception or an assertion error), or it can return to its caller. Give two examples of library methods (standard or the library methods used in this book) that return some result to their callers when called with invalid parameters, and give two examples of library methods that terminate.

★★   **Exercise R8.19.** Consider a `CashRegister` class with methods

　　• `public void enterPayment(int coinCount, Coin coinType)`

　　• `public double getTotalPayment()`

Give a reasonable postcondition of the `enterPayment` method. What preconditions would you need so that the `CashRegister` class can ensure that postcondition?

★★   **Exercise R8.20.** Consider the following method that is intended to swap the values of two floating-point numbers:

```
public static void falseSwap(double a, double b)
{
   double temp = a;
   a = b;
   b = temp;
}

public static void main(String[] args)
{
   double x = 3;
   double y = 4;
   falseSwap(x, y);
   System.out.println(x + " " + y);
}
```

Why doesn't the method swap the contents of x and y?

★★★   **Exercise R8.21.** How can you write a method that swaps two floating-point numbers? *Hint:* `Point2D.Double`.

★★   **Exercise R8.22.** Draw a memory diagram that shows why the following method can't swap two `BankAccount` objects:

```
public static void falseSwap(BankAccount a, BankAccount b)
{
   BankAccount temp = a;
   a = b;
   b = temp;
}
```

★ **Exercise R8.23.** Consider an enhancement of the Die class of Chapter 6 with a static field

```
public class Die
{
    public Die(int s) { . . . }
    public int cast() { . . . }
    private int sides;
    private static Random generator = new Random();
}
```

Draw a memory diagram that shows three dice:

```
Die d4 = new Die(4);
Die d6 = new Die(6);
Die d8 = new Die(8);
```

Be sure to indicate the values of the sides and generator fields.

★ **Exercise R8.24.** Try compiling the following program. Explain the error message that you get.

```
public class Print13
{
    public void print(int x)
    {
        System.out.println(x);
    }

    public static void main(String[] args)
    {
        int n = 13;
        print(n);
    }
}
```

★ **Exercise R8.25.** Look at the methods in the Integer class. Which are static? Why?

★★ **Exercise R8.26.** Look at the methods in the String class (but ignore the ones that take a parameter of type char[]). Which are static? Why?

★★ **Exercise R8.27.** The in and out fields of the System class are public static fields of the System class. Is that good design? If not, how could you improve on it?

★★ **Exercise R8.28.** In the following class, the variable n occurs in multiple scopes. Which declarations of n are legal and which are illegal?

```
public class X
{
    public int f()
    {
        int n = 1;
        return n;
    }

    public int g(int k)
    {
```

```
        int a;
        for (int n = 1; n <= k; n++)
            a = a + n;
        return a;
    }

    public int h(int n)
    {
        int b;
        for (int n = 1; n <= 10; n++)
            b = b + n;
        return b + n;
    }

    public int k(int n)
    {
        if (n < 0)
        {
            int k = -n;
            int n = (int) (Math.sqrt(k));
            return n;
        }
        else return n;
    }

    public int m(int k)
    {
        int a;
        for (int n = 1; n <= k; n++)
            a = a + n;
        for (int n = k; n >= 1; n++)
            a = a + n;
        return a;
    }

    private int n;
}
```

★ **Exercise R8.29.** What is a qualified name? What is an unqualified name?

★★ **Exercise R8.30.** When you access an unqualified name in a method, what does that access mean? Discuss both instance and static features.

★★ **Exercise R8.31.** Every Java program can be rewritten to avoid import statements. Explain how, and rewrite RectangleComponent.java from Chapter 2 to avoid import statements.

★ **Exercise R8.32.** What is the default package? Have you used it before this chapter in your programming?

★★T **Exercise R8.33.** What does JUnit do when a test method throws an exception? Try it out and report your findings.

Additional review exercises are available in WileyPLUS.

PROGRAMMING EXERCISES

★★ **Exercise P8.1.** Implement the Coin class described in Section 8.2. Modify the CashRegister class so that coins can be added to the cash register, by supplying a method

```
void enterPayment(int coinCount, Coin coinType)
```

The caller needs to invoke this method multiple times, once for each type of coin that is present in the payment.

★★ **Exercise P8.2.** Modify the giveChange method of the CashRegister class so that it returns the number of coins of a particular type to return:

```
int giveChange(Coin coinType)
```

The caller needs to invoke this method for each coin type, in decreasing value.

★ **Exercise P8.3.** Real cash registers can handle both bills and coins. Design a single class that expresses the commonality of these concepts. Redesign the CashRegister class and provide a method for entering payments that are described by your class. Your primary challenge is to come up with a good name for this class.

★ **Exercise P8.4.** Enhance the BankAccount class by adding preconditions for the constructor and the deposit method that require the amount parameter to be at least zero, and a precondition for the withdraw method that requires amount to be a value between 0 and the current balance. Use assertions to test the preconditions.

★★ **Exercise P8.5.** Write static methods

- public static double sphereVolume(double r)
- public static double sphereSurface(double r)
- public static double cylinderVolume(double r, double h)
- public static double cylinderSurface(double r, double h)
- public static double coneVolume(double r, double h)
- public static double coneSurface(double r, double h)

that compute the volume and surface area of a sphere with radius r, a cylinder with circular base with radius r and height h, and a cone with circular base with radius r and height h. Place them into a class Geometry. Then write a program that prompts the user for the values of r and h, calls the six methods, and prints the results.

★★ **Exercise P8.6.** Solve Exercise P8.5 by implementing classes Sphere, Cylinder, and Cone. Which approach is more object-oriented?

★★★ **Exercise P8.7.** Write methods

```
public static double perimeter(Ellipse2D.Double e);
public static double area(Ellipse2D.Double e);
```

that compute the area and the perimeter of the ellipse e. Add these methods to a class Geometry. The challenging part of this assignment is to find and implement an accurate formula for the perimeter. Why does it make sense to use a static method in this case?

★★ **Exercise P8.8.** Write methods

```
public static double angle(Point2D.Double p, Point2D.Double q)
public static double slope(Point2D.Double p, Point2D.Double q)
```

that compute the angle between the x-axis and the line joining two points, measured in degrees, and the slope of that line. Add the methods to the class Geometry. Supply suitable preconditions. Why does it make sense to use a static method in this case?

★★★ **Exercise P8.9.** Write methods

```
public static boolean isInside(Point2D.Double p, Ellipse2D.Double e)
public static boolean isOnBoundary(Point2D.Double p, Ellipse2D.Double e)
```

that test whether a point is inside or on the boundary of an ellipse. Add the methods to the class Geometry.

★ **Exercise P8.10.** Write a method

```
public static int readInt(
        Scanner in, String prompt, String error, int min, int max)
```

that displays the prompt string, reads an integer, and tests whether it is between the minimum and maximum. If not, print an error message and repeat reading the input. Add the method to a class Input.

★★ **Exercise P8.11.** Consider the following algorithm for computing x^n for an integer n. If $n < 0$, x^n is $1/x^{-n}$. If n is positive and even, then $x^n = (x^{n/2})^2$. If n is positive and odd, then $x^n = x^{n-1} \cdot x$. Implement a static method double intPower(double x, int n) that uses this algorithm. Add it to a class called Numeric.

★★ **Exercise P8.12.** Improve the Needle class of Chapter 6. Turn the generator field into a static field so that all needles share a single random number generator.

★★ **Exercise P8.13.** Implement a Coin and CashRegister class as described in Exercise P8.1. Place the classes into a package called money. Keep the CashRegisterTester class in the default package.

★ **Exercise P8.14.** Place a BankAccount class in a package whose name is derived from your e-mail address, as described in Section 8.9. Keep the BankAccountTester class in the default package.

★★T **Exercise P8.15.** Provide a JUnit test class BankTest with three test methods, each of which tests a different method of the Bank class in Chapter 7.

★★T **Exercise P8.16.** Provide JUnit test class TaxReturnTest with three test methods that test different tax situations for the Tax class in Chapter 5.

★G **Exercise P8.17.** Write methods

- public static void drawH(Graphics2D g2, Point2D.Double p);
- public static void drawE(Graphics2D g2, Point2D.Double p);

- `public static void drawL(Graphics2D g2, Point2D.Double p);`
- `public static void drawO(Graphics2D g2, Point2D.Double p);`

that show the letters H, E, L, O on the graphics window, where the point p is the top-left corner of the letter. Then call the methods to draw the words "HELLO" and "HOLE" on the graphics display. Draw lines and ellipses. Do not use the drawString method. Do not use System.out.

★★G **Exercise P8.18.** Repeat Exercise P8.15 by designing classes LetterH, LetterE, LetterL, and LetterO, each with a constructor that takes a Point2D.Double parameter (the top-left corner) and a method draw(Graphics2D g2).Which solution is more object-oriented?

Additional programming exercises are available in WileyPLUS.

PROGRAMMING PROJECTS

★★★ **Project 8.1.** Implement a program that prints paychecks for a group of student assistants. Deduct federal and Social Security taxes. (You may want to use the tax computation used in Chapter 5. Find out about Social Security taxes on the Internet.) Your program should prompt for the names, hourly wages, and hours worked of each student.

★★★ **Project 8.2.** For faster sorting of letters, the United States Postal Service encourages companies that send large volumes of mail to use a bar code denoting the ZIP code (see Figure 7).

The encoding scheme for a five-digit ZIP code is shown in Figure 8. There are full-height frame bars on each side. The five encoded digits are followed by a check digit, which is computed as follows: Add up all digits, and choose the check digit to make the sum a multiple of 10. For example, the sum of the digits in the ZIP code 95014 is 19, so the check digit is 1 to make the sum equal to 20.

```
*************** ECRLOT ** C057

CODE C671RTS2
JOHN DOE                      C057
1009 FRANKLIN BLVD
SUNNYVALE      CA 95014 – 5143
```

Figure 7 A Postal Bar Code

Figure 8 Encoding for Five-Digit Bar Codes

Each digit of the ZIP code, and the check digit, is encoded according to the following table:

	7	4	2	1	0
1	0	0	0	1	1
2	0	0	1	0	1
3	0	0	1	1	0
4	0	1	0	0	1
5	0	1	0	1	0
6	0	1	1	0	0
7	1	0	0	0	1
8	1	0	0	1	0
9	1	0	1	0	0
0	1	1	0	0	0

where 0 denotes a half bar and 1 a full bar. Note that they represent all combinations of two full and three half bars. The digit can be computed easily from the bar code using the column weights 7, 4, 2, 1, 0. For example, 01100 is

$$0 \cdot 7 + 1 \cdot 4 + 1 \cdot 2 + 0 \cdot 1 + 0 \cdot 0 = 6$$

The only exception is 0, which would yield 11 according to the weight formula.

Write a program that asks the user for a ZIP code and prints the bar code. Use : for half bars, | for full bars. For example, 95014 becomes

```
||:|:::|:|:||::::::||:|::|:::|||
```

(Alternatively, write a graphical application that draws real bars.)

Your program should also be able to carry out the opposite conversion: Translate bars into their ZIP code, reporting any errors in the input format or a mismatch of the digits.

ANSWERS TO SELF-CHECK QUESTIONS

1. Look for nouns in the problem description.
2. Yes (ChessBoard) and no (MovePiece).
3. Some of its features deal with payments, others with coin values.

4. None of the coin operations require the `CashRegister` class.

5. If a class doesn't depend on another, it is not affected by interface changes in the other class.

6. It is an accessor—calling `substring` doesn't modify the string on which the method is invoked. In fact, all methods of the `String` class are accessors.

7. No—`translate` is a mutator.

8. It is a side effect; this kind of side effect is common in object-oriented programming.

9. Yes—the method affects the state of the `Scanner` parameter.

10. Then you don't have to worry about checking for invalid values—it becomes the caller's responsibility.

11. No—you can take any action that is convenient for you.

12. `Math m = new Math(); y = m.sqrt(x);`

13. In an object-oriented solution, the `main` method would construct objects of classes `Game`, `Player`, and the like. Most methods would be instance methods that depend on the state of these objects.

14. `System.in` and `System.out`.

15. Yes, it works. Static methods can access static fields of the same class. But it is a terrible idea. As your programming tasks get more complex, you will want to use objects and classes to organize your programs.

16. The scope of `amount` is the entire `deposit` method. The scope of `newBalance` starts at the point at which the variable is defined and extends to the end of the method.

17. It starts at the beginning of the class and ends at the end of the class.

18. (a) No; (b) Yes; (c) Yes; (d) No

19. No—you simply use fully qualified names for all other classes, such as `java.util.Random` and `java.awt.Rectangle`.

20. `/home/me/cs101/hw1/problem1` or, on Windows, `c:\me\cs101\hw1\problem1`.

21. Here is one possible answer, using the JUnit 4 style.

```
public class EarthquakeTest
{
   @Test public void testLevel4()
   {
      Earthquake quake = new Earthquake(4);
      Assert.assertEquals("Felt by many people, no destruction",
            quake.getDescription());
   }
}
```

22. It is a tolerance threshold for comparing floating-point numbers. We want the equality test to pass if there is a small roundoff error.

Interfaces and Polymorphism

CHAPTER GOALS

- To learn about interfaces
- To be able to convert between class and interface references
- To understand the concept of polymorphism
- To appreciate how interfaces can be used to decouple classes
- To learn how to implement helper classes as inner classes
- To understand how inner classes access variables from the surrounding scope
- G To implement event listeners in graphical applications

In order to increase programming productivity, we want to be able to *reuse* software components in multiple projects. However, some adaptations are often required to make reuse possible. In this chapter, you will learn an important strategy for separating the reusable part of a computation from the parts that vary in each reuse scenario. The reusable part invokes methods of an *interface*. It is combined with a class that implements the interface methods. To produce a different application, you simply plug in another class that implements the same methods. The program's behavior varies according to the class that was plugged in—this phenomenon is called *polymorphism*.

CHAPTER CONTENTS

9.1 Using Interfaces for Code Reuse

Use interface types to make code more reusable.

It is often possible to make code more general and more reusable by focusing on the essential operations that are carried out. *Interface types* are used to express these common operations.

Consider the DataSet class of Chapter 6. We used that class to compute the average and maximum of a set of input values. However, the class was suitable only for computing the average of a set of *numbers*. If we wanted to process bank accounts to find the bank account with the highest balance, we would have to modify the class, like this:

```
public class DataSet // Modified for BankAccount objects
{
   . . .
   public void add(BankAccount x)
   {
      sum = sum + x.getBalance();
      if (count == 0 || maximum.getBalance() < x.getBalance())
         maximum = x;
      count++;
   }

   public BankAccount getMaximum()
   {
```

```
        return maximum;
    }

    private double sum;
    private BankAccount maximum;
    private int count;
}
```

Or suppose we wanted to find the coin with the highest value among a set of coins. We would need to modify the DataSet class again.

```
public class DataSet // Modified for Coin objects
{
    . . .
    public void add(Coin x)
    {
        sum = sum + x.getValue();
        if (count == 0  || maximum.getValue() < x.getValue())
            maximum = x;
        count++;
    }

    public Coin getMaximum()
    {
        return maximum;
    }

    private double sum;
    private Coin maximum;
    private int count;
}
```

Clearly, the fundamental mechanics of analyzing the data is the same in all cases, but the details of measurement differ.

Suppose that the various classes agree on a single method getMeasure that obtains the measure to be used in the data analysis. For bank accounts, getMeasure returns the balance. For coins, getMeasure returns the coin value, and so on. Then we can implement a single reusable DataSet class whose add method looks like this:

```
sum = sum + x.getMeasure();
if (count == 0 || maximum.getMeasure() < x.getMeasure())
    maximum = x;
count++;
```

What is the type of the variable x? Ideally, x should refer to any class that has a getMeasure method.

> A Java interface type declares a set of methods and their signatures.

In Java, an *interface type* is used to specify required operations. We will define an interface type that we call Measurable:

```
public interface Measurable
{
    double getMeasure();
}
```

The interface declaration lists all methods that the interface type requires. The Measurable interface type requires a single method, but in general, an interface type can require multiple methods.

Note that the Measurable type is not a type in the standard library—it is a type that was created specifically for this book, in order to make the DataSet class more reusable.

An interface type is similar to a class, but there are several important differences:

> Unlike a class, an interface type provides no implementation.

- All methods in an interface type are *abstract;* that is, they have a name, parameters, and a return type, but they don't have an implementation.
- All methods in an interface type are automatically public.
- An interface type does not have instance fields.

Now we can use the interface type Measurable to declare the variables x and maximum.

```java
public class DataSet
{
    . . .
    public void add(Measurable x)
    {
        sum = sum + x.getMeasure();
        if (count == 0  || maximum.getMeasure() < x.getMeasure())
            maximum = x;
        count++;
    }

    public Measurable getMaximum()
    {
        return maximum;
    }

    private double sum;
    private Measurable maximum;
    private int count;
}
```

> Use the implements keyword to indicate that a class implements an interface type.

This DataSet class is usable for analyzing objects of any class that *implements* the Measurable interface. A class implements an interface type if it declares the interface in an implements clause. It should then implement the method or methods that the interface requires.

```java
class ClassName implements Measurable
{
    public double getMeasure()
    {
        Implementation
    }

    Additional methods and fields
}
```

A class can implement more than one interface type. Of course, the class must then define all the methods that are required by all the interfaces it implements.

Let us modify the BankAccount class to implement the Measurable interface.

```
public class BankAccount implements Measurable
{
    public double getMeasure()
    {
        return balance;
    }
    . . .
}
```

Note that the class must declare the method as public, whereas the interface need not—all methods in an interface are public.

Similarly, it is an easy matter to modify the Coin class to implement the Measurable interface.

```
public class Coin implements Measurable
{
    public double getMeasure()
    {
        return value;
    }
    . . .
}
```

In summary, the Measurable interface expresses what all measurable objects have in common. This commonality makes the DataSet class reusable. Objects of the DataSet class can be used to analyze collections of objects of *any* class that implements the Measurable interface. Following is a test program that illustrates that fact.

> Interfaces can reduce the coupling between classes.

Figure 1 shows the relationships between the Measurable interface, the classes that implement the interface, and the DataSet class that uses the interface. In the UML notation, interfaces are tagged with a "stereotype" indicator «interface». A dotted arrow with a triangular

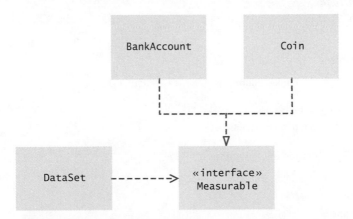

Figure 1 UML Diagram of the DataSet Class and the Classes that Implement the Measurable Interface

tip denotes the *"is-a"* relationship between a class and an interface. You have to look carefully at the arrow tips—a dotted line with an open arrow tip (⇾) denotes the *"uses"* relationship or dependency.

This diagram shows that the DataSet class depends only on the Measurable interface. It is decoupled from the BankAccount and Coin classes.

SYNTAX 9.1 Defining an Interface

```
public interface InterfaceName
{
    method signatures
}
```

Example:

```
public interface Measurable
{
    double getMeasure();
}
```

Purpose:

To define an interface and its method signatures. The methods are automatically public.

SYNTAX 9.2 Implementing an Interface

```
public class ClassName
        implements InterfaceName, InterfaceName, . . .
{
    methods
    fields
}
```

Example:

```
public class BankAccount implements Measurable
{
    // Other BankAccount methods
    public double getMeasure()
    {
        // Method implementation
    }
}
```

Purpose:

To define a new class that implements the methods of an interface

ch09/measure1/DataSetTester.java

```
1  /**
2      This program tests the DataSet class.
3  */
4  public class DataSetTester
5  {
6     public static void main(String[] args)
7     {
8        DataSet bankData = new DataSet();
9
10       bankData.add(new BankAccount(0));
11       bankData.add(new BankAccount(10000));
12       bankData.add(new BankAccount(2000));
13
14       System.out.println("Average balance: "
15             + bankData.getAverage());
16       System.out.println("Expected: 4000");
17       Measurable max = bankData.getMaximum();
18       System.out.println("Highest balance: "
19             + max.getMeasure());
20       System.out.println("Expected: 10000");
21
22       DataSet coinData = new DataSet();
23
24       coinData.add(new Coin(0.25, "quarter"));
25       coinData.add(new Coin(0.1, "dime"));
26       coinData.add(new Coin(0.05, "nickel"));
27
28       System.out.println("Average coin value: "
29             + coinData.getAverage());
30       System.out.println("Expected: 0.133");
31       max = coinData.getMaximum();
32       System.out.println("Highest coin value: "
33             + max.getMeasure());
34       System.out.println("Expected: 0.25");
35    }
36 }
```

Output

```
Average balance: 4000.0
Expected: 4000
Highest balance: 10000.0
Expected: 10000
Average coin value: 0.13333333333333333
Expected: 0.133
Highest coin value: 0.25
Expected: 0.25
```

SELF CHECK

1. Suppose you want to use the DataSet class to find the Country object with the largest population. What condition must the Country class fulfill?

2. Why can't the add method of the DataSet class have a parameter of type Object?

COMMON ERROR 9.1

Forgetting to Define Implementing Methods as Public

The methods in an interface are not declared as public, because they are public by default. However, the methods in a class are not public by default—their default access level is "package" access, which we discuss in Chapter 10. It is a common error to forget the public keyword when defining a method from an interface:

```
public class BankAccount implements Measurable
{
    double getMeasure() // Oops—should be public
    {
        return balance;
    }
    . . .
}
```

Then the compiler complains that the method has a weaker access level, namely package access instead of public access. The remedy is to declare the method as public.

ADVANCED TOPIC 9.1

Constants in Interfaces

Interfaces cannot have instance fields, but it is legal to specify *constants*. For example, the SwingConstants interface defines various constants, such as SwingConstants.NORTH, SwingConstants.EAST, and so on.

When defining a constant in an interface, you can (and should) omit the keywords public static final, because all fields in an interface are automatically public static final. For example,

```
public interface SwingConstants
{
    int NORTH = 1;
    int NORTHEAST = 2;
    int EAST = 3;
    . . .
}
```

9.2 Converting Between Class and Interface Types

Interfaces are used to express the commonality between classes. In this section, we discuss when it is legal to convert between class and interface types.

Have a close look at the call

```
bankData.add(new BankAccount(10000));
```

from the test program of the preceding section. Here we pass an object of type BankAccount to the add method of the DataSet class. However, that method has a parameter of type Measurable:

```
public void add(Measurable x)
```

Is it legal to convert from the BankAccount type to the Measurable type?

> You can convert from a class type to an interface type, provided the class implements the interface.

In Java, such a type conversion is legal. You can convert from a class type to the type of any interface that the class implements. For example,

```
BankAccount account = new BankAccount(10000);
Measurable x = account; // OK
```

Alternatively, x can refer to a Coin object, provided the Coin class has been modified to implement the Measurable interface.

```
Coin dime = new Coin(0.1, "dime");
Measurable x = dime; // Also OK
```

Thus, when you have an object variable of type Measurable, you don't actually know the exact type of the object to which x refers. All you know is that the object has a getMeasure method.

However, you cannot convert between unrelated types:

```
Measurable x = new Rectangle(5, 10, 20, 30); // Error
```

That assignment is an error, because the Rectangle class doesn't implement the Measurable interface.

Occasionally, it happens that you convert an object to an interface reference and you need to convert it back. This happens in the getMaximum method of the DataSet class. The DataSet stores the object with the largest measure, *as a* Measurable *reference*.

```
DataSet coinData = new DataSet();
coinData.add(new Coin(0.25, "quarter"));
coinData.add(new Coin(0.1, "dime"));
coinData.add(new Coin(0.05, "nickel"));
Measurable max = coinData.getMaximum();
```

Now what can you do with the max reference? *You* know it refers to a Coin object, but the compiler doesn't. For example, you cannot call the getName method:

```
String coinName = max.getName(); // Error
```

That call is an error, because the Measurable type has no getName method.

> You need a cast to convert from an interface type to a class type.

However, as long as you are absolutely sure that max refers to a Coin object, you can use the *cast* notation to convert it back:

```
Coin maxCoin = (Coin) max;
String name = maxCoin.getName();
```

If you are wrong, and the object doesn't actually refer to a coin, your program will throw an exception and terminate.

This cast notation is the same notation that you saw in Chapter 4 to convert between number types. For example, if x is a floating-point number, then (int) x is the integer part of the number. The intent is similar—to convert from one type to another. However, there is one big difference between casting of number types and casting of class types. When casting number types, you *lose information*, and you use the cast to tell the compiler that you agree to the information loss. When casting object types, on the other hand, you *take a risk* of causing an exception, and you tell the compiler that you agree to that risk.

SELF CHECK

3. Can you use a cast (BankAccount) x to convert a Measurable variable x to a BankAccount reference?

4. If both BankAccount and Coin implement the Measurable interface, can a Coin reference be converted to a BankAccount reference?

COMMON ERROR 9.2

Trying to Instantiate an Interface

You can define variables whose type is an interface, for example:

```
Measurable x;
```

However, you can *never* construct an interface:

```
Measurable x = new Measurable(); // Error
```

Interfaces aren't classes. There are no objects whose types are interfaces. If an interface variable refers to an object, then the object must belong to some class—a class that implements the interface:

```
Measurable x = new BankAccount(); // OK
```

9.3 Polymorphism

When multiple classes implement the same interface, each class implements the methods of the interface in different ways. How is the correct method executed when the interface method is invoked? We will answer that question in this section.

It is worth emphasizing once again that it is perfectly legal—and in fact very common—to have variables whose type is an interface, such as

```
Measurable x;
```

Just remember that the object to which x refers doesn't have type Measurable. In fact, *no object* has type Measurable. Instead, the type of the object is some class that implements the Measurable interface, such as BankAccount or Coin.

Note that x can refer to objects of *different* types during its lifetime. Here the variable x first contains a reference to a bank account, then a reference to a coin.

```
x = new BankAccount(10000); // OK
x = new Coin(0.1, "dime"); // OK
```

What can you do with an interface variable, given that you don't know the class of the object that it references? You can invoke the methods of the interface:

```
double m = x.getMeasure();
```

The DataSet class took advantage of this capability by computing the measure of the added object, without worrying exactly what kind of object was added.

Now let's think through the call to the getMeasure method more carefully. *Which* getMeasure method? The BankAccount and Coin classes provide two *different* implementations of that method. How did the correct method get called if the caller didn't even know the exact class to which x belongs?

The Java virtual machine makes a special effort to locate the correct method that belongs to the class of the actual object. That is, if x refers to a BankAccount object, then the BankAccount.getMeasure method is called. If x refers to a Coin object, then the Coin.getMeasure method is called. This means that one method call

```
double m = x.getMeasure();
```

can call different methods depending on the momentary contents of x.

> Polymorphism denotes the principle that behavior can vary depending on the actual type of an object.

The principle that the actual type of the object determines the method to be called is called *polymorphism*. The term "polymorphism" comes from the Greek words for "many shapes". The same computation works for objects of many shapes, and adapts itself to the nature of the objects. In Java, all instance methods are polymorphic.

When you see a polymorphic method call, such as x.getMeasure(), there are several possible getMeasure methods that can be called. You have already seen another case in which the same method name can refer to different methods, namely when a method name is *overloaded:* that is, when a single class has several methods with the same name but different parameter types. For example, you can have two constructors BankAccount() and BankAccount(double). The compiler selects the appropriate method when compiling the program, simply by looking at the types of the parameters:

```
account = new BankAccount();
    // Compiler selects BankAccount()
account = new BankAccount(10000);
    // Compiler selects BankAccount(double)
```

Early binding of methods occurs if the compiler selects a method from several possible candidates. Late binding occurs if the method selection takes place when the program runs.

There is an important difference between polymorphism and overloading. The compiler picks an overloaded method when translating the program, before the program ever runs. This method selection is called *early binding*. However, when selecting the appropriate getMeasure method in a call x.getMeasure(), the compiler does not make any decision when translating the method. The program has to run before anyone can know what is stored in x. Therefore, the virtual machine, and not the compiler, selects the appropriate method. This method selection is called *late binding*.

SELF CHECK

5. Why is it impossible to construct a Measurable object?
6. Why can you nevertheless declare a variable whose type is Measurable?
7. What do overloading and polymorphism have in common? Where do they differ?

9.4 Using Interfaces for Callbacks

In this section, we discuss how the DataSet class can be made even more reusable by supplying a different interface type. This type of interface provides a "callback" mechanism, allowing the DataSet class to call back a specific method when it needs more information.

To understand why a further improvement to the DataSet class is desirable, consider these limitations of the Measurable interface:

- You can add the Measurable interface only to classes under your control. If you want to process a set of Rectangle objects, you cannot make the Rectangle class implement another interface—it is a system class, which you cannot change.

- You can measure an object in only one way. If you want to analyze a set of savings accounts both by bank balance and by interest rate, you are stuck.

Therefore, let us rethink the DataSet class. The data set needs to measure the objects that are added. When the objects are required to be of type Measurable, the responsibility of measuring lies with the added objects themselves, which is the cause of the limitations that we noted. It would be better if another object could carry out the measurement. Let's move the measurement method into a different interface:

```
public interface Measurer
{
    double measure(Object anObject);
}
```

The measure method measures an object and returns its measurement. Here we use the fact that all objects can be converted to the type Object, the "lowest common denominator" of all classes in Java. We will discuss the Object type in greater detail in Chapter 10.

The improved DataSet class is constructed with a Measurer object (that is, an object of some class that implements the Measurer interface). That object is saved in a measurer instance field and used to carry out the measurements, like this:

```java
public void add(Object x)
{
    sum = sum + measurer.measure(x);
    if (count == 0 || measurer.measure(maximum) < measurer.measure(x))
        maximum = x;
    count++;
}
```

The DataSet class simply makes a callback to the measure method whenever it needs to measure any object.

Now you can define measurers to take on any kind of measurement. For example, here is how you can measure rectangles by area. Define a class

```java
public class RectangleMeasurer implements Measurer
{
    public double measure(Object anObject)
    {
        Rectangle aRectangle = (Rectangle) anObject;
        double area = aRectangle.getWidth() * aRectangle.getHeight();
        return area;
    }
}
```

Note that the measure method must accept a parameter of type Object, even though this particular measurer just wants to measure rectangles. The method signature must match the signature of the measure method in the Measurer interface. Therefore, the Object parameter is cast to the Rectangle type:

```java
Rectangle aRectangle = (Rectangle) anObject;
```

What can you do with a RectangleMeasurer? You need it for a DataSet that compares rectangles by area. Construct an object of the RectangleMeasurer class and pass it to the DataSet constructor.

```java
Measurer m = new RectangleMeasurer();
DataSet data = new DataSet(m);
```

Next, add rectangles to the data set.

```java
data.add(new Rectangle(5, 10, 20, 30));
data.add(new Rectangle(10, 20, 30, 40));
. . .
```

The data set will ask the RectangleMeasurer object to measure the rectangles. In other words, the data set uses the RectangleMeasurer object to carry out callbacks.

Figure 2 shows the UML diagram of the classes and interfaces of this solution. As in Figure 1, the DataSet class is decoupled from the Rectangle class whose objects it processes. However, unlike in Figure 1, the Rectangle class is no longer coupled with another class. Instead, to process rectangles, you have to come up

Figure 2   UML Diagram of the DataSet Class and the Measurer Interface

with a small "helper" class `RectangleMeasurer`. This helper class has only one purpose: to tell the `DataSet` how to measure its objects.

ch09/measure2/DataSet.java

```java
1   /**
2       Computes the average of a set of data values.
3   */
4   public class DataSet
5   {
6       /**
7           Constructs an empty data set with a given measurer.
8           @param aMeasurer  the measurer that is used to measure data values
9       */
10      public DataSet(Measurer aMeasurer)
11      {
12          sum = 0;
13          count = 0;
14          maximum = null;
15          measurer = aMeasurer;
16      }
17
18      /**
19          Adds a data value to the data set.
20          @param x  a data value
21      */
22      public void add(Object x)
23      {
24          sum = sum + measurer.measure(x);
25          if (count == 0
26              || measurer.measure(maximum) < measurer.measure(x))
27              maximum = x;
28          count++;
29      }
30
```

```
31      /**
32          Gets the average of the added data.
33          @return the average or 0 if no data has been added
34      */
35      public double getAverage()
36      {
37          if (count == 0) return 0;
38          else return sum / count;
39      }
40
41      /**
42          Gets the largest of the added data.
43          @return the maximum or 0 if no data has been added
44      */
45      public Object getMaximum()
46      {
47          return maximum;
48      }
49
50      private double sum;
51      private Object maximum;
52      private int count;
53      private Measurer measurer;
54  }
```

ch09/measure2/DataSetTester2.java

```
1   import java.awt.Rectangle;
2
3   /**
4       This program demonstrates the use of a Measurer.
5   */
6   public class DataSetTester2
7   {
8       public static void main(String[] args)
9       {
10          Measurer m = new RectangleMeasurer();
11
12          DataSet data = new DataSet(m);
13
14          data.add(new Rectangle(5, 10, 20, 30));
15          data.add(new Rectangle(10, 20, 30, 40));
16          data.add(new Rectangle(20, 30, 5, 15));
17
18          System.out.println("Average area: " + data.getAverage());
19          System.out.println("Expected: 625");
20
21          Rectangle max = (Rectangle) data.getMaximum();
22          System.out.println("Maximum area rectangle: " + max);
23          System.out.println("Expected: java.awt.Rectangle[
24              x=10,y=20,width=30,height=40]");
25      }
26  }
```

ch09/measure2/Measurer.java

```
1  /**
2     Describes any class whose objects can measure other objects.
3  */
4  public interface Measurer
5  {
6     /**
7        Computes the measure of an object.
8        @param anObject  the object to be measured
9        @return  the measure
10    */
11    double measure(Object anObject);
12 }
```

ch09/measure2/RectangleMeasurer.java

```
1  import java.awt.Rectangle;
2
3  /**
4     Objects of this class measure rectangles by area.
5  */
6  public class RectangleMeasurer implements Measurer
7  {
8     public double measure(Object anObject)
9     {
10       Rectangle aRectangle = (Rectangle) anObject;
11       double area = aRectangle.getWidth() * aRectangle.getHeight();
12       return area;
13    }
14 }
```

Output

```
Average area: 625
Expected: 625
Maximum area rectangle: java.awt.Rectangle[x=10,y=20,width=30,height=40]
Expected: java.awt.Rectangle[x=10,y=20,width=30,height=40]
```

SELF CHECK

8. Suppose you want to use the DataSet class of Section 9.1 to find the longest String from a set of inputs. Why can't this work?

9. How can you use the DataSet class of this section to find the longest String from a set of inputs?

10. Why does the measure method of the Measurer interface have one more parameter than the getMeasure method of the Measurable interface?

9.5 Inner Classes

The RectangleMeasurer class is a very trivial class. We need this class only because the DataSet class needs an object of some class that implements the Measurer interface. When you have a class that serves a very limited purpose, such as this one, you can declare the class inside the method that needs it:

```
public class DataSetTester3
{
    public static void main(String[] args)
    {
        class RectangleMeasurer implements Measurer
        {
            . . .
        }

        Measurer m = new RectangleMeasurer();
        DataSet data = new DataSet(m);
        . . .
    }
}
```

> An inner class is declared inside another class. Inner classes are commonly used for tactical classes that should not be visible elsewhere in a program.

Such a class is called an *inner class*. An inner class is any class that is defined inside another class. This arrangement signals to the reader of your program that the RectangleMeasurer class is not interesting beyond the scope of this method. Since an inner class inside a method is not a publicly accessible feature, you don't need to document it as thoroughly.

You can also define an inner class inside an enclosing class, but outside of its methods. Then the inner class is available to all methods of the enclosing class.

SYNTAX 9.3 Inner Classes

Declared inside a method:

```
class OuterClassName
{
    method signature
    {
        . . .
        class InnerClassName
        {
            methods
            fields
        }
        . . .
    }
    . . .
}
```

Declared inside the class:

```
class OuterClassName
{
    methods
    fields
    accessSpecifier class InnerClassName
    {
        methods
        fields
    }
    . . .
}
```

Example:

```
public class Tester
{
   public static void main(String[] args)
   {
      class RectangleMeasurer implements Measurer
      {
         . . .
      }
      . . .
   }
}
```

Purpose:

To define an inner class whose scope is restricted to a single method or the methods of a single class

When you compile the source files for a program that uses inner classes, have a look at the class files in your program directory—you will find that the inner classes are stored in files with curious names, such as DataSetTester3$1$Rectangle-Measurer.class. The exact names aren't important. The point is that the compiler turns an inner class into a regular class file.

ch09/measure3/DataSetTester3.java

```
1   import java.awt.Rectangle;
2
3   /**
4       This program demonstrates the use of an inner class.
5   */
6   public class DataSetTester3
7   {
8      public static void main(String[] args)
9      {
10        class RectangleMeasurer implements Measurer
11        {
12           public double measure(Object anObject)
13           {
14              Rectangle aRectangle = (Rectangle) anObject;
15              double area
16                 = aRectangle.getWidth() * aRectangle.getHeight();
17              return area;
18           }
19        }
20
21        Measurer m = new RectangleMeasurer();
22
23        DataSet data = new DataSet(m);
24
25        data.add(new Rectangle(5, 10, 20, 30));
```

```
26          data.add(new Rectangle(10, 20, 30, 40));
27          data.add(new Rectangle(20, 30, 5, 15));
28
29          System.out.println("Average area: " + data.getAverage());
30          System.out.println("Expected: 625");
31
32          Rectangle max = (Rectangle) data.getMaximum();
33          System.out.println("Maximum area rectangle: " + max);
34          System.out.println("Expected: java.awt.Rectangle[
35              x=10,y=20,width=30,height=40]");
36      }
37  }
```

SELF CHECK

11. Why would you use an inner class instead of a regular class?
12. How many class files are produced when you compile the DataSetTester3 program?

ADVANCED TOPIC 9.2

Anonymous Classes

An entity is *anonymous* if it does not have a name. In a program, something that is only used once doesn't usually need a name. For example, you can replace

```
Coin aCoin = new Coin(0.1, "dime");
data.add(aCoin);
```

with

```
data.add(new Coin(0.1, "dime"));
```

if the coin is not used elsewhere in the same method. The object new Coin(0.1, "dime") is an *anonymous object*. Programmers like anonymous objects, because they don't have to go through the trouble of coming up with a name. If you have struggled with the decision whether to call a coin c, dime, or aCoin, you'll understand this sentiment.

Inner classes often give rise to a similar situation. After a single object of the Rectangle-Measurer has been constructed, the class is never used again. In Java, it is possible to define *anonymous classes* if all you ever need is a single object of the class.

```
public static void main(String[] args)
{
    // Construct an object of an anonymous class
    Measurer m = new Measurer()
        // Class definition starts here
        {
            public double measure(Object anObject)
            {
                Rectangle aRectangle = (Rectangle) anObject;
                double area = aRectangle.getWidth() * aRectangle.getHeight();
                return area;
```

```
        }
    };

    DataSet data = new DataSet(m);
    . . .
}
```

This means: Construct an object of a class that implements the `Measurer` interface by defining the `measure` method as specified. Many programmers like this style, but we will not use it in this book.

RANDOM FACT 9.1

Operating Systems

Without an operating system, a computer would not be useful. Minimally, you need an operating system to locate files and to start programs. The programs that you run need services from the operating system to access devices and to interact with other programs. Operating systems on large computers need to provide more services than those on personal computers do.

Here are some typical services:

- *Program loading.* Every operating system provides some way of launching application programs. The user indicates what program should be run, usually by typing the name of the program or by clicking on an icon. The operating system locates the program code, loads it into memory, and starts it.

- *Managing files.* A storage device, such as a hard disk is, electronically, simply a device capable of storing a huge sequence of zeroes and ones. It is up to the operating system to bring some structure to the storage layout and organize it into files, folders, and so on. The operating system also needs to impose some amount of security and redundancy into the file system so that a power outage does not jeopardize the contents of an entire hard disk. Some operating systems do a better job in this regard than others.

- *Virtual memory.* RAM is expensive, and few computers have enough RAM to hold all programs and their data that a user would like to run simultaneously. Most operating systems extend the available memory by storing some data on the hard disk. The application programs do not realize whether a particular data item is in memory or in the virtual memory disk storage. When a program accesses a data item that is currently not in RAM, the processor senses this and notifies the operating system. The operating system swaps the needed data from the hard disk into RAM, simultaneously swapping out a memory block of equal size that had not been accessed for some time.

- *Handling multiple users.* The operating systems of large and powerful computers allow simultaneous access by multiple users. Each user is connected to the computer through a separate terminal. The operating system authenticates users by checking that each one has a valid account and password. It gives each user a small slice of processor time, then serves the next user.

- *Multitasking.* Even if you are the sole user of a computer, you may want to run multiple applications—for example, to read your e-mail in one window and run the Java compiler in another. The operating system is responsible for dividing processor time between the applications you are running, so that each can make progress.

A Graphical Software Environment for the Linux Operating System

- *Printing.* The operating system queues up the print requests that are sent by multiple applications. This is necessary to make sure that the printed pages do not contain a mixture of words sent simultaneously from separate programs.
- *Windows.* Many operating systems present their users with a desktop made up of multiple windows. The operating system manages the location and appearance of the window frames; the applications are responsible for the interiors.
- *Fonts.* To render text on the screen and the printer, the shapes of characters must be defined. This is especially important for programs that can display multiple type styles and sizes. Modern operating systems contain a central font repository.
- *Communicating between programs.* The operating system can facilitate the transfer of information between programs. That transfer can happen through *cut and paste* or *interprocess communication.* Cut and paste is a user-initiated data transfer in which the user copies data from one application into a transfer buffer (often called a "clipboard") managed by the operating system and inserts the buffer's contents into another application. Interprocess communication is initiated by applications that transfer data without direct user involvement.
- *Networking.* The operating system provides protocols and services for enabling applications to reach information on other computers attached to the network.

Today, the most popular operating systems for personal computers are Linux (see figure), the Macintosh OS, and Microsoft Windows.

9.6 Events, Event Sources, and Event Listeners

In the applications that you have written so far, user input was under control of the *program*. The program asked the user for input in a specific order. For example, a program might ask the user to supply first a name, then a dollar amount. But the programs that you use every day on your computer don't work like that. In a program with a modern graphical user interface, the *user* is in control. The user can use both the mouse and the keyboard and can manipulate many parts of the user interface in any desired order. For example, the user can enter information into text fields, pull down menus, click buttons, and drag scroll bars in any order. The program must react to the user commands, in whatever order they arrive. Having to deal with many possible inputs in random order is quite a bit harder than simply forcing the user to supply input in a fixed order.

> User interface events include key presses, mouse moves, button clicks, menu selections, and so on.

In the following sections, you will learn how to write Java programs that can react to user interface events, such as button pushes and mouse clicks. The Java windowing toolkit has a very sophisticated mechanism that allows a program to specify the events in which it is interested and which objects to notify when one of these events occurs.

Whenever the user of a graphical program types characters or uses the mouse anywhere inside one of the windows of the program, the Java window manager sends a notification to the program that an *event* has occurred. The window manager generates huge numbers of events. For example, whenever the mouse moves a tiny interval over a window, a "mouse move" event is generated. Events are also generated when the user presses a key, clicks a button, or selects a menu item.

> An event listener belongs to a class that is provided by the application programmer. Its methods describe the actions to be taken when an event occurs.

Most programs don't want to be flooded by boring events. For example, when a button is clicked with the mouse, the mouse moves over the button, then the mouse button is pressed, and finally the button is released. Rather than receiving lots of irrelevant mouse events, a program can indicate that it only cares about button clicks, not about the underlying mouse events. However, if the mouse input is used for drawing shapes on a virtual canvas, it is necessary to closely track mouse events.

Every program must indicate which events it needs to receive. It does that by installing *event listener* objects. An event listener object belongs to a class that you define. The methods of your event listener classes contain the instructions that you want to have executed when the events occur.

> Event sources report on events. When an event occurs, the event source notifies all event listeners.

To install a listener, you need to know the *event source*. The event source is the user interface component that generates a particular event. You add an event listener object to the appropriate event sources. Whenever the event occurs, the event source calls the appropriate methods of all attached event listeners.

Use JButton components for buttons. Attach an ActionListener to each button.

This sounds somewhat abstract, so let's run through an extremely simple program that prints a message whenever a button is clicked. Button listeners must belong to a class that implements the Action-Listener interface:

```
public interface ActionListener
{
    void actionPerformed(ActionEvent event);
}
```

This particular interface has a single method, actionPerformed. It is your job to supply a class whose actionPerformed method contains the instructions that you want executed whenever the button is clicked. Here is a very simple example of such a listener class:

ch09/button1/ClickListener.java

```
1  import java.awt.event.ActionEvent;
2  import java.awt.event.ActionListener;
3
4  /**
5     An action listener that prints a message.
6  */
7  public class ClickListener implements ActionListener
8  {
9      public void actionPerformed(ActionEvent event)
10     {
11         System.out.println("I was clicked.");
12     }
13 }
```

We ignore the event parameter of the actionPerformed method—it contains additional details about the event, such as the time at which it occurred.

Once the listener class has been defined, we need to construct an object of the class and add it to the button:

```
ActionListener listener = new ClickListener();
button.addActionListener(listener);
```

Whenever the button is clicked, it calls

```
listener.actionPerformed(event);
```

As a result, the message is printed.

You can think of the actionPerformed method as another example of a callback, similar to the measure method of the Measurer class. The windowing toolkit calls the actionPerformed method whenever the button is pressed, whereas the DataSet calls the measure method whenever it needs to measure an object.

You can test this program out by opening a console window, starting the Button-Viewer program from that console window, clicking the button, and watching the messages in the console window (see Figure 3).

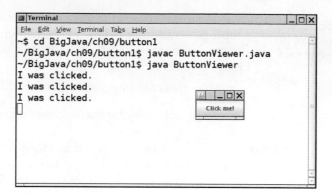

Figure 3   Implementing an Action Listener

ch09/button1/ButtonViewer.java

```
1   import java.awt.event.ActionListener;
2   import javax.swing.JButton;
3   import javax.swing.JFrame;
4
5   /**
6       This program demonstrates how to install an action listener.
7   */
8   public class ButtonViewer
9   {
10      public static void main(String[] args)
11      {
12         JFrame frame = new JFrame();
13         JButton button = new JButton("Click me!");
14         frame.add(button);
15
16         ActionListener listener = new ClickListener();
17         button.addActionListener(listener);
18
19         frame.setSize(FRAME_WIDTH, FRAME_HEIGHT);
20         frame.setDefaultCloseOperation(JFrame.EXIT_ON_CLOSE);
21         frame.setVisible(true);
22      }
23
24      private static final int FRAME_WIDTH = 100;
25      private static final int FRAME_HEIGHT = 60;
26   }
```

SELF CHECK

13. Which objects are the event source and the event listener in the ButtonViewer program?

14. Why is it legal to assign a ClickListener object to a variable of type ActionListener?

COMMON ERROR 9.3

Modifying the Signature in the Implementing Method

When you implement an interface, you must define each method *exactly* as it is specified in the interface. Accidentally making small changes to the parameter or return types is a common error. Here is the classic example,

```
class MyListener implements ActionListener
{
    public void actionPerformed()
    // Oops . . . forgot ActionEvent parameter
    {
        . . .
    }
}
```

As far as the compiler is concerned, this class has two methods:

```
public void actionPerformed(ActionEvent event)
public void actionPerformed()
```

The first method is undefined. The compiler will complain that the method is missing. You have to read the error message carefully and pay attention to the parameter and return types to find your error.

9.7 Using Inner Classes for Listeners

In the preceding section, you saw how the code that is executed when a button is clicked is placed into a listener class. It is common to implement listener classes as inner classes like this:

```
JButton button = new JButton(". . .");

// This inner class is declared in the same method as the button variable
class MyListener implements ActionListener
{
    . . .
};

ActionListener listener = new MyListener();
button.addActionListener(listener);
```

There are two reasons for this arrangement. First, it places the trivial listener class exactly where it is needed, without cluttering up the remainder of the project. Moreover, inner classes have a very attractive feature: Their methods can access variables that are defined in surrounding blocks. In this regard, method definitions of inner classes behave similarly to nested blocks.

Recall that a *block* is a statement group enclosed by braces. If a block is nested inside another, the inner block has access to all variables from the surrounding block:

```
{   // Surrounding block
    BankAccount account = new BankAccount();
    if (. . .)
    {   // Inner block
        . . .
        // OK to access variable from surrounding block
        account.deposit(interest);
        . . .
    }   // End of inner block
    . . .
}   // End of surrounding block
```

> Methods of an inner class can access local variables from surrounding blocks and fields from surrounding classes.

The same nesting works for inner classes. Except for some technical restrictions, which we will examine later in this section, the methods of an inner class can access the variables from the enclosing scope. This feature is very useful when implementing event handlers. It allows the inner class to access variables without having to pass them as constructor or method parameters.

Let's look at an example. Suppose we want to add interest to a bank account whenever a button is clicked.

```
JButton button = new JButton("Add Interest");
final BankAccount account = new BankAccount(INITIAL_BALANCE);

// This inner class is declared in the same method as the account and button variables.
class AddInterestListener implements ActionListener
{
    public void actionPerformed(ActionEvent event)
    {
        // The listener method accesses the account variable
        // from the surrounding block
        double interest = account.getBalance()
                * INTEREST_RATE / 100;
        account.deposit(interest);
    }
};

ActionListener listener = new AddInterestListener();
button.addActionListener(listener);
```

> Local variables that are accessed by an inner-class method must be declared as final.

There is a technical wrinkle. An inner class can access surrounding *local* variables only if they are declared as final. That sounds like a restriction, but it is usually not an issue in practice. Keep in mind that an object variable is final when the variable always refers to the same object. The state of the object can change, but the variable can't refer to a different object. For example, in our program, we never intended to have the account variable refer to multiple bank accounts, so there was no harm in declaring it as final.

An inner class can also access *fields* of the surrounding class, again with a restriction. The field must belong to the object that constructed the inner class object. If the inner class object was created inside a static method, it can only access static surrounding fields.

Here is the source code for the program.

ch09/button2/InvestmentViewer1.java

```
1   import java.awt.event.ActionEvent;
2   import java.awt.event.ActionListener;
3   import javax.swing.JButton;
4   import javax.swing.JFrame;
5
6   /**
7      This program demonstrates how an action listener can access
8      a variable from a surrounding block.
9   */
10  public class InvestmentViewer1
11  {
12     public static void main(String[] args)
13     {
14        JFrame frame = new JFrame();
15
16        // The button to trigger the calculation
17        JButton button = new JButton("Add Interest");
18        frame.add(button);
19
20        // The application adds interest to this bank account
21        final BankAccount account = new BankAccount(INITIAL_BALANCE);
22
23        class AddInterestListener implements ActionListener
24        {
25           public void actionPerformed(ActionEvent event)
26           {
27              // The listener method accesses the account variable
28              // from the surrounding block
29              double interest = account.getBalance()
30                 * INTEREST_RATE / 100;
31              account.deposit(interest);
32              System.out.println("balance: " + account.getBalance());
33           }
34        }
35
36        ActionListener listener = new AddInterestListener();
37        button.addActionListener(listener);
38
39        frame.setSize(FRAME_WIDTH, FRAME_HEIGHT);
40        frame.setDefaultCloseOperation(JFrame.EXIT_ON_CLOSE);
41        frame.setVisible(true);
42     }
43
44     private static final double INTEREST_RATE = 10;
45     private static final double INITIAL_BALANCE = 1000;
```

```
46
47        private static final int FRAME_WIDTH = 120;
48        private static final int FRAME_HEIGHT = 60;
49    }
```

Output

```
balance: 1100.0
balance: 1210.0
balance: 1331.0
balance: 1464.1
```

SELF CHECK

15. Why would an inner class method want to access a variable from a surrounding scope?

16. If an inner class accesses a local variable from a surrounding scope, what special rule applies?

9.8 Building Applications with Buttons

In this section, you will learn how to structure a graphical application that contains buttons. We will put a button to work in our simple investment viewer program. Whenever the button is clicked, interest is added to a bank account, and the new balance is displayed (see Figure 4).

First, we construct an object of the JButton class. Pass the button label to the constructor:

```
JButton button = new JButton("Add Interest");
```

We also need a user interface component that displays a message, namely the current bank balance. Such a component is called a *label*. You pass the initial message string to the JLabel constructor, like this:

```
JLabel label = new JLabel("balance: " + account.getBalance());
```

Figure 4   An Application with a Button

Use a JPanel container to group multiple user-interface components together.

The frame of our application contains both the button and the label. However, we cannot simply add both components directly to the frame—they would be placed on top of each other. The solution is to put them into a *panel*, a container for other user-interface components, and then add the panel to the frame:

```
JPanel panel = new JPanel();
panel.add(button);
panel.add(label);
frame.add(panel);
```

Now we are ready for the hard part—the event listener that handles button clicks. As in the preceding section, it is necessary to define a class that implements the ActionListener interface, and to place the button action into the actionPerformed method. Our listener class adds interest and displays the new balance:

```
class AddInterestListener implements ActionListener
{
    public void actionPerformed(ActionEvent event)
    {
        double interest = account.getBalance() * INTEREST_RATE / 100;
        account.deposit(interest);
        label.setText("balance: " + account.getBalance());
    }
}
```

You often install event listeners as inner classes so that they can have access to the surrounding fields, methods, and final variables.

There is just a minor technicality. The actionPerformed method manipulates the account and label variables. These are local variables of the main method of the investment viewer program, not instance fields of the AddInterestListener class. We therefore need to declare the account and label variables as final so that the actionPerformed method can access them.

Let's put the pieces together.

```
public static void main(String[] args)
{
    . . .
    JButton button = new JButton("Add Interest");
    final BankAccount account = new BankAccount(INITIAL_BALANCE);
    final JLabel label = new JLabel("balance: " + account.getBalance());

    class AddInterestListener implements ActionListener
    {
        public void actionPerformed(ActionEvent event)
        {
            double interest = account.getBalance()
                * INTEREST_RATE / 100;
            account.deposit(interest);
            label.setText("balance: " + account.getBalance());
        }
    }

    ActionListener listener = new AddInterestListener();
    button.addActionListener(listener);
```

. . .
```
    }
```

With a bit of practice, you will learn to glance at this code and translate it into plain English: "When the button is clicked, add interest and set the label text."

Here is the complete program. It demonstrates how to add multiple components to a frame, by using a panel, and how to implement listeners as inner classes.

ch09/button3/InvestmentViewer2.java

```java
1  import java.awt.event.ActionEvent;
2  import java.awt.event.ActionListener;
3  import javax.swing.JButton;
4  import javax.swing.JFrame;
5  import javax.swing.JLabel;
6  import javax.swing.JPanel;
7  import javax.swing.JTextField;
8
9  /**
10     This program displays the growth of an investment.
11  */
12  public class InvestmentViewer2
13  {
14     public static void main(String[] args)
15     {
16        JFrame frame = new JFrame();
17
18        // The button to trigger the calculation
19        JButton button = new JButton("Add Interest");
20
21        // The application adds interest to this bank account
22        final BankAccount account = new BankAccount(INITIAL_BALANCE);
23
24        // The label for displaying the results
25        final JLabel label = new JLabel(
26           "balance: " + account.getBalance());
27
28        // The panel that holds the user interface components
29        JPanel panel = new JPanel();
30        panel.add(button);
31        panel.add(label);
32        frame.add(panel);
33
34        class AddInterestListener implements ActionListener
35        {
36           public void actionPerformed(ActionEvent event)
37           {
38              double interest = account.getBalance()
39                 * INTEREST_RATE / 100;
40              account.deposit(interest);
41              label.setText(
42                 "balance: " + account.getBalance());
43           }
44        }
45
```

```
46          ActionListener listener = new AddInterestListener();
47          button.addActionListener(listener);
48
49          frame.setSize(FRAME_WIDTH, FRAME_HEIGHT);
50          frame.setDefaultCloseOperation(JFrame.EXIT_ON_CLOSE);
51          frame.setVisible(true);
52       }
53
54       private static final double INTEREST_RATE = 10;
55       private static final double INITIAL_BALANCE = 1000;
56
57       private static final int FRAME_WIDTH = 400;
58       private static final int FRAME_HEIGHT = 100;
59    }
```

SELF CHECK

17. How do you place the "balance: . . ." message to the left of the "Add Interest" button?

18. Why was it not necessary to declare the button variable as final?

COMMON ERROR 9.4

Forgetting to Attach a Listener

If you run your program and find that your buttons seem to be dead, double-check that you attached the button listener. The same holds for other user interface components. It is a surprisingly common error to program the listener class and the event handler action without actually attaching the listener to the event source.

PRODUCTIVITY HINT 9.1

Don't Use a Container as a Listener

In this book, we use inner classes for event listeners. That approach works for many different event types. Once you master the technique, you don't have to think about it anymore. Many development environments automatically generate code with inner classes, so it is a good idea to be familiar with them.

However, some programmers bypass the event listener classes and instead turn a container (such as a panel or frame) into a listener. Here is a typical example. The actionPerformed method is added to the viewer class. That is, the viewer implements the ActionListener interface.

```
public class InvestmentViewer
      implements ActionListener // This approach is not recommended
   {
```

```
        public InvestmentViewer()
        {
            JButton button = new JButton("Add Interest");
            button.addActionListener(this);
            . . .
        }

        public void actionPerformed(ActionEvent event)
        {
        }
        . . .
    }
```

Now the `actionPerformed` method is a part of the `InvestmentViewer` class rather than part of a separate listener class. The listener is installed as `this`.

This technique has two major flaws. First, it separates the button definition from the button action. Also, it doesn't *scale* well. If the viewer class contains two buttons that each generate action events, then the `actionPerformed` method must investigate the event source, which leads to code that is tedious and error-prone.

9.9 Processing Timer Events

In this section we will study timer events and show how they allow you to implement simple animations.

The `Timer` class in the `javax.swing` package generates a sequence of action events, spaced apart at even time intervals. (You can think of a timer as an invisible button that is automatically clicked.) This is useful whenever you want to have an object updated in regular intervals. For example, in an animation, you may want to update a scene ten times per second and redisplay the image, to give the illusion of movement.

> A timer generates timer events at fixed intervals.

When you use a timer, you specify the frequency of the events and an object of a class that implements the `ActionListener` interface. Place whatever action you want to occur inside the `actionPerformed` method. Finally, start the timer.

```
class MyListener implements ActionListener
{
    public void actionPerformed(ActionEvent event)
    {
        // This action will be executed at each timer event
        Place listener action here
    }
}

MyListener listener = new MyListener();
Timer t = new Timer(interval, listener);
t.start();
```

Then the timer calls the `actionPerformed` method of the `listener` object every interval milliseconds.

Our sample program will display a moving rectangle. We first supply a `RectangleComponent` class with a `moveBy` method that moves the rectangle by a given amount.

ch09/timer/RectangleComponent.java

```java
1  import java.awt.Graphics;
2  import java.awt.Graphics2D;
3  import java.awt.Rectangle;
4  import javax.swing.JComponent;
5
6  /**
7     This component displays a rectangle that can be moved.
8  */
9  public class RectangleComponent extends JComponent
10 {
11    public RectangleComponent()
12    {
13       // The rectangle that the paint method draws
14       box = new Rectangle(BOX_X, BOX_Y,
15             BOX_WIDTH, BOX_HEIGHT);
16    }
17
18    public void paintComponent(Graphics g)
19    {
20       super.paintComponent(g);
21       Graphics2D g2 = (Graphics2D) g;
22
23       g2.draw(box);
24    }
25
26    /**
27       Moves the rectangle by a given amount.
28       @param x the amount to move in the x-direction
29       @param y the amount to move in the y-direction
30    */
31    public void moveBy(int dx, int dy)
32    {
33       box.translate(dx, dy);
34       repaint();
35    }
36
37    private Rectangle box;
38
39    private static final int BOX_X = 100;
40    private static final int BOX_Y = 100;
41    private static final int BOX_WIDTH = 20;
42    private static final int BOX_HEIGHT = 30;
43 }
```

The repaint method causes a component to repaint itself. Call this method whenever you modify the shapes that the paintComponent method draws.

Note the call to repaint in the moveBy method. This call is necessary to ensure that the component is repainted after the state of the rectangle object has been changed. Keep in mind that the component object does not contain the pixels that show the drawing. The component merely contains a Rectangle object, which itself contains four coordinate values. Calling translate updates the rectangle coordinate values. The call to repaint forces a call to the paintComponent method. The paintComponent method redraws the component, causing the rectangle to appear at the updated location.

The actionPerformed method of the timer listener simply calls component.moveBy(1, 1). This moves the rectangle one pixel down and to the right. Since the actionPerformed method is called many times per second, the rectangle appears to move smoothly across the frame.

ch09/timer/RectangleMover.java

```
 1  import java.awt.event.ActionEvent;
 2  import java.awt.event.ActionListener;
 3  import javax.swing.JFrame;
 4  import javax.swing.Timer;
 5
 6  /**
 7     This program moves the rectangle.
 8  */
 9  public class RectangleMover
10  {
11     public static void main(String[] args)
12     {
13        JFrame frame = new JFrame();
14
15        frame.setSize(FRAME_WIDTH, FRAME_HEIGHT);
16        frame.setTitle("An animated rectangle");
17        frame.setDefaultCloseOperation(JFrame.EXIT_ON_CLOSE);
18
19        final RectangleComponent component = new RectangleComponent();
20        frame.add(component);
21
22        frame.setVisible(true);
23
24        class TimerListener implements ActionListener
25        {
26           public void actionPerformed(ActionEvent event)
27           {
28              component.moveBy(1, 1);
29           }
30        }
31
32        ActionListener listener = new TimerListener();
33
34        final int DELAY = 100; // Milliseconds between timer ticks
35        Timer t = new Timer(DELAY, listener);
36        t.start();
```

```
37      }
38
39      private static final int FRAME_WIDTH = 300;
40      private static final int FRAME_HEIGHT = 400;
41   }
```

SELF CHECK

19. Why does a timer require a listener object?

20. What would happen if you omitted the call to `repaint` in the `moveBy` method?

COMMON ERROR 9.5

Forgetting to Repaint

You have to be careful when your event handlers change the data in a painted component. When you make a change to the data, the component is not automatically painted with the new data. You must tell the Swing framework that the component needs to be repainted, by calling the `repaint` method either in the event handler or in the component's mutator methods. Your component's `paintComponent` method will then be invoked at an opportune moment, with an appropriate `Graphics` object. Note that you should not call the `paintComponent` method directly.

This is a concern only for your own painted components. When you make a change to a standard Swing component such as a `JLabel`, the component is automatically repainted.

9.10 Mouse Events

You use a mouse listener to capture mouse events.

If you write programs that show drawings, and you want users to manipulate the drawings with a mouse, then you need to process mouse events. Mouse events are more complex than button clicks or timer ticks.

A mouse listener must implement the `MouseListener` interface, which contains the following five methods:

```
public interface MouseListener
{
   void mousePressed(MouseEvent event);
       // Called when a mouse button has been pressed on a component
   void mouseReleased(MouseEvent event);
       // Called when a mouse button has been released on a component
   void mouseClicked(MouseEvent event);
       // Called when the mouse has been clicked on a component
```

```
void mouseEntered(MouseEvent event);
   // Called when the mouse enters a component
void mouseExited(MouseEvent event);
   // Called when the mouse exits a component
}
```

The mousePressed and mouseReleased methods are called whenever a mouse button is pressed or released. If a button is pressed and released in quick succession, and the mouse has not moved, then the mouseClicked method is called as well. The mouseEntered and mouseExited methods can be used to paint a user-interface component in a special way whenever the mouse is pointing inside it.

The most commonly used method is mousePressed. Users generally expect that their actions are processed as soon as the mouse button is pressed.

You add a mouse listener to a component by calling the addMouseListener method:

```
public class MyMouseListener implements MouseListener
{
   // Implements five methods
}

MouseListener listener = new MyMouseListener();
component.addMouseListener(listener);
```

In our sample program, a user clicks on a component containing a rectangle. Whenever the mouse button is pressed, the rectangle is moved to the mouse location. We first enhance the RectangleComponent class and add a moveTo method to move the rectangle to a new position.

ch09/mouse/RectangleComponent.java

```
1   import java.awt.Graphics;
2   import java.awt.Graphics2D;
3   import java.awt.Rectangle;
4   import javax.swing.JComponent;
5
6   /**
7      This component displays a rectangle that can be moved.
8   */
9   public class RectangleComponent extends JComponent
10  {
11     public RectangleComponent()
12     {
13        // The rectangle that the paint method draws
14        box = new Rectangle(BOX_X, BOX_Y,
15           BOX_WIDTH, BOX_HEIGHT);
16     }
17
18     public void paintComponent(Graphics g)
19     {
20        super.paintComponent(g);
21        Graphics2D g2 = (Graphics2D) g;
22
```

```
23        g2.draw(box);
24    }
25
26    /**
27        Moves the rectangle to the given location.
28        @param x the x-position of the new location
29        @param y the y-position of the new location
30    */
31    public void moveTo(int x, int y)
32    {
33        box.setLocation(x, y);
34        repaint();
35    }
36
37    private Rectangle box;
38
39    private static final int BOX_X = 100;
40    private static final int BOX_Y = 100;
41    private static final int BOX_WIDTH = 20;
42    private static final int BOX_HEIGHT = 30;
43 }
```

Note the call to repaint in the moveTo method. As explained in the preceding section, this call causes the component to repaint itself and show the rectangle in the new position.

Now, add a mouse listener to the component. Whenever the mouse is pressed, the listener moves the rectangle to the mouse location.

```
class MousePressListener implements MouseListener
{
    public void mousePressed(MouseEvent event)
    {
        int x = event.getX();
        int y = event.getY();
        component.moveTo(x, y);
    }

    // Do-nothing methods
    public void mouseReleased(MouseEvent event) {}
    public void mouseClicked(MouseEvent event) {}
    public void mouseEntered(MouseEvent event) {}
    public void mouseExited(MouseEvent event) {}
}
```

It often happens that a particular listener specifies actions only for one or two of the listener methods. Nevertheless, all five methods of the interface must be implemented. The unused methods are simply implemented as do-nothing methods.

Go ahead and run the RectangleComponentViewer program. Whenever you click the mouse inside the frame, the top left corner of the rectangle moves to the mouse pointer (see Figure 5).

Figure 5 Clicking the Mouse Moves the Rectangle

ch09/mouse/RectangleComponentViewer.java

```java
1  import java.awt.event.MouseListener;
2  import java.awt.event.MouseEvent;
3  import javax.swing.JFrame;
4
5  /**
6     This program displays a RectangleComponent.
7  */
8  public class RectangleComponentViewer
9  {
10    public static void main(String[] args)
11    {
12       final RectangleComponent component = new RectangleComponent();
13
14       // Add mouse press listener
15
16       class MousePressListener implements MouseListener
17       {
18          public void mousePressed(MouseEvent event)
19          {
20             int x = event.getX();
21             int y = event.getY();
22             component.moveTo(x, y);
23          }
24
25          // Do-nothing methods
26          public void mouseReleased(MouseEvent event) {}
27          public void mouseClicked(MouseEvent event) {}
28          public void mouseEntered(MouseEvent event) {}
29          public void mouseExited(MouseEvent event) {}
```

```
30              }
31
32              MouseListener listener = new MousePressListener();
33              component.addMouseListener(listener);
34
35              JFrame frame = new JFrame();
36              frame.add(component);
37
38              frame.setSize(FRAME_WIDTH, FRAME_HEIGHT);
39              frame.setDefaultCloseOperation(JFrame.EXIT_ON_CLOSE);
40              frame.setVisible(true);
41          }
42
43      private static final int FRAME_WIDTH = 300;
44      private static final int FRAME_HEIGHT = 400;
45  }
```

SELF CHECK

21. Why was the moveBy method in the RectangleComponent replaced with a moveTo method?

22. Why must the MousePressListener class supply five methods?

ADVANCED TOPIC 9.3

Event Adapters

In the preceding section you saw how to install a mouse listener into a mouse event source and how the listener methods are called when an event occurs. Usually, a program is not interested in all listener notifications. For example, a program may only be interested in mouse clicks and may not care that these mouse clicks are composed of "mouse pressed" and "mouse released" events. Of course, the program could supply a listener that defines all those methods in which it has no interest as "do-nothing" methods, for example:

```
class MouseClickListener implements MouseListener
{
    public void mouseClicked(MouseEvent event)
    {
        // Mouse click action here
    }

    // Four do-nothing methods
    public void mouseEntered(MouseEvent event) {}
    public void mouseExited(MouseEvent event) {}
    public void mousePressed(MouseEvent event) {}
    public void mouseReleased(MouseEvent event) {}
}
```

This is boring. For that reason, some friendly soul has created a MouseAdapter class that implements the MouseListener interface such that all methods do nothing. You can *extend* that class, inheriting the do-nothing methods and overriding the methods that you care about, like this:

```
class MouseClickListener extends MouseAdapter
{
    public void mouseClicked(MouseEvent event)
    {
        // Mouse click action here
    }
}
```

See Chapter 10 for more information on the process of extending classes.

Random Fact 9.2

Programming Languages

Many hundreds of programming languages exist today, which is actually quite surprising. The idea behind a high-level programming language is to provide a medium for programming that is independent from the instruction set of a particular processor, so that one can move programs from one computer to another without rewriting them. Moving a program from one programming language to another is a difficult process, however, and it is rarely done. Thus, it seems that there would be little use for so many programming languages.

Unlike human languages, programming languages are created with specific purposes. Some programming languages make it particularly easy to express tasks from a particular problem domain. Some languages specialize in database processing; others in "artificial intelligence" programs that try to infer new facts from a given base of knowledge; others in multimedia programming. The Pascal language was purposefully kept simple because it was designed as a teaching language. The C language was developed to be translated efficiently into fast machine code, with a minimum of housekeeping overhead. The C++ language builds on C by adding features for object-oriented programming. The Java language was designed for securely deploying programs across the Internet.

In the early 1970s the U.S. Department of Defense (DoD) was seriously concerned about the high cost of the software components of its weapons equipment. It was estimated that more than half of the total DoD budget was spent on the development of this *embedded-systems* software—that is, software that is embedded in some machinery, such as an airplane or missile, to control it. One of the perceived problems was the great diversity of programming languages that were used to produce that software. Many of these languages, such as TACPOL, CMS-2, SPL/1, and JOVIAL, were virtually unknown outside the defense sector.

In 1976 a committee of computer scientists and defense industry representatives was asked to evaluate existing programming languages. The committee was to determine whether any of them could be made the DoD standard for all future military programming. To nobody's surprise, the committee decided that a new language would need to be created. Contractors were then invited to submit designs for such a new language. Of 17 initial proposals, four were chosen to develop their languages. To ensure an unbiased evaluation, the languages received code names: Red (by Intermetrics), Green (by CII Honeywell Bull), Blue (by Softech), and Yellow (by SRI International). All four languages were based on Pascal. The Green language emerged as the winner in 1979. It was named Ada in honor of the world's first programmer, Ada Lovelace (see Random Fact 14.1).

The Ada language was roundly derided by academics as a typical bloated Defense Department product. Military contractors routinely sought, and obtained, exemptions from the requirement that they had to use Ada on their projects. Outside the defense industry, few companies used Ada. Perhaps that is unfair. Ada had been *designed* to be complex enough to be useful for many applications, whereas other, more popular languages, notably C++, have *grown* to be just as complex and ended up being unmanageable.

The initial version of the C language was designed around 1972. Unlike Ada, C is a simple language that lets you program "close to the machine". It is also quite unsafe. Because different compiler writers added different features, the language actually sprouted various dialects. Some programming instructions were understood by one compiler but rejected by another. Such divergence is an immense pain to a programmer who wants to move code from one computer to another, and an effort got underway to iron out the differences and come up with a standard version of C. The design process ended in 1989 with the completion of the ANSI (American National Standards Institute) Standard. In the meantime, Bjarne Stroustrup of AT&T added features of the language Simula (an object-oriented language designed for carrying out simulations) to C. The resulting language was called C++. From 1985 until today, C++ has grown by the addition of many features, and a standardization process was completed in 1998. C++ has been enormously popular because programmers can take their existing C code and move it to C++ with only minimal changes. In order to keep compatibility with existing code, every innovation in C++ had to work around the existing language constructs, yielding a language that is powerful but somewhat cumbersome to use.

In 1995, Java was designed to be conceptually simpler and more internally consistent than C++, while retaining the syntax that is familiar to millions of C and C++ programmers. The Java *language* was a great design success. It is indeed clean and simple. As for the Java *library,* you know from your own experience that it is neither.

Keep in mind that a programming language is only part of the technology for writing programs. To be successful, a programming language needs feature-rich libraries, powerful tools, and a community of knowledgeable and enthusiastic users. Several very well-designed programming languages have withered on the vine, whereas other programming languages whose design was merely "good enough" have thrived in the marketplace.

CHAPTER SUMMARY

1. Use interface types to make code more reusable.

2. A Java interface type declares a set of methods and their signatures.

3. Unlike a class, an interface type provides no implementation.

4. Use the `implements` keyword to indicate that a class implements an interface type.

5. Interfaces can reduce the coupling between classes.

6. You can convert from a class type to an interface type, provided the class implements the interface.

7. You need a cast to convert from an interface type to a class type.

8. Polymorphism denotes the principle that behavior can vary depending on the actual type of an object.

9. Early binding of methods occurs if the compiler selects a method from several possible candidates. Late binding occurs if the method selection takes place when the program runs.

10. An inner class is declared inside another class. Inner classes are commonly used for tactical classes that should not be visible elsewhere in a program.

11. User interface events include key presses, mouse moves, button clicks, menu selections, and so on.

12. An event listener belongs to a class that is provided by the application programmer. Its methods describe the actions to be taken when an event occurs.

13. Event sources report on events. When an event occurs, the event source notifies all event listeners.

14. Use `JButton` components for buttons. Attach an `ActionListener` to each button.

15. Methods of an inner class can access local variables from surrounding blocks and fields from surrounding classes.

16. Local variables that are accessed by an inner-class method must be declared as `final`.

17. Use a `JPanel` container to group multiple user-interface components together.

18. You often install event listeners as inner classes so that they can have access to the surrounding fields, methods, and final variables.

19. A timer generates timer events at fixed intervals.

20. The repaint method causes a component to repaint itself. Call this method whenever you modify the shapes that the paintComponent method draws.

21. You use a mouse listener to capture mouse events.

CLASSES, OBJECTS, AND METHODS INTRODUCED IN THIS CHAPTER

```
java.awt.Component
    addMouseListener
    repaint
java.awt.Container
    add
java.awt.Rectangle
    setLocation
java.awt.event.ActionListener
    actionPerformed
java.awt.event.MouseEvent
    getX
    getY
java.awt.event.MouseListener
    mouseClicked
    mouseEntered
    mouseExited
    mousePressed
    mouseReleased
javax.swing.AbstractButton
    addActionListener
javax.swing.JButton
javax.swing.JLabel
javax.swing.JPanel
javax.swing.Timer
    start
    stop
```

REVIEW EXERCISES

★ **Exercise R9.1.** Suppose C is a class that implements the interfaces I and J. Which of the following assignments require a cast?

```
C c = . . .;
I i = . . .;
J j = . . .;
```

a. c = i;

b. j = c;

c. i = j;

★ **Exercise R9.2.** Suppose C is a class that implements the interfaces I and J, and suppose i is declared as

```
I i = new C();
```

Which of the following statements will throw an exception?

a. C c = (C) i;

b. J j = (J) i;

c. i = (I) null;

★ **Exercise R9.3.** Suppose the class Sandwich implements the Edible interface, and you are given the variable definitions

```
Sandwich sub = new Sandwich();
Rectangle cerealBox = new Rectangle(5, 10, 20, 30);
Edible e = null;
```

Which of the following assignment statements are legal?

a. e = sub;

b. sub = e;

c. sub = (Sandwich) e;

d. sub = (Sandwich) cerealBox;

e. e = cerealBox;

f. e = (Edible) cerealBox;

g. e = (Rectangle) cerealBox;

h. e = (Rectangle) null;

★★ **Exercise R9.4.** How does a cast such as (BankAccount) x differ from a cast of number values such as (int) x?

★★ **Exercise R9.5.** The classes Rectangle2D.Double, Ellipse2D.Double, and Line2D.Double implement the Shape interface. The Graphics2D class depends on the Shape interface but not on the rectangle, ellipse, and line classes. Draw a UML diagram denoting these facts.

★★ **Exercise R9.6.** Suppose r contains a reference to a new Rectangle(5, 10, 20, 30). Which of the following assignments is legal? (Look inside the API documentation to check which interfaces the Rectangle class implements.)

a. Rectangle a = r;

b. Shape b = r;

c. String c = r;

d. ActionListener d = r;

e. Measurable e = r;

f. Serializable f = r;

g. Object g = r;

★★ **Exercise R9.7.** Classes such as `Rectangle2D.Double`, `Ellipse2D.Double` and
`Line2D.Double` implement the `Shape` interface. The `Shape` interface has a method

```
Rectangle getBounds()
```

that returns a rectangle completely enclosing the shape. Consider the method call:

```
Shape s = . . .;
Rectangle r = s.getBounds();
```

Explain why this is an example of polymorphism.

★★★ **Exercise R9.8.** In Java, a method call such as `x.f()` uses late binding—the exact
method to be called depends on the type of the object to which x refers. Give two
kinds of method calls that use early binding in Java.

★★ **Exercise R9.9.** Suppose you need to process an array of employees to find the average
and the highest salaries. Discuss what you need to do to use the implementation of
the `DataSet` class in Section 9.1 (which processes `Measurable` objects). What do you
need to do to use the second implementation (in Section 9.4)? Which is easier?

★★★ **Exercise R9.10.** What happens if you add a `String` object to the implementation of
the `DataSet` class in Section 9.1? What happens if you add a `String` object to a
`DataSet` object of the implementation in Section 9.4 that uses a `RectangleMeasurer`
class?

★ **Exercise R9.11.** How would you reorganize the `DataSetTester3` program if you
needed to make `RectangleMeasurer` into a top-level class (that is, not an inner class)?

★★ **Exercise R9.12.** What is a callback? Can you think of another use for a callback for
the `DataSet` class? (*Hint:* Exercise P9.8.)

★★ **Exercise R9.13.** Consider this top-level and inner class. Which variables can the f
method access?

```
public class T
{
   public void m(final int x, int y)
   {
      int a;
      final int b;

      class C implements I
      {
         public void f()
         {
            . . .
         }
      }

      final int c;
      . . .
   }

   private int t;
}
```

★★ **Exercise R9.14.** What happens when an inner class tries to access a non-final local variable? Try it out and explain your findings.

★★★G **Exercise R9.15.** How would you reorganize the InvestmentViewer1 program if you needed to make AddInterestListener into a top-level class (that is, not an inner class)?

★G **Exercise R9.16.** What is an event object? An event source? An event listener?

★G **Exercise R9.17.** From a programmer's perspective, what is the most important difference between the user interfaces of a console application and a graphical application?

★G **Exercise R9.18.** What is the difference between an ActionEvent and a MouseEvent?

★★G **Exercise R9.19.** Why does the ActionListener interface have only one method, whereas the MouseListener has five methods?

★★G **Exercise R9.20.** Can a class be an event source for multiple event types? If so, give an example.

★★G **Exercise R9.21.** What information does an action event object carry? What additional information does a mouse event object carry?

★★★G **Exercise R9.22.** Why are we using inner classes for event listeners? If Java did not have inner classes, could we still implement event listeners? How?

★★G **Exercise R9.23.** What is the difference between the paintComponent and repaint methods?

★G **Exercise R9.24.** What is the difference between a frame and a panel?

Additional review exercises are available in WileyPLUS.

PROGRAMMING EXERCISES

★ **Exercise P9.1.** Have the Die class of Chapter 6 implement the Measurable interface. Generate dice, cast them, and add them to the implementation of the DataSet class in Section 9.1. Display the average.

★ **Exercise P9.2.** Define a class Quiz that implements the Measurable interface. A quiz has a score and a letter grade (such as B+). Use the implementation of the DataSet class in Section 9.1 to process a collection of quizzes. Display the average score and the quiz with the highest score (both letter grade and score).

★ **Exercise P9.3.** A person has a name and a height in centimeters. Use the implementation of the DataSet class in Section 9.4 to process a collection of Person objects. Display the average height and the name of the tallest person.

★ **Exercise P9.4.** Modify the implementation of the DataSet class in Section 9.1 (the one processing Measurable objects) to also compute the minimum data element.

★ **Exercise P9.5.** Modify the implementation of the DataSet class in Section 9.4 (the one using a Measurer object) to also compute the minimum data element.

★ **Exercise P9.6.** Using a different Measurer object, process a set of Rectangle objects to find the rectangle with the largest perimeter.

★★★ **Exercise P9.7.** Enhance the DataSet class so that it can either be used with a Measurer object or for processing Measurable objects. *Hint:* Supply a default constructor that implements a Measurer that processes Measurable objects.

★★ **Exercise P9.8.** Define an interface Filter as follows:

```
public interface Filter
{
    boolean accept(Object x);
}
```

Modify the implementation of the DataSet class in Section 9.4 to use both a Measurer and a Filter object. Only objects that the filter accepts should be processed. Demonstrate your modification by having a data set process a collection of bank accounts, filtering out all accounts with balances less than $1,000.

★★ **Exercise P9.9.** Look up the definition of the standard Comparable interface in the API documentation. Modify the DataSet class of Section 9.1 to accept Comparable objects. With this interface, it is no longer meaningful to compute the average. The DataSet class should record the minimum and maximum data values. Test your modified DataSet class by adding a number of String objects. (The String class implements the Comparable interface.)

★ **Exercise P9.10.** Modify the Coin class to have it implement the Comparable interface.

★★★ **Exercise P9.11.** The System.out.printf method has predefined formats for printing integers, floating-point numbers, and other data types. But it is also extensible. If you use the S format, you can print any class that implements the Formattable interface. That interface has a single method:

```
void formatTo(Formatter formatter, int flags, int width, int precision)
```

In this exercise, you should make the BankAccount class implement the Formattable interface. Ignore the flags and precision and simply format the bank balance, using the given width. In order to achieve this task, you need to get an Appendable reference like this:

```
Appendable a = formatter.out();
```

Appendable is another interface with a method

```
void append(CharSequence sequence)
```

CharSequence is yet another interface that is implemented by (among others) the String class. Construct a string by first converting the bank balance into a string and then padding it with spaces so that it has the desired width. Pass that string to the append method.

★★★   **Exercise P9.12.** Enhance the formatTo method of Exercise P9.11 by taking into account the precision.

★★G   **Exercise P9.13.** Write a method randomShape that randomly generates objects implementing the Shape interface: some mixture of rectangles, ellipses, and lines, with random positions. Call it 10 times and draw all of them.

★G   **Exercise P9.14.** Enhance the ButtonViewer program so that it prints a message "I was clicked *n* times!" whenever the button is clicked. The value *n* should be incremented with each click.

★★G   **Exercise P9.15.** Enhance the ButtonViewer program so that it has two buttons, each of which prints a message "I was clicked *n* times!" whenever the button is clicked. Each button should have a separate click count.

★★G   **Exercise P9.16.** Enhance the ButtonViewer program so that it has two buttons labeled A and B, each of which prints a message "Button *x* was clicked!", where *x* is A or B.

★★★G   **Exercise P9.17.** Implement a ButtonViewer program as in Exercise P9.16, using only a single listener class.

★G   **Exercise P9.18.** Enhance the ButtonViewer program so that it prints the time at which the button was clicked.

★★★G   **Exercise P9.19.** Implement the AddInterestListener in the InvestmentViewer1 program as a regular class (that is, not an inner class). *Hint:* Store a reference to the bank account. Add a constructor to the listener class that sets the reference.

★★★G   **Exercise P9.20.** Implement the AddInterestListener in the InvestmentViewer2 program as a regular class (that is, not an inner class). *Hint:* Store references to the bank account and the label in the listener. Add a constructor to the listener class that sets the references.

★★G   **Exercise P9.21.** Write a program that uses a timer to print the current time once a second. *Hint:* The following code prints the current time:

```
Date now = new Date();
System.out.println(now);
```

The Date class is in the java.util package.

★★★G   **Exercise P9.22.** Change the RectangleComponent for the animation program in Section 9.9 so that the rectangle bounces off the edges of the component rather than simply moving outside.

★★G   **Exercise P9.23.** Write a program that animates a car so that it moves across a frame.

★★★G   **Exercise P9.24.** Write a program that animates two cars moving across a frame in opposite directions (but at different heights so that they don't collide.)

★★G   **Exercise P9.25.** Change the RectangleComponent for the mouse listener program in Section 9.10 so that a new rectangle is added to the component whenever the mouse is clicked. *Hint:* Keep an ArrayList<Rectangle> and draw all rectangles in the paintComponent method.

★★G **Exercise P9.26.** Write a program that demonstrates the growth of a roach population. Start with two roaches and double the number of roaches with each button click.

Additional programming exercises are available in WileyPLUS.

PROGRAMMING PROJECTS

★★★ **Project 9.1.** Design an interface MoveableShape that can be used as a generic mechanism for animating a shape. A moveable shape must have two methods: move and draw. Write a generic AnimationPanel that paints and moves any MoveableShape (or array list of MoveableShape objects if you covered Chapter 7). Supply moveable rectangle and car shapes.

★★★ **Project 9.2.** Your task is to design a general program for managing board games with two players. Your program should be flexible enough to handle games such as tic-tac-toe, chess, or the Game of Nim of Project 6.2.

Design an interface Game that describes a board game. Think about what your program needs to do. It asks the first player to input a move—a string in a game-specific format, such as Be3 in chess. Your program knows nothing about specific games, so the Game interface must have a method such as

```
boolean isValidMove(String move)
```

Once the move is found to be valid, it needs to be executed—the interface needs another method executeMove. Next, your program needs to check whether the game is over. If not, the other player's move is processed. You should also provide some mechanism for displaying the current state of the board.

Design the Game interface and provide two implementations of your choice—such as Nim and Chess (or TicTacToe if you are less ambitious). Your GamePlayer class should manage a Game reference without knowing which game is played, and process the moves from both players. Supply two programs that differ only in the initialization of the Game reference.

ANSWERS TO SELF-CHECK QUESTIONS

1. It must implement the Measurable interface, and its getMeasure method must return the population.

2. The Object class doesn't have a getMeasure method, and the add method invokes the getMeasure method.

3. Only if x actually refers to a BankAccount object.

4. No—a Coin reference can be converted to a Measurable reference, but if you attempt to cast that reference to a BankAccount, an exception occurs.

5. Measurable is an interface. Interfaces have no fields and no method implementations.

6. That variable never refers to a Measurable object. It refers to an object of some class—a class that implements the Measurable interface.

7. Both describe a situation where one method name can denote multiple methods. However, overloading is resolved early by the compiler, by looking at the types of the parameter variables. Polymorphism is resolved late, by looking at the type of the implicit parameter object just before making the call.

8. The String class doesn't implement the Measurable interface.

9. Implement a class StringMeasurer that implements the Measurer interface.

10. A measurer measures an object, whereas getMeasure measures "itself", that is, the implicit parameter.

11. Inner classes are convenient for insignificant classes. Also, their methods can access variables and fields from the surrounding scope.

12. Four: one for the outer class, one for the inner class, and two for the DataSet and Measurer classes.

13. The button object is the event source. The listener object is the event listener.

14. The ClickListener class implements the ActionListener interface.

15. Direct access is simpler than the alternative—passing the variable as a parameter to a constructor or method.

16. The local variable must be declared as final.

17. First add label to the panel, then add button.

18. The actionPerformed method does not access that variable.

19. The timer needs to call some method whenever the time interval expires. It calls the actionPerformed method of the listener object.

20. The moved rectangles won't be painted, and the rectangle will appear to be stationary until the frame is repainted for an external reason.

21. Because you know the current mouse position, not the amount by which the mouse has moved.

22. It implements the MouseListener interface, which has five methods.

Inheritance

CHAPTER GOALS

- To learn about inheritance
- To understand how to inherit and override superclass methods
- To be able to invoke superclass constructors
- To learn about protected and package access control
- To understand the common superclass Object and how to override its toString and equals methods
- G To use inheritance for customizing user interfaces

In this chapter, we discuss the important concept of inheritance. Specialized classes can be created that inherit behavior from more general classes. You will learn how to implement inheritance in Java, and how to make use of the Object class—the most general class in the inheritance hierarchy.

CHAPTER CONTENTS

10.1 An Introduction to Inheritance

> Inheritance is a
> mechanism for extending
> existing classes by adding
> methods and fields.

Inheritance is a mechanism for enhancing existing classes. If you need to implement a new class and a class representing a more general concept is already available, then the new class can inherit from the existing class. For example, suppose you need to define a class SavingsAccount to model an account that pays a fixed interest rate on deposits. You already have a class BankAccount, and a savings account is a special case of a bank account. In this case, it makes sense to use the language construct of inheritance. Here is the syntax for the class definition:

```
class SavingsAccount extends BankAccount
{
    new methods
    new instance fields
}
```

In the SavingsAccount class definition you specify only new methods and instance fields. The SavingsAccount class *automatically inherits* all methods and instance fields of the BankAccount class. For example, the deposit method automatically applies to savings accounts:

```
SavingsAccount collegeFund = new SavingsAccount(10);
    // Savings account with 10% interest
collegeFund.deposit(500);
    // OK to use BankAccount method with SavingsAccount object
```

> The more general class is called a superclass. The more specialized class that inherits from the superclass is called the subclass.

We must introduce some more terminology here. The more general class that forms the basis for inheritance is called the *superclass*. The more specialized class that inherits from the superclass is called the *subclass*. In our example, BankAccount is the superclass and Savings-Account is the subclass.

> Every class extends the Object class either directly or indirectly.

In Java, every class that does not specifically extend another class is a subclass of the class Object. For example, the BankAccount class extends the class Object. The Object class has a small number of methods that make sense for all objects, such as the toString method, which you can use to obtain a string that describes the state of an object.

Figure 1 is a class diagram showing the relationship between the three classes Object, BankAccount, and SavingsAccount. In a class diagram, you denote inheritance by a solid arrow with a "hollow triangle" tip that points to the superclass.

Figure 1
An Inheritance Diagram

Inheriting from a class differs from implementing an interface: The subclass inherits behavior and state from the superclass.

You may wonder at this point in what way inheritance differs from implementing an interface. An interface is not a class. It has *no state and no behavior*. It merely tells you which methods you should implement. A superclass has state and behavior, and the subclasses inherit them.

One important reason for inheritance is *code reuse*. By inheriting an existing class, you do not have to replicate the effort that went into designing and perfecting that class. For example, when implementing the SavingsAccount class, you can rely on the withdraw, deposit, and getBalance methods of the BankAccount class without touching them.

One advantage of inheritance is code reuse.

Let's see how savings account objects are different from BankAccount objects. We will set an interest rate in the constructor, and we need a method to apply that interest periodically. That is, in addition to the three methods that can be applied to every account, there is an additional method addInterest. The new method and instance field must be defined in the subclass.

When defining a subclass, you specify added instance fields, added methods, and changed or overridden methods.

```java
public class SavingsAccount extends BankAccount
{
    public SavingsAccount(double rate)
    {
        Constructor implementation
    }

    public void addInterest()
    {
        Method implementation
    }

    private double interestRate;
}
```

Figure 2 shows the layout of a SavingsAccount object. It inherits the balance instance field from the BankAccount superclass, and it gains one additional instance field: interestRate.

Next, you need to implement the new addInterest method. The method computes the interest due on the current balance and deposits that interest to the account.

Figure 2 Layout of a Subclass Object

SYNTAX 10.1 Inheritance

```
class SubclassName extends SuperclassName
{
   methods
   instance fields
}
```

Example:

```
public class SavingsAccount extends BankAccount
{
   public SavingsAccount(double rate)
   {
      interestRate = rate;
   }

   public void addInterest()
   {
      double interest = getBalance() * interestRate / 100;
      deposit(interest);
   }

   private double interestRate;
}
```

Purpose:

To define a new class that inherits from an existing class, and define the methods and instance fields that are added in the new class

```
public class SavingsAccount extends BankAccount
{
   public SavingsAccount(double rate)
   {
      interestRate = rate;
   }

   public void addInterest()
   {
      double interest = getBalance() * interestRate / 100;
      deposit(interest);
   }

   private double interestRate;
}
```

You may wonder why the addInterest method calls the getBalance and deposit methods rather than directly updating the balance field of the superclass. This is a consequence of encapsulation. The balance field was defined as private in the BankAccount class. The addInterest method is defined in the SavingsAccount class. It does not have the right to access a private field of another class.

Note how the `addInterest` method calls the `getBalance` and `deposit` methods of the superclass without specifying an implicit parameter. This means that the calls apply to the same object, that is, the implicit parameter of the `addInterest` method. For example, if you call

```
collegeFund.addInterest();
```

then the following instructions are executed:

```
double interest = collegeFund.getBalance()
      * collegeFund.interestRate / 100;
collegeFund.deposit(interest);
```

In other words, the statements in the `addInterest` method are a shorthand for the following statements:

```
double interest = this.getBalance()
      * this.interestRate / 100;
this.deposit(interest);
```

(Recall that the `this` variable holds a reference to the implicit parameter.)

SELF CHECK

1. Which instance fields does an object of class `SavingsAccount` have?
2. Name four methods that you can apply to `SavingsAccount` objects.
3. If the class `Manager` extends the class `Employee`, which class is the superclass and which is the subclass?

COMMON ERROR 10.1

Confusing Super- and Subclasses

If you compare an object of type `SavingsAccount` with an object of type `BankAccount`, then you find that

- The keyword `extends` suggests that the `SavingsAccount` object is an extended version of a `BankAccount`.

- The `SavingsAccount` object is larger; it has an added instance field `interestRate`.

- The `SavingsAccount` object is more capable; it has an `addInterest` method.

It seems a superior object in every way. So why is `SavingsAccount` called the *subclass* and `BankAccount` the *superclass*?

The *super/sub* terminology comes from set theory. Look at the set of all bank accounts. Not all of them are `SavingsAccount` objects; some of them are other kinds of bank accounts. Therefore, the set of `SavingsAccount` objects is a *subset* of the set of all `BankAccount` objects, and the set of `BankAccount` objects is a *superset* of the set of `SavingsAccount` objects. The more specialized objects in the subset have a richer state and more capabilities.

10.2 Inheritance Hierarchies

In the real world, you often categorize concepts into *hierarchies.* Hierarchies are frequently represented as trees, with the most general concepts at the root of the hierarchy and more specialized ones towards the branches. Figure 3 shows a typical example.

Sets of classes can form complex inheritance hierarchies.

In Java it is equally common to group classes in complex *inheritance hierarchies.* The classes representing the most general concepts are near the root, more specialized classes towards the branches. For example, Figure 4 shows part of the hierarchy of Swing user interface components in Java.

When designing a hierarchy of classes, you ask yourself which features and behaviors are common to all the classes that you are designing. Those common properties are collected in a superclass. For example, all user interface components have a width and height, and the getWidth and getHeight methods of the JComponent class return the component's dimensions. More specialized properties can be found in subclasses. For example, buttons can have text and icon labels. The class AbstractButton, but not the superclass JComponent, has methods to set and get the button text and icon, and instance fields to store them. The individual button classes (such as JButton, JRadioButton, and JCheckBox) inherit these properties. In fact, the AbstractButton class was created to express the commonality among these buttons.

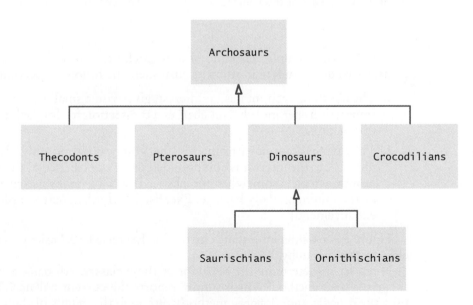

Figure 3   A Part of the Hierarchy of Ancient Reptiles

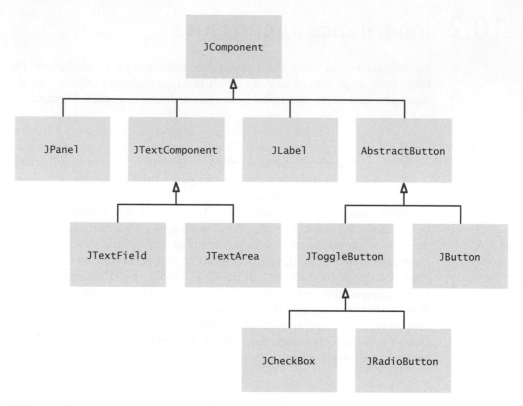

Figure 4 A Part of the Hierarchy of Swing User Interface Components

We will use a simpler example of a hierarchy in our study of inheritance concepts. Consider a bank that offers its customers the following account types:

1. The checking account has no interest, gives you a small number of free transactions per month, and charges a transaction fee for each additional transaction.

2. The savings account earns interest that compounds monthly. (In our implementation, the interest is compounded using the balance of the last day of the month, which is somewhat unrealistic. Typically, banks use either the average or the minimum daily balance. Exercise P10.1 asks you to implement this enhancement.)

Figure 5 shows the inheritance hierarchy. Exercise P10.2 asks you to add another class to this hierarchy.

Next, let us determine the behavior of these classes. All bank accounts support the getBalance method, which simply reports the current balance. They also support the deposit and withdraw methods, although the details of the implementation differ. For example, a checking account must keep track of the number of transactions to account for the transaction fees.

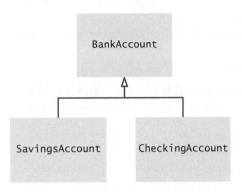

Figure 5   Inheritance Hierarchy for Bank Account Classes

The checking account needs a method `deductFees` to deduct the monthly fees and to reset the transaction counter. The `deposit` and `withdraw` methods must be redefined to count the transactions.

The savings account needs a method `addInterest` to add interest.

To summarize: The subclasses support all methods from the superclass, but their implementations may be modified to match the specialized purposes of the subclasses. In addition, subclasses are free to introduce additional methods.

SELF CHECK

4. What is the purpose of the `JTextComponent` class in Figure 4?
5. Which instance field will we need to add to the `CheckingAccount` class?

10.3 Inheriting Instance Fields and Methods

When you form a subclass of a given class, you can specify additional instance fields and methods. In this section we will discuss this process in detail.

When defining the methods for a subclass, there are three possibilities.

1. You can *override* methods from the superclass. If you specify a method with the same *signature* (that is, the same name and the same parameter types), it overrides the method of the same name in the superclass. Whenever the method is applied to an object of the subclass type, the overriding method, and not the original method, is executed. For example, `Checking-Account.deposit` overrides `BankAccount.deposit`.

2. You can *inherit* methods from the superclass. If you do not explicitly override a superclass method, you automatically inherit it. The superclass method can be applied to the subclass objects. For example, the `SavingsAccount` class inherits the `BankAccount.getBalance` method.

3. You can define new methods. If you define a method that did not exist in the superclass, then the new method can be applied only to subclass objects. For example, `SavingsAccount.addInterest` is a new method that does not exist in the superclass `BankAccount`.

The situation for instance fields is quite different. You can never override instance fields. For fields in a subclass, there are only two cases:

1. The subclass inherits all fields from the superclass. All instance fields from the superclass are automatically inherited. For example, all subclasses of the `BankAccount` class inherit the instance field `balance`.

2. Any new instance fields that you define in the subclass are present only in subclass objects. For example, the subclass `SavingsAccount` defines a new instance field `interestRate`.

What happens if you define a new field with the same name as a superclass field? For example, can you define another field named `balance` in the `SavingsAccount` class? This is legal but extremely undesirable. Each `SavingsAccount` object would have *two* instance fields of the same name. The two fields can hold different values, which is likely to lead to confusion—see Common Error 10.2.

We already implemented the `BankAccount` and `SavingsAccount` classes. Now we will implement the subclass `CheckingAccount` so that you can see in detail how methods and instance fields are inherited. Recall that the `BankAccount` class has three methods and one instance field:

```
public class BankAccount
{
   public double getBalance() { . . . }
   public void deposit(double amount) { . . . }
   public void withdraw(double amount) { . . . }

   private double balance;
}
```

The `CheckingAccount` class has an added method `deductFees` and an added instance field `transactionCount`, and it overrides the `deposit` and `withdraw` methods to increment the transaction count:

```
public class CheckingAccount extends BankAccount
{
   public void deposit(double amount) { . . . }
   public void withdraw(double amount) { . . . }
   public void deductFees() { . . . }

   private int transactionCount;
}
```

Each object of class `CheckingAccount` has two instance fields:

• `balance` (inherited from `BankAccount`)

• `transactionCount` (new to `CheckingAccount`)

You can apply four methods to `CheckingAccount` objects:

- `getBalance()` (inherited from `BankAccount`)
- `deposit(double amount)` (overrides `BankAccount` method)
- `withdraw(double amount)` (overrides `BankAccount` method)
- `deductFees()` (new to `CheckingAccount`)

Next, let us implement these methods. The `deposit` method increments the transaction count and deposits the money:

```
public class CheckingAccount extends BankAccount
{
    public void deposit(double amount)
    {
        transactionCount++;
        // Now add amount to balance
        . . .
    }
    . . .
}
```

Now we have a problem. We can't simply add `amount` to `balance`:

```
public class CheckingAccount extends BankAccount
{
    public void deposit(double amount)
    {
        transactionCount++;
        // Now add amount to balance
        balance = balance + amount; // Error
    }
    . . .
}
```

A subclass has no access to private fields of its superclass.

Although every `CheckingAccount` object has a `balance` instance field, that instance field is *private* to the superclass `BankAccount`. Subclass methods have no more access rights to the private data of the superclass than any other methods. If you want to modify a private superclass field, you must use a public method of the superclass.

How can we add the deposit amount to the balance, using the public interface of the `BankAccount` class? There is a perfectly good method for that purpose—namely, the `deposit` method of the `BankAccount` class. So we must invoke the `deposit` method on some object. On which object? The checking account into which the money is deposited—that is, the implicit parameter of the `deposit` method of the `Checking-Account` class. To invoke another method on the implicit parameter, you don't specify the parameter but simply write the method name, like this:

```
public class CheckingAccount extends BankAccount
{
    public void deposit(double amount)
    {
        transactionCount++;
        // Now add amount to balance
        deposit(amount); // Not complete
```

```
      }
   }    . . .
```

But this won't quite work. The compiler interprets

```
   deposit(amount);
```

as

```
   this.deposit(amount);
```

The this parameter is of type CheckingAccount. There is a method called deposit in the CheckingAccount class. Therefore, that method will be called—but that is just the method we are currently writing! The method will call itself over and over, and the program will die in an infinite recursion (discussed in Chapter 13).

> Use the super keyword to call a method of the superclass.

Instead, we must be specific that we want to invoke only the *superclass's* deposit method. There is a special keyword super for this purpose:

```
public class CheckingAccount extends BankAccount
{
   public void deposit(double amount)
   {
      transactionCount++;
      // Now add amount to balance
      super.deposit(amount);
   }
   . . .
}
```

This version of the deposit method is correct. To deposit money into a checking account, update the transaction count and call the deposit method of the superclass.

The remaining methods are now straightforward.

```
public class CheckingAccount extends BankAccount
{
   . . .
   public void withdraw(double amount)
   {
      transactionCount++;
      // Now subtract amount from balance
      super.withdraw(amount);
   }

   public void deductFees()
   {
      if (transactionCount > FREE_TRANSACTIONS)
      {
         double fees = TRANSACTION_FEE
               * (transactionCount - FREE_TRANSACTIONS);
         super.withdraw(fees);
      }
      transactionCount = 0;
   }
   . . .
   private static final int FREE_TRANSACTIONS = 3;
   private static final double TRANSACTION_FEE = 2.0;
}
```

SYNTAX 10.2 Calling a Superclass Method

super.*methodName*(*parameters*);

Example:

```
public void deposit(double amount)
{
   transactionCount++;
   super.deposit(amount);
}
```

Purpose:

To call a method of the superclass instead of the method of the current class

---

SELF CHECK

6. Why does the withdraw method of the CheckingAccount class call super.withdraw?

7. Why does the deductFees method set the transaction count to zero?

COMMON ERROR 10.2

Shadowing Instance Fields

A subclass has no access to the private instance fields of the superclass. For example, the methods of the CheckingAccount class cannot access the balance field:

```
public class CheckingAccount extends BankAccount
{
   public void deposit(double amount)
   {
      transactionCount++;
      balance = balance + amount; // Error
   }
   . . .
}
```

It is a common beginner's error to "solve" this problem by adding *another* instance field with the same name.

```
public class CheckingAccount extends BankAccount
{
   public void deposit(double amount)
   {
```

```
            transactionCount++;
            balance = balance + amount;
        }
        . . .
        private double balance; // Don't
    }
```

Sure, now the deposit method compiles, but it doesn't update the correct balance! Such a CheckingAccount object has two instance fields, both named balance (see Figure 6). The getBalance method of the superclass retrieves one of them, and the deposit method of the subclass updates the other.

Figure 6   Shadowing Instance Fields

COMMON ERROR 10.3

Failing to Invoke the Superclass Method

A common error in extending the functionality of a superclass method is to forget the super. qualifier. For example, to withdraw money from a checking account, update the transaction count and then withdraw the amount:

```
public void withdraw(double amount)
{
    transactionCount++;
    withdraw(amount);
    // Error—should be super.withdraw(amount)
}
```

Here withdraw(amount) refers to the withdraw method applied to the implicit parameter of the method. The implicit parameter is of type CheckingAccount, and the CheckingAccount class has a withdraw method, so that method is called. Of course, that calls the current method all over again, which will call itself yet again, over and over, until the program runs out of memory. Instead, you must precisely identify which withdraw method you want to call.

Another common error is to forget to call the superclass method altogether. Then the functionality of the superclass mysteriously vanishes.

10.4 Subclass Construction

In this section, we discuss the implementation of constructors in subclasses. As an example, let us define a constructor to set the initial balance of a checking account.

We want to invoke the `BankAccount` constructor to set the balance to the initial balance. There is a special instruction to call the superclass constructor from a subclass constructor. You use the keyword super, followed by the construction parameters in parentheses:

```
public class CheckingAccount extends BankAccount
{
    public CheckingAccount(double initialBalance)
    {
        // Construct superclass
        super(initialBalance);
        // Initialize transaction count
        transactionCount = 0;
    }
    . . .
}
```

> To call the superclass constructor, you use the super keyword in the first statement of the subclass constructor.

When the keyword super is followed by a parenthesis, it indicates a call to the superclass constructor. When used in this way, the constructor call must be *the first statement of the subclass constructor.* If super is followed by a period and a method name, on the other hand, it indicates a call to a superclass method, as you saw in the preceding section. Such a call can be made anywhere in any subclass method.

SYNTAX 10.3 Calling a Superclass Constructor

```
accessSpecifier ClassName(parameterType parameterName, . . .)
{
    super(parameters);
    . . .
}
```

Example:

```
public CheckingAccount(double initialBalance)
{
    super(initialBalance);
    transactionCount = 0;
}
```

Purpose:

To invoke the constructor of the superclass. Note that this statement must be the first statement of the subclass constructor.

The dual use of the super keyword is analogous to the dual use of the this keyword (see Advanced Topic 3.1).

If a subclass constructor does not call the superclass constructor, the superclass is constructed with its default constructor (that is, the constructor that has no parameters). However, if all constructors of the superclass require parameters, then the compiler reports an error.

For example, you can implement the CheckingAccount constructor without calling the superclass constructor. Then the BankAccount class is constructed with its default constructor, which sets the balance to zero. Of course, then the CheckingAccount constructor must explicitly deposit the initial balance.

Most commonly, however, subclass constructors have some parameters that they pass on to the superclass and others that they use to initialize subclass fields.

SELF CHECK

8. Why didn't the SavingsAccount constructor in Section 10.1 call its superclass constructor?

9. When you invoke a superclass method with the super keyword, does the call have to be the first statement of the subclass method?

10.5 Converting Between Subclass and Superclass Types

It is often necessary to convert a subclass type to a superclass type. Occasionally, you need to carry out the conversion in the opposite direction. This section discusses the conversion rules.

> Subclass references can be converted to superclass references.

The class SavingsAccount extends the class BankAccount. In other words, a SavingsAccount object is a special case of a BankAccount object. Therefore, a reference to a SavingsAccount object can be converted to a BankAccount reference.

```
SavingsAccount collegeFund = new SavingsAccount(10);
BankAccount anAccount = collegeFund;
```

Furthermore, all references can be converted to the type Object.

```
Object anObject = collegeFund;
```

Now the three object references stored in collegeFund, anAccount, and anObject all refer to the same object of type SavingsAccount (see Figure 7).

However, the object reference anAccount knows less than the full story about the object to which it refers. Because anAccount is an object of type BankAccount, you can use the deposit and withdraw methods to change the balance of the savings account. You cannot use the addInterest method, though—it is not a method of the BankAccount superclass:

Figure 7   Variables of Different Types Refer to the Same Object

```
anAccount.deposit(1000); // OK
anAccount.addInterest();
      // No—not a method of the class to which anAccount belongs
```

And, of course, the variable anObject knows even less. You can't even apply the deposit method to it—deposit is not a method of the Object class.

Conversion of references is different from a numerical conversion, such as a conversion from an integer to a floating-point number. If you convert an integer, say 4, into the double value 4.0, then the representation changes: the double value 4.0 uses a different sequence of bits than the int value 4. However, when you convert a SavingsAccount reference to a BankAccount reference, then the value of the reference stays the same—it is the memory location of the object. However, after conversion, less information is known about the object. We only know that it is a bank account. It might be a plain bank account, a savings account, or another kind of bank account.

Why would anyone *want* to know less about an object and store a reference in an object field of a superclass? This can happen if you want to *reuse code* that knows about the superclass but not the subclass. Here is a typical example. Consider a transfer method that transfers money from one account to another:

```
public void transfer(double amount, BankAccount other)
{
   withdraw(amount);
   other.deposit(amount);
}
```

You can use this method to transfer money from one bank account to another:

```
BankAccount momsAccount = . . . ;
BankAccount harrysAccount = . . . ;
momsAccount.transfer(1000, harrysAccount);
```

You can *also* use the method to transfer money into a CheckingAccount:

```
CheckingAccount harrysChecking = . . . ;
momsAccount.transfer(1000, harrysChecking);
      // OK to pass a CheckingAccount reference to a method expecting a BankAccount
```

The transfer method expects a reference to a BankAccount, and it gets a reference to the subclass CheckingAccount. Fortunately, rather than complaining about a type mismatch, the compiler simply copies the subclass reference harrysChecking to the superclass reference other. The transfer method doesn't actually know that, in this case, `other` refers to a `CheckingAccount` reference. It knows only that `other` is a `BankAccount`, and it doesn't need to know anything else. All it cares about is that the other object can carry out the `deposit` method.

Very occasionally, you need to carry out the opposite conversion, from a superclass reference to a subclass reference. For example, you may have a variable of type `Object`, and you know that it actually holds a `BankAccount` reference. In that case, you can use a cast to convert the type:

```
BankAccount anAccount = (BankAccount) anObject;
```

However, this cast is somewhat dangerous. If you are wrong, and `anObject` actually refers to an object of an unrelated type, then an exception is thrown.

> The `instanceof` operator tests whether an object belongs to a particular type.

To protect against bad casts, you can use the `instanceof` operator. It tests whether an object belongs to a particular type. For example,

```
anObject instanceof BankAccount
```

returns `true` if the type of `anObject` is convertible to `BankAccount`. This happens if `anObject` refers to an actual `BankAccount` or a subclass such as `SavingsAccount`. Using the `instanceof` operator, a safe cast can be programmed as follows:

```
if (anObject instanceof BankAccount)
{
    BankAccount anAccount = (BankAccount) anObject;
    . . .
}
```

SYNTAX 10.4 The instanceof Operator

object `instanceof` *TypeName*

Example:

```
if (anObject instanceof BankAccount)
{
    BankAccount anAccount = (BankAccount) anObject;
    . . .
}
```

Purpose:

To return `true` if the *object* is an instance of *TypeName* (or one of its subtypes), and `false` otherwise

SELF CHECK

10. Why did the second parameter of the `transfer` method have to be of type `BankAccount` and not, for example, `SavingsAccount`?

11. Why can't we change the second parameter of the `transfer` method to the type `Object`?

10.6 Polymorphism

In Java, the type of a variable does not completely determine the type of the object to which it refers. For example, a variable of type BankAccount can hold a reference to an actual BankAccount object or a subclass object such as SavingsAccount. You already encountered this phenomenon in Chapter 9 with variables whose type was an interface. A variable whose type is Measurable holds a reference to an object of a class that implements the Measurable interface, perhaps a Coin object or an object of an entirely different class.

What happens when you invoke a method? For example,

```
BankAccount anAccount = new CheckingAccount();
anAccount.deposit(1000);
```

Which deposit method is called? The anAccount parameter has type BankAccount, so it would appear as if BankAccount.deposit is called. On the other hand, the CheckingAccount class provides its own deposit method that updates the transaction count. The anAccount field actually refers to an object of the subclass Checking-Account, so it would be appropriate if the CheckingAccount.deposit method were called instead.

In Java, method calls *are always determined by the type of the actual object*, not the type of the object reference. That is, if the actual object has the type Checking-Account, then the CheckingAccount.deposit method is called. It does not matter that the object reference is stored in a field of type BankAccount. As we discussed in Chapter 9, the ability to refer to objects of multiple types with varying behavior is called *polymorphism*.

If polymorphism is so powerful, why not store all account references in variables of type Object? This does not work because the compiler needs to check that only legal methods are invoked. The Object type does not define a deposit method—the BankAccount type (at least) is required to make a call to the deposit method.

Have another look at the transfer method to see polymorphism at work. Here is the implementation of the method:

```
public void transfer(double amount, BankAccount other)
{
   withdraw(amount);
   other.deposit(amount);
}
```

Suppose you call

```
anAccount.transfer(1000, anotherAccount);
```

Two method calls are the result:

```
anAccount.withdraw(1000);
anotherAccount.deposit(1000);
```

Depending on the actual types of anAccount and anotherAccount, different versions of the withdraw and deposit methods are called.

If you look into the implementation of the transfer method, it may not be immediately obvious that the first method call

```
withdraw(amount);
```

depends on the type of an object. However, that call is a shortcut for

```
this.withdraw(amount);
```

The this parameter holds a reference to the implicit parameter, which can refer to a BankAccount or a subclass object.

The following program calls the polymorphic withdraw and deposit methods. You should manually calculate what the program should print for each account balance, and confirm that the correct methods have in fact been called.

ch10/accounts/AccountTester.java

```java
1  /**
2      This program tests the BankAccount class and
3      its subclasses.
4  */
5  public class AccountTester
6  {
7      public static void main(String[] args)
8      {
9          SavingsAccount momsSavings
10             = new SavingsAccount(0.5);
11
12         CheckingAccount harrysChecking
13             = new CheckingAccount(100);
14
15         momsSavings.deposit(10000);
16
17         momsSavings.transfer(2000, harrysChecking);
18         harrysChecking.withdraw(1500);
19         harrysChecking.withdraw(80);
20
21         momsSavings.transfer(1000, harrysChecking);
22         harrysChecking.withdraw(400);
23
24         // Simulate end of month
25         momsSavings.addInterest();
26         harrysChecking.deductFees();
27
28         System.out.println("Mom's savings balance: "
29             + momsSavings.getBalance());
30         System.out.println("Expected: 7035");
31
32         System.out.println("Harry's checking balance: "
33             + harrysChecking.getBalance());
34         System.out.println("Expected: 1116");
35     }
36 }
```

ch10/accounts/BankAccount.java

```
 1  /**
 2      A bank account has a balance that can be changed by
 3      deposits and withdrawals.
 4  */
 5  public class BankAccount
 6  {
 7      /**
 8          Constructs a bank account with a zero balance.
 9      */
10      public BankAccount()
11      {
12         balance = 0;
13      }
14
15      /**
16          Constructs a bank account with a given balance.
17          @param initialBalance the initial balance
18      */
19      public BankAccount(double initialBalance)
20      {
21         balance = initialBalance;
22      }
23
24      /**
25          Deposits money into the bank account.
26          @param amount the amount to deposit
27      */
28      public void deposit(double amount)
29      {
30         balance = balance + amount;
31      }
32
33      /**
34          Withdraws money from the bank account.
35          @param amount the amount to withdraw
36      */
37      public void withdraw(double amount)
38      {
39         balance = balance - amount;
40      }
41
42      /**
43          Gets the current balance of the bank account.
44          @return the current balance
45      */
46      public double getBalance()
47      {
48         return balance;
49      }
50
```

```
51    /**
52        Transfers money from the bank account to another account.
53        @param amount  the amount to transfer
54        @param other  the other account
55    */
56    public void transfer(double amount, BankAccount other)
57    {
58        withdraw(amount);
59        other.deposit(amount);
60    }
61
62    private double balance;
63 }
```

ch10/accounts/CheckingAccount.java

```
1    /**
2        A checking account that charges transaction fees.
3    */
4    public class CheckingAccount extends BankAccount
5    {
6        /**
7            Constructs a checking account with a given balance.
8            @param initialBalance  the initial balance
9        */
10       public CheckingAccount(double initialBalance)
11       {
12           // Construct superclass
13           super(initialBalance);
14
15           // Initialize transaction count
16           transactionCount = 0;
17       }
18
19       public void deposit(double amount)
20       {
21           transactionCount++;
22           // Now add amount to balance
23           super.deposit(amount);
24       }
25
26       public void withdraw(double amount)
27       {
28           transactionCount++;
29           // Now subtract amount from balance
30           super.withdraw(amount);
31       }
32
33       /**
34           Deducts the accumulated fees and resets the
35           transaction count.
36       */
```

```
37    public void deductFees()
38    {
39       if (transactionCount > FREE_TRANSACTIONS)
40       {
41          double fees = TRANSACTION_FEE *
42                (transactionCount - FREE_TRANSACTIONS);
43          super.withdraw(fees);
44       }
45       transactionCount = 0;
46    }
47
48    private int transactionCount;
49
50    private static final int FREE_TRANSACTIONS = 3;
51    private static final double TRANSACTION_FEE = 2.0;
52 }
```

ch10/accounts/SavingsAccount.java

```
1  /**
2      An account that earns interest at a fixed rate.
3  */
4  public class SavingsAccount extends BankAccount
5  {
6     /**
7         Constructs a bank account with a given interest rate.
8         @param rate the interest rate
9     */
10    public SavingsAccount(double rate)
11    {
12       interestRate = rate;
13    }
14
15    /**
16        Adds the earned interest to the account balance.
17    */
18    public void addInterest()
19    {
20       double interest = getBalance() * interestRate / 100;
21       deposit(interest);
22    }
23
24    private double interestRate;
25 }
```

Output

```
Mom's savings balance: 7035.0
Expected: 7035
Harry's checking balance: 1116.0
Expected: 1116
```

SELF CHECK

12. If `a` is a variable of type `BankAccount` that holds a non-null reference, what do you know about the object to which `a` refers?

13. If `a` refers to a checking account, what is the effect of calling `a.transfer(1000, a)`?

ADVANCED TOPIC 10.1

Abstract Classes

When you extend an existing class, you have the choice whether or not to redefine the methods of the superclass. Sometimes, it is desirable to *force* programmers to redefine a method. That happens when there is no good default for the superclass, and only the subclass programmer can know how to implement the method properly.

Here is an example. Suppose the First National Bank of Java decides that every account type must have some monthly fees. Therefore, a `deductFees` method should be added to the `BankAccount` class:

```
public class BankAccount
{
    public void deductFees() { . . . }
    . . .
}
```

But what should this method do? Of course, we could have the method do nothing. But then a programmer implementing a new subclass might simply forget to implement the deductFees method, and the new account would inherit the do-nothing method of the superclass. There is a better way—declare the `deductFees` method as an *abstract method:*

```
public abstract void deductFees();
```

> An abstract method is a method whose implementation is not specified.

An abstract method has no implementation. This forces the implementors of subclasses to specify concrete implementations of this method. (Of course, some subclasses might decide to implement a do-nothing method, but then that is their choice—not a silently inherited default.)

You cannot construct objects of classes with abstract methods. For example, once the `BankAccount` class has an abstract method, the compiler will flag an attempt to create a `new BankAccount()` as an error. Of course, if the `CheckingAccount` subclass overrides the deductFees method and supplies an implementation, then you can create `CheckingAccount` objects.

> An abstract class is a class that cannot be instantiated.

A class for which you cannot create objects is called an *abstract class.* A class for which you can create objects is sometimes called a *concrete class.* In Java, you must declare all abstract classes with the keyword **abstract**:

```
public abstract class BankAccount
{
    public abstract void deductFees();
    . . .
}
```

A class that defines an abstract method, or that inherits an abstract method without overriding it, *must* be declared as abstract. You can also declare classes with no abstract methods as abstract. Doing so prevents programmers from creating instances of that class but allows them to create their own subclasses.

Note that you cannot construct an *object* of an abstract class, but you can still have an *object reference* whose type is an abstract class. Of course, the actual object to which it refers must be an instance of a concrete subclass:

```
BankAccount anAccount; // OK
anAccount = new BankAccount(); // Error—BankAccount is abstract
anAccount = new SavingsAccount(); // OK
anAccount = null; // OK
```

The reason for using abstract classes is to force programmers to create subclasses. By specifying certain methods as abstract, you avoid the trouble of coming up with useless default methods that others might inherit by accident.

Abstract classes differ from interfaces in an important way—they can have instance fields, and they can have concrete methods and constructors.

ADVANCED TOPIC 10.2

Final Methods and Classes

In Advanced Topic 10.1 you saw how you can force other programmers to create subclasses of abstract classes and override abstract methods. Occasionally, you may want to do the opposite and *prevent* other programmers from creating subclasses or from overriding certain methods. In these situations, you use the final keyword. For example, the String class in the standard Java library has been declared as

```
public final class String { . . . }
```

That means that nobody can extend the String class.

The String class is meant to be *immutable*—string objects can't be modified by any of their methods. Since the Java language does not enforce this, the class designers did. Nobody can create subclasses of String; therefore, you know that all String references can be copied without the risk of mutation.

You can also declare individual methods as final:

```
public class SecureAccount extends BankAccount
{
    . . .
    public final boolean checkPassword(String password)
    {
        . . .
    }
}
```

This way, nobody can override the checkPassword method with another method that simply returns true.

10.7 Access Control

Java has four levels of controlling access to fields, methods, and classes:

- `public` access
- `private` access
- `protected` access (see Advanced Topic 10.3)
- package access (the default, when no access modifier is given)

You have already used the `private` and `public` modifiers extensively. Private features can be accessed only by the methods of their own class. Public features can be accessed by methods of all classes. We will discuss protected access in Advanced Topic 10.3—we will not need it in this book.

> A field or method that is not declared as public, private, or protected can be accessed by all classes in the same package, which is usually not desirable.

If you do not supply an access control modifier, then the default is *package access.* That is, all methods of classes in the same package can access the feature. For example, if a class is declared as `public`, then all other classes in all packages can use it. But if a class is declared without an access modifier, then only the other classes in the same package can use it. Package access is a good default for classes, but it is extremely unfortunate for fields. Instance and static fields of classes should always be `private`. There are a few exceptions:

- Public constants (`public static final` fields) are useful and safe.
- Some objects, such as `System.out`, need to be accessible to all programs and therefore should be public.
- Very occasionally, several classes in a package must collaborate very closely. In that case, it may make sense to give some fields package access. But inner classes are usually a better solution—you have seen examples in Chapter 9.

It is a common error to *forget* the keyword `private`, thereby opening up a potential security hole. For example, at the time of this writing, the `Window` class in the `java.awt` package contained the following declaration:

```
public class Window extends Container
{
   String warningString;
   . . .
}
```

The programmer was careless and didn't make the field private. There actually was no good reason to grant package access to the `warningString` field—no other class accesses it. It is a security risk. Packages are not closed entities—any programmer can make a new class, add it to the `java.awt` package, and gain access to the `warningString` fields of all `Window` objects! (Actually, this possibility bothered the Java implementors so much that recent versions of the virtual machine refuse to load unknown classes whose package name starts with "java.". Your own packages, however, do not enjoy this protection.)

Package access for fields is rarely useful, and most fields are given package access by accident because the programmer simply forgot the `private` keyword.

Methods should generally be `public` or `private`. We recommend avoiding the use of package-visible methods.

Classes and interfaces can have public or package access. Classes that are generally useful should have public access. Classes that are used for implementation reasons should have package access. You can hide them even better by turning them into inner classes; you saw examples of inner classes in Chapter 9. There are a few examples of public inner classes, such as the `Ellipse2D.Double` class that you saw in Chapter 2 (Section 2.13). However, in general, inner classes should not be public.

SELF CHECK

14. What is a common reason for defining package-visible instance fields?
15. If a class with a public constructor has package access, who can construct objects of it?

COMMON ERROR 10.4

Accidental Package Access

It is very easy to forget the `private` modifier for instance fields.

```
public class BankAccount
{
    . . .
    double balance; // Package access really intended?
}
```

Most likely, this was just an oversight. The programmer probably never intended to grant access to this field to other classes in the same package. The compiler won't complain, of course. Much later, some other programmer may take advantage of the access privilege, either out of convenience or out of evil intent. This is a serious problem, and you must get into the habit of scanning your field declarations for missing `private` modifiers.

COMMON ERROR 10.5

Making Inherited Methods Less Accessible

If a superclass declares a method to be publicly accessible, you cannot override it to be more private. For example,

```
public class BankAccount
{
    public void withdraw(double amount) { . . . }
    . . .
```

```
    }
    public class CheckingAccount extends BankAccount
    {
        private void withdraw(double amount) { . . . }
            // Error—subclass method cannot be more private
        . . .
    }
```

The compiler does not allow this, because the increased privacy would be an illusion. Anyone can still call the method through a superclass reference:

```
    BankAccount account = new CheckingAccount();
    account.withdraw(100000); // Calls CheckingAccount.withdraw
```

Because of polymorphism, the subclass method is called.

These errors are usually an oversight. If you forget the `public` modifier, your subclass method has package access, which is more restrictive. Simply restore the `public` modifier, and the error will go away.

ADVANCED TOPIC 10.3

Protected Access

We ran into a hurdle when trying to implement the `deposit` method of the `CheckingAccount` class. That method needed access to the `balance` instance field of the superclass. Our remedy was to use the appropriate method of the superclass to set the balance.

Java offers another solution to this problem. The superclass can declare an instance field as *protected:*

```
    public class BankAccount
    {
        . . .
        protected double balance;
    }
```

> Protected features can be accessed by all subclasses and all classes in the same package.

Protected data in an object can be accessed by the methods of the object's class and all its subclasses. For example, `CheckingAccount` inherits from `BankAccount`, so its methods can access the protected instance fields of the `BankAccount` class. Furthermore, protected data can be accessed by all methods of classes in the same package.

Some programmers like the `protected` access feature because it seems to strike a balance between absolute protection (making all fields private) and no protection at all (making all fields public). However, experience has shown that protected fields are subject to the same kinds of problems as public fields. The designer of the superclass has no control over the authors of subclasses. Any of the subclass methods can corrupt the superclass data. Furthermore, classes with protected fields are hard to modify. Even if the author of the superclass would like to change the data implementation, the protected fields cannot be changed, because someone somewhere out there might have written a subclass whose code depends on them.

In Java, protected fields have another drawback—they are accessible not just by subclasses, but also by other classes in the same package.

It is best to leave all data private. If you want to grant access to the data to subclass methods only, consider making the *accessor* method protected.

10.8 Object: The Cosmic Superclass

In Java, every class that is defined without an explicit extends clause automatically extends the class Object. That is, the class Object is the direct or indirect superclass of *every* class in Java (see Figure 8).

Of course, the methods of the Object class are very general. Here are the most useful ones:

Method	Purpose
String toString()	Returns a string representation of the object
boolean equals(Object otherObject)	Tests whether the object equals another object
Object clone()	Makes a full copy of an object

It is a good idea for you to override these methods in your classes.

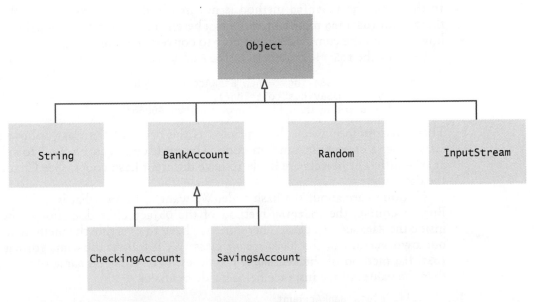

Figure 8 The Object Class Is the Superclass of Every Java Class

10.8.1 Overriding the toString Method

Define the toString
method to yield a string
that describes the object
state.

The toString method returns a string representation for each object.
It is used for debugging. For example,

```
Rectangle box = new Rectangle(5, 10, 20, 30);
String s = box.toString();
    // Sets s to "java.awt.Rectangle[x=5,y=10,width=20,height=30]"
```

In fact, this toString method is called whenever you concatenate a string with an
object. Consider the concatenation

```
"box=" + box;
```

On one side of the + concatenation operator is a string, but on the other side is an
object reference. The Java compiler automatically invokes the toString method to
turn the object into a string. Then both strings are concatenated. In this case, the
result is the string

```
"box=java.awt.Rectangle[x=5,y=10,width=20,height=30]"
```

The compiler can invoke the toString method, because it knows that *every* object
has a toString method: Every class extends the Object class, and that class defines
toString.

As you know, numbers are also converted to strings when they are concatenated
with other strings. For example,

```
int age = 18;
String s = "Harry's age is " + age;
    // Sets s to "Harry's age is 18"
```

In this case, the toString method is not involved. Numbers are not objects, and
there is no toString method for them. There is only a small set of primitive types,
however, and the compiler knows how to convert them to strings.

Let's try the toString method for the BankAccount class:

```
BankAccount momsSavings = new BankAccount(5000);
String s = momsSavings.toString();
    // Sets s to something like "BankAccount@d24606bf"
```

That's disappointing—all that's printed is the name of the class, followed by the
hash code, a seemingly random code. The hash code can be used to tell objects
apart—different objects are likely to have different hash codes. (See Chapter 16 for
the details.)

We don't care about the hash code. We want to know what is inside the object.
But, of course, the toString method of the Object class does not know what is
inside the BankAccount class. Therefore, we have to override the method and supply
our own version in the BankAccount class. We'll follow the same format that the
toString method of the Rectangle class uses: first print the name of the class, and
then the values of the instance fields inside brackets.

```
public class BankAccount
{
```

```
    . . .
    public String toString()
    {
        return "BankAccount[balance=" + balance + "]";
    }
}
```

This works better:

```
BankAccount momsSavings = new BankAccount(5000);
String s = momsSavings.toString();
    // Sets s to "BankAccount[balance=5000]"
```

PRODUCTIVITY HINT 10.1

Supply toString in All Classes

If you have a class whose toString() method returns a string that describes the object state, then you can simply call System.out.println(x) whenever you need to inspect the current state of an object x. This works because the println method of the PrintStream class invokes x.toString() when it needs to print an object, which is extremely helpful if there is an error in your program and the objects don't behave the way you think they should. You can simply insert a few print statements and peek inside the object state during the program run. Some debuggers can even invoke the toString method on objects that you inspect.

Sure, it is a bit more trouble to write a toString method when you aren't sure your program ever needs one—after all, it might work correctly on the first try. Then again, many programs don't work on the first try. As soon as you find out that yours doesn't, consider adding those toString methods to help you debug the program.

ADVANCED TOPIC 10.4

Inheritance and the toString Method

You just saw how to write a toString method: Form a string consisting of the class name and the names and values of the instance fields. However, if you want your toString method to be usable by subclasses of your class, you need to work a bit harder. Instead of hardcoding the class name, you should call the getClass method to obtain a *class* object, an object of the Class class that describes classes and their properties. Then invoke the getName method to get the name of the class:

```
public String toString()
{
    return getClass().getName() + "[balance="
        + balance + "]";
}
```

Then the toString method prints the correct class name when you apply it to a subclass, say a SavingsAccount.

```
SavingsAccount momsSavings = . . . ;
System.out.println(momsSavings);
// Prints "SavingsAccount[balance=10000]"
```

Of course, in the subclass, you should override toString and add the values of the subclass instance fields. Note that you must call super.toString to get the superclass field values—the subclass can't access them directly.

```
public class SavingsAccount extends BankAccount
{
    public String toString()
    {
        return super.toString() +
            "[interestRate=" + interestRate + "]";
    }
}
```

Now a savings account is converted to a string such as SavingsAccount[balance=10000][interestRate=5]. The brackets show which fields belong to the superclass.

10.8.2 Overriding the equals Method

Define the equals method to test whether two objects have equal state.

The equals method is called whenever you want to compare whether two objects have the same contents:

```
if (coin1.equals(coin2)) . . .
        // Contents are the same—see Figure 9
```

This is different from the test with the == operator, which tests whether the two references are to the *same object*:

```
if (coin1 == coin2) . . .
        // Objects are the same—see Figure 10
```

Figure 9   Two References to Equal Objects

Figure 10 Two References to the Same Object

Let us implement the equals method for the Coin class. You need to override the equals method of the Object class:

```
public class Coin
{
   . . .
   public boolean equals(Object otherObject)
   {
      . . .
   }
   . . .
}
```

Now you have a slight problem. The Object class knows nothing about coins, so it defines the otherObject parameter of the equals method to have the type Object. When redefining the method, you are not allowed to change the object signature. Cast the parameter to the class Coin:

```
Coin other = (Coin) otherObject;
```

Then you can compare the two coins.

```
public boolean equals(Object otherObject)
{
   Coin other = (Coin) otherObject;
   return name.equals(other.name)
         && value == other.value;
}
```

Note that you must use equals to compare object fields, but use == to compare number fields.

When you override the equals method, you should also override the hashCode method so that equal objects have the same hash code—see Chapter 16 for details.

SELF CHECK

16. Should the call x.equals(x) always return true?

17. Can you implement equals in terms of toString? Should you?

COMMON ERROR 10.6

Defining the equals Method with the Wrong Parameter Type

Consider the following, seemingly simpler, version of the equals method for the Coin class:

```java
public boolean equals(Coin other) // Don't do this!
{
    return name.equals(other.name) && value == other.value;
}
```

Here, the parameter of the equals method has the type Coin, not Object.

Unfortunately, this method *does not override* the equals method in the Object class. Instead, the Coin class now has two different equals methods:

```java
boolean equals(Coin other) // Defined in the Coin class
boolean equals(Object otherObject) // Inherited from the Object class
```

This is error-prone because the wrong equals method can be called. For example, consider these variable definitions:

```java
Coin aCoin = new Coin(0.25, "quarter");
Object anObject = new Coin(0.25, "quarter");
```

The call aCoin.equals(anObject) calls the second equals method, which returns false.

The remedy is to ensure that you use the Object type for the explicit parameter of the equals method.

ADVANCED TOPIC 10.5

Inheritance and the equals Method

You just saw how to write an equals method: Cast the otherObject parameter to the type of your class, and then compare the fields of the implicit parameter and the other parameter.

But what if someone called coin1.equals(x) where x wasn't a Coin object? Then the bad cast would generate an exception, and the program would die. Therefore, you first want to test whether otherObject really is an instance of the Coin class. The easiest test would be with the instanceof operator. However, that test is not specific enough. It would be possible for otherObject to belong to some subclass of Coin. To rule out that possibility, you should test whether the two objects belong to the *same class*. If not, return false.

```java
if (getClass() != otherObject.getClass()) return false;
```

Moreover, the Java language specification [1] demands that the equals method return false when otherObject is null.

Here is an improved version of the equals method that takes these two points into account:

```java
public boolean equals(Object otherObject)
{
    if (otherObject == null) return false;
    if (getClass() != otherObject.getClass())
        return false;

    Coin other = (Coin) otherObject;
    return name.equals(other.name) && value == other.value;
```

```
      }
```

When you define equals in a subclass, you should first call equals in the superclass, like this:

```
public CollectibleCoin extends Coin
{
   . . .

   public boolean equals(Object otherObject)
   {
      if (!super.equals(otherObject)) return false;

      CollectibleCoin other = (CollectibleCoin) otherObject;
      return year == other.year;
   }
   private int year;
}
```

10.8.3 The clone Method

You know that copying an object reference simply gives you two references to the same object:

```
BankAccount account = new BankAccount(1000);
BankAccount account2 = account;
account2.deposit(500);
   // Now both account and account2 refer to a bank account with a balance of 1500
```

> The clone method makes a new object with the same state as an existing object.

What can you do if you actually want to make a copy of an object? That is the purpose of the clone method. The clone method must return a *new* object that has an identical state to the existing object (see Figure 11).

Figure 11
Cloning Objects

Implementing the clone method is quite a bit more difficult than implementing the toString or equals methods—see Advanced Topic 10.6 for details.

Let us suppose that someone has implemented the clone method for the BankAccount class. Here is how to call it:

```
BankAccount clonedAccount = (BankAccount) account.clone();
```

The return type of the clone method is the class Object. When you call the method, you must use a cast to convince the compiler that account.clone() really has the same type as clonedAccount.

COMMON ERROR 10.7

Forgetting to Clone

In Java, object fields contain references to objects, not actual objects. This can be convenient for giving *two names to the same object:*

```
BankAccount harrysChecking = new BankAccount();
BankAccount slushFund = harrysChecking;
    // Use Harry's checking account for the slush fund
slushFund.deposit(80000)
    // A lot of money ends up in Harry's checking account
```

However, if you don't intend two references to refer to the same object, then this is a problem. In that case, you should use the clone method:

```
BankAccount slushFund = (BankAccount) harrysChecking.clone();
```

QUALITY TIP 10.1

Clone Mutable Instance Fields in Accessor Methods

Consider the following class:

```
public class Customer
{
    public Customer(String aName)
    {
        name = aName;
        account = new BankAccount();
    }

    public String getName()
    {
        return name;
    }

    public BankAccount getAccount();
    {
        return account;
```

```
      }

      private String name;
      private BankAccount account;
}
```

This class looks very boring and normal, but the getAccount method has a curious property. It *breaks encapsulation,* because anyone can modify the object state without going through the public interface:

```
Customer harry = new Customer("Harry Handsome");
BankAccount account = harry.getAccount();
   // Anyone can withdraw money!
account.withdraw(100000);
```

Maybe that wasn't what the designers of the class had in mind? Maybe they wanted class users only to inspect the account? In such a situation, you should *clone* the object reference:

```
public BankAccount getAccount();
{
    return (BankAccount) account.clone();
}
```

Do you also need to clone the getName method? No—that method returns a string, and strings are immutable. It is safe to give out a reference to an immutable object.

ADVANCED TOPIC 10.6

Implementing the clone Method

The Object.clone method is the starting point for the clone methods in your own classes. It creates a new object of the same type as the original object. It also automatically copies the instance fields from the original object to the cloned object. Here is a first attempt to implement the clone method for the BankAccount class:

```
public class BankAccount
{
    . . .
    public Object clone()
    {
       // Not complete
       Object clonedAccount = super.clone();
       return clonedAccount;
    }
}
```

However, this Object.clone method must be used with care. It only shifts the problem of cloning by one level; it does not completely solve it. Specifically, if an object contains a reference to another object, then the Object.clone method makes a copy of that object reference, not a clone of that object. The figure below shows how the Object.clone method works with a Customer object that has references to a String object and a BankAccount object. As you can see, the Object.clone method copies the references to the cloned Customer object and does not clone the objects to which they refer. Such a copy is called a *shallow copy*.

The `Object.clone` Method Makes a Shallow Copy

There is a reason why the `Object.clone` method does not systematically clone all sub-objects. In some situations, it is unnecessary. For example, if an object contains a reference to a string, there is no harm in copying the string reference, because Java string objects can never change their contents. The `Object.clone` method does the right thing if an object contains only numbers, Boolean values, and strings. But it must be used with caution when an object contains references to other objects.

For that reason, there are two safeguards built into the `Object.clone` method to ensure that it is not used accidentally. First, the method is declared `protected` (see Advanced Topic 10.3). This prevents you from accidentally calling `x.clone()` if the class to which x belongs hasn't redefined `clone` to be public.

As a second precaution, `Object.clone` checks that the object being cloned implements the `Cloneable` interface. If not, it throws an exception. The `Object.clone` method looks like this:

```
public class Object
{
   protected Object clone()
         throws CloneNotSupportedException
   {
      if (this instanceof Cloneable)
      {
         // Copy the instance fields
         . . .
      }
      else
         throw new CloneNotSupportedException();
   }
}
```

Unfortunately, all that safeguarding means that the legitimate callers of `Object.clone()` pay a price—they must catch that exception *even if their class implements* `Cloneable`.

```
public class BankAccount implements Cloneable
{
```

```
    . . .
    public Object clone()
    {
       try
       {
          return super.clone();
       }
       catch (CloneNotSupportedException e)
       {
          // Can't happen because we implement Cloneable but we still must catch it.
          return null;
       }
    }
}
```

If an object contains a reference to another mutable object, then you must call clone for that reference. For example, suppose the Customer class has an instance field of class Bank-Account. You can implement Customer.clone as follows:

```
public class Customer implements Cloneable
{
    . . .
    public Object clone()
    {
       try
       {
          Customer cloned = (Customer) super.clone();
          cloned.account = (BankAccount) account.clone();
          return cloned;
       }
       catch(CloneNotSupportedException e)
       {
          // Can't happen because we implement Cloneable
          return null;
       }
    }

    private String name;
    private BankAccount account;
}
```

ADVANCED TOPIC 10.7

Enumerated Types Revisited

In Advanced Topic 5.3, we introduced the concept of an enumerated type: a type with a finite number of values. An example is

```
public enum FilingStatus { SINGLE, MARRIED }
```

In Java, enumerated types are classes with special properties. They have a finite number of instances, namely the objects defined inside the braces. For example, there are exactly two objects of the FilingStatus class: FilingStatus.SINGLE and FilingStatus.MARRIED. Since FilingStatus has no public constructor, it is impossible to construct additional objects.

Enumeration classes extend the Enum class, from which they inherit toString and clone methods. The toString method returns a string that equals the object's name. For example, FilingStatus.SINGLE.toString() returns "SINGLE". The clone method returns the given object *without making a copy*. After all, it should not be possible to generate new objects of an enumeration class.

The Enum class inherits the equals method from its superclass, Object. Thus, two enumeration constants are only considered equal when they are identical.

You can add your own methods and constructors to an enumeration class, for example

```
public enum CoinType
{
    PENNY(0.01), NICKEL(0.05), DIME(0.1), QUARTER(0.25);
    CoinType(double aValue) { value = aValue; }
    public double getValue() { return value; }
    private double value;
}
```

This CoinType class has exactly four instances: CoinType.PENNY, CoinType.NICKEL, CoinType.DIME, and CoinType.QUARTER. If you have one of these four CoinType objects, you can apply the getValue method to obtain the coin's value.

Note that there is a major philosophical difference between this CoinType class and the Coin class that we have discussed elsewhere in this chapter. A Coin object represents a particular coin. You can construct as many Coin objects as you like. Different Coin objects can be equal to another. We consider two Coin objects equal when their names and values match. However, CoinType describes a type of coins, not an individual coin. The four CoinType objects are distinct from each other.

RANDOM FACT 10.1

Scripting Languages

Suppose you work for an office where you must help with the bookkeeping. Suppose that every sales person sends in a weekly spreadsheet with sales figures. One of your jobs is to copy and paste the individual figures into a master spreadsheet and then copy and paste the totals into a word processor document that gets e-mailed to several managers. This kind of repetitive work can be intensely boring. Can you automate it?

It would be a real challenge to write a Java program that can help you—you'd have to know how to read a spreadsheet file, how to format a word processor document, and how to send e-mail.

Fortunately, many office software packages include *scripting languages*. These are programming languages that are integrated with the software for the purpose of automating repetitive tasks. The best-known of these scripting languages is Visual Basic Script, which is a part of the Microsoft Office suite. The Macintosh operating system has a language called AppleScript for the same purpose.

In addition, scripting languages are available for many other purposes. JavaScript is used for web pages. (There is no relationship between Java and JavaScript—the name JavaScript was chosen for marketing reasons.) Tcl (short for "tool control language" and pronounced

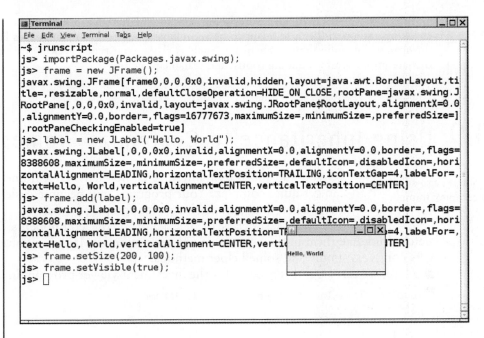

Scripting Java Classes with JavaScript

"tickle") is an open source scripting language that has been ported to many platforms and is often used for scripting software test procedures. Shell scripts are used for automating software configuration, backup procedures, and other system administration tasks.

Scripting languages have two features that makes them easier to use than full-fledged programming languages such as Java. First, they are *interpreted.* The interpreter program reads each line of program code and executes it immediately without compiling it first. That makes experimenting much more fun—you get immediate feedback. Also, scripting languages are usually *loosely typed,* meaning you don't have to declare the types of variables. Every variable can hold values of any type. For example, the Scripting Java Classes with JavaScript figure shows a scripting session with the JavaScript implementation that is included in Java 6. This version of JavaScript allows you to manipulate Java objects. The script stores frame and label objects in variables that are declared without types. It then calls methods that are executed immediately, without compilation. The frame pops up as soon as the line with the set-Visible command is entered. (If you use an earlier version of Java, you can achieve the same effect with the Rhino scripting engine. You can download Rhino from the Mozilla web site [2]). In recent years, authors of computer viruses have discovered how scripting languages simplify their lives. The famous "love bug" is a Visual Basic Script program that is sent as an attachment to an e-mail. The e-mail has an enticing subject line "I love you" and asks the recipient to click on an attachment masquerading as a love letter. In fact, the attachment is a script file that is executed when the user clicks on it. The script creates some damage on the recipient's computer and then, through the power of the scripting language, uses the Outlook e-mail client to mail itself to all addresses found in the address book. Try programming that in Java! By the way, the person suspected of authoring that virus was a student who had submitted a proposal to write a thesis researching how to write such programs. Perhaps not surprisingly, the proposal was rejected by the faculty.

> Why do we still need Java if scripting is easy and fun? Scripts often have poor error checking and are difficult to adapt to new circumstances. Scripting languages lack many of the structuring and safety mechanisms (such as classes and type checking by the compiler) that are important for building robust and scalable programs.

10.9 Using Inheritance to Customize Frames

Define a JFrame subclass for a complex frame.

As you add more user interface components to a frame, the frame can get quite complex. Your programs will become easier to understand when you use inheritance for complex frames.

Design a subclass of JFrame. Store the components as instance fields. Initialize them in the constructor of your subclass. If the initialization code gets complex, simply add some helper methods.

Here, we carry out this process for the investment viewer program in Chapter 9.

```java
public class InvestmentFrame extends JFrame
{
   public InvestmentFrame()
   {
      account = new BankAccount(INITIAL_BALANCE);

      // Use instance fields for components
      label = new JLabel("balance: " + account.getBalance());

      // Use helper methods
      createButton();
      createPanel();

      setSize(FRAME_WIDTH, FRAME_HEIGHT);
   }

   private void createButton()
   {
      ActionListener listener = new AddInterestListener();
      button.addActionListener(listener);
      button = new JButton("Add Interest");
   }

   private void createPanel()
   {
      panel = new JPanel();
      panel.add(button);
      panel.add(label);
      add(panel);
   }

   private JButton button;
   private JLabel label;
   private JPanel panel;
   private BankAccount account;
```

```
   }
```

This approach differs from the programs in Chapter 9. In those programs, we simply configured the frame in the main method of a viewer class.

It is a bit more work to provide a separate class for the frame. However, the frame class makes it easier to organize the code that constructs the user-interface elements. We will use this approach for all examples in this chapter.

Of course, we still need a class with a main method:

```java
public class InvestmentViewer2
{
   public static void main(String[] args)
   {
      JFrame frame = new InvestmentFrame();
      frame.setDefaultCloseOperation(JFrame.EXIT_ON_CLOSE);
      frame.setVisible(true);
   }
}
```

SELF CHECK

18. How many Java source files are required by the investment viewer application when we use inheritance to define the frame class?

19. Why does the InvestmentFrame constructor call setSize(FRAME_WIDTH, FRAME_HEIGHT), whereas the main method of the investment viewer class in Chapter 9 called frame.setSize(FRAME_WIDTH, FRAME_HEIGHT)?

ADVANCED TOPIC 10.8

Adding the main Method to the Frame Class

Have another look at the InvestmentFrame and InvestmentViewer2 classes. Some programmers prefer to combine these two classes, by adding the main method to the frame class:

```java
public class InvestmentFrame extends JFrame
{
   public static void main(String[] args)
   {
      JFrame frame = new InvestmentFrame();
      frame.setDefaultCloseOperation(JFrame.EXIT_ON_CLOSE);
      frame.setVisible(true);
   }

   public InvestmentFrame()
   {
      account = new BankAccount(INITIAL_BALANCE);

      // Use instance fields for components
      label = new JLabel("balance: " + account.getBalance());
```

```
        // Use helper methods
        createButton();
        createPanel();

        setSize(FRAME_WIDTH, FRAME_HEIGHT);
    }
    . . .
}
```

This is a convenient shortcut that you will find in many programs, but it does muddle the responsibilities between the frame class and the program. Therefore, we do not use this approach in this book.

10.10 Processing Text Input

A graphical application can receive text input by calling the showInputDialog method of the JOptionPane class, but popping up a separate dialog box for each input is not a natural user interface. Most graphical programs collect text input through *text fields* (see Figure 12). In this section, you will learn how to add text fields to a graphical application, and how to read what the user types into them.

> Use JTextField components to provide space for user input. Place a JLabel next to each text field.

The JTextField class provides a text field. When you construct a text field, you need to supply the width—the approximate number of characters that you expect the user to type.

```
final int FIELD_WIDTH = 10;
final JTextField rateField = new JTextField(FIELD_WIDTH);
```

Users can type additional characters, but then a part of the contents of the field becomes invisible.

You will want to label each text field so that the user knows what to type into it. Construct a JLabel object for each label:

```
JLabel rateLabel = new JLabel("Interest Rate: ");
```

You want to give the user an opportunity to enter all information into the text fields before processing it. Therefore, you should supply a button that the user can press to indicate that the input is ready for processing.

When that button is clicked, its actionPerformed method reads the user input from the text fields, using the getText method of the JTextField class. The getText

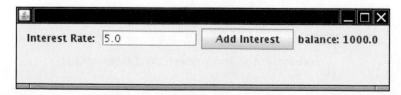

Figure 12   An Application with a Text Field

method returns a String object. In our sample program, we turn the string into a number, using the Double.parseDouble method:

```
class AddInterestListener implements ActionListener
{
   public void actionPerformed(ActionEvent event)
   {
      double rate = Double.parseDouble(rateField.getText());
      . . .
   }
}
```

The following application is a useful prototype for a graphical user-interface front end for arbitrary calculations. You can easily modify it for your own needs. Place other input components into the frame. Change the contents of the actionPerformed method to carry out other calculations. Display the result in a label.

ch10/textfield/InvestmentViewer3.java

```
1  import javax.swing.JFrame;
2
3  /**
4     This program displays the growth of an investment.
5  */
6  public class InvestmentViewer3
7  {
8     public static void main(String[] args)
9     {
10        JFrame frame = new InvestmentFrame();
11        frame.setDefaultCloseOperation(JFrame.EXIT_ON_CLOSE);
12        frame.setVisible(true);
13     }
14  }
```

ch10/textfield/InvestmentFrame.java

```
1  import java.awt.event.ActionEvent;
2  import java.awt.event.ActionListener;
3  import javax.swing.JButton;
4  import javax.swing.JFrame;
5  import javax.swing.JLabel;
6  import javax.swing.JPanel;
7  import javax.swing.JTextField;
8
9  /**
10     A frame that shows the growth of an investment with variable interest.
11  */
12  public class InvestmentFrame extends JFrame
13  {
14     public InvestmentFrame()
15     {
16        account = new BankAccount(INITIAL_BALANCE);
17
18        // Use instance fields for components
19        resultLabel = new JLabel("balance: " + account.getBalance());
```

```
20
21          // Use helper methods
22          createTextField();
23          createButton();
24          createPanel();
25
26          setSize(FRAME_WIDTH, FRAME_HEIGHT);
27       }
28
29       private void createTextField()
30       {
31          rateLabel = new JLabel("Interest Rate: ");
32
33          final int FIELD_WIDTH = 10;
34          rateField = new JTextField(FIELD_WIDTH);
35          rateField.setText("" + DEFAULT_RATE);
36       }
37
38       private void createButton()
39       {
40          button = new JButton("Add Interest");
41
42          class AddInterestListener implements ActionListener
43          {
44             public void actionPerformed(ActionEvent event)
45             {
46                double rate = Double.parseDouble(
47                     rateField.getText());
48                double interest = account.getBalance()
49                     * rate / 100;
50                account.deposit(interest);
51                resultLabel.setText(
52                     "balance: " + account.getBalance());
53             }
54          }
55
56          ActionListener listener = new AddInterestListener();
57          button.addActionListener(listener);
58       }
59
60       private void createPanel()
61       {
62          panel = new JPanel();
63          panel.add(rateLabel);
64          panel.add(rateField);
65          panel.add(button);
66          panel.add(resultLabel);
67          add(panel);
68       }
69
70       private JLabel rateLabel;
71       private JTextField rateField;
72       private JButton button;
73       private JLabel resultLabel;
```

```
74      private JPanel panel;
75      private BankAccount account;
76
77      private static final int FRAME_WIDTH = 500;
78      private static final int FRAME_HEIGHT = 200;
79
80      private static final double DEFAULT_RATE = 5;
81      private static final double INITIAL_BALANCE = 1000;
82 }
```

SELF CHECK

20. What happens if you omit the first JLabel object?

21. If a text field holds an integer, what expression do you use to read its contents?

10.11 Text Areas

> Use a JTextArea to show multiple lines of text.

In Section 10.10, you saw how to construct text fields. A text field holds a single line of text. To display multiple lines of text, use the JTextArea class.

When constructing a text area, you can specify the number of rows and columns:

```
final int ROWS = 10;
final int COLUMNS = 30;
JTextArea textArea = new JTextArea(ROWS, COLUMNS);
```

Use the setText method to set the text of a text field or text area. The append method adds text to the end of a text area. Use newline characters to separate lines, like this:

```
textArea.append(account.getBalance() + "\n");
```

If you want to use a text field or text area for display purposes only, call the setEditable method like this

```
textArea.setEditable(false);
```

Now the user can no longer edit the contents of the field, but your program can still call setText and append to change it.

As shown in Figure 4, the JTextField and JTextArea classes are subclasses of the class JTextComponent. The methods setText and setEditable are defined in the JTextComponent class and inherited by JTextField and JTextArea. However, the append method is defined in the JTextArea class.

> You can add scroll bars to any component with a JScrollPane.

To add scroll bars to a text area, use a JScrollPane, like this:

```
JTextArea textArea = new JTextArea(ROWS, COLUMNS);
JScrollPane scrollPane = new JScrollPane(textArea);
```

Then add the scroll pane to the panel. Figure 13 shows the result.

The following sample program puts these concepts together. A user can enter numbers into the interest rate text field and then click on the "Add Interest" button).

Figure 13   The Investment Application with a Text Area

The interest rate is applied, and the updated balance is appended to the text area. The text area has scroll bars and is not editable.

This program is similar to the previous investment viewer program, but it keeps track of all the bank balances, not just the last one.

ch10/textarea/InvestmentFrame.java

```java
1   import java.awt.event.ActionEvent;
2   import java.awt.event.ActionListener;
3   import javax.swing.JButton;
4   import javax.swing.JFrame;
5   import javax.swing.JLabel;
6   import javax.swing.JPanel;
7   import javax.swing.JScrollPane;
8   import javax.swing.JTextArea;
9   import javax.swing.JTextField;
10
11  /**
12      A frame that shows the growth of an investment with variable interest.
13  */
14  public class InvestmentFrame extends JFrame
15  {
16     public InvestmentFrame()
17     {
18        account = new BankAccount(INITIAL_BALANCE);
19        resultArea = new JTextArea(AREA_ROWS, AREA_COLUMNS);
20        resultArea.setEditable(false);
21
22        // Use helper methods
23        createTextField();
24        createButton();
25        createPanel();
26
27        setSize(FRAME_WIDTH, FRAME_HEIGHT);
28     }
29
30     private void createTextField()
31     {
32        rateLabel = new JLabel("Interest Rate: ");
33
```

```
34              final int FIELD_WIDTH = 10;
35              rateField = new JTextField(FIELD_WIDTH);
36              rateField.setText("" + DEFAULT_RATE);
37          }
38
39      private void createButton()
40      {
41          button = new JButton("Add Interest");
42
43          class AddInterestListener implements ActionListener
44          {
45              public void actionPerformed(ActionEvent event)
46              {
47                  double rate = Double.parseDouble(
48                      rateField.getText());
49                  double interest = account.getBalance()
50                      * rate / 100;
51                  account.deposit(interest);
52                  resultArea.append(account.getBalance() + "\n");
53              }
54          }
55
56          ActionListener listener = new AddInterestListener();
57          button.addActionListener(listener);
58      }
59
60      private void createPanel()
61      {
62          panel = new JPanel();
63          panel.add(rateLabel);
64          panel.add(rateField);
65          panel.add(button);
66          JScrollPane scrollPane = new JScrollPane(resultArea);
67          panel.add(scrollPane);
68          add(panel);
69      }
70
71      private JLabel rateLabel;
72      private JTextField rateField;
73      private JButton button;
74      private JTextArea resultArea;
75      private JPanel panel;
76      private BankAccount account;
77
78      private static final int FRAME_WIDTH = 400;
79      private static final int FRAME_HEIGHT = 250;
80
81      private static final int AREA_ROWS = 10;
82      private static final int AREA_COLUMNS = 30;
83
84      private static final double DEFAULT_RATE = 5;
85      private static final double INITIAL_BALANCE = 1000;
86  }
```

22. What is the difference between a text field and a text area?

23. Why did the InvestmentFrame program call resultArea.setEditable(false)?

24. How would you modify the InvestmentFrame program if you didn't want to use scroll bars?

How To 10.1

Implementing a Graphical User Interface (GUI)

A GUI program allows users to supply inputs and specify actions. The InvestmentViewer3 program has only one input and one action. More sophisticated programs have more interesting user interactions, but the basic principles are the same.

Step 1　Enumerate the actions that your program needs to carry out.

For example, the investment viewer has a single action, to add interest. Other programs may have different actions, perhaps for making deposits, inserting coins, and so on.

Step 2　For each action, enumerate the inputs that you need.

For example, the investment viewer has a single input: the interest rate. Other programs may have different inputs, such as amounts of money, product quantities, and so on.

Step 3　For each action, enumerate the outputs that you need to show.

The investment viewer has a single output: the current balance. Other programs may show different quantities, messages, and so on.

Step 4　Supply the user interface components.

Right now, you need to use buttons for actions, text fields for inputs, and labels for outputs. In Chapter 18, you will see many more user-interface components that can be used for actions and inputs. In Chapter 3, you learned how to implement your own components to produce graphical output, such as charts or drawings.

　　Add the required buttons, text fields, and other components to a frame. In this chapter, you have seen how to lay out very simple user interfaces, by adding all components to a single panel and adding the panel to the frame. Chapter 18 shows you how you can achieve more complex layouts.

Step 5　Supply event handler classes.

For each button, you need to add an object of a listener class. The listener classes must implement the ActionListener interface. Supply a class for each action (or group of related actions), and put the instructions for the action in the actionPerformed method.

```
class Button1Listener implements ActionListener
{
   public void actionPerformed(ActionEvent event)
   {
      // button1 action goes here
      . . .
   }
}
```

Remember to declare any local variables accessed by the listener methods as final.

Step 6   Make listener objects and attach them to the event sources.

For action events, the event source is a button or other user-interface component, or a timer. You need to add a listener object to each event source, like this:

```
ActionListener listener1 = new Button1Listener();
button1.addActionListener(listener1);
```

COMMON ERROR 10.8

By Default, Components Have Zero Width and Height

The sample GUI programs of this chapter display results in a label or text area. Sometimes, you want to use a graphical component such as a chart. You add the chart component to the panel:

```
panel.add(textField);
panel.add(button);
panel.add(chartComponent);
```

However, the default size for a component is 0 by 0 pixels, and the chart component will not be visible. The remedy is to call the setPreferredSize method, like this:

```
chartComponent.setPreferredSize(new Dimension(CHART_WIDTH, CHART_HEIGHT));
```

GUI components such as buttons and text fields know how to compute their preferred size, but you must set the preferred size of components on which you paint.

PRODUCTIVITY HINT 10.2

Code Reuse

Suppose you are given the task of writing another graphical user-interface program that reads input from a couple of text fields and displays the result of some calculations in a label or text area. You don't have to start from scratch. Instead, you can—and often should—*reuse* the outline of an existing program, such as the foregoing InvestmentFrame class.

To reuse program code, simply make a copy of a program file and give the copy a new name. For example, you may want to copy InvestmentFrame.java to a file TaxReturn-Frame.java. Then remove the code that is clearly specific to the old problem, but leave the outline in place. That is, keep the panel, text field, event listener, and so on. Fill in the code for your new calculations. Finally, rename classes, buttons, frame titles, and so on.

Once you understand the principles behind event listeners, frames, and panels, there is no need to rethink them every time. Reusing the structure of a working program makes your work more efficient.

However, reuse by "copy and rename" is still a mechanical and somewhat error-prone approach. It is even better to package reusable program structures into a set of common classes. The inheritance mechanism lets you design classes for reuse without copy and paste.

CHAPTER SUMMARY

1. Inheritance is a mechanism for extending existing classes by adding methods and fields.

2. The more general class is called a superclass. The more specialized class that inherits from the superclass is called the subclass.

3. Every class extends the `Object` class either directly or indirectly.

4. Inheriting from a class differs from implementing an interface: The subclass inherits behavior and state from the superclass.

5. One advantage of inheritance is code reuse.

6. When defining a subclass, you specify added instance fields, added methods, and changed or overridden methods.

7. Sets of classes can form complex inheritance hierarchies.

8. A subclass has no access to private fields of its superclass.

9. Use the `super` keyword to call a method of the superclass.

10. To call the superclass constructor, you use the `super` keyword in the first statement of the subclass constructor.

11. Subclass references can be converted to superclass references.

12. The `instanceof` operator tests whether an object belongs to a particular type.

13. An abstract method is a method whose implementation is not specified.

14. An abstract class is a class that cannot be instantiated.

15. A field or method that is not declared as `public`, `private`, or `protected` can be accessed by all classes in the same package, which is usually not desirable.

16. Protected features can be accessed by all subclasses and all classes in the same package.

17. Define the `toString` method to yield a string that describes the object state.

18. Define the `equals` method to test whether two objects have equal state.

19. The `clone` method makes a new object with the same state as an existing object.

20. Define a `JFrame` subclass for a complex frame.

21. Use `JTextField` components to provide space for user input. Place a `JLabel` next to each text field.

22. Use a `JTextArea` to show multiple lines of text.

23. You can add scroll bars to any component with a `JScrollPane`.

FURTHER READING

1. James Gosling, Bill Joy, Guy Steele, and Gilad Bracha, *The Java Language Specification*, 3rd edition, Addison-Wesley, 2005.

2. `http://www.mozilla.org/rhino`   The Rhino interpreter for the JavaScript language.

CLASSES, OBJECTS, AND METHODS INTRODUCED IN THIS CHAPTER

```
java.awt.Component
    setPreferredSize
java.awt.Dimension
java.lang.Cloneable
java.lang.CloneNotSupportedException
java.lang.Object
    clone
    toString
javax.swing.JTextArea
    append
javax.swing.JTextField
javax.swing.text.JTextComponent
    getText
    isEditable
    setEditable
    setText
```

REVIEW EXERCISES

★ **Exercise R10.1.** What is the balance of b after the following operations?

```
SavingsAccount b = new SavingsAccount(10);
b.deposit(5000);
b.withdraw(b.getBalance() / 2);
b.addInterest();
```

★ **Exercise R10.2.** Describe all constructors of the SavingsAccount class. List all methods that are inherited from the BankAccount class. List all methods that are added to the SavingsAccount class.

★★ **Exercise R10.3.** Can you convert a superclass reference into a subclass reference? A subclass reference into a superclass reference? If so, give examples. If not, explain why not.

★★ **Exercise R10.4.** Identify the superclass and the subclass in each of the following pairs of classes.

    a. Employee, Manager

    b. Polygon, Triangle

    c. GraduateStudent, Student

    d. Person, Student

    e. Employee, GraduateStudent

    f. BankAccount, CheckingAccount

    g. Vehicle, Car

    h. Vehicle, Minivan

    i. Car, Minivan

    j. Truck, Vehicle

★ **Exercise R10.5.** Suppose the class Sub extends the class Sandwich. Which of the following assignments are legal?

```
Sandwich x = new Sandwich();
Sub y = new Sub();
```

    a. x = y;   **c.** y = new Sandwich();

    b. y = x;   **d.** x = new Sub();

★ **Exercise R10.6.** Draw an inheritance diagram that shows the inheritance relationships between the classes:

    • Person   • Instructor

    • Employee   • Classroom

    • Student   • Object

★★ **Exercise R10.7.** In an object-oriented traffic simulation system, we have the following classes:

    • Vehicle   • PickupTruck

    • Car   • SportUtilityVehicle

    • Truck   • Minivan

    • Sedan   • Bicycle

    • Coupe   • Motorcycle

Draw an inheritance diagram that shows the relationships between these classes.

★★ **Exercise R10.8.** What inheritance relationships would you establish among the following classes?

    • Student

    • Professor

    • TeachingAssistant

    • Employee

- Secretary
- DepartmentChair
- Janitor
- SeminarSpeaker
- Person
- Course
- Seminar
- Lecture
- ComputerLab

★★★ **Exercise R10.9.** Which of these conditions returns true? Check the Java documentation for the inheritance patterns.

a. `Rectangle r = new Rectangle(5, 10, 20, 30);`

b. `if (r instanceof Rectangle) . . .`

c. `if (r instanceof Point) . . .`

d. `if (r instanceof Rectangle2D.Double) . . .`

e. `if (r instanceof RectangularShape) . . .`

f. `if (r instanceof Object) . . .`

g. `if (r instanceof Shape) . . .`

★★ **Exercise R10.10.** Explain the two meanings of the super keyword. Explain the two meanings of the this keyword. How are they related?

★★★ **Exercise R10.11.** (Tricky.) Consider the two calls

```
public class D extends B
{
    public void f()
    {
        this.g(); // 1
    }
    public void g()
    {
        super.g(); // 2
    }
    . . .
}
```

Which of them is an example of polymorphism?

★★★ **Exercise R10.12.** Consider this program:

```
public class AccountPrinter
{
    public static void main(String[] args)
    {
        SavingsAccount momsSavings
            = new SavingsAccount(0.5);
```

```
            CheckingAccount harrysChecking
                = new CheckingAccount(0);

            . . .
            endOfMonth(momsSavings);
            endOfMonth(harrysChecking);
            printBalance(momsSavings);
            printBalance(harrysChecking);
        }

        public static void endOfMonth(SavingsAccount savings)
        {
            savings.addInterest();
        }

        public static void endOfMonth(CheckingAccount checking)
        {
            checking.deductFees();
        }

        public static void printBalance(BankAccount account)
        {
            System.out.println("The balance is $"
                + account.getBalance());
        }
    }
```

Are the calls to the endOfMonth methods resolved by early binding or late binding? Inside the printBalance method, is the call to getBalance resolved by early binding or late binding?

★ **Exercise R10.13.** Explain the terms *shallow copy* and *deep copy*.

★ **Exercise R10.14.** What access attribute should instance fields have? What access attribute should static fields have? How about static final fields?

★ **Exercise R10.15.** What access attribute should instance methods have? Does the same hold for static methods?

★★ **Exercise R10.16.** The fields System.in and System.out are static public fields. Is it possible to overwrite them? If so, how?

★★ **Exercise R10.17.** Why are public fields dangerous? Are public static fields more dangerous than public instance fields?

★G **Exercise R10.18.** What is the difference between a label, a text field, and a text area?

★★G **Exercise R10.19.** Name a method that is defined in JTextArea, a method that JTextArea inherits from JTextComponent, and a method that JTextArea inherits from JComponent.

Additional review exercises are available in WileyPLUS.

PROGRAMMING EXERCISES

★ **Exercise P10.1.** Enhance the addInterest method of the SavingsAccount class to compute the interest on the *minimum* balance since the last call to addInterest. *Hint:* You need to modify the withdraw method as well, and you need to add an instance field to remember the minimum balance.

★★ **Exercise P10.2.** Add a TimeDepositAccount class to the bank account hierarchy. The time deposit account is just like a savings account, but you promise to leave the money in the account for a particular number of months, and there is a penalty for early withdrawal. Construct the account with the interest rate and the number of months to maturity. In the addInterest method, decrement the count of months. If the count is positive during a withdrawal, charge the withdrawal penalty.

★ **Exercise P10.3.** Implement a subclass Square that extends the Rectangle class. In the constructor, accept the *x*- and *y*-positions of the *center* and the side length of the square. Call the setLocation and setSize methods of the Rectangle class. Look up these methods in the documentation for the Rectangle class. Also supply a method getArea that computes and returns the area of the square. Write a sample program that asks for the center and side length, then prints out the square (using the toString method that you inherit from Rectangle) and the area of the square.

★ **Exercise P10.4.** Implement a superclass Person. Make two classes, Student and Instructor, that inherit from Person. A person has a name and a year of birth. A student has a major, and an instructor has a salary. Write the class definitions, the constructors, and the methods toString for all classes. Supply a test program that tests these classes and methods.

★★ **Exercise P10.5.** Make a class Employee with a name and salary. Make a class Manager inherit from Employee. Add an instance field, named department, of type String. Supply a method toString that prints the manager's name, department, and salary. Make a class Executive inherit from Manager. Supply appropriate toString methods for all classes. Supply a test program that tests these classes and methods.

★ **Exercise P10.6.** Write a superclass Worker and subclasses HourlyWorker and SalariedWorker. Every worker has a name and a salary rate. Write a method computePay(int hours) that computes the weekly pay for every worker. An hourly worker gets paid the hourly wage for the actual number of hours worked, if hours is at most 40. If the hourly worker worked more than 40 hours, the excess is paid at time and a half. The salaried worker gets paid the hourly wage for 40 hours, no matter what the actual number of hours is. Supply a test program that uses polymorphism to test these classes and methods.

★★★ **Exercise P10.7.** Reorganize the bank account classes as follows. In the BankAccount class, introduce an abstract method endOfMonth with no implementation. Rename the addInterest and deductFees methods into endOfMonth in the subclasses. Which classes are now abstract and which are concrete? Write a static method void test(BankAccount account) that makes five transactions and then calls endOfMonth. Test it with instances of all concrete account classes.

★★★G Exercise P10.8. Implement an abstract class Vehicle and concrete subclasses Car and Truck. A vehicle has a position on the screen. Write methods draw that draw cars and trucks as follows:

Car   Truck

Then write a method randomVehicle that randomly generates Vehicle references, with an equal probability for constructing cars and trucks, with random positions. Call it 10 times and draw all of them.

★G Exercise P10.9. Write a graphical application front end for a bank account class. Supply text fields and buttons for depositing and withdrawing money, and for displaying the current balance in a label.

★G Exercise P10.10. Write a graphical application front end for an Earthquake class. Supply a text field and button for entering the strength of the earthquake. Display the earthquake description in a label.

★G Exercise P10.11. Write a graphical application front end for a DataSet class. Supply text fields and buttons for adding floating-point values, and display the current minimum, maximum, and average in a label.

★G Exercise P10.12. Write an application with three labeled text fields, one each for the initial amount of a savings account, the annual interest rate, and the number of years. Add a button "Calculate" and a read-only text area to display the result, namely, the balance of the savings account after the end of each year.

★★G Exercise P10.13. In the application from Exercise P10.12, replace the text area with a bar chart that shows the balance after the end of each year.

★★★G Exercise P10.14. Write a program that contains a text field, a button "Add Value", and a component that draws a bar chart of the numbers that a user typed into the text field.

★★G Exercise P10.15. Write a program that prompts the user for an integer and then draws as many rectangles at random positions in a component as the user requested.

★G Exercise P10.16. Write a program that prompts the user to enter the x- and y-positions of the center and a radius. When the user clicks a "Draw" button, draw a circle with that center and radius in a component.

★★G Exercise P10.17. Write a program that allows the user to specify a circle by typing the radius in a text field and then clicking on the center. Note that you don't need a "Draw" button.

★★★G Exercise P10.18. Write a program that allows the user to specify a circle with two mouse presses, the first one on the center and the second on a point on the periphery. *Hint:* In the mouse press handler, you must keep track of whether you already received the center point in a previous mouse press.

★★★G **Exercise P10.19.** Write a program that draws a clock face with a time that the user enters in two text fields (one for the hours, one for the minutes).

Hint: You need to determine the angles of the hour hand and the minute hand. The angle of the minute hand is easy: The minute hand travels 360 degrees in 60 minutes. The angle of the hour hand is harder; it travels 360 degrees in 12 × 60 *minutes*.

★★G **Exercise P10.20.** Write a program that asks the user to enter an integer n, and then draws an n-by-n grid.

Additional programming exercises are available in WileyPLUS.

PROGRAMMING PROJECTS

★★★ **Project 10.1.** Your task is to program robots with varying behaviors. The robots try to escape a maze, such as the following:

A robot has a position and a method void move(Maze m) that modifies the position. Provide a common superclass Robot whose move method does nothing. Provide subclasses RandomRobot, RightHandRuleRobot, and MemoryRobot. Each of these robots has a different strategy for escaping. The RandomRobot simply makes random moves. The RightHandRuleRobot moves around the maze so that it's right hand always touches a wall. The MemoryRobot remembers all positions that it has previously occupied and never goes back to a position that it knows to be a dead end.

★★★ **Project 10.2.** Implement the toString, equals, and clone methods for all subclasses of the BankAccount class, as well as the Bank class of Chapter 7. Write unit tests that verify that your methods work correctly. Be sure to test a Bank that holds objects from a mixture of account classes.

ANSWERS TO SELF-CHECK QUESTIONS

1. Two instance fields: `balance` and `interestRate`.
2. `deposit`, `withdraw`, `getBalance`, and `addInterest`.
3. `Manager` is the subclass; `Employee` is the superclass.
4. To express the common behavior of text fields and text components.
5. We need a counter that counts the number of withdrawals and deposits.
6. It needs to reduce the balance, and it cannot access the `balance` field directly.
7. So that the count can reflect the number of transactions for the following month.
8. It was content to use the default constructor of the superclass, which sets the balance to zero.
9. No—this is a requirement only for constructors. For example, the `Checking-Account.deposit` method first increments the transaction count, then calls the superclass method.
10. We want to use the method for all kinds of bank accounts. Had we used a parameter of type `SavingsAccount`, we couldn't have called the method with a `CheckingAccount` object.
11. We cannot invoke the `deposit` method on a variable of type `Object`.
12. The object is an instance of `BankAccount` or one of its subclasses.
13. The balance of a is unchanged, and the transaction count is incremented twice.
14. Accidentally forgetting the `private` modifer.
15. Any methods of classes in the same package.
16. It certainly should—unless, of course, x is `null`.
17. If `toString` returns a string that describes all instance fields, you can simply call `toString` on the implicit and explicit parameters, and compare the results. However, comparing the fields is more efficient than converting them into strings.
18. Three: `InvestmentFrameViewer`, `InvestmentFrame`, and `BankAccount`.
19. The `InvestmentFrame` constructor adds the panel to *itself*.
20. Then the text field is not labeled, and the user will not know its purpose.
21. `Integer.parseInt(textField.getText())`
22. A text field holds a single line of text; a text area holds multiple lines.
23. The text area is intended to display the program output. It does not collect user input.
24. Don't construct a `JScrollPane` and add the `resultArea` object directly to the frame.

Input/Output and Exception Handling

CHAPTER GOALS

- To be able to read and write text files
- To learn how to throw exceptions
- To be able to design your own exception classes
- To understand the difference between checked and unchecked exceptions
- To learn how to catch exceptions
- To know when and where to catch an exception

This chapter starts with a discussion of file input and output. Whenever you read or write data, potential errors are to be expected. A file may have been corrupted or deleted, or it may be stored on another computer that was just disconnected from the network. In order to deal with these issues, you need to know about exception handling. The remainder of this chapter tells you how your programs can report exceptional conditions, and how they can recover when an exceptional condition has occurred.

CHAPTER CONTENTS

11.1 Reading and Writing Text Files

We begin this chapter by discussing the common task of reading and writing files that contain text. Examples are files that are created with a simple text editor, such as Windows Notepad, as well as Java source code and HTML files.

The simplest mechanism for reading text is to use the Scanner class. You already know how to use a Scanner for reading console input. To read input from a disk file, first construct a FileReader object with the name of the input file, then use the FileReader to construct a Scanner object:

```
FileReader reader = new FileReader("input.txt");
Scanner in = new Scanner(reader);
```

> When reading text files, use the Scanner class.

This Scanner object reads text from the file input.txt. You can use the Scanner methods (such as next, nextLine, nextInt, and nextDouble) to read data from the input file.

To write output to a file, you construct a PrintWriter object with the given file name, for example

> When writing text files, use the PrintWriter class and the print/println methods.

```
PrintWriter out = new PrintWriter("output.txt");
```

If the output file already exists, it is emptied before the new data are written into it. If the file doesn't exist, an empty file is created.

Use the familiar print and println methods to send numbers, objects, and strings to a PrintWriter:

```
out.println(29.95);
out.println(new Rectangle(5, 10, 15, 25));
out.println("Hello, World!");
```

The print and println methods convert numbers to their decimal string representations and use the toString method to convert objects to strings.

You must close all files when you are done processing them.

When you are done processing a file, be sure to *close* the Scanner or PrintWriter:

```
in.close();
out.close();
```

If your program exits without closing the PrintWriter, not all of the output may be written to the disk file.

The following program puts these concepts to work. It reads all lines of an input file and sends them to the output file, preceded by *line numbers*. If the input file is

```
Mary had a little lamb
Whose fleece was white as snow.
And everywhere that Mary went,
The lamb was sure to go!
```

then the program produces the output file

```
/* 1 */ Mary had a little lamb
/* 2 */ Whose fleece was white as snow.
/* 3 */ And everywhere that Mary went,
/* 4 */ The lamb was sure to go!
```

The line numbers are enclosed in /* */ delimiters so that the program can be used for numbering Java source files.

There one additional issue that we need to tackle. When the input or output file doesn't exist, a FileNotFoundException can occur. The compiler insists that we tell it what the program should do when that happens. (In this regard, the FileNot-FoundException is different from the exceptions that you have already encountered. We will discuss this difference in detail in Section 11.3.) In our sample program, we take the easy way out and acknowledge that the main method should simply be terminated if the exception occurs. We label the main method like this:

```
public static void main(String[] args) throws FileNotFoundException
```

You will see in the following sections how to deal with exceptions in a more professional way.

ch11/fileio/LineNumberer.java

```
1   import java.io.FileReader;
2   import java.io.FileNotFoundException;
3   import java.io.PrintWriter;
4   import java.util.Scanner;
5
6   public class LineNumberer
7   {
8      public static void main(String[] args)
9            throws FileNotFoundException
10     {
11        Scanner console = new Scanner(System.in);
12        System.out.print("Input file: ");
13        String inputFileName = console.next();
14        System.out.print("Output file: ");
15        String outputFileName = console.next();
16
```

```
17        FileReader reader = new FileReader(inputFileName);
18        Scanner in = new Scanner(reader);
19        PrintWriter out = new PrintWriter(outputFileName);
20        int lineNumber = 1;
21
22        while (in.hasNextLine())
23        {
24           String line = in.nextLine();
25           out.println("/* " + lineNumber + " */ " + line);
26           lineNumber++;
27        }
28
29        out.close();
30     }
31  }
```

SELF CHECK

1. What happens when you supply the same name for the input and output files to the LineNumberer program?

2. What happens when you supply the name of a nonexistent input file to the LineNumberer program?

COMMON ERROR 11.1

Backslashes in File Names

When you specify a file name as a constant string, and the name contains backslash characters (as in a Windows file name), you must supply each backslash twice:

```
in = new FileReader("c:\\homework\\input.dat");
```

Recall that a single backslash inside quoted strings is an *escape character* that is combined with another character to form a special meaning, such as \n for a newline character. The \\ combination denotes a single backslash.

When a user supplies a file name to a program, however, the user should not type the backslash twice.

ADVANCED TOPIC 11.1

File Dialog Boxes

> The JFileChooser dialog box allows users to select a file by navigating through directories.

In a program with a graphical user interface, you will want to use a file dialog box (such as the one shown in the figure below) whenever the users of your program need to pick a file. The JFileChooser class implements a file dialog box for the Swing user interface toolkit.

A `JFileChooser` Dialog Box

> A `File` object describes a file or directory.

The `JFileChooser` class relies on another class, `File`, which describes disk files and directories. For example,

```
File inputFile = new File("input.txt");
```

describes the file `input.txt` in the current directory. The `File` class has methods to delete or rename the file. The file does not actually have to exist—you may want to pass the `File` object to an output stream or writer so that the file can be created. The `exists` method returns `true` if the file already exists.

> You can pass a `File` object to the constructor of a file reader, writer, or stream.

You cannot directly use a `File` object for reading or writing. You still need to construct a file reader or writer from the `File` object. Simply pass the `File` object in the constructor.

```
FileReader in = new FileReader(inputFile);
```

The `JFileChooser` class has many options to fine-tune the display of the dialog box, but in its most basic form it is quite simple: Construct a file chooser object; then call the `showOpenDialog` or `showSaveDialog` method. Both methods show the same dialog box, but the button for selecting a file is labeled "Open" or "Save", depending on which method you call.

For better placement of the dialog box on the screen, you can specify the user interface component over which to pop up the dialog box. If you don't care where the dialog box pops up, you can simply pass `null`. These methods return either `JFileChooser.APPROVE_OPTION`, if the user has chosen a file, or `JFileChooser.CANCEL_OPTION`, if the user canceled the selection. If a file was chosen, then you call the `getSelectedFile` method to obtain a `File` object that describes the file. Here is a complete example:

```
JFileChooser chooser = new JFileChooser();
FileReader in = null;
if (chooser.showOpenDialog(null) == JFileChooser.APPROVE_OPTION)
{
   File selectedFile = chooser.getSelectedFile();
   reader = new FileReader(selectedFile);
   . . .
}
```

ADVANCED TOPIC 11.2

Command Line Arguments

Depending on the operating system and Java development system used, there are different methods of starting a program—for example, by selecting "Run" in the compilation environment, by clicking on an icon, or by typing the name of the program at a prompt in a terminal or shell window. The latter method is called "invoking the program from the command line". When you use this method, you must type the name of the program, but you can also type in additional information that the program can use. These additional strings are called *command line arguments*.

For example, it is convenient to specify the input and output file names for the Line-Numberer program on the command line:

```
java LineNumberer input.txt numbered.txt
```

> When you launch a program from the command line, you can specify arguments after the program name. The program can access these strings by processing the args parameter of the main method.

The strings that are typed after the Java program name are placed into the args parameter of the main method. (Now you finally know the use of the args parameter that you have seen in so many programs!)

For example, with the given program invocation, the args parameter of the LineNumberer.main method has the following contents:

- args[0] is "input.txt"
- args[1] is "output.txt"

The main method can then process these parameters, for example:

```
if (args.length >= 1)
    inputFileName = args[0];
```

It is entirely up to the program what to do with the command line argument strings. It is customary to interpret strings starting with a hyphen (-) as options and other strings as file names. For example, we may want to enhance the LineNumberer program so that a -c option places line numbers inside comment delimiters; for example

```
java LineNumberer -c HelloWorld.java HelloWorld.txt
```

If the -c option is missing, the delimiters should not be included. Here is how the main method can analyze the command line arguments:

```
for (String a : args)
{
    if (a.startsWith("-")) // It's an option
    {
        if (a.equals("-c")) useCommentDelimiters = true;
    }
    else if (inputFileName == null) inputFileName = a;
    else if (outputFileName == null) outputFileName = a;
}
```

Should you support command line interfaces for your programs, or should you instead supply a graphical user interface with file chooser dialog boxes? For a casual and infrequent user, the graphical user interface is much better. The user interface guides the user along and makes it possible to navigate the application without much knowledge. But for a frequent user, graphical user interfaces have a major drawback—they are hard to automate. If you need to process hundreds of files every day, you could spend all your time typing file names into file chooser dialog boxes. But it is not difficult to call a program multiple times automatically with different command line arguments. Productivity Hint 7.1 discusses how to use shell scripts (also called batch files) for this purpose.

11.2 Throwing Exceptions

There are two main aspects to exception handling: *reporting* and *recovery*. A major challenge of error handling is that the point of reporting is usually far apart from the point of recovery. For example, the get method of the ArrayList class may detect that a nonexistent element is being accessed, but it does not have enough information to decide what to do about this failure. Should the user be asked to try a different operation? Should the program be aborted after saving the user's work? The logic for these decisions is contained in a different part of the program code.

In Java, *exception handling* provides a flexible mechanism for passing control from the point of error reporting to a competent recovery handler. In the remainder of this chapter, we will look into the details of this mechanism.

When you detect an error condition, your job is really easy. You just throw an appropriate exception object, and you are done. For example, suppose someone tries to withdraw too much money from a bank account.

> To signal an exceptional condition, use the throw statement to throw an exception object.

```
public class BankAccount
{
   public void withdraw(double amount)
   {
      if (amount > balance)
         // Now what?
      . . .
   }
   . . .
}
```

First look for an appropriate exception class. The Java library provides many classes to signal all sorts of exceptional conditions. Figure 1 shows the most useful ones.

Look around for an exception type that might describe your situation. How about the IllegalStateException? Is the bank account in an illegal state for the withdraw operation? Not really—some withdraw operations could succeed. Is the parameter value illegal? Indeed it is. It is just too large. Therefore, let's throw an IllegalArgumentException. (The term *argument* is an alternative term for a parameter value.)

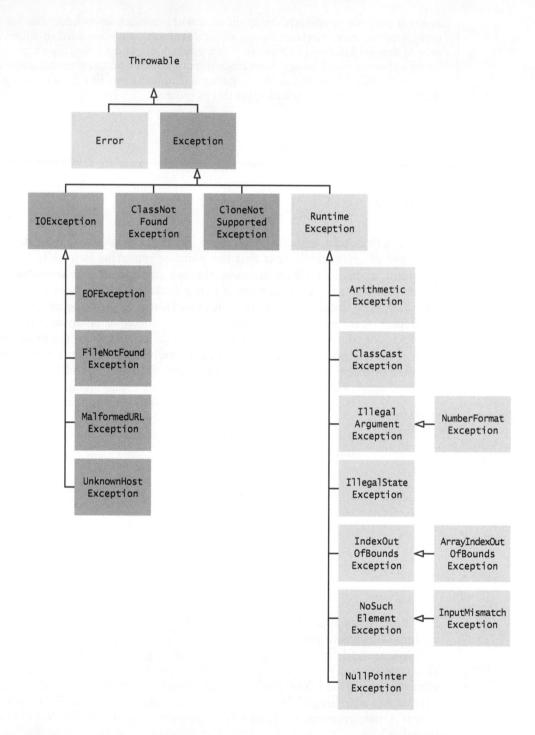

Figure 1 The Hierarchy of Exception Classes

```
public class BankAccount
{
    public void withdraw(double amount)
    {
        if (amount > balance)
        {
            IllegalArgumentException exception
                = new IllegalArgumentException("Amount exceeds balance");
            throw exception;
        }
        balance = balance - amount;
    }
    . . .
}
```

Actually, you don't have to store the exception object in a variable. You can just throw the object that the new operator returns:

```
throw new IllegalArgumentException("Amount exceeds balance");
```

When you throw an exception, the current method terminates immediately.

When you throw an exception, execution does not continue with the next statement but with an *exception handler*. For now, we won't worry about the handling of the exception. That is the topic of Section 11.4.

SYNTAX 11.1 Throwing an Exception

---

throw *exceptionObject*;

Example:

throw new IllegalArgumentException();

Purpose:

To throw an exception and transfer control to a handler for this exception type

---

SELF CHECK

3. How should you modify the deposit method to ensure that the balance is never negative?

4. Suppose you construct a new bank account object with a zero balance and then call withdraw(10). What is the value of balance afterwards?

11.3 Checked and Unchecked Exceptions

> There are two kinds of exceptions: checked and unchecked. Unchecked exceptions extend the class RuntimeException or Error.

Java exceptions fall into two categories, called *checked* and *unchecked* exceptions. When you call a method that throws a checked exception, the compiler checks that you don't ignore it. You must tell the compiler what you are going to do about the exception if it is ever thrown. For example, all subclasses of IOException are checked exceptions. On the other hand, the compiler does not require you to keep track of unchecked exceptions. Exceptions, such as NumberFormatException, IllegalArgumentException, and NullPointerException, are unchecked exceptions. More generally, all exceptions that belong to subclasses of RuntimeException are unchecked, and all other subclasses of the class Exception are checked. (In Figure 1, the checked exceptions are shaded in a darker color.) There is a second category of internal errors that are reported by throwing objects of type Error. One example is the OutOfMemoryError, which is thrown when all available memory has been used up. These are fatal errors that happen rarely and are beyond your control. They too are unchecked.

> Checked exceptions are due to external circumstances that the programmer cannot prevent. The compiler checks that your program handles these exceptions.

Why have two kinds of exceptions? A checked exception describes a problem that is likely to occur at times, no matter how careful you are. The unchecked exceptions, on the other hand, are your fault. For example, an unexpected end of file can be caused by forces beyond your control, such as a disk error or a broken network connection. But you are to blame for a NullPointerException, because your code was wrong when it tried to use a null reference.

The compiler doesn't check whether you handle a NullPointer-Exception, because you should test your references for null before using them rather than install a handler for that exception. The compiler does insist that your program be able to handle error conditions that you cannot prevent.

Actually, those categories aren't perfect. For example, the Scanner.nextInt method throws an unchecked InputMismatchException if a user enters an input that is not an integer. A checked exception would have been more appropriate because the programmer cannot prevent users from entering incorrect input. (The designers of the Scanner class made this choice to make the class easy to use for beginning programmers.)

As you can see from Figure 1, the majority of checked exceptions occur when you deal with input and output. That is a fertile ground for external failures beyond your control—a file might have been corrupted or removed, a network connection might be overloaded, a server might have crashed, and so on. Therefore, you will need to deal with checked exceptions principally when programming with files and streams.

You have seen how to use the Scanner class to read data from a file, by passing a FileReader object to the Scanner constructor:

```
String filename = . . .;
FileReader reader = new FileReader(filename);
Scanner in = new Scanner(reader);
```

However, the FileReader constructor can throw a FileNotFoundException. The FileNotFoundException is a checked exception, so you need to tell the compiler what you are going to do about it. You have two choices. You can handle the exception, using the techniques that you will see in Section 11.4. Or you can simply tell the compiler that you are aware of this exception and that you want your method to be terminated when it occurs. The method that reads input rarely knows what to do about an unexpected error, so that is usually the better option.

To declare that a method should be terminated when a checked exception occurs within it, tag the method with a throws specifier.

```
public class DataSet
{
   public void read(String filename) throws FileNotFoundException
   {
      FileReader reader = new FileReader(filename);
      Scanner in = new Scanner(reader);
      . . .
   }
   . . .
}
```

Add a throws specifier to a method that can throw a checked exception.

The throws clause in turn signals the caller of your method that it may encounter a FileNotFoundException. Then the caller needs to make the same decision—handle the exception, or tell its caller that the exception may be thrown.

If your method can throw checked exceptions of different types, you separate the exception class names by commas:

```
public void read(String filename)
      throws IOException, ClassNotFoundException
```

Always keep in mind that exception classes form an inheritance hierarchy. For example, FileNotFoundException is a subclass of IOException. Thus, if a method can throw both an IOException and a FileNotFoundException, you only tag it as throws IOException.

It sounds somehow irresponsible not to handle an exception when you know that it happened. Actually, though, it is usually best not to catch an exception if you don't know how to remedy the situation. After all, what can you do in a low-level read method? Can you tell the user? How? By sending a message to System.out? You don't know whether this method is called in a graphical program or an embedded system (such as a vending machine), where the user may never see System.out. And even if your users can see your error message, how do you know that they can understand English? Your class may be used to build an application for users in another country. If you can't tell the user, can you patch up the data and keep going? How? If you set a variable to zero, null or an empty string, that may just cause the program to break later, with much greater mystery.

Of course, some methods in the program know how to communicate with the user or take other remedial action. By allowing the exception to reach those methods, you make it possible for the exception to be processed by a competent handler.

SYNTAX 11.2 Exception Specification

accessSpecifier returnType methodName(parameterType parameterName, . . .)
    throws *ExceptionClass, ExceptionClass, . . .*

Example:

```
public void read(FileReader in)
    throws IOException
```

Purpose:

To indicate the checked exceptions that this method can throw

SELF CHECK

5. Suppose a method calls the `FileReader` constructor and the read method of the `FileReader` class, which can throw an `IOException`. Which `throws` specification should you use?

6. Why is a `NullPointerException` not a checked exception?

11.4 Catching Exceptions

In a method that is ready to handle a particular exception type, place the statements that can cause the exception inside a `try` block, and the handler inside a `catch` clause.

Every exception should be handled somewhere in your program. If an exception has no handler, an error message is printed, and your program terminates. That may be fine for a student program. But you would not want a professionally written program to die just because some method detected an unexpected error. Therefore, you should install exception handlers for all exceptions that your program might throw.

You install an exception handler with the `try/catch` statement. Each `try` block contains one or more statements that may cause an exception. Each `catch` clause contains the handler for an exception type. Here is an example:

```
try
{
    String filename = . . .;
    FileReader reader = new FileReader(filename);
    Scanner in = new Scanner(reader);
    String input = in.next();
    int value = Integer.parseInt(input);
    . . .
}
catch (IOException exception)
{
    exception.printStackTrace();
}
```

```
catch (NumberFormatException exception)
{
    System.out.println("Input was not a number");
}
```

Three exceptions may be thrown in this try block: The `FileReader` constructor can throw a `FileNotFoundException`, `Scanner.next` can throw a `NoSuchElementException`, and `Integer.parseInt` can throw a `NumberFormatException`.

SYNTAX 11.3 General try Block

```
try
{
    statement
    statement
    . . .
}
catch (ExceptionClass exceptionObject)
{
    statement
    statement
    . . .
}
catch (ExceptionClass exceptionObject)
{
    statement
    statement
    . . .
}
. . .
```

Example:

```
try
{
    System.out.println("How old are you?");
    int age = in.nextInt();
    System.out.println("Next year, you'll be " + (age + 1));
}
catch (InputMismatchException exception)
{
    exception.printStackTrace();
}
```

Purpose:

To execute one or more statements that may generate exceptions. If an exception occurs and it matches one of the catch clauses, execute the first one that matches. If no exception occurs, or an exception is thrown that doesn't match any catch clause, then skip the catch clauses.

If any of these exceptions is actually thrown, then the rest of the instructions in the try block are skipped. Here is what happens for the various exception types:

- If a FileNotFoundException is thrown, then the catch clause for the IOException is executed. (Recall that FileNotFoundException is a subclass of IOException.)
- If a NumberFormatException occurs, then the second catch clause is executed.
- A NoSuchElementException is *not caught* by any of the catch clauses. The exception remains thrown until it is caught by another try block.

When the catch (IOException exception) block is executed, then some method in the try block has failed with an IOException. The variable exception contains a reference to the exception object that was thrown. The catch clause can analyze that object to find out more details about the failure. For example, you can get a printout of the chain of method calls that lead to the exception, by calling

```
exception.printStackTrace()
```

In these sample catch clauses, we merely inform the user of the source of the problem. A better way of dealing with the exception would be to give the user another chance to provide a correct input—see Section 11.7 for a solution.

It is important to remember that you should place catch clauses only in methods in which you can competently handle the particular exception type.

SELF CHECK

7. Suppose the file with the given file name exists and has no contents. Trace the flow of execution in the try block in this section.

8. Is there a difference between catching checked and unchecked exceptions?

QUALITY TIP 11.1

Throw Early, Catch Late

> It is better to declare that a method throws a checked exception than to handle the exception poorly.

When a method notices a problem that it cannot solve, it is generally better to throw an exception rather than try to come up with an imperfect fix (such as doing nothing or returning a default value).

Conversely, a method should only catch an exception if it can really remedy the situation. Otherwise, the best remedy is simply to have the exception propagate to its caller, allowing it to be caught by a competent handler.

These principles can be summarized with the slogan "throw early, catch late".

Do Not Squelch Exceptions

When you call a method that throws a checked exception and you haven't specified a handler, the compiler complains. In your eagerness to continue your work, it is an understandable impulse to shut the compiler up by squelching the exception:

```
try
{
    FileReader reader = new FileReader(filename);
    // Compiler complained about FileNotFoundException
    . . .
}
catch (Exception e) {} // So there!
```

The do-nothing exception handler fools the compiler into thinking that the exception has been handled. In the long run, this is clearly a bad idea. Exceptions were designed to transmit problem reports to a competent handler. Installing an incompetent handler simply hides an error condition that could be serious.

11.5 The finally Clause

Occasionally, you need to take some action whether or not an exception is thrown. The finally construct is used to handle this situation. Here is a typical situation.

It is important to close a PrintWriter to ensure that all output is written to the file. In the following code segment, we open a writer, call one or more methods, and then close the writer:

```
PrintWriter out = new PrintWriter(filename);
writeData(out);
out.close(); // May never get here
```

Now suppose that one of the methods before the last line throws an exception. Then the call to close is never executed! Solve this problem by placing the call to close inside a finally clause:

```
PrintWriter out = new PrintWriter(filename);
try
{
    writeData(out);
}
finally
{
    out.close();
}
```

Once a try block is entered, the statements in a finally clause are guaranteed to be executed, whether or not an exception is thrown.

In a normal case, there will be no problem. When the try block is completed, the finally clause is executed, and the writer is closed. However, if an exception occurs, the finally clause is also executed before the exception is passed to its handler.

Use the finally clause whenever you need to do some clean up, such as closing a file, to ensure that the clean up happens no matter how the method exits.

It is also possible to have a finally clause following one or more catch clauses. Then the code in the finally clause is executed whenever the try block is exited in any of three ways:

1. After completing the last statement of the try block

2. After completing the last statement of a catch clause, if this try block caught an exception

3. When an exception was thrown in the try block and not caught

SYNTAX 11.4 finally Clause

```
try
{
    statement
    statement
    . . .
}
finally
{
    statement
    statement
    . . .
}
```

Example:

```
PrintWriter out = new PrintWriter(filename);
try
{
    writeData(out);
}
finally
{
    out.close();
}
```

Purpose:

To ensure that the statements in the finally clause are executed whether or not the statements in the try block throw an exception

However, we recommend that you don't mix catch and finally clauses in the same try block — see Quality Tip 11.3.

SELF CHECK

9. Why was the out variable declared outside the try block?
10. Suppose the file with the given name does not exist. Trace the flow of execution of the code segment in this section.

QUALITY TIP 11.3

Do Not Use catch and finally in the Same try Statement

It is tempting to combine catch and finally clauses, but the resulting code can be hard to understand. Instead, you should use a try/finally statement to close resources and a separate try/catch statement to handle errors. For example,

```
try
{
   PrintWriter out = new PrintWriter(filename);
   try
   {
      // Write output
   }
   finally
   {
      out.close();
   }
}
catch (IOException exception)
{
   // Handle exception
}
```

Note that the nested statements work correctly if the call out.close() throws an exception—see Exercise R11.18.

11.6 Designing Your Own Exception Types

Sometimes none of the standard exception types describe your particular error condition well enough. In that case, you can design your own exception class. Consider a bank account. Let's report an InsufficientFundsException when an attempt is made to withdraw an amount from a bank account that exceeds the current balance.

```
if (amount > balance)
{
```

```
        throw new InsufficientFundsException(
            "withdrawal of " + amount + " exceeds balance of " + balance);
    }
```

> You can design your own exception types—subclasses of Exception or RuntimeException.

Now you need to define the InsufficientFundsException class. Should it be a checked or an unchecked exception? Is it the fault of some external event, or is it the fault of the programmer? We take the position that the programmer could have prevented the exceptional condition—after all, it would have been an easy matter to check whether amount <= account.getBalance() before calling the withdraw method. Therefore, the exception should be an unchecked exception and extend the RuntimeException class or one of its subclasses.

It is customary to provide two constructors for an exception class: a default constructor and a constructor that accepts a message string describing the reason for the exception. Here is the definition of the exception class.

```
public class InsufficientFundsException
        extends RuntimeException
{
    public InsufficientFundsException() {}

    public InsufficientFundsException(String message)
    {
        super(message);
    }
}
```

When the exception is caught, its message string can be retrieved using the getMessage method of the RunTimeException class.

SELF CHECK

11. What is the purpose of the call super(message) in the second Insufficient-FundsException constructor?

12. Suppose you read bank account data from a file. Contrary to your expectation, the next input value is not of type double. You decide to implement a BadData-Exception. Which exception class should you extend?

QUALITY TIP 11.4

Do Throw Specific Exceptions

When throwing an exception, you should choose an exception class that describes the situation as closely as possible. For example, it would be a bad idea to simply throw a Runtime-Exception object when a bank account has insufficient funds. This would make it far too difficult to catch the exception. After all, if you caught all exceptions of type Runtime-Exception, your catch clause would also be activated by exceptions of the type NullPointer-Exception, ArrayIndexOutOfBoundsException, and so on. You would then need to carefully examine the exception object and attempt to deduce whether the exception was caused by insufficient funds.

> If the standard library does not have an exception class that describes your particular error situation, simply define a new exception class.

11.7 Case Study: A Complete Example

This section walks through a complete example of a program with exception handling. The program asks a user for the name of a file. The file is expected to contain data values. The first line of the file contains the total number of values, and the remaining lines contain the data. A typical input file looks like this:

```
3
1.45
-2.1
0.05
```

What can go wrong? There are two principal risks.

- The file might not exist.
- The file might have data in the wrong format.

Who can detect these faults? The `FileReader` constructor will throw an exception when the file does not exist. The methods that process the input values need to throw an exception when they find an error in the data format.

What exceptions can be thrown? The `FileReader` constructor throws a `FileNot-FoundException` when the file does not exist, which is very appropriate in our situation. The `close` method of the `FileReader` class can throw an `IOException`. Finally, when the file data is in the wrong format, we will throw a `BadDataException`, a custom checked exception class. We use a checked exception because corruption of a data file is beyond the control of the programmer.

Who can remedy the faults that the exceptions report? Only the `main` method of the `DataAnalyzer` program interacts with the user. It catches the exceptions, prints appropriate error messages, and gives the user another chance to enter a correct file.

ch11/data/DataAnalyzer.java

```
1   import java.io.FileNotFoundException;
2   import java.io.IOException;
3   import java.util.Scanner;
4
5   /**
6      This program reads a file containing numbers and analyzes its contents.
7      If the file doesn't exist or contains strings that are not numbers, an
8      error message is displayed.
9   */
10  public class DataAnalyzer
11  {
12     public static void main(String[] args)
13     {
```

```
14          Scanner in = new Scanner(System.in);
15          DataSetReader reader = new DataSetReader();
16
17          boolean done = false;
18          while (!done)
19          {
20             try
21             {
22                System.out.println("Please enter the file name: ");
23                String filename = in.next();
24
25                double[] data = reader.readFile(filename);
26                double sum = 0;
27                for (double d : data) sum = sum + d;
28                System.out.println("The sum is " + sum);
29                done = true;
30             }
31             catch (FileNotFoundException exception)
32             {
33                System.out.println("File not found.");
34             }
35             catch (BadDataException exception)
36             {
37                System.out.println("Bad data: " + exception.getMessage());
38             }
39             catch (IOException exception)
40             {
41                exception.printStackTrace();
42             }
43          }
44       }
45    }
```

The first two catch clauses in the main method give a human-readable error report if the file was not found or bad data was encountered. However, if another IOException occurs, then we print the stack trace so that a programmer can diagnose the problem.

The following readFile method of the DataSetReader class constructs the Scanner object and calls the readData method. It is completely unconcerned with any exceptions. If there is a problem with the input file, it simply passes the exception to its caller.

```
public double[] readFile(String filename)
      throws IOException, BadDataException
{
   FileReader reader = new FileReader(filename);
   try
   {
      Scanner in = new Scanner(reader);
      readData(in);
   }
   finally
   {
```

```
            reader.close();
         }
         return data;
      }
```

Note how the `finally` clause ensures that the file is closed even when an exception occurs.

Also note that the `throws` specifier of the `readFile` method need not include the `FileNotFoundException` class because it is a subclass of `IOException`.

Next, here is the `readData` method of the `DataSetReader` class. It reads the number of values, constructs an array, and calls `readValue` for each data value.

```
private void readData(Scanner in) throws BadDataException
{
   if (!in.hasNextInt())
      throw new BadDataException("Length expected");
   int numberOfValues = in.nextInt();
   data = new double[numberOfValues];

   for (int i = 0; i < numberOfValues; i++)
      readValue(in, i);

   if (in.hasNext())
      throw new BadDataException("End of file expected");
}
```

This method checks for two potential errors. The file might not start with an integer, or it might have additional data after reading all values.

However, this method makes no attempt to catch any exceptions. Plus, if the `readValue` method throws an exception—which it will if there aren't enough values in the file—the exception is simply passed on to the caller.

Here is the `readValue` method:

```
private void readValue(Scanner in, int i) throws BadDataException
{
   if (!in.hasNextDouble())
      throw new BadDataException("Data value expected");
   data[i] = in.nextDouble();
}
```

To see the exception handling at work, look at a specific error scenario.

1. `DataAnalyzer.main` calls `DataSetReader.readFile`.
2. `readFile` calls `readData`.
3. `readData` calls `readValue`.
4. `readValue` doesn't find the expected value and throws a `BadDataException`.
5. `readValue` has no handler for the exception and terminates immediately.
6. `readData` has no handler for the exception and terminates immediately.
7. `readFile` has no handler for the exception and terminates immediately after executing the `finally` clause and closing the file.
8. `DataAnalyzer.main` has a handler for a `BadDataException`. That handler prints a message to the user. Afterwards, the user is given another chance to enter a file

name. Note that the statements computing the sum of the values have been skipped.

This example shows the separation between error detection (in the DataSetReader. readValue method) and error handling (in the DataAnalyzer.main method). In between the two are the readData and readFile methods, which just pass exceptions along.

ch11/data/DataSetReader.java

```
1   import java.io.FileReader;
2   import java.io.IOException;
3   import java.util.Scanner;
4
5   /**
6       Reads a data set from a file. The file must have the format
7       numberOfValues
8       value1
9       value2
10      . . .
11  */
12  public class DataSetReader
13  {
14      /**
15          Reads a data set.
16          @param filename the name of the file holding the data
17          @return the data in the file
18      */
19      public double[] readFile(String filename)
20              throws IOException, BadDataException
21      {
22          FileReader reader = new FileReader(filename);
23          try
24          {
25              Scanner in = new Scanner(reader);
26              readData(in);
27          }
28          finally
29          {
30              reader.close();
31          }
32          return data;
33      }
34
35      /**
36          Reads all data.
37          @param in the scanner that scans the data
38      */
39      private void readData(Scanner in) throws BadDataException
40      {
41          if (!in.hasNextInt())
42              throw new BadDataException("Length expected");
43          int numberOfValues = in.nextInt();
```

```
44            data = new double[numberOfValues];
45
46            for (int i = 0; i < numberOfValues; i++)
47                readValue(in, i);
48
49            if (in.hasNext())
50                throw new BadDataException("End of file expected");
51        }
52
53        /**
54            Reads one data value.
55            @param in  the scanner that scans the data
56            @param i  the position of the value to read
57        */
58        private void readValue(Scanner in, int i) throws BadDataException
59        {
60            if (!in.hasNextDouble())
61                throw new BadDataException("Data value expected");
62            data[i] = in.nextDouble();
63        }
64
65        private double[] data;
66    }
```

ch11/data/BadDataException.java

```
1    /**
2        This class reports bad input data.
3    */
4    public class BadDataException extends Exception
5    {
6        public BadDataException() {}
7        public BadDataException(String message)
8        {
9            super(message);
10       }
11   }
```

SELF CHECK

13. Why doesn't the DataSetReader.readFile method catch any exceptions?

14. Suppose the user specifies a file that exists and is empty. Trace the flow of execution.

RANDOM FACT 11.1

The Ariane Rocket Incident

The European Space Agency (ESA), Europe's counterpart to NASA, had developed a rocket model called Ariane that it had successfully used several times to launch satellites and scientific experiments into space. However, when a new version, the Ariane 5, was launched on June 4, 1996, from ESA's launch site in Kourou, French Guiana, the rocket veered off course about 40 seconds after liftoff. Flying at an angle of more than 20 degrees, rather than straight up, exerted such an aerodynamic force that the boosters separated, which triggered the automatic self-destruction mechanism. The rocket blew itself up.

The ultimate cause of this accident was an unhandled exception! The rocket contained two identical devices (called inertial reference systems) that processed flight data from measuring devices and turned the data into information about the rocket position. The onboard computer used the position information for controlling the boosters. The same inertial reference systems and computer software had worked fine on the Ariane 4.

However, due to design changes to the rocket, one of the sensors measured a larger acceleration force than had been encountered in the Ariane 4. That value, expressed as a floating-point value, was stored in a 16-bit integer (like a short variable in Java). Unlike Java, the Ada language, used for the device software, generates an exception if a floating-point number is too large to be converted to an integer. Unfortunately, the programmers of the device had decided that this situation would never happen and didn't provide an exception handler.

When the overflow did happen, the exception was triggered and, because there was no handler, the device shut itself off. The onboard computer sensed the failure and switched over to the backup device. However, that device had shut itself off for exactly the same reason, something that the designers of the rocket had not expected. They figured that the devices might fail for mechanical reasons, and the chances of two devices having the same mechanical failure was considered remote. At that point, the rocket was without reliable position information and went off course.

Perhaps it would have been better if the software hadn't been so thorough? If it had ignored the overflow, the device wouldn't have been shut off. It would have computed bad data. But then the device would have reported wrong position data, which could have been just as fatal. Instead, a correct implementation should have caught overflow exceptions and come up with some strategy to recompute the flight data. Clearly, giving up was not a reasonable option in this context.

The Explosion of the Ariane Rocket

> The advantage of the exception-handling mechanism is that it makes these issues explicit to programmers—something to think about when you curse the Java compiler for complaining about uncaught exceptions.

CHAPTER SUMMARY

1. When reading text files, use the `Scanner` class.

2. When writing text files, use the `PrintWriter` class and the `print`/`println` methods.

3. You must close all files when you are done processing them.

4. The `JFileChooser` dialog box allows users to select a file by navigating through directories.

5. A `File` object describes a file or directory.

6. You can pass a `File` object to the constructor of a file reader, writer, or stream.

7. When you launch a program from the command line, you can specify arguments after the program name. The program can access these strings by processing the `args` parameter of the `main` method.

8. To signal an exceptional condition, use the `throw` statement to throw an exception object.

9. When you throw an exception, the current method terminates immediately.

10. There are two kinds of exceptions: checked and unchecked. Unchecked exceptions extend the class `RuntimeException` or `Error`.

11. Checked exceptions are due to external circumstances that the programmer cannot prevent. The compiler checks that your program handles these exceptions.

12. Add a `throws` specifier to a method that can throw a checked exception.

13. In a method that is ready to handle a particular exception type, place the statements that can cause the exception inside a `try` block, and the handler inside a `catch` clause.

14. It is better to declare that a method throws a checked exception than to handle the exception poorly.

15. Once a `try` block is entered, the statements in a `finally` clause are guaranteed to be executed, whether or not an exception is thrown.

16. You can design your own exception types—subclasses of `Exception` or `RuntimeException`.

CLASSES, OBJECTS, AND METHODS INTRODUCED IN THIS CHAPTER

```
java.io.EOFException
java.io.File
   exists
java.io.FileNotFoundException
java.io.FileReader
java.io.IOException
java.io.PrintWriter
   close
   print
   println
java.lang.Error
java.lang.IllegalArgumentException
java.lang.IllegalStateException
java.lang.NullPointerException
```

```
java.lang.NumberFormatException
java.lang.RuntimeException
java.lang.Throwable
   getMessage
   printStackTrace
java.util.InputMismatchException
java.util.NoSuchElementException
java.util.Scanner
   close
javax.swing.JFileChooser
   getSelectedFile
   showOpenDialog
   showSaveDialog
```

REVIEW EXERCISES

★★ **Exercise R11.1.** What happens if you try to open a file for reading that doesn't exist? What happens if you try to open a file for writing that doesn't exist?

★★★ **Exercise R11.2.** What happens if you try to open a file for writing, but the file or device is write-protected (sometimes called read-only)? Try it out with a short test program.

★ **Exercise R11.3.** How do you open a file whose name contains a backslash, like c:\temp\output.dat?

★★★ **Exercise R11.4.** What is a command line? How can a program read its command line arguments?

★★ **Exercise R11.5.** Give two examples of programs on your computer that read arguments from the command line.

★★ **Exercise R11.6.** If a program Woozle is started with the command

```
java Woozle -Dname=piglet -I\eeyore -v heff.txt a.txt lump.txt
```

what are the values of args[0], args[1], and so on?

★★ **Exercise R11.7.** What is the difference between throwing an exception and catching an exception?

★★ **Exercise R11.8.** What is a checked exception? What is an unchecked exception? Is a NullPointerException checked or unchecked? Which exceptions do you need to declare with the throws keyword?

★ **Exercise R11.9.** Why don't you need to declare that your method might throw a NullPointerException?

★★ **Exercise R11.10.** When your program executes a throw statement, which statement is executed next?

★ **Exercise R11.11.** What happens if an exception does not have a matching catch clause?

★ **Exercise R11.12.** What can your program do with the exception object that a catch clause receives?

★ **Exercise R11.13.** Is the type of the exception object always the same as the type declared in the catch clause that catches it?

★ **Exercise R11.14.** What kind of values can you throw? Can you throw a string? An integer?

★★ **Exercise R11.15.** What is the purpose of the finally clause? Give an example of how it can be used.

★★★ **Exercise R11.16.** What happens when an exception is thrown, the code of a finally clause executes, and that code throws an exception of a different kind than the original one? Which one is caught by a surrounding catch clause? Write a sample program to try it out.

★★ **Exercise R11.17.** Which exceptions can the next and nextInt methods of the Scanner class throw? Are they checked exceptions or unchecked exceptions?

★★★ **Exercise R11.18.** Suppose the catch clause in the example of Quality Tip 11.3 had been moved to the inner try block, eliminating the outer try block. Does the modified code work correctly if (a) the FileReader constructor throws an exception and (b) the close method throws an exception?

★★ **Exercise R11.19.** Suppose the program in Section 11.7 reads a file containing the following values:

```
0
1
2
3
```

What is the outcome? How could the program be improved to give a more accurate error report?

★★ **Exercise R11.20.** Can the readFile method in Section 11.7 throw a NullPointer-Exception? If so, how?

Additional review exercises are available in WileyPLUS.

PROGRAMMING EXERCISES

★★ **Exercise P11.1.** Write a program that asks a user for a file name and prints the number of characters, words, and lines in that file.

★★ **Exercise P11.2.** Write a program that asks the user for a file name and counts the number of characters, words, and lines in that file. Then the program asks for the name of the next file. When the user enters a file that doesn't exist, the program prints the total counts of characters, words, and lines in all processed files and exits.

★★ **Exercise P11.3.** Write a program `CopyFile` that copies one file to another. The file names are specified on the command line. For example,

```
java CopyFile report.txt report.sav
```

★★ **Exercise P11.4.** Write a program that *concatenates* the contents of several files into one file. For example,

```
java CatFiles chapter1.txt chapter2.txt chapter3.txt book.txt
```

makes a long file, `book.txt`, that contains the contents of the files `chapter1.txt`, `chapter2.txt`, and `chapter3.txt`. The output file is always the last file specified on the command line.

★★ **Exercise P11.5.** Write a program `Find` that searches all files specified on the command line and prints out all lines containing a keyword. For example, if you call

```
java Find ring report.txt address.txt Homework.java
```

then the program might print

```
report.txt: has broken up an international ring of DVD bootleggers that
address.txt: Kris Kringle, North Pole
address.txt: Homer Simpson, Springfield
Homework.java: String filename;
```

The keyword is always the first command line argument.

★★ **Exercise P11.6.** Write a program that checks the spelling of all words in a file. It should read each word of a file and check whether it is contained in a word list. A word list is available on most UNIX systems in the file `/usr/dict/words`. (If you don't have access to a UNIX system, your instructor should be able to get you a copy.) The program should print out all words that it cannot find in the word list.

★★ **Exercise P11.7.** Write a program that replaces each line of a file with its reverse. For example, if you run

```
java Reverse HelloPrinter.java
```

then the contents of `HelloPrinter.java` are changed to

```
retnirPolleH ssalc cilbup
{
)sgra ][gnirtS(niam diov citats cilbup
{
wodniw elosnoc eht ni gniteerg a yalpsiD //

;)"!dlroW ,olleH"(nltnirp.tuo.metsyS
}
}
```

Of course, if you run `Reverse` twice on the same file, you get back the original file.

★★★ **Exercise P11.8.** Write a program that replaces all tab characters '\t' in a file with the *appropriate* number of spaces. By default, the distance between tab columns should be 3 (the value we use in this book for Java programs) but it can be changed by the user. Expand tabs to the number of spaces necessary to move to the next tab column. That may be *less* than three spaces. For example, consider the line containing "\t|\t||\t|". The first tab is changed to three spaces, the second to two spaces, and the third to one space. Your program should be executed as

```
java TabExpander filename
```

or
```
java -t tabwidth filename
```

★ **Exercise P11.9.** Modify the BankAccount class to throw an IllegalArgumentException when the account is constructed with a negative balance, when a negative amount is deposited, or when an amount that is not between 0 and the current balance is withdrawn. Write a test program that causes all three exceptions to occur and that catches them all.

★★ **Exercise P11.10.** Repeat Exercise P11.9, but throw exceptions of three exception types that you define.

★★ **Exercise P11.11.** Write a program that asks the user to input a set of floating-point values. When the user enters a value that is not a number, give the user a second chance to enter the value. After two chances, quit reading input. Add all correctly specified values and print the sum when the user is done entering data. Use exception handling to detect improper inputs.

★★ **Exercise P11.12.** Repeat Exercise P11.11, but give the user as many chances as necessary to enter a correct value. Quit the program only when the user enters a blank input.

★ **Exercise P11.13.** Modify the DataSetReader class so that you do not call hasNextInt or hasNextDouble. Simply have nextInt and nextDouble throw an InputMismatchException or NoSuchElementException and catch it in the main method.

★★ **Exercise P11.14.** Write a program that reads in a set of coin descriptions from a file. The input file has the format

```
coinName1 coinValue1
coinName2 coinValue2
. . .
```

Add a method
```
void read(Scanner in) throws IOException
```
to the Coin class. Throw an exception if the current line is not properly formatted. Then implement a method
```
static ArrayList<Coin> readFile(String filename) throws IOException
```
In the main method, call readFile. If an exception is thrown, give the user a chance to select another file. If you read all coins successfully, print the total value.

★★★   **Exercise P11.15.** Design a class `Bank` that contains a number of bank accounts. Each account has an account number and a current balance. Add an `accountNumber` field to the `BankAccount` class. Store the bank accounts in an array list. Write a `readFile` method of the `Bank` class for reading a file with the format

```
accountNumber1   balance1
accountNumber2   balance2
. . .
```

Implement read methods for the `Bank` and `BankAccount` classes. Write a sample program to read in a file with bank accounts, then print the account with the highest balance. If the file is not properly formatted, give the user a chance to select another file.

Additional programming exercises are available in WileyPLUS.

PROGRAMMING PROJECTS

★★★   **Project 11.1.** You can read the contents of a web page with this sequence of commands.

```
String address = "http://java.sun.com/index.html";
URL u = new URL(address);
URLConnection connection = u.openConnection();
InputStream stream = connection.getInputStream();
Scanner in = new Scanner(stream);
. . .
```

Some of these methods may throw exceptions—check out the API documentation. Design a class `LinkFinder` that finds all hyperlinks of the form

```
<a href="link">link text</a>
```

Throw an exception if you find a malformed hyperlink. Extra credit if your program can follow the links that it finds and find links in those web pages as well. (This is the method that search engines such as Google use to find web sites.)

ANSWERS TO SELF-CHECK QUESTIONS

1. When the PrintWriter object is created, the output file is emptied. Sadly, that is the same file as the input file. The input file is now empty and the while loop exits immediately.

2. The program throws and catches a FileNotFoundException, prints an error message, and terminates.

3. Throw an exception if the amount being deposited is less than zero.

4. The balance is still zero because the last statement of the withdraw method was never executed.

5. The specification throws IOException is sufficient because FileNotFound-Exception is a subclass of IOException.

6. Because programmers should simply check for null pointers instead of trying to handle a NullPointerException.

7. The FileReader constructor succeeds, and in is constructed. Then the call in.next() throws a NoSuchElementException, and the try block is aborted. None of the catch clauses match, so none are executed. If none of the enclosing method calls catch the exception, the program terminates.

8. No—you catch both exception types in the same way, as you can see from the code example on page 508. Recall that IOException is a checked exception and NumberFormatException is an unchecked exception.

9. If it had been declared inside the try block, its scope would only have extended to the end of the try block, and the finally clause could not have closed it.

10. The FileReader constructor throws an exception. The finally clause is executed. Since reader is null, the call to close is not executed. Next, a catch clause that matches the FileNotFoundException is located. If none exists, the program terminates.

11. To pass the exception message string to the RuntimeException superclass.

12. Exception or IOException are both good choices. Because file corruption is beyond the control of the programmer, this should be a checked exception, so it would be wrong to extend RuntimeException.

13. It would not be able to do much with them. The DataSetReader class is a reusable class that may be used for systems with different languages and different user interfaces. Thus, it cannot engage in a dialog with the program user.

14. DataAnalyzer.main calls DataSetReader.readFile, which calls readData. The call in.hasNextInt() returns false, and readData throws a BadDataException. The readFile method doesn't catch it, so it propagates back to main, where it is caught.

Object-Oriented Design

CHAPTER GOALS

- To learn about the software life cycle

- To learn how to discover new classes and methods

- To understand the use of CRC cards for class discovery

- To be able to identify inheritance, aggregation, and dependency relationships between classes

- To master the use of UML class diagrams to describe class relationships

- To learn how to use object-oriented design to build complex programs

To implement a software system successfully, be it as simple as your next homework project or as complex as the next air traffic monitoring system, some amount of planning, design, and testing is required. In fact, for larger projects, the amount of time spent on planning is much higher than the amount of time spent on programming and testing.

If you find that most of your homework time is spent in front of the computer, keying in code and fixing bugs, you are probably spending more time on your homework than you should. You could cut down your total time by spending more on the planning and design phase. This chapter tells you how to approach these tasks in a systematic manner, using the object-oriented design methodology.

CHAPTER CONTENTS

12.1 The Software Life Cycle

> The life cycle of software encompasses all activities from initial analysis until obsolescence.

In this section we will discuss the *software life cycle*: the activities that take place between the time a software program is first conceived and the time it is finally retired.

A software project usually starts because a customer has a problem and is willing to pay money to have it solved. The Department of Defense, the customer of many programming projects, was an early proponent of a *formal process* for software development. A formal

> A formal process for software development describes phases of the development process and gives guidelines for how to carry out the phases.

process identifies and describes different phases and gives guidelines for carrying out the phases and when to move from one phase to the next.

Many software engineers break the development process down into the following five phases:

- Analysis
- Design
- Implementation
- Testing
- Deployment

In the *analysis* phase, you decide *what* the project is supposed to accomplish; you do not think about *how* the program will accomplish its tasks. The output of the analysis phase is a *requirements document*, which describes in complete detail what the program will be able to do once it is completed. Part of this requirements document can be a user manual that tells how the user will operate the program to derive the promised benefits. Another part sets performance criteria—how many inputs the program must be able to handle in what time, or what its maximum memory and disk storage requirements are.

In the *design* phase, you develop a plan for how you will implement the system. You discover the structures that underlie the problem to be solved. When you use object-oriented design, you decide what classes you need and what their most important methods are. The output of this phase is a description of the classes and methods, with diagrams that show the relationships among the classes.

In the *implementation* phase, you write and compile program code to implement the classes and methods that were discovered in the design phase. The output of this phase is the completed program.

In the *testing* phase, you run tests to verify that the program works correctly. The output of this phase is a report describing the tests that you carried out and their results.

In the *deployment* phase, the users of the program install it and use it for its intended purpose.

> The waterfall model of software development describes a sequential process of analysis, design, implementation, testing, and deployment.

When formal development processes were first established in the early 1970s, software engineers had a very simple visual model of these phases. They postulated that one phase would run to completion, its output would spill over to the next phase, and the next phase would begin. This model is called the *waterfall model* of software development (see Figure 1).

In an ideal world the waterfall model has a lot of appeal: You figure out what to do; then you figure out how to do it; then you do it; then you verify that you did it right; then you hand the product to the customer. When rigidly applied, though, the waterfall model simply did not work. It was very difficult to come up with a perfect requirement specification. It was quite common

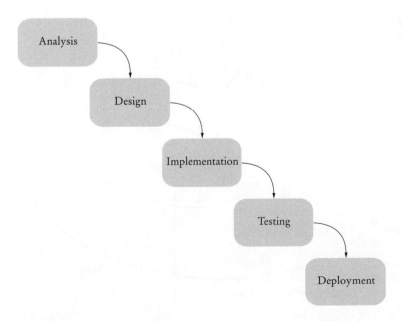

Figure 1 The Waterfall Model

to discover in the design phase that the requirements were inconsistent or that a small change in the requirements would lead to a system that was both easier to design and more useful for the customer, but the analysis phase was over, so the designers had no choice—they had to take the existing requirements, errors and all. This problem would repeat itself during implementation. The designers may have thought they knew how to solve the problem as efficiently as possible, but when the design was actually implemented, it turned out that the resulting program was not as fast as the designers had thought. The next transition is one with which you are surely familiar. When the program was handed to the quality assurance department for testing, many bugs were found that would best be fixed by reimplementing, or maybe even redesigning, the program, but the waterfall model did not allow for this. Finally, when the customers received the finished product, they were often not at all happy with it. Even though the customers typically were very involved in the analysis phase, often they themselves were not sure exactly what they needed. After all, it can be very difficult to describe how you want to use a product that you have never seen before. But when the customers started using the program, they began to realize what they would have liked. Of course, then it was too late, and they had to live with what they got.

> The spiral model of software development describes an iterative process in which design and implementation are repeated.

Having some level of iteration is clearly necessary. There simply must be a mechanism to deal with errors from the preceding phase. A *spiral model*, originally proposed by Barry Boehm in 1988, breaks the development process down into multiple phases (see Figure 2). Early phases focus on the construction of *prototypes*. A prototype is a small system that shows some aspects of the final system. Because prototypes model only a part of a system and do not need to withstand

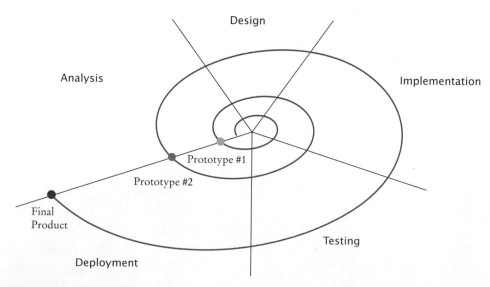

Figure 2 A Spiral Model

Figure 3   Activity Levels in the Rational Unified Process Methodology [1]

customer abuse, they can be implemented quickly. It is common to build a *user interface prototype* that shows the user interface in action. This gives customers an early chance to become more familiar with the system and to suggest improvements before the analysis is complete. Other prototypes can be built to validate interfaces with external systems, to test performance, and so on. Lessons learned from the development of one prototype can be applied to the next iteration of the spiral.

By building in repeated trials and feedback, a development process that follows the spiral model has a greater chance of delivering a satisfactory system. However, there is also a danger. If engineers believe that they don't have to do a good job because they can always do another iteration, then there will be many iterations, and the process will take a very long time to complete.

Figure 3 shows activity levels in the "Rational Unified Process", a development process methodology by the inventors of UML. The details are not important, but as you can see, this is a complex process involving multiple iterations.

> Extreme Programming is a development methodology that strives for simplicity by removing formal structure and focusing on best practices.

Even complex development processes with many iterations have not always met with success. In 1999, Kent Beck published an influential book [2] on *Extreme Programming*, a development methodology that strives for simplicity by cutting out most of the formal trappings of a traditional development methodolgy and instead focusing on a set of *practices*:

- *Realistic planning:* Customers are to make business decisions, programmers are to make technical decisions. Update the plan when it conflicts with reality.

- *Small releases:* Release a useful system quickly, then release updates on a very short cycle.

- *Metaphor:* All programmers should have a simple shared story that explains the system under development.
- *Simplicity:* Design everything to be as simple as possible instead of preparing for future complexity.
- *Testing:* Both programmers and customers are to write test cases. The system is continuously tested.
- *Refactoring:* Programmers are to restructure the system continuously to improve the code and eliminate duplication.
- *Pair programming:* Put programmers together in pairs, and require each pair to write code on a single computer.
- *Collective ownership:* All programmers have permission to change all code as it becomes necessary.
- *Continuous integration:* Whenever a task is completed, build the entire system and test it.
- *40-hour week:* Don't cover up unrealistic schedules with bursts of heroic effort.
- *On-site customer:* An actual customer of the system is to be accessible to team members at all times.
- *Coding standards:* Programmers are to follow standards that emphasize self-documenting code.

Many of these practices are common sense. Others, such as the pair programming requirement, are surprising. Beck claims that the value of the Extreme Programming approach lies in the synergy of these practices—the sum is bigger than the parts.

In your first programming course, you will not develop systems that are so complex that you need a full-fledged methodology to solve your homework problems. This introduction to the development process should, however, show you that successful software development involves more than just coding. In the remainder of this chapter we will have a closer look at the *design phase* of the software development process.

SELF CHECK

1. Suppose you sign a contract, promising that you will, for an agreed-upon price, design, implement, and test a software package exactly as it has been specified in a requirements document. What is the primary risk you and your customer are facing with this business arrangement?
2. Does Extreme Programming follow a waterfall or a spiral model?
3. What is the purpose of the "on-site customer" in Extreme Programming?

RANDOM FACT 12.1

Programmer Productivity

If you talk to your friends in this programming class, you will find that some of them consistently complete their assignments much more quickly than others. Perhaps they have more experience. However, even when programmers with the same education and experience are compared, wide variations in competence are routinely observed and measured. It is not uncommon to have the best programmer in a team be five to ten times as productive as the worst, using any of a number of reasonable measures of productivity [3].

That is a staggering range of performance among trained professionals. In a marathon race, the best runner will not run five to ten times faster than the slowest one. Software product managers are acutely aware of these disparities. The obvious solution is, of course, to hire only the best programmers, but even in recent periods of economic slowdown the demand for good programmers has greatly outstripped the supply.

Fortunately for all of us, joining the rank of the best is not necessarily a question of raw intellectual power. Good judgment, experience, broad knowledge, attention to detail, and superior planning are at least as important as mental brilliance. These skills can be acquired by individuals who are genuinely interested in improving themselves.

Even the most gifted programmer can deal with only a finite number of details in a given time period. Suppose a programmer can implement and debug one method every two hours, or one hundred methods per month. (This is a generous estimate. Few programmers are this productive.) If a task requires 10,000 methods (which is typical for a medium-sized program), then a single programmer would need 100 months to complete the job. Such a project is sometimes expressed as a "100-man-month" project. But as Fred Brooks explains in his famous book [4], the concept of "man-month" is a myth. One cannot trade months for programmers. One hundred programmers cannot finish the task in one month. In fact, 10 programmers probably couldn't finish it in 10 months. First of all, the 10 programmers need to learn about the project before they can get productive. Whenever there is a problem with a particular method, both the author and its users need to meet and discuss it, taking time away from all of them. A bug in one method may have other programmers twiddling their thumbs until it is fixed.

It is difficult to estimate these inevitable delays. They are one reason why software is often released later than originally promised. What is a manager to do when the delays mount? As Brooks points out, adding more personnel will make a late project even later, because the productive people have to stop working and train the newcomers.

You will experience these problems when you work on your first team project with other students. Be prepared for a major drop in productivity, and be sure to set ample time aside for team communications.

There is, however, no alternative to teamwork. Most important and worthwhile projects transcend the ability of one single individual. Learning to function well in a team is just as important as becoming a competent programmer.

12.2 Discovering Classes

In the design phase of software development, your task is to discover structures that make it possible to implement a set of tasks on a computer. When you use the object-oriented design process, you carry out the following tasks:

In object-oriented design, you discover classes, determine the responsibilities of classes, and describe the relationships between classes.

1. Discover classes.

2. Determine the responsibilities of each class.

3. Describe the relationships between the classes.

A class represents some useful concept. You have seen classes for concrete entities, such as bank accounts, ellipses, and products. Other classes represent abstract concepts, such as streams and windows.

A simple rule for finding classes is to look for *nouns* in the task description. For example, suppose your job is to print an invoice such as the one in Figure 4. Obvious classes that come to mind are Invoice, LineItem, and Customer. It is a good idea to keep a list of *candidate classes* on a whiteboard or a sheet of paper. As you brainstorm, simply put all ideas for classes onto the list. You can always cross out the ones that weren't useful after all.

INVOICE

Sam's Small Appliances
100 Main Street
Anytown, CA 98765

Item	Qty	Price	Total
Toaster	3	$29.95	$89.85
Hair Dryer	1	$24.95	$24.95
Car Vacuum	2	$19.99	$39.98

AMOUNT DUE: **$154.78**

Figure 4   An Invoice

When finding classes, keep the following points in mind:

- A class represents a set of objects with the same behavior. Entities with multiple occurrences in your problem description, such as customers or products, are good candidates for objects. Find out what they have in common, and design classes to capture those commonalities.

- Some entities should be represented as objects, others as primitive types. For example, should an address be an object of an Address class, or should it simply be a string? There is no perfect answer—it depends on the task that you want to solve. If your software needs to analyze addresses (for example, to determine shipping costs), then an Address class is an appropriate design. However, if your software will never need such a capability, you should not waste time on an overly complex design. It is your job to find a balanced design; one that is not too limiting or excessively general.

- Not all classes can be discovered in the analysis phase. Most complex programs need classes for tactical purposes, such as file or database access, user interfaces, control mechanisms, and so on.

- Some of the classes that you need may already exist, either in the standard library or in a program that you developed previously. You also may be able to use inheritance to extend existing classes into classes that match your needs.

Once a set of classes has been identified, you need to define the behavior for each class. That is, you need to find out what methods each object needs to carry out to solve the programming problem. A simple rule for finding these methods is to look for *verbs* in the task description, and then match the verbs to the appropriate objects. For example, in the invoice program, a class needs to compute the amount due. Now you need to figure out *which class* is responsible for this method. Do customers compute what they owe? Do invoices total up the amount due? Do the items total themselves up? The best choice is to make "compute amount due" the responsibility of the Invoice class.

An excellent way to carry out this task is the "CRC card method."

> A CRC card describes a class, its responsibilities, and its collaborating classes.

CRC stands for "classes", "responsibilities", "collaborators", and in its simplest form, the method works as follows. Use an index card for each *class* (see Figure 5). As you think about verbs in the task description that indicate methods, you pick the card of the class that you think should be responsible, and write that *responsibility* on the card. For each responsibility, you record which other classes are needed to fulfill it. Those classes are the *collaborators*.

For example, suppose you decide that an invoice should compute the amount due. Then you write "compute amount due" on the left-hand side of an index card with the title Invoice.

If a class can carry out that responsibility by itself, do nothing further. But if the class needs the help of other classes, write the names of these collaborators on the right-hand side of the card.

To compute the total, the invoice needs to ask each line item about its total price. Therefore, the LineItem class is a collaborator.

Figure 5   A CRC Card

This is a good time to look up the index card for the LineItem class. Does it have a "get total price" method? If not, add one.

How do you know that you are on the right track? For each responsibility, ask yourself how it can actually be done, using the responsibilities written on the various cards. Many people find it helpful to group the cards on a table so that the collaborators are close to each other, and to simulate tasks by moving a token (such as a coin) from one card to the next to indicate which object is currently active.

Keep in mind that the responsibilities that you list on the CRC card are on a *high level*. Sometimes a single responsibility may need two or more Java methods for carrying it out. Some researchers say that a CRC card should have no more than three distinct responsibilities.

The CRC card method is informal on purpose, so that you can be creative and discover classes and their properties. Once you find that you have settled on a good set of classes, you will want to know how they are related to each other. Can you find classes with common properties, so that some responsibilities can be taken care of by a common superclass? Can you organize classes into clusters that are independent of each other? Finding class relationships and documenting them with diagrams is the topic of the next section.

SELF CHECK

4. Suppose the invoice is to be saved to a file. Name a likely collaborator.
5. Looking at the invoice in Figure 4, what is a likely responsibility of the Customer class?
6. What do you do if a CRC card has ten responsibilities?

12.3 Relationships Between Classes

When designing a program, it is useful to document the relationships between classes. This helps you in a number of ways. For example, if you find classes with common behavior, you can save effort by placing the common behavior into a superclass. If you know that some classes are *not* related to each other, you can assign different programmers to implement each of them, without worrying that one of them has to wait for the other.

You have seen the inheritance relationship between classes many times in this book. Inheritance is a very important relationship, but, as it turns out, it is not the only useful relationship, and it can be overused.

Inheritance is a relationship between a more general class (the superclass) and a more specialized class (the subclass). This relationship is often described as the *is-a* relationship. Every truck is a vehicle. Every savings account is a bank account. Every circle is an ellipse (with equal width and height).

> Inheritance (the *is-a* relationship) is sometimes inappropriately used when the *has-a* relationship would be more appropriate.

Inheritance is sometimes abused, however. For example, consider a Tire class that describes a car tire. Should the class Tire be a subclass of a class Circle? It sounds convenient. There are quite a few useful methods in the Circle class—for example, the Tire class may inherit methods that compute the radius, perimeter, and center point, which should come in handy when drawing tire shapes. Though it may be convenient for the programmer, this arrangement makes no sense conceptually. It isn't true that every tire is a circle. Tires are car parts, whereas circles are geometric objects. There is a relationship between tires and circles, though. A tire *has a* circle as its boundary. Java lets us model that relationship, too. Use an instance field:

```
public class Tire
{
   . . .
   private String rating;
   private Circle boundary;
}
```

The technical term for this relationship is *aggregation*. Each Tire aggregates a Circle object. In general, a class aggregates another class if its objects have objects of the other class.

> Aggregation (the *has-a* relationship) denotes that objects of one class contain references to objects of another class.

Here is another example. Every car *is a* vehicle. Every car *has a* tire (in fact, it has four or, if you count the spare, five). Thus, you would use inheritance from Vehicle and use aggregation of Tire objects:

```
public class Car extends Vehicle
{
   . . .
   private Tire[] tires;
}
```

Figure 6
UML Notation for
Inheritance and Aggregation

In this book, we use the UML notation for class diagrams. You have already seen many examples of the UML notation for inheritance—an arrow with an open triangle pointing to the superclass. In the UML notation, aggregation is denoted by a solid line with a diamond-shaped symbol next to the aggregating class. Figure 6 shows a class diagram with an inheritance and an aggregation relationship.

Dependency is another name for the "uses" relationship.

The aggregation relationship is related to the *dependency* relationship, which you saw in Chapter 8. Recall that a class depends on another if one of its methods *uses* an object of the other class in some way.

For example, many of our applications depend on the Scanner class, because they use a Scanner object to read input.

Aggregation is a stronger form of dependency. If a class has objects of another class, it certainly uses the other class. However, the converse is not true. For example, a class may use the Scanner class without ever defining an instance field of class Scanner. The class may simply construct a local variable of type Scanner, or its methods may receive Scanner objects as parameters. This use is not aggregation because the objects of the class don't contain Scanner objects—they just create or receive them for the duration of a single method.

You need to be able to distinguish the UML notations for inheritance, interface implementation, aggregation, and dependency.

Generally, you need aggregation when an object needs to remember another object *between method calls.*

As you saw in Chapter 8, the UML notation for dependency is a dashed line with an open arrow that points to the dependent class.

The arrows in the UML notation can get confusing. Table 1 shows a summary of the four UML relationship symbols that we use in this book.

Table 1 UML Relationship Symbols

Relationship	Symbol	Line Style	Arrow Tip
Inheritance	——————▷	Solid	Triangle
Interface Implementation	- - - - - - -▷	Dotted	Triangle
Aggregation	◇———————	Solid	Diamond
Dependency	- - - - - - -→	Dotted	Open

SELF CHECK

7. Consider the `Bank` and `BankAccount` classes of Chapter 7. How are they related?

8. Consider the `BankAccount` and `SavingsAccount` objects of Chapter 10. How are they related?

9. Consider the `BankAccountTester` class of Chapter 3. Which classes does it depend on?

HOW TO 12.1

CRC Cards and UML Diagrams

Before writing code for a complex problem, you need to design a solution. The methodology introduced in this chapter suggests that you follow a design process that is composed of the following tasks:

1. Discover classes.
2. Determine the responsibilities of each class.
3. Describe the relationships between the classes.

CRC cards and UML diagrams help you discover and record this information.

Step 1 Discover classes.

Highlight the nouns in the problem description. Make a list of the nouns. Cross out those that don't seem reasonable candidates for classes.

Step 2 Discover responsibilities.

Make a list of the major tasks that your system needs to fulfill. From those tasks, pick one that is not trivial and that is intuitive to you. Find a class that is responsible for carrying out that task. Make an index card and write the name and the task on it. Now ask yourself how an object of the class can carry out the task. It probably needs help from other objects. Then make CRC cards for the classes to which those objects belong and write the responsibilities on them.

Don't be afraid to cross out, move, split, or merge responsibilities. Rip up cards if they become too messy. This is an informal process.

You are done when you have walked through all major tasks and are satisfied that they can all be solved with the classes and responsibilities that you discovered.

Step 3 Describe relationships.

Make a class diagram that shows the relationships between all the classes that you discovered.

Start with inheritance—the *is-a* relationship between classes. Is any class a specialization of another? If so, draw inheritance arrows. Keep in mind that many designs, especially for simple programs, don't use inheritance extensively.

The "collaborators" column of the CRC cards tell you which classes use others. Draw usage arrows for the collaborators on the CRC cards.

Some dependency relationships give rise to aggregations. For each of the dependency relationships, ask yourself: How does the object locate its collaborator? Does it navigate to it directly because it stores a reference? In that case, draw an aggregation arrow. Or is the collaborator a method parameter or return value? Then simply draw a dependency arrow.

ADVANCED TOPIC 12.1

Attributes and Methods in UML Diagrams

Sometimes it is useful to indicate class *attributes* and *methods* in a class diagram. An *attribute* is an externally observable property that objects of a class have. For example, `name` and `price` would be attributes of the `Product` class. Usually, attributes correspond to instance variables. But they don't have to—a class may have a different way of organizing its data. For example, a `GregorianCalendar` object from the Java library has attributes `day`, `month`, and `year`, and it would be appropriate to draw a UML diagram that shows these attributes. However, the class doesn't actually have instance fields that store these quantities. Instead, it internally represents all dates by counting the milliseconds from January 1, 1970—an implementation detail that a class user certainly doesn't need to know about.

You can indicate attributes and methods in a class diagram by dividing a class rectangle into three compartments, with the class name in the top, attributes in the middle, and methods in the bottom (see Attributes and Methods in a Class Diagram). You need not list *all* attributes and methods in a particular diagram. Just list the ones that are helpful to understand whatever point you are making with a particular diagram.

Also, don't list as an attribute what you also draw as an aggregation. If you denote by aggregation the fact that a `Car` has `Tire` objects, don't add an attribute `tires`.

Attributes and Methods in a Class Diagram

ADVANCED TOPIC 12.2

Multiplicities

Some designers like to write *multiplicities* at the end(s) of an aggregation relationship to denote how many objects are aggregated. The notations for the most common multiplicities are:

- any number (zero or more): *
- one or more: 1..*
- zero or one: 0..1
- exactly one: 1

The figure below shows that a customer has one or more bank accounts.

An Aggregation Relationship with Multiplicities

ADVANCED TOPIC 12.3

Aggregation and Association

Some designers find the aggregation or *has-a* terminology unsatisfactory. For example, consider customers of a bank. Does the bank "have" customers? Do the customers "have" bank accounts, or does the bank "have" them? Which of these "has" relationships should be modeled by aggregation? This line of thinking can lead us to premature implementation decisions.

Early in the design phase, it makes sense to use a more general relationship between classes called *association*. A class is associated with another if you can *navigate* from objects of one class to objects of the other class. For example, given a Bank object, you can navigate to Customer objects, perhaps by accessing an instance field, or by making a database lookup.

The UML notation for an association relationship is a solid line, with optional arrows that show in which directions you can navigate the relationship. You can also add words to the line ends to further explain the nature of the relationship. An Association Relationship shows that you can navigate from Bank objects to Customer objects, but you cannot navigate the other way around. That is, in this particular design, the Customer class has no mechanism to determine in which banks it keeps its money.

An Association Relationship

> Frankly, the differences between aggregation and association are confusing, even to experienced designers. If you find the distinction helpful, by all means use the relationship that you find most appropriate. But don't spend time pondering subtle differences between these concepts. From the practical point of view of a Java programmer, it is useful to know when objects of one class manage objects of another class. The aggregation or *has-a* relationship accurately describes this phenomenon.

12.4 Case Study: Printing an Invoice

In this chapter, we discuss a five-part development process that is particularly well suited for beginning programmers:

1. Gather requirements.
2. Use CRC cards to find classes, responsibilities, and collaborators.
3. Use UML diagrams to record class relationships.
4. Use javadoc to document method behavior.
5. Implement your program.

There isn't a lot of notation to learn. The class diagrams are simple to draw. The deliverables of the design phase are obviously useful for the implementation phase—you simply take the source files and start adding the method code. Of course, as your projects get more complex, you will want to learn more about formal design methods. There are many techniques to describe object scenarios, call sequencing, the large-scale structure of programs, and so on, that are very beneficial even for relatively simple projects. *The Unified Modeling Language User Guide* [1] gives a good overview of these techniques.

In this section, we will walk through the object-oriented design technique with a very simple example. In this case, the methodology may feel overblown, but it is a good introduction to the mechanics of each step. You will then be better prepared for the more complex example that follows.

12.4.1 Requirements

The task of this program is to print out an invoice. An invoice describes the charges for a set of products in certain quantities. (We omit complexities such as dates, taxes, and invoice and customer numbers.) The program simply prints the billing address, all line items, and the amount due. Each line item contains the description and unit price of a product, the quantity ordered, and the total price.

```
            I N V O I C E

Sam's Small Appliances
100 Main Street
Anytown, CA 98765

Description              Price  Qty  Total
Toaster                  29.95   3   89.85
Hair dryer               24.95   1   24.95
Car vacuum               19.99   2   39.98

AMOUNT DUE: $154.78
```

Also, in the interest of simplicity, we do not provide a user interface. We just supply a test program that adds line items to the invoice and then prints it.

12.4.2 CRC Cards

First, you need to discover classes. Classes correspond to nouns in the requirements description. In this problem, it is pretty obvious what the nouns are:

```
Invoice
Address
LineItem
Product
Description
Price
Quantity
Total
Amount Due
```

(Of course, Toaster doesn't count—it is the description of a LineItem object and therefore a data value, not the name of a class.)

Description and price are fields of the Product class. What about the quantity? The quantity is not an attribute of a Product. Just as in the printed invoice, let's have a class LineItem that records the product and the quantity (such as "3 toasters").

The total and amount due are computed—not stored anywhere. Thus, they don't lead to classes.

After this process of elimination, we are left with four candidates for classes:

```
Invoice
Address
LineItem
Product
```

Each of them represents a useful concept, so let's make them all into classes.

The purpose of the program is to print an invoice. However, the Invoice class won't necessarily know whether to display the output in System.out, in a text area, or in a file. Therefore, let's relax the task slightly and make the invoice responsible for *formatting* the invoice. The result is a string (containing multiple lines) that can be printed out or displayed. Record that responsibility on a CRC card:

Invoice	
format the invoice	

How does an invoice format itself? It must format the billing address, format all line items, and then add the amount due. How can the invoice format an address? It can't—that really is the responsibility of the Address class. This leads to a second CRC card:

Address	
format the address	

Similarly, formatting of a line item is the responsibility of the LineItem class.

The format method of the Invoice class calls the format methods of the Address and LineItem classes. Whenever a method uses another class, you list that other class as a collaborator. In other words, Address and LineItem are collaborators of Invoice:

Invoice	
format the invoice	Address
	LineItem

When formatting the invoice, the invoice also needs to compute the total amount due. To obtain that amount, it must ask each line item about the total price of the item.

How does a line item obtain that total? It must ask the product for the unit price, and then multiply it by the quantity. That is, the Product class must reveal the unit price, and it is a collaborator of the LineItem class.

Finally, the invoice must be populated with products and quantities, so that it makes sense to format the result. That too is a responsibility of the Invoice class.

We now have a set of CRC cards that completes the CRC card process.

Product	
get description	
get unit price	

LineItem	
format the item	Product
get total price	

Invoice	
format the invoice	Address
add a product and quantity	LineItem
	Product

12.4.3 UML Diagrams

The dependency relationships come from the collaboration column on the CRC cards. Each class depends on the classes with which it collaborates. In our example, the Invoice class collaborates with the Address, LineItem, and Product classes. The LineItem class collaborates with the Product class.

Now ask yourself which of these dependencies are actually aggregations. How does an invoice know about the address, line item, and product objects with which it collaborates? An invoice object must hold references to the address and the line items when it formats the invoice. But an invoice object need not hold a reference to a product object when adding a product. The product is turned into a line item, and then it is the item's responsibility to hold a reference to it.

Therefore, the Invoice class aggregates the Address and LineItem classes. The LineItem class aggregates the Product class. However, there is no *has-a* relationship between an invoice and a product. An invoice doesn't store products directly—they are stored in the LineItem objects.

There is no inheritance in this example.

Figure 7 shows the class relationships that we discovered.

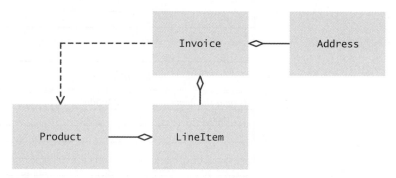

Figure 7   The Relationships Between the Invoice Classes

12.4.4 Method Documentation

Use javadoc comments (with the method bodies left blank) to record the behavior of classes.

The final step of the design phase is to write the documentation of the discovered classes and methods. Simply write a Java source file for each class, write the method comments for those methods that you have discovered, and leave the bodies of the methods blank.

```
/**
    Describes an invoice for a set of purchased products.
*/
public class Invoice
{
```

```java
/**
    Adds a charge for a product to this invoice.
    @param aProduct the product that the customer ordered
    @param quantity the quantity of the product
*/
public void add(Product aProduct, int quantity)
{
}

/**
    Formats the invoice.
    @return the formatted invoice
*/
public String format()
{
}
}

/**
    Describes a quantity of an article to purchase and its price.
*/
public class LineItem
{
    /**
        Computes the total cost of this line item.
        @return the total price
    */
    public double getTotalPrice()
    {
    }

    /**
        Formats this item.
        @return a formatted string of this line item
    */
    public String format()
    {
    }
}

/**
    Describes a product with a description and a price.
*/
public class Product
{
    /**
        Gets the product description.
        @return the description
    */
    public String getDescription()
    {
    }
```

```
    /**
        Gets the product price.
        @return the unit price
    */
    public double getPrice()
    {
    }
}

/**
    Describes a mailing address.
*/
public class Address
{
    /**
        Formats the address.
        @return the address as a string with three lines
    */
    public String format()
    {
    }
}
```

Then run the javadoc program to obtain a prettily formatted version of your documentation in HTML format (see Figure 8).

This approach for documenting your classes has a number of advantages. You can share the HTML documentation with others if you work in a team. You use a format that is immediately useful—Java source files that you can carry into the implementation phase. And, most importantly, you supply the comments of the key methods—a task that less prepared programmers leave for later, and then often neglect for lack of time.

12.4.5 Implementation

Finally, you are ready to implement the classes.

You already have the method signatures and comments from the previous step. Now look at the UML diagram to add instance fields. Aggregated classes yield instance fields. Start with the Invoice class. An invoice aggregates Address and LineItem. Every invoice has one billing address, but it can have many line items. To store multiple LineItem objects, you can use an array list. Now you have the instance fields of the Invoice class:

```
public class Invoice
{
    . . .
    private Address billingAddress;
    private ArrayList<LineItem> items;
}
```

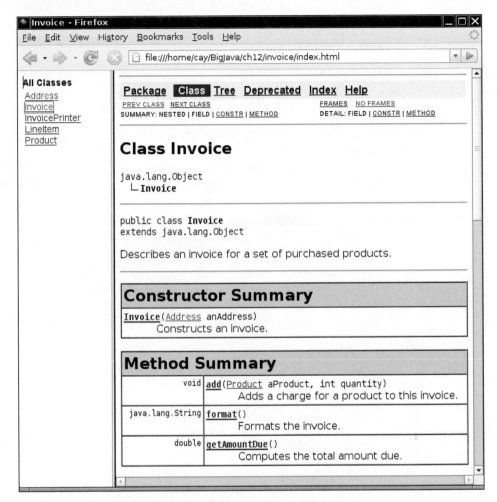

Figure 8 The Class Documentation in HTML Format

A line item needs to store a `Product` object and the product quantity. That leads to the following instance fields:

```
public class LineItem
{
   . . .
   private int quantity;
   private Product theProduct;
}
```

The methods themselves are now very easy. Here is a typical example. You already know what the `getTotalPrice` method of the `LineItem` class needs to do—get the unit price of the product and multiply it with the quantity.

```
/**
    Computes the total cost of this line item.
    @return the total price
*/
public double getTotalPrice()
{
    return theProduct.getPrice() * quantity;
}
```

We will not discuss the other methods in detail—they are equally straightforward. Finally, you need to supply constructors, another routine task.

Here is the entire program. It is a good practice to go through it in detail and match up the classes and methods against the CRC cards and UML diagram.

ch12/invoice/InvoicePrinter.java

```
1  /**
2      This program demonstrates the invoice classes by
3      printing a sample invoice.
4  */
5  public class InvoicePrinter
6  {
7     public static void main(String[] args)
8     {
9        Address samsAddress
10           = new Address("Sam's Small Appliances",
11           "100 Main Street", "Anytown", "CA", "98765");
12
13        Invoice samsInvoice = new Invoice(samsAddress);
14        samsInvoice.add(new Product("Toaster", 29.95), 3);
15        samsInvoice.add(new Product("Hair dryer", 24.95), 1);
16        samsInvoice.add(new Product("Car vacuum", 19.99), 2);
17
18        System.out.println(samsInvoice.format());
19     }
20  }
```

ch12/invoice/Invoice.java

```
1  import java.util.ArrayList;
2
3  /**
4      Describes an invoice for a set of purchased products.
5  */
6  public class Invoice
7  {
8     /**
9         Constructs an invoice.
10         @param anAddress the billing address
11     */
12     public Invoice(Address anAddress)
13     {
```

```
14          items = new ArrayList<LineItem>();
15          billingAddress = anAddress;
16       }
17
18       /**
19           Adds a charge for a product to this invoice.
20           @param aProduct the product that the customer ordered
21           @param quantity the quantity of the product
22       */
23       public void add(Product aProduct, int quantity)
24       {
25          LineItem anItem = new LineItem(aProduct, quantity);
26          items.add(anItem);
27       }
28
29       /**
30           Formats the invoice.
31           @return the formatted invoice
32       */
33       public String format()
34       {
35          String r = "                       I N V O I C E\n\n"
36                + billingAddress.format()
37                + String.format("\n\n%-30s%8s%5s%8s\n",
38                "Description", "Price", "Qty", "Total");
39
40          for (LineItem i : items)
41          {
42             r = r + i.format() + "\n";
43          }
44
45          r = r + String.format("\nAMOUNT DUE: $%8.2f", getAmountDue());
46
47          return r;
48       }
49
50       /**
51           Computes the total amount due.
52           @return the amount due
53       */
54       public double getAmountDue()
55       {
56          double amountDue = 0;
57          for (LineItem i : items)
58          {
59             amountDue = amountDue + i.getTotalPrice();
60          }
61          return amountDue;
62       }
63
64       private Address billingAddress;
65       private ArrayList<LineItem> items;
66    }
```

ch12/invoice/LineItem.java

```
1   /**
2       Describes a quantity of an article to purchase.
3   */
4   public class LineItem
5   {
6       /**
7           Constructs an item from the product and quantity.
8           @param aProduct the product
9           @param aQuantity the item quantity
10      */
11      public LineItem(Product aProduct, int aQuantity)
12      {
13          theProduct = aProduct;
14          quantity = aQuantity;
15      }
16
17      /**
18          Computes the total cost of this line item.
19          @return the total price
20      */
21      public double getTotalPrice()
22      {
23          return theProduct.getPrice() * quantity;
24      }
25
26      /**
27          Formats this item.
28          @return a formatted string of this line item
29      */
30      public String format()
31      {
32          return String.format("%-30s%8.2f%5d%8.2f",
33              theProduct.getDescription(), theProduct.getPrice(),
34              quantity, getTotalPrice());
35      }
36
37      private int quantity;
38      private Product theProduct;
39  }
```

ch12/invoice/Product.java

```
1   /**
2       Describes a product with a description and a price.
3   */
4   public class Product
5   {
6       /**
7           Constructs a product from a description and a price.
8           @param aDescription the product description
9           @param aPrice the product price
10      */
11      public Product(String aDescription, double aPrice)
```

```
12    {
13        description = aDescription;
14        price = aPrice;
15    }
16
17    /**
18        Gets the product description.
19        @return the description
20    */
21    public String getDescription()
22    {
23        return description;
24    }
25
26    /**
27        Gets the product price.
28        @return the unit price
29    */
30    public double getPrice()
31    {
32        return price;
33    }
34
35    private String description;
36    private double price;
37 }
```

ch12/invoice/Address.java

```
1  /**
2      Describes a mailing address.
3  */
4  public class Address
5  {
6      /**
7          Constructs a mailing address.
8          @param aName the recipient name
9          @param aStreet the street
10         @param aCity the city
11         @param aState the two-letter state code
12         @param aZip the ZIP postal code
13     */
14     public Address(String aName, String aStreet,
15             String aCity, String aState, String aZip)
16     {
17         name = aName;
18         street = aStreet;
19         city = aCity;
20         state = aState;
21         zip = aZip;
22     }
23
```

```
24      /**
25          Formats the address.
26          @return  the address as a string with three lines
27      */
28      public String format()
29      {
30          return name + "\n" + street + "\n"
31                  + city + ", " + state + " " + zip;
32      }
33
34      private String name;
35      private String street;
36      private String city;
37      private String state;
38      private String zip;
39  }
```

SELF CHECK

10. Which class is responsible for computing the amount due? What are its collaborators for this task?

11. Why do the format methods return String objects instead of directly printing to System.out?

12.5 Case Study: An Automatic Teller Machine

12.5.1 Requirements

The purpose of this project is to design a simulation of an automatic teller machine (ATM). The ATM is used by the customers of a bank. Each customer has two accounts: a checking account and a savings account. Each customer also has a customer number and a personal identification number (PIN); both are required to gain access to the accounts. (In a real ATM, the customer number would be recorded on the magnetic strip of the ATM card. In this simulation, the customer will need to type it in.) With the ATM, customers can select an account (checking or savings). The balance of the selected account is displayed. Then the customer can deposit and withdraw money. This process is repeated until the customer chooses to exit.

The details of the user interaction depend on the user interface that we choose for the simulation. We will develop two separate interfaces: a graphical interface that closely mimics an actual ATM (see Figure 9), and a text-based interface that allows you to test the ATM and bank classes without being distracted by GUI programming.

In the GUI interface, the ATM has a keypad to enter numbers, a display to show messages, and a set of buttons, labeled A, B, and C, whose function depends on the state of the machine.

Figure 9
Graphical User Interface
for the Automatic Teller Machine

Specifically, the user interaction is as follows. When the ATM starts up, it expects a user to enter a customer number. The display shows the following message:

```
Enter customer number
A = OK
```

The user enters the customer number on the keypad and presses the A button. The display message changes to

```
Enter PIN
A = OK
```

Next, the user enters the PIN and presses the A button again. If the customer number and ID match those of one of the customers in the bank, then the customer can proceed. If not, the user is again prompted to enter the customer number.

If the customer has been authorized to use the system, then the display message changes to

```
Select Account
A = Checking
B = Savings
C = Exit
```

If the user presses the C button, the ATM reverts to its original state and asks the next user to enter a customer number.

If the user presses the A or B buttons, the ATM remembers the selected account, and the display message changes to

```
Balance = balance of selected account
Enter amount and select transaction
A = Withdraw
B = Deposit
C = Cancel
```

If the user presses the A or B buttons, the value entered in the keypad is withdrawn from or deposited into the selected account. (This is just a simulation, so no money is dispensed and no deposit is accepted.) Afterwards, the ATM reverts to the preceding state, allowing the user to select another account or to exit.

If the user presses the C button, the ATM reverts to the preceding state without executing any transaction.

In the text-based interaction, we read input from System.in instead of the buttons. Here is a typical dialog:

```
Enter account number: 1
Enter PIN: 1234
A=Checking, B=Savings, C=Quit: A
Balance=0.0
A=Deposit, B=Withdrawal, C=Cancel: A
Amount: 1000
A=Checking, B=Savings, C=Quit: C
```

In our solution, only the user interface classes are affected by the choice of user interface. The remainder of the classes can be used for both solutions—they are decoupled from the user interface.

Because this is a simulation, the ATM does not actually communicate with a bank. It simply loads a set of customer numbers and PINs from a file. All accounts are initialized with a zero balance.

12.5.2 CRC Cards

We will again follow the recipe of Section 12.2 and show how to discover classes, responsibilities, and relationships and how to obtain a detailed design for the ATM program.

Recall that the first rule for finding classes is "Look for nouns in the problem description". Here is a list of the nouns:

```
ATM
User
Keypad
Display
Display message
Button
State
Bank account
Checking account
Savings account
Customer
Customer number
PIN
Bank
```

Of course, not all of these nouns will become names of classes, and we may yet discover the need for classes that aren't in this list, but it is a good start.

Users and customers represent the same concept in this program. Let's use a class Customer. A customer has two bank accounts, and we will require that a Customer object should be able to locate these accounts. (Another possible design would make the Bank class responsible for locating the accounts of a given customer—see Exercise P12.9.)

A customer also has a customer number and a PIN. We can, of course, require that a customer object give us the customer number and the PIN. But perhaps that isn't so secure. Instead, simply require that a customer object, when given a customer number and a PIN, will tell us whether it matches its own information or not.

Customer
get accounts
match number and PIN

A bank contains a collection of customers. When a user walks up to the ATM and enters a customer number and PIN, it is the job of the bank to find the matching customer. How can the bank do this? It needs to check for each customer whether its customer number and PIN match. Thus, it needs to call the *match number and PIN* method of the Customer class that we just discovered. Because the *find customer* method calls a Customer method, it collaborates with the Customer class. We record that fact in the right-hand column of the CRC card.

When the simulation starts up, the bank must also be able to read account information from a file.

Bank	
find customer	Customer
read customers	

The BankAccount class is our familiar class with methods to get the balance and to deposit and withdraw money.

In this program there is nothing that distinguishes checking accounts from savings accounts. The ATM does not add interest or deduct fees. Therefore, we decide not to implement separate subclasses for checking and savings accounts.

Finally, we are left with the ATM class itself. An important notion of the ATM is the *state*. The current machine state determines the text of the prompts and the function of the buttons. For example, when you first log in, you use the A and B buttons to select an account. Next, you use the same buttons to choose between deposit and withdrawal. The ATM must remember the current state so that it can correctly interpret the buttons.

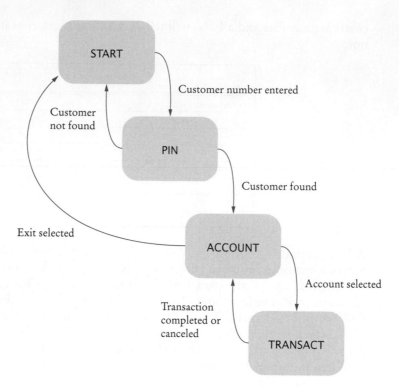

Figure 10 State Diagram for the ATM Class

There are four states:

1. START: Enter customer ID

2. PIN: Enter PIN

3. ACCOUNT: Select account

4. TRANSACT: Select transaction

To understand how to move from one state to the next, it is useful to draw a *state diagram* (Figure 10). The UML notation has standardized shapes for state diagrams. Draw states as rectangles with rounded corners. Draw state changes as arrows, with labels that indicate the reason for the change.

The user must type a valid customer number and PIN. Then the ATM can ask the bank to find the customer. This calls for a *select customer* method. It collaborates with the bank, asking the bank for the customer that matches the customer number and PIN. Next, there must be a *select account* method that asks the current customer for the checking or savings account. Finally, the ATM must carry out the selected transaction on the current account.

ATM	
manage state	Customer
select customer	Bank
select account	BankAccount
execute transaction	

Of course, discovering these classes and methods was not as neat and orderly as it appears from this discussion. When I designed these classes for this book, it took me several trials and many torn cards to come up with a satisfactory design. It is also important to remember that there is seldom one best design.

This design has several advantages. The classes describe clear concepts. The methods are sufficient to implement all necessary tasks. (I mentally walked through every ATM usage scenario to verify that.) There are not too many collaboration dependencies between the classes. Thus, I was satisfied with this design and proceeded to the next step.

12.5.3 UML Diagrams

Figure 11 shows the relationships between these classes, using the graphical user interface. (The console user interface uses a single class ATMSimulator instead of the ATMFrame and Keypad classes.)

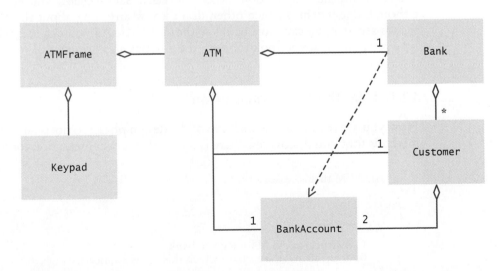

Figure 11   Relationships Between the ATM Classes

To draw the dependencies, use the "collaborator" columns from the CRC cards. Looking at those columns, you find that the dependencies are as follows:

- ATM uses Bank, Customer, and BankAccount.
- Bank uses Customer.
- Customer uses BankAccount.

It is easy to see some of the aggregation relationships. A bank has customers, and each customer has two bank accounts.

Does the ATM class aggregate Bank? To answer this question, ask yourself whether an ATM object needs to store a reference to a bank object. Does it need to locate the same bank object across multiple method calls? Indeed it does. Therefore, aggregation is the appropriate relationship.

Does an ATM aggregate customers? Clearly, the ATM is not responsible for storing all of the bank's customers. That's the bank's job. But in our design, the ATM remembers the *current* customer. If a customer has logged in, subsequent commands refer to the same customer. The ATM needs to either store a reference to the customer, or ask the bank to look up the object whenever it needs the current customer. It is a design decision: either store the object, or look it up when needed. We will decide to store the current customer object. That is, we will use aggregation. Note that the choice of aggregation is not an automatic consequence of the problem description—it is a design decision.

Similarly, we will decide to store the current bank account (checking or savings) that the user selects. Therefore, we have an aggregation relationship between ATM and BankAccount.

The class diagram is a good tool to visualize dependencies. Look at the GUI classes. They are completely independent from the rest of the ATM system. You can replace the GUI with a console interface, and you can take out the Keypad class and use it in another application. Also, the Bank, BankAccount, and Customer classes, although dependent on each other, don't know anything about the ATM class. That makes sense—you can have banks without ATMs. As you can see, when you analyze relationships, you look for both the absence and presence of relationships.

12.5.4 Method Documentation

Now you are ready for the final step of the design phase: to document the classes and methods that you discovered. Here is a part of the documentation for the ATM class:

```
/**
    An ATM that accesses a bank.
*/
public class ATM
{
    /**
        Constructs an ATM for a given bank.
        @param aBank  the bank to which this ATM connects
    */
    public ATM(Bank aBank) { }
```

```
    /**
        Sets the current customer number
        and sets state to PIN.
        (Precondition: state is START)
        @param number  the customer number
    */
    public void setCustomerNumber(int number) { }

    /**
        Finds customer in bank.
        If found sets state to ACCOUNT, else to START.
        (Precondition: state is PIN)
        @param pin  the PIN of the current customer
    */
    public void selectCustomer(int pin) { }

    /**
        Sets current account to checking or savings. Sets
        state to TRANSACT.
        (Precondition: state is ACCOUNT or TRANSACT)
        @param account  one of CHECKING or SAVINGS
    */
    public void selectAccount(int account) { }

    /**
        Withdraws amount from current account.
        (Precondition: state is TRANSACT)
        @param value  the amount to withdraw
    */
    public void withdraw(double value) { }
    . . .
}
```

Then run the javadoc utility to turn this documentation into HTML format.

For conciseness, we omit the documentation of the other classes.

12.5.5 Implementation

Finally, the time has come to implement the ATM simulator. The implementation phase is very straightforward and should take *much less time than the design phase*.

A good strategy for implementing the classes is to go "bottom-up". Start with the classes that don't depend on others, such as Keypad and BankAccount. Then implement a class such as Customer that depends only on the BankAccount class. This "bottom-up" approach allows you to test your classes individually. You will find the implementations of these classes at the end of this section.

The most complex class is the ATM class. In order to implement the methods, you need to define the necessary instance variables. From the class diagram, you can tell that the ATM has a bank object. It becomes an instance variable of the class:

```
public class ATM
{
```

```
      . . .
      private Bank theBank;
}
```

From the description of the ATM states, it is clear that we require additional instance variables to store the current state, customer, and bank account.

```
public class ATM
{  . . .
   private int state;
   private Customer currentCustomer;
   private BankAccount currentAccount;
   . . .
}
```

Most methods are very straightforward to implement. Consider the selectCustomer method. From the design documentation, we have the description

```
/**
   Finds customer in bank.
   If found sets state to ACCOUNT, else to START.
   (Precondition: state is PIN)
   @param pin the PIN of the current customer
*/
```

This description can be almost literally translated to Java instructions:

```
public void selectCustomer(int pin)
{
   assert state == PIN;
   currentCustomer = theBank.findCustomer(customerNumber, pin);
   if (currentCustomer == null)
      state = START;
   else
      state = ACCOUNT;
}
```

We won't go through a method-by-method description of the ATM program. You should take some time and compare the actual implementation against the CRC cards and the UML diagram.

ch12/atm/ATM.java

```
 1  /**
 2     An ATM that accesses a bank.
 3  */
 4  public class ATM
 5  {
 6     /**
 7        Constructs an ATM for a given bank.
 8        @param aBank the bank to which this ATM connects
 9     */
10     public ATM(Bank aBank)
11     {
12        theBank = aBank;
13        reset();
14     }
```

```
15
16      /**
17          Resets the ATM to the initial state.
18      */
19      public void reset()
20      {
21          customerNumber = -1;
22          currentAccount = null;
23          state = START;
24      }
25
26      /**
27          Sets the current customer number
28          and sets state to PIN.
29          (Precondition: state is START)
30          @param number the customer number
31      */
32      public void setCustomerNumber(int number)
33      {
34          assert state == START;
35          customerNumber = number;
36          state = PIN;
37      }
38
39      /**
40          Finds customer in bank.
41          If found, sets state to ACCOUNT, else to START.
42          (Precondition: state is PIN)
43          @param pin the PIN of the current customer
44      */
45      public void selectCustomer(int pin)
46      {
47          assert state == PIN;
48          currentCustomer = theBank.findCustomer(customerNumber, pin);
49          if (currentCustomer == null)
50              state = START;
51          else
52              state = ACCOUNT;
53      }
54
55      /**
56          Sets current account to checking or savings. Sets
57          state to TRANSACT.
58          (Precondition: state is ACCOUNT or TRANSACT)
59          @param account one of CHECKING or SAVINGS
60      */
61      public void selectAccount(int account)
62      {
63          assert state == ACCOUNT || state == TRANSACT;
64          if (account == CHECKING)
65              currentAccount = currentCustomer.getCheckingAccount();
66          else
67              currentAccount = currentCustomer.getSavingsAccount();
68          state = TRANSACT;
```

```
69      }
70
71      /**
72          Withdraws amount from current account.
73          (Precondition: state is TRANSACT)
74          @param value  the amount to withdraw
75      */
76      public void withdraw(double value)
77      {
78          assert state == TRANSACT;
79          currentAccount.withdraw(value);
80      }
81
82      /**
83          Deposits amount to current account.
84          (Precondition: state is TRANSACT)
85          @param value  the amount to deposit
86      */
87      public void deposit(double value)
88      {
89          assert state == TRANSACT;
90          currentAccount.deposit(value);
91      }
92
93      /**
94          Gets the balance of the current account.
95          (Precondition: state is TRANSACT)
96          @return  the balance
97      */
98      public double getBalance()
99      {
100         assert state == TRANSACT;
101         return currentAccount.getBalance();
102     }
103
104     /**
105         Moves back to the previous state.
106     */
107     public void back()
108     {
109         if (state == TRANSACT)
110            state = ACCOUNT;
111         else if (state == ACCOUNT)
112            state = PIN;
113         else if (state == PIN)
114            state = START;
115     }
116
117     /**
118         Gets the current state of this ATM.
119         @return  the current state
120     */
121     public int getState()
122     {
```

```
123            return state;
124        }
125
126        private int state;
127        private int customerNumber;
128        private Customer currentCustomer;
129        private BankAccount currentAccount;
130        private Bank theBank;
131
132        public static final int START = 1;
133        public static final int PIN = 2;
134        public static final int ACCOUNT = 3;
135        public static final int TRANSACT = 4;
136
137        public static final int CHECKING = 1;
138        public static final int SAVINGS = 2;
139    }
```

ch12/atm/Bank.java

```
1    import java.io.FileReader;
2    import java.io.IOException;
3    import java.util.ArrayList;
4    import java.util.Scanner;
5
6    /**
7        A bank contains customers with bank accounts.
8    */
9    public class Bank
10   {
11       /**
12           Constructs a bank with no customers.
13       */
14       public Bank()
15       {
16           customers = new ArrayList<Customer>();
17       }
18
19       /**
20           Reads the customer numbers and pins
21           and initializes the bank accounts.
22           @param filename the name of the customer file
23       */
24       public void readCustomers(String filename)
25               throws IOException
26       {
27           Scanner in = new Scanner(new FileReader(filename));
28           while (in.hasNext())
29           {
30               int number = in.nextInt();
31               int pin = in.nextInt();
32               Customer c = new Customer(number, pin);
33               addCustomer(c);
```

```
34          }
35          in.close();
36       }
37
38       /**
39          Adds a customer to the bank.
40          @param c the customer to add
41       */
42       public void addCustomer(Customer c)
43       {
44          customers.add(c);
45       }
46
47       /**
48          Finds a customer in the bank.
49          @param aNumber a customer number
50          @param aPin a personal identification number
51          @return the matching customer, or null if no customer
52          matches
53       */
54       public Customer findCustomer(int aNumber, int aPin)
55       {
56          for (Customer c : customers)
57          {
58             if (c.match(aNumber, aPin))
59                return c;
60          }
61          return null;
62       }
63
64       private ArrayList<Customer> customers;
65    }
```

ch12/atm/Customer.java

```
1    /**
2       A bank customer with a checking and a savings account.
3    */
4    public class Customer
5    {
6       /**
7          Constructs a customer with a given number and PIN.
8          @param aNumber the customer number
9          @param aPin the personal identification number
10      */
11      public Customer(int aNumber, int aPin)
12      {
13         customerNumber = aNumber;
14         pin = aPin;
15         checkingAccount = new BankAccount();
16         savingsAccount = new BankAccount();
17      }
18
```

```
19      /**
20          Tests if this customer matches a customer number
21          and PIN.
22          @param aNumber a customer number
23          @param aPin a personal identification number
24          @return true if the customer number and PIN match
25      */
26      public boolean match(int aNumber, int aPin)
27      {
28          return customerNumber == aNumber && pin == aPin;
29      }
30
31      /**
32          Gets the checking account of this customer.
33          @return the checking account
34      */
35      public BankAccount getCheckingAccount()
36      {
37          return checkingAccount;
38      }
39
40      /**
41          Gets the savings account of this customer.
42          @return the checking account
43      */
44      public BankAccount getSavingsAccount()
45      {
46          return savingsAccount;
47      }
48
49      private int customerNumber;
50      private int pin;
51      private BankAccount checkingAccount;
52      private BankAccount savingsAccount;
53  }
```

The following class implements a console user interface for the ATM.

ch12/atm/ATMSimulator.java

```
1   import java.io.IOException;
2   import java.util.Scanner;
3
4   /**
5       A text-based simulation of an automatic teller machine.
6   */
7   public class ATMSimulator
8   {
9       public static void main(String[] args)
10      {
11          ATM theATM;
12          try
13          {
```

```
14              Bank theBank = new Bank();
15              theBank.readCustomers("customers.txt");
16              theATM = new ATM(theBank);
17           }
18           catch(IOException e)
19           {
20              System.out.println("Error opening accounts file.");
21              return;
22           }
23
24           Scanner in = new Scanner(System.in);
25
26           while (true)
27           {
28              int state = theATM.getState();
29              if (state == ATM.START)
30              {
31                 System.out.print("Enter customer number: ");
32                 int number = in.nextInt();
33                 theATM.setCustomerNumber(number);
34              }
35              else if (state == ATM.PIN)
36              {
37                 System.out.print("Enter PIN: ");
38                 int pin = in.nextInt();
39                 theATM.selectCustomer(pin);
40              }
41              else if (state == ATM.ACCOUNT)
42              {
43                 System.out.print("A=Checking, B=Savings, C=Quit: ");
44                 String command = in.next();
45                 if (command.equalsIgnoreCase("A"))
46                    theATM.selectAccount(ATM.CHECKING);
47                 else if (command.equalsIgnoreCase("B"))
48                    theATM.selectAccount(ATM.SAVINGS);
49                 else if (command.equalsIgnoreCase("C"))
50                    theATM.reset();
51                 else
52                    System.out.println("Illegal input!");
53              }
54              else if (state == ATM.TRANSACT)
55              {
56                 System.out.println("Balance=" + theATM.getBalance());
57                 System.out.print("A=Deposit, B=Withdrawal, C=Cancel: ");
58                 String command = in.next();
59                 if (command.equalsIgnoreCase("A"))
60                 {
61                    System.out.print("Amount: ");
62                    double amount = in.nextDouble();
63                    theATM.deposit(amount);
64                    theATM.back();
65                 }
66                 else if (command.equalsIgnoreCase("B"))
67                 {
```

```
68                        System.out.print("Amount: ");
69                        double amount = in.nextDouble();
70                        theATM.withdraw(amount);
71                        theATM.back();
72                     }
73                     else if (command.equalsIgnoreCase("C"))
74                        theATM.back();
75                     else
76                        System.out.println("Illegal input!");
77               }
78           }
79        }
80  }
```

Output

```
Enter account number: 1
Enter PIN: 1234
A=Checking, B=Savings, C=Quit: A
Balance=0.0
A=Deposit, B=Withdrawal, C=Cancel: A
Amount: 1000
A=Checking, B=Savings, C=Quit: C
. . .
```

Here are the user interface classes for the GUI version of the user interface.

ch12/atm/ATMViewer.java

```
1  import java.io.IOException;
2  import javax.swing.JFrame;
3  import javax.swing.JOptionPane;
4
5  /**
6      A graphical simulation of an automatic teller machine.
7  */
8  public class ATMViewer
9  {
10     public static void main(String[] args)
11     {
12        ATM theATM;
13
14        try
15        {
16           Bank theBank = new Bank();
17           theBank.readCustomers("customers.txt");
18           theATM = new ATM(theBank);
19        }
20        catch(IOException e)
21        {
22           JOptionPane.showMessageDialog(null,
23               "Error opening accounts file.");
24           return;
```

```
25            }
26
27            JFrame frame = new ATMFrame(theATM);
28            frame.setTitle("First National Bank of Java");
29            frame.setDefaultCloseOperation(JFrame.EXIT_ON_CLOSE);
30            frame.setVisible(true);
31        }
32    }
```

ch12/atm/ATMFrame.java

```
1    import java.awt.FlowLayout;
2    import java.awt.GridLayout;
3    import java.awt.event.ActionEvent;
4    import java.awt.event.ActionListener;
5    import javax.swing.JButton;
6    import javax.swing.JFrame;
7    import javax.swing.JPanel;
8    import javax.swing.JTextArea;
9
10   /**
11       A frame displaying the components of an ATM.
12   */
13   public class ATMFrame extends JFrame
14   {
15       /**
16           Constructs the user interface of the ATM frame.
17       */
18       public ATMFrame(ATM anATM)
19       {
20           theATM = anATM;
21
22           // Construct components
23           pad = new KeyPad();
24
25           display = new JTextArea(4, 20);
26
27           aButton = new JButton("  A  ");
28           aButton.addActionListener(new AButtonListener());
29
30           bButton = new JButton("  B  ");
31           bButton.addActionListener(new BButtonListener());
32
33           cButton = new JButton("  C  ");
34           cButton.addActionListener(new CButtonListener());
35
36           // Add components
37
38           JPanel buttonPanel = new JPanel();
39           buttonPanel.add(aButton);
40           buttonPanel.add(bButton);
41           buttonPanel.add(cButton);
42
```

```
43          setLayout(new FlowLayout());
44          add(pad);
45          add(display);
46          add(buttonPanel);
47          showState();
48
49          setSize(FRAME_WIDTH, FRAME_HEIGHT);
50       }
51
52       /**
53          Updates display message.
54       */
55       public void showState()
56       {
57          int state = theATM.getState();
58          pad.clear();
59          if (state == ATM.START)
60             display.setText("Enter customer number\nA = OK");
61          else if (state == ATM.PIN)
62             display.setText("Enter PIN\nA = OK");
63          else if (state == ATM.ACCOUNT)
64             display.setText("Select Account\n"
65                   + "A = Checking\nB = Savings\nC = Exit");
66          else if (state == ATM.TRANSACT)
67             display.setText("Balance = "
68                   + theATM.getBalance()
69                   + "\nEnter amount and select transaction\n"
70                   + "A = Withdraw\nB = Deposit\nC = Cancel");
71       }
72
73       private class AButtonListener implements ActionListener
74       {
75          public void actionPerformed(ActionEvent event)
76          {
77             int state = theATM.getState();
78             if (state == ATM.START)
79                theATM.setCustomerNumber((int) pad.getValue());
80             else if (state == ATM.PIN)
81                theATM.selectCustomer((int) pad.getValue());
82             else if (state == ATM.ACCOUNT)
83                theATM.selectAccount(ATM.CHECKING);
84             else if (state == ATM.TRANSACT)
85             {
86                theATM.withdraw(pad.getValue());
87                theATM.back();
88             }
89             showState();
90          }
91       }
92
93       private class BButtonListener implements ActionListener
94       {
95          public void actionPerformed(ActionEvent event)
96          {
```

```
 97            int state = theATM.getState();
 98            if (state == ATM.ACCOUNT)
 99               theATM.selectAccount(ATM.SAVINGS);
100            else if (state == ATM.TRANSACT)
101            {
102               theATM.deposit(pad.getValue());
103               theATM.back();
104            }
105            showState();
106         }
107      }
108
109      private class CButtonListener implements ActionListener
110      {
111         public void actionPerformed(ActionEvent event)
112         {
113            int state = theATM.getState();
114            if (state == ATM.ACCOUNT)
115               theATM.reset();
116            else if (state == ATM.TRANSACT)
117               theATM.back();
118            showState();
119         }
120      }
121
122      private JButton aButton;
123      private JButton bButton;
124      private JButton cButton;
125
126      private KeyPad pad;
127      private JTextArea display;
128
129      private ATM theATM;
130
131      private static final int FRAME_WIDTH = 300;
132      private static final int FRAME_HEIGHT = 300;
133   }
```

This class uses layout managers to arrange the text field and the keypad buttons. See Chapter 18 for more information about layout managers.

ch12/atm/KeyPad.java

```
1   import java.awt.BorderLayout;
2   import java.awt.GridLayout;
3   import java.awt.event.ActionEvent;
4   import java.awt.event.ActionListener;
5   import javax.swing.JButton;
6   import javax.swing.JPanel;
7   import javax.swing.JTextField;
8
```

```
 9  /**
10      A component that lets the user enter a number, using
11      a keypad labeled with digits.
12  */
13  public class KeyPad extends JPanel
14  {
15      /**
16          Constructs the keypad panel.
17      */
18      public KeyPad()
19      {
20          setLayout(new BorderLayout());
21
22          // Add display field
23
24          display = new JTextField();
25          add(display, "North");
26
27          // Make button panel
28
29          buttonPanel = new JPanel();
30          buttonPanel.setLayout(new GridLayout(4, 3));
31
32          // Add digit buttons
33
34          addButton("7");
35          addButton("8");
36          addButton("9");
37          addButton("4");
38          addButton("5");
39          addButton("6");
40          addButton("1");
41          addButton("2");
42          addButton("3");
43          addButton("0");
44          addButton(".");
45
46          // Add clear entry button
47
48          clearButton = new JButton("CE");
49          buttonPanel.add(clearButton);
50
51          class ClearButtonListener implements ActionListener
52          {
53              public void actionPerformed(ActionEvent event)
54              {
55                  display.setText("");
56              }
57          }
58          ActionListener listener = new ClearButtonListener();
59
60          clearButton.addActionListener(new
61                  ClearButtonListener());
62
```

```
63          add(buttonPanel, "Center");
64       }
65
66       /**
67          Adds a button to the button panel.
68          @param label the button label
69       */
70       private void addButton(final String label)
71       {
72          class DigitButtonListener implements ActionListener
73          {
74             public void actionPerformed(ActionEvent event)
75             {
76
77                // Don't add two decimal points
78                if (label.equals(".")
79                      && display.getText().indexOf(".") != -1)
80                   return;
81
82                // Append label text to button
83                display.setText(display.getText() + label);
84             }
85          }
86
87          JButton button = new JButton(label);
88          buttonPanel.add(button);
89          ActionListener listener = new DigitButtonListener();
90          button.addActionListener(listener);
91       }
92
93       /**
94          Gets the value that the user entered.
95          @return the value in the text field of the keypad
96       */
97       public double getValue()
98       {
99          return Double.parseDouble(display.getText());
100      }
101
102      /**
103         Clears the display.
104      */
105      public void clear()
106      {
107         display.setText("");
108      }
109
110      private JPanel buttonPanel;
111      private JButton clearButton;
112      private JTextField display;
113   }
```

In this chapter, you learned a systematic approach for building a relatively complex program. However, object-oriented design is definitely not a spectator sport. To really learn how to design and implement programs, you have to gain experience by repeating this process with your own projects. It is quite possible that you don't immediately home in on a good solution and that you need to go back and reorganize your classes and responsibilities. That is normal and only to be expected. The purpose of the object-oriented design process is to spot these problems in the design phase, when they are still easy to rectify, instead of in the implementation phase, when massive reorganization is more difficult and time consuming.

SELF CHECK

12. Why does the Bank class in this example not store an array list of bank accounts?

13. Suppose the requirements change—you need to save the current account balances to a file after every transaction and reload them when the program starts. What is the impact of this change on the design?

RANDOM FACT 12.2

Software Development—Art or Science?

There has been a long discussion whether the discipline of computing is a science or not. We call the field "computer science", but that doesn't mean much. Except possibly for librarians and sociologists, few people believe that library science and social science are scientific endeavors.

A scientific discipline aims to discover certain fundamental principles dictated by the laws of nature. It operates on the *scientific method:* by posing hypotheses and testing them with experiments that are repeatable by other workers in the field. For example, a physicist may have a theory on the makeup of nuclear particles and attempt to confirm or refute that theory by running experiments in a particle collider. If an experiment cannot be confirmed, such as the "cold fusion" research in the early 1990s, then the theory dies a quick death.

Some software developers indeed run experiments. They try out various methods of computing certain results or of configuring computer systems, and measure the differences in performance. However, their aim is not to discover laws of nature.

Some computer scientists discover fundamental principles. One class of fundamental results, for instance, states that it is impossible to write certain kinds of computer programs, no matter how powerful the computing equipment is. For example, it is impossible to write a program that takes as its input any two Java program files and as its output prints whether or not these two programs always compute the same results. Such a program would be very handy for grading student homework, but nobody, no matter how clever, will ever be able to write one that works for all input files. However, the majority of computer scientists are not researching the limits of computation.

Some people view software development as an *art* or *craft*. A programmer who writes elegant code that is easy to understand and runs with optimum efficiency can indeed be considered a good craftsman. Calling it an art is perhaps far-fetched, because an art object requires an audience to appreciate it, whereas the program code is generally hidden from the program user.

Others call software development an *engineering discipline*. Just as mechanical engineering is based on the fundamental mathematical principles of statics, computing has certain mathematical foundations. There is more to mechanical engineering than mathematics, such as knowledge of materials and of project planning. The same is true for computing. A *software engineer* needs to know about planning, budgeting, design, test automation, documentation, and source code control, in addition to computer science subjects, such as programming, algorithm design, and database technologies.

In one somewhat worrisome aspect, software development does not have the same standing as other engineering disciplines. There is little agreement as to what constitutes professional conduct in the computer field. Unlike the scientist, whose main responsibility is the search for truth, the software developer must strive to satisfy the conflicting demands of quality, safety, and economy. Engineering disciplines have professional organizations that hold their members to standards of conduct. The computer field is so new that in many cases we simply don't know the correct method for achieving certain tasks. That makes it difficult to set professional standards.

What do you think? From your limited experience, do you consider software development an art, a craft, a science, or an engineering activity?

CHAPTER SUMMARY

1. The life cycle of software encompasses all activities from initial analysis until obsolescence.

2. A formal process for software development describes phases of the development process and gives guidelines for how to carry out the phases.

3. The waterfall model of software development describes a sequential process of analysis, design, implementation, testing, and deployment.

4. The spiral model of software development describes an iterative process in which design and implementation are repeated.

5. Extreme Programming is a development methodology that strives for simplicity by removing formal structure and focusing on best practices.

6. In object-oriented design, you discover classes, determine the responsibilities of classes, and describe the relationships between classes.

7. A CRC card describes a class, its responsibilities, and its collaborating classes.

8. Inheritance (the *is-a* relationship) is sometimes inappropriately used when the *has-a* relationship would be more appropriate.

9. Aggregation (the *has-a* relationship) denotes that objects of one class contain references to objects of another class.

10. Dependency is another name for the "uses" relationship.

11. You need to be able to distinguish the UML notations for inheritance, interface implementation, aggregation, and dependency.

12. Use javadoc comments (with the method bodies left blank) to record the behavior of classes.

FURTHER READING

1. Grady Booch, James Rumbaugh, and Ivar Jacobson, *The Unified Modeling Language User Guide,* Addison-Wesley, 1999.

2. Kent Beck, *Extreme Programming Explained,* Addison-Wesley, 1999.

3. W. H. Sackmann, W. J. Erikson, and E. E. Grant, "Exploratory Experimental Studies Comparing Online and Offline Programming Performance", *Communications of the ACM, vol. 11, no. 1* (January 1968), pp. 3–11.

4. F. Brooks, *The Mythical Man-Month,* Addison-Wesley, 1975.

REVIEW EXERCISES

★ **Exercise R12.1.** What is the software life cycle?

★★ **Exercise R12.2.** List the steps in the process of object-oriented design that this chapter recommends for student use.

★ **Exercise R12.3.** Give a rule of thumb for how to find classes when designing a program.

★ **Exercise R12.4.** Give a rule of thumb for how to find methods when designing a program.

★★ **Exercise R12.5.** After discovering a method, why is it important to identify the object that is *responsible* for carrying out the action?

★ **Exercise R12.6.** What relationship is appropriate between the following classes: aggregation, inheritance, or neither?

    a. University–Student

    b. Student–TeachingAssistant

    c. Student–Freshman

    d. Student–Professor

    e. Car–Door

    f. Truck–Vehicle

    g. Traffic–TrafficSign

    h. TrafficSign–Color

★★ **Exercise R12.7.** Every BMW is a vehicle. Should a class BMW inherit from the class Vehicle? BMW is a vehicle manufacturer. Does that mean that the class BMW should inherit from the class VehicleManufacturer?

★★ **Exercise R12.8.** Some books on object-oriented programming recommend using inheritance so that the class Circle extends the class Point. Then the Circle class inherits the setLocation method from the Point superclass. Explain why the setLocation method need not be redefined in the subclass. Why is it nevertheless not a good idea to have Circle inherit from Point? Conversely, would inheriting Point from Circle fulfill the *is-a* rule? Would it be a good idea?

★   **Exercise R12.9.** Write CRC cards for the Coin and CashRegister classes described in Section 8.2.

★   **Exercise R12.10.** Write CRC cards for the Bank and BankAccount classes in Section 7.2.

★★   **Exercise R12.11.** Draw a UML diagram for the Coin and CashRegister classes described in Section 8.2.

★★★   **Exercise R12.12.** A file contains a set of records describing countries. Each record consists of the name of the country, its population, and its area. Suppose your task is to write a program that reads in such a file and prints

- The country with the largest area
- The country with the largest population
- The country with the largest population density (people per square kilometer)

Think through the problems that you need to solve. What classes and methods will you need? Produce a set of CRC cards, a UML diagram, and a set of javadoc comments.

★★★   **Exercise R12.13.** Discover classes and methods for generating a student report card that lists all classes, grades, and the grade point average for a semester. Produce a set of CRC cards, a UML diagram, and a set of javadoc comments.

★★★   **Exercise R12.14.** Consider a quiz grading system that grades student responses to quizzes. A quiz consists of questions. There are different types of questions, including essay questions and multiple-choice questions. Students turn in submissions for quizzes, and the grading system grades them. Draw a UML diagram for classes Quiz, Question, EssayQuestion, MultipleChoiceQuestion, Student, and Submission.

Additional review exercises are available in WileyPLUS.

PROGRAMMING EXERCISES

★★   **Exercise P12.1.** Enhance the invoice-printing program by providing for two kinds of line items: One kind describes products that are purchased in certain numerical quantities (such as "3 toasters"), another describes a fixed charge (such as "shipping: $5.00"). *Hint:* Use inheritance. Produce a UML diagram of your modified implementation.

★★   **Exercise P12.2.** The invoice-printing program is somewhat unrealistic because the formatting of the LineItem objects won't lead to good visual results when the prices and quantities have varying numbers of digits. Enhance the format method in two ways: Accept an int[] array of column widths as a parameter. Use the NumberFormat class to format the currency values.

★★ **Exercise P12.3.** The invoice-printing program has an unfortunate flaw—it mixes "business logic", the computation of total charges, and "presentation", the visual appearance of the invoice. To appreciate this flaw, imagine the changes that would be necessary to draw the invoice in HTML for presentation on the Web. Reimplement the program, using a separate `InvoiceFormatter` class to format the invoice. That is, the `Invoice` and `LineItem` methods are no longer responsible for formatting. However, they will acquire other responsibilities, because the `Invoice-Formatter` class needs to query them for the values that it requires.

★★★ **Exercise P12.4.** Write a program that teaches arithmetic to your younger brother. The program tests addition and subtraction. In level 1 it tests only addition of numbers less than 10 whose sum is less than 10. In level 2 it tests addition of arbitrary one-digit numbers. In level 3 it tests subtraction of one-digit numbers with a non-negative difference. Generate random problems and get the player input. The player gets up to two tries per problem. Advance from one level to the next when the player has achieved a score of five points.

★★★ **Exercise P12.5.** Design a simple e-mail messaging system. A message has a recipient, a sender, and a message text. A mailbox can store messages. Supply a number of mailboxes for different users and a user interface for users to log in, send messages to other users, read their own messages, and log out. Follow the design process that was described in this chapter.

★★ **Exercise P12.6.** Write a program that simulates a vending machine. Products can be purchased by inserting coins with a value at least equal to the cost of the product. A user selects a product from a list of available products, adds coins, and either gets the product or gets the coins returned if insufficient money was supplied or if the product is sold out. The machine does not give change if too much money was added. Products can be restocked and money removed by an operator. Follow the design process that was described in this chapter. Your solution should include a class `VendingMachine` that is not coupled with the `Scanner` or `PrintStream` classes.

★★★ **Exercise P12.7.** Write a program to design an appointment calendar. An appointment includes the date, starting time, ending time, and a description; for example,

```
Dentist 2007/10/1 17:30 18:30
CS1 class 2007/10/2 08:30 10:00
```

Supply a user interface to add appointments, remove canceled appointments, and print out a list of appointments for a particular day. Follow the design process that was described in this chapter. Your solution should include a class `Appointment-Calendar` that is not coupled with the `Scanner` or `PrintStream` classes.

★★★ **Exercise P12.8.** *Airline seating.* Write a program that assigns seats on an airplane. Assume the airplane has 20 seats in first class (5 rows of 4 seats each, separated by an aisle) and 90 seats in economy class (15 rows of 6 seats each, separated by an aisle). Your program should take three commands: add passengers, show seating, and quit. When passengers are added, ask for the class (first or economy), the number of passengers traveling together (1 or 2 in first class; 1 to 3 in economy), and the seating preference (aisle or window in first class; aisle, center, or window in economy).

Then try to find a match and assign the seats. If no match exists, print a message. Your solution should include a class `Airplane` that is not coupled with the `Scanner` or `PrintSream` classes. Follow the design process that was described in this chapter.

★★   **Exercise P12.9.** Modify the implementations of the classes in the ATM example so that the bank manages a collection of bank accounts and a separate collection of customers. Allow joint accounts in which some accounts can have more than one customer.

★★★   **Exercise P12.10.** Write a program that administers and grades quizzes. A quiz consists of questions. There are four types of questions: text questions, number questions, choice questions with a single answer, and choice questions with multiple answers. When grading a text question, ignore leading or trailing spaces and letter case. When grading a numeric question, accept a response that is approximately the same as the answer.

A quiz is specified in a text file. Each question starts with a letter indicating the question type (T, N, S, M), followed by a line containing the question text. The next line of a non-choice question contains the answer. Choice questions have a list of choices that is terminated by a blank line. Each choice starts with + (correct) or - (incorrect). Here is a sample file:

```
T
Which Java keyword is used to define a subclass?
extends
S
What is the original name of the Java language?
- *7
- C--
+ Oak
- Gosling

M
Which of the following types are supertypes of Rectangle?
- PrintStream
+ Shape
+ RectangularShape
+ Object
- String

N
What is the square root of 2?
1.41421356
```

Your program should read in a quiz file, prompt the user for responses to all questions, and grade the responses. Follow the design process that was described in this chapter.

★★★G   **Exercise P12.11.** Implement a program to teach your baby sister to read the clock. In the game, present an analog clock, such as the one in Figure 12. Generate random times and display the clock. Accept guesses from the player. Reward the player for correct guesses. After two incorrect guesses, display the correct answer and make a new random time. Implement several levels of play. In level 1, only show full hours. In level 2, show quarter hours. In level 3, show five-minute multiples, and in level 4, show any number of minutes. After a player has achieved five correct guesses at one level, advance to the next level.

Figure 12   An Analog Clock

★★★G   **Exercise P12.12.** Write a program that can be used to design a suburban scene, with houses, streets, and cars. Users can add houses and cars of various colors to a street. Write more specific requirements that include a detailed description of the user interface. Then, discover classes and methods, provide UML diagrams, and implement your program.

★★★G   **Exercise P12.13.** Write a simple graphics editor that allows users to add a mixture of shapes (ellipses, rectangles, and lines in different colors) to a panel. Supply commands to load and save the picture. Discover classes, supply a UML diagram, and implement your program.

Additional programming exercises are available in WileyPLUS.

PROGRAMMING PROJECTS

★★★   **Project 12.1.** Produce a requirements document for a program that allows a company to send out personalized mailings, either by e-mail or through the postal service. Template files contain the message text, together with variable fields (such as Dear [Title] [Last Name] . . .). A database (stored as a text file) contains the field values for each recipient. Use HTML as the output file format. Then design and implement the program.

★★★   **Project 12.2.** Write a tic-tac-toe game that allows a human player to play against the computer. Your program will play many turns against a human opponent, and it will learn. When it is the computer's turn, the computer randomly selects an empty field, except that it won't ever choose a losing combination. For that purpose, your program must keep an array of losing combinations. Whenever the human wins, the immediately preceding combination is stored as losing. For example, suppose that x = computer and o = human. Suppose the current combination is

```
 O | X | X
---+---+---
   | O |
---+---+---
   |   |
```

Now it is the human's turn, who will of course choose

```
 O | X | X
---+---+---
   | O |
---+---+---
   |   | O
```

The computer should then remember the preceding combination

```
 O | X | X
---+---+---
   | O |
---+---+---
   |   |
```

as a losing combination. As a result, the computer will never again choose that combination from

```
 O | X |
---+---+---
   | O |
---+---+---
   |   |
```

or

```
 O |   | X
---+---+---
   | O |
---+---+---
   |   |
```

Discover classes and supply a UML diagram before you begin to program.

ANSWERS TO SELF-CHECK QUESTIONS

1. It is unlikely that the customer did a perfect job with the requirements document. If you don't accommodate changes, your customer may not like the outcome. If you charge for the changes, your customer may not like the cost.

2. An "extreme" spiral model, with lots of iterations.

3. To give frequent feedback as to whether the current iteration of the product fits customer needs.

4. `FileWriter`

5. To produce the shipping address of the customer.

6. Reword the responsibilities so that they are at a higher level, or come up with more classes to handle the responsibilities.

7. Through aggregation. The bank manages bank account objects.

8. Through inheritance.

9. The `BankAccount`, `System`, and `PrintStream` classes.

10. The `Invoice` class is responsible for computing the amount due. It collaborates with the `LineItem` class.

11. This design decision reduces coupling. It enables us to reuse the classes when we want to show the invoice in a dialog box or on a web page.

12. The bank needs to store the list of customers so that customers can log in. We need to locate all bank accounts of a customer, and we chose to simply store them in the customer class. In this program, there is no further need to access bank accounts.

13. The `Bank` class needs to have an additional responsibility: to load and save the accounts. The bank can carry out this responsibility because it has access to the customer objects and, through them, to the bank accounts.

Recursion

CHAPTER GOALS

- To learn about the method of recursion

- To understand the relationship between recursion and iteration

- To analyze problems that are much easier to solve by recursion than by iteration

- To learn to "think recursively"

- To be able to use recursive helper methods

- To understand when the use of recursion affects the efficiency of an algorithm

The **method of** recursion is a powerful technique to break up complex computational problems into simpler ones. The term "recursion" refers to the fact that the same computation recurs, or occurs repeatedly, as the problem is solved. Recursion is often the most natural way of thinking about a problem, and there are some computations that are very difficult to perform without recursion. This chapter shows you simple and complex examples of recursion and teaches you how to "think recursively".

CHAPTER CONTENTS

13.1 Triangle Numbers

We begin this chapter with a very simple example that demonstrates the power of thinking recursively. In this example, we will look at triangle shapes such as the ones from Section 6.3. We'd like to compute the area of a triangle of width n, assuming that each [] square has area 1. This value is sometimes called the nth *triangle number*. For example, as you can tell from looking at

```
[]
[][]
[][][]
```

the third triangle number is 6.

You may know that there is a very simple formula to compute these numbers, but you should pretend for now that you don't know about it. The ultimate purpose of this section is not to compute triangle numbers, but to learn about the concept of recursion in a simple situation.

Here is the outline of the class that we will develop:

```java
public class Triangle
{
   public Triangle(int aWidth)
   {
      width = aWidth;
   }

   public int getArea()
   {
      . . .
   }

   private int width;
}
```

If the width of the triangle is 1, then the triangle consists of a single square, and its area is 1. Let's take care of this case first.

```
public int getArea()
{
    if (width == 1) return 1;
    . . .
}
```

To deal with the general case, consider this picture.

```
[]
[][]
[][][]
[][][][]
```

Suppose we knew the area of the smaller, colored triangle. Then we could easily compute the area of the larger triangle as

```
smallerArea + width
```

How can we get the smaller area? Let's make a smaller triangle and ask it!

```
Triangle smallerTriangle = new Triangle(width - 1);
int smallerArea = smallerTriangle.getArea();
```

Now we can complete the getArea method:

```
public int getArea()
{
    if (width == 1) return 1;
    Triangle smallerTriangle = new Triangle(width - 1);
    int smallerArea = smallerTriangle.getArea();
    return smallerArea + width;
}
```

A recursive computation solves a problem by using the solution of the same problem with simpler values.

Here is an illustration of what happens when we compute the area of a triangle of width 4.

- The getArea method makes a smaller triangle of width 3.
  - It calls getArea on that triangle.
    - That method makes a smaller triangle of width 2.
      - It calls getArea on that triangle.
        - That method makes a smaller triangle of width 1.
          - It calls getArea on that triangle.
          - That method returns 1.
        - The method returns smallerArea + width = 1 + 2 = 3.
      - The method returns smallerArea + width = 3 + 3 = 6.
  - The method returns smallerArea + width = 6 + 4 = 10.

This solution has one remarkable aspect. To solve the area problem for a triangle of a given width, we use the fact that we can solve the same problem for a lesser width. This is called a *recursive* solution.

The call pattern of a *recursive method* looks complicated, and the key to the successful design of a recursive method is *not to think about it.* Instead, look at the getArea method one more time and notice how utterly reasonable it is. If the width is 1, then, of course, the area is 1. The next part is just as reasonable. Compute the area of the smaller triangle *and don't think about why that works*. Then the area of the larger triangle is clearly the sum of the smaller area and the width.

There are two key requirements to make sure that the recursion is successful:

- Every recursive call must simplify the computation in some way.

- There must be special cases to handle the simplest computations directly.

> For a recursion to terminate, there must be special cases for the simplest values.

The `getArea` method calls itself again with smaller and smaller width values. Eventually the width must reach 1, and there is a special case for computing the area of a triangle with width 1. Thus, the `getArea` method always succeeds.

Actually, you have to be careful. What happens when you call the area of a triangle with width –1? It computes the area of a triangle with width –2, which computes the area of a triangle with width –3, and so on. To avoid this, the `getArea` method should return 0 if the width is ≤ 0.

Recursion is not really necessary to compute the triangle numbers. The area of a triangle equals the sum

```
1 + 2 + 3 + . . . + width
```

Of course, we can program a simple loop:

```
double area = 0;
for (int i = 1; i <= width; i++)
   area = area + i;
```

Many simple recursions can be computed as loops. However, loop equivalents for more complex recursions—such as the one in our next example—can be complex.

Actually, in this case, you don't even need a loop to compute the answer. The sum of the first n integers can be computed as

$$1 + 2 + \cdots + n = n \times (n+1)/2$$

Thus, the area equals

```
width * (width + 1) / 2
```

Therefore, neither recursion nor a loop is required to solve this problem. The recursive solution is intended as a "warm-up" to introduce you to the concept of recursion.

ch13/triangle/Triangle.java

```
 1  /**
 2      A triangular shape composed of stacked unit squares like this:
 3      []
 4      [][]
 5      [][][]
 6      . . .
 7  */
 8  public class Triangle
 9  {
```

```
10    /**
11        Constructs a triangular shape.
12        @param aWidth the width (and height) of the triangle
13    */
14    public Triangle(int aWidth)
15    {
16        width = aWidth;
17    }
18
19    /**
20        Computes the area of the triangle.
21        @return the area
22    */
23    public int getArea()
24    {
25        if (width <= 0) return 0;
26        if (width == 1) return 1;
27        Triangle smallerTriangle = new Triangle(width - 1);
28        int smallerArea = smallerTriangle.getArea();
29        return smallerArea + width;
30    }
31
32    private int width;
33 }
```

ch13/triangle/TriangleTester.java

```
1  public class TriangleTester
2  {
3      public static void main(String[] args)
4      {
5          Triangle t = new Triangle(10);
6          int area = t.getArea();
7          System.out.println("Area: " + area);
8          System.out.println("Expected: 55");
9      }
10 }
```

Output

```
Enter width: 10
Area: 55
Expected: 55
```

SELF CHECK

1. Why is the statement if (width == 1) return 1; in the getArea method unnecessary?

2. How would you modify the program to recursively compute the area of a square?

COMMON ERROR 13.1

Infinite Recursion

A common programming error is an infinite recursion: a method calling itself over and over with no end in sight. The computer needs some amount of memory for bookkeeping for each call. After some number of calls, all memory that is available for this purpose is exhausted. Your program shuts down and reports a "stack fault".

Infinite recursion happens either because the parameter values don't get simpler or because a special terminating case is missing. For example, suppose the getArea method computes the area of a triangle with width 0. If it wasn't for the special test, the method would have constructed triangles with width –1, –2, –3, and so on.

13.2 Permutations

We will now turn to a more complex example of recursion that would be difficult to program with a simple loop. We will design a class that lists all permutations of a string. A *permutation* is simply a rearrangement of the letters. For example, the string "eat" has six permutations (including the original string itself):

```
"eat"
"eta"
"aet"
"ate"
"tea"
"tae"
```

As in the preceding section, we will define a class that is in charge of computing the answer. In this case, the answer is not a single number but a collection of permuted strings. Here is our class:

```
public class PermutationGenerator
{
    public PermutationGenerator(String aWord) { . . . }
    ArrayList<String> getPermutations() { . . . }
}
```

Here is the test program that prints out all permutations of the string "eat":

ch13/permute/PermutationGeneratorDemo.java

```
1  import java.util.ArrayList;
2
3  /**
4      This program demonstrates the permutation generator.
5  */
6  public class PermutationGeneratorDemo
7  {
```

```
 8      public static void main(String[] args)
 9      {
10          PermutationGenerator generator
11                  = new PermutationGenerator("eat");
12          ArrayList<String> permutations = generator.getPermutations();
13          for (String s : permutations)
14          {
15              System.out.println(s);
16          }
17      }
18  }
```

Output

```
eat
eta
aet
ate
tea
tae
```

Now we need a way to generate the permutations recursively. Consider the string "eat". Let's simplify the problem. First, we'll generate all permutations that start with the letter 'e', then those that start with 'a', and finally those that start with 't'. How do we generate the permutations that start with 'e'? We need to know the permutations of the substring "at". But that's the same problem—to generate all permutations—with a simpler input, namely the shorter string "at". Thus, we can use recursion. Generate the permutations of the substring "at". They are

```
"at"
"ta"
```

For each permutation of that substring, prepend the letter 'e' to get the permutations of "eat" that start with 'e', namely

```
"eat"
"eta"
```

Now let's turn our attention to the permutations of "eat" that start with 'a'. We need to produce the permutations of the remaining letters, "et". They are:

```
"et"
"te"
```

We add the letter 'a' to the front of the strings and obtain

```
"aet"
"ate"
```

We generate the permutations that start with 't' in the same way.

That's the idea. The implementation is fairly straightforward. In the get-Permutations method, we loop through all positions in the word to be permuted.

For each of them, we compute the shorter word that is obtained by removing the ith letter:

```
String shorterWord = word.substring(0, i) + word.substring(i + 1);
```

We construct a permutation generator to get the permutations of the shorter word, and ask it to give us all permutations of the shorter word.

```
PermutationGenerator shorterPermutationGenerator
      = new PermutationGenerator(shorterWord);
ArrayList<String> shorterWordPermutations
      = shorterPermutationGenerator.getPermutations();
```

Finally, we add the removed letter to the front of all permutations of the shorter word.

```
for (String s : shorterWordPermutations)
{
    result.add(word.charAt(i) + s);
}
```

As always, we have to provide a special case for the simplest strings. The simplest possible string is the empty string, which has a single permutation—itself.

Here is the complete PermutationGenerator class.

ch13/permute/PermutationGenerator.java

```
 1  import java.util.ArrayList;
 2
 3  /**
 4      This class generates permutations of a word.
 5  */
 6  public class PermutationGenerator
 7  {
 8      /**
 9          Constructs a permutation generator.
10          @param aWord  the word to permute
11      */
12      public PermutationGenerator(String aWord)
13      {
14          word = aWord;
15      }
16
17      /**
18          Gets all permutations of a given word.
19      */
20      public ArrayList<String> getPermutations()
21      {
22          ArrayList<String> result = new ArrayList<String>();
23
24          // The empty string has a single permutation: itself
25          if (word.length() == 0)
26          {
27              result.add(word);
28              return result;
29          }
```

```
30
31          // Loop through all character positions
32          for (int i = 0; i < word.length(); i++)
33          {
34              // Form a simpler word by removing the ith character
35              String shorterWord = word.substring(0, i)
36                      + word.substring(i + 1);
37
38              // Generate all permutations of the simpler word
39              PermutationGenerator shorterPermutationGenerator
40                      = new PermutationGenerator(shorterWord);
41              ArrayList<String> shorterWordPermutations
42                      = shorterPermutationGenerator.getPermutations();
43
44              // Add the removed character to the front of
45              // each permutation of the simpler word
46              for (String s : shorterWordPermutations)
47              {
48                  result.add(word.charAt(i) + s);
49              }
50          }
51          // Return all permutations
52          return result;
53      }
54
55      private String word;
56 }
```

Compare the PermutationGenerator and Triangle classes. Both of them work on the same principle. When they work on a more complex input, they first solve the problem for a simpler input. Then they combine the result for the simpler input with additional work to deliver the results for the more complex input. There really is no particular complexity behind that process as long as you think about the solution on that level only. However, behind the scenes, the simpler input creates even simpler input, which creates yet another simplification, and so on, until one input is so simple that the result can be obtained without further help. It is interesting to think about this process, but it can also be confusing. What's important is that you can focus on the one level that matters—putting a solution together from the slightly simpler problem, ignoring the fact that it also uses recursion to get its results.

SELF CHECK

3. What are all permutations of the four-letter word beat?
4. Our recursion for the permutation generator stops at the empty string. What simple modification would make the recursion stop at strings of length 0 or 1?

COMMON ERROR 13.2

Tracing Through Recursive Methods

Debugging a recursive method can be somewhat challenging. When you set a breakpoint in a recursive method, the program stops as soon as that program line is encountered in *any call to the recursive method.* Suppose you want to debug the recursive getArea method of the Triangle class. Debug the TriangleTester program and run until the beginning of the getArea method. Inspect the width instance variable. It is 10.

Remove the breakpoint and now run until the statement return smallerArea + width; (see Figure 1). When you inspect width again, its value is 2! That makes no sense. There was no instruction that changed the value of width. Is that a bug with the debugger?

No. The program stopped in the first recursive call to getArea that reached the return statement. If you are confused, look at the *call stack* (top left in the figure). You will see that nine calls to getArea are pending.

You can debug recursive methods with the debugger. You just need to be particularly careful, and watch the call stack to understand which nested call you currently are in.

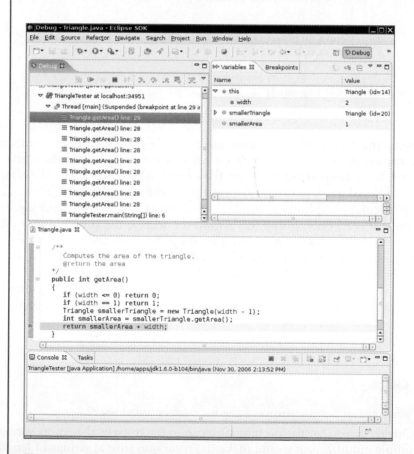

Figure 1 Debugging a Recursive Method

How To 13.1

Thinking Recursively

To solve a problem recursively requires a different mindset than to solve it by programming loops. In fact, it helps if you are, or pretend to be, a bit lazy and like others to do most of the work for you. If you need to solve a complex problem, pretend that "someone else" will do most of the heavy lifting and solve the problem for all simpler inputs. Then you only need to figure out how you can turn the solutions with simpler inputs into a solution for the whole problem.

To illustrate the method of recursion, let us consider the following problem. We want to test whether a sentence is a *palindrome*—a string that is equal to itself when you reverse all characters. Typical examples of palindromes are

- A man, a plan, a canal—Panama!

- Go hang a salami, I'm a lasagna hog

and, of course, the oldest palindrome of all:

- Madam, I'm Adam

When testing for a palindrome, we match upper- and lowercase letters, and ignore all spaces and punctuation marks.

We want to implement the isPalindrome method in the following class:

```java
public class Sentence
{
   /**
       Constructs a sentence.
       @param aText a string containing all characters of the sentence
   */
   public Sentence(String aText)
   {
      text = aText;
   }

   /**
       Tests whether this sentence is a palindrome.
       @return true if this sentence is a palindrome, false otherwise
   */
   public boolean isPalindrome()
   {
      . . .
   }

   private String text;
}
```

Step 1 Consider various ways to simplify inputs.

In your mind, fix a particular input or set of inputs for the problem that you want to solve.

Think how you can simplify the inputs in such a way that the same problem can be applied to the simpler input.

When you consider simpler inputs, you may want to remove just a little bit from the original input—maybe remove one or two characters from a string, or remove a small portion of a geometric shape. But sometimes it is more useful to cut the input in half and then see what it means to solve the problem for both halves.

In the palindrome test problem, the input is the string that we need to test. How can you simplify the input? Here are several possibilities:

- Remove the first character.
- Remove the last character.
- Remove both the first and last characters.
- Remove a character from the middle.
- Cut the string into two halves.

These simpler inputs are all potential inputs for the palindrome test.

Step 2   Combine solutions with simpler inputs into a solution of the original problem.

In your mind, consider the solutions of your problem for the simpler inputs that you discovered in Step 1. Don't worry *how* those solutions are obtained. Simply have faith that the solutions are readily available. Just say to yourself: These are simpler inputs, so someone else will solve the problem for me.

Now think how you can turn the solution for the simpler inputs into a solution for the input that you are currently thinking about. Maybe you need to add a small quantity, related to the quantity that you lopped off to arrive at the simpler input. Maybe you cut the original input in half and have solutions for each half. Then you may need to add both solutions to arrive at a solution for the whole.

Consider the methods for simplifying the inputs for the palindrome test. Cutting the string in half doesn't seem a good idea. If you cut

```
"Madam, I'm Adam"
```

in half, you get two strings:

```
"Madam, I"
```

and

```
"'m Adam"
```

Neither of them is a palindrome. Cutting the input in half and testing whether the halves are palindromes seems a dead end.

The most promising simplification is to remove the first *and* last characters.

Removing the M at the front and the m at the back yields

```
"adam, I'm Ada"
```

Suppose you can verify that the shorter string is a palindrome. Then *of course* the original string is a palindrome—we put the same letter in the front and the back. That's extremely promising. A word is a palindrome if

- The first and last letters match (ignoring letter case)

and

- The word obtained by removing the first and last letters is a palindrome.

Again, don't worry how the test works for the shorter string. It just works.

There is one other case to consider. What if the first or last letter of the word is not a letter? For example, the string

```
"A man, a plan, a canal, Panama!"
```

ends in a ! character, which does not match the A in the front. But we should ignore non-letters when testing for palindromes. Thus, when the last character is not a letter but the first character is a letter, it doesn't make sense to remove both the first and the last characters. That's not a problem. Remove only the last character. If the shorter string is a palindrome, then it stays a palindrome when you attach a nonletter.

The same argument applies if the first character is not a letter. Now we have a complete set of cases.

- If the first and last characters are both letters, then check whether they match. If so, remove both and test the shorter string.
- Otherwise, if the last character isn't a letter, remove it and test the shorter string.
- Otherwise, the first character isn't a letter. Remove it and test the shorter string.

In all three cases, you can use the solution to the simpler problem to arrive at a solution to your problem.

Step 3   Find solutions to the simplest inputs.

A recursive computation keeps simplifying its inputs. Eventually it arrives at very simple inputs. To make sure that the recursion comes to a stop, you must deal with the simplest inputs separately. Come up with special solutions for them, which is usually very easy.

However, sometimes you get into philosophical questions dealing with *degenerate* inputs: empty strings, shapes with no area, and so on. Then you may want to investigate a slightly larger input that gets reduced to such a trivial input and see what value you should attach to the degenerate inputs so that the simpler value, when used according to the rules you discovered in Step 2, yields the correct answer.

Let's look at the simplest strings for the palindrome test:

- Strings with two characters
- Strings with a single character
- The empty string

We don't have to come up with a special solution for strings with two characters. Step 2 still applies to those strings—either or both of the characters are removed. But we do need to worry about strings of length 0 and 1. In those cases, Step 2 can't apply. There aren't two characters to remove.

The empty string is a palindrome—it's the same string when you read it backwards. If you find that too artificial, consider a string "mm". According to the rule discovered in Step 2, this string is a palindrome if the first and last characters of that string match and the remainder—that is, the empty string—is also a palindrome. Therefore, it makes sense to consider the empty string a palindrome.

A string with a single letter, such as "I", is a palindrome. How about the case in which the character is not a letter, such as "!"? Removing the ! yields the empty string, which is a palindrome. Thus, we conclude that all strings of length 0 or 1 are palindromes.

Step 4   Implement the solution by combining the simple cases and the reduction step.

Now you are ready to implement the solution. Make separate cases for the simple inputs that you considered in Step 3. If the input isn't one of the simplest cases, then implement the logic you discovered in Step 2.

Here is the isPalindrome method.

```
public boolean isPalindrome()
{
```

```
int length = text.length();

// Separate case for shortest strings.
if (length <= 1) return true;

// Get first and last characters, converted to lowercase.
char first = Character.toLowerCase(text.charAt(0));
char last = Character.toLowerCase(text.charAt(length - 1));

if (Character.isLetter(first) && Character.isLetter(last))
{
    // Both are letters.
    if (first == last)
    {
        // Remove both first and last character.
        Sentence shorter = new Sentence(text.substring(1, length - 1));
        return shorter.isPalindrome();
    }
    else
        return false;
}
else if (!Character.isLetter(last))
{
    // Remove last character.
    Sentence shorter = new Sentence(text.substring(0, length - 1));
    return shorter.isPalindrome();
}
else
{
    // Remove first character.
    Sentence shorter = new Sentence(text.substring(1));
    return shorter.isPalindrome();
}
}
```

13.3 Recursive Helper Methods

Sometimes it is easier to find a recursive solution if you make a slight change to the original problem.

Sometimes it is easier to find a recursive solution if you change the original problem slightly. Then the original problem can be solved by calling a recursive helper method.

Here is a typical example. Consider the palindrome test of How To 13.1. It is a bit inefficient to construct new Sentence objects in every step. Now consider the following change in the problem. Rather than testing whether the entire sentence is a palindrome, let's check whether a substring is a palindrome:

```
/**
    Tests whether a substring of the sentence is a palindrome.
    @param start the index of the first character of the substring
    @param end the index of the last character of the substring
    @return true if the substring is a palindrome
*/
public boolean isPalindrome(int start, int end)
```

This method turns out to be even easier to implement than the original test. In the recursive calls, simply adjust the start and end parameters to skip over matching letter pairs and characters that are not letters. There is no need to construct new Sentence objects to represent the shorter strings.

```
public boolean isPalindrome(int start, int end)
{
    // Separate case for substrings of length 0 and 1.
    if (start >= end) return true;

    // Get first and last characters, converted to lowercase.
    char first = Character.toLowerCase(text.charAt(start));
    char last = Character.toLowerCase(text.charAt(end));

    if (Character.isLetter(first) && Character.isLetter(last))
    {
        if (first == last)
        {
            // Test substring that doesn't contain the matching letters.
            return isPalindrome(start + 1, end - 1);
        }
        else
            return false;
    }
    else if (!Character.isLetter(last))
    {
        // Test substring that doesn't contain the last character.
        return isPalindrome(start, end - 1);
    }
    else
    {
        // Test substring that doesn't contain the first character.
        return isPalindrome(start + 1, end);
    }
}
```

You should still supply a method to solve the whole problem—the user of your method shouldn't have to know about the trick with the substring positions. Simply call the helper method with positions that test the entire string:

```
public boolean isPalindrome()
{
    return isPalindrome(0, text.length() - 1);
}
```

Note that this call is *not* a recursive method. The isPalindrome() method calls the helper method isPalindrome(int, int). In this example, we use overloading to define two methods with the same name. The isPalindrome method without parameters is the method that we expect the public to use. The second method, with two `int` parameters, is the recursive helper method. If you prefer, you can avoid overloaded methods by choosing a different name for the helper method, such as `substringIsPalindrome`.

Use the technique of recursive helper methods whenever it is easier to solve a recursive problem that is slightly different from the original problem.

SELF CHECK

5. Do we have to give the same name to both `isPalindrome` methods?
6. When does the recursive `isPalindrome` method stop calling itself?

13.4 The Efficiency of Recursion

As you have seen in this chapter, recursion can be a powerful tool to implement complex algorithms. On the other hand, recursion can lead to algorithms that perform poorly. In this section, we will analyze the question of when recursion is beneficial and when it is inefficient.

Consider the Fibonacci sequence introduced in Exercise P6.4: a sequence of numbers defined by the equation

$$f_1 = 1$$
$$f_2 = 1$$
$$f_n = f_{n-1} + f_{n-2}$$

That is, each value of the sequence is the sum of the two preceding values. The first ten terms of the sequence are

$$1, 1, 2, 3, 5, 8, 13, 21, 34, 55$$

It is easy to extend this sequence indefinitely. Just keep appending the sum of the last two values of the sequence. For example, the next entry is $34 + 55 = 89$.

We would like to write a function that computes f_n for any value of n. Let us translate the definition directly into a recursive method:

ch13/fib/RecursiveFib.java

```
1  import java.util.Scanner;
2
3  /**
4     This program computes Fibonacci numbers using a recursive
5     method.
6  */
```

```
 7  public class RecursiveFib
 8  {
 9     public static void main(String[] args)
10     {
11        Scanner in = new Scanner(System.in);
12        System.out.print("Enter n: ");
13        int n = in.nextInt();
14
15        for (int i = 1; i <= n; i++)
16        {
17           long f = fib(i);
18           System.out.println("fib(" + i + ") = " + f);
19        }
20     }
21
22     /**
23        Computes a Fibonacci number.
24        @param n  an integer
25        @return  the nth Fibonacci number
26     */
27     public static long fib(int n)
28     {
29        if (n <= 2) return 1;
30        else return fib(n - 1) + fib(n - 2);
31     }
32  }
```

Output

```
Enter n: 50
fib(1) = 1
fib(2) = 1
fib(3) = 2
fib(4) = 3
fib(5) = 5
fib(6) = 8
fib(7) = 13
. . .
fib(50) = 12586269025
```

That is certainly simple, and the method will work correctly. But watch the output closely as you run the test program. The first few calls to the fib method are quite fast. For larger values, though, the program pauses an amazingly long time between outputs.

That makes no sense. Armed with pencil, paper, and a pocket calculator you could calculate these numbers pretty quickly, so it shouldn't take the computer anywhere near that long.

To find out the problem, let us insert *trace messages* into the method:

ch13/fib/RecursiveFibTracer.java

```java
1   import java.util.Scanner;
2
3   /**
4      This program prints trace messages that show how often the
5      recursive method for computing Fibonacci numbers calls itself.
6   */
7   public class RecursiveFibTracer
8   {
9      public static void main(String[] args)
10     {
11        Scanner in = new Scanner(System.in);
12        System.out.print("Enter n: ");
13        int n = in.nextInt();
14
15        long f = fib(n);
16
17        System.out.println("fib(" + n + ") = " + f);
18     }
19
20     /**
21        Computes a Fibonacci number.
22        @param n  an integer
23        @return  the nth Fibonacci number
24     */
25     public static long fib(int n)
26     {
27        System.out.println("Entering fib: n = " + n);
28        long f;
29        if (n <= 2) f = 1;
30        else f = fib(n - 1) + fib(n - 2);
31        System.out.println("Exiting fib: n = " + n
32              + " return value = " + f);
33        return f;
34     }
35  }
```

Output

```
Enter n: 6
Entering fib: n = 6
Entering fib: n = 5
Entering fib: n = 4
Entering fib: n = 3
Entering fib: n = 2
Exiting fib: n = 2 return value = 1
Entering fib: n = 1
Exiting fib: n = 1 return value = 1
Exiting fib: n = 3 return value = 2
Entering fib: n = 2
Exiting fib: n = 2 return value = 1
Exiting fib: n = 4 return value = 3
```

```
Entering fib: n = 3
Entering fib: n = 2
Exiting fib: n = 2 return value - 1
Entering fib: n = 1
Exiting fib: n = 1 return value = 1
Exiting fib: n = 3 return value = 2
Exiting fib: n = 5 return value = 5
Entering fib: n = 4
Entering fib: n = 3
Entering fib: n = 2
Exiting fib: n = 2 return value = 1
Entering fib: n = 1
Exiting fib: n = 1 return value = 1
Exiting fib: n = 3 return value = 2
Entering fib: n - 2
Exiting fib: n = 2 return value = 1
Exiting fib: n = 4 return value = 3
Exiting fib: n = 6 return value = 8
fib(6) = 8
```

Figure 2 shows the call tree for computing fib(6). Now it is becoming apparent why the method takes so long. It is computing the same values over and over. For example, the computation of fib(6) calls fib(4) twice and fib(3) three times. That is very different from the computation we would do with pencil and paper. There we would just write down the values as they were computed and add up the last two to get the next one until we reached the desired entry; no sequence value would ever be computed twice.

If we imitate the pencil-and-paper process, then we get the following program.

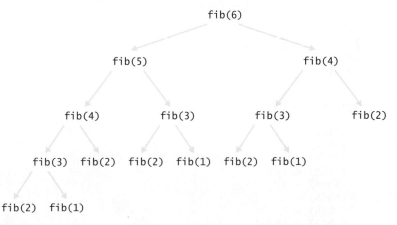

Figure 2   Call Pattern of the Recursive fib Method

ch13/fib/LoopFib.java

```java
1   import java.util.Scanner;
2
3   /**
4       This program computes Fibonacci numbers using an iterative method.
5   */
6   public class LoopFib
7   {
8      public static void main(String[] args)
9      {
10        Scanner in = new Scanner(System.in);
11        System.out.print("Enter n: ");
12        int n = in.nextInt();
13
14        for (int i = 1; i <= n; i++)
15        {
16           long f = fib(i);
17           System.out.println("fib(" + i + ") = " + f);
18        }
19     }
20
21     /**
22         Computes a Fibonacci number.
23         @param n an integer
24         @return the nth Fibonacci number
25     */
26     public static long fib(int n)
27     {
28        if (n <= 2) return 1;
29        long fold = 1;
30        long fold2 = 1;
31        long fnew = 1;
32        for (int i = 3; i <= n; i++)
33        {
34           fnew = fold + fold2;
35           fold2 = fold;
36           fold = fnew;
37        }
38        return fnew;
39     }
40   }
```

Output

```
Enter n: 50
fib(1) = 1
fib(2) = 1
fib(3) = 2
fib(4) = 3
fib(5) = 5
fib(6) = 8
fib(7) = 13
. . .
fib(50) = 12586269025
```

This method runs *much* faster than the recursive version.

In this example of the fib method, the recursive solution was easy to program because it exactly followed the mathematical definition, but it ran far more slowly than the iterative solution, because it computed many intermediate results multiple times.

Can you always speed up a recursive solution by changing it into a loop? Frequently, the iterative and recursive solution have essentially the same performance. For example, here is an iterative solution for the palindrome test.

```java
public boolean isPalindrome()
{
   int start = 0;
   int end = text.length() - 1;
   while (start < end)
   {
      char first = Character.toLowerCase(text.charAt(start));
      char last = Character.toLowerCase(text.charAt(end);

      if (Character.isLetter(first) && Character.isLetter(last))
      {
         // Both are letters.
         if (first == last)
         {
            start++;
            end--;
         }
         else
            return false;
      }
      if (!Character.isLetter(last))
         end--;
      if (!Character.isLetter(first))
         start++;
   }
   return true;
}
```

This solution keeps two index variables: start and end. The first index starts at the beginning of the string and is advanced whenever a letter has been matched or a nonletter has been ignored. The second index starts at the end of the string and moves toward the beginning. When the two index variables meet, the iteration stops.

Both the iteration and the recursion run at about the same speed. If a palindrome has n characters, the iteration executes the loop between $n/2$ and n times, depending on how many of the characters are letters, since one or both index variables are moved in each step. Similarly, the recursive solution calls itself between $n/2$ and n times, because one or two characters are removed in each step.

> Occasionally, a recursive solution runs much slower than its iterative counterpart. However, in most cases, the recursive solution is only slightly slower.

In such a situation, the iterative solution tends to be a bit faster, because each recursive method call takes a certain amount of processor time. In principle, it is possible for a smart compiler to avoid recursive method calls if they follow simple patterns, but most compilers don't do that. From that point of view, an iterative solution is preferable.

There are quite a few problems that are dramatically easier to solve recursively than iteratively. For example, it is not at all obvious how you can come up with a nonrecursive solution for the permutation generator. As Exercise P13.11 shows, it is possible to avoid the recursion, but the resulting solution is quite complex (and no faster).

> In many cases, a recursive solution is easier to understand and implement correctly than an iterative solution.

Often, recursive solutions are easier to understand and implement correctly than their iterative counterparts. There is a certain elegance and economy of thought to recursive solutions that makes them more appealing. As the computer scientist (and creator of the Ghost-Script interpreter for the PostScript graphics description language) L. Peter Deutsch put it: "To iterate is human, to recurse divine."

SELF CHECK

7. You can compute the factorial function either with a loop, using the definition that $n! = 1 \times 2 \times \ldots \times n$, or recursively, using the definition that $0! = 1$ and $n! = (n - 1)! \times n$. Is the recursive approach inefficient in this case?

8. Why isn't it easy to develop an iterative solution for the permutation generator?

RANDOM FACT 13.1

The Limits of Computation

Have you ever wondered how your instructor or grader makes sure your programming homework is correct? In all likelihood, they look at your solution and perhaps run it with some test inputs. But usually they have a correct solution available. That suggests that there might be an easier way. Perhaps they could feed your program and their correct program into a "program comparator", a computer program that analyzes both programs and determines whether they both compute the same results. Of course, your solution and the program that is known to be correct need not be identical—what matters is that they produce the same output when given the same input.

How could such a program comparator work? Well, the Java compiler knows how to read a program and make sense of the classes, methods, and statements. So it seems plausible that someone could, with some effort, write a program that reads two Java programs, analyzes what they do, and determines whether they solve the same task. Of course, such a program would be very attractive to instructors, because it could automate the grading process. Thus, even though no such program exists today, it might be tempting to try to develop one and sell it to universities around the world.

However, before you start raising venture capital for such an effort, you should know that theoretical computer scientists have proven that it is impossible to develop such a program, *no matter how hard you try*.

There are quite a few of these unsolvable problems. The first one, called the *halting problem,* was discovered by the British researcher Alan Turing in 1936 (see photo below). Because his research occurred before the first actual computer was constructed, Turing had to devise a theoretical device, the *Turing machine,* to explain how computers could work. The Turing machine consists of a long magnetic tape, a read/write head, and a program that

Alan Turing

has numbered instructions of the form: "If the current symbol under the head is *x*, then replace it with *y*, move the head one unit left or right, and continue with instruction *n*" (see A Turing Machine). Interestingly enough, with only these instructions, you can program just as much as with Java, even though it is incredibly tedious to do so. Theoretical computer scientists like Turing machines because they can be described using nothing more than the laws of mathematics.

Program

Instruction number	If tape symbol is	Replace with	Then move head	Then go to instruction
1	0	2	right	2
1	1	1	left	4
2	0	0	right	2
2	1	1	right	2
2	2	0	left	3
3	0	0	left	3
3	1	1	left	3
3	2	2	right	1
4	1	1	right	5
4	2	0	left	4

Control unit

Read/write head

Tape

A Turing Machine

Expressed in terms of Java, the halting problem states: "It is impossible to write a program with two inputs, namely the source code of an arbitrary Java program *P* and a string *I*, and that decides whether the program *P*, when executed with the input *I*, will halt without getting into an infinite loop". Of course, for some kinds of programs and inputs, it is possible to decide whether the program halts with the given input. The halting problem asserts that it is impossible to come up with a single decision-making algorithm that works with all programs and inputs. Note that you can't simply run the program *P* on the input *I* to settle this question. If the program runs for 1,000 days, you don't know that the program is in an infinite loop. Maybe you just have to wait another day for it to stop.

Such a "halt checker", if it could be written, might also be useful for grading homework. An instructor could use it to screen student submissions to see if they get into an infinite loop with a particular input, and then stop checking them. However, as Turing demonstrated, such a program cannot be written. His argument is ingenious and quite simple.

Suppose a "halt checker" program existed. Let's call it *H*. From *H*, we will develop another program, the "killer" program *K*. *K* does the following computation. Its input is a string containing the source code for a program *R*. It then applies the halt checker on the input program *R* and the input string *R*. That is, it checks whether the program *R* halts if its input is its own source code. It sounds bizarre to feed a program to itself, but it isn't impossible. For example, the Java compiler is written in Java, and you can use it to compile itself. Or, as a simpler example, a word counting program can count the words in its own source code.

When *K* gets the answer from *H* that *R* halts when applied to itself, it is programmed to enter an infinite loop. Otherwise *K* exits. In Java, the program might look like this:

```java
public class Killer
{
    public static void main(String[] args)
    {
        String r = read program input;
        HaltChecker checker = new HaltChecker();
        if (checker.check(r, r))
            while (true) { } // Infinite loop
        else
            return;
    }
}
```

Now ask yourself: What does the halt checker answer when asked whether *K* halts when given *K* as the input? Maybe it finds out that *K* gets into an infinite loop with such an input. But wait, that can't be right. That would mean that `checker.check(r, r)` returns `false` when r is the program code of *K*. As you can plainly see, in that case, the `killer` method returns, so *K* didn't get into an infinite loop. That shows that *K* must halt when analyzing itself, so `checker.check(r, r)` should return `true`. But then the `killer` method doesn't terminate—it goes into an infinite loop. That shows that it is logically impossible to implement a program that can check whether *every* program halts on a particular input.

It is sobering to know that there are *limits* to computing. There are problems that no computer program, no matter how ingenious, can answer.

Theoretical computer scientists are working on other research involving the nature of computation. One important question that remains unsettled to this day deals with problems that in practice are very time-consuming to solve. It may be that these problems are intrinsically hard, in which case it would be pointless to try to look for better algorithms. Such theoretical research can have important practical applications. For example, right now, nobody knows whether the most common encryption schemes used today could be broken by discovering a new algorithm (see Random Fact 19.1 for more information on encryption algorithms). Knowing that no fast algorithms exist for breaking a particular code could make us feel more comfortable about the security of encryption.

13.5 Mutual Recursions

> In a mutual recursion, a set of cooperating methods calls each other repeatedly.

In the preceding examples, a method called itself to solve a simpler problem. Sometimes, a set of cooperating methods calls each other in a recursive fashion. In this section, we will explore a typical situation of such a mutual recursion. This technique is significantly more advanced than the simple recursion that we discussed in the preceding sections. Feel free to skip this section if this is your first exposure to recursion.

We will develop a program that can compute the values of arithmetic expressions such as

```
3+4*5
(3+4)*5
1-(2-(3-(4-5)))
```

Computing such an expression is complicated by the fact that * and / bind more strongly than + and -, and that parentheses can be used to group subexpressions.

Figure 3 shows a set of *syntax diagrams* that describes the syntax of these expressions. To see how the syntax diagrams work, consider the expression 3+4*5. When

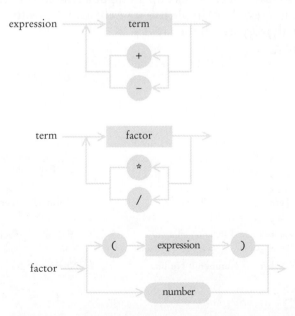

Figure 3 Syntax Diagrams for Evaluating an Expression

you enter the *expression* syntax diagram, the arrow points directly to *term*, giving you no alternative but to enter the *term* syntax diagram. The arrow points to *factor*, again giving you no choice. You enter the *factor* diagram, and now you have two choices: to follow the top branch or the bottom branch. Because the first input token is the number 3 and not a (, you must follow the bottom branch. You accept the input token because it matches the *number*. Follow the arrow out of *number* to the end of *factor*. Just like in a method call, you now back up, returning to the end of the *factor* element of the *term* diagram. Now you have another choice—to loop back in the *term* diagram, or to exit. The next input token is a +, and it matches neither the * or the / that would be required to loop back. So you exit, returning to *expression*. Again, you have a choice, to loop back or to exit. Now the + matches one of the choices in the loop. Accept the + in the input and move back to the *term* element.

In this fashion, an expression is broken down into a sequence of terms, separated by + or -, each term is broken down into a sequence of factors, each separated by * or /, and each factor is either a parenthesized expression or a number. You can draw this breakdown as a tree. Figure 4 shows how the expressions 3+4*5 and (3+4)*5 are derived from the syntax diagram.

Why do the syntax diagrams help us compute the value of the tree? If you look at the syntax trees, you will see that they accurately represent which operations should be carried out first. In the first tree, 4 and 5 should be multiplied, and then the result should be added to 3. In the second tree, 3 and 4 should be added, and the result should be multiplied by 5.

At the end of this section, you will find the implementation of the Evaluator class, which evaluates these expressions. The Evaluator makes use of an Expression-Tokenizer class, which breaks up an input string into tokens—numbers, operators, and parentheses. (For simplicity, we only accept positive integers as numbers, and we don't allow spaces in the input.)

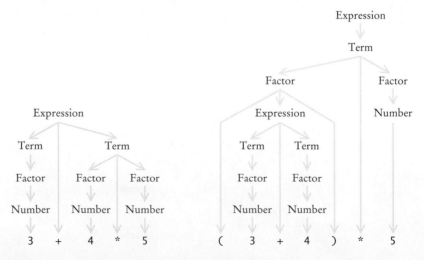

Figure 4   Syntax Trees for Two Expressions

When you call nextToken, the next input token is returned as a string. We also supply another method, peekToken, which allows you to see the next token without consuming it. To see why the peekToken method is necessary, consider the syntax diagram of the factor type. If the next token is a "*" or "/", you want to continue adding and subtracting terms. But if the next token is another character, such as a "+" or "-", you want to stop without actually consuming it, so that the token can be considered later.

To compute the value of an expression, we implement three methods: getExpressionValue, getTermValue, and getFactorValue. The getExpressionValue method first calls getTermValue to get the value of the first term of the expression. Then it checks whether the next input token is one of + or -. If so, it calls getTermValue again and adds or subtracts it.

```java
public int getExpressionValue()
{
   int value = getTermValue();
   boolean done = false;
   while (!done)
   {
      String next = tokenizer.peekToken();
      if ("+".equals(next) || "-".equals(next))
      {
         tokenizer.nextToken(); // Discard "+" or "-"
         int value2 = getTermValue();
         if ("+".equals(next)) value = value + value2;
         else value = value - value2;
      }
      else done = true;
   }
   return value;
}
```

The getTermValue method calls getFactorValue in the same way, multiplying or dividing the factor values.

Finally, the getFactorValue method checks whether the next input is a number, or whether it begins with a (token. In the first case, the value is simply the value of the number. However, in the second case, the getFactorValue method makes a recursive call to getExpressionValue. Thus, the three methods are mutually recursive.

```java
public int getFactorValue()
{
   int value;
   String next = tokenizer.peekToken();
   if ("(".equals(next))
   {
      tokenizer.nextToken(); // Discard "("
      value = getExpressionValue();
      tokenizer.nextToken(); // Discard ")"
   }
   else
      value = Integer.parseInt(tokenizer.nextToken());
   return value;
}
```

To see the mutual recursion clearly, trace through the expression (3+4)*5:

- getExpressionValue calls getTermValue
  - getTermValue calls getFactorValue
    - getFactorValue consumes the (input
    - getFactorValue calls getExpressionValue
      - getExpressionValue returns eventually with the value of 7, having consumed 3 + 4. This is the recursive call.
    - getFactorValue consumes the) input
    - getFactorValue returns 7
  - getTermValue consumes the inputs * and 5 and returns 35
- getExpressionValue returns 35

As always with a recursive solution, you need to ensure that the recursion terminates. In this situation, that is easy to see. If getExpressionValue calls itself, the second call works on a shorter subexpression than the original expression. At each recursive call, at least some of the tokens of the input string are consumed, so eventually the recursion must come to an end.

ch13/expr/Evaluator.java

```
1   /**
2       A class that can compute the value of an arithmetic expression.
3   */
4   public class Evaluator
5   {
6       /**
7           Constructs an evaluator.
8           @param anExpression a string containing the expression
9           to be evaluated
10      */
11      public Evaluator(String anExpression)
12      {
13          tokenizer = new ExpressionTokenizer(anExpression);
14      }
15
16      /**
17          Evaluates the expression.
18          @return the value of the expression
19      */
20      public int getExpressionValue()
21      {
22          int value = getTermValue();
23          boolean done = false;
24          while (!done)
25          {
26              String next = tokenizer.peekToken();
27              if ("+".equals(next) || "-".equals(next))
28              {
```

```
29            tokenizer.nextToken(); // Discard "+" or "-"
30            int value2 = getTermValue();
31            if ("+".equals(next)) value = value + value2;
32            else value = value - value2;
33         }
34         else done = true;
35      }
36      return value;
37   }
38
39   /**
40      Evaluates the next term found in the expression.
41      @return the value of the term
42   */
43   public int getTermValue()
44   {
45      int value = getFactorValue();
46      boolean done = false;
47      while (!done)
48      {
49         String next = tokenizer.peekToken();
50         if ("*".equals(next) || "/".equals(next))
51         {
52            tokenizer.nextToken();
53            int value2 = getFactorValue();
54            if ("*".equals(next)) value = value * value2;
55            else value = value / value2;
56         }
57         else done = true;
58      }
59      return value;
60   }
61
62   /**
63      Evaluates the next factor found in the expression.
64      @return the value of the factor
65   */
66   public int getFactorValue()
67   {
68      int value;
69      String next = tokenizer.peekToken();
70      if ("(".equals(next))
71      {
72         tokenizer.nextToken(); // Discard "("
73         value = getExpressionValue();
74         tokenizer.nextToken(); // Discard ")"
75      }
76      else
77         value = Integer.parseInt(tokenizer.nextToken());
78      return value;
79   }
80
81   private ExpressionTokenizer tokenizer;
82 }
```

ch13/expr/ExpressionTokenizer.java

```java
1   /**
2       This class breaks up a string describing an expression
3       into tokens: numbers, parentheses, and operators.
4   */
5   public class ExpressionTokenizer
6   {
7       /**
8           Constructs a tokenizer.
9           @param anInput the string to tokenize
10      */
11      public ExpressionTokenizer(String anInput)
12      {
13          input = anInput;
14          start = 0;
15          end = 0;
16          nextToken();
17      }
18
19      /**
20          Peeks at the next token without consuming it.
21          @return the next token or null if there are no more tokens
22      */
23      public String peekToken()
24      {
25          if (start >= input.length()) return null;
26          else return input.substring(start, end);
27      }
28
29      /**
30          Gets the next token and moves the tokenizer to the following token.
31          @return the next token or null if there are no more tokens
32      */
33      public String nextToken()
34      {
35          String r = peekToken();
36          start = end;
37          if (start >= input.length()) return r;
38          if (Character.isDigit(input.charAt(start)))
39          {
40              end = start + 1;
41              while (end < input.length()
42                      && Character.isDigit(input.charAt(end)))
43                  end++;
44          }
45          else
46              end = start + 1;
47          return r;
48      }
49
50      private String input;
51      private int start;
52      private int end;
53  }
```

ch13/expr/ExpressionCalculator.java

```
1  import java.util.Scanner;
2
3  /**
4     This program calculates the value of an expression
5     consisting of numbers, arithmetic operators, and parentheses.
6  */
7  public class ExpressionCalculator
8  {
9     public static void main(String[] args)
10    {
11       Scanner in = new Scanner(System.in);
12       System.out.print("Enter an expression: ");
13       String input = in.nextLine();
14       Evaluator e = new Evaluator(input);
15       int value = e.getExpressionValue();
16       System.out.println(input + "=" + value);
17    }
18 }
```

Output

```
Enter an expression: 3+4*5
3+4*5=23
```

SELF CHECK

9. What is the difference between a term and a factor? Why do we need both concepts?

10. Why does the expression parser use mutual recursion?

11. What happens if you try to parse the illegal expression 3+4*)5? Specifically, which method throws an exception?

CHAPTER SUMMARY

1. A recursive computation solves a problem by using the solution of the same problem with simpler values.

2. For a recursion to terminate, there must be special cases for the simplest values.

3. Sometimes it is easier to find a recursive solution if you make a slight change to the original problem.

4. Occasionally, a recursive solution runs much slower than its iterative counterpart. However, in most cases, the recursive solution is only slightly slower.

5. In many cases, a recursive solution is easier to understand and implement correctly than an iterative solution.

6. In a mutual recursion, a set of cooperating methods calls each other repeatedly.

REVIEW EXERCISES

★ **Exercise R13.1.** Define the terms
   a. Recursion
   b. Iteration
   c. Infinite recursion
   d. Recursive helper method

★★ **Exercise R13.2.** Outline, but do not implement, a recursive solution for finding the smallest value in an array.

★★ **Exercise R13.3.** Outline, but do not implement, a recursive solution for sorting an array of numbers. *Hint:* First find the smallest value in the array.

★★ **Exercise R13.4.** Outline, but do not implement, a recursive solution for generating all subsets of the set $\{1, 2, \ldots, n\}$.

★★★ **Exercise R13.5.** Exercise P13.12 shows an iterative way of generating all permutations of the sequence $(0, 1, \ldots, n - 1)$. Explain why the algorithm produces the correct result.

★ **Exercise R13.6.** Write a recursive definition of x^n, where $n \geq 0$, similar to the recursive definition of the Fibonacci numbers. *Hint:* How do you compute x^n from x^{n-1}? How does the recursion terminate?

★★ **Exercise R13.7.** Improve upon Exercise R13.6 by computing x^n as $(x^{n/2})^2$ if n is even. Why is this approach significantly faster? (*Hint:* Compute x^{1023} and x^{1024} both ways.)

★ **Exercise R13.8.** Write a recursive definition of $n! = 1 \times 2 \times \ldots \times n$, similar to the recursive definition of the Fibonacci numbers.

★★ **Exercise R13.9.** Find out how often the recursive version of fib calls itself. Keep a static variable fibCount and increment it once in every call of fib. What is the relationship between fib(n) and fibCount?

★★★ **Exercise R13.10.** How many moves are required in the "Towers of Hanoi" problem of Exercise P13.13 to move n disks? *Hint:* As explained in the exercise,

$$\text{moves}(1) = 1$$
$$\text{moves}(n) = 2 \cdot \text{moves}(n - 1) + 1$$

Additional review exercises are available in WileyPLUS.

PROGRAMMING EXERCISES

★ **Exercise P13.1.** Write a recursive method void reverse() that reverses a sentence. For example:

```
Sentence greeting = new Sentence("Hello!");
greeting.reverse();
System.out.println(greeting.getText());
```

prints the string "!olleH". Implement a recursive solution by removing the first character, reversing a sentence consisting of the remaining text, and combining the two.

★★ **Exercise P13.2.** Redo Exercise P13.1 with a recursive helper method that reverses a substring of the message text.

★ **Exercise P13.3.** Implement the reverse method of Exercise P13.1 as an iteration.

★★ **Exercise P13.4.** Use recursion to implement a method boolean find(String t) that tests whether a string is contained in a sentence:

```
Sentence s = new Sentence("Mississippi!");
boolean b = s.find("sip"); // Returns true
```

Hint: If the text starts with the string you want to match, then you are done. If not, consider the sentence that you obtain by removing the first character.

★★ **Exercise P13.5.** Use recursion to implement a method int indexOf(String t) that returns the starting position of the first substring of the text that matches t. Return –1 if t is not a substring of s. For example,

```
Sentence s = new Sentence("Mississippi!");
int n = s.indexOf("sip"); // Returns 6
```

Hint: This is a bit trickier than the preceding problem, because you must keep track of how far the match is from the beginning of the sentence. Make that value a parameter of a helper method.

★ **Exercise P13.6.** Using recursion, find the largest element in an array.

```
public class DataSet
{
    public DataSet(int[] values, int first, int last) { . . . }
    public int getMaximum() { . . . }
    . . .
}
```

Hint: Find the largest element in the subset containing all but the last element. Then compare that maximum to the value of the last element.

★ **Exercise P13.7.** Using recursion, compute the sum of all values in an array.

```
public class DataSet
{
```

```
              public DataSet(int[] values, int first, int last) { . . . }
              public int getSum() { . . . }
                  . . .
          }
```

★★ **Exercise P13.8.** Using recursion, compute the area of a polygon. Cut off a triangle and use the fact that a triangle with corners (x_1, y_1), (x_2, y_2), (x_3, y_3) has area

$$\frac{\left| x_1 y_2 + x_2 y_3 + x_3 y_1 - y_1 x_2 - y_2 x_3 - y_3 x_1 \right|}{2}$$

★★★ **Exercise P13.9.** Implement a SubstringGenerator that generates all substrings of a string. For example, the substrings of the string "rum" are the seven strings

"r", "ru", "rum", "u", "um", "m", ""

Hint: First enumerate all substrings that start with the first character. There are *n* of them if the string has length *n*. Then enumerate the substrings of the string that you obtain by removing the first character.

★★★ **Exercise P13.10.** Implement a SubsetGenerator that generates all subsets of the characters of a string. For example, the subsets of the characters of the string "rum" are the eight strings

"rum", "ru", "rm", "r", "um", "u", "m", ""

Note that the subsets don't have to be substrings—for example, "rm" isn't a substring of "rum".

★★★ **Exercise P13.11.** In this exercise, you will change the PermutationGenerator of Section 13.2 (which computed all permutations at once) to a PermutationIterator (which computes them one at a time.)

```
public class PermutationIterator
{
   public PermutationIterator(String s) { . . . }
   public String nextPermutation() { . . . }
   public boolean hasMorePermutations() { . . . }
}
```

Here is how you would print out all permutations of the string "eat":

```
PermutationIterator iter = new PermutationIterator("eat");
while (iter.hasMorePermutations())
   System.out.println(iter.nextPermutation());
```

Now we need a way to iterate through the permutations recursively. Consider the string "eat". As before, we'll generate all permutations that start with the letter 'e', then those that start with 'a', and finally those that start with 't'. How do we generate the permutations that start with 'e'? Make another PermutationIterator object (called tailIterator) that iterates through the permutations of the substring "at". In the nextPermutation method, simply ask tailIterator what *its* next permutation is, and then add the 'e' at the front. However, there is one special case. When the tail generator runs out of permutations, all permutations that start with the current letter have been enumerated. Then

- Increment the current position.
- Compute the tail string that contains all letters except for the current one.
- Make a new permutation iterator for the tail string.

You are done when the current position has reached the end of the string.

★★★ **Exercise P13.12.** The following class generates all permutations of the numbers $0, 1, 2, \ldots, n - 1$, without using recursion.

```java
public class NumberPermutationIterator
{
   public NumberPermutationIterator(int n)
   {
      a = new int[n];
      done = false;
      for (int i = 0; i < n; i++) a[i] = i;
   }

   public int[] nextPermutation()
   {
      if (a.length <- 1) return a;

      for (int i = a.length - 1; i > 0; i--)
      {
         if (a[i - 1] < a[i])
         {
            int j = a.length - 1;
            while (a[i - 1] > a[j]) j--;
            swap(i - 1, j);
            reverse(i, a.length - 1);
            return a;
         }
      }
      return a;
   }

   public boolean hasMorePermutations()
   {
      if (a.length <= 1) return false;
      for (int i = a.length - 1; i > 0; i--)
      {
         if (a[i - 1] < a[i]) return true;
      }
      return false;
```

```
        }

        public void swap(int i, int j)
        {
            int temp = a[i];
            a[i] = a[j];
            a[j] = temp;
        }

        public void reverse(int i, int j)
        {
            while (i < j) { swap(i, j); i++; j--; }
        }
        private int[] a;
    }
```

The algorithm uses the fact that the set to be permuted consists of distinct numbers. Thus, you cannot use the same algorithm to compute the permutations of the characters in a string. You can, however, use this class to get all permutations of the character positions and then compute a string whose ith character is word.charAt(a[i]). Use this approach to reimplement the PermutationIterator of Exercise P13.11 without recursion.

★★ **Exercise P13.13.** *Towers of Hanoi.* This is a well-known puzzle. A stack of disks of decreasing size is to be transported from the leftmost peg to the rightmost peg. The middle peg can be used as temporary storage (see Figure 5). One disk can be moved at one time, from any peg to any other peg. You can place smaller disks only on top of larger ones, not the other way around.

Write a program that prints the moves necessary to solve the puzzle for *n* disks. (Ask the user for *n* at the beginning of the program.) Print moves in the form

```
Move disk from peg 1 to peg 3
```

Hint: Implement a class DiskMover. The constructor takes

- The source peg from which to move the disks (1, 2, or 3)
- The target peg to which to move the disks (1, 2, or 3)
- The number of disks to move

Figure 5   Towers of Hanoi

A disk mover that moves a single disk from one peg to another simply has a nextMove method that returns a string

```
Move disk from peg source to peg target
```

A disk mover with more than one disk to move must work harder. It needs another DiskMover to help it. In the constructor, construct a DiskMover(source, other, disks - 1) where other is the peg other than from and target.

The nextMove asks that disk mover for its next move until it is done. The effect is to move the first disks - 1 disks to the other peg. Then the nextMove method issues a command to move a disk from the from peg to the to peg. Finally, it constructs another disk mover DiskMover(other, target, disks - 1) that generates the moves that move the disks from the other peg to the target peg.

Hint: It helps to keep track of the state of the disk mover:

- BEFORE_LARGEST: The helper mover moves the smaller pile to the other peg.
- LARGEST: Move the largest disk from the source to the destination.
- AFTER_LARGEST: The helper mover moves the smaller pile from the other peg to the target.
- DONE: All moves are done.

Test your program as follows:

```
DiskMover mover = new DiskMover(1, 3, n);
while (mover.hasMoreMoves())
    System.out.println(mover.nextMove());
```

★★★ **Exercise P13.14.** *Escaping a Maze.* You are currently located inside a maze. The walls of the maze are indicated by asterisks (*).

```
*  *******
*     *  *
*  *****  *
*  *  *   *
*  *  ***  *
*  *   *   *
*** *  *  *
*      *  *
*******  *
```

Use the following recursive approach to check whether you can escape from the maze: If you are at an exit, return true. Recursively check whether you can escape from one of the empty neighboring locations without visiting the current location. This method merely tests whether there is a path out of the maze. Extra credit if you can print out a path that leads to an exit.

★★★G **Exercise P13.15.** *The Koch Snowflake.* A snowflake-like shape is recursively defined as follows. Start with an equilateral triangle:

◁

Next, increase the size by a factor of three and replace each straight line with four line segments.

Repeat the process.

Write a program that draws the iterations of this curve. Supply a button that, when clicked, produces the next iteration.

★★ **Exercise P13.16.** The recursive computation of Fibonacci numbers can be speeded up significantly by keeping track of the values that have already been computed. Provide an implementation of the `fib` method that uses this strategy. Whenever you return a new value, also store it in an auxiliary array. However, before embarking on a computation, consult the array to find whether the result has already been computed. Compare the running time of your improved implementation with that of the original recursive implementation and the loop implementation.

Additional programming exercises are available in WileyPLUS.

PROGRAMMING PROJECTS

★★★ **Project 13.1.** Enhance the expression parser of Section 13.5 to handle more sophisticated expressions, such as exponents, and mathematical functions, such as `sqrt` or `sin`.

★★★G **Project 13.2.** Implement a graphical version of the Towers of Hanoi program (see Exercise P13.13). Every time the user clicks on a button labeled "Next", draw the next move.

ANSWERS TO SELF-CHECK QUESTIONS

1. Suppose we omit the statement. When computing the area of a triangle with width 1, we compute the area of the triangle with width 0 as 0, and then add 1, to arrive at the correct area.

2. You would compute the smaller area recursively, then return
   `smallerArea + width + width - 1`.

   [] [] [] []
   [] [] [] []
   [] [] [] []
   [] [] [] []

   Of course, it would be simpler to compute the area simply as `width * width`. The results are identical because

   $$1 + 0 + 2 + 1 + 3 + 2 + \cdots + n + n - 1 = \frac{n(n+1)}{2} + \frac{(n-1)n}{2} = n^2.$$

3. They are b followed by the six permutations of eat, e followed by the six permutations of bat, a followed by the six permutations of bet, and t followed by the six permutations of bea.

4. Simply change `if (word.length() == 0)` to `if (word.length() <= 1)`, because a word with a single letter is also its sole permutation.

5. No—the first one could be given a different name such as `substringIsPalindrome`.

6. When `start >= end`, that is, when the investigated string is either empty or has length 1.

7. No, the recursive solution is about as efficient as the iterative approach. Both require $n - 1$ multiplications to compute $n!$.

8. An iterative solution would have a loop whose body computes the next permutation from the previous ones. But there is no obvious mechanism for getting the next permutation. For example, if you already found permutations eat, eta, and aet, it is not clear how you use that information to get the next permutation. Actually, there is an ingenious mechanism for doing just that, but it is far from obvious—see Exercise P13.12.

9. Factors are combined by multiplicative operators (* and /), terms are combined by additive operators (+, -). We need both so that multiplication can bind more strongly than addition.

10. To handle parenthesized expressions, such as 2+3*(4+5). The subexpression 4+5 is handled by a recursive call to `getExpressionValue`.

11. The `Integer.parseInt` call in `getFactorValue` throws an exception when it is given the string ")".

Sorting and Searching

CHAPTER GOALS

- To study several sorting and searching algorithms
- To appreciate that algorithms for the same task can differ widely in performance
- To understand the big-Oh notation
- To learn how to estimate and compare the performance of algorithms
- To learn how to measure the running time of a program

One of the most common tasks in data processing is sorting. For example, a collection of employees may need to be printed out in alphabetical order or sorted by salary. We will study several sorting methods in this chapter and compare their performance. This is by no means an exhaustive treatment of the subject of sorting. You will likely revisit this topic at a later time in your computer science studies. A good overview of the many sorting methods available can be found in [1].

Once a sequence of objects is sorted, one can locate individual objects rapidly. We will study the *binary search* algorithm, which carries out this fast lookup.

CHAPTER CONTENTS

14.1 Selection Sort

In this section, we show you the first of several sorting algorithms. A *sorting algorithm* rearranges the elements of a collection so that they are stored in sorted order. To keep the examples simple, we will discuss how to sort an array of integers before going on to sorting strings or more complex data. Consider the following array a:

11 9 17 5 12

> The selection sort algorithm sorts an array by repeatedly finding the smallest element of the unsorted tail region and moving it to the front.

An obvious first step is to find the smallest element. In this case the smallest element is 5, stored in a[3]. We should move the 5 to the beginning of the array. Of course, there is already an element stored in a[0], namely 11. Therefore we cannot simply move a[3] into a[0] without moving the 11 somewhere else. We don't yet know where the 11 should end up, but we know for certain that it should not be in a[0]. We simply get it out of the way by *swapping* it with a[3].

Now the first element is in the correct place. In the foregoing figure, the darker color indicates the portion of the array that is already sorted.

Next we take the minimum of the remaining entries a[1] . . . a[4]. That minimum value, 9, is already in the correct place. We don't need to do anything in this case and can simply extend the sorted area by one to the right:

5 9 17 11 12

Repeat the process. The minimum value of the unsorted region is 11, which needs to be swapped with the first value of the unsorted region, 17:

Now the unsorted region is only two elements long, but we keep to the same successful strategy. The minimum value is 12, and we swap it with the first value, 17.

That leaves us with an unprocessed region of length 1, but of course a region of length 1 is always sorted. We are done.

Let us program this algorithm. For this program, as well as the other programs in this chapter, we will use a utility method to generate an array with random entries. We place it into a class ArrayUtil so that we don't have to repeat the code in every example. To show the array, we call the static toString method of the Arrays class in the Java library and print the resulting string.

This algorithm will sort any array of integers. If speed were not an issue, or if there simply were no better sorting method available, we could stop the discussion of sorting right here. As the next section shows, however, this algorithm, while entirely correct, shows disappointing performance when run on a large data set.

Advanced Topic 14.1 discusses insertion sort, another simple (and similarly inefficient) sorting algorithm.

ch14/selsort/SelectionSorter.java

```
1   /**
2        This class sorts an array, using the selection sort
3        algorithm.
4   */
5   public class SelectionSorter
6   {
7        /**
8             Constructs a selection sorter.
9             @param anArray the array to sort
10       */
11       public SelectionSorter(int[] anArray)
12       {
13            a = anArray;
14       }
15
16       /**
17            Sorts the array managed by this selection sorter.
18       */
19       public void sort()
20       {
21            for (int i = 0; i < a.length - 1; i++)
22            {
23                 int minPos = minimumPosition(i);
```

```
24              swap(minPos, i);
25          }
26      }
27
28      /**
29          Finds the smallest element in a tail range of the array.
30          @param from  the first position in a to compare
31          @return  the position of the smallest element in the
32          range a[from] . . . a[a.length - 1]
33      */
34      private int minimumPosition(int from)
35      {
36          int minPos = from;
37          for (int i = from + 1; i < a.length; i++)
38              if (a[i] < a[minPos]) minPos = i;
39          return minPos;
40      }
41
42      /**
43          Swaps two entries of the array.
44          @param i  the first position to swap
45          @param j  the second position to swap
46      */
47      private void swap(int i, int j)
48      {
49          int temp = a[i];
50          a[i] = a[j];
51          a[j] = temp;
52      }
53
54      private int[] a;
55  }
```

ch14/selsort/SelectionSortDemo.java

```
1   import java.util.Arrays;
2
3   /**
4       This program demonstrates the selection sort algorithm by
5       sorting an array that is filled with random numbers.
6   */
7   public class SelectionSortDemo
8   {
9       public static void main(String[] args)
10      {
11          int[] a = ArrayUtil.randomIntArray(20, 100);
12          System.out.println(Arrays.toString(a));
13
14          SelectionSorter sorter = new SelectionSorter(a);
15          sorter.sort();
16
17          System.out.println(Arrays.toString(a));
18      }
19  }
```

ch14/selsort/ArrayUtil.java

```java
1   import java.util.Random;
2
3   /**
4       This class contains utility methods for array manipulation.
5   */
6   public class ArrayUtil
7   {
8       /**
9           Creates an array filled with random values.
10          @param length the length of the array
11          @param n the number of possible random values
12          @return an array filled with length numbers between
13          0 and n - 1
14      */
15      public static int[] randomIntArray(int length, int n)
16      {
17          int[] a = new int[length];
18          for (int i = 0; i < a.length; i++)
19              a[i] = generator.nextInt(n);
20
21          return a;
22      }
23
24      private static Random generator = new Random();
25  }
```

Typical Output

```
[65, 46, 14, 52, 38, 2, 96, 39, 14, 33, 13, 4, 24, 99, 89, 77, 73, 87, 36, 81]
[2, 4, 13, 14, 14, 24, 33, 36, 38, 39, 46, 52, 65, 73, 77, 81, 87, 89, 96, 99]
```

SELF CHECK

1. Why do we need the temp variable in the swap method? What would happen if you simply assigned a[i] to a[j] and a[j] to a[i]?

2. What steps does the selection sort algorithm go through to sort the sequence 6 5 4 3 2 1?

14.2 Profiling the Selection Sort Algorithm

To measure the performance of a program, you could simply run it and measure how long it takes by using a stopwatch. However, most of our programs run very quickly, and it is not easy to time them accurately in this way. Furthermore, when a program takes a noticeable time to run, a certain amount of that time may simply be used for loading the program from disk into memory (for which we should not penalize it) or for screen output (whose speed depends on the computer model, even for computers with identical CPUs). We will instead create a StopWatch class.

This class works like a real stopwatch. You can start it, stop it, and read out the elapsed time. The class uses the System.currentTimeMillis method, which returns the milliseconds that have elapsed since midnight at the start of January 1, 1970. Of course, you don't care about the absolute number of seconds since this historical moment, but the *difference* of two such counts gives us the number of milliseconds of a time interval. Here is the code for the StopWatch class:

ch14/selsort/StopWatch.java

```
 1  /**
 2        A stopwatch accumulates time when it is running. You can
 3        repeatedly start and stop the stopwatch. You can use a
 4        stopwatch to measure the running time of a program.
 5  */
 6  public class StopWatch
 7  {
 8      /**
 9          Constructs a stopwatch that is in the stopped state
10          and has no time accumulated.
11      */
12      public StopWatch()
13      {
14          reset();
15      }
16
17      /**
18          Starts the stopwatch. Time starts accumulating now.
19      */
20      public void start()
21      {
22          if (isRunning) return;
23          isRunning = true;
24          startTime = System.currentTimeMillis();
25      }
26
27      /**
28          Stops the stopwatch. Time stops accumulating and is
29          is added to the elapsed time.
30      */
31      public void stop()
32      {
33          if (!isRunning) return;
34          isRunning = false;
35          long endTime = System.currentTimeMillis();
36          elapsedTime = elapsedTime + endTime - startTime;
37      }
38
39      /**
40          Returns the total elapsed time.
41          @return the total elapsed time
42      */
43      public long getElapsedTime()
44      {
45          if (isRunning)
```

```
46          {
47              long endTime = System.currentTimeMillis();
48              return elapsedTime + endTime - startTime;
49          }
50          else
51              return elapsedTime;
52      }
53
54      /**
55          Stops the watch and resets the elapsed time to 0.
56      */
57      public void reset()
58      {
59          elapsedTime = 0;
60          isRunning = false;
61      }
62
63      private long elapsedTime;
64      private long startTime;
65      private boolean isRunning;
66  }
```

Here is how we will use the stopwatch to measure the performance of the sorting algorithm:

ch14/selsort/SelectionSortTimer.java

```
1   import java.util.Scanner;
2
3   /**
4       This program measures how long it takes to sort an
5       array of a user-specified size with the selection
6       sort algorithm.
7   */
8   public class SelectionSortTimer
9   {
10      public static void main(String[] args)
11      {
12          Scanner in = new Scanner(System.in);
13          System.out.print("Enter array size: ");
14          int n = in.nextInt();
15
16          // Construct random array
17
18          int[] a = ArrayUtil.randomIntArray(n, 100);
19          SelectionSorter sorter = new SelectionSorter(a);
20
21          // Use stopwatch to time selection sort
22
23          StopWatch timer = new StopWatch();
24
25          timer.start();
26          sorter.sort();
27          timer.stop();
```

```
28
29          System.out.println("Elapsed time: "
30              + timer.getElapsedTime() + " milliseconds");
31      }
32  }
```

Output

```
Enter array size: 100000
Elapsed time: 27880 milliseconds
```

By starting to measure the time just before sorting, and stopping the stopwatch just after, you don't count the time it takes to initialize the array or the time during which the program waits for the user to type in n.

Here are the results of some sample runs:

n	Milliseconds
10,000	786
20,000	2,148
30,000	4,796
40,000	9,192
50,000	13,321
60,000	19,299

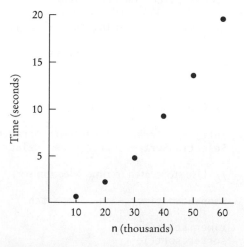

Figure 1   Time Taken by Selection Sort

These measurements were obtained with a Pentium processor with a clock speed of 2 GHz, running Java 6 on the Linux operating system. On another computer the actual numbers will look different, but the relationship between the numbers will be the same. Figure 1 shows a plot of the measurements. As you can see, doubling the size of the data set more than doubles the time needed to sort it.

SELF CHECK

3. Approximately how many seconds would it take to sort a data set of 80,000 values?
4. Look at the graph in Figure 1. What mathematical shape does it resemble?

14.3 Analyzing the Performance of the Selection Sort Algorithm

Let us count the number of operations that the program must carry out to sort an array with the selection sort algorithm. We don't actually know how many machine operations are generated for each Java instruction or which of those instructions are more time-consuming than others, but we can make a simplification. We will simply count how often an array element is *visited*. Each visit requires about the same amount of work by other operations, such as incrementing subscripts and comparing values.

Let n be the size of the array. First, we must find the smallest of n numbers. To achieve that, we must visit n array elements. Then we swap the elements, which takes two visits. (You may argue that there is a certain probability that we don't need to swap the values. That is true, and one can refine the computation to reflect that observation. As we will soon see, doing so would not affect the overall conclusion.) In the next step, we need to visit only $n - 1$ elements to find the minimum. In the following step, $n - 2$ elements are visited to find the minimum. The last step visits two elements to find the minimum. Each step requires two visits to swap the elements. Therefore, the total number of visits is

$$n + 2 + (n - 1) + 2 + \cdots + 2 + 2 = n + (n - 1) + \cdots + 2 + (n - 1) \cdot 2$$
$$= 2 + \cdots + (n - 1) + n + (n - 1) \cdot 2$$
$$= \frac{n(n + 1)}{2} - 1 + (n - 1) \cdot 2$$

because

$$1 + 2 + \cdots + (n - 1) + n = \frac{n(n + 1)}{2}$$

After multiplying out and collecting terms of n, we find that the number of visits is

$$\tfrac{1}{2}n^2 + \tfrac{5}{2}n - 3$$

We obtain a quadratic equation in n. That explains why the graph of Figure 1 looks approximately like a parabola.

Now let us simplify the analysis further. When you plug in a large value for n (for example, 1,000 or 2,000), then $\frac{1}{2}n^2$ is 500,000 or 2,000,000. The lower term, $\frac{5}{2}n - 3$, doesn't contribute much at all; it is only 2,497 or 4,997, a drop in the bucket compared to the hundreds of thousands or even millions of comparisons specified by the $\frac{1}{2}n^2$ term. We will just ignore these lower-level terms. Next, we will ignore the constant factor $\frac{1}{2}$. We are not interested in the actual count of visits for a single n. We want to compare the ratios of counts for different values of n. For example, we can say that sorting an array of 2,000 numbers requires four times as many visits as sorting an array of 1,000 numbers:

$$\frac{\left(\frac{1}{2} \cdot 2000^2\right)}{\left(\frac{1}{2} \cdot 1000^2\right)} = 4$$

The factor $\frac{1}{2}$ cancels out in comparisons of this kind. We will simply say, "The number of visits is of order n^2". That way, we can easily see that the number of comparisons increases fourfold when the size of the array doubles: $(2n)^2 = 4n^2$.

To indicate that the number of visits is of order n^2, computer scientists often use *big-Oh notation:* The number of visits is $O(n^2)$. This is a convenient shorthand.

> Computer scientists use the big-Oh notation $f(n) = O(g(n))$ to express that the function f grows no faster than the function g.

In general, the expression $f(n) = O(g(n))$ means that f grows no faster than g, or, more formally, that for all n larger than some threshold, the ratio $f(n)/g(n) \leq C$ for some constant value C. The function g is usually chosen to be very simple, such as n^2 in our example.

To turn an exact expression such as

$$\frac{1}{2}n^2 + \frac{5}{2}n - 3$$

into big-Oh notation, simply locate the fastest-growing term, n^2, and ignore its constant coefficient, no matter how large or small it may be.

We observed before that the actual number of machine operations, and the actual number of microseconds that the computer spends on them, is approximately proportional to the number of element visits. Maybe there are about 10 machine operations (increments, comparisons, memory loads, and stores) for every element visit. The number of machine operations is then approximately $10 \times \frac{1}{2}n^2$. Again, we aren't interested in the coefficient, so we can say that the number of machine operations, and hence the time spent on the sorting, is of the order of n^2 or $O(n^2)$.

> Selection sort is an $O(n^2)$ algorithm. Doubling the data set means a fourfold increase in processing time.

The sad fact remains that doubling the size of the array causes a fourfold increase in the time required for sorting it with selection sort. When the size of the array increases by a factor of 100, the sorting time increases by a factor of 10,000. To sort an array of a million entries, (for example, to create a telephone directory) takes 10,000 times as long as sorting 10,000 entries. If 10,000 entries can be sorted in about 1/2 of a second (as in our example), then sorting one million entries requires well over an hour. We will see in the next section how one can dramatically improve the performance of the sorting process by choosing a more sophisticated algorithm.

SELF CHECK

5. If you increase the size of a data set tenfold, how much longer does it take to sort it with the selection sort algorithm?
6. How large does n need to be so that $\frac{1}{2}n^2$ is bigger than $\frac{5}{2}n - 3$?

ADVANCED TOPIC 14.1

Insertion Sort

Insertion sort is another simple sorting algorithm. In this algorithm, we assume that the initial sequence

```
a[0] a[1] . . . a[k]
```

of an array is already sorted. (When the algorithm starts, we set k to 0.) We enlarge the initial sequence by inserting the next array element, a[k + 1], at the proper location. When we reach the end of the array, the sorting process is complete.

For example, suppose we start with the array

| 11 | 9 | 16 | 5 | 7 |

Of course, the initial sequence of length 1 is already sorted. We now add a[1], which has the value 9. The element needs to be inserted before the element 11. The result is

| 9 | 11 | 16 | 5 | 7 |

Next, we add a[2], which has the value 16. As it happens, the element does not have to be moved.

| 9 | 11 | 16 | 5 | 7 |

We repeat the process, inserting a[3] or 5 at the very beginning of the initial sequence.

| 5 | 9 | 11 | 16 | 7 |

Finally, a[4] or 7 is inserted in its correct position, and the sorting is completed.

The following class implements the insertion sort algorithm:

```java
public class InsertionSorter
{
   /**
      Constructs an insertion sorter.
      @param anArray the array to sort
   */
   public InsertionSorter(int[] anArray)
   {
      a = anArray;
   }
```

```
/**
    Sorts the array managed by this insertion sorter.
*/
public void sort()
{
    for (int i = 1; i < a.length; i++)
    {
        int next = a[i];
        // Find the insertion location
        // Move all larger elements up
        int j = i;
        while (j > 0 && a[j - 1] > next)
        {
            a[j] = a[j - 1];
            j--;
        }
        // Insert the element
        a[j] = next;
    }
}

private int[] a;
}
```

How efficient is this algorithm? Let n denote the size of the array. We carry out $n - 1$ iterations. In the kth iteration, we have a sequence of k elements that is already sorted, and we need to insert a new element into the sequence. For each insertion, we need to visit the elements of the initial sequence until we have found the location in which the new element can be inserted. Then we need to move up the remaining elements of the sequence. Thus, $k + 1$ array elements are visited. Therefore, the total number of visits is

$$2 + 3 + \cdots + n = \frac{n(n + 1)}{2} - 1$$

> Insertion sort is an $O(n^2)$ algorithm.

We conclude that insertion sort is an $O(n^2)$ algorithm, on the same order of efficiency as selection sort.

Insertion sort has one desirable property: Its performance is $O(n)$ if the array is already sorted—see Exercise R14.13. This is a useful property in practical applications, in which data sets are often partially sorted.

ADVANCED TOPIC 14.2

Oh, Omega, and Theta

We have used the big-Oh notation somewhat casually in this chapter, to describe the growth behavior of a function. Strictly speaking, $f(n) = O(g(n))$ means that f grows *no faster* than g. But it is permissible for f to grow much slower. Thus, it is technically correct to state that $f(n) = n^2 + 5n - 3$ is $O(n^3)$ or even $O(n^{10})$.

Computer scientists have invented additional notation to describe the growth behavior of functions more accurately. The expression

$$f(n) = \Omega(g(n))$$

means that f grows at least as fast as g, or, formally, that for all n larger than some threshold, the ratio $f(n)/g(n) \geq C$ for some constant value C. (The Ω symbol is the capital Greek letter omega.) For example, $f(n) = n^2 + 5n - 3$ is $\Omega(n^2)$ or even $\Omega(n)$.

The expression

$$f(n) = \Theta(g(n))$$

means that f and g grow at the same rate—that is, both $f(n) = O(g(n))$ and $f(n) = \Omega(g(n))$ hold. (The Θ symbol is the capital Greek letter theta.)

The Θ notation gives the most precise description of growth behavior. For example, $f(n) = n^2 + 5n - 3$ is $\Theta(n^2)$ but not $\Theta(n)$ or $\Theta(n^3)$.

The Ω and Θ notation is very important for the precise analysis of algorithms. However, in casual conversation it is common to stick with big-Oh, while still giving as good an estimate as one can.

14.4 Merge Sort

In this section, you will learn about the merge sort algorithm, a much more efficient algorithm than selection sort. The basic idea behind merge sort is very simple.

Suppose we have an array of 10 integers. Let us engage in a bit of wishful thinking and hope that the first half of the array is already perfectly sorted, and the second half is too, like this:

| 5 | 9 | 10 | 12 | 17 | 1 | 8 | 11 | 20 | 32 |

Now it is simple to *merge* the two sorted arrays into one sorted array, by taking a new element from either the first or the second subarray, and choosing the smaller of the elements each time:

5 9 10 12 17 1 8 11 20 32	1
5 9 10 12 17 1 8 11 20 32	1 5
5 9 10 12 17 1 8 11 20 32	1 5 8
5 9 10 12 17 1 8 11 20 32	1 5 8 9
5 9 10 12 17 1 8 11 20 32	1 5 8 9 10
5 9 10 12 17 1 8 11 20 32	1 5 8 9 10 11
5 9 10 12 17 1 8 11 20 32	1 5 8 9 10 11 12
5 9 10 12 17 1 8 11 20 32	1 5 8 9 10 11 12 17
5 9 10 12 17 1 8 11 20 32	1 5 8 9 10 11 12 17 20
5 9 10 12 17 1 8 11 20 32	1 5 8 9 10 11 12 17 20 32

In fact, you probably performed this merging before when you and a friend had to sort a pile of papers. You and the friend split the pile in half, each of you sorted your half, and then you merged the results together.

The merge sort algorithm sorts an array by cutting the array in half, recursively sorting each half, and then merging the sorted halves.

That is all well and good, but it doesn't seem to solve the problem for the computer. It still must sort the first and second halves of the array, because it can't very well ask a few buddies to pitch in. As it turns out, though, if the computer keeps dividing the array into smaller and smaller subarrays, sorting each half and merging them back together, it carries out dramatically fewer steps than the selection sort requires.

Let us write a MergeSorter class that implements this idea. When the MergeSorter sorts an array, it makes two arrays, each half the size of the original, and sorts them recursively. Then it merges the two sorted arrays together:

```java
public void sort()
{
   if (a.length <= 1) return;
   int[] first = new int[a.length / 2];
   int[] second = new int[a.length - first.length];
   System.arraycopy(a, 0, first, 0, first.length);
   System.arraycopy(a,
       first.length, second, 0, second.length);
   MergeSorter firstSorter = new MergeSorter(first);
   MergeSorter secondSorter = new MergeSorter(second);
   firstSorter.sort();
   secondSorter.sort();
   merge(first, second);
}
```

The merge method is tedious but quite straightforward. You will find it in the code that follows.

ch14/mergesort/MergeSorter.java

```java
1   /**
2       This class sorts an array, using the merge sort algorithm.
3   */
4   public class MergeSorter
5   {
6      /**
7          Constructs a merge sorter.
8          @param anArray the array to sort
9      */
10     public MergeSorter(int[] anArray)
11     {
12        a = anArray;
13     }
14
15     /**
16         Sorts the array managed by this merge sorter.
17     */
18     public void sort()
19     {
20        if (a.length <= 1) return;
21        int[] first = new int[a.length / 2];
22        int[] second = new int[a.length - first.length];
```

```
23        System.arraycopy(a, 0, first, 0, first.length);
24        System.arraycopy(a, first.length, second, 0, second.length);
25        MergeSorter firstSorter = new MergeSorter(first);
26        MergeSorter secondSorter = new MergeSorter(second);
27        firstSorter.sort();
28        secondSorter.sort();
29        merge(first, second);
30     }
31
32     /**
33        Merges two sorted arrays into the array managed by this
34        merge sorter.
35        @param first the first sorted array
36        @param second the second sorted array
37     */
38     private void merge(int[] first, int[] second)
39     {
40        // Merge both halves into the temporary array
41
42        int iFirst = 0;
43           // Next element to consider in the first array
44        int iSecond = 0;
45           // Next element to consider in the second array
46        int j = 0;
47           // Next open position in a
48
49        // As long as neither iFirst nor iSecond past the end, move
50        // the smaller element into a
51        while (iFirst < first.length && iSecond < second.length)
52        {
53           if (first[iFirst] < second[iSecond])
54           {
55              a[j] = first[iFirst];
56              iFirst++;
57           }
58           else
59           {
60              a[j] = second[iSecond];
61              iSecond++;
62           }
63           j++;
64        }
65
66        // Note that only one of the two calls to arraycopy below
67        // copies entries
68
69        // Copy any remaining entries of the first array
70        System.arraycopy(first, iFirst, a, j, first.length - iFirst);
71
72        // Copy any remaining entries of the second half
73        System.arraycopy(second, iSecond, a, j, second.length - iSecond);
74     }
75
76     private int[] a;
77  }
```

ch14/mergesort/MergeSortDemo.java

```
 1  import java.util.Arrays;
 1
 1  /**
 2     This program demonstrates the merge sort algorithm by
 3     sorting an array that is filled with random numbers.
 4  */
 5  public class MergeSortDemo
 6  {
 7     public static void main(String[] args)
 8     {
 9        int[] a = ArrayUtil.randomIntArray(20, 100);
10        System.out.println(Arrays.toString(a));
11        MergeSorter sorter = new MergeSorter(a);
12        sorter.sort();
13        System.out.println(Arrays.toString(a));
14     }
15  }
```

Typical Output

```
[8, 81, 48, 53, 46, 70, 98, 42, 27, 76, 33, 24, 2, 76, 62, 89, 90, 5, 13, 21]
[2, 5, 8, 13, 21, 24, 27, 33, 42, 46, 48, 53, 62, 70, 76, 76, 81, 89, 90, 98]
```

SELF CHECK

7. Why does only one of the two arraycopy calls at the end of the merge method do any work?

8. Manually run the merge sort algorithm on the array 8 7 6 5 4 3 2 1.

14.5 Analyzing the Merge Sort Algorithm

The merge sort algorithm looks a lot more complicated than the selection sort algorithm, and it appears that it may well take much longer to carry out these repeated subdivisions. However, the timing results for merge sort look much better than those for selection sort (see table on next page).

Figure 2 shows a graph comparing both sets of performance data. That is a tremendous improvement. To understand why, let us estimate the number of array element visits that are required to sort an array with the merge sort algorithm. First, let us tackle the merge process that happens after the first and second halves have been sorted.

Each step in the merge process adds one more element to a. That element may come from first or second, and in most cases the elements from the two halves must be compared to see which one to take. Let us count that as 3 visits (one for a and one each for first and second) per element, or $3n$ visits total, where n denotes the length of a. Moreover, at the beginning, we had to copy from a to first and second, yielding another $2n$ visits, for a total of $5n$.

n	Merge Sort (milliseconds)	Selection Sort (milliseconds)
10,000	40	786
20,000	73	2,148
30,000	134	4,796
40,000	170	9,192
50,000	192	13,321
60,000	205	19,299

If we let $T(n)$ denote the number of visits required to sort a range of n elements through the merge sort process, then we obtain

$$T(n) = T\left(\frac{n}{2}\right) + T\left(\frac{n}{2}\right) + 5n$$

because sorting each half takes $T(n/2)$ visits. Actually, if n is not even, then we have one subarray of size $(n-1)/2$ and one of size $(n+1)/2$. Although it turns out that this detail does not affect the outcome of the computation, we will nevertheless assume for now that n is a power of 2, say $n = 2^m$. That way, all subarrays can be evenly divided into two parts.

Figure 2
Merge Sort Timing (blue) versus Selection Sort (red)

Unfortunately, the formula

$$T(n) = 2T\left(\frac{n}{2}\right) + 5n$$

does not clearly tell us the relationship between n and $T(n)$. To understand the relationship, let us evaluate $T(n/2)$, using the same formula:

$$T\left(\frac{n}{2}\right) = 2T\left(\frac{n}{4}\right) + 5\frac{n}{2}$$

Therefore

$$T(n) = 2 \times 2T\left(\frac{n}{4}\right) + 5n + 5n$$

Let us do that again:

$$T\left(\frac{n}{4}\right) = 2T\left(\frac{n}{8}\right) + 5\frac{n}{4}$$

hence

$$T(n) = 2 \times 2 \times 2T\left(\frac{n}{8}\right) + 5n + 5n + 5n$$

This generalizes from 2, 4, 8, to arbitrary powers of 2:

$$T(n) = 2^k T\left(\frac{n}{2^k}\right) + 5nk$$

Recall that we assume that $n = 2^m$; hence, for $k = m$,

$$T(n) = 2^m T\left(\frac{n}{2^m}\right) + 5nm$$
$$= nT(1) + 5nm$$
$$= n + 5n\log_2(n)$$

Because $n = 2^m$, we have $m = \log_2(n)$.

To establish the growth order, we drop the lower-order term n and are left with $5n\log_2(n)$. We drop the constant factor 5. It is also customary to drop the base of the logarithm, because all logarithms are related by a constant factor. For example,

$$\log_2(x) = \log_{10}(x)/\log_{10}(2) \approx \log_{10}(x) \times 3.32193$$

Hence we say that merge sort is an $O(n \log(n))$ algorithm.

Merge sort is an $O(n \log(n))$ algorithm. The $n \log(n)$ function grows much more slowly than n^2.

Is the $O(n \log(n))$ merge sort algorithm better than the $O(n^2)$ selection sort algorithm? You bet it is. Recall that it took $100^2 = 10,000$ times as long to sort a million records as it took to sort 10,000 records with the $O(n^2)$ algorithm. With the $O(n \log(n))$ algorithm, the ratio is

$$\frac{1,000,000 \log(1,000,000)}{10,000 \log(10,000)} = 100 \left(\frac{6}{4} \right) = 150$$

Suppose for the moment that merge sort takes the same time as selection sort to sort an array of 10,000 integers, that is, 3/4 of a second on the test machine. (Actually, it is much faster than that.) Then it would take about 0.75×150 seconds, or under 2 minutes, to sort a million integers. Contrast that with selection sort, which would take over 2 hours for the same task. As you can see, even if it takes you several hours to learn about a better algorithm, that can be time well spent.

In this chapter we have barely begun to scratch the surface of this interesting topic. There are many sorting algorithms, some with even better performance than the merge sort algorithm, and the analysis of these algorithms can be quite challenging. If you are a computer science major, you may revisit these important issues in a later computer science class.

The Arrays class implements a sorting method that you should use for your Java programs.

However, when you write Java programs, you don't have to implement your own sorting algorithm. The Arrays class contains static sort methods to sort arrays of integers and floating-point numbers. For example, you can sort an array of integers simply as

```
int[] a = . . .;
Arrays.sort(a);
```

That sort method uses the quicksort algorithm—see Advanced Topic 14.3 for more information about that algorithm.

SELF CHECK

9. Given the timing data for the merge sort algorithm in the table at the beginning of this section, how long would it take to sort an array of 100,000 values?

10. Suppose you have an array double[] values in a Java program. How would you sort it?

ADVANCED TOPIC 14.3

The Quicksort Algorithm

Quicksort is a commonly used algorithm that has the advantage over merge sort that no temporary arrays are required to sort and merge the partial results.

The quicksort algorithm, like merge sort, is based on the strategy of divide and conquer. To sort a range a[from] . . . a[to] of the array a, first rearrange the elements in the range so that no element in the range a[from] . . . a[p] is larger than any element in the range a[p + 1] . . . a[to]. This step is called *partitioning* the range.

For example, suppose we start with a range

| 5 | 3 | 2 | 6 | 4 | 1 | 3 | 7 |

Here is a partitioning of the range. Note that the partitions aren't yet sorted.

| 3 | 3 | 2 | 1 | 4 | | 6 | 5 | 7 |

You'll see later how to obtain such a partition. In the next step, sort each partition, by recursively applying the same algorithm on the two partitions. That sorts the entire range, because the largest element in the first partition is at most as large as the smallest element in the second partition.

| 1 | 2 | 3 | 3 | 4 | | 5 | 6 | 7 |

Quicksort is implemented recursively as follows:

```
public void sort(int from, int to)
{
   if (from >= to) return;
   int p = partition(from, to);
   sort(from, p);
   sort(p + 1, to);
}
```

Let us return to the problem of partitioning a range. Pick an element from the range and call it the *pivot*. There are several variations of the quicksort algorithm. In the simplest one, we'll pick the first element of the range, a[from], as the pivot.

Now form two regions a[from] . . . a[i], consisting of values at most as large as the pivot and a[j] . . . a[to], consisting of values at least as large as the pivot. The region a[i + 1] . . . a[j - 1] consists of values that haven't been analyzed yet. (See Partitioning a Range.) At the beginning, both the left and right areas are empty; that is, i = from - 1 and j = to + 1.

Partitioning a Range

Extending the Partitions

Then keep incrementing i while a[i] < pivot and keep decrementing j while a[j] > pivot. Extending the Partitions shows i and j when that process stops.

Now swap the values in positions i and j, increasing both areas once more. Keep going while i < j. Here is the code for the partition method:

```
private int partition(int from, int to)
{
   int pivot = a[from];
   int i = from - 1;
   int j = to + 1;
   while (i < j)
   {
      i++; while (a[i] < pivot) i++;
      j--; while (a[j] > pivot) j--;
      if (i < j) swap(i, j);
   }
   return j;
}
```

On average, the quicksort algorithm is an $O(n \log(n))$ algorithm. Because it is simpler, it runs faster than merge sort in most cases. There is just one unfortunate aspect to the quicksort algorithm. Its *worst-case* runtime behavior is $O(n^2)$. Moreover, if the pivot element is chosen as the first element of the region, that worst-case behavior occurs when the input set is already sorted—a common situation in practice. By selecting the pivot element more cleverly, we can make it extremely unlikely for the worst-case behavior to occur. Such "tuned" quicksort algorithms are commonly used, because their performance is generally excellent. For example, as was mentioned, the sort method in the Arrays class uses a quicksort algorithm.

Another improvement that is commonly made in practice is to switch to insertion sort when the array is short, because the total number of operations of insertion sort is lower for short arrays. The Java library makes that switch if the array length is less than 7.

RANDOM FACT 14.1

The First Programmer

Before pocket calculators and personal computers existed, navigators and engineers used mechanical adding machines, slide rules, and tables of logarithms and trigonometric functions to speed up computations. Unfortunately, the tables—for which values had to be computed by hand—were notoriously inaccurate. The mathematician Charles Babbage (1791–1871) had the insight that if a machine could be constructed that produced printed tables automatically, both calculation and typesetting errors could be avoided. Babbage set out to develop a machine for this purpose, which he called a *Difference Engine* because it used successive differences to compute polynomials. For example, consider the function $f(x) = x^3$. Write down the values for $f(1)$, $f(2)$, $f(3)$, and so on. Then take the *differences* between successive values:

```
1
        7
8
        19
27
        37
64
        61
125
        91
216
```

Repeat the process, taking the difference of successive values in the second column, and then repeat once again:

```
1
        7
8               12
        19              6
27              18
        37              6
64              24
        61              6
125             30
        91
216
```

Now the differences are all the same. You can retrieve the function values by a pattern of additions—you need to know the values at the fringe of the pattern and the constant difference. This method was very attractive, because mechanical addition machines had been known for some time. They consisted of cog wheels, with 10 cogs per wheel, to represent

Babbage's Difference Engine

digits, and mechanisms to handle the carry from one digit to the next. Mechanical multiplication machines, on the other hand, were fragile and unreliable. Babbage built a successful prototype of the Difference Engine (see the Babbage's Difference Engine figure) and, with his own money and government grants, proceeded to build the table-printing machine. However, because of funding problems and the difficulty of building the machine to the required precision, it was never completed.

While working on the Difference Engine, Babbage conceived of a much grander vision that he called the *Analytical Engine*. The Difference Engine was designed to carry out a limited set of computations—it was no smarter than a pocket calculator is today. But Babbage realized that such a machine could be made *programmable* by storing programs as well as data. The internal storage of the Analytical Engine was to consist of 1,000 registers of 50 decimal digits each. Programs and constants were to be stored on punched cards—a technique that was, at that time, commonly used on looms for weaving patterned fabrics.

Ada Augusta, Countess of Lovelace (1815–1852), the only child of Lord Byron, was a friend and sponsor of Charles Babbage. Ada Lovelace was one of the first people to realize the potential of such a machine, not just for computing mathematical tables but for processing data that were not numbers. She is considered by many the world's first programmer. The Ada programming language, a language developed for use in U.S. Department of Defense projects (see Random Fact 9.2), was named in her honor.

14.6 Searching

Suppose you need to find the telephone number of your friend. You look up his name in the telephone book, and naturally you can find it quickly, because the telephone book is sorted alphabetically. Quite possibly, you may never have thought how important it is that the telephone book is sorted. To see that, think of the following problem: Suppose you have a telephone number and you must know to what party it belongs. You could of course call that number, but suppose nobody picks up on the other end. You could look through the telephone book, a number at a time, until you find the number. That would obviously be a tremendous amount of work, and you would have to be desperate to attempt that.

This thought experiment shows the difference between a search through an unsorted data set and a search through a sorted data set. The following two sections will analyze the difference formally.

> A linear search examines all values in an array until it finds a match or reaches the end.

If you want to find a number in a sequence of values that occur in arbitrary order, there is nothing you can do to speed up the search. You must simply look through all elements until you have found a match or until you reach the end. This is called a *linear* or *sequential search*.

> A linear search locates a value in an array in $O(n)$ steps.

How long does a linear search take? If we assume that the element v is present in the array a, then the average search visits $n/2$ elements, where n is the length of the array. If it is not present, then all n elements must be inspected to verify the absence. Either way, a linear search is an $O(n)$ algorithm.

Here is a class that performs linear searches through an array a of integers. When searching for the value v, the search method returns the first index of the match, or -1 if v does not occur in a.

ch14/linsearch/LinearSearcher.java

```
1   /**
2       A class for executing linear searches through an array.
3   */
4   public class LinearSearcher
5   {
6       /**
7           Constructs the LinearSearcher.
8           @param anArray an array of integers
9       */
10      public LinearSearcher(int[] anArray)
11      {
12          a = anArray;
13      }
14
15      /**
16          Finds a value in an array, using the linear search
17          algorithm.
18          @param v the value to search
19          @return the index at which the value occurs, or -1
20          if it does not occur in the array
21      */
22      public int search(int v)
23      {
24          for (int i = 0; i < a.length; i++)
25          {
26              if (a[i] == v)
27                  return i;
28          }
29          return -1;
30      }
31
32      private int[] a;
33  }
```

ch14/linsearch/LinearSearchDemo.java

```
1   import java.util.Arrays;
2   import java.util.Scanner;
3
4   /**
5       This program demonstrates the linear search algorithm.
6   */
7   public class LinearSearchDemo
8   {
9       public static void main(String[] args)
10      {
11          int[] a = ArrayUtil.randomIntArray(20, 100);
12          System.out.println(Arrays.toString(a));
```

```
13        LinearSearcher searcher = new LinearSearcher(a);
14
15        Scanner in = new Scanner(System.in);
16
17        boolean done = false;
18        while (!done)
19        {
20           System.out.print("Enter number to search for, -1 to quit: ");
21           int n = in.nextInt();
22           if (n == -1)
23              done = true;
24           else
25           {
26              int pos = searcher.search(n);
27              System.out.println("Found in position " + pos);
28           }
29        }
30     }
31 }
```

Typical Output

```
[46, 99, 45, 57, 64, 95, 81, 69, 11, 97, 6, 85, 61, 88, 29, 65, 83, 88, 45, 88]
Enter number to search for, -1 to quit: 11
Found in position 8
```

SELF CHECK

11. Suppose you need to look through 1,000,000 records to find a telephone number. How many records do you expect to search before finding the number?

12. Why can't you use a "for each" loop for (int element : a) in the search method?

14.7 Binary Search

Now let us search for an item in a data sequence that has been previously sorted. Of course, we could still do a linear search, but it turns out we can do much better than that.

Consider the following sorted array a. The data set is:

[0][1][2][3][4][5][6][7]

| 1 | 5 | 8 | 9 | 12 | 17 | 20 | 32 |

We would like to see whether the value 15 is in the data set. Let's narrow our search by finding whether the value is in the first or second half of the array. The last point in the first half of the data set, a[3], is 9, which is smaller than the value we are looking for. Hence, we should look in the second half of the array for a match, that is, in the sequence:

```
[0][1][2][3][4][5][6][7]
 1  5  8  9  12 17 20 32
```

Now the last value of the first half of this sequence is 17; hence, the value must be located in the sequence:

```
[0][1][2][3][4][5][6][7]
 1  5  8  9  12 17 20 32
```

The last value of the first half of this very short sequence is 12, which is smaller than the value that we are searching, so we must look in the second half:

```
[0][1][2][3][4][5][6][7]
 1  5  8  9  12 17 20 32
```

> A binary search locates a value in a sorted array by determining whether the value occurs in the first or second half, then repeating the search in one of the halves.

It is trivial to see that we don't have a match, because 15 ≠ 17. If we wanted to insert 15 into the sequence, we would need to insert it just before a[5].

This search process is called a *binary search*, because we cut the size of the search in half in each step. That cutting in half works only because we know that the sequence of values is sorted.

The following class implements binary searches in a sorted array of integers. The search method returns the position of the match if the search succeeds, or –1 if v is not found in a.

ch14/binsearch/BinarySearcher.java

```
1  /**
2     A class for executing binary searches through an array.
3  */
4  public class BinarySearcher
5  {
6     /**
7        Constructs a BinarySearcher.
8        @param anArray a sorted array of integers
9     */
10    public BinarySearcher(int[] anArray)
11    {
12       a = anArray;
13    }
14
15    /**
16       Finds a value in a sorted array, using the binary
17       search algorithm.
18       @param v the value to search
19       @return the index at which the value occurs, or -1
20       if it does not occur in the array
21    */
```

```
22      public int search(int v)
23      {
24         int low = 0;
25         int high = a.length - 1;
26         while (low <= high)
27         {
28            int mid = (low + high) / 2;
29            int diff = a[mid] - v;
30
31            if (diff == 0) // a[mid] == v
32               return mid;
33            else if (diff < 0) // a[mid] < v
34               low = mid + 1;
35            else
36               high = mid - 1;
37         }
38         return -1;
39      }
40
41      private int[] a;
42   }
```

Let us determine the number of visits of array elements required to carry out a search. We can use the same technique as in the analysis of merge sort. Because we look at the middle element, which counts as one comparison, and then search either the left or the right subarray, we have

$$T(n) = T\left(\frac{n}{2}\right) + 1$$

Using the same equation,

$$T\left(\frac{n}{2}\right) = T\left(\frac{n}{4}\right) + 1$$

By plugging this result into the original equation, we get

$$T(n) = T\left(\frac{n}{4}\right) + 2$$

That generalizes to

$$T(n) = T\left(\frac{n}{2^k}\right) + k$$

As in the analysis of merge sort, we make the simplifying assumption that n is a power of 2, $n = 2^m$, where $m = \log_2(n)$. Then we obtain

$$T(n) = 1 + \log_2(n)$$

Therefore, binary search is an $O(\log(n))$ algorithm.

A binary search locates a value in an array in $O(\log(n))$ steps.

That result makes intuitive sense. Suppose that n is 100. Then after each search, the size of the search range is cut in half, to 50, 25, 12, 6, 3, and 1. After seven comparisons we are done. This agrees with our formula, because $\log_2(100) \approx 6.64386$, and indeed the next larger power of 2 is $2^7 = 128$.

Because a binary search is so much faster than a linear search, is it worthwhile to sort an array first and then use a binary search? It depends. If you search the array only once, then it is more efficient to pay for an $O(n)$ linear search than for an $O(n \log(n))$ sort and an $O(\log(n))$ binary search. But if you will be making many searches in the same array, then sorting it is definitely worthwhile.

The `Arrays` class contains a static `binarySearch` method that implements the binary search algorithm, but with a useful enhancement. If a value is not found in the array, then the returned value is not -1, but $-k - 1$, where k is the position before which the element should be inserted. For example,

```
int[] a = { 1, 4, 9 };
int v = 7;
int pos = Arrays.binarySearch(a, v);
    // Returns -3; v should be inserted before position 2
```

SELF CHECK

13. Suppose you need to look through a sorted array with 1,000,000 elements to find a value. Using the binary search algorithm, how many records do you expect to search before finding the value?

14. Why is it useful that the `Arrays.binarySearch` method indicates the position where a missing element should be inserted?

15. Why does `Arrays.binarySearch` return $-k - 1$ and not $-k$ to indicate that a value is not present and should be inserted before position k?

14.8 Sorting Real Data

In this chapter we have studied how to search and sort arrays of integers. Of course, in application programs, there is rarely a need to search through a collection of integers. However, it is easy to modify these techniques to search through real data.

The `sort` method of the Arrays class sorts objects of classes that implement the Comparable interface.

The `Arrays` class supplies a static `sort` method for sorting arrays of objects. However, the `Arrays` class cannot know how to compare arbitrary objects. Suppose, for example, that you have an array of `Coin` objects. It is not obvious how the coins should be sorted. You could sort them by their names, or by their values. The `Arrays.sort` method cannot make that decision for you. Instead, it requires that the objects belong to classes that implement the `Comparable` interface. That interface has a single method:

```
public interface Comparable
{
```

```
    int compareTo(Object otherObject);
}
```

The call

```
a.compareTo(b)
```

must return a negative number if a should come before b, 0 if a and b are the same, and a positive number otherwise.

Several classes in the standard Java library, such as the String and Date classes, implement the Comparable interface.

You can implement the Comparable interface for your own classes as well. For example, to sort a collection of coins, the Coin class would need to implement this interface and define a compareTo method:

```
public class Coin implements Comparable
{
    . . .
    public int compareTo(Object otherObject)
    {
        Coin other = (Coin) otherObject;
        if (value < other.value) return -1;
        if (value == other.value) return 0;
        return 1;
    }
    . . .
}
```

When you implement the compareTo method of the Comparable interface, you must make sure that the method defines a *total ordering relationship*, with the following three properties:

- *Antisymmetric:* If a.compareTo(b) $\leq$ 0, then b.compareTo(a) $\geq$ 0
- *Reflexive:* a.compareTo(a) = 0
- *Transitive:* If a.compareTo(b) $\leq$ 0 and b.compareTo(c) $\leq$ 0, then a.compareTo(c) $\leq$ 0

Once your Coin class implements the Comparable interface, you can simply pass an array of coins to the Arrays.sort method:

```
Coin[] coins = new Coin[n];
// Add coins
. . .
Arrays.sort(coins);
```

> The Collections class contains a sort method that can sort array lists.

If the coins are stored in an ArrayList, use the Collections.sort method instead; it uses the merge sort algorithm:

```
ArrayList<Coin> coins = new ArrayList<Coin>();
// Add coins
. . .
Collections.sort(coins);
```

As a practical matter, you should use the sorting and searching methods in the Arrays and Collections classes and not those that you write yourself. The library algorithms have been fully debugged and optimized. Thus, the primary purpose of this chapter was not to teach you how to implement practical sorting and searching algorithms. Instead, you have learned something more important, namely that different algorithms can vary widely in performance, and that it is worthwhile to learn more about the design and analysis of algorithms.

SELF CHECK

16. Why can't the Arrays.sort method sort an array of Rectangle objects?
17. What steps would you need to take to sort an array of BankAccount objects by increasing balance?

COMMON ERROR 14.1

The compareTo Method Can Return Any Integer, Not Just –1, 0, and 1

The call a.compareTo(b) is allowed to return *any* negative integer to denote that a should come before b, not necessarily the value –1. That is, the test

```
if (a.compareTo(b) == -1) // ERROR!
```

is generally wrong. Instead, you should test

```
if (a.compareTo(b) < 0) // OK
```

Why would a compareTo method ever want to return a number other than –1, 0, or 1? Sometimes, it is convenient to just return the difference of two integers. For example, the compareTo method of the String class compares characters in matching positions:

```
char c1 = charAt(i);
char c2 = other.charAt(i);
```

If the characters are different, then the method simply returns their difference:

```
if (c1 != c2) return c1 - c2;
```

This difference is a negative number if c1 is less than c2, but it is not necessarily the number –1.

ADVANCED TOPIC 14.4

The Parameterized Comparable Interface

As of Java version 5.0, the Comparable interface is a parameterized type, similar to the ArrayList type:

```
public interface Comparable<T>
{
    int compareTo(T other)
}
```

The type parameter specifies the type of the objects that this class is willing to accept for comparison. Usually, this type is the same as the class type itself. For example, the Coin class would implement Comparable<Coin>, like this:

```
public class Coin implements Comparable<Coin>
{
    . . .
    public int compareTo(Coin other)
    {
        if (value < other.value) return -1;
        if (value == other.value) return 0;
        return 1;
    }
    . . .
}
```

The type parameter has a significant advantage: You need not use a cast to convert an Object parameter into the desired type.

ADVANCED TOPIC 14.5

The Comparator Interface

Sometimes, you want so sort an array or array list of objects, but the objects don't belong to a class that implements the Comparable interface. Or, perhaps, you want to sort the array in a different order. For example, you may want to sort coins by name rather than by value.

You wouldn't want to change the implementation of a class just in order to call Arrays.sort. Fortunately, there is an alternative. One version of the Arrays.sort method does not require that the objects belong to classes that implement the Comparable interface. Instead, you can supply arbitrary objects. However, you must also provide a *comparator* object whose job is to compare objects. The comparator object must belong to a class that implements the Comparator interface. That interface has a single method, compare, which compares two objects.

As of Java version 5.0, the Comparator interface is a parameterized type. The type parameter specifies the type of the compare parameters. For example, Comparator<Coin> looks like this:

```
public interface Comparator<Coin>
{
    int compare(Coin a, Coin b);
}
```

The call

```
comp.compare(a, b)
```

must return a negative number if a should come before b, 0 if a and b are the same, and a positive number otherwise. (Here, comp is an object of a class that implements Comparator<Coin>.)

For example, here is a Comparator class for coins:

```
public class CoinComparator implements Comparator<Coin>
{
    public int compare(Coin a, Coin b)
    {
        if (a.getValue() < b.getValue()) return -1;
        if (a.getValue() == b.getValue()) return 0;
        return 1;
    }
}
```

To sort an array of coins by value, call

```
Arrays.sort(coins, new CoinComparator());
```

CHAPTER SUMMARY

1. The selection sort algorithm sorts an array by repeatedly finding the smallest element of the unsorted tail region and moving it to the front.

2. Computer scientists use the big-Oh notation $f(n) = O(g(n))$ to express that the function f grows no faster than the function g.

3. Selection sort is an $O(n^2)$ algorithm. Doubling the data set means a fourfold increase in processing time.

4. Insertion sort is an $O(n^2)$ algorithm.

5. The merge sort algorithm sorts an array by cutting the array in half, recursively sorting each half, and then merging the sorted halves.

6. Merge sort is an $O(n \log(n))$ algorithm. The $n \log(n)$ function grows much more slowly than n^2.

7. The Arrays class implements a sorting method that you should use for your Java programs.

8. A linear search examines all values in an array until it finds a match or reaches the end.

9. A linear search locates a value in an array in $O(n)$ steps.

10. A binary search locates a value in a sorted array by determining whether the value occurs in the first or second half, then repeating the search in one of the halves.

11. A binary search locates a value in an array in $O(\log(n))$ steps.

12. The sort method of the Arrays class sorts objects of classes that implement the Comparable interface.

13. The Collections class contains a sort method that can sort array lists.

FURTHER READING

1. Michael T. Goodrich and Roberto Tamassia, *Data Structures and Algorithms in Java, 3rd edition*, John Wiley & Sons, 2003.

CLASSES, OBJECTS, AND METHODS INTRODUCED IN THIS CHAPTER

```
java.lang.Comparable<T>
    compareTo
java.lang.System
    currentTimeMillis
java.util.Arrays
    binarySearch
    sort
    toString
java.util.Collections
    binarySearch
    sort
java.util.Comparator<T>
    compare
```

REVIEW EXERCISES

★★ **Exercise R14.1.** *Checking against off-by-one errors.* When writing the selection sort algorithm of Section 14.1, a programmer must make the usual choices of < against <=, a.length against a.length - 1, and from against from + 1. This is a fertile ground for off-by-one errors. Conduct code walkthroughs of the algorithm with arrays of length 0, 1, 2, and 3 and check carefully that all index values are correct.

★ **Exercise R14.2.** What is the difference between searching and sorting?

★★ **Exercise R14.3.** For the following expressions, what is the order of the growth of each?

  a. $n^2 + 2n + 1$

  b. $n^{10} + 9n^9 + 20n^8 + 145n^7$

  c. $(n + 1)^4$

  d. $(n^2 + n)^2$

  e. $n + 0.001n^3$

  f. $n^3 - 1000n^2 + 10^9$

  g. $n + \log(n)$

  h. $n^2 + n \log(n)$

  i. $2^n + n^2$

  j. $\dfrac{n^3 + 2n}{n^2 + 0.75}$

★ **Exercise R14.4.** We determined that the actual number of visits in the selection sort algorithm is

$$T(n) = \tfrac{1}{2}n^2 + \tfrac{5}{2}n - 3$$

We characterized this method as having $O(n^2)$ growth. Compute the actual ratios

$$T(2{,}000)/T(1{,}000)$$
$$T(4{,}000)/T(1{,}000)$$
$$T(10{,}000)/T(1{,}000)$$

and compare them with

$$f(2{,}000)/f(1{,}000)$$
$$f(4{,}000)/f(1{,}000)$$
$$f(10{,}000)/f(1{,}000)$$

where $f(n) = n^2$.

★ **Exercise R14.5.** Suppose algorithm A takes 5 seconds to handle a data set of 1,000 records. If the algorithm A is an $O(n)$ algorithm, how long will it take to handle a data set of 2,000 records? Of 10,000 records?

★★ **Exercise R14.6.** Suppose an algorithm takes 5 seconds to handle a data set of 1,000 records. Fill in the following table, which shows the approximate growth of the execution times depending on the complexity of the algorithm.

	$O(n)$	$O(n^2)$	$O(n^3)$	$O(n \log(n))$	$O(2^n)$
1,000	5	5	5	5	5
2,000					
3,000		45			
10,000					

For example, because $3{,}000^2/1{,}000^2 = 9$, the algorithm would take 9 times as long, or 45 seconds, to handle a data set of 3,000 records.

★★ **Exercise R14.7.** Sort the following growth rates from slowest to fastest growth.

$O(n)$ $O(n \log(n))$

$O(n^3)$ $O(2^n)$

$O(n^n)$ $O(\sqrt{n})$

$O(\log(n))$ $O(n\sqrt{n})$

$O(n^2 \log(n))$ $O(n^{\log(n)})$

★ **Exercise R14.8.** What is the growth rate of the standard algorithm to find the minimum value of an array? Of finding both the minimum and the maximum?

★ **Exercise R14.9.** What is the growth rate of the following method?

```java
public static int count(int[] a, int c)
{
    int count = 0;

    for (int i = 0; i < a.length; i++)
    {
        if (a[i] == c) count++;
    }
    return count;
}
```

★★ **Exercise R14.10.** Your task is to remove all duplicates from an array. For example, if the array has the values

4 7 11 4 9 5 11 7 3 5

then the array should be changed to

4 7 11 9 5 3

Here is a simple algorithm. Look at a[i]. Count how many times it occurs in a. If the count is larger than 1, remove it. What is the growth rate of the time required for this algorithm?

★★ **Exercise R14.11.** Consider the following algorithm to remove all duplicates from an array. Sort the array. For each element in the array, look at its next neighbor to decide whether it is present more than once. If so, remove it. Is this a faster algorithm than the one in Exercise R14.10?

★★★ **Exercise R14.12.** Develop an $O(n \log (n))$ algorithm for removing duplicates from an array if the resulting array must have the same ordering as the original array.

★★★ **Exercise R14.13.** Why does insertion sort perform significantly better than selection sort if an array is already sorted?

★★★ **Exercise R14.14.** Consider the following speedup of the insertion sort algorithm of Advanced Topic 14.1. For each element, use the enhanced binary search algorithm that yields the insertion position for missing elements. Does this speedup have a significant impact on the efficiency of the algorithm?

Additional review exercises are available in WileyPLUS.

PROGRAMMING EXERCISES

★ **Exercise P14.1.** Modify the selection sort algorithm to sort an array of integers in descending order.

★ **Exercise P14.2.** Modify the selection sort algorithm to sort an array of coins by their value.

★★   **Exercise P14.3.** Write a program that generates the table of sample runs of the selection sort times automatically. The program should ask for the smallest and largest value of n and the number of measurements and then make all sample runs.

★   **Exercise P14.4.** Modify the merge sort algorithm to sort an array of strings in lexicographic order.

★★★   **Exercise P14.5.** Write a telephone lookup program. Read a data set of 1,000 names and telephone numbers from a file that contains the numbers in random order. Handle lookups by name and also reverse lookups by phone number. Use a binary search for both lookups.

★★   **Exercise P14.6.** Implement a program that measures the performance of the insertion sort algorithm described in Advanced Topic 14.1.

★★★   **Exercise P14.7.** Write a program that sorts an ArrayList<Coin> in decreasing order so that the most valuable coin is at the beginning of the array. Use a Comparator.

★★   **Exercise P14.8.** Consider the binary search algorithm in Section 14.7. If no match is found, the search method returns −1. Modify the method so that if a is not found, the method returns $-k - 1$, where k is the position before which the element should be inserted. (This is the same behavior as Arrays.binarySearch.)

★★   **Exercise P14.9.** Implement the sort method of the merge sort algorithm without recursion, where the length of the array is a power of 2. First merge adjacent regions of size 1, then adjacent regions of size 2, then adjacent regions of size 4, and so on.

★★★   **Exercise P14.10.** Implement the sort method of the merge sort algorithm without recursion, where the length of the array is an arbitrary number. Keep merging adjacent regions whose size is a power of 2, and pay special attention to the last area whose size is less.

★★★   **Exercise P14.11.** Use insertion sort and the binary search from Exercise P14.8 to sort an array as described in Exercise R14.14. Implement this algorithm and measure its performance.

★   **Exercise P14.12.** Supply a class Person that implements the Comparable interface. Compare persons by their names. Ask the user to input 10 names and generate 10 Person objects. Using the compareTo method, determine the first and last person among them and print them.

★★   **Exercise P14.13.** Sort an array list of strings by increasing *length*. *Hint:* Supply a Comparator.

★★★   **Exercise P14.14.** Sort an array list of strings by increasing length, and so that strings of the same length are sorted lexicographically. *Hint:* Supply a Comparator.

Additional programming exercises are available in WileyPLUS.

PROGRAMMING PROJECTS

★★★ **Project 14.1.** Write a program that keeps an appointment book. Make a class Appointment that stores a description of the appointment, the appointment day, the starting time, and the ending time. Your program should keep the appointments in a sorted array list. Users can add appointments and print out all appointments for a given day. When a new appointment is added, use binary search to find where it should be inserted in the array list. Do not add it if it conflicts with another appointment.

★★★G **Project 14.2.** Implement a *graphical animation* of sorting and searching algorithms. Fill an array with a set of random numbers between 1 and 100. Draw each array element as a bar, as in Figure 3. Whenever the algorithm changes the array, wait for the user to click a button, then call the repaint method.

Animate selection sort, merge sort, and binary search. In the binary search animation, highlight the currently inspected element and the current values of from and to.

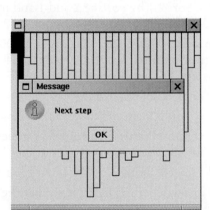

Figure 3
Graphical Animation

ANSWERS TO SELF-CHECK QUESTIONS

1. Dropping the temp variable would not work. Then a[i] and a[j] would end up being the same value.

2. 1 | 5 4 3 2 6, 1 2 | 4 3 5 6, 1 2 3 4 5 6

3. Four times as long as 40,000 values, or about 50 seconds.

4. A parabola.

5. It takes about 100 times longer.

6. If n is 4, then $\frac{1}{2}n^2$ is 8 and $\frac{5}{2}n - 3$ is 7.

7. When the preceding while loop ends, the loop condition must be false, that is, iFirst >= first.length or iSecond >= second.length (De Morgan's Law). Then first.length - iFirst <= 0 or iSecond.length - iSecond <= 0.

8. First sort 8 7 6 5. Recursively, first sort 8 7. Recursively, first sort 8. It's sorted. Sort 7. It's sorted. Merge them: 7 8. Do the same with 6 5 to get 5 6. Merge them to 5 6 7 8. Do the same with 4 3 2 1: Sort 4 3 by sorting 4 and 3 and merging them to 3 4. Sort 2 1 by sorting 2 and 1 and merging them to 1 2. Merge 3 4 and 1 2 to 1 2 3 4. Finally, merge 5 6 7 8 and 1 2 3 4 to 1 2 3 4 5 6 7 8.

9. Approximately $100{,}000 \cdot \log(100{,}000) / 50{,}000 \cdot \log(50{,}000) = 2 \cdot 5 / 4.7 = 2.13$ times the time required for 50,000 values. That's $2.13 \cdot 97$ milliseconds or approximately 207 milliseconds.

10. By calling Arrays.sort(values).

11. On average, you'd make 500,000 comparisons.

12. The search method returns the index at which the match occurs, not the data stored at that location.

13. You would search about 20. (The binary log of 1,024 is 10.)

14. Then you know where to insert it so that the array stays sorted, and you can keep using binary search.

15. Otherwise, you would not know whether a value is present when the method returns 0.

16. The Rectangle class does not implement the Comparable interface.

17. The BankAccount class needs to implement the Comparable interface. Its compareTo method must compare the bank balances.

An Introduction to Data Structures

CHAPTER GOALS

- To learn how to use the linked lists provided in the standard library
- To be able to use iterators to traverse linked lists
- To understand the implementation of linked lists
- To distinguish between abstract and concrete data types
- To know the efficiency of fundamental operations of lists and arrays
- To become familiar with the stack and queue types

Up to this point, we used arrays as a one-size-fits-all mechanism for collecting objects. However, computer scientists have developed many different data structures that have varying performance tradeoffs. In this chapter, you will learn about the *linked list*, a data structure that allows you to add and remove elements efficiently, without moving any existing elements. You will also learn about the distinction between concrete and abstract data types. An abstract type spells out what fundamental operations should be supported efficiently, but it leaves the implementation unspecified. The stack and queue types, introduced at the end of this chapter, are examples of abstract types.

CHAPTER CONTENTS

15.1 Using Linked Lists

A *linked list* is a data structure used for collecting a sequence of objects, which allows efficient addition and removal of elements in the middle of the sequence.

To understand the need for such a data structure, imagine a program that maintains a sequence of employee objects, sorted by the last names of the employees. When a new employee is hired, an object needs to be inserted into the sequence. Unless the company happened to hire employees in dictionary order, the new object probably needs to be inserted somewhere near the middle of the sequence. If we use an array to store the objects, then all objects following the new hire must be moved toward the end.

Conversely, if an employee leaves the company, the object must be removed, and the hole in the sequence needs to be closed up by moving all objects that come after it. Moving a large number of values can involve a substantial amount of processing time. We would like to structure the data in a way that minimizes this cost.

> A linked list consists of a number of nodes, each of which has a reference to the next node.

Rather than storing the values in an array, a linked list uses a sequence of *nodes*. Each node stores a value and a reference to the next node in the sequence (see Figure 1). When you insert a new node into a linked list, only the neighboring node references need to be updated. The same is true when you remove a node. What's the catch? Linked lists allow speedy insertion and removal, but element access can be slow.

> Adding and removing elements in the middle of a linked list is efficient.

For example, suppose you want to locate the fifth element. You must first traverse the first four. This is a problem if you need to access the elements in arbitrary order. The term "random access" is used in computer science to describe an access pattern in which elements are accessed in arbitrary (not necessarily random) order. In contrast, sequential access visits the elements in sequence. For example, a binary search requires random access, whereas a linear search requires sequential access.

> Visiting the elements of a linked list in sequential order is efficient, but random access is not.

Of course, if you mostly visit all elements in sequence (for example, to display or print the elements), the inefficiency of random access is not a problem. You use linked lists when you are concerned about the efficiency of inserting or removing elements and you rarely need element access in random order.

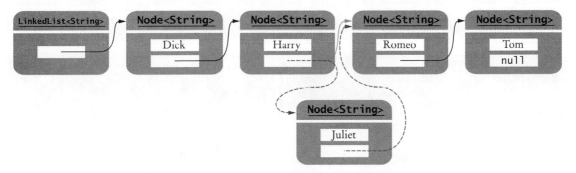

Figure 1 Inserting an Element into a Linked List

The Java library provides a linked list class. In this section you will learn how to use the library class. In the next section you will peek under the hood and see how some of its key methods are implemented.

The LinkedList class in the java.util package is a generic class, just like the ArrayList class. That is, you specify the type of the list elements in angle brackets, such as LinkedList<String> or LinkedList<Product>.

The following methods give you direct access to the first and the last element in the list. Here, E is the element type of LinkedList<E>.

```
void addFirst(E element)
void addLast(E element)
E getFirst()
E getLast()
E removeFirst()
E removeLast()
```

How do you add and remove elements in the middle of the list? The list will not give you references to the nodes. If you had direct access to them and somehow messed them up, you would break the linked list. As you will see in the next section, where you implement some of the linked list operations yourself, keeping all links between nodes intact is not trivial.

> You use a list iterator to access elements inside a linked list.

Instead, the Java library supplies a ListIterator type. A list iterator encapsulates a position anywhere inside the linked list (see Figure 2).

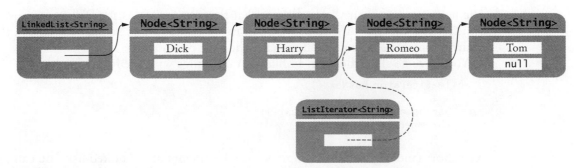

Figure 2 A List Iterator

Initial ListIterator position

After calling next

After inserting J

Figure 3   A Conceptual View of the List Iterator

Conceptually, you should think of the iterator as pointing between two elements, just as the cursor in a word processor points between two characters (see Figure 3). In the conceptual view, think of each element as being like a letter in a word processor, and think of the iterator as being like the blinking cursor between letters.

You obtain a list iterator with the listIterator method of the LinkedList class:

```
LinkedList<String> employeeNames = . . .;
ListIterator<String> iterator = employeeNames.listIterator();
```

Note that the iterator class is also a generic type. A ListIterator<String> iterates through a list of strings; a ListIterator<Product> visits the elements in a LinkedList<Product>.

Initially, the iterator points before the first element. You can move the iterator position with the next method:

```
iterator.next();
```

The next method throws a NoSuchElementException if you are already past the end of the list. You should always call the method hasNext before calling next—it returns true if there is a next element.

```
if (iterator.hasNext())
   iterator.next();
```

The next method returns the element that the iterator is passing. When you use a ListIterator<String>, the return type of the next method is String. In general, the return type of the next method matches the type parameter.

You traverse all elements in a linked list of strings with the following loop:

```
while (iterator.hasNext())
{
   String name = iterator.next();
   Do something with name
}
```

As a shorthand, if your loop simply visits all elements of the linked list, you can use the "for each" loop:

```
for (String name : employeeNames)
{
    Do something with name
}
```

Then you don't have to worry about iterators at all. Behind the scenes, the `for` loop uses an iterator to visit all list elements (see Advanced Topic 15.1).

The nodes of the `LinkedList` class store two links: one to the next element and one to the previous one. Such a list is called a *doubly linked list*. You can use the `previous` and `hasPrevious` methods of the `ListIterator` interface to move the iterator position backwards.

The `add` method adds an object after the iterator, then moves the iterator position past the new element.

```
iterator.add("Juliet");
```

You can visualize insertion to be like typing text in a word processor. Each character is inserted after the cursor, and then the cursor moves past the inserted character (see Figure 3). Most people never pay much attention to this—you may want to try it out and watch carefully how your word processor inserts characters.

The `remove` method removes the object that was returned by the last call to `next` or `previous`. For example, the following loop removes all names that fulfill a certain condition:

```
while (iterator.hasNext())
{
    String name = iterator.next();
    if (name fulfills condition)
        iterator.remove();
}
```

You have to be careful when calling `remove`. It can be called only once after calling `next` or `previous`, and you cannot call it immediately after a call to `add`. If you call the method improperly, it throws an `IllegalStateException`.

Here is a sample program that inserts strings into a list and then iterates through the list, adding and removing elements. Finally, the entire list is printed. The comments indicate the iterator position.

ch15/uselist/ListTester.java

```
1   import java.util.LinkedList;
2   import java.util.ListIterator;
3
4   /**
5       A program that tests the LinkedList class.
6   */
7   public class ListTester
8   {
9       public static void main(String[] args)
10      {
11          LinkedList<String> staff = new LinkedList<String>();
12          staff.addLast("Dick");
13          staff.addLast("Harry");
```

```
14        staff.addLast("Romeo");
15        staff.addLast("Tom");
16
17        // | in the comments indicates the iterator position
18
19        ListIterator<String> iterator
20             = staff.listIterator(); // |DHRT
21        iterator.next(); // D|HRT
22        iterator.next(); // DH|RT
23
24        // Add more elements after second element
25
26        iterator.add("Juliet"); // DHJ|RT
27        iterator.add("Nina"); // DHJN|RT
28
29        iterator.next(); // DHJNR|T
30
31        // Remove last traversed element
32
33        iterator.remove(); // DHJN|T
34
35        // Print all elements
36
37        for (String name : staff)
38           System.out.print(iterator.next() + " ");
39        System.out.println();
40        System.out.println("Expected: Dick Harry Juliet Nina Tom");
41    }
42 }
```

Output

```
Dick Harry Juliet Nina Tom
Expected: Dick Harry Juliet Nina Tom
```

SELF CHECK

1. Do linked lists take more storage space than arrays of the same size?
2. Why don't we need iterators with arrays?

ADVANCED TOPIC 15.1

The Iterable Interface and the "For Each" Loop

You can use the "for each" loop

     for (*Type variable* : *collection*)

with any of the collection classes in the standard Java library. This includes the ArrayList and LinkedList classes as well as the library classes which will be discussed in Chapter 16. In fact, the "for each" loop can be used with any class that implements the Iterable interface:

```
public interface Iterable<E>
{
    Iterator<E> iterator();
}
```

The interface has a type parameter E, denoting the element type of the collection. The single method, iterator, yields an object that implements the Iterator interface.

```
public interface Iterator<E>
{
    boolean hasNext();
    E next();
    void remove();
}
```

The ListIterator interface that you saw in the preceding section is a subinterface of Iterator with additional methods (such as add and previous).

The compiler translates a "for each" loop into an equivalent loop that uses an iterator. The loop

```
for (Type variable : collection)
    body
```

is equivalent to

```
Iterator<Type> iter = collection.iterator();
while (iter.hasNext())
{
    Type variable = iter.next();
    body
}
```

The ArrayList and LinkedList classes implement the Iterable interface. If your own classes implement the Iterable interface, you can use them with the "for each" loop as well—see Exercise P15.15.

15.2 Implementing Linked Lists

In the last section you saw how to use the linked list class supplied by the Java library. In this section, we will look at the implementation of a simplified version of this class. This shows you how the list operations manipulate the links as the list is modified.

To keep this sample code simple, we will not implement all methods of the linked list class. We will implement only a singly linked list, and the list class will supply direct access only to the first list element, not the last one. Our list will not use a type parameter. We will simply store raw Object values and insert casts when retrieving them. The result will be a fully functional list class that shows how the links are updated in the add and remove operations and how the iterator traverses the list.

A Node object stores an object and a reference to the next node. Because the methods of both the linked list class and the iterator class have frequent access to the Node instance variables, we do not make the instance variables private. Instead, we make Node a private inner class of the LinkedList class. Because none of the list methods returns a Node object, it is safe to leave the instance variables public.

```java
public class LinkedList
{
   . . .
   private class Node
   {
      public Object data;
      public Node next;
   }
}
```

The LinkedList class holds a reference first to the first node (or null, if the list is completely empty).

```java
public class LinkedList
{
   public LinkedList()
   {
      first = null;
   }

   public Object getFirst()
   {
      if (first == null)
         throw new NoSuchElementException();
      return first.data;
   }


   . . .
   private Node first;
}
```

Now let us turn to the addFirst method (see Figure 4). When a new node is added to the list, it becomes the head of the list, and the node that was the old list head becomes its next node:

```java
public class LinkedList
{
   . . .
   public void addFirst(Object element)
   {
      Node newNode = new Node();        ❶
      newNode.data = element;
      newNode.next = first;             ❷
      first = newNode;                  ❸
   }
   . . .
}
```

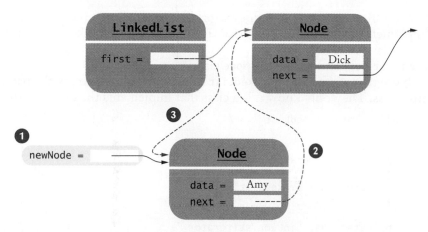

Figure 4 Adding a Node to the Head of a Linked List

Removing the first element of the list works as follows. The data of the first node are saved and later returned as the method result. The successor of the first node becomes the first node of the shorter list (see Figure 5). Then there are no further references to the old node, and the garbage collector will eventually recycle it.

```
public class LinkedList
{
   . . .
   public Object removeFirst()
   {
      if (first == null)
         throw new NoSuchElementException();
      Object element = first.data;
      first = first.next; ❶
      return element;
   }
   . . .
}
```

Next, let us turn to the iterator class. The ListIterator interface in the standard library defines nine methods. We omit four of them (the methods that move the iterator backwards and the methods that report an integer index of the iterator).

Figure 5 Removing the First Node from a Linked List

Our `LinkedList` class defines a private inner class `LinkedListIterator`, which implements the simplified `ListIterator` interface. Because `LinkedListIterator` is an inner class, it has access to the private features of the `LinkedList` class—in particular, the `first` field and the private `Node` class.

Note that clients of the `LinkedList` class don't actually know the name of the iterator class. They only know it is a class that implements the `ListIterator` interface.

```java
public class LinkedList
{
   . . .
   public ListIterator listIterator()
   {
      return new LinkedListIterator();
   }

   private class LinkedListIterator
      implements ListIterator
   {
      public LinkedListIterator()
      {
         position = null;
         previous = null;
      }

      . . .
      private Node position;
      private Node previous;
   }
   . . .
}
```

Each iterator object has a reference `position` to the last visited node. We also store a reference to the last node before that. We will need that reference to adjust the links properly in the `remove` method.

The next method is simple. The `position` reference is advanced to `position.next`, and the old position is remembered in `previous`. There is a special case, however—if the iterator points before the first element of the list, then the old `position` is `null`, and `position` must be set to `first`.

```java
private class LinkedListIterator
   implements ListIterator
{
   . . .
   public Object next()
   {
      if (!hasNext())
         throw new NoSuchElementException();
      previous = position; // Remember for remove

      if (position == null)
         position = first;
      else
         position = position.next;

      return position.data;
```

```
      }
      . . .
}
```

The next method is supposed to be called only when the iterator is not yet at the end of the list. The iterator is at the end if the list is empty (that is, first == null) or if there is no element after the current position (position.next == null).

```
private class LinkedListIterator
   implements ListIterator
{
   . . .
   public boolean hasNext()
   {
      if (position == null)
         return first != null;
      else
         return position.next != null;
   }
   . . .
}
```

Implementing operations that modify a linked list is challenging—you need to make sure that you update all node references correctly.

Removing the last visited node is more involved. If the element to be removed is the first element, we just call removeFirst. Otherwise, an element in the middle of the list must be removed, and the node preceding it needs to have its next reference updated to skip the removed element (see Figure 6). If the previous reference equals position, then this call to remove does not immediately follow a call to next, and we throw an IllegalStateException.

Figure 6   Removing a Node from the Middle of a Linked List

According to the definition of the remove method, it is illegal to call remove twice in a row. Therefore, the remove method sets the previous reference to position.

```java
private class LinkedListIterator
    implements ListIterator
{
    . . .
    public void remove()
    {
        if (previous == position)
            throw new IllegalStateException();
        if (position == first)
        {
            removeFirst();
        }
        else
        {
            previous.next = position.next;   ❶
        }
        position = previous;   ❷
    }
    . . .
}
```

The set method changes the data stored in the previously visited element. Its implementation is straightforward because our linked lists can be traversed in only one direction. The linked-list implementation of the standard library must keep track of

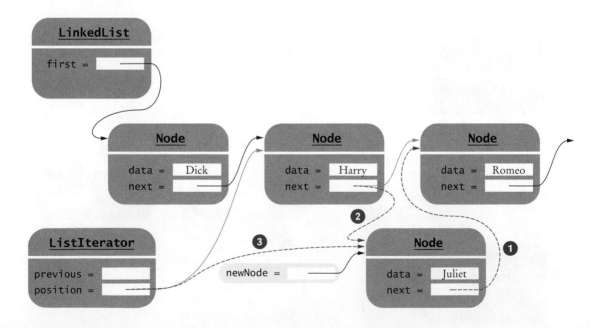

Figure 7 Adding a Node to the Middle of a Linked List

whether the last iterator movement was forward or backward. For that reason, the standard library forbids a call to the set method following an add or remove method. We do not enforce that restriction.

```
public void set(Object element)
{
    if (position == null)
        throw new NoSuchElementException();
    position.data = element;
}
```

Finally, the most complex operation is the addition of a node. You insert the new node after the current position, and set the successor of the new node to the successor of the current position (see Figure 7).

```
private class LinkedListIterator
    implements ListIterator
{
    . . .
    public void add(Object element)
    {
        if (position == null)
        {
            addFirst(element);
            position = first;
        }
        else
        {
            Node newNode = new Node();
            newNode.data = element;
            newNode.next = position.next;      ❶
            position.next = newNode;           ❷
            position = newNode;                ❸
        }
        previous = position;
    }
    . . .
}
```

At the end of this section is the complete implementation of our LinkedList class.

You now know how to use the LinkedList class in the Java library, and you have had a peek "under the hood" to see how linked lists are implemented.

ch15/impllist/LinkedList.java

```
 1  import java.util.NoSuchElementException;
 2
 3  /**
 4     A linked list is a sequence of nodes with efficient
 5     element insertion and removal. This class
 6     contains a subset of the methods of the standard
 7     java.util.LinkedList class.
 8  */
 9  public class LinkedList
10  {
```

```
11    /**
12        Constructs an empty linked list.
13    */
14    public LinkedList()
15    {
16        first = null;
17    }
18
19    /**
20        Returns the first element in the linked list.
21        @return the first element in the linked list
22    */
23    public Object getFirst()
24    {
25        if (first == null)
26            throw new NoSuchElementException();
27        return first.data;
28    }
29
30    /**
31        Removes the first element in the linked list.
32        @return the removed element
33    */
34    public Object removeFirst()
35    {
36        if (first == null)
37            throw new NoSuchElementException();
38        Object element = first.data;
39        first = first.next;
40        return element;
41    }
42
43    /**
44        Adds an element to the front of the linked list.
45        @param element the element to add
46    */
47    public void addFirst(Object element)
48    {
49        Node newNode = new Node();
50        newNode.data = element;
51        newNode.next = first;
52        first = newNode;
53    }
54
55    /**
56        Returns an iterator for iterating through this list.
57        @return an iterator for iterating through this list
58    */
59    public ListIterator listIterator()
60    {
61        return new LinkedListIterator();
62    }
63
```

```
64      private Node first;
65
66      private class Node
67      {
68          public Object data;
69          public Node next;
70      }
71
72      private class LinkedListIterator implements ListIterator
73      {
74          /**
75              Constructs an iterator that points to the front
76              of the linked list.
77          */
78          public LinkedListIterator()
79          {
80              position = null;
81              previous = null;
82          }
83
84          /**
85              Moves the iterator past the next element.
86              @return the traversed element
87          */
88          public Object next()
89          {
90              if (!hasNext())
91                  throw new NoSuchElementException();
92              previous = position; // Remember for remove

94              if (position == null)
95                  position = first;
96              else
97                  position = position.next;

99              return position.data;
100         }
101
102         /**
103             Tests if there is an element after the iterator
104             position.
105             @return true if there is an element after the iterator
106             position
107         */
108         public boolean hasNext()
109         {
110             if (position == null)
111                 return first != null;
112             else
113                 return position.next != null;
114         }
115
```

```
116    /**
117        Adds an element before the iterator position
118        and moves the iterator past the inserted element.
119        @param element the element to add
120    */
121    public void add(Object element)
122    {
123       if (position == null)
124       {
125          addFirst(element);
126          position = first;
127       }
128       else
129       {
130          Node newNode = new Node();
131          newNode.data = element;
132          newNode.next = position.next;
133          position.next = newNode;
134          position = newNode;
135       }
136       previous = position;
137    }
138
139    /**
140        Removes the last traversed element. This method may
141        only be called after a call to the next() method.
142    */
143    public void remove()
144    {
145       if (previous == position)
146          throw new IllegalStateException();
147
148       if (position == first)
149       {
150          removeFirst();
151       }
152       else
153       {
154          previous.next = position.next;
155       }
156       position = previous;
157    }
158
159    /**
160        Sets the last traversed element to a different
161        value.
162        @param element the element to set
163    */
164    public void set(Object element)
165    {
166       if (position == null)
167          throw new NoSuchElementException();
168       position.data = element;
169    }
```

```
170
171         private Node position;
172         private Node previous;
173     }
174 }
```

ch15/impllist/ListIterator.java

```
1  /**
2      A list iterator allows access to a position in a linked list.
3      This interface contains a subset of the methods of the
4      standard java.util.ListIterator interface. The methods for
5   ·  backward traversal are not included.
6  */
7  public interface ListIterator
8  {
9      /**
10         Moves the iterator past the next element.
11         @return the traversed element
12      */
13      Object next();
14
15      /**
16         Tests if there is an element after the iterator
17         position.
18         @return true if there is an element after the iterator
19         position
20      */
21      boolean hasNext();
22
23      /**
24         Adds an element before the iterator position
25         and moves the iterator past the inserted element.
26         @param element the element to add
27      */
28      void add(Object element);
29
30      /**
31         Removes the last traversed element. This method may
32         only be called after a call to the next() method.
33      */
34      void remove();
35
36      /**
37         Sets the last traversed element to a different
38         value.
39         @param element the element to set
40      */
41      void set(Object element);
42  }
```

3. Trace through the addFirst method when adding an element to an empty list.
4. Conceptually, an iterator points between elements (see Figure 3). Does the position reference point to the element to the left or to the element to the right?
5. Why does the add method have two separate cases?

ADVANCED TOPIC 15.2

Static Inner Classes

You first saw the use of inner classes for event handlers. Inner classes are useful in that context, because their methods have the privilege of accessing private data members of outer-class objects. The same is true for the LinkedListIterator inner class in the sample code for this section. The iterator needs to access the first instance variable of its linked list.

However, the Node inner class has no need to access the outer class. In fact, it has no methods. Thus, there is no need to store a reference to the outer list class with each Node object. To suppress the outer-class reference, you can declare the inner class as static:

```
public class LinkedList
{
    . . .
    private static class Node
    {
        . . .
    }
}
```

The purpose of the keyword static in this context is to indicate that the inner-class objects do not depend on the outer-class objects that generate them. In particular, the methods of a static inner class cannot access the outer-class instance variables. Declaring the inner class static is efficient, because its objects do not store an outer-class reference.

However, the LinkedListIterator class cannot be a static inner class. It frequently references the first element of the enclosing LinkedList.

15.3 Abstract and Concrete Data Types

There are two ways of looking at a linked list. One way is to think of the concrete implementation of such a list as a sequence of node objects with links between them (see Figure 8).

On the other hand, you can think of the *abstract* concept of the linked list. In the abstract, a linked list is an ordered sequence of data items that can be traversed with an iterator (see Figure 9).

> An abstract data type defines the fundamental operations on the data but does not specify an implementation.

Similarly, there are two ways of looking at an array list. Of course, an array list has a concrete implementation: a partially filled array of object references (see Figure 10). But you don't usually think about

Figure 8 A Concrete View of a Linked List

Figure 9 An Abstract View of a Linked List

the concrete implementation when using an array list. You take the abstract point of view. An array list is an ordered sequence of data items, each of which can be accessed by an integer index (see Figure 11).

The concrete implementations of a linked list and an array list are quite different. The abstractions, on the other hand, seem to be similar at first glance. To see the difference, consider the public interfaces stripped down to their minimal essentials.

Figure 10 A Concrete View of an Array List

Figure 11 An Abstract View of an Array List

An array list allows *random access* to all elements. You specify an integer index, and you can get or set the corresponding element.

```
public class ArrayList
{
    public Object get(int index) { . . . }
    public void set(int index, Object element) { . . . }
    . . .
}
```

With a linked list, on the other hand, element access is a bit more complex. A linked list allows sequential access. You need to ask the linked list for an iterator. Using that iterator, you can easily traverse the list elements one at a time. But if you want to go to a particular element, say the 100th one, you first have to skip all elements before it.

```
public class LinkedList
{
    public ListIterator listIterator() { . . . }
    . . .
}

public interface ListIterator
{
    Object next();
    boolean hasNext();
    void add(Object element);
    void remove();
    void set(Object element);
    . . .
}
```

Here we show only the *fundamental* operations on array lists and linked lists. Other operations can be composed from these fundamental operations. For example, you can add or remove an element in an array list by moving all elements beyond the insertion or removal index, calling get and set multiple times.

Of course, the ArrayList class has methods to add and remove elements in the middle, even if they are slow. Conversely, the LinkedList class has get and set methods that let you access any element in the linked list, albeit very inefficiently, by performing repeated sequential accesses.

In fact, the term ArrayList signifies that its implementors wanted to combine the interfaces of an array and a list. Somewhat confusingly, both the ArrayList and the LinkedList class implement an interface called List that defines operations both for random access and for sequential access.

That terminology is not in common use outside the Java library. Instead, let us adopt a more traditional terminology. We will call the abstract types *array* and *list*. The Java library provides concrete implementations ArrayList and LinkedList for these abstract types. Other concrete implementations are possible in other libraries. In fact, Java arrays are another implementation of the abstract array type.

To understand an abstract data type completely, you need to know not just its fundamental operations but also their relative efficiency.

Table 1 Efficiency of Operations for Arrays and Lists

Operation	Array	List
Random access	$O(1)$	$O(n)$
Linear traversal step	$O(1)$	$O(1)$
Add/remove an element	$O(n)$	$O(1)$

An abstract list is an ordered sequence of items that can be traversed sequentially and that allows for insertion and removal of elements at any position.

In a linked list, an element can be added or removed in constant time (assuming that the iterator is already in the right position). A fixed number of node references need to be modified to add or remove a node, regardless of the size of the list. Using the big-Oh notation, an operation that requires a bounded amount of time, regardless of the total number of elements in the structure, is denoted as $O(1)$. Random access in an array list also takes $O(1)$ time.

Adding or removing an arbitrary element in an array takes $O(n)$ time, where n is the size of the array list, because on average $n/2$ elements need to be moved. Random access in a linked list takes $O(n)$ time because on average $n/2$ elements need to be skipped.

An abstract array is an ordered sequence of items with random access via an integer index.

Table 1 shows this information for arrays and lists.

Why consider abstract types at all? If you implement a particular algorithm, you can tell what operations you need to carry out on the data structures that your algorithm manipulates. You can then determine the abstract type that supports those operations efficiently, without being distracted by implementation details.

For example, suppose you have a sorted collection of items and you want to locate items using the binary search algorithm (see Section 14.7). That algorithm makes a random access to the middle of the collection, followed by other random accesses. Thus, fast random access is essential for the algorithm to work correctly. Once you know that an array supports fast random access and a linked list does not, you then look for concrete implementations of the abstract array type. You won't be fooled into using a LinkedList, even though the LinkedList class actually provides get and set methods.

In the next section, you will see additional examples of abstract data types.

SELF CHECK

6. What is the advantage of viewing a type abstractly?

7. How would you sketch an abstract view of a doubly linked list? A concrete view?

8. How much slower is the binary search algorithm for a linked list compared to the linear search algorithm?

15.4 Stacks and Queues

In this section we will consider two common abstract data types that allow insertion and removal of items at the ends only, not in the middle. A *stack* lets you insert and remove elements at only one end, traditionally called the *top* of the stack. To visualize a stack, think of a stack of books (see Figure 12).

> A stack is a collection of items with "last in first out" retrieval.

New items can be added to the top of the stack. Items are removed at the top of the stack as well. Therefore, they are removed in the order that is opposite from the order in which they have been added, called *last in, first out* or *LIFO* order. For example, if you add items A, B, and C and then remove them, you obtain C, B, and A. Traditionally, the addition and removal operations are called push and pop.

> A queue is a collection of items with "first in first out" retrieval.

A *queue* is similar to a stack, except that you add items to one end of the queue (the *tail*) and remove them from the other end of the queue (the *head*). To visualize a queue, simply think of people lining up (see Figure 13). People join the tail of the queue and wait until they have reached the head of the queue. Queues store items in a *first in, first out* or *FIFO* fashion. Items are removed in the same order in which they have been added.

There are many uses of queues and stacks in computer science. The Java graphical user interface system keeps an event queue of all events, such as mouse and keyboard events. The events are inserted into the queue whenever the operating system notifies the application of the event. Another thread of control removes them from the queue and passes them to the appropriate event listeners. Another example is a print queue. A printer may be accessed by several applications, perhaps running on different computers. If each of the applications tried to access the printer at the same time, the printout would be garbled. Instead, each application places all bytes that need to be sent to the printer into a file and inserts that file into the print queue. When the printer is done printing one file, it retrieves the next one from the queue. Therefore, print jobs are printed using the "first in, first out" rule, which is a fair arrangement for users of the shared printer.

Figure 12   A Stack of Books

Figure 13 A Queue

Stacks are used when a "last in, first out" rule is required. For example, consider an algorithm that attempts to find a path through a maze. When the algorithm encounters an intersection, it pushes the location on the stack, and then it explores the first branch. If that branch is a dead end, it returns to the location at the top of the stack. If all branches are dead ends, it pops the location off the stack, revealing a previously encountered intersection. Another important example is the *run-time stack* that a processor or virtual machine keeps to organize the variables of nested methods. Whenever a new method is called, its parameters and local variables are pushed onto a stack. When the method exits, they are popped off again. This stack makes recursive method calls possible.

There is a Stack class in the Java library that implements the abstract stack type and the push and pop operations. The following sample code shows how to use that class.

```
Stack<String> s = new Stack<String>();
s.push("A");
s.push("B");
s.push("C");
// The following loop prints C, B, and A
while (s.size() > 0)
   System.out.println(s.pop());
```

The Stack class in the Java library uses an array to implement a stack. Exercise P15.11 shows how to use a linked list instead.

The implementations of a queue in the standard library are designed for use with multithreaded programs. However, it is simple to implement a basic queue yourself:

```java
public class LinkedListQueue
{
   /**
      Constructs an empty queue that uses a linked list.
   */
   public LinkedListQueue()
   {
      list = new LinkedList();
   }

   /**
      Adds an element to the tail of the queue.
      @param element the element to add
   */
   public void add(Object element)
   {
      list.addLast(element);
   }

   /**
      Removes an element from the head of the queue.
      @return the removed element
   */
   public Object remove()
   {
      return list.removeFirst();
   }

   /**
      Gets the number of elements in the queue.
      @return the size
   */
   int size()
   {
      return list.size();
   }

   private LinkedList list;
}
```

You would definitely not want to use an ArrayList to implement a queue. Removing the first element of an array list is inefficient—all other elements must be moved towards the beginning. However, Exercise P15.12 shows you how to implement a queue efficiently as a "circular" array, in which all elements stay at the position at which they were inserted, but the index values that denote the head and tail of the queue change when elements are added and removed.

In this chapter, you have seen the two most fundamental abstract data types, arrays and lists, and their concrete implementations. You also learned about the stack and queue types. In the next chapter, you will see additional data types that require more sophisticated implementation techniques.

9. Draw a sketch of the abstract queue type, similar to Figures 9 and 11.
10. Why wouldn't you want to use a stack to manage print jobs?

RANDOM FACT 15.1

Standardization

You encounter the benefits of standardization every day. When you buy a light bulb, you can be assured that it fits the socket without having to measure the socket at home and the light bulb in the store. In fact, you may have experienced how painful the lack of standards can be if you have ever purchased a flashlight with nonstandard bulbs. Replacement bulbs for such a flashlight can be difficult and expensive to obtain.

Programmers have a similar desire for standardization. Consider the important goal of platform independence for Java programs. After you compile a Java program into class files, you can execute the class files on any computer that has a Java virtual machine. For this to work, the behavior of the virtual machine has to be strictly defined. If virtual machines don't all behave exactly the same way, then the slogan of "write once, run anywhere" turns into "write once, debug everywhere". In order for multiple implementors to create compatible virtual machines, the virtual machine needed to be *standardized*. That is, someone needed to create a definition of the virtual machine and its expected behavior.

Who creates standards? Some of the most successful standards have been created by volunteer groups such as the Internet Engineering Task Force (IETF) and the World Wide Web Consortium (W3C). You can find the Requests for Comment (RFC) that standardize many of the Internet protocols at the IETF site, http://www.ietf.org/rfc.html. For example, RFC 822 standardizes the format of e-mail, and RFC 2616 defines the Hypertext Transmission Protocol (HTTP) that is used to serve web pages to browsers. The W3C standardizes the Hypertext Markup Language (HTML), the format for web pages—see http://www.w3c.org. These standards have been instrumental in the creation of the World Wide Web as an open platform that is not controlled by any one company.

Many programming languages, such as C++ and Scheme, have been standardized by independent standards organizations, such as the American National Standards Institute (ANSI) and the International Organization for Standardization—called ISO for short (not an acronym; see http://www.iso.ch/iso/en/aboutiso/introduction/whatisISO.html). ANSI and ISO are associations of industry professionals who develop standards for everything from car tires and credit card shapes to programming languages.

The process of standardizing the C++ language turned out to be very painstaking and time-consuming, and the standards organization followed a rigorous process to ensure fairness and to avoid being influenced by companies with vested interests.

When a company invents a new technology, it has an interest in its invention becoming a standard, so that other vendors produce tools that work with the invention and thus increase its likelihood of success. On the other hand, by handing over the invention to a standards committee, especially one that insists on a fair process, the company may lose control over the standard. For that reason, Sun Microsystems, the inventor of Java, never agreed to have a third-party organization standardize the Java language. They run their own standardization process, involving other companies but refusing to relinquish control. Another unfortunate but common tactic is to create a weak standard. For example, Netscape and Microsoft chose the European Computer Manufacturers Association (ECMA) to standardize the JavaScript language (see Random Fact 10.1). ECMA was willing to settle for something less than truly useful, standardizing the behavior of the core language and just a few of its libraries. Because most useful JavaScript programs need to use more libraries than those defined in the standard, programmers still go through a lot of tedious trial and error to write JavaScript code that runs identically on different browsers.

Often, competing standards are developed by different coalitions of vendors. For example, at the time of this writing, hardware vendors are in disagreement whether to use the HD DVD or Blu-Ray standard for high-density video disks. As Grace Hopper, the famous computer science pioneer, observed: "The great thing about standards is that there are so many to choose from".

Of course, many important pieces of technology aren't standardized at all. Consider the Windows operating system. Although Windows is often called a de-facto standard, it really is no standard at all. Nobody has ever attempted to define formally what the Windows operating system should do. The behavior changes at the whim of its vendor. That suits Microsoft just fine, because it makes it impossible for a third party to create its own version of Windows.

As a computer professional, there will be many times in your career when you need to make a decision whether to support a particular standard. Consider a simple example. In this chapter, we use the LinkedList class from the standard Java library. However, many computer scientists dislike this class because the interface muddies the distinction between abstract lists and arrays, and the iterators are clumsy to use. Should you use the LinkedList class in your own code, or should you implement a better list? If you do the former, you have to deal with a design that is less than optimal. If you do the latter, other programmers may have a hard time understanding your code because they aren't familiar with your list class.

CHAPTER SUMMARY

1. A linked list consists of a number of nodes, each of which has a reference to the next node.

2. Adding and removing elements in the middle of a linked list is efficient.

3. Visiting the elements of a linked list in sequential order is efficient, but random access is not.

4. You use a list iterator to access elements inside a linked list.

5. Implementing operations that modify a linked list is challenging—you need to make sure that you update all node references correctly.

6. An abstract data type defines the fundamental operations on the data but does not specify an implementation.

7. An abstract list is an ordered sequence of items that can be traversed sequentially and that allows for insertion and removal of elements at any position.

8. An abstract array is an ordered sequence of items with random access via an integer index.

9. A stack is a collection of items with "last in first out" retrieval.

10. A queue is a collection of items with "first in first out" retrieval.

CLASSES, OBJECTS, AND METHODS INTRODUCED IN THIS CHAPTER

java.util.Collection<E>
   add
   contains
   iterator
   remove
   size
java.util.Iterator<E>
   hasNext
   next
   remove
java.util.LinkedList<E>
   addFirst
   addLast
   getFirst
   getLast
   removeFirst
   removeLast

java.util.List<E>
   listIterator
java.util.ListIterator<E>
   add
   hasPrevious
   previous
   set

REVIEW EXERCISES

★ **Exercise R15.1.** Explain what the following code prints. Draw pictures of the linked list after each step. Just draw the forward links, as in Figure 1.

```
LinkedList<String> staff = new LinkedList<String>();
staff.addFirst("Harry");
staff.addFirst("Dick");
staff.addFirst("Tom");
System.out.println(staff.removeFirst());
System.out.println(staff.removeFirst());
System.out.println(staff.removeFirst());
```

★ **Exercise R15.2.** Explain what the following code prints. Draw pictures of the linked list after each step. Just draw the forward links, as in Figure 1.

```
LinkedList<String> staff = new LinkedList<String>();
staff.addFirst("Harry");
staff.addFirst("Dick");
staff.addFirst("Tom");
System.out.println(staff.removeLast());
System.out.println(staff.removeFirst());
System.out.println(staff.removeLast());
```

★ **Exercise R15.3.** Explain what the following code prints. Draw pictures of the linked list after each step. Just draw the forward links, as in Figure 1.

```
LinkedList<String> staff = new LinkedList<String>();
staff.addFirst("Harry");
staff.addLast("Dick");
staff.addFirst("Tom");
System.out.println(staff.removeLast());
System.out.println(staff.removeFirst());
System.out.println(staff.removeLast());
```

★ **Exercise R15.4.** Explain what the following code prints. Draw pictures of the linked list and the iterator position after each step.

```
LinkedList<String> staff = new LinkedList<String>();
ListIterator<String> iterator = staff.listIterator();
iterator.add("Tom");
iterator.add("Dick");
iterator.add("Harry");
iterator = staff.listIterator();
if (iterator.next().equals("Tom"))
    iterator.remove();
while (iterator.hasNext())
    System.out.println(iterator.next());
```

★ **Exercise R15.5.** Explain what the following code prints. Draw pictures of the linked list and the iterator position after each step.

```
LinkedList<String> staff = new LinkedList<String>();
ListIterator<String> iterator = staff.listIterator();
iterator.add("Tom");
iterator.add("Dick");
iterator.add("Harry");
iterator = staff.listIterator();
iterator.next();
iterator.next();
iterator.add("Romeo");
iterator.next();
iterator.add("Juliet");
iterator = staff.listIterator();
iterator.next();
iterator.remove();
while (iterator.hasNext())
    System.out.println(iterator.next());
```

★★ **Exercise R15.6.** The linked list class in the Java library supports operations addLast and removeLast. To carry out these operations efficiently, the LinkedList class has an added reference last to the last node in the linked list. Draw a "before/after" diagram of the changes of the links in a linked list under the addLast and removeLast methods.

★★ **Exercise R15.7.** The linked list class in the Java library supports bidirectional iterators. To go backward efficiently, each Node has an added reference, previous, to the predecessor node in the linked list. Draw a "before/after" diagram of the changes of the links in a linked list under the addFirst and removeFirst methods that shows how the previous links need to be updated.

★★ **Exercise R15.8.** What advantages do lists have over arrays? What disadvantages do they have?

★★ **Exercise R15.9.** Suppose you needed to organize a collection of telephone numbers for a company division. There are currently about 6,000 employees, and you know that the phone switch can handle at most 10,000 phone numbers. You expect several hundred lookups against the collection every day. Would you use an array or a list to store the information?

★★ **Exercise R15.10.** Suppose you needed to keep a collection of appointments. Would you use a list or an array of Appointment objects?

★ **Exercise R15.11.** Suppose you write a program that models a card deck. Cards are taken from the top of the deck and given out to players. As cards are returned to the deck, they are placed on the bottom of the deck. Would you store the cards in a stack or a queue?

★ **Exercise R15.12.** Suppose the strings "A" ... "Z" are pushed onto a stack. Then they are popped off the stack and pushed onto a second stack. Finally, they are all popped off the second stack and printed. In which order are the strings printed?

Additional review exercises are available in WileyPLUS.

PROGRAMMING EXERCISES

★★ **Exercise P15.1.** Using only the public interface of the linked list class, write a method

```
public static void downsize(LinkedList<String> staff)
```

that removes every other employee from a linked list.

★★ **Exercise P15.2.** Using only the public interface of the linked list class, write a method

```
public static void reverse(LinkedList<String> staff)
```

that reverses the entries in a linked list.

★★★ **Exercise P15.3.** Add a method reverse to our implementation of the LinkedList class that reverses the links in a list. Implement this method by directly rerouting the links, not by using an iterator.

★ **Exercise P15.4.** Add a method size to our implementation of the LinkedList class that computes the number of elements in the list, by following links and counting the elements until the end of the list is reached.

★ **Exercise P15.5.** Add a currentSize field to our implementation of the LinkedList class. Modify the add and remove methods of both the linked list and the list iterator to update the currentSize field so that it always contains the correct size. Change the size method of the preceding exercise so that it simply returns the value of this instance variable.

★★ **Exercise P15.6.** The linked list class of the standard library has an add method that allows efficient insertion at the end of the list. Implement this method for the LinkedList class in Section 15.2. Add an instance field to the linked list class that points to the last node in the list. Make sure the other mutator methods update that field.

★★★ **Exercise P15.7.** Repeat Exercise P15.6, but use a different implementation strategy. Remove the reference to the first node in the LinkedList class, and make the next reference of the last node point to the first node, so that all nodes form a cycle. Such an implementation is called a *circular linked list*.

★★★ **Exercise P15.8.** Reimplement the LinkedList class of Section 15.2 so that the Node and LinkedListIterator classes are not inner classes.

★★★ **Exercise P15.9.** Add a previous field to the Node class in Section 15.2, and supply previous and hasPrevious methods in the iterator.

★★ **Exercise P15.10.** The standard Java library implements a Stack class, but in this exercise you are asked to provide your own implementation. Do not implement type parameters. Use an Object[] array to hold the stack elements. When the array fills up, allocate an array of twice the size and copy the values to the larger array.

★ **Exercise P15.11.** Implement a Stack class by using a linked list to store the elements. Do not implement type parameters.

★★ **Exercise P15.12.** Implement a queue as a *circular array* as follows: Use two index variables head and tail that contain the index of the next element to be removed and the next element to be added. After an element is removed or added, the index is incremented (see Figure 14).

After a while, the tail element will reach the top of the array. Then it "wraps around" and starts again at 0—see Figure 15. For that reason, the array is called "circular".

```java
public class CircularArrayQueue
{
    public CircularArrayQueue(int capacity) { . . . }
    public void add(Object x) { . . . }
    public Object remove() { . . . }
    public int size() { . . . }
    private int head;
    private int tail;
    private int theSize;
    private Object[] elements;
}
```

This implementation supplies a *bounded* queue—it can eventually fill up. See the next exercise on how to remove that limitation.

Figure 14
Adding and Removing
Queue Elements

Figure 15
A Queue That Wraps Around
the End of the Array

★★★ **Exercise P15.13.** The queue in Exercise P15.12 can fill up if more elements are added than the array can hold. Improve the implementation as follows. When the array fills up, allocate a larger array, copy the values to the larger array, and assign it to the elements instance variable. *Hint:* You can't just copy the elements into the same position of the new array. Move the head element to position 0 instead.

★★ **Exercise P15.14.** Modify the insertion sort algorithm of Advanced Topic 14.1 to sort a linked list.

★★ **Exercise P15.15.** Modify the Invoice class of Chapter 12 so that it implements the Iterable<LineItem> interface. Then demonstrate how an Invoice object can be used in a "for each" loop.

★★G **Exercise P15.16.** Write a program to display a linked list graphically. Draw each element of the list as a box, and indicate the links with line segments. Draw an iterator as in Figure 3. Supply buttons to move the iterator and to add and remove elements.

Additional programming exercises are available in WileyPLUS.

PROGRAMMING PROJECTS

★★★ **Project 15.1.** Implement a class Polynomial that describes a polynomial such as

$$p(x) = 5x^{10} + 9x^7 - x - 10$$

Store a polynomial as a linked list of terms. A term contains the coefficient and the power of x. For example, you would store $p(x)$ as

$$(5, 10), (9, 7), (-1, 1), (-10, 0)$$

Supply methods to add, multiply, and print polynomials, and to compute the derivative of a polynomial.

★★★   **Project 15.2.** Make the list implementation of this chapter as powerful as the implementation of the Java library. (Do not implement type parameters, though.)

- Provide bidirectional iteration.
- Make Node a static inner class.
- Implement the standard List and ListIterator interfaces and provide the missing methods. (*Tip:* You may find it easier to extend AbstractList instead of implementing all List methods from scratch.)

★★★   **Project 15.3.** Implement the following algorithm for the evaluation of arithmetic expressions.

Each operator has a *precedence*. The + and - operators have the lowest precedence, * and / have a higher (and equal) precedence, and ∧ (which denotes "raising to a power" in this exercise) has the highest. For example,

```
3 * 4 ∧ 2 + 5
```

should mean the same as

```
(3 * (4 ∧ 2)) + 5
```

with a value of 53.

In your algorithm, use two stacks. One stack holds numbers, the other holds operators. When you encounter a number, push it on the number stack. When you encounter an operator, push it on the operator stack if it has higher precedence than the operator on the top of the stack. Otherwise, pop an operator off the operator stack, pop two numbers off the number stack, and push the result of the computation on the number stack. Repeat until the top of the operator stack has lower precedence. At the end of the expression, clear the stack in the same way. For example, here is how the expression 3 * 4 ∧ 2 + 5 is evaluated:

Expression: 3 * 4 ∧ 2 + 5			
❶ Remaining expression:	* 4 ∧ 2 + 5	Number stack 3	Operator stack
❷ Remaining expression:	4 ∧ 2 + 5	Number stack 3	Operator stack *
❸ Remaining expression:	∧ 2 + 5	Number stack 4 3	Operator stack *
❹ Remaining expression:	2 + 5	Number stack 4 3	Operator stack ∧ *

	Remaining expression:		Number stack	Operator stack
5	Remaining expression:	+ 5	2 4 3	 ∧ *
6	Remaining expression:	+ 5	16 3	 *
7	Remaining expression:	5	48	+
8	Remaining expression:		5 48	 +
9	Remaining expression:		53	

You should enhance this algorithm to deal with parentheses. Also, make sure that subtractions and divisions are carried out in the correct order. For example, 12 - 5 - 3 should yield 4.

ANSWERS TO SELF-CHECK QUESTIONS

1. Yes, for two reasons. You need to store the node references, and each node is a separate object. (There is a fixed overhead to store each object in the virtual machine.)
2. An integer index can be used to access any array location.
3. When the list is empty, first is null. A new Node is allocated. It's data field is set to the newly inserted object. It's next field is set to null because first is null. The first field is set to the new node. The result is a linked list of length 1.
4. It points to the element to the left. You can see that by tracing out the first call to next. It leaves position to point to the first node.
5. If position is null, we must be at the head of the list, and inserting an element requires updating the first reference. If we are in the middle of the list, the first reference should not be changed.
6. You can focus on the essential characteristics of the data type without being distracted by implementation details.
7. The abstract view would be like Figure 9, but with arrows in both directions. The concrete view would be like Figure 8, but with references to the previous node added to each node.

8. To locate the midde element takes $n/2$ steps. To locate the middle of the sub-interval to the left or right takes another $n/4$ steps. The next lookup takes $n/8$ steps. Thus, we expect almost n steps to locate an element. At this point, you are better off just making a linear search that, on average, takes $n/2$ steps.

9.

10. Stacks use a "last in, first out" discipline. If you are the first one to submit a print job and lots of people add print jobs before the printer has a chance to deal with your job, they get their printouts first, and you have to wait until all other jobs are completed.

Chapter

16

Advanced
Data Structures

CHAPTER GOALS

- To learn about the set and map data types
- To understand the implementation of hash tables
- To be able to program hash functions
- To learn about binary trees
- To be able to use tree sets and tree maps
- To become familiar with the heap data structure
- To learn how to implement the priority queue data type
- To understand how to use heaps for sorting

In this chapter we study data structures that are more complex than arrays or lists. These data structures take control of organizing their elements, rather than keeping them in a fixed position. In return, they can offer better performance for adding, removing, and finding elements.

You will learn about the abstract set and map data types and the implementations that the standard library offers for these abstract types. You will see how two completely different implementations—hash tables and trees—can be used to implement these abstract types efficiently.

CHAPTER CONTENTS

16.1 Sets

In the preceding chapter you encountered two important data structures: arrays and lists. Both have one characteristic in common: These data structures keep the elements in the same order in which you inserted them. However, in many applications, you don't really care about the order of the elements in a collection. For example, a server may keep a collection of objects representing available printers (see Figure 1). The order of the objects doesn't really matter.

Figure 1   A Set of Printers

A set is an unordered collection of distinct elements. Elements can be added, located, and removed.

In mathematics, such an unordered collection is called a *set*. You have probably learned some set theory in a course in mathematics, and you may know that sets are a fundamental mathematical notion.

But what does that mean for data structures? If the data structure is no longer responsible for remembering the order of element insertion, can it give us better performance for some of its operations? It turns out that it can indeed, as you will see later in this chapter.

Let's list the fundamental operations on a set:

- Adding an element
- Removing an element
- Containment testing (does the set contain a given object?)
- Listing all elements (in arbitrary order)

Sets don't have duplicates. Adding a duplicate of an element that is already present is silently ignored.

In mathematics, a set rejects duplicates. If an object is already in the set, an attempt to add it again is ignored. That's useful in many programming situations as well. For example, if we keep a set of available printers, each printer should occur at most once in the set. Thus, we will interpret the add and remove operations of sets just as we do in mathematics: Adding an element has no effect if the element is already in the set, and attempting to remove an element that isn't in the set is silently ignored.

Of course, we could use a linked list to implement a set. But adding, removing, and containment testing would be relatively slow, because they all have to do a linear search through the list. (Adding requires a search through the list to make sure that we don't add a duplicate.) As you will see later in this chapter, there are data structures that can handle these operations much more quickly.

The HashSet and TreeSet classes both implement the Set interface.

In fact, there are two different data structures for this purpose, called *hash tables* and *trees*. The standard Java library provides set implementations based on both data structures, called HashSet and TreeSet. Both of these data structures implement the Set interface (see Figure 2).

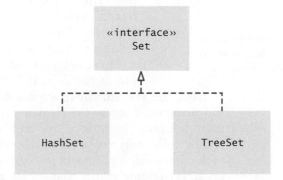

Figure 2
Set Classes and Interfaces in the Standard Library

You will see later in this chapter when it is better to choose a hash set over a tree set. For now, let's look at an example where we choose a hash set. To keep the example simple, we'll store only strings, not Printer objects.

```
Set<String> names = new HashSet<String>();
```

Note that we store the reference to the HashSet<String> object in a Set<String> variable. After you construct the collection object, the implementation no longer matters; only the interface is important.

Adding and removing set elements is straightforward:

```
names.add("Romeo");
names.remove("Juliet");
```

The contains method tests whether an element is contained in the set:

```
if (names.contains("Juliet")) . . .
```

> An iterator visits all elements in a set.

Finally, to list all elements in the set, get an iterator. As with list iterators, you use the next and hasNext methods to step through the set.

```
Iterator<String> iter = names.iterator();
while (iter.hasNext())
{
    String name = iter.next();
    Do something with name
}
```

Or, as with arrays and lists, you can use the "for each" loop instead of explicitly using an iterator:

```
for (String name : names)
{
    Do something with name
}
```

> A set iterator does not visit the elements in the order in which you inserted them. The set implementation rearranges the elements so that it can locate them quickly.

> You cannot add an element to a set at an iterator position.

Note that the elements are *not* visited in the order in which you inserted them. Instead, they are visited in the order in which the HashSet keeps them for rapid execution of its methods.

There is an important difference between the Iterator that you obtain from a set and the ListIterator that a list yields. The ListIterator has an add method to add an element at the list iterator position. The Iterator interface has no such method. It makes no sense to add an element at a particular position in a set, because the set can order the elements any way it likes. Thus, you always add elements directly to a set, never to an iterator of the set.

However, you can remove a set element at an iterator position, just as you do with list iterators.

Also, the Iterator interface has no previous method to go backwards through the elements. Because the elements are not ordered, it is not meaningful to distinguish between "going forward" and "going backward".

The following test program allows you to add and remove set elements. After each command, it prints out the current contents of the set. When you run this program, try adding strings that are already contained in the set and removing strings that aren't present in the set.

ch16/set/SetDemo.java

```java
1   import java.util.HashSet;
2   import java.util.Scanner;
3   import java.util.Set;
4
5   /**
6       This program demonstrates a set of strings. The user
7       can add and remove strings.
8   */
9   public class SetDemo
10  {
11     public static void main(String[] args)
12     {
13        Set<String> names = new HashSet<String>();
14        Scanner in = new Scanner(System.in);
15
16        boolean done = false;
17        while (!done)
18        {
19           System.out.print("Add name, Q when done: ");
20           String input = in.next();
21           if (input.equalsIgnoreCase("Q"))
22              done = true;
23           else
24           {
25              names.add(input);
26              print(names);
27           }
28        }
29
30        done = false;
31        while (!done)
32        {
33           System.out.print("Remove name, Q when done: ");
34           String input = in.next();
35           if (input.equalsIgnoreCase("Q"))
36              done = true;
37           else
38           {
39              names.remove(input);
40              print(names);
41           }
42        }
43     }
44
45     /**
46         Prints the contents of a set of strings.
47         @param s a set of strings
48     */
49     private static void print(Set<String> s)
50     {
51        System.out.print("{ ");
52        for (String element : s)
53        {
```

```
54            System.out.print(element);
55            System.out.print(" ");
56        }
57        System.out.println("}");
58    }
59 }
```

Output

```
Add name, Q when done: Dick
{ Dick }
Add name, Q when done: Tom
{ Tom Dick }
Add name, Q when done: Harry
{ Harry Tom Dick }
Add name, Q when done: Tom
{ Harry Tom Dick }
Add name, Q when done: Q
Remove name, Q when done: Tom
{ Harry Dick }
Remove name, Q when done: Jerry
{ Harry Dick }
Remove name, Q when done: Q
```

SELF CHECK

1. Arrays and lists remember the order in which you added elements; sets do not. Why would you want to use a set instead of an array or list?

2. Why are set iterators different from list iterators?

QUALITY TIP 16.1

Use Interface References to Manipulate Data Structures

It is considered good style to store a reference to a HashSet or TreeSet in a variable of type Set.

```
Set<String> names = new HashSet<String>();
```

This way, you have to change only one line if you decide to use a TreeSet instead.

Also, methods that operate on sets should specify parameters of type Set:

```
public static void print(Set<String> s)
```

Then the method can be used for all set implementations.

In theory, we should make the same recommendation for linked lists, namely to save LinkedList references in variables of type List. However, in the Java library, the List interface is common to both the ArrayList and the LinkedList class. In particular, it has get and set methods for random access, even though these methods are very inefficient for linked lists. You can't write efficient code if you don't know whether random access is efficient or not. This is plainly a serious design error in the standard library, and I cannot recommend using the List interface for that reason. (To see just how embarrassing that error is, have a look at the source code for the binarySearch method of the Collections class. That method takes a List parameter, but binary search makes no sense for a linked list. The code then clumsily tries to discover whether the list is a linked list, and then switches to a linear search!)

The Set interface and the Map interface, which you will see in the next section, are well-designed, and you should use them.

16.2 Maps

A map keeps associations between key and value objects.

A map is a data type that keeps associations between *keys* and *values*. Figure 3 gives a typical example: a map that associates names with colors. This map might describe the favorite colors of various people.

Mathematically speaking, a map is a function from one set, the *key set*, to another set, the *value set*. Every key in the map has a unique value, but a value may be associated with several keys.

The HashMap and TreeMap classes both implement the Map interface.

Just as there are two kinds of set implementations, the Java library has two implementations for maps: HashMap and TreeMap. Both of them implement the Map interface (see Figure 4).

After constructing a HashMap or TreeMap, you should store the reference to the map object in a Map reference:

```
Map<String, Color> favoriteColors = new HashMap<String, Color>();
```

Figure 3 A Map

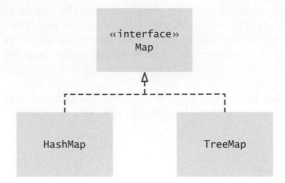

Figure 4
Map Classes and Interfaces in
the Standard Library

Use the put method to add an association:

```
favoriteColors.put("Juliet", Color.PINK);
```

You can change the value of an existing association, simply by calling put again:

```
favoriteColors.put("Juliet", Color.RED);
```

The get method returns the value associated with a key.

```
Color julietsFavoriteColor = favoriteColors.get("Juliet");
```

If you ask for a key that isn't associated with any values, then the get method returns null.

To remove a key and its associated value, use the remove method:

```
favoriteColors.remove("Juliet");
```

> To find all keys and values in a map, iterate through the key set and find the values that correspond to the keys.

Sometimes you want to enumerate all keys in a map. The keySet method yields the set of keys. You can then ask the key set for an iterator and get all keys. From each key, you can find the associated value with the get method. Thus, the following instructions print all key/value pairs in a map m:

```
Set<String> keySet = m.keySet();
for (String key : keySet)
{
    Color value = m.get(key);
    System.out.println(key + "->" + value);
}
```

The following sample program shows a map in action.

ch16/map/MapDemo.java

```
1  import java.awt.Color;
2  import java.util.HashMap;
3  import java.util.Map;
4  import java.util.Set;
5
```

```
 6  /**
 7        This program demonstrates a map that maps names to colors.
 8  */
 9  public class MapDemo
10  {
11     public static void main(String[] args)
12     {
13        Map<String, Color> favoriteColors
14              = new HashMap<String, Color>();
15        favoriteColors.put("Juliet", Color.PINK);
16        favoriteColors.put("Romeo", Color.GREEN);
17        favoriteColors.put("Adam", Color.BLUE);
18        favoriteColors.put("Eve", Color.PINK);
19
20        Set<String> keySet - favoriteColors.keySet();
21        for (String key : keySet)
22        {
23           Color value = favoriteColors.get(key);
24           System.out.println(key + "->" + value);
25        }
26     }
27  }
```

Output

```
Romeo->java.awt.Color[r=0,g=255,b=0]
Eve->java.awt.Color[r=255,g=175,b=175]
Adam->java.awt.Color[r=0,g=0,b=255]
Juliet->java.awt.Color[r=255,g=175,b=175]
```

SELF CHECK

3. What is the difference between a set and a map?
4. Why is the collection of the keys of a map a set?

16.3 Hash Tables

In this section, you will see how the technique of *hashing* can be used to find elements in a data structure quickly, without making a linear search through all elements. Hashing gives rise to the *hash table,* which can be used to implement sets and maps.

A hash function computes an integer value from an object.

A *hash function* is a function that computes an integer value, the *hash code,* from an object, in such a way that different objects are likely to yield different hash codes. The Object class has a hashCode method that other classes need to redefine. The call

```
int h = x.hashCode();
```

computes the hash code of the object x.

Table 1   Sample Strings and Their Hash Codes

String	Hash Code
"Adam"	2035631
"Eve"	70068
"Harry"	69496448
"Jim"	74478
"Joe"	74656
"Juliet"	−2065036585
"Katherine"	2079199209
"Sue"	83491

A good hash function minimizes *collisions*—identical hash codes for different objects.

It is possible for two or more distinct objects to have the same hash code; this is called a *collision*. A good hash function minimizes collisions. For example, the String class defines a hash function for strings that does a good job of producing different integer values for different strings. Table 1 shows some examples of strings and their hash codes. You will see in Section 16.4 how these values are obtained.

Section 16.4 explains how you should redefine the hashCode method for other classes.

A hash code is used as an array index into a hash table. In the simplest implementation of a hash table, you could make an array and insert each object at the location of its hash code (see Figure 5).

Figure 5
A Simplistic Implementation of a Hash Table

Then it is a very simple matter to find out whether an object is already present in the set or not. Compute its hash code and check whether the array position with that hash code is already occupied. This doesn't require a search through the entire array!

However, there are two problems with this simplistic approach. First, it is not possible to allocate an array that is large enough to hold all possible integer index positions. Therefore, we must pick an array of some reasonable size and then reduce the hash code to fall inside the array:

```
int h = x.hashCode();
if (h < 0) h = -h;
h = h % size;
```

Furthermore, it is possible that two different objects have the same hash code. After reducing the hash code modulo a smaller array size, it becomes even more likely that several objects will collide and need to share a position in the array.

> A hash table can be implemented as an array of *buckets*—sequences of nodes that hold elements with the same hash code.

To store multiple objects in the same array position, use short node sequences for the elements with the same hash code (see Figure 6). These node sequences are called *buckets*.

Now the algorithm for finding an object x in a hash table is quite simple.

1. Compute the hash code and reduce it modulo the table size. This gives an index h into the hash table.

2. Iterate through the elements of the bucket at position h. For each element of the bucket, check whether it is equal to x.

3. If a match is found among the elements of that bucket, then x is in the set. Otherwise, it is not.

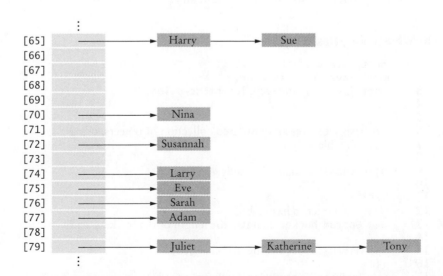

Figure 6   A Hash Table with Buckets to Store Elements with the Same Hash Code

> If there are no or only a few collisions, then adding, locating, and removing hash table elements takes constant or $O(1)$ time.

In the best case, in which there are no collisions, all buckets either are empty or have a single element. Then checking for containment takes constant or $O(1)$ time.

More generally, for this algorithm to be effective, the bucket sizes must be small. If the table length is small, then collisions are unavoidable, and each bucket will get quite full. Then the linear search through a bucket is time-consuming. In the worst case, where all elements end up in the same bucket, a hash table degenerates into a linked list!

> The table size should be a prime number, larger than the expected number of elements.

In order to reduce the chance for collisions, you should make a hash table somewhat larger than the number of elements that you expect to insert. An excess capacity of about 30 percent is typically recommended. According to some researchers, the hash table size should be chosen to be a prime number to minimize the number of collisions.

Adding an element is a simple extension of the algorithm for finding an object. First compute the hash code to locate the bucket in which the element should be inserted. Try finding the object in that bucket. If it is already present, do nothing. Otherwise, insert it.

Removing an element is equally simple. First compute the hash code to locate the bucket in which the element should be inserted. Try finding the object in that bucket. If it is present, remove it. Otherwise, do nothing.

As long as there are few collisions, an element can also be added or removed in constant or $O(1)$ time.

At the end of this section you will find the code for a simple implementation of a hash set. That implementation takes advantage of the AbstractSet class, which already implements most of the methods of the Set interface.

In this implementation you must specify the size of the hash table. In the standard library, you don't need to supply a table size. If the hash table gets too full, a new table of twice the size is created, and all elements are inserted into the new table.

ch16/hashtable/HashSet.java

```java
1   import java.util.AbstractSet;
2   import java.util.Iterator;
3   import java.util.NoSuchElementException;
4
5   /**
6       A hash set stores an unordered collection of objects, using
7       a hash table.
8   */
9   public class HashSet extends AbstractSet
10  {
11      /**
12          Constructs a hash table.
13          @param bucketsLength the length of the buckets array
14      */
15      public HashSet(int bucketsLength)
16      {
17          buckets = new Node[bucketsLength];
18          size = 0;
```

```
19      }
20
21      /**
22         Tests for set membership.
23         @param x an object
24         @return true if x is an element of this set
25      */
26      public boolean contains(Object x)
27      {
28         int h = x.hashCode();
29         if (h < 0) h = -h;
30         h = h % buckets.length;
31
32         Node current = buckets[h];
33         while (current != null)
34         {
35            if (current.data.equals(x)) return true;
36            current = current.next;
37         }
38         return false;
39      }
40
41      /**
42         Adds an element to this set.
43         @param x an object
44         @return true if x is a new object, false if x was
45         already in the set
46      */
47      public boolean add(Object x)
48      {
49         int h = x.hashCode();
50         if (h < 0) h = -h;
51         h = h % buckets.length;
52
53         Node current = buckets[h];
54         while (current != null)
55         {
56            if (current.data.equals(x))
57               return false; // Already in the set
58            current = current.next;
59         }
60         Node newNode = new Node();
61         newNode.data = x;
62         newNode.next = buckets[h];
63         buckets[h] = newNode;
64         size++;
65         return true;
66      }
67
68      /**
69         Removes an object from this set.
70         @param x an object
71         @return true if x was removed from this set, false
72         if x was not an element of this set
73      */
```

```
 74      public boolean remove(Object x)
 75      {
 76         int h = x.hashCode();
 77         if (h < 0) h = -h;
 78         h = h % buckets.length;
 79
 80         Node current = buckets[h];
 81         Node previous = null;
 82         while (current != null)
 83         {
 84            if (current.data.equals(x))
 85            {
 86               if (previous == null) buckets[h] = current.next;
 87               else previous.next = current.next;
 88               size--;
 89               return true;
 90            }
 91            previous = current;
 92            current = current.next;
 93         }
 94         return false;
 95      }
 96
 97      /**
 98         Returns an iterator that traverses the elements of this set.
 99         @return a hash set iterator
100      */
101      public Iterator iterator()
102      {
103         return new HashSetIterator();
104      }
105
106      /**
107         Gets the number of elements in this set.
108         @return the number of elements
109      */
110      public int size()
111      {
112         return size;
113      }
114
115      private Node[] buckets;
116      private int size;
117
118      private class Node
119      {
120         public Object data;
121         public Node next;
122      }
123
124      private class HashSetIterator implements Iterator
125      {
126         /**
127            Constructs a hash set iterator that points to the
128            first element of the hash set.
```

```
129          */
130          public HashSetIterator()
131          {
132             current = null;
133             bucket = -1;
134             previous = null;
135             previousBucket = -1;
136          }
137
138          public boolean hasNext()
139          {
140             if (current != null && current.next != null)
141                return true;
142             for (int b = bucket + 1; b < buckets.length; b++)
143                if (buckets[b] != null) return true;
144             return false;
145          }
146
147          public Object next()
148          {
149             previous = current;
150             previousBucket = bucket;
151             if (current == null || current.next == null)
152             {
153                // Move to next bucket
154                bucket++;
155
156                while (bucket < buckets.length
157                      && buckets[bucket] == null)
158                   bucket++;
159                if (bucket < buckets.length)
160                   current = buckets[bucket];
161                else
162                   throw new NoSuchElementException();
163             }
164             else // Move to next element in bucket
165                current = current.next;
166             return current.data;
167          }
168
169          public void remove()
170          {
171             if (previous != null && previous.next == current)
172                previous.next = current.next;
173             else if (previousBucket < bucket)
174                buckets[bucket] = current.next;
175             else
176                throw new IllegalStateException();
177             current = previous;
178             bucket = previousBucket;
179          }
180
181          private int bucket;
182          private Node current;
```

```
183          private int previousBucket;
184          private Node previous;
185      }
186  }
```

ch16/hashtable/HashSetDemo.java

```java
1  import java.util.Iterator;
2  import java.util.Set;
3
4  /**
5      This program demonstrates the hash set class.
6  */
7  public class HashSetDemo
8  {
9      public static void main(String[] args)
10     {
11        Set names = new HashSet(101); // 101 is a prime
12
13        names.add("Sue");
14        names.add("Harry");
15        names.add("Nina");
16        names.add("Susannah");
17        names.add("Larry");
18        names.add("Eve");
19        names.add("Sarah");
20        names.add("Adam");
21        names.add("Tony");
22        names.add("Katherine");
23        names.add("Juliet");
24        names.add("Romeo");
25        names.remove("Romeo");
26        names.remove("George");
27
28        Iterator iter = names.iterator();
29        while (iter.hasNext())
30            System.out.println(iter.next());
31     }
32  }
```

Output

```
Harry
Sue
Nina
Susannah
Larry
Eve
Sarah
Adam
Juliet
Katherine
Tony
```

5. If a hash function returns 0 for all values, will the HashSet work correctly?

6. What does the hasNext method of the HashSetIterator do when it has reached the end of a bucket?

16.4 Computing Hash Codes

A hash function computes an integer hash code from an object, so that different objects are likely to have different hash codes. Let us first look at how you can compute a hash code from a string. Clearly, you need to combine the character values of the string to yield some integer. You could, for example, add up the character values:

```
int h = 0;
for (int i = 0; i < s.length(); i++)
    h = h + s.charAt(i);
```

However, that would not be a good idea. It doesn't scramble the character values enough. Strings that are permutations of another (such as "eat" and "tea") all have the same hash code.

Here is the method the standard library uses to compute the hash code for a string.

```
final int HASH_MULTIPLIER = 31;
int h = 0;
for (int i = 0; i < s.length(); i++)
    h = HASH_MULTIPLIER * h + s.charAt(i);
```

For example, the hash code of "eat" is

```
31 * (31 * 'e' + 'a') + 't' = 100184
```

The hash code of "tea" is quite different, namely

```
31 * (31 * 't' + 'e') + 'a' = 114704
```

(Use the Unicode table from Appendix B to look up the character values: 'a' is 97, 'e' is 101, and 't' is 116.)

> Define hashCode methods for your own classes by combining the hash codes for the instance variables.

For your own classes, you should make up a hash code that combines the hash codes of the instance fields in a similar way. For example, let us define a hashCode method for the Coin class. There are two instance fields: the coin name and the coin value. First, compute their hash code. You know how to compute the hash code of a string. To compute the hash code of a floating-point number, first wrap the floating-point number into a Double object, and then compute its hash code.

```
class Coin
{
    public int hashCode()
    {
        int h1 = name.hashCode();
        int h2 = new Double(value).hashCode();
        . . .
```

```
        }
    }
```

Then combine the two hash codes.

```
final int HASH_MULTIPLIER = 29;
int h = HASH_MULTIPLIER * h1 + h2;
return h;
```

Use a prime number as the hash multiplier—it scrambles the values better.

If you have more than two instance fields, then combine their hash codes as follows:

```
int h = HASH_MULTIPLIER * h1 + h2;
h = HASH_MULTIPLIER * h + h3;
h = HASH_MULTIPLIER * h + h4;
. . .
return h;
```

If one of the instance fields is an integer, just use the field value as its hash code.

> Your hashCode method must be compatible with the equals method.

When you add objects of your class into a hash table, you need to double-check that the hashCode method is *compatible* with the equals method of your class. Two objects that are equal must yield the same hash code:

- If x.equals(y), then x.hashCode() == y.hashCode()

After all, if x and y are equal to each other, then you don't want to insert both of them into a set—sets don't store duplicates. But if their hash codes are different, x and y may end up in different buckets, and the add method would never notice that they are actually duplicates.

Of course, the converse of the compatibility condition is generally not true. It is possible for two objects to have the same hash code without being equal.

For the Coin class, the compatibility condition holds. We define two coins to be equal to each other if their names and values are equal. In that case, their hash codes will also be equal, because the hash code is computed from the hash codes of the name and value fields.

You get into trouble if your class defines an equals method but not a hashCode method. Suppose we forget to define a hashCode method for the Coin class. Then it inherits the hash code method from the Object superclass. That method computes a hash code from the *memory location* of the object. The effect is that any two objects are very likely to have a different hash code.

```
Coin coin1 = new Coin(0.25, "quarter");
Coin coin2 = new Coin(0.25, "quarter");
```

Now coin1.hashCode() is derived from the memory location of coin1, and coin2.hashCode() is derived from the memory location of coin2. Even though coin1.equals(coin2) is true, their hash codes differ.

However, if you define *neither* equals *nor* hashCode, then there is no problem. The equals method of the Object class considers two objects equal only if their memory location is the same. That is, the Object class has compatible equals and hashCode methods. Of course, then the notion of equality is very restricted: Only identical objects are considered equal. That is not necessarily a bad notion of equality: If you want to collect a set of coins in a purse, you may not want to lump coins of equal value together.

Whenever you use a hash set, you need to make sure that an appropriate hash function exists for the type of the objects that you add to the set. Check the equals method of your class. It tells you when two objects are considered equal. There are two possibilities. Either equals has been defined or it has not been defined. If equals has not been defined, only identical objects are considered equal. In that case, don't define hashCode either. However, if the equals method has been defined, look at its implementation. Typically, two objects are considered equal if some or all of the instance fields are equal. Sometimes, not all instance fields are used in the comparison. Two Student objects may be considered equal if their studentID fields are equal. Define the hashCode method to combine the hash codes of the fields that are compared in the equals method.

In a hash map, only the keys are hashed.

When you use a HashMap, only the keys are hashed. They need compatible hashCode and equals methods. The values are never hashed or compared. The reason is simple—the map only needs to find, add, and remove keys quickly.

What can you do if the objects of your class have equals and hashCode methods defined that don't work for your situation, or if you don't want to define an appropriate hashCode method? Maybe you can use a TreeSet or TreeMap instead. Trees are the subject of the next section.

ch16/hashcode/Coin.java

```
1  /**
2     A coin with a monetary value.
3  */
4  public class Coin
5  {
6     /**
7        Constructs a coin.
8        @param aValue the monetary value of the coin
9        @param aName the name of the coin
10    */
11    public Coin(double aValue, String aName)
12    {
13       value = aValue;
14       name = aName;
15    }
16
17    /**
18       Gets the coin value.
19       @return the value
20    */
21    public double getValue()
22    {
23       return value;
24    }
25
```

```
26     /**
27         Gets the coin name.
28         @return the name
29     */
30     public String getName()
31     {
32         return name;
33     }
34
35     public boolean equals(Object otherObject)
36     {
37         if (otherObject == null) return false;
38         if (getClass() != otherObject.getClass()) return false;
39         Coin other = (Coin) otherObject;
40         return value == other.value && name.equals(other.name);
41     }
42
43     public int hashCode()
44     {
45         int h1 = name.hashCode();
46         int h2 = new Double(value).hashCode();
47         final int HASH_MULTIPLIER = 29;
48         int h = HASH_MULTIPLIER * h1 + h2;
49         return h;
50     }
51
52     public String toString()
53     {
54         return "Coin[value=" + value + ",name=" + name + "]";
55     }
56
57     private double value;
58     private String name;
59 }
```

ch16/hashcode/CoinHashCodePrinter.java

```
1  import java.util.HashSet;
2  import java.util.Set;
3
4  /**
5      A program that prints hash codes of coins.
6  */
7  public class CoinHashCodePrinter
8  {
9      public static void main(String[] args)
10     {
11         Coin coin1 = new Coin(0.25, "quarter");
12         Coin coin2 = new Coin(0.25, "quarter");
13         Coin coin3 = new Coin(0.05, "nickel");
14
15         System.out.println("hash code of coin1="
16             + coin1.hashCode());
```

```
17        System.out.println("hash code of coin2="
18             + coin2.hashCode());
19        System.out.println("hash code of coin3="
20             + coin3.hashCode());
21
22        Set<Coin> coins = new HashSet<Coin>();
23        coins.add(coin1);
24        coins.add(coin2);
25        coins.add(coin3);
26
27        for (Coin c : coins)
28             System.out.println(c);
29    }
30 }
```

Output

```
hash code of coin1=-1513525892
hash code of coin2=-1513525892
hash code of coin3=-1768365211
Coin[value=0.25,name=quarter]
Coin[value=0.05,name=nickel]
```

SELF CHECK

7. What is the hash code of the string "to"?

8. What is the hash code of new Integer(13)?

COMMON ERROR 16.1

Forgetting to Define hashCode

When putting elements into a hash table, make sure that the hashCode method is defined. (The only exception is that you don't need to define hashCode if equals isn't defined. In that case, distinct objects of your class are considered different, even if they have matching contents.)

If you forget to implement the hashCode method, then you inherit the hashCode method of the Object class. That method computes a hash code of the memory location of the object. For example, suppose that you do *not* define the hashCode method of the Coin class. Then the following code is likely to fail:

```
Set<Coin> coins = new HashSet<Coin>();
coins.add(new Coin(0.25, "quarter"));
// The following comparison will probably fail if hashCode not defined
if (coins.contains(new Coin(0.25, "quarter"))
    System.out.println("The set contains a quarter.");
```

The two Coin objects are constructed at different memory locations, so the hashCode method of the Object class will probably compute different hash codes for them. (As always with hash codes, there is a small chance that the hash codes happen to collide.) Then the contains method will inspect the wrong bucket and never find the matching coin.

The remedy is to define a hashCode method in the Coin class.

16.5 Binary Search Trees

A set implementation is allowed to rearrange its elements in any way it chooses so that it can find elements quickly. Suppose a set implementation *sorts* its entries. Then it can use *binary search* to locate elements quickly. Binary search takes $O(\log(n))$ steps, where n is the size of the set. For example, binary search in an array of 1,000 elements is able to locate an element in about 10 steps by cutting the size of the search interval in half in each step.

There is just one wrinkle with this idea. We can't use an array to store the elements of a set, because insertion and removal in an array is slow; an $O(n)$ operation.

In this section we will introduce the simplest of many *treelike* data structures that computer scientists have invented to overcome that problem. Binary search trees allow fast insertion and removal of elements, and they are specially designed for fast searching.

> A binary tree consists of nodes, each of which has at most two child nodes.

A linked list is a one-dimensional data structure. Every node has a reference to a single successor node. You can imagine that all nodes are arranged in line. In contrast, a *tree* is made of nodes that have references to multiple nodes, called the child nodes. Because the child nodes can also have children, the data structure has a tree-like appearance. It is traditional to draw the tree upside down, like a family tree or hierarchy chart (see Figure 7). In a *binary tree*, every node has at most two children (called the *left* and *right children*); hence the name *binary*.

> All nodes in a binary search tree fulfill the property that the descendants to the left have smaller data values than the node data value, and the descendants to the right have larger data values.

Finally, a *binary search tree* is carefully constructed to have the following important property:

- The data values of *all* descendants to the left of *any* node are less than the data value stored in that node, and *all* descendants to the right have greater data values.

The tree in Figure 7 has this property. To verify the binary search property, you must check each node. Consider the node "Juliet". All descendants to the left have data before "Juliet". All descendants on the right have data after "Juliet". Move on to "Eve". There is a single descendant to the left, with data "Adam" before "Eve", and a single descendant to the right, with data "Harry" after "Eve". Check the remaining nodes in the same way.

Figure 8 shows a binary tree that is not a binary search tree. Look carefully—the root node passes the test, but its two children do not.

Let us implement these tree classes. Just as you needed classes for lists and their nodes, you need one class for the tree, containing a reference to the *root node,* and a separate class for the nodes. Each node contains two references (to the left and right child nodes) and a data field. At the fringes of the tree, one or two of the child references are null. The data field has type Comparable, not Object, because you must be able to compare the values in a binary search tree in order to place them into the correct position.

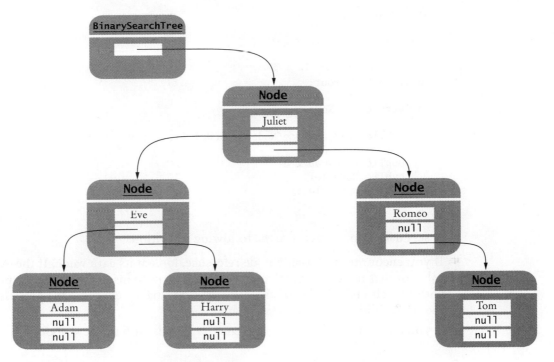

Figure 7 A Binary Search Tree

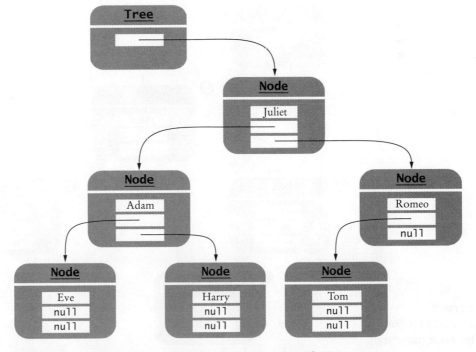

Figure 8 A Binary Tree That Is Not a Binary Search Tree

```
public class BinarySearchTree
{
    public BinarySearchTree() { . . . }
    public void add(Comparable obj) { . . . }
    . . .
    private Node root;

    private class Node
    {
        public void addNode(Node newNode) { . . . }
        . . .
        public Comparable data;
        public Node left;
        public Node right;
    }
}
```

To insert data into the tree, use the following algorithm:

- If you encounter a non-null node reference, look at its data value. If the data value of that node is larger than the one you want to insert, continue the process with the left child. If the existing data value is smaller, continue the process with the right child.

- If you encounter a null node reference, replace it with the new node.

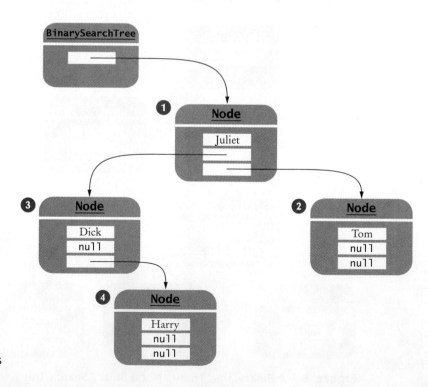

Figure 9
Binary Search Tree
After Four Insertions

For example, consider the tree in Figure 9. It is the result of the following statements:

```
BinarySearchTree tree = new BinarySearchTree();
tree.add("Juliet");  ❶
tree.add("Tom");       ❷
tree.add("Dick");    ❸
tree.add("Harry");      ❹
```

We want to insert a new element Romeo into it.

```
tree.add("Romeo");  ❺
```

Start with the root, Juliet. Romeo comes after Juliet, so you move to the right subtree. You encounter the node Tom. Romeo comes before Tom, so you move to the left subtree. But there is no left subtree. Hence, you insert a new Romeo node as the left child of Tom (see Figure 10).

You should convince yourself that the resulting tree is still a binary search tree. When Romeo is inserted, it must end up as a right descendant of Juliet—that is what the binary search tree condition means for the root node Juliet. The root node doesn't care where in the right subtree the new node ends up. Moving along to Tom, the right child of Juliet, all it cares about is that the new node Romeo ends up somewhere on its left. There is nothing to its left, so Romeo becomes the new left child, and the resulting tree is again a binary search tree.

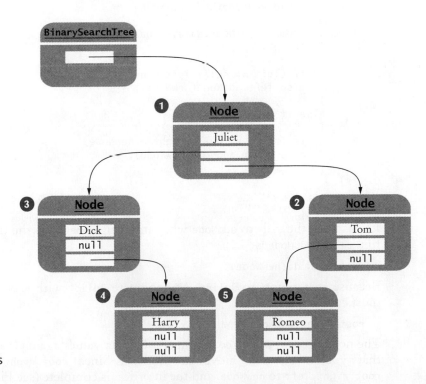

Figure 10
Binary Search Tree
After Five Insertions

Here is the code for the add method of the BinarySearchTree class:

```
public class BinarySearchTree
{
   . . .
   public void add(Comparable obj)
   {
      Node newNode = new Node();
      newNode.data = obj;
      newNode.left = null;
      newNode.right = null;
      if (root == null) root = newNode;
      else root.addNode(newNode);
   }
   . . .
}
```

If the tree is empty, simply set its root to the new node. Otherwise, you know that the new node must be inserted somewhere within the nodes, and you can ask the root node to perform the insertion. That node object calls the addNode method of the Node class, which checks whether the new object is less than the object stored in the node. If so, the element is inserted in the left subtree; if not, it is inserted in the right subtree:

```
private class Node
{
   . . .
   public void addNode(Node newNode)
   {
      int comp = newNode.data.compareTo(data);
      if (comp < 0)
      {
         if (left == null) left = newNode;
         else left.addNode(newNode);
      }
      else if (comp > 0)
      {
         if (right == null) right = newNode;
         else right.addNode(newNode);
      }
   }
   . . .
}
```

Let us trace the calls to addNode when inserting Romeo into the tree in Figure 9. The first call to addNode is

```
root.addNode(newNode)
```

Because root points to Juliet, you compare Juliet with Romeo and find that you must call

```
root.right.addNode(newNode)
```

The node root.right is Tom. Compare the data values again (Tom vs. Romeo) and find that you must now move to the left. Since root.right.left is null, set root.right.left to newNode, and the insertion is complete (see Figure 10).

Unlike a linked list or an array, and like a hash table, a binary tree has no *insert positions.* You cannot select the position where you would like to insert an element into a binary search tree. The data structure is *self-organizing;* that is, each element finds its own place.

We will now discuss the removal algorithm. Our task is to remove a node from the tree. Of course, we must first *find* the node to be removed. That is a simple matter, due to the characteristic property of a binary search tree. Compare the data value to be removed with the data value that is stored in the root node. If it is smaller, keep looking in the left subtree. Otherwise, keep looking in the right subtree.

Let us now assume that we have located the node that needs to be removed. First, let us consider an easy case, when that node has only one child (see Figure 11).

To remove the node, simply modify the parent link that points to the node so that it points to the child instead.

If the node to be removed has no children at all, then the parent link is simply set to null.

> When removing a node with only one child from a binary search tree, the child replaces the node to be removed.

The case in which the node to be removed has two children is more challenging. Rather than removing the node, it is easier to replace its data value with the next larger value in the tree. That replacement preserves the binary search tree property. (Alternatively, you could use the largest element of the left subtree—see Exercise P16.16).

> When removing a node with two children from a binary search tree, replace it with the smallest node of the right subtree.

To locate the next larger value, go to the right subtree and find its smallest data value. Keep following the left child links. Once you reach a node that has no left child, you have found the node containing the smallest data value of the subtree. Now remove that node—it is easily removed because it has at most one child to the right. Then store its data value in the original node that was slated for removal. Figure 12 shows the details. You will find the complete code at the end of this section.

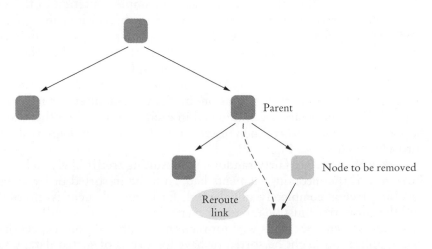

Figure 11 Removing a Node with One Child

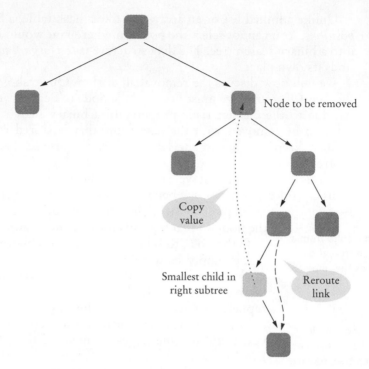

Node to be removed

Copy
value

Reroute
link

Smallest child in
right subtree

Figure 12   Removing a Node with Two Children

At the end of this section, you will find the source code for the `BinarySearchTree` class. It contains the `add` and `remove` methods that we just described, as well as a `find` method that tests whether a value is present in a binary search tree, and a `print` method that we will analyze in the following section.

> If a binary search tree is balanced, then adding an element takes $O(\log(n))$ time.

Now that you have seen the implementation of this complex data structure, you may well wonder whether it is any good. Like nodes in a list, nodes are allocated one at a time. No existing elements need to be moved when a new element is inserted in the tree; that is an advantage. How fast insertion is, however, depends on the shape of the tree. If the tree is *balanced*—that is, if each node has approximately as many descendants on the left as on the right—then insertion is very fast, because about half of the nodes are eliminated in each step. On the other hand, if the tree happens to be *unbalanced*, then insertion can be slow—perhaps as slow as insertion into a linked list. (See Figure 13.)

If new elements are fairly random, the resulting tree is likely to be well balanced. However, if the incoming elements happen to be in sorted order already, then the resulting tree is completely unbalanced. Each new element is inserted at the end, and the entire tree must be traversed every time to find that end!

Binary search trees work well for random data, but if you suspect that the data in your application might be sorted or have long runs of sorted data, you should not use a binary search tree. There are more sophisticated tree structures whose methods

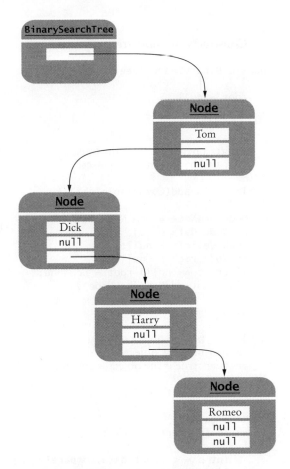

Figure 13 An Unbalanced Binary Search Tree

keep trees balanced at all times. In these tree structures, one can guarantee that finding, adding, and removing elements takes $O(\log(n))$ time. To learn more about those advanced data structures, you may want to enroll in a course about data structures.

The standard Java library uses *red-black trees*, a special form of balanced binary trees, to implement sets and maps. You will see in Section 16.7 what you need to do to use the TreeSet and TreeMap classes. For information on how to implement a red-black tree yourself, see [1].

ch16/tree/BinarySearchTree.java

```
1  /**
2      This class implements a binary search tree whose
3      nodes hold objects that implement the Comparable
4      interface.
5  */
6  public class BinarySearchTree
7  {
```

```
 8      /**
 9          Constructs an empty tree.
10      */
11      public BinarySearchTree()
12      {
13          root = null;
14      }
15
16      /**
17          Inserts a new node into the tree.
18          @param obj  the object to insert
19      */
20      public void add(Comparable obj)
21      {
22          Node newNode = new Node();
23          newNode.data = obj;
24          newNode.left = null;
25          newNode.right = null;
26          if (root == null) root = newNode;
27          else root.addNode(newNode);
28      }
29
30   /**
31          Tries to find an object in the tree.
32          @param obj the object to find
33          @return true if the object is contained in the tree
34      */
35      public boolean find(Comparable obj)
36      {
37          Node current = root;
38          while (current != null)
39          {
40              int d = current.data.compareTo(obj);
41              if (d == 0) return true;
42              else if (d > 0) current = current.left;
43              else current = current.right;
44          }
45          return false;
46      }
47
48      /**
49          Tries to remove an object from the tree. Does nothing
50          if the object is not contained in the tree.
51          @param obj  the object to remove
52      */
53      public void remove(Comparable obj)
54      {
55          // Find node to be removed
56
57          Node toBeRemoved = root;
58          Node parent = null;
59          boolean found = false;
60          while (!found && toBeRemoved != null)
61          {
```

```
 62            int d = toBeRemoved.data.compareTo(obj);
 63            if (d == 0) found = true;
 64            else
 65            {
 66               parent = toBeRemoved;
 67               if (d > 0) toBeRemoved = toBeRemoved.left;
 68               else toBeRemoved = toBeRemoved.right;
 69            }
 70         }
 71
 72         if (!found) return;
 73
 74         // toBeRemoved contains obj
 75
 76         // If one of the children is empty, use the other
 77
 78         if (toBeRemoved.left == null || toBeRemoved.right == null)
 79         {
 80            Node newChild;
 81            if (toBeRemoved.left == null)
 82               newChild = toBeRemoved.right;
 83            else
 84               newChild = toBeRemoved.left;
 85
 86            if (parent == null) // Found in root
 87               root = newChild;
 88            else if (parent.left == toBeRemoved)
 89               parent.left = newChild;
 90            else
 91               parent.right = newChild;
 92            return;
 93         }
 94
 95         // Neither subtree is empty
 96
 97         // Find smallest element of the right subtree
 98
 99         Node smallestParent = toBeRemoved;
100         Node smallest = toBeRemoved.right;
101         while (smallest.left != null)
102         {
103            smallestParent = smallest;
104            smallest = smallest.left;
105         }
106
107         // smallest contains smallest child in right subtree
108
109         // Move contents, unlink child
110
111         toBeRemoved.data = smallest.data;
112         smallestParent.left = smallest.right;
113      }
114
```

```
115    /**
116        Prints the contents of the tree in sorted order.
117    */
118    public void print()
119    {
120        if (root != null)
121            root.printNodes();
122        System.out.println();
123    }
124
125    private Node root;
126
127    /**
128        A node of a tree stores a data item and references
129        to the child nodes to the left and to the right.
130    */
131    private class Node
132    {
133        /**
134            Inserts a new node as a descendant of this node.
135            @param newNode  the node to insert
136        */
137        public void addNode(Node newNode)
138        {
139            int comp = newNode.data.compareTo(data);
140            if (comp < 0)
141            {
142                if (left == null) left = newNode;
143                else left.addNode(newNode);
144            }
145            if (comp > 0)
146            {
147                if (right == null) right = newNode;
148                else right.addNode(newNode);
149            }
150        }
151
152        /**
153            Prints this node and all of its descendants
154            in sorted order.
155        */
156        public void printNodes()
157        {
158            if (left != null)
159                left.printNodes();
160            System.out.println(data + " ");
161            if (right != null)
162                right.printNodes();
163        }
164
165        public Comparable data;
166        public Node left;
167        public Node right;
168    }
169 }
```

9. What is the difference between a tree, a binary tree, and a balanced binary tree?
10. Give an example of a string that, when inserted into the tree of Figure 10, becomes a right child of Romeo.

16.6 Tree Traversal

Now that the data are inserted in the tree, what can you do with them? It turns out to be surprisingly simple to print all elements in sorted order. You *know* that all data in the left subtree of any node must come before the node and before all data in the right subtree. That is, the following algorithm will print the elements in sorted order:

1. Print the left subtree.
2. Print the data.
3. Print the right subtree.

Let's try this out with the tree in Figure 10. The algorithm tells us to

1. Print the left subtree of Juliet; that is, Dick and descendants.
2. Print Juliet.
3. Print the right subtree of Juliet; that is, Tom and descendants.

How do you print the subtree starting at Dick?

1. Print the left subtree of Dick. There is nothing to print.
2. Print Dick.
3. Print the right subtree of Dick, that is, Harry.

That is, the left subtree of Juliet is printed as

```
Dick Harry
```

The right subtree of Juliet is the subtree starting at Tom. How is it printed? Again, using the same algorithm:

1. Print the left subtree of Tom, that is, Romeo.
2. Print Tom.
3. Print the right subtree of Tom. There is nothing to print.

Thus, the right subtree of Juliet is printed as

```
Romeo Tom
```

Now put it all together: the left subtree, Juliet, and the right subtree:

```
Dick Harry Juliet Romeo Tom
```

The tree is printed in sorted order.

Let us implement the print method. You need a worker method printNodes of the Node class:

```java
private class Node
{
   . . .
   public void printNodes()
   {
      if (left != null)
         left.printNodes();
      System.out.print(data + " ");

      if (right != null)
         right.printNodes();
   }
   . . .
}
```

To print the entire tree, start this recursive printing process at the root, with the following method of the BinarySearchTree class.

```java
public class BinarySearchTree
{
   . . .
   public void print()
   {
      if (root != null)
         root.printNodes();
      System.out.println();
   }
   . . .
}
```

> Tree traversal schemes include preorder traversal, inorder traversal, and postorder traversal.

This visitation scheme is called *inorder traversal*. There are two other traversal schemes, called *preorder traversal* and *postorder traversal*.

In preorder traversal,

- Visit the root
- Visit the left subtree
- Visit the right subtree

In postorder traversal,

- Visit the left subtree
- Visit the right subtree
- Visit the root

These two visitation schemes will not print the tree in sorted order. However, they are important in other applications of binary trees. Here is an example.

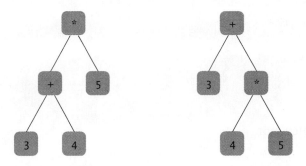

Figure 14   Expression Trees

In Chapter 13, we presented an algorithm for parsing arithmetic expressions such as

```
(3 + 4) * 5
3 + 4 * 5
```

It is customary to draw these expressions in tree form—see Figure 14. If all operators have two arguments, then the resulting tree is a binary tree. Its leaves store numbers, and its interior nodes store operators.

Note that the expression trees describe the order in which the operators are applied.

This order becomes visible when applying the postorder traversal of the expression tree. The first tree yields

```
3 4 + 5 *
```

whereas the second tree yields

```
3 4 5 * +
```

> Postorder traversal of an expression tree yields the instructions for evaluating the expression on a stack-based calculator.

You can interpret these sequences as instructions for a stack-based calculator. A number means:

• Push the number on the stack.

An operator means:

• Pop the top two numbers off the stack.

• Apply the operator to these two numbers.

• Push the result back on the stack.

Figure 15 shows the computation sequences for the two expressions.

This observation yields an algorithm for evaluating arithmetic expressions. First, turn the expression into a tree. Then carry out a postorder traversal of the

Figure 15
A Stack-Based Calculator

expression tree and apply the operations in the given order. The result is the value of the expression.

SELF CHECK

11. What are the inorder traversals of the two trees in Figure 14?
12. Are the trees in Figure 14 binary search trees?

RANDOM FACT 16.1

Reverse Polish Notation

In the 1920s, the Polish mathematician Jan Łukasiewicz realized that it is possible to dispense with parentheses in arithmetic expressions, provided that you write the operators *before* their arguments. For example,

Standard Notation	Łukasiewicz Notation
3 + 4	+ 3 4
3 + 4 * 5	+ 3 * 4 5
3 * (4 + 5)	* 3 + 4 5
(3 + 4) * 5	* + 3 4 5
3 + 4 + 5	+ + 3 4 5

The Łukasiewicz notation might look strange to you, but that is just an accident of history. Had earlier mathematicians realized its advantages, schoolchildren today would not learn an inferior notation with arbitrary precedence rules and parentheses.

Of course, an entrenched notation is not easily displaced, even when it has distinct disadvantages, and Łukasiewicz's discovery did not cause much of a stir for about 50 years.

However, in 1972, Hewlett-Packard introduced the HP 35 calculator that used *reverse Polish notation* or RPN. RPN is simply Łukasiewicz's notation in reverse, with the operators after their arguments. For example, to compute 3 + 4 * 5, you enter 3 4 5 * +. RPN calculators have no keys labeled with parentheses or an equals symbol. There is just a key labeled ENTER to push a number onto a stack. For that reason, Hewlett-Packard's marketing department used to refer to their product as "the calculators that have no equal". Indeed, the Hewlett-Packard calculators were a great advance over competing models that were unable to handle algebraic notation, leaving users with no other choice but to write intermediate results on paper.

Over time, developers of high-quality calculators have adapted to the standard algebraic notation rather than forcing its users to learn a new notation. However, those users who have made the effort to learn RPN tend to be fanatic proponents, and to this day, some Hewlett-Packard calculator models still support it.

16.7 Using Tree Sets and Tree Maps

Both the HashSet and the TreeSet classes implement the Set interface. Thus, if you need a set of objects, you have a choice.

> The TreeSet class uses a form of balanced binary tree that guarantees that adding and removing an element takes $O(\log(n))$ time.

If you have a good hash function for your objects, then hashing is usually faster than tree-based algorithms. But the balanced trees used in the TreeSet class can *guarantee* reasonable performance, whereas the HashSet is entirely at the mercy of the hash function.

If you don't want to define a hash function, then a tree set is an attractive option. Tree sets have another advantage: The iterators visit elements in *sorted order* rather than the completely random order given by the hash codes.

> To use a tree set, the elements must be comparable.

To use a TreeSet, your objects must belong to a class that implements the Comparable interface or you must supply a Comparator object. That is the same requirement that you saw in Section 14.8 for using the sort and binarySearch methods in the standard library.

To use a TreeMap, the same requirement holds for the *keys*. There is no requirement for the values.

For example, the String class implements the Comparable interface. The compareTo method compares strings in dictionary order. Thus, you can form tree sets of strings, and use strings as keys for tree maps.

If the class of the tree set elements doesn't implement the Comparable interface, or the sort order of the compareTo method isn't the one you want, then you can define your own comparison by supplying a Comparator object to the TreeSet or TreeMap constructor. For example,

```
Comparator comp = new CoinComparator();
Set s = new TreeSet(comp);
```

As described in Advanced Topic 14.5, a Comparator object compares two elements and returns a negative integer if the first is less than the second, zero if they are identical, and a positive value otherwise. The example program at the end of this section constructs a TreeSet of Coin objects, using the coin comparator of Advanced Topic 14.5.

ch16/treeset/TreeSetTester.java

```java
1   import java.util.Comparator;
2   import java.util.Set;
3   import java.util.TreeSet;
4
5   /**
6      A program to a test a tree set with a comparator for coins.
7   */
8   public class TreeSetTester
9   {
10     public static void main(String[] args)
11     {
12        Coin coin1 = new Coin(0.25, "quarter");
13        Coin coin2 = new Coin(0.25, "quarter");
14        Coin coin3 = new Coin(0.01, "penny");
15        Coin coin4 = new Coin(0.05, "nickel");
16
17        class CoinComparator implements Comparator<Coin>
18        {
19           public int compare(Coin first, Coin second)
20           {
21              if (first.getValue() < second.getValue()) return -1;
22              if (first.getValue() == second.getValue()) return 0;
23              return 1;
24           }
25        }
26
27        Comparator<Coin> comp = new CoinComparator();
28        Set<Coin> coins = new TreeSet<Coin>(comp);
29        coins.add(coin1);
30        coins.add(coin2);
31        coins.add(coin3);
32        coins.add(coin4);
33
34        for (Coin c : coins)
35           System.out.print(c.getValue() + " ");
36        System.out.println("Expected: 0.01 0.05 0.25");
37     }
38  }
```

Output

```
0.01 0.05 0.25
Expected: 0.01 0.05 0.25
```

SELF CHECK

13. When would you choose a tree set over a hash set?

14. Suppose we define a coin comparator whose `compare` method always returns 0. Would the `TreeSet` function correctly?

HOW TO 16.1

Choosing a Container

Suppose you need to store objects in a container. You have now seen a number of different data structures. This How To reviews how to pick an appropriate container for your application.

Step 1 Determine how you access the elements.

You store elements in a container so that you can later retrieve them. How do you want to access individual elements? You have several choices.

- It doesn't matter. Elements are always accessed "in bulk", by visiting all elements and doing something with them.
- Access by key. Elements are accessed by a special key. *Example:* Retrieve a bank account by the account number.
- Access by integer index. Elements have a position that is naturally an integer or a pair of integers. *Example:* A piece on a chess board is accessed by a row and column index.

If you need keyed access, use a map. If you need access by integer index, use an array list or array. For an index pair, use a two-dimensional array.

Step 2 Determine whether element order matters.

When you retrieve elements from a container, do you care about the order in which they are retrieved? You have several choices.

- It doesn't matter. As long as you get to visit all elements, you don't care in which order.
- Elements must be sorted.
- Elements must be in the same order in which they were inserted.

To keep elements sorted, use a `TreeSet`. To keep elements in the order in which you inserted them, use a `LinkedList`, `ArrayList`, or array.

Step 3 Determine which operations must be fast.

You have several choices.

- It doesn't matter. You collect so few elements that you aren't concerned about speed.
- Adding and removing elements must be fast.
- Finding elements must be fast.

Linked lists allow you to add and remove elements efficiently, provided you are already near the location of the change. Changing either end of the linked list is always fast.

If you need to find an element quickly, use a set.

At this point, you should have narrowed down your selection to a particular container. If you answered "It doesn't matter" for each of the choices, then just use an `ArrayList`. It's a simple container that you already know well.

Step 4 For sets and maps, choose between hash tables and trees.

If you decided that you need a set or map, you need to pick a particular implementation, either a hash table or a tree.

If your elements (or keys, in case of a map) are strings, use a hash table. It's more efficient.

If your elements or keys belong to a type that someone else defined, check whether the class implements its own `hashCode` and `equals` methods. The inherited `hashCode` method of the `Object` class takes only the object's memory address into account, not its contents. If there is no satisfactory `hashCode` method, then you must use a tree.

If your elements or keys belong to your own class, you usually want to use hashing. Define a `hashCode` and compatible `equals` method.

Step 5 If you use a tree, decide whether to supply a comparator.

Look at the class of the elements or keys that the tree manages. Does that class implement the `Comparable` interface? If so, is the sort order given by the `compareTo` method the one you want? If yes, then you don't need to do anything further. If no, then you must define a class that implements the `Comparator` interface and define the `compare` method. Supply an object of the comparator class to the `TreeSet` or `TreeMap` constructor.

RANDOM FACT 16.2

Software Piracy

As you read this, you have written a few computer programs, and you have experienced firsthand how much effort it takes to write even the humblest of programs. Writing a real software product, such as a financial application or a computer game, takes a lot of time and money. Few people, and fewer companies, are going to spend that kind of time and money if they don't have a reasonable chance to make more money from their effort. (Actually, some companies give away their software in the hope that users will upgrade to more elaborate paid versions. Other companies give away the software that enables users to read and use files but sell the software needed to create those files. Finally, there are individuals who donate their time, out of enthusiasm, and produce programs that you can copy freely.)

When selling software, a company must rely on the honesty of its customers. It is an easy matter for an unscrupulous person to make copies of computer programs without paying for them. In most countries that is illegal. Most governments provide legal protection, such as copyright laws and patents, to encourage the development of new products. Countries that tolerate widespread piracy have found that they have an ample cheap supply of foreign software, but no local manufacturers willing to design good software for their own citizens, such as word processors in the local script or financial programs adapted to the local tax laws.

When a mass market for software first appeared, vendors were enraged by the money they lost through piracy. They tried to fight back by various schemes to ensure that only the legitimate owner could use the software. Some manufacturers used *key disks:* disks with special patterns of holes burned in by a laser, which couldn't be copied. Others used *dongles:*

devices that are attached to a printer port. Legitimate users hated these measures. They paid for the software, but they had to suffer through the inconvenience of inserting a key disk every time they started the software or having multiple dongles stick out from their computer. In the United States, market pressures forced most vendors to give up on these copy protection schemes, but they are still commonplace in other parts of the world.

Because it is so easy and inexpensive to pirate software, and the chance of being found out is minimal, you have to make a moral choice for yourself. If a package that you would really like to have is too expensive for your budget, do you steal it, or do you stay honest and get by with a more affordable product?

Of course, piracy is not limited to software. The same issues arise for other digital products as well. You may have had the opportunity to obtain copies of songs or movies without payment. Or you may have been frustrated by a copy protection device on your music player that made it difficult for you to listen to songs that you paid for. Admittedly, it can be difficult to have a lot of sympathy for a musical ensemble whose publisher charges a lot of money for what seems to have been very little effort on their part, at least when compared to the effort that goes into designing and implementing a software package. Nevertheless, it seems only fair that artists and authors receive some compensation for their efforts. How to pay artists, authors, and programmers fairly, without burdening honest customers, is an unsolved problem at the time of this writing, and many computer scientists are engaged in research in this area.

16.8 Priority Queues

In Section 15.4, you encountered two common abstract data types: stacks and queues. Another important abstract data type, the *priority queue*, collects elements, each of which has a *priority*. A typical example of a priority queue is a collection of work requests, some of which may be more urgent than others.

> When removing an element from a priority queue, the element with the highest priority is retrieved.

Unlike a regular queue, the priority queue does not maintain a first-in, first-out discipline. Instead, elements are retrieved according to their priority. In other words, new items can be inserted in any order. But whenever an item is removed, that item has highest priority.

It is customary to give low values to high priorities, with priority 1 denoting the highest priority. The priority queue extracts the *minimum* element from the queue.

For example, consider this sample code:

```
PriorityQueue<WorkOrder> q = new PriorityQueue<WorkOrder>;
q.add(new WorkOrder(3, "Shampoo carpets"));
q.add(new WorkOrder(1, "Fix overflowing sink"));
q.add(new WorkOrder(2, "Order cleaning supplies"));
```

When calling q.remove() for the first time, the work order with priority 1 is removed. The next call to q.remove() removes the work order whose priority is highest among those remaining in the queue—in our example, the work order with priority 2.

The standard Java library supplies a PriorityQueue class that is ready for you to use. Later in this chapter, you will learn how to supply your own implementation.

Keep in mind that the priority queue is an *abstract* data type. You do not know how a priority queue organizes its elements. There are several concrete data structures that can be used to implement priority queues.

Of course, one implementation comes to mind immediately. Just store the elements in a linked list, adding new elements to the head of the list. The `remove` method then traverses the linked list and removes the element with the highest priority. In this implementation, adding elements is quick, but removing them is slow.

Another implementation strategy is to keep the elements in sorted order, for example in a binary search tree. Then it is an easy matter to locate and remove the largest element. However, another data structure, called a heap, is even more suitable for implementing priority queues.

16.9 Heaps

> A heap is an almost complete tree in which the values of all nodes are at most as large as those of their descendants.

A *heap* (or, for greater clarity, *min-heap*) is a binary tree with two special properties.

1. A heap is *almost complete:* all nodes are filled in, except the last level may have some nodes missing toward the right (see Figure 16).

2. The tree fulfills the *heap property:* all nodes store values that are at most as large as the values stored in their descendants (see Figure 17).

It is easy to see that the heap property ensures that the smallest element is stored in the root.

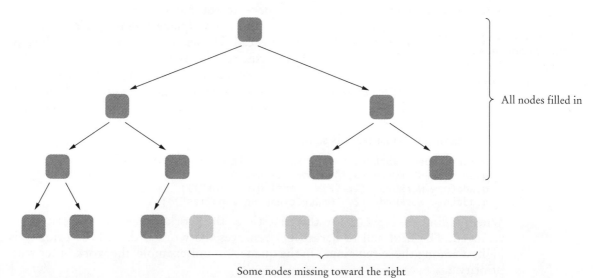

All nodes filled in

Some nodes missing toward the right

Figure 16   An Almost Complete Tree

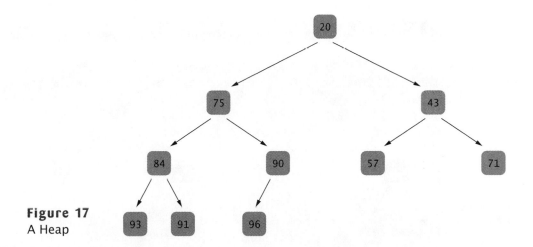

Figure 17
A Heap

A heap is superficially similar to a binary search tree, but there are two important differences.

1. The shape of a heap is very regular. Binary search trees can have arbitrary shapes.

2. In a heap, the left and right subtrees both store elements that are larger than the root element. In contrast, in a binary search tree, smaller elements are stored in the left subtree and larger elements are stored in the right subtree.

Suppose we have a heap and want to insert a new element. Afterwards, the heap property should again be fulfilled. The following algorithm carries out the insertion (see Figure 18).

1. First, add a vacant slot to the end of the tree.

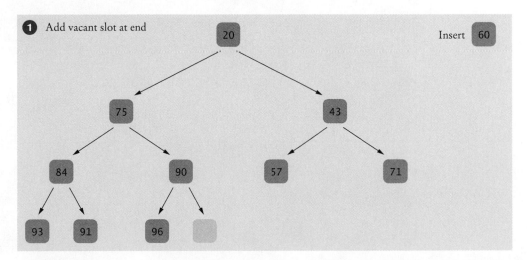

Figure 18 Inserting an Element into a Heap

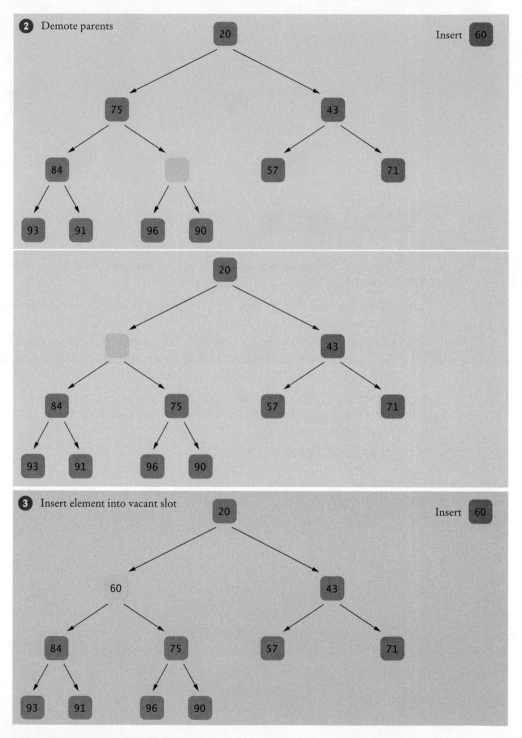

Figure 18 (continued)   Inserting an Element into a Heap

2. Next, demote the parent of the empty slot if it is larger than the element to be inserted. That is, move the parent value into the vacant slot, and move the vacant slot up. Repeat this demotion as long as the parent of the vacant slot is larger than the element to be inserted. (See Figure 18 continued.)

3. At this point, either the vacant slot is at the root, or the parent of the vacant slot is smaller than the element to be inserted. Insert the element into the vacant slot.

We will not consider an algorithm for removing an arbitrary node from a heap. The only node that we will remove is the root node, which contains the minimum of all of the values in the heap. Figure 19 shows the algorithm in action.

1. Extract the root node value.

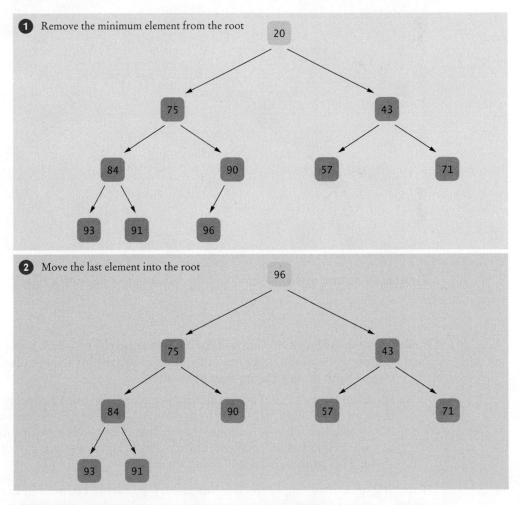

Figure 19   Removing the Minimum Value from a Heap

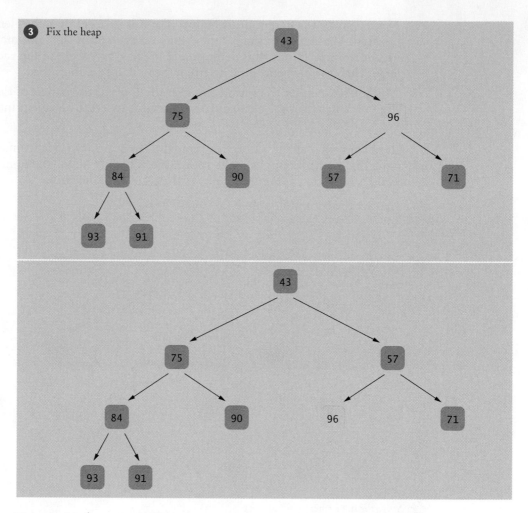

Figure 19 (continued) Removing the Minimum Value from a Heap

2. Move the value of the last node of the heap into the root node, and remove the last node. Now the heap property may be violated for the root node, because one or both of its children may be smaller.

3. Promote the smaller child of the root node. (See Figure 19 continued.) Now the root node again fulfills the heap property. Repeat this process with the demoted child. That is, promote the smaller of its children. Continue until the demoted child has no smaller children. The heap property is now fulfilled again. This process is called "fixing the heap".

Inserting and removing heap elements is very efficient. The reason lies in the balanced shape of a heap. The insertion and removal operations visit at most h nodes, where h is the height of the tree. A heap of height h contains at least $2^{h\ 1}$ elements, but less than 2^h elements. In other words, if n is the number of elements, then

$$2^{h-1} \le n < 2^h$$

or

$$h - 1 \le \log_2(n) < h$$

Inserting or removing a heap element is an $O(\log(n))$ operation.

This argument shows that the insertion and removal operations in a heap with n elements take $O(\log(n))$ steps.

Contrast this finding with the situation of binary search trees. When a binary search tree is unbalanced, it can degenerate into a linked list, so that in the worst case insertion and removal are $O(n)$ operations.

The regular layout of a heap makes it possible to store heap nodes efficiently in an array.

Heaps have another major advantage. Because of the regular layout of the heap nodes, it is easy to store the node values in an array. First store the first layer, then the second, and so on (see Figure 20). For convenience, we leave the 0 element of the array empty. Then the child nodes of the node with index i have index $2 \cdot i$ and $2 \cdot i + 1$, and the parent node of the node with index i has index $i/2$. For example, as you can see in Figure 20, the children of node 4 are nodes 8 and 9, and the parent is node 2.

Storing the heap values in an array may not be intuitive, but it is very efficient. There is no need to allocate individual nodes or to store the links to the child nodes. Instead, child and parent positions can be determined by very simple computations.

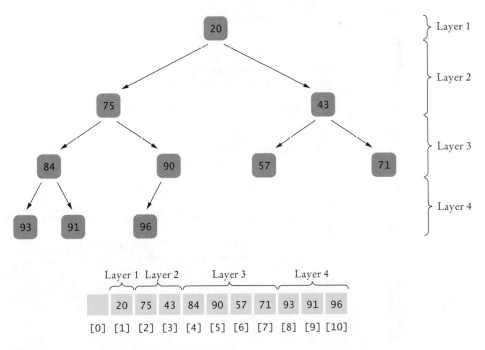

Figure 20 Storing a Heap in an Array

The program at the end of this section contains an implementation of a heap. For greater clarity, the computation of the parent and child index positions is carried out in methods getParentIndex, getLeftChildIndex, and getRightChildIndex. For greater efficiency, the method calls could be avoided by using expressions index / 2, 2 * index, and 2 * index + 1 directly.

In this section, we have organized our heaps such that the smallest element is stored in the root. It is also possible to store the largest element in the root, simply by reversing all comparisons in the heap-building algorithm. If there is a possibility of misunderstanding, it is best to refer to the data structures as min-heap or max-heap.

The test program demonstrates how to use a min-heap as a priority queue.

ch16/pqueue/MinHeap.java

```
1   import java.util.*;
2
3   /**
4       This class implements a heap.
5   */
6   public class MinHeap
7   {
8       /**
9           Constructs an empty heap.
10      */
11      public MinHeap()
12      {
13          elements = new ArrayList<Comparable>();
14          elements.add(null);
15      }
16
17      /**
18          Adds a new element to this heap.
19          @param newElement the element to add
20      */
21      public void add(Comparable newElement)
22      {
23          // Add a new leaf
24          elements.add(null);
25          int index = elements.size() - 1;
26
27          // Demote parents that are larger than the new element
28          while (index > 1
29                  && getParent(index).compareTo(newElement) > 0)
30          {
31              elements.set(index, getParent(index));
32              index = getParentIndex(index);
33          }
34
35          // Store the new element in the vacant slot
36          elements.set(index, newElement);
37      }
38
```

```
39    /**
40        Gets the minimum element stored in this heap.
41        @return the minimum element
42    */
43    public Comparable peek()
44    {
45        return elements.get(1);
46    }
47
48    /**
49        Removes the minimum element from this heap.
50        @return the minimum element
51    */
52    public Comparable remove()
53    {
54        Comparable minimum = elements.get(1);
55
56        // Remove last element
57        int lastIndex = elements.size() - 1;
58        Comparable last = elements.remove(lastIndex);
59
60        if (lastIndex > 1)
61        {
62            elements.set(1, last);
63            fixHeap();
64        }
65
66        return minimum;
67    }
68
69    /**
70        Turns the tree back into a heap, provided only the root
71        node violates the heap condition.
72    */
73    private void fixHeap()
74    {
75        Comparable root = elements.get(1);
76
77        int lastIndex = elements.size() - 1;
78        // Promote children of removed root while they are larger than last
79
80        int index = 1;
81        boolean more = true;
82        while (more)
83        {
84            int childIndex = getLeftChildIndex(index);
85            if (childIndex <= lastIndex)
86            {
87                // Get smaller child
88
89                // Get left child first
90                Comparable child = getLeftChild(index);
91
```

```
 92                        // Use right child instead if it is smaller
 93                        if (getRightChildIndex(index) <= lastIndex
 94                                && getRightChild(index).compareTo(child) < 0)
 95                        {
 96                            childIndex = getRightChildIndex(index);
 97                            child = getRightChild(index);
 98                        }
 99
100                        // Check if larger child is smaller than root
101                        if (child.compareTo(root) < 0)
102                        {
103                            // Promote child
104                            elements.set(index, child);
105                            index = childIndex;
106                        }
107                        else
108                        {
109                            // root  is smaller than both children
110                            more = false;
111                        }
112                    }
113                    else
114                    {
115                        // No children
116                        more = false;
117                    }
118                }
119
120                // Store root element in vacant slot
121                elements.set(index, root);
122            }
123
124            /**
125                Returns the number of elements in this heap.
126            */
127            public int size()
128            {
129                return elements.size() - 1;
130            }
131
132            /**
133                Returns the index of the left child.
134                @param index  the index of a node in this heap
135                @return  the index of the left child of the given node
136            */
137            private static int getLeftChildIndex(int index)
138            {
139                return 2 * index;
140            }
141
142            /**
143                Returns the index of the right child.
144                @param index  the index of a node in this heap
145                @return  the index of the right child of the given node
146            */
```

```
147     private static int getRightChildIndex(int index)
148     {
149        return 2 * index + 1;
150     }
151
152     /**
153        Returns the index of the parent.
154        @param index  the index of a node in this heap
155        @return  the index of the parent of the given node
156     */
157     private static int getParentIndex(int index)
158     {
159        return index / 2;
160     }
161
162     /**
163        Returns the value of the left child.
164        @param index  the index of a node in this heap
165        @return  the value of the left child of the given node
166     */
167     private Comparable getLeftChild(int index)
168     {
169        return elements.get(2 * index);
170     }
171
172     /**
173        Returns the value of the right child.
174        @param index  the index of a node in this heap
175        @return  the value of the right child of the given node
176     */
177     private Comparable getRightChild(int index)
178     {
179        return elements.get(2 * index + 1);
180     }
181
182     /**
183        Returns the value of the parent.
184        @param index  the index of a node in this heap
185        @return  the value of the parent of the given node
186     */
187     private Comparable getParent(int index)
188     {
189        return elements.get(index / 2);
190     }
191
192     private ArrayList<Comparable> elements;
193  }
```

ch16/pqueue/HeapDemo.java

```
1   /**
2      This program demonstrates the use of a heap as a priority queue.
3   */
4   public class HeapDemo
```

```
 5  {
 6     public static void main(String[] args)
 7     {
 8        MinHeap q = new MinHeap();
 9        q.add(new WorkOrder(3, "Shampoo carpets"));
10        q.add(new WorkOrder(7, "Empty trash"));
11        q.add(new WorkOrder(8, "Water plants"));
12        q.add(new WorkOrder(10, "Remove pencil sharpener shavings"));
13        q.add(new WorkOrder(6, "Replace light bulb"));
14        q.add(new WorkOrder(1, "Fix broken sink"));
15        q.add(new WorkOrder(9, "Clean coffee maker"));
16        q.add(new WorkOrder(2, "Order cleaning supplies"));
17
18        while (q.size() > 0)
19           System.out.println(q.remove());
20     }
21  }
```

ch16/pqueue/WorkOrder.java

```
 1  /**
 2      This class encapsulates a work order with a priority.
 3  */
 4  public class WorkOrder implements Comparable
 5  {
 6     /**
 7         Constructs a work order with a given priority and description.
 8         @param aPriority the priority of this work order
 9         @param aDescription the description of this work order
10     */
11     public WorkOrder(int aPriority, String aDescription)
12     {
13        priority = aPriority;
14        description = aDescription;
15     }
16
17     public String toString()
18     {
19        return "priority=" + priority + ", description=" + description;
20     }
21
22     public int compareTo(Object otherObject)
23     {
24        WorkOrder other = (WorkOrder) otherObject;
25        if (priority < other.priority) return -1;
26        if (priority > other.priority) return 1;
27        return 0;
28     }
29
30     private int priority;
31     private String description;
32  }
```

Output

```
priority=1, description=Fix broken sink
priority=2, description=Order cleaning supplies
priority=3, description=Shampoo carpets
priority=6, description=Replace light bulb
priority=7, description=Empty trash
priority=8, description=Water plants
priority=9, description=Clean coffee maker
priority=10, description=Remove pencil sharpener shavings
```

SELF CHECK

15. The software that controls the events in a user interface keeps the events in a data structure. Whenever an event such as a mouse move or repaint request occurs, the event is added. Events are retrieved according to their importance. What abstract data type is appropriate for this application?

16. Could we store a binary search tree in an array so that we can quickly locate the children by looking at array locations 2 * index and 2 * index + 1?

16.10 The Heapsort Algorithm

> The heapsort algorithm is based on inserting elements into a heap and removing them in sorted order.

Heaps are not only useful for implementing priority queues, they also give rise to an efficient sorting algorithm, heapsort. In its simplest form, the algorithm works as follows. First insert all elements to be sorted into the heap, then keep extracting the minimum.

> Heapsort is an $O(n \log(n))$ algorithm.

This algorithm is an $O(n \log(n))$ algorithm: each insertion and removal is $O(\log(n))$, and these steps are repeated n times, once for each element in the sequence that is to be sorted.

The algorithm can be made a bit more efficient. Rather than inserting the elements one at a time, we will start with a sequence of values in an array. Of course, that array does not represent a heap. We will use the procedure of "fixing the heap" that you encountered in the preceding section as part of the element removal algorithm. "Fixing the heap" operates on a binary tree whose child trees are heaps but whose root value may not be smaller than the descendants. The procedure turns the tree into a heap, by repeatedly promoting the smallest child value, moving the root value to its proper location.

Of course, we cannot simply apply this procedure to the initial sequence of unsorted values—the child trees of the root are not likely to be heaps. But we can first fix small subtrees into heaps, then fix larger trees. Because trees of size 1 are automatically heaps, we can begin the fixing procedure with the subtrees whose roots are located in the next-to-lowest level of the tree.

The sorting algorithm uses a generalized fixHeap method that fixes a subtree with a given root index:

```
void fixHeap(int rootIndex, int lastIndex)
```

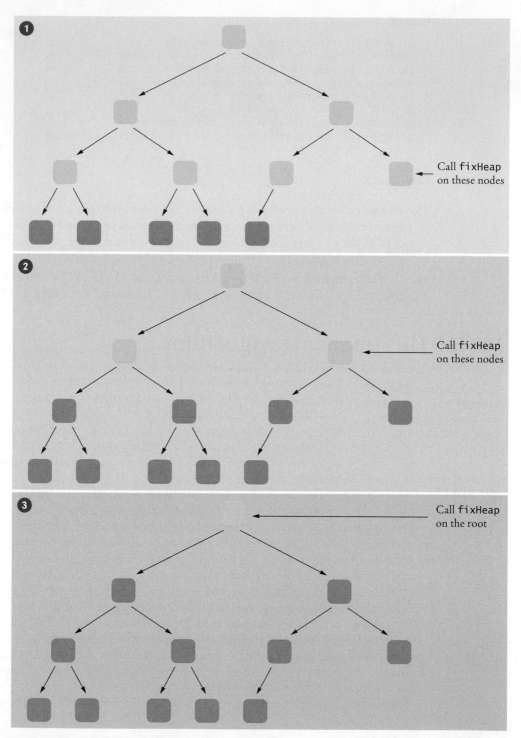

Call fixHeap
on these nodes

Call fixHeap
on these nodes

Call fixHeap
on the root

Figure 21   Turning a Tree into a Heap

Here, lastIndex is the index of the last node in the full tree. The fixHeap method needs to be invoked on all subtrees whose roots are in the next-to-last level. Then the subtrees whose roots are in the next level above are fixed, and so on. Finally, the fixup is applied to the root node, and the tree is turned into a heap (see Figure 21).

That repetition can be programmed easily. Start with the *last* node on the next-to-lowest level and work toward the left. Then go to the next higher level. The node index values then simply run backwards from the index of the last node to the index of the root.

```
int n = a.length - 1;
for (int i = (n - 1) / 2; i >= 0; i--)
    fixHeap(i, n);
```

Note that the loop ends with index 0. When working with a given array, we don't have the luxury of skipping the 0 entry. We consider the 0 entry the root and adjust the formulas for computing the child and parent index values.

After the array has been turned into a heap, we repeatedly remove the root element. Recall from the preceding section that removing the root element is achieved by placing the last element of the tree in the root and calling the fixHeap method.

Rather than moving the root element into a separate array, we will *swap* the root element with the last element of the tree and then reduce the tree length. Thus, the removed root ends up in the last position of the array, which is no longer needed by the heap. In this way, we can use the same array both to hold the heap (which gets shorter with each step) and the sorted sequence (which gets longer with each step).

There is just a minor inconvenience. When we use a min-heap, the sorted sequence is accumulated in reverse order, with the smallest element at the end of the array. We could reverse the sequence after sorting is complete. However, it is easier to use a max-heap rather than a min-heap in the heapsort algorithm. With this modification, the largest value is placed at the end of the array after the first step. After the next step, the next-largest value is swapped from the heap root to the second position from the end, and so on (see Figure 22).

The following class implements the heapsort algorithm.

Figure 22   Using Heapsort to Sort an Array

ch16/heapsort/HeapSorter.java

```java
1    /**
2        This class applies the heapsort algorithm to sort an array.
3    */
4    public class HeapSorter
5    {
6        /**
7            Constructs a heap sorter that sorts a given array.
8            @param anArray an array of integers
9        */
10       public HeapSorter(int[] anArray)
11       {
12           a = anArray;
13       }
14
15       /**
16           Sorts the array managed by this heap sorter.
17       */
18       public void sort()
19       {
20           int n = a.length - 1;
21           for (int i = (n - 1) / 2; i >= 0; i--)
22               fixHeap(i, n);
23           while (n > 0)
24           {
25               swap(0, n);
26               n--;
27               fixHeap(0, n);
28           }
29       }
30
31       /**
32           Ensures the heap property for a subtree, provided its
33           children already fulfill the heap property.
34           @param rootIndex the index of the subtree to be fixed
35           @param lastIndex the last valid index of the tree that
36           contains the subtree to be fixed
37       */
38       private void fixHeap(int rootIndex, int lastIndex)
39       {
40           // Remove root
41           int rootValue = a[rootIndex];
42
43           // Promote children while they are larger than the root
44
45           int index = rootIndex;
46           boolean more = true;
47           while (more)
48           {
49               int childIndex = getLeftChildIndex(index);
50               if (childIndex <= lastIndex)
51               {
52                   // Use right child instead if it is larger
53                   int rightChildIndex = getRightChildIndex(index);
```

```
54              if (rightChildIndex <= lastIndex
55                  && a[rightChildIndex] > a[childIndex])
56              {
57                  childIndex = rightChildIndex;
58              }
59
60              if (a[childIndex] > rootValue)
61              {
62                  // Promote child
63                  a[index] = a[childIndex];
64                  index = childIndex;
65              }
66              else
67              {
68                  // Root value is larger than both children
69                  more = false;
70              }
71          }
72          else
73          {
74              // No children
75              more = false;
76          }
77      }
78
79      // Store root value in vacant slot
80      a[index] = rootValue;
81   }
82
83   /**
84      Swaps two entries of the array.
85      @param i the first position to swap
86      @param j the second position to swap
87   */
88   private void swap(int i, int j)
89   {
90      int temp = a[i];
91      a[i] = a[j];
92      a[j] = temp;
93   }
94
95   /**
96      Returns the index of the left child.
97      @param index the index of a node in this heap
98      @return the index of the left child of the given node
99   */
100  private static int getLeftChildIndex(int index)
101  {
102     return 2 * index + 1;
103  }
104
```

```
105     /**
106         Returns the index of the right child.
107         @param index  the index of a node in this heap
108         @return  the index of the right child of the given node
109     */
110     private static int getRightChildIndex(int index)
111     {
112         return 2 * index + 2;
113     }
114
115     private int[] a;
116 }
```

SELF CHECK

17. Which algorithm requires less storage, heapsort or merge sort?

18. Why are the computations of the left child index and the right child index in the HeapSorter different than in MinHeap?

CHAPTER SUMMARY

1. A set is an unordered collection of distinct elements. Elements can be added, located, and removed.

2. Sets don't have duplicates. Adding a duplicate of an element that is already present is silently ignored.

3. The HashSet and TreeSet classes both implement the Set interface.

4. An iterator visits all elements in a set.

5. A set iterator does not visit the elements in the order in which you inserted them. The set implementation rearranges the elements so that it can locate them quickly.

6. You cannot add an element to a set at an iterator position.

7. A map keeps associations between key and value objects.

8. The HashMap and TreeMap classes both implement the Map interface.

9. To find all keys and values in a map, iterate through the key set and find the values that correspond to the keys.

10. A hash function computes an integer value from an object.

11. A good hash function minimizes *collisions*—identical hash codes for different objects.

12. A hash table can be implemented as an array of *buckets*—sequences of nodes that hold elements with the same hash code.

13. If there are no or only a few collisions, then adding, locating, and removing hash table elements takes constant or $O(1)$ time.

14. The table size should be a prime number, larger than the expected number of elements.

15. Define `hashCode` methods for your own classes by combining the hash codes for the instance variables.

16. Your `hashCode` method must be compatible with the `equals` method.

17. In a hash map, only the keys are hashed.

18. A binary tree consists of nodes, each of which has at most two child nodes.

19. All nodes in a binary search tree fulfill the property that the descendants to the left have smaller data values than the node data value, and the descendants to the right have larger data values.

20. When removing a node with only one child from a binary search tree, the child replaces the node to be removed.

21. When removing a node with two children from a binary search tree, replace it with the smallest node of the right subtree.

22. If a binary search tree is balanced, then adding an element takes $O(\log(n))$ time.

23. Tree traversal schemes include preorder traversal, inorder traversal, and post-order traversal.

24. Postorder traversal of an expression tree yields the instructions for evaluating the expression on a stack-based calculator.

25. The `TreeSet` class uses a form of balanced binary trees that guarantees that adding and removing an element takes $O(\log(n))$ time.

26. To use a tree set, the elements must be comparable.

27. When removing an element from a priority queue, the element with the highest priority is retrieved.

28. A heap is an almost complete tree in which the values of all nodes are at most as large as those of their descendants.

29. Inserting or removing a heap element is an $O(\log(n))$ operation.

30. The regular layout of a heap makes it possible to store heap nodes efficiently in an array.

31. The heapsort algorithm is based on inserting elements into a heap and removing them in sorted order.

32. Heapsort is an $O(n \log(n))$ algorithm.

CLASSES, OBJECTS, AND METHODS INTRODUCED IN THIS CHAPTER

```
java.util.Collection<E>
    contains
    remove
    size
java.util.HashMap<K, V>
java.util.HashSet<K, V>
java.util.Map<K, V>
    get
    keySet
    put
    remove
java.util.PriorityQueue<E>
    remove
java.util.Set<E>
java.util.TreeMap<K, V>
java.util.TreeSet<K, V>
```

FURTHER READING

1. Thomas H. Cormen, Charles E. Leiserson, Ronald L. Rivest, and Clifford Stein, *Introduction to Algorithms*, 2nd edition, MIT Press, 2001.

REVIEW EXERCISES

★ **Exercise R16.1.** What is the difference between a set and a map?

★ **Exercise R16.2.** What implementations does the Java library provide for the abstract set type?

★★ **Exercise R16.3.** What are the fundamental operations on the abstract set type? What additional methods does the Set interface provide? (Look up the interface in the API documentation.)

★★ **Exercise R16.4.** The union of two sets *A* and *B* is the set of all elements that are contained in *A, B,* or both. The intersection is the set of all elements that are contained in *A* and *B.* How can you compute the union and intersection of two sets, using the four fundamental set operations described on page 701?

★★ **Exercise R16.5.** How can you compute the union and intersection of two sets, using some of the methods that the java.util.Set interface provides? (Look up the interface in the API documentation.)

★ **Exercise R16.6.** Can a map have two keys with the same value? Two values with the same key?

★ **Exercise R16.7.** A map can be implemented as a set of (*key, value*) pairs. Explain.

★★ **Exercise R16.8.** When implementing a map as a hash set of (*key, value*) pairs, how is the hash code of a pair computed?

★ **Exercise R16.9.** Verify the hash codes of the strings "Jim" and "Joe" in Table 1.

★ **Exercise R16.10.** From the hash codes in Table 1, show that Figure 6 accurately shows the locations of the strings if the hash table size is 101.

★ **Exercise R16.11.** What is the difference between a binary tree and a binary search tree? Give examples of each.

★ **Exercise R16.12.** What is the difference between a balanced tree and an unbalanced tree? Give examples of each.

★ **Exercise R16.13.** The following elements are inserted into a binary search tree. Make a drawing that shows the resulting tree after each insertion.

```
Adam
Eve
Romeo
Juliet
Tom
Dick
Harry
```

★★ **Exercise R16.14.** Insert the elements of Exercise R16.13 in opposite order. Then determine how the BinarySearchTree.print method prints out both the tree from Exercise R16.13 and this tree. Explain how the printouts are related.

★★ **Exercise R16.15.** Consider the following tree. In which order are the nodes printed by the BinarySearchTree.print method?

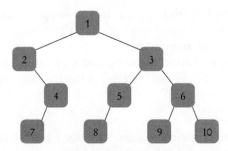

★★ **Exercise R16.16.** Could a priority queue be implemented efficiently as a binary search tree? Give a detailed argument for your answer.

★★★ **Exercise R16.17.** Will preorder, inorder, or postorder traversal print a heap in sorted order? Why or why not?

★★★   **Exercise R16.18.** Prove that a heap of height h contains at least 2^{h-1} elements but less than 2^h elements.

★★★   **Exercise R16.19.** Suppose the heap nodes are stored in an array, starting with index 1. Prove that the child nodes of the heap node with index i have index $2 \cdot i$ and $2 \cdot i + 1$, and the parent heap node of the node with index i has index $i/2$.

★★   **Exercise R16.20.** Simulate the heapsort algorithm manually to sort the array

    11 27 8 14 45 6 24 81 29 33

Show all steps.

Additional review exercises are available in WileyPLUS.

PROGRAMMING EXERCISES

★   **Exercise P16.1.** Write a program that reads text from System.in and breaks it up into individual words. Insert the words into a tree set. At the end of the input file, print all words, followed by the size of the resulting set. This program determines how many unique words a text file has.

★   **Exercise P16.2.** Insert the 13 standard colors that the Color class predefines (that is, Color.PINK, Color.GREEN, and so on) into a set. Prompt the user to enter a color by specifying red, green, and blue integer values between 0 and 255. Then tell the user whether the resulting color is in the set.

★★★   **Exercise P16.3.** Add a debug method to the HashSet implementation in Section 16.3 that prints the nonempty buckets of the hash table. Run the test program at the end of Section 16.3. Call the debug method after all additions and removals and verify that Figure 6 accurately represents the state of the hash table.

★★   **Exercise P16.4.** Write a program that keeps a map in which both keys and values are strings—the names of students and their course grades. Prompt the user of the program to add or remove students, to modify grades, or to print all grades. The printout should be sorted by name and formatted like this:

    Carl: B+
    Joe: C
    Sarah: A

★★★   **Exercise P16.5.** Reimplement Exercise P16.4 so that the keys of the map are objects of class Student. A student should have a first name, a last name, and a unique integer ID. For grade changes and removals, lookup should be by ID. The printout should be sorted by last name. If two students have the same last name, then use the first name as tie breaker. If the first names are also identical, then use the integer ID. *Hint:* Use two maps.

★★   **Exercise P16.6.** Supply compatible `hashCode` and `equals` methods to the `Student` class described in Exercise P16.5. Test the hash code by adding `Student` objects to a hash set.

  ★   **Exercise P16.7.** Supply compatible `hashCode` and `equals` methods to the `BankAccount` class of Chapter 7. Test the `hashCode` method by printing out hash codes and by adding `BankAccount` objects to a hash set.

★★   **Exercise P16.8.** Design an `IntTree` class that stores only integers, not objects. Support the same methods as the `BinarySearchTree` class in the book.

★★   **Exercise P16.9.** Design a data structure `IntSet` that can hold a set of integers. Hide the private implementation: a binary search tree of `Integer` objects. Provide the following methods:

- A constructor to make an empty set
- `void add(int x)` to add x if it is not present
- `void remove(int x)` to remove x if it is present
- `void print()` to print all elements currently in the set
- `boolean find(int x)` to test whether x is present

★★   **Exercise P16.10.** Reimplement the set class from Exercise P16.9 by using a `TreeSet<Integer>`. In addition to the methods specified in Exercise P16.9, supply an `iterator` method yielding an object that supports *only* the `hasNext`/`next` methods.

The `next` method should return an `int`, not an object. For that reason, you cannot simply return the iterator of the tree set.

  ★   **Exercise P16.11.** Reimplement the set class from Exercise P16.9 by using a `TreeSet<Integer>`. In addition to the methods specified in Exercise P16.9, supply methods

```
IntSet union(IntSet other)
IntSet intersection(IntSet other)
```

that compute the union and intersection of two sets.

★★   **Exercise P16.12.** Implement the *sieve of Eratosthenes:* a method for computing prime numbers, known to the ancient Greeks. Choose an n. This method will compute all prime numbers up to n. First insert all numbers from 2 to n into a set. Then erase all multiples of 2 (except 2); that is, 4, 6, 8, 10, 12, ... Erase all multiples of 3; that is, 6, 9, 12, 15, ... Go up to $\sqrt{n}$. Then print the set.

  ★   **Exercise P16.13.** Write a method of the `BinarySearchTree` class

```
Comparable smallest()
```

that returns the smallest element of a tree. You will also need to add a method to the `Node` class.

★★★   **Exercise P16.14.** Change the `BinarySearchTree.print` method to print the tree as a tree shape. You can print the tree sideways. Extra credit if you instead display the tree with the root node centered on the top.

★   **Exercise P16.15.** Implement methods that use preorder and postorder traversal to print the elements in a binary search tree.

★★★   **Exercise P16.16.** In the `BinarySearchTree` class, modify the `remove` method so that a node with two children is replaced by the largest child of the left subtree.

★★   **Exercise P16.17.** Suppose an interface `Visitor` has a single method

```
void visit(Object obj)
```

Supply methods

```
void inOrder(Visitor v)
void preOrder(Visitor v)
void postOrder(Visitor v)
```

to the `BinarySearchTree` class. These methods should visit the tree nodes in the specified traversal order and apply the `visit` method to the data of the visited node.

★★   **Exercise P16.18.** Apply Exercise P16.17 to compute the average value of the elements in a binary search tree filled with `Integer` objects. That is, supply an object of an appropriate class that implements the `Visitor` interface.

★★   **Exercise P16.19.** Modify the implementation of the `MinHeap` class so that the parent and child index positions and elements are computed directly, without calling helper methods.

★★★   **Exercise P16.20.** Modify the implementation of the `MinHeap` class so that the 0 element of the array is not wasted.

★   **Exercise P16.21.** Time the results of heapsort and merge sort. Which algorithm behaves better in practice?

Additional programming exercises are available in WileyPLUS.

PROGRAMMING PROJECTS

★★★   **Project 16.1.** Implement a `BinaryTreeSet` class that uses a `TreeSet` to store its elements. You will need to implement an iterator that iterates through the nodes in sorted order. This iterator is somewhat complex, because sometimes you need to backtrack. You can either add a reference to the parent node in each `Node` object, or have your iterator object store a stack of the visited nodes.

★★★   **Project 16.2.** Implement an expression evaluator that uses a parser to build an expression tree, such as in Section 16.6. (Note that the resulting tree is a binary tree but not a binary search tree.) Then use postorder traversal to evaluate the expression, using a stack for the intermediate results.

★★★   **Project 16.3.** Program an animation of the heapsort algorithm, displaying the tree graphically and stopping after each call to `fixHeap`.

ANSWERS TO SELF-CHECK QUESTIONS

1. Efficient set implementations can quickly test whether a given element is a member of the set.

2. Sets do not have an ordering, so it doesn't make sense to add an element at a particular iterator position, or to traverse a set backwards.

3. A set stores elements. A map stores associations between keys and values.

4. The ordering does not matter, and you cannot have duplicates.

5. Yes, the hash set will work correctly. All elements will be inserted into a single bucket.

6. It locates the next bucket in the bucket array and points to its first element.

7. $31 \times 116 + 111 = 3707$.

8. 13.

9. In a tree, each node can have any number of children. In a binary tree, a node has at most two children. In a balanced binary tree, all nodes have approximately as many descendants to the left as to the right.

10. For example, Sarah. Any string between Romeo and Tom will do.

11. For both trees, the inorder traversal is 3 + 4 * 5.

12. No—for example, consider the children of +. Even without looking up the Unicode codes for 3, 4, and +, it is obvious that + isn't between 3 and 4.

13. When it is desirable to visit the set elements in sorted order.

14. No—it would never be able to tell two coins apart. Thus, it would think that all coins are duplicates of the first.

15. A priority queue is appropriate because we want to get the important events first, even if they have been inserted later.

16. Yes, but a binary search tree isn't almost filled, so there may be holes in the array. We could indicate the missing nodes with null elements.

17. Heapsort requires less storage because it doesn't need an auxiliary array.

18. The MinHeap wastes the 0 entry to make the formulas more intuitive. When sorting an array, we don't want to waste the 0 entry, so we adjust the formulas instead.

Java Language Coding Guidelines

Introduction

This coding style guide is a simplified version of one that has been used with good success both in industrial practice and for college courses.

A style guide is a set of mandatory requirements for layout and formatting. Uniform style makes it easier for you to read code from your instructor and classmates. You will really appreciate that if you do a team project. It is also easier for your instructor and your grader to grasp the essence of your programs quickly.

A style guide makes you a more productive programmer because it *reduces gratuitous choice*. If you don't have to make choices about trivial matters, you can spend your energy on the solution of real problems.

In these guidelines, several constructs are plainly outlawed. That doesn't mean that programmers using them are evil or incompetent. It does mean that the constructs are not essential and can be expressed just as well or even better with other language constructs.

If you already have programming experience, in Java or another language, you may be initially uncomfortable at giving up some fond habits. However, it is a sign of professionalism to set aside personal preferences in minor matters and to compromise for the benefit of your group.

These guidelines are necessarily somewhat dull. They also mention features that you may not yet have seen in class. Here are the most important highlights:

- Tabs are set every three spaces.
- Variable and method names are lowercase, with occasional upperCase characters in the middle.
- Class names start with an Uppercase letter.
- Constant names are UPPERCASE, with an occasional UNDER_SCORE.
- There are spaces after keywords and surrounding binary operators.
- Braces must line up horizontally or vertically.
- No magic numbers may be used.
- Every method, except for `main` and overridden library methods, must have a comment.
- At most 30 lines of code may be used per method.
- No `continue` or `break` is allowed.
- All non-`final` variables must be private.

Note to the instructor: Of course, many programmers and organizations have strong feelings about coding style. If this style guide is incompatible with your own preferences or with local custom, please feel free to modify it. For that purpose, this coding style guide is available in electronic form in the WileyPLUS course, or from the companion web site for this book at `http://www.wiley.com/college/horstmann`.

Source Files

Each Java program is a collection of one or more source files. The executable program is obtained by compiling these files. Organize the material in each file as follows:

- `package` statement, if appropriate
- `import` statements
- A comment explaining the purpose of this file
- A `public` class
- Other classes, if appropriate

The comment explaining the purpose of this file should be in the format recognized by the `javadoc` utility. Start with a `/**`, and use the `@author` and `@version` tags:

```
/**
   COPYRIGHT (C) 2007 Harry Hacker. All Rights Reserved.
   Classes to manipulate widgets.
   Solves CS101 homework assignment #3
   @author  Harry Hacker
   @version  1.01 2007-02-15
*/
```

Classes

Each class should be preceded by a class comment explaining the purpose of the class.

First list all public features, then all private features.

Within the public and private sections, use the following order:

1. Constructors
2. Instance methods
3. Static methods
4. Instance fields
5. Static fields
6. Inner classes

Leave a blank line after every method.

All non-`final` variables must be private. (However, instance variables of a private inner class may be public.) Methods and final variables can be either public or private, as appropriate.

All features must be tagged `public` or `private`. Do not use the default visibility (that is, package visibility) or the `protected` attribute.

Avoid static variables (except `final` ones) whenever possible. In the rare instance that you need static variables, you are permitted one static variable per class.

Methods

Every method (except for `main`) starts with a comment in `javadoc` format.

```
/**
    Convert calendar date into Julian day.
    Note: This algorithm is from Press et al., Numerical Recipes
    in C, 2nd ed., Cambridge University Press, 1992.
    @param day  day of the date to be converted
    @param month  month of the date to be converted
    @param year  year of the date to be converted
    @return  the Julian day number that begins at noon of the
    given calendar date.
*/
public static int getJulianDayNumber(int day, int month, int year)
{
    . . .
}
```

Parameter names must be explicit, especially if they are integers or Boolean:

```
public Employee remove(int d, double s)
    // Huh?
public Employee remove(int department, double severancePay)
    // OK
```

Methods must have at most 30 lines of code. The method signature, comments, blank lines, and lines containing only braces are not included in this count. This rule forces you to break up complex computations into separate methods.

Variables and Constants

Do not define all variables at the beginning of a block:

```
{
   double xold; // Don't
   double xnew;
   boolean more;
   . . .
}
```

Define each variable just before it is used for the first time:

```
{
   . . .
   double xold = Integer.parseInt(input);
   boolean more = false;
   while (more)
   {
      double xnew = (xold + a / xold) / 2;
      . . .
   }
   . . .
}
```

Do not define two variables on the same line:

```
int dimes = 0, nickels = 0; // Don't
```

Instead, use two separate definitions:

```
int dimes = 0; // OK
int nickels = 0;
```

In Java, constants must be defined with the keyword `final`. If the constant is used by multiple methods, declare it as `static final`. It is a good idea to define static final variables as `private` if no other class has an interest in them.

Do not use *magic numbers!* A magic number is a numeric constant embedded in code, without a constant definition. Any number except −1, 0, 1, and 2 is considered magic:

```
if (p.getX() < 300) // Don't
```

Use `final` variables instead:

```
final double WINDOW_WIDTH = 300;
. . .
if (p.getX() < WINDOW_WIDTH) // OK
```

Even the most reasonable cosmic constant is going to change one day. You think there are 365 days per year? Your customers on Mars are going to be pretty unhappy about your silly prejudice. Make a constant

```
public static final int DAYS_PER_YEAR = 365;
```

so that you can easily produce a Martian version without trying to find all the 365s, 364s, 366s, 367s, and so on, in your code.

When declaring array variables, group the [ ] with the type, not the variable.

```
int[] values; // OK
int values[]; // Ugh—this is an ugly holdover from C
```

When using collections, use type parameters and not "raw" types.

```
ArrayList<String> names = new ArrayList<String>(); // OK
ArrayList names = new ArrayList(); // Not OK
```

Control Flow

The if Statement

Avoid the "if . . . if . . . else" trap. The code

```
if ( . . . )
    if ( . . . ) . . .;
else . . .;
```

will not do what the indentation level suggests, and it can take hours to find such a bug. Always use an extra pair of { . . . } when dealing with "if . . . if . . . else":

```
if ( . . . )
{
    if ( . . . ) . . .;
} // { . . . } are necessary
else . . .;

if ( . . . )
{
    if ( . . . ) . . .;
    else . . .;
} // { . . . } not necessary, but they keep you out of trouble
```

The for Statement

Use for loops only when a variable runs from somewhere to somewhere with some constant increment/decrement:

```
for (int i = 0; i < a.length; i++)
    System.out.println(a[i]);
```

Or, even better, use the "for each" loop:

```
for (int e : a)
    System.out.println(e);
```

Do not use the for loop for weird constructs such as

```
for (a = a / 2; count < ITERATIONS; System.out.println(xnew))
    // Don't
```

Make such a loop into a `while` loop. That way, the sequence of instructions is much clearer.

```
a = a / 2;
while (count < ITERATIONS) // OK
{
    . . .
    System.out.println(xnew);
}
```

Nonlinear Control Flow

Avoid the `switch` statement, because it is easy to fall through accidentally to an unwanted case. Use `if/else` instead.

Avoid the `break` or `continue` statements. Use another `boolean` variable to control the execution flow.

Exceptions

Do not tag a method with an overly general exception specification:

```
Widget readWidget(Reader in) throws Exception // Bad
```

Instead, specifically declare any checked exceptions that your method may throw:

```
Widget readWidget(Reader in)
        throws IOException, MalformedWidgetException // Good
```

Do not "squelch" exceptions:

```
try
{
    double price = in.readDouble();
}
catch (Exception e)
{ } // Bad
```

Beginners often make this mistake "to keep the compiler happy". If the current method is not appropriate for handling the exception, simply use a `throws` specification and let one of its callers handle it.

Lexical Issues

Naming Conventions

The following rules specify when to use upper- and lowercase letters in identifier names.

- All variable and method names and all data fields of classes are in lowercase (maybe with an occasional upperCase in the middle); for example, `firstPlayer`.
- All constants are in uppercase (maybe with an occasional UNDER_SCORE); for example, `CLOCK_RADIUS`.

- All class and interface names start with uppercase and are followed by lowercase letters (maybe with an occasional UpperCase letter); for example, `BankTeller`.
- Generic type variables are in uppercase, usually a single letter.

Names must be reasonably long and descriptive. Use `firstPlayer` instead of `fp`. No drppng f vwls. Local variables that are fairly routine can be short (`ch`, `i`) as long as they are really just boring holders for an input character, a loop counter, and so on. Also, do not use `ctr`, `c`, `cntr`, `cnt`, `c2` for variables in your method. Surely these variables all have specific purposes and can be named to remind the reader of them (for example, `current`, `next`, `previous`, `result`, ...). However, it is customary to use single-letter names, such as `T` or `E` for generic types.

Indentation and White Space

Use tab stops every three columns. That means you will need to change the tab stop setting in your editor!

Use blank lines freely to separate parts of a method that are logically distinct.

Use a blank space around every binary operator:

```
x1 = (-b - Math.sqrt(b * b - 4 * a * c)) / (2 * a);
// Good

x1=(-b-Math.sqrt(b*b-4*a*c))/(2*a);
// Bad
```

Leave a blank space after (and not before) each comma or semicolon. Do not leave a space before or after a parenthesis or bracket in an expression. Leave spaces around the (. . .) part of an `if`, `while`, `for`, or `catch` statement.

```
if (x == 0) y - 0;

f(a, b[i]);
```

Every line must fit in 80 columns. If you must break a statement, add an indentation level for the continuation:

```
a[n] = .............................................
       + .................;
```

Start the indented line with an operator (if possible).

If the condition in an `if` or `while` statement must be broken, be sure to brace the body in, even if it consists of only one statement:

```
if ( ..................................................
      && ..................
      || .......... )
{
   . . .
}
```

If it weren't for the braces, it would be hard to separate the continuation of the condition visually from the statement to be executed.

Braces

Opening and closing braces must line up, either horizontally or vertically:

```
while (i < n) { System.out.println(a[i]); i++; }

while (i < n)
{
   System.out.println(a[i]);
   i++;
}
```

Some programmers don't line up vertical braces but place the { behind the keyword:

```
while (i < n) { // DON'T
   System.out.println(a[i]);
   i++;
}
```

Doing so makes it hard to check that the braces match.

Unstable Layout

Some programmers take great pride in lining up certain columns in their code:

```
firstRecord = other.firstRecord;
lastRecord  = other.lastRecord;
cutoff      = other.cutoff;
```

This is undeniably neat, but the layout is not stable under change. A new variable name that is longer than the preallotted number of columns requires that you move all entries around:

```
firstRecord = other.firstRecord;
lastRecord  = other.lastRecord;
cutoff      = other.cutoff;
marginalFudgeFactor = other.marginalFudgeFactor;
```

This is just the kind of trap that makes you decide to use a short variable name like mff instead. Use a simple layout that is easy to maintain as your programs change.

The Basic Latin and Latin-1 Subsets of Unicode

This appendix lists the Unicode characters that are most commonly used for processing Western European languages. A complete listing of Unicode characters can be found at http://unicode.org.

Table 1 Selected Control Characters			
Character	**Code**	**Decimal**	**Escape Sequence**
Tab	'\u0009'	9	'\t'
Newline	'\u000A'	10	'\n'
Return	'\u000D'	13	'\r'
Space	'\u0020'	32	

Table 2 The Basic Latin (ASCII) Subset of Unicode

Char.	Code	Dec.	Char.	Code	Dec.	Char.	Code	Dec.
			@	'\u0040'	64	`	'\u0060'	96
!	'\u0021'	33	A	'\u0041'	65	a	'\u0061'	97
"	'\u0022'	34	B	'\u0042'	66	b	'\u0062'	98
#	'\u0023'	35	C	'\u0043'	67	c	'\u0063'	99
$	'\u0024'	36	D	'\u0044'	68	d	'\u0064'	100
%	'\u0025'	37	E	'\u0045'	69	e	'\u0065'	101
&	'\u0026'	38	F	'\u0046'	70	f	'\u0066'	102
'	'\u0027'	39	G	'\u0047'	71	g	'\u0067'	103
(	'\u0028'	40	H	'\u0048'	72	h	'\u0068'	104
)	'\u0029'	41	I	'\u0049'	73	i	'\u0069'	105
*	'\u002A'	42	J	'\u004A'	74	j	'\u006A'	106
+	'\u002B'	43	K	'\u004B'	75	k	'\u006B'	107
,	'\u002C'	44	L	'\u004C'	76	l	'\u006C'	108
-	'\u002D'	45	M	'\u004D'	77	m	'\u006D'	109
.	'\u002E'	46	N	'\u004E'	78	n	'\u006E'	110
/	'\u002F'	47	O	'\u004F'	79	o	'\u006F'	111
0	'\u0030'	48	P	'\u0050'	80	p	'\u0070'	112
1	'\u0031'	49	Q	'\u0051'	81	q	'\u0071'	113
2	'\u0032'	50	R	'\u0052'	82	r	'\u0072'	114
3	'\u0033'	51	S	'\u0053'	83	s	'\u0073'	115
4	'\u0034'	52	T	'\u0054'	84	t	'\u0074'	116
5	'\u0035'	53	U	'\u0055'	85	u	'\u0075'	117
6	'\u0036'	54	V	'\u0056'	86	v	'\u0076'	118
7	'\u0037'	55	W	'\u0057'	87	w	'\u0077'	119
8	'\u0038'	56	X	'\u0058'	88	x	'\u0078'	120
9	'\u0039'	57	Y	'\u0059'	89	y	'\u0079'	121
:	'\u003A'	58	Z	'\u005A'	90	z	'\u007A'	122
;	'\u003B'	59	[	'\u005B'	91	{	'\u007B'	123
<	'\u003C'	60	\	'\u005C'	92	|	'\u007C'	124
=	'\u003D'	61	]	'\u005D'	93	}	'\u007D'	125
>	'\u003E'	62	^	'\u005E'	94	~	'\u007E'	126
?	'\u003F'	63	_	'\u005F'	95			

Table 3   The Latin-1 Subset of Unicode

Char.	Code	Dec.	Char.	Code	Dec.	Char.	Code	Dec.
			À	'\u00C0'	192	à	'\u00E0'	224
¡	'\u00A1'	161	Á	'\u00C1'	193	á	'\u00E1'	225
¢	'\u00A2'	162	Â	'\u00C2'	194	â	'\u00E2'	226
£	'\u00A3'	163	Ã	'\u00C3'	195	ã	'\u00E3'	227
¤	'\u00A4'	164	Ä	'\u00C4'	196	ä	'\u00E4'	228
¥	'\u00A5'	165	Å	'\u00C5'	197	å	'\u00E5'	229
¦	'\u00A6'	166	Æ	'\u00C6'	198	æ	'\u00E6'	230
§	'\u00A7'	167	Ç	'\u00C7'	199	ç	'\u00E7'	231
¨	'\u00A8'	168	È	'\u00C8'	200	è	'\u00E8'	232
©	'\u00A9'	169	É	'\u00C9'	201	é	'\u00E9'	233
ª	'\u00AA'	170	Ê	'\u00CA'	202	ê	'\u00EA'	234
«	'\u00AB'	171	Ë	'\u00CB'	203	ë	'\u00EB'	235
¬	'\u00AC'	172	Ì	'\u00CC'	204	ì	'\u00EC'	236
	'\u00AD'	173	Í	'\u00CD'	205	í	'\u00ED'	237
®	'\u00AE'	174	Î	'\u00CE'	206	î	'\u00EE'	238
¯	'\u00AF'	175	Ï	'\u00CF'	207	ï	'\u00EF'	239
°	'\u00B0'	176	Ð	'\u00D0'	208	ð	'\u00F0'	240
±	'\u00B1'	177	Ñ	'\u00D1'	209	ñ	'\u00F1'	241
²	'\u00B2'	178	Ò	'\u00D2'	210	ò	'\u00F2'	242
³	'\u00B3'	179	Ó	'\u00D3'	211	ó	'\u00F3'	243
´	'\u00B4'	180	Ô	'\u00D4'	212	ô	'\u00F4'	244
µ	'\u00B5'	181	Õ	'\u00D5'	213	õ	'\u00F5'	245
¶	'\u00B6'	182	Ö	'\u00D6'	214	ö	'\u00F6'	246
·	'\u00B7'	183	×	'\u00D7'	215	÷	'\u00F7'	247
¸	'\u00B8'	184	Ø	'\u00D8'	216	ø	'\u00F8'	248
¹	'\u00B9'	185	Ù	'\u00D9'	217	ù	'\u00F9'	249
º	'\u00BA'	186	Ú	'\u00DA'	218	ú	'\u00FA'	250
»	'\u00BB'	187	Û	'\u00DB'	219	û	'\u00FB'	251
¼	'\u00BC'	188	Ü	'\u00DC'	220	ü	'\u00FC'	252
½	'\u00BD'	189	Ý	'\u00DD'	221	ý	'\u00FD'	253
¾	'\u00BE'	190	Þ	'\u00DE'	222	þ	'\u00FE'	254
¿	'\u00BF'	191	ß	'\u00DF'	223	ÿ	'\u00FF'	255

The Java Library

This appendix lists all classes and methods from the standard Java library that are used in this book.

In the following inheritance hierarchy, superclasses that are not used in this book are shown in parentheses. Some classes implement interfaces not covered in this book; they are omitted. Classes are sorted first by package, then alphabetically within a package. Interfaces are in italics.

```
java.awt.Shape
java.lang.Cloneable
java.lang.Object
   java.awt.Color
   java.awt.Component
      java.awt.Container
         javax.swing.JComponent
            javax.swing.AbstractButton
               javax.swing.JButton
            javax.swing.JFileChooser
            javax.swing.JLabel
            javax.swing.JPanel
            javax.swing.JOptionPane
            javax.swing.text.JTextComponent
               javax.swing.JTextArea
               javax.swing.JTextField
         (java.awt.Panel)
            java.applet.Applet
               javax.swing.JApplet
      (java.awt.Window)
         java.awt.Frame
            javax.swing.JFrame
   (java.awt.Dimension2D)
      java.awt.Dimension implements Cloneable
```

```
java.awt.Graphics
   java.awt.Graphics2D
java.awt.event.MouseAdapter implements MouseListener
java.awt.geom.Line2D implements Cloneable, Shape
   java.awt.geom.Line2D.Double
java.awt.geom.Point2D implements Cloneable
   java.awt.geom.Point2D.Double
java.awt.geom.RectangularShape implements Cloneable, Shape
  (java.awt.geom.Rectangle2D)
      java.awt.Rectangle
   java.awt.geom.Ellipse2D
      java.awt.geom.Ellipse2D.Double
java.io.File implements Comparable
java.io.OutputStream
  (java.io.FilterOutputStream)
      java.io.PrintStream
java.io.Reader
  (java.io.InputStreamReader)
      java.io.FileReader
java.io.Writer
   java.io.PrintWriter
java.lang.Boolean
java.lang.Character implements Comparable
java.lang.Math
(java.lang.Number)
   java.math.BigDecimal implements Comparable
   java.math.BigInteger implements Comparable
   java.lang.Double implements Comparable
   java.lang.Integer implements Comparable
java.lang.String implements Comparable
java.lang.System
java.lang.Throwable
   java.lang.Error
   java.lang.Exception
      java.lang.CloneNotSupportedException
      java.io.IOException
         java.io.EOFException
         java.io.FileNotFoundException
      java.lang.RuntimeException
         java.lang.IllegalArgumentException
            java.lang.NumberFormatException
         java.lang.IllegalStateException
         java.util.NoSuchElementException
            java.util.InputMismatchException
         java.lang.NullPointerException
(java.util.AbstractCollection<E>)
   java.util.AbstractList<E>
     (java.util.AbstractSequentialList<E>)
         java.util.LinkedList<E> implements Cloneable, List<E>
      java.util.ArrayList<E> implements Cloneable, List<E>
   (java.util.AbstractQueue<E>)
      java.util.PriorityQueue<E>
   (java.util.AbstractSet<E>)
      java.util.HashSet<E> implements Cloneable, Set<E>
      java.util.TreeSet<E> implements Cloneable, SortedSet<E>
(java.util.AbstractMap<K, V>)
   java.util.HashMap<K, V> implements Cloneable, Map<K, V>
   java.util.TreeMap<K, V> implements Cloneable, Map<K, V>
```

Package java.applet

```
            java.util.Arrays
            java.util.Collections
            java.util.Calendar
               java.util.GregorianCalendar
            java.util.EventObject
              (java.awt.AWTEvent)
                    java.awt.event.ActionEvent
                  (java.awt.event.ComponentEvent)
                     (java.awt.event.InputEvent)
                         java.awt.event.MouseEvent
            java.util.Random
            java.util.Scanner
            java.util.logging.Level
            java.util.logging.Logger
            javax.swing.Timer
       java.lang.Comparable<T>
       java.util.Collection<E>
          java.util.List<E>
          java.util.Set<E>
              java.util.SortedSet<E>
       java.util.Comparator<T>
      (java.util.EventListener)
          java.awt.event.ActionListener
          java.awt.event.MouseListener
       java.util.Iterator<E>
          java.util.ListIterator<E>
       java.util.Map<K, V>
```

In the following descriptions, the phrase "this object" ("this component", "this container", and so forth) means the object (component, container, and so forth) on which the method is invoked (the implicit parameter, this).

Package java.applet

Class java.applet.Applet

- void **destroy**()
  This method is called when the applet is about to be terminated, after the last call to stop.

- void **init**()
  This method is called when the applet has been loaded, before the first call to start. Applets override this method to carry out applet-specific initialization and to read applet parameters.

- void **start**()
  This method is called after the init method and each time the applet is revisited.

- void **stop**()
  This method is called whenever the user has stopped watching this applet.

Package java.awt

Class java.awt.Color

- `Color(int red, int green, int blue)`
  This creates a color with the specified red, green, and blue values between 0 and 255.
  Parameters: red The red component
  green The green component
  blue The blue component

Class java.awt.Component

- `void addMouseListener(MouseListener listener)`
  This method adds a mouse listener to the component.
  Parameters: listener The mouse listener to be added
- `int getHeight()`
  This method gets the height of this component.
  Returns: The height in pixels.
- `int getWidth()`
  This method gets the width of this component.
  Returns: The width in pixels.
- `void repaint()`
  This method repaints this component by scheduling a call to the paint method.
- `void setPreferredSize(Dimension preferredSize)`
  This method sets the preferred size of this component.
- `void setSize(int width, int height)`
  This method sets the size of this component.
  Parameters: width the component width
  height the component height
- `void setVisible(boolean visible)`
  This method shows or hides the component.
  Parameters: visible true to show the component, or false to hide it

Class java.awt.Container

- `void add(Component c)`
- `void add(Component c, Object position)`
  These methods add a component to the end of this container. If a position is given, the layout manager is called to position the component.
  Parameters: c The component to be added
  position An object expressing position information for the layout manager

Class java.awt.Dimension

- Dimension(int width, int height)

This constructs a Dimension object with the given width and height.

Parameters: width The width

height The height

Class java.awt.Frame

- void setTitle(String title)

This method sets the frame title.

Parameters: title The title to be displayed in the border of the frame

Class java.awt.Graphics

- void setColor(Color c)

This method sets the current color. From now on, all graphics operations use this color.

Parameters: c The new drawing color

Class java.awt.Graphics2D

- void draw(Shape s)

This method draws the outline of the given shape. Many classes—among them Rectangle and Line2D.Double—implement the Shape interface.

Parameters: s The shape to be drawn

- void drawString(String s, int x, int y)
- void drawString(String s, float x, float y)

These methods draw a string in the current font.

Parameters: s The string to draw

x, y The basepoint of the first character in the string

- void fill(Shape s)

This method draws the given shape and fills it with the current color.

Parameters: s The shape to be filled

Class java.awt.Rectangle

- Rectangle()

This constructs a rectangle whose top left corner is at (0, 0) and whose width and height are both zero.

- Rectangle(int x, int y, int width, int height)

This constructs a rectangle with given top-left corner and size.

Parameters: x,y The top-left corner

width The width

height The height

- double getHeight()
- double getWidth()

These methods get the height and width of the rectangle.

- double **getX**()
- double **getY**()
  These methods get the *x*- and *y*-coordinates of the top-left corner of the rectangle.
- Rectangle **intersection**(Rectangle other)
  This method computes the intersection of this rectangle with the specified rectangle.
  Parameters: other A rectangle
  Returns: The largest rectangle contained in both this and other
- void **setLocation**(int x, int y)
  This method moves this rectangle to a new location.
  Parameters: x,y The new top-left corner
- void **translate**(int dx, int dy)
  This method moves this rectangle.
  Parameters: dx The distance to move along the *x*-axis
                  dy The distance to move along the *y*-axis
- Rectangle **union**(Rectangle other)
  This method computes the union of this rectangle with the specified rectangle. This is not the set-theoretic union but the smallest rectangle that contains both this and other.
  Parameters: other A rectangle
  Returns: The smallest rectangle containing both this and other

Interface java.awt.Shape

The Shape interface describes shapes that can be drawn and filled by a Graphics2D object.

Package java.awt.event

Interface java.awt.event.ActionListener

- void **actionPerformed**(ActionEvent e)
  The event source calls this method when an action occurs.

Class java.awt.event.MouseEvent

- int **getX**()
  This method returns the horizontal position of the mouse as of the time the event occurred.
  Returns: The *x*-position of the mouse
- int **getY**()
  This method returns the vertical position of the mouse as of the time the event occurred.
  Returns: The *y*-position of the mouse

Interface java.awt.event.MouseListener

- void **mouseClicked**(MouseEvent e)

  This method is called when the mouse has been clicked (that is, pressed and released in quick succession).

- void **mouseEntered**(MouseEvent e)

  This method is called when the mouse has entered the component to which this listener was added.

- void **mouseExited**(MouseEvent e)

  This method is called when the mouse has exited the component to which this listener was added.

- void **mousePressed**(MouseEvent e)

  This method is called when a mouse button has been pressed.

- void **mouseReleased**(MouseEvent e)

  This method is called when a mouse button has been released.

Package java.awt.geom

Class java.awt.geom.Ellipse2D.Double

- Ellipse2D.Double(double x, double y, double w, double h)

  This constructs an ellipse from the specified coordinates.

  Parameters: x, y The top-left corner of the bounding rectangle

              w The width of the bounding rectangle

              h The height of the bounding rectangle

Class java.awt.geom.Line2D

- double **getX1**()
- double **getX2**()
- double **getY1**()
- double **getY2**()

  These methods get the requested coordinate of an endpoint of this line.

  Returns: The *x*- or *y*-coordinate of the first or second endpoint

- void **setLine**(double x1, double y1, double x2, double y2)

  This methods sets the endpoints of this line.

  Parameters: x1, y1 A new endpoint of this line

              x2, y2 The other new endpoint

Class java.awt.geom.Line2D.Double

- **Line2D.Double**(double x1, double y1, double x2, double y2)
  This constructs a line from the specified coordinates.
  Parameters: x1, y1 One endpoint of the line
  x2, y2 The other endpoint
- **Line2D.Double**(Point2D p1, Point2D p2)
  This constructs a line from the two endpoints.
  Parameters: p1, p2 The endpoints of the line

Class java.awt.geom.Point2D

- double **getX**()
- double **getY**()
  These methods get the requested coordinates of this point.
  Returns: The *x*- or *y*-coordinate of this point
- void **setLocation**(double x, double y)
  This method sets the *x*- and *y*-coordinates of this point.
  Parameters: x, y The new location of this point

Class java.awt.geom.Point2D.Double

- **Point2D.Double**(double x, double y)
  This constructs a point with the specified coordinates.
  Parameters: x, y The coordinates of the point

Class java.awt.geom.RectangularShape

- int **getHeight**()
- int **getWidth**()
  These methods get the height or width of the bounding rectangle of this rectangular shape.
  Returns: The height or width, respectively
- double **getCenterX**()
- double **getCenterY**()
- double **getMaxX**()
- double **getMaxY**()
- double **getMinX**()
- double **getMinY**()
  These methods get the requested coordinate value of the corners or center of the bounding rectangle of this shape.
  Returns: The center, maximum, or minimum *x*- and *y*-coordinates

Package java.io

Class java.io.EOFException

- `EOFException(String message)`
  This constructs an "end of file" exception object.
  Parameters: `message` The detail message

Class java.io.File

- `File(String name)`
  This constructs a File object that describes a file (which may or may not exist) with the given name.
  Parameters: `name` The name of the file
- `boolean exists()`
  This method checks whether there is a file in the local file system that matches this `File` object.
  Returns: `true` if there is a matching file, `false` otherwise

Class java.io.FileNotFoundException

This exception is thrown when a file could not be opened.

Class java.io.FileReader

- `FileReader(File f)`
  This constructs a file reader and opens the chosen file. If the file cannot be opened for reading, a `FileNotFoundException` is thrown.
  Parameters: `f` The file to be opened for reading
- `FileReader(String name)`
  This constructs a file reader and opens the named file. If the file cannot be opened for reading, a `FileNotFoundException` is thrown.
  Parameters: `name` The name of the file to be opened for reading

Class java.io.InputStreamReader

- `InputStreamReader(InputStream in)`
  This constructs a reader from a specified input stream.
  Parameters: `in` The stream to read from

Class java.io.IOException

This type of exception is thrown when an input/output error is encountered.

Class java.io.PrintStream

- `void print(int x)`
- `void print(double x)`

- void **print**(Object x)
- void **print**(String x)
- void **println**()
- void **println**(int x)
- void **println**(double x)
- void **println**(Object x)
- void **println**(String x)

These methods print a value to this print stream. The println methods print a newline after the value. Objects are printed by converting them to strings with their toString methods.

Parameters: x   The value to be printed

- PrintStream **printf**(Sting format, Object... values)

This method prints the format string, substituting the given values for placeholders that start with %.

Parameters: format   The format string

values   The values to be printed. You can supply any number of values

Returns: The implicit parameter

Class java.io.PrintWriter

- **PrintWriter**(String name)

This constructs a print writer and opens the named file. If the file cannot be opened for writing, a FileNotFoundException is thrown.

Parameters: name   The name of the file to be opened for writing

- **PrintWriter**(Writer out)

This constructs a print writer from a specified writer (such as a FileWriter).

Parameters: out   The writer to write output to

- void **close**()

This method closes this writer and releases any associated system resources.

- void **print**(int x)
- void **print**(double x)
- void **print**(Object x)
- void **print**(String x)
- void **println**()
- void **println**(int x)
- void **println**(double x)
- void **println**(Object x)
- void **println**(String x)

These methods print a value to this print writer. The println methods print a newline after the value. Objects are printed by converting them to strings with their toString methods.

Parameters: x   The value to be printed

Package java.lang

Class java.lang.Boolean

- **Boolean**(boolean value)
  This constructs a wrapper object for a boolean value.
  Parameters: value The value to store in this object
- boolean **booleanValue**()
  This method returns the boolean value stored in this Boolean object.
  Returns: The Boolean value of this object

Class java.lang.Character

- static boolean **isDigit**(ch)
  This method tests whether a given character is a Unicode digit.
  Parameters: ch The character to test
  Returns: true if the character is a digit
- static boolean **isLetter**(ch)
  This method tests whether a given character is a Unicode letter.
  Parameters: ch The character to test
  Returns: true if the character is a letter
- static boolean **isLowerCase**(ch)
  This method tests whether a given character is a lowercase Unicode letter.
  Parameters: ch The character to test
  Returns: true if the character is a lowercase letter
- static boolean **isUpperCase**(ch)
  This method tests whether a given character is an uppercase Unicode letter.
  Parameters: ch The character to test
  Returns: true if the character is an uppercase letter

Interface java.lang.Cloneable

A class implements this interface to indicate that the Object.clone method is allowed to make a shallow copy of its instance variables.

Class java.lang.CloneNotSupportedException

This exception is thrown when a program tries to use Object.clone to make a shallow copy of an object of a class that does not implement the Cloneable interface.

Interface java.lang.Comparable<T>

- int **compareTo**(T other)
  This method compares this object with the other object.
  Parameters: other The object to be compared
  Returns: A negative integer if this object is less than the other, zero if they are equal, or a positive integer otherwise

Class java.lang.Double

- **Double**(double value)
  This constructs a wrapper object for a double-precision floating-point number.
  Parameters: value   The value to store in this object
- double **doubleValue**()
  This method returns the floating-point value stored in this Double wrapper object.
  Returns: The value stored in the object.
- static double **parseDouble**(String s)
  This method returns the floating-point number that the string represents. If the string cannot be interpreted as a number, a NumberFormatException is thrown.
  Parameters: s   The string to be parsed
  Returns: The value represented by the string parameter

Class java.lang.Error

This is the superclass for all unchecked system errors.

Class java.lang.IllegalArgumentException

- **IllegalArgumentException**()
  This constructs an IllegalArgumentException with no detail message.

Class java.lang.IllegalStateException

This exception is thrown if the state of an object indicates that a method cannot currently be applied.

Class java.lang.Integer

- **Integer**(int value)
  This constructs a wrapper object for an integer.
  Parameters: value   The value to store in this object
- int **intValue**()
  This method returns the integer value stored in this wrapper object.
  Returns: The value stored in the object
- static int **parseInt**(String s)
  This method returns the integer that the string represents. If the string cannot be interpreted as an integer, a NumberFormatException is thrown.
  Parameters: s   The string to be parsed
  Returns: The value represented by the string parameter
- static Integer **parseInt**(String s, int base)
  This method returns the integer value that the string represents in a given number system. If the string cannot be interpreted as an integer, a NumberFormatException is thrown.
  Parameters: s   The string to be parsed
  base   The base of the number system (such as 2 or 16)
  Returns: The value represented by the string parameter

- `static String` **toString**`(int i)`
- `static String` **toString**`(int i, int base)`
  This method creates a string representation of an integer in a given number system. If no base is given, a decimal representation is created.
  Parameters: i   An integer number

              base   The base of the number system (such as 2 or 16)
  Returns: A string representation of the number parameter in the specified number system
- `static final int` `MAX_VALUE`
  This constant is the largest value of type `int`.
- `static final int` `MIN_VALUE`
  This constant is the smallest (negative) value of type `int`.

Class `java.lang.Math`

- `static double` **abs**`(double x)`
  This method returns the absolute value $|x|$.
  Parameters: x   A floating-point value
  Returns: The absolute value of the parameter
- `static double` **acos**`(double x)`
  This method returns the angle with the given cosine, $\cos^{-1} x \in [0, \pi]$.
  Parameters: x   A floating-point value between -1 and 1
  Returns: The arc cosine of the parameter, in radians
- `static double` **asin**`(double x)`
  This method returns the angle with the given sine, $\sin^{-1} x \in [-\pi/2, \pi/2]$.
  Parameters: x   A floating-point value between -1 and 1
  Returns: The arc sine of the parameter, in radians
- `static double` **atan**`(double x)`
  This method returns the angle with the given tangent, $\tan^{-1} x$ $(-\pi/2, \pi/2)$.
  Parameters: x   A floating-point value
  Returns: The arc tangent of the parameter, in radians
- `static double` **atan2**`(double y, double x)`
  This method returns the arc tangent, $\tan^{-1}(y/x) \in (-\pi, \pi)$. If x can equal zero, or if it is necessary to distinguish "northwest" from "southeast" and "northeast" from "southwest", use this method instead of `atan(y/x)`.
  Parameters: y,x   Two floating-point values
  Returns: The angle, in radians, between the points $(0,0)$ and (x,y)
- `static double` **ceil**`(double x)`
  This method returns the smallest integer $\geq x$ (as a `double`).
  Parameters: x   A floating-point value
  Returns: The "ceiling integer" of the parameter
- `static double` **cos**`(double radians)`
  This method returns the cosine of an angle given in radians.
  Parameters: radians   An angle, in radians
  Returns: The cosine of the parameter

- `static double exp(double x)`
  This method returns the value e^x, where e is the base of the natural logarithms.
  Parameters: x   A floating-point value
  Returns: e^x

- `static double floor(double x)`
  This method returns the largest integer $\leq x$ (as a double).
  Parameters: x   A floating-point value
  Returns: The "floor integer" of the parameter

- `static double log(double x)`
  This method returns the natural (base e) logarithm of x, $\ln x$.
  Parameters: x   A number greater than 0.0
  Returns: The natural logarithm of the parameter

- `static int max(int x, int y)`

- `static double max(double x, double y)`
  These methods return the larger of the given parameter values.
  Parameters: x, y   Two integers or floating-point values
  Returns: The maximum of the parameter values

- `static int min(int x, int y)`

- `static double min(double x, double y)`
  These methods return the smaller of the given parameter values.
  Parameters: x, y   Two integers or floating-point values
  Returns: The minimum of the parameter values

- `static double pow(double x, double y)`
  This method returns the value x^y ($x > 0$, or $x = 0$ and $y > 0$, or $x < 0$ and y is an integer).
  Parameters: x, y   Two floating-point values
  Returns: The value of the first parameter raised to the power of the second parameter

- `static long round(double x)`
  This method returns the closest long integer to the parameter.
  Parameters: x   A floating-point value
  Returns: The value of the parameter rounded to the nearest long value.

- `static double sin(double radians)`
  This method returns the sine of an angle given in radians.
  Parameters: radians   An angle, in radians
  Returns: The sine of the parameter.

- `static double sqrt(double x)`
  This method returns the square root of x, $\sqrt{x}$.
  Parameters: x   A nonnegative floating-point value
  Returns: The square root of the parameter

- `static double tan(double radians)`
  This method returns the tangent of an angle given in radians.
  Parameters: radians   An angle, in radians
  Returns: The tangent of the parameter

- `static double` **`toDegrees`**`(double radian)`
  This method converts radians to degrees.
  Parameters: `radians` An angle, in radians
  Returns: The angle in degrees
- `static double` **`toRadians`**`(double degrees)`
  This methods converts degrees to radians.
  Parameters: `degrees` An angle, in degrees
  Returns: The angle in radians
- `static final double E`
  This constant is the value of e, the base of the natural logarithms.
- `static final double PI`
  This constant is the value of π.

Class java.lang.NullPointerException

This exception is thrown when a program tries to use an object through a `null` reference.

Class java.lang.NumberFormatException

This exception is thrown when a program tries to parse the numerical value of a string that is not a number.

Class java.lang.Object

- `protected Object` **`clone`**`()`
  This constructs and returns a shallow copy of this object whose instance variables are copies of the instance variables of this object. If an instance variable of the object is an object reference itself, only the reference is copied, not the object itself. However, if the class does not implement the `Cloneable` interface, a `CloneNotSupportedException` is thrown. Subclasses should redefine this method to make a deep copy.
  Returns: A copy of this object
- `boolean` **`equals`**`(Object other)`
  This method tests whether `this` and the other object are equal. This method tests only whether the object references are to the same object. Subclasses should redefine this method to compare the instance variables.
  Parameters: `other` The object with which to compare
  Returns: `true` if the objects are equal, `false` otherwise
- `String` **`toString`**`()`
  This method returns a string representation of this object. This method produces only the class name and locations of the objects. Subclasses should redefine this method to print the instance variables.
  Returns: A string describing this object

Class java.lang.RuntimeException

This is the superclass for all unchecked exceptions.

Class `java.lang.String`

- `int compareTo(String other)`

  This method compares this string and the other string lexicographically.

  Parameters: `other` The other string to be compared

  Returns: A value less than 0 if this string is lexicographically less than the other, 0 if the strings are equal, and a value greater than 0 otherwise.

- `boolean equals(String other)`
- `boolean equalsIgnoreCase(String other)`

  These methods test whether two strings are equal, or whether they are equal when letter case is ignored.

  Parameters: `other` The other string to be compared

  Returns: `true` if the strings are equal

- `static String format(String format, Object... values)`

  This method formats the given string by substituting placeholders that start with `%` with the given values.

  Parameters: `format` The string with the placeholders

  `values` The values to be substituted for the placeholders

  Returns: The formatted string, with the placeholders replaced by the given values

- `int length()`

  This method returns the length of this string.

  Returns: The count of characters in this string

- `String replace(String match, String replacement)`

  This methods replaces matching substrings with a given replacement.

  Parameters: `match` The string whose matches are to be replaced

  `replacement` The string with which matching substrings are replaced

  Returns: A string that is identical to this string, with all matching substrings replaced by the given replacement

- `String substring(int begin)`
- `String substring(int begin, int pastEnd)`

  These methods return a new string that is a substring of this string, made up of all characters starting at position `begin` and up to either position `pastEnd - 1`, if it is given, or the end of the string.

  Parameters: `begin` The beginning index, inclusive

  `pastEnd` The ending index, exclusive

  Returns: The specified substring

- `String toLowerCase()`

  This method returns a new string that consists of all characters in this string converted to lowercase.

  Returns: A string with all characters in this string converted to lowercase

- `String toUpperCase()`

  This method returns a new string that consists of all characters in this string converted to uppercase.

  Returns: A string with all characters in this string converted to uppercase

Class `java.lang.System`

- `static void arraycopy(`
  `        Object from, int fromStart, Object to, int toStart, int count)`

  This method copies values from one array to the other. (The array parameters are of type `Object` because you can convert an array of numbers to an `Object` but not to an `Object[]`.)

  Parameters: `from` The source array

  `fromStart` Start position in the source array

  `to` The destination array

  `toStart` Start position in the destination data

  `count` The number of array elements to be copied

- `static long currentTimeMillis()`

  This method returns the difference, measured in milliseconds, between the current time and midnight, Universal Time, January 1, 1970.

  Returns: The current time in milliseconds

- `static void exit(int status)`

  This method terminates the program.

  Parameters: `status` Exit status. A nonzero status code indicates abnormal termination

- `static final InputStream in`

  This object is the "standard input" stream. Reading from this stream typically reads keyboard input.

- `static final PrintStream out`

  This object is the "standard output" stream. Printing to this stream typically sends output to the console window.

Class `java.lang.Throwable`

This is the superclass of exceptions and errors.

- `Throwable()`

  This constructs a `Throwable` with no detail message.

- `String getMessage()`

  This method gets the message that describes the exception or error.

  Returns: The message

- `void printStackTrace()`

  This method prints a stack trace to the "standard error" stream. The stack trace contains a printout of this object and of all calls that were pending at the time it was created.

Package `java.math`

Class `java.math.BigDecimal`

- `BigDecimal(String value)`

  This constructs an arbitrary-precision floating-point number from the digits in the given string.

  Parameters: `value` A string representing the floating-point number

- BigDecimal **add**(BigDecimal other)
- BigDecimal **multiply**(BigDecimal other)
- BigDecimal **subtract**(BigDecimal other)

These methods return a BigDecimal whose value is the sum, difference, product, or quotient of this number and the other.

Parameters: other The other number

Returns: The result of the arithmetic operation

Class java.math.BigInteger

- **BigInteger**(String value)

This constructs an arbitrary-precision integer from the digits in the given string.

Parameters: value A string representing an arbitrary-precision integer

- BigInteger **add**(BigInteger other)
- BigInteger **divide**(BigInteger other)
- BigInteger **mod**(BigInteger other)
- BigInteger **multiply**(BigInteger other)
- BigInteger **subtract**(BigInteger other)

These methods return a BigInteger whose value is the sum, difference, product, quotient, or remainder of this number and the other.

Parameters: other The other number

Returns: The result of the arithmetic operation

Package java.util

Class java.util.ArrayList<E>

- ArrayList()

This constructs an empty array list.

- boolean **add**(E element)

This method appends an element to the end of this array list.

Parameters: element The element to add

Returns: true (This method returns a value because it overrides a method in the List interface.)

- void **add**(int index, E element)

This method inserts an element into this array list.

Parameters: index Insert position

element The element to insert

- E **get**(int index)

This method gets the element at the specified position in this array list.

Parameters: index Position of the element to return

Returns: The requested element

- E **remove**(int index)

  This method removes the element at the specified position in this array list and returns it.

  Parameters: index   Position of the element to remove

  Returns: The removed element

- E **set**(int index, E element)

  This method replaces the element at a specified position in this array list.

  Parameters: index   Position of element to replace

  element   Element to be stored at the specified position

  Returns: The element previously at the specified position

- int **size**()

  This method returns the number of elements in this array list.

  Returns: The number of elements in this array list

Class java.util.Arrays

- static int **binarySearch**(Object[] a, Object key)

  This method searches the specified array for the specified object using the binary search algorithm. The array elements must implement the Comparable interface. The array must be sorted in ascending order.

  Parameters: a   The array to be searched

  key   The value to be searched for

  Returns: The position of the search key, if it is contained in the array; otherwise, $-index - 1$, where *index* is the position where the element may be inserted

- static void **sort**(Object[] a)

  This method sorts the specified array of objects into ascending order. Its elements must implement the Comparable interface.

  Parameters: a   The array to be sorted

Class java.util.Calendar

- int **get**(int field)

  This method returns the value of the given field.

  Parameters: One of Calendar.YEAR, Calendar.MONTH, Calendar.DAY_OF_MONTH, Calendar.HOUR, Calendar.MINUTE, Calendar.SECOND, or Calendar.MILLISECOND

Interface java.util.Collection<E>

- boolean **add**(E element)

  This method adds an element to this collection.

  Parameters: element   The element to add

  Returns: true if adding the element changes the collection

- boolean **contains**(E element)

  This method tests whether an element is present in this collection.

  Parameters: element   The element to find

  Returns: true if the element is contained in the collection

- Iterator **iterator**()
  This method returns an iterator that can be used to traverse the elements of this collection.
  Returns: An object of a class implementing the Iterator interface
- boolean **remove**(E element)
  This method removes an element from this collection.
  Parameters: element The element to remove
  Returns: true if removing the element changes the collection
- int **size**()
  This method returns the number of elements in this collection.
  Returns: The number of elements in this collection

Class java.util.Collections

- static <T> int **binarySearch**(List<T> a, T key)
  This method searches the specified list for the specified object using the binary search algorithm. The list elements must implement the Comparable interface. The list must be sorted in ascending order.
  Parameters: a The list to be searched
  key The value to be searched for
  Returns: The position of the search key, if it is contained in the list; otherwise, $-index - 1$, where *index* is the position where the element may be inserted
- static <T> void **sort**(T[] a)
  This method sorts the specified list of objects into ascending order. Its elements must implement the Comparable interface.
  Parameters: a The list to be sorted

Interface java.util.Comparator<T>

- int **compare**(T first, T second)
  This method compares the given objects.
  Parameters: first, second The objects to be compared
  Returns: A negative integer if the first object is less than the second, zero if they are equal, or a positive integer otherwise

Class java.util.EventObject

- Object **getSource**()
  This method returns a reference to the object on which this event initially occurred.
  Returns: The source of this event

Class java.util.GregorianCalendar

- GregorianCalendar()
  This constructs a calendar object that represents the current date and time.
- GregorianCalendar(int year, int month, int day)
  This constructs a calendar object that represents the start of the given date.
  Parameters: year, month, day The given date

Class java.util.HashMap<K, V>

- HashMap<K, V>()

  This constructs an empty hash map.

Class java.util.HashSet<K, V>

- HashSet<K, V>()

  This constructs an empty hash set.

Class java.util.InputMismatchException

This exception is thrown if the next available input item does not match the type of the requested item.

Interface java.util.Iterator<E>

- boolean hasNext()

  This method checks whether the iterator is past the end of the list.

  Returns: true if the iterator is not yet past the end of the list

- E next()

  This method moves the iterator over the next element in the linked list. This method throws an exception if the iterator is past the end of the list.

  Returns: The object that was just skipped over

- void remove()

  This method removes the element that was returned by the last call to next or previous. This method throws an exception if there was an add or remove operation after the last call to next or previous.

Class java.util.LinkedList<E>

- void addFirst(E element)
- void addLast(E element)

  These methods add an element before the first or after the last element in this list.

  Parameters: element The element to be added

- E getFirst()
- E getLast()

  These methods return a reference to the specified element from this list.

  Returns: The first or last element

- E removeFirst()
- E removeLast()

  These methods remove the specified element from this list.

  Returns: A reference to the removed element

Interface java.util.List<E>

- ListIterator<E> listIterator()

  This method gets an iterator to visit the elements in this list.

  Returns: An iterator that points before the first element in this list

Interface java.util.ListIterator<E>

Objects implementing this interface are created by the listIterator methods of list classes.

- void **add**(E element)

This method adds an element after the iterator position and moves the iterator after the new element.

Parameters: element The element to be added

- boolean **hasPrevious**()

This method checks whether the iterator is before the first element of the list.

Returns: true if the iterator is not before the first element of the list

- E **previous**()

This method moves the iterator over the previous element in the linked list. This method throws an exception if the iterator is before the first element of the list.

Returns: The object that was just skipped over

- void **set**(E element)

This method replaces the element that was returned by the last call to next or previous. This method throws an exception if there was an add or remove operation after the last call to next or previous.

Parameters: element The element that replaces the old list element

Interface java.util.Map<K, V>

- V **get**(K key)

Gets the value associated with a key in this map.

Parameters: key The key for which to find the associated value

Returns: The value associated with the key, or null if the key is not present in the table

- Set<K> **keySet**()

This method returns all keys in the table of this map.

Returns: A set of all keys in the table of this map

- V **put**(K key, V value)

This method associates a value with a key in this map.

Parameters: key The lookup key

value The value to associate with the key

Returns: The value previously associated with the key, or null if the key was not present in the table

- V **remove**(K key)

This method removes a key and its associated value from this map.

Parameters: key The lookup key

Returns: The value previously associated with the key, or null if the key was not present in the table

Class java.util.NoSuchElementException

This exception is thrown if an attempt is made to retrieve a value that does not exist.

Class java.util.PriorityQueue<E>

- PriorityQueue<E>()

  This constructs an empty priority queue. The element type E must implement the Comparable interface.

- E remove()

  This method removes the smallest element in the priority queue.

  Returns: The removed value

Class java.util.Random

- Random()

  This constructs a new random number generator.

- double nextDouble()

  This method returns the next pseudorandom, uniformly distributed floating-point number between 0.0 (inclusive) and 1.0 (exclusive) from this random number generator's sequence.

  Returns: The next pseudorandom floating-point number

- int nextInt(int n)

  This method returns the next pseudorandom, uniformly distributed integer between 0 (inclusive) and the specified value (exclusive) drawn from this random number generator's sequence.

  Parameters: n Number of values to draw from

  Returns: The next pseudorandom integer

Class java.util.Scanner

- Scanner(InputStream in)
- Scanner(Reader in)

  These construct a scanner that reads from the given input stream or reader.

  Parameters: in The input stream or reader from which to read

- void close()

  This method closes this scanner and releases any associated system resources.

- boolean hasNext()
- boolean hasNextDouble()
- boolean hasNextInt()
- boolean hasNextLine()

  These methods test whether it is possible to read any non-empty string, a floating-point value, an integer, or a line, as the next item.

  Returns: true if it is possible to read an item of the requested type, false otherwise (either because the end of the file has been reached, or because a number type was tested and the next item is not a number)

- `String` **next**`()`
- `double` **nextDouble**`()`
- `int` **nextInt**`()`
- `String` **nextLine**`()`

  These methods read the next whitespace-delimited string, floating-point value, integer, or line.

  Returns: The string that was read

Interface java.util.Set<E>

This interface describes a collection that contains no duplicate elements.

Class java.util.TreeMap<K, V>

- `TreeMap<K, V>()`

  This constructs an empty tree map. The iterator of a `TreeMap` visits entries in sorted order.

Class java.util.TreeSet<K, V>

- `TreeSet<K, V>()`

  This constructs an empty tree set.

Package java.util.logging

Class java.util.logging.Level

- `static final int ALL`

  This value indicates logging of all messages.
- `static final int INFO`

  This value indicates informational logging.
- `static final int NONE`

  This value indicates logging of no messages.

Class java.util.logging.Logger

- `static Logger` **getLogger**`(String id)`

  This method gets the logger for a given ID. Use the ID `"global"` to get the default global logger.

  Parameters: `id` the logger ID such as `"global"` or `"com.mycompany.mymodule"`

  Returns: The logger with the given ID
- `void` **info**`(String message)`

  This method logs an informational message.

  Parameters: `message` The message to log
- `void` **setLevel**`(Level aLevel)`

  This method sets the logging level. Logging messages with a lesser severity than the current level are ignored.

  Parameters: `aLevel` The minimum level for logging messages

Package javax.swing

Class javax.swing.AbstractButton

- void **addActionListener**(ActionListener listener)
  This method adds an action listener to the button.
  Parameters: listener The action listener to be added

Class javax.swing.JButton

- **JButton**(String label)
  This constructs a button with the given label.
  Parameters: label The button label

Class javax.swing.JComponent

- protected void **paintComponent**(Graphics g)
  Override this method to paint the surface of a component. Your method needs to call
  super.paintComponent(g).
  Parameters: g The graphics context used for drawing

Class javax.swing.JFileChooser

- **JFileChooser**()
  This constructs a file chooser.
- File **getSelectedFile**()
  This method gets the selected file from this file chooser.
  Returns: The selected file
- int **showOpenDialog**(Component parent)
  This method displays an "Open File" file chooser dialog box.
  Parameters: parent The parent component or null
  Returns: The return state of this file chooser after it has been closed by the user:
  either APPROVE_OPTION or CANCEL_OPTION. If APPROVE_OPTION is returned, call
  getSelectedFile()on this file chooser to get the file
- int **showSaveDialog**(Component parent)
  This method displays a "Save File" file chooser dialog box.
  Parameters: parent The parent component or null
  Returns: The return state of the file chooser after it has been closed by the user:
  either APPROVE_OPTION or CANCEL_OPTION

Class javax.swing.JFrame

- void **setDefaultCloseOperation**(int operation)

  This method sets the default action for closing the frame.

  Parameters: operation   The desired close operation. Choose among
  DO_NOTHING_ON_CLOSE, HIDE_ON_CLOSE (the default), DISPOSE_ON_CLOSE,
  or EXIT_ON_CLOSE

- static final int EXIT_ON_CLOSE

  This value indicates that when the user closes this frame, the application is to exit.

Class javax.swing.JLabel

- **JLabel**(String text)

- **JLabel**(String text, int alignment)

  These containers create a JLabel instance with the specified text and horizontal alignment.

  Parameters: text   The label text to be displayed by the label

  alignment   One of SwingConstants.LEFT, SwingConstants.CENTER, or
  SwingConstants.RIGHT

Class javax.swing.JOptionPane

- static String **showInputDialog**(Object prompt)

  This method brings up a modal input dialog box, which displays a prompt and waits for
  the user to enter an input in a text field, preventing the user from doing anything else in
  this program.

  Parameters: prompt   The prompt to display

  Returns: The string that the user typed

- static void **showMessageDialog**(Component parent, Object message)

  This method brings up a confirmation dialog box that displays a message and waits for the
  user to confirm it.

  Parameters: parent   The parent component or null

  message   The message to display

Class javax.swing.JPanel

This class is a component without decorations. It can be used as an invisible container for
other components.

Class javax.swing.JTextArea

- **JTextArea**()

  This constructs an empty text area.

- **JTextArea**(int rows, int columns)

  This constructs an empty text area with the specified number of rows and columns.

  Parameters: rows   The number of rows

  columns   The number of columns

- void **append**(String text)
  This method appends text to this text area.
  Parameters: text The text to append

Class javax.swing.JTextField

- JTextField()
  This constructs an empty text field.
- JTextField(int columns)
  This constructs an empty text field with the specified number of columns.
  Parameters: columns The number of columns

Class javax.swing.Timer

- Timer(int millis, ActionListener listener)
  This constructs a timer that notifies an action listener whenever a time interval has elapsed.
  Parameters: millis The number of milliseconds between timer notifications
  listener The object to be notified when the time interval has elapsed
- void **start**()
  This method starts the timer. Once the timer has started, it begins notifying its listener.
- void **stop**()
  This method stops the timer. Once the timer has stopped, it no longer notifies its listener.

Package javax.swing.text

Class javax.swing.text.JTextComponent

- String **getText**()
  This method returns the text contained in this text component.
  Returns: The text
- boolean **isEditable**()
  This method checks whether this text component is editable.
  Returns: true if the component is editable
- void **setEditable**(boolean state)
  This method is used to make this text component editable or not.
  Parameters: state true to make editable, false to disable editing
- void **setText**(String text)
  This method sets the text of this text component to the specified text. If the text is empty, the old text is deleted.
  Parameters: text The new text to be set

Glossary

Abstract array An ordered sequence of items that can be efficiently accessed at random through an integer index.

Abstract class A class that cannot be instantiated.

Abstract list An ordered sequence of items that can be traversed sequentially and that allows for efficient insertion and removal of elements at any position.

Abstract method A method with a name, parameter types, and return type but without an implementation.

Abstraction The process of finding the essential feature set for a building block of a program such as a class.

Access specifier A keyword that indicates the accessibility of a feature, such as `private` or `public`.

Accessor method A method that accesses an object but does not change it.

Actual parameter The expression supplied for a formal parameter of a method by the caller.

ADT (Abstract Data Type) A specification of the fundamental operations that characterize a data type, without supplying an implementation.

Aggregation The *has-a* relationship between classes.

Algorithm An unambiguous, executable, and terminating specification of a way to solve a problem.

Anonymous class A class that does not have a name.

Anonymous object An object that is not stored in a named variable.

API (Application Programming Interface) A code library for building programs.

Applet A graphical Java program that executes inside a web browser or applet viewer.

Argument An actual parameter in a method call, or one of the values combined by an operator.

Array A collection of values of the same type stored in contiguous memory locations, each of which can be accessed by an integer index.

Array list   A Java class that implements a dynamically growable array of objects.

Assertion   A claim that a certain condition holds in a particular program location.

Assignment   Placing a new value into a variable.

Association   A relationship between classes in which one can navigate from objects of one class to objects of the other class, usually by following object references.

Asymmetric bounds   Bounds that include the starting index but not the ending index.

Attribute   A named property that an object is responsible for maintaining.

Auto-boxing   Automatically converting a primitive type value into a wrapper type object.

Balanced tree   A tree in which each subtree has the property that the number of descendants to the left is approximately the same as the number of descendants to the right.

Big-Oh notation   The notation $g(n) = O(f(n))$, which denotes that the function g grows at a rate that is bounded by the growth rate of the function f with respect to n. For example, $10n^2 + 100n - 1000 = O(n^2)$.

Binary file   A file in which values are stored in their binary representation and cannot be read as text.

Binary operator   An operator that takes two arguments, for example + in $x + y$.

Binary search   A fast algorithm to find a value in a sorted array. It narrows the search down to half of the array in every step.

Binary search tree   A binary tree in which *each* subtree has the property that all left descendants are smaller than the value stored in the root, and all right descendants are larger.

Binary tree   A tree in which each node has at most two child nodes.

Bit   Binary digit; the smallest unit of information, having two possible values: 0 and 1. A data element consisting of n bits has 2^n possible values.

Black-box testing   Testing a method without knowing its implementation.

Block   A group of statements bracketed by {}.

Boolean operator   See **Logical operator**

Boolean type   A type with two possible values: true and false.

Border layout   A layout management scheme in which components are placed into the center or one of the four borders of their container.

Boundary test case   A test case involving values that are at the outer boundary of the set of legal values. For example, if a function is expected to work for all nonnegative integers, then 0 is a boundary test case.

Bounds error   Trying to access an array element that is outside the legal range.

Breakpoint   A point in a program, specified in a debugger, at which the debugger stops executing the program and lets the user inspect the program state.

break statement   A statement that terminates a loop or switch statement.

Bucket   In a hash table, a set of values with the same hash code.

Buffer A temporary storage location for holding values that have been produced (for example, characters typed by the user) and are waiting to be consumed (for example, read a line at a time).

Buffered input Input that is gathered in batches, for example, a line at a time.

Bug A programming error.

Byte A number made up of eight bits. Essentially all currently manufactured computers use a byte as the smallest unit of storage in memory.

Bytecode Instructions for the Java virtual machine.

Call by reference A method call mechanism in which the method receives the location in memory of a variable supplied as an actual parameter. Call by reference enables a method to change the contents of the original variable so that the change remains in effect after the method returns.

Call by value A method call mechanism in which the method receives a copy of the contents of a variable supplied as an actual parameter. Java uses only call by value. If a parameter variable's type is a class, its value is an object reference, so the method can alter that object but cannot make the parameter variable refer to a different object.

Call stack The ordered set of all methods that currently have been called but not yet terminated, starting with the current method and ending with main.

Case sensitive Distinguishing upper- and lowercase characters.

Cast Explicitly converting a value from one type to a different type. For example, the cast from a floating-point number x to an integer is expressed in Java by the cast notation (int) x.

catch clause A part of a try block that is executed when a matching exception is thrown by any statement in the try block.

Character A single letter, digit, or symbol.

Check box A user interface component that can be used for a binary selection.

Checked exception An exception that the compiler checks. All checked exceptions must be declared or caught.

Class A programmer-defined data type.

Class method See **Static method**

Class path The set of directories and archives that the virtual machine searches for class files.

Cloning Making a copy of an object whose state can be modified independently of the original object.

Cohesion A class is cohesive if its features support a single abstraction.

Collaborator A class on which another class depends.

Combo box A user interface component that combines a text field with a drop-down list of selections.

Command line The line the user types to start a program in DOS or UNIX or a command window in Windows. It consists of the program name followed by any necessary arguments.

Comment   An explanation to help the human reader understand a section of a program; ignored by the compiler.

Compiler   A program that translates code in a high-level language (such as Java) to machine instructions (such as bytecode for the Java virtual machine).

Compile-time error   An error that is detected when a program is compiled.

Component   See **User interface component**

Compound statement   A statement such as `if` or `while` that is made up of several parts such as a condition and a body.

Concatenation   Placing one string after another to form a new string.

Concrete class   A class that can be instantiated.

Console program   A Java program that does not have a graphical window. A console program reads input from the keyboard and writes output to the terminal screen.

Constant   A value that cannot be changed by a program. In Java, constants are defined with the keyword `final`.

Construction   Setting a newly allocated object to an initial state.

Constructor   A method that initializes a newly instantiated object.

Container   A user interface component that can hold other components and present them together to the user. Also, a data structure, such as a list, that can hold a collection of objects and present them individually to a program.

Content pane   The part of a Swing frame that holds the user interface components of the frame.

Coupling   The degree to which classes are related to each other by dependency.

CPU (Central Processing Unit)   The part of a computer that executes the machine instructions.

CRC card   An index card representing a class and listing its responsibilities and collaborating classes.

De Morgan's Law   A law about logical operations that describes how to negate expressions formed with *and* and *or* operations.

Debugger   A program that lets a user run another program one or a few steps at a time, stop execution, and inspect the variables in order to analyze it for bugs.

Default constructor   A constructor that is invoked with no parameters.

Dependency   The *uses* relationship between classes, in which one class needs services provided by another class.

Dictionary ordering   See **Lexicographic ordering**

Directory   A structure on a disk that can hold files or other directories; also called a folder.

Documentation comment   A comment in a source file that can be automatically extracted into the program documentation by a program such as `javadoc`.

Dot notation   The notation *object.method(parameters)* or *object.field* used to invoke a method or access a field.

Doubly linked list   A linked list in which each link has a reference to both its predecessor and successor links.

Early binding   Choosing at compile time among several methods with the same name but different parameter types.

Editor   A program for writing and modifying text files.

Encapsulation   The hiding of implementation details.

End of file   The condition that is true when all characters of a file have been read. Note that there is no special "end of file character". When composing a file on the keyboard, you may need to type a special character to tell the operating system to end the file, but that character is not part of the file.

Enumerated type   A type with a finite number of values, each of which has its own symbolic name.

Escape character   A character in text that is not taken literally but has a special meaning when combined with the character or characters that follow it. The \ character is an escape character in Java strings.

Event class   A class that contains information about an event, such as its source.

Event adapter   A class that implements an event listener interface by defining all methods to do nothing.

Event handler   A method that is executed when an event occurs.

Event listener   An object that is notified by an event source when an event occurs.

Event source   An object that can notify other classes of events.

Exception   A class that signals a condition that prevents the program from continuing normally. When such a condition occurs, an object of the exception class is thrown.

Exception handler   A sequence of statements that is given control when an exception of a particular type has been thrown and caught.

Explicit parameter   A parameter of a method other than the object on which the method is invoked.

Expression   A syntactical construct that is made up of constants, variables, method calls, and operators combining them.

Extension   The last part of a file name, which specifies the file type. For example, the extension .java denotes a Java file.

Extreme Programming   A development methodology that strives for simplicity, by removing formal structure and focusing on best practices.

Fibonacci numbers   The sequence of numbers 1, 1, 2, 3, 5, 8, 13, . . ., in which every term is the sum of its two predecessors.

File   A sequence of bytes that is stored on disk.

File pointer   The position within a random-access file of the next byte to be read or written. It can be moved so as to access any byte in the file.

finally clause   A part of a try block that is executed no matter how the try block is exited.

Flag   See **Boolean type**

Floating-point number   A number that can have a fractional part.

Flow layout   A layout management scheme in which components are laid out left to right.

Flushing a stream   Sending all characters that are still held in a buffer to its destination.

Folder   See **Directory**

Font   A set of character shapes in a particular style and size.

Formal parameter   A variable in a method definition; it is initialized with an actual parameter value when the method is called.

Frame   A window with a border and a title bar.

Garbage collection   Automatic reclamation of memory occupied by objects that are no longer referenced.

Generic class   A class with one or more type parameters.

Generic method   A method with one or more type parameters.

Generic programming   Providing program components that can be reused in a wide variety of situations.

goto statement   A statement that transfers control to some other statement, which is tagged with a label. Java does not have a goto statement.

Graphics context   A class through which a programmer can cause shapes to appear on a window or off-screen bitmap.

grep   The "global regular expression print" search program, useful for finding all strings matching a pattern in a set of files.

Grid layout   A layout management scheme in which components are placed into a two-dimensional grid.

GUI (Graphical User Interface)   A user interface in which the user supplies inputs through graphical components such as buttons, menus, and text fields.

Hash code   A value that is computed by a hash function.

Hash collision   Two different objects for which a hash function computes identical values.

Hash function   A function that computes an integer value from an object in such a way that different objects are likely to yield different values.

Hash table   A data structure in which elements are mapped to array positions according to their hash function values.

Hashing   Applying a hash function to a set of objects.

Heap   A balanced binary tree that is used for implementing sorting algorithms and priority queues.

Heapsort algorithm   A sorting algorithm that inserts the values to be sorted into a heap.

HTML (Hypertext Markup Language)   The language in which web pages are described.

IDE (Integrated Development Environment)   A programming environment that includes an editor, compiler, and debugger.

Immutable class   A class without a mutator method.

Implementing an interface   See **Realizing an interface**

Implicit parameter   The object on which a method is invoked. For example, in the call x.f(y), the object x is the implicit parameter of the method f.

Importing a class or package   Indicating the intention of referring to a class, or all classes in a package, by the simple name rather than the qualified name.

Inheritance   The *is-a* relationship between a more general superclass and a more specialized subclass.

Initialization   Setting a variable to a well-defined value when it is created.

Inner class   A class that is defined inside another class.

Instance method   A method with an implicit parameter; that is, a method that is invoked on an instance of a class.

Instance of a class   An object whose type is that class.

Instance field   A variable defined in a class for which every object of the class has its own value.

Instantiation of a class   Construction of an object of that class.

Integer   A number that cannot have a fractional part.

Integer division   Taking the quotient of two integers and discarding the remainder. In Java the / symbol denotes integer division if both arguments are integers. For example, 11/4 is 2, not 2.75.

Interface   A type with no instance variables, only abstract methods and constants.

Internet   A worldwide collection of networks, routing equipment, and computers using a common set of protocols that define how participants interact with each other.

Interpreter   A program that reads a set of codes and carries out the commands specified by them.

Iterator   An object that can inspect all elements in a container such as a linked list.

javadoc   The documentation generator in the Java SDK. It extracts documentation comments from Java source files and produces a set of linked HTML files.

JDK   The Java software development kit that contains the Java compiler and related development tools.

Join   A database query that involves multiple tables.

JVM   The Java Virtual Machine

Late binding   Choosing at run time among several methods with the same name invoked on objects belonging to subclasses of the same superclass.

Layout manager   A class that arranges user interface components inside a container.

Lazy evaluation   Deferring the computation of a value until it is needed, thereby avoiding the computation if the value is never needed.

Legacy code   Software that has existed for a long time and that continues to operate.

Lexicographic ordering   Ordering strings in the same order as in a dictionary, by skipping all matching characters and comparing the first nonmatching characters of both strings. For example, "orbit" comes before "orchid" in lexicographic ordering. Note that in Java, unlike a dictionary, the ordering is case-sensitive: Z comes before a.

Library   A set of precompiled classes that can be included in programs.

Linear search   Searching a container (such as an array or list) for an object by inspecting each element in turn.

Linked list   A data structure that can hold an arbitrary number of objects, each of which is stored in a link object, which contains a pointer to the next link.

Local variable   A variable whose scope is a block.

Logging   Sending messages that trace the progress of a program to a file or window.

Logical operator   An operator that can be applied to Boolean values. Java has three logical operators: &&, ||, and !.

Logic error   An error in a syntactically correct program that causes it to act differently from its specification.

Loop   A sequence of instructions that is executed repeatedly.

Loop and a half   A loop whose termination decision is neither at the beginning nor at the end.

Loop invariant   A statement about the program state that is preserved when the statements in the loop are executed once.

Machine code   Instructions that can be executed directly by the CPU.

Magic number   A number that appears in a program without explanation.

main method   The method that is first called when a Java application executes.

Map   A data structure that keeps associations between key and value objects.

Markup   Information about data that is added as humanly readable instructions. An example is the tagging of HTML documents with elements such as <h1> or <b>.

Member   A method, field, or type defined inside a class.

Memory location   A value that specifies the location of data in computer memory.

Merge sort   A sorting algorithm that first sorts two halves of a data structure and then merges the sorted subarrays together.

Method   A sequence of statements that has a name, may have formal parameters, and may return a value. A method can be invoked any number of times, with different values for its parameters.

Method signature   The name of a method and the types of its parameters.

Mutator method   A method that changes the state of an object.

Mutual recursion   Cooperating methods that call each other.

Name clash   Accidentally using the same name to denote two program features in a way that cannot be resolved by the compiler.

Negative test case   A test case that is expected to fail. For example, when testing a root-finding program, an attempt to compute the square root of −1 is a negative test case.

Nested block   A block that is contained inside another block.

Nested loop   A loop that is contained in another loop.

new operator   An operator that allocates new objects.

Newline   The '\n' character, which indicates the end of a line.

Null reference   A reference that does not refer to any object.

Object   A value of a class type.

Object-oriented design   Designing a program by discovering objects, their properties, and their relationships.

Object reference   A value that denotes the location of an object in memory. In Java, a variable whose type is a class contains a reference to an object of that class.

Off-by-one error   A common programming error in which a value is one larger or smaller than it should be.

Opening a file   Preparing a file for reading or writing.

Operating system   The software that launches application programs and provides services (such as a file system) for those programs.

Operator   A symbol denoting a mathematical or logical operation, such as + or &&.

Operator associativity   The rule that governs in which order operators of the same precedence are executed. For example, in Java the - operator is left-associative because a - b - c is interpreted as (a - b) - c, and = is right-associative because a = b = c is interpreted as a = (b = c).

Operator precedence   The rule that governs which operator is evaluated first. For example, in Java the && operator has a higher precedence than the || operator. Hence a || b && c is interpreted as a || (b && c).

Oracle   A program that predicts how another program should behave.

Overloading   Giving more than one meaning to a method name.

Overriding   Redefining a method in a subclass.

Package   A collection of related classes. The import statement is used to access one or more classes in a package.

Package access   Accessibility by methods of classes in the same package.

Panel   A user interface component with no visual appearance. It can be used to group other components.

Parallel arrays   Arrays of the same length, in which corresponding elements are logically related.

Parameter   An item of information that is specified to a method when the method is called. For example, in the call System.out.println("Hello, World!"), the parameters are the implicit parameter System.out and the explicit parameter "Hello, World!".

Parameter passing   Specifying expressions to be actual parameter values for a method when it is called.

Parameter variable   A variable of a method that is initialized with a parameter value when the method is called.

Partially-filled array   An array that is not filled to capacity, together with a companion variable that indicates the number of elements actually stored.

Permutation   A rearrangement of a set of values.

Polymorphism   Selecting a method among several methods that have the same name on the basis of the actual types of the implicit parameters.

Positive test case   A test case that a method is expected to handle correctly.

Postcondition   A condition that is true after a method has been called.

Postfix operator   A unary operator that is written after its argument.

Precondition   A condition that must be true when a method is called if the method is to work correctly.

Predicate method   A method that returns a Boolean value.

Prefix operator   A unary operator that is written before its argument.

Primitive type   In Java, a number type or `boolean`.

Priority queue   An abstract data type that enables efficient insertion of elements and efficient removal of the smallest element.

Private feature   A feature that is accessible only by methods of the same class or an inner class.

Project   A collection of source files and their dependencies.

Prompt   A string that tells the user to provide input.

Protected feature   A feature that is accessible by a class, its inner classes, its subclasses, and the other classes in the same package.

Pseudorandom number   A number that appears to be random but is generated by a mathematical formula.

Public feature   A feature that is accessible by all classes.

Public interface   The features (methods, fields, and nested types) of a class that are accessible to all clients.

Qualified name   A name that is made unambiguous because it starts with the package name.

Queue   A collection of items with "first in, first out" retrieval.

Quicksort   A generally fast sorting algorithm that picks an element, called the pivot, partitions the sequence into the elements smaller than the pivot and those larger than the pivot, and then recursively sorts the subsequences.

Radio button   A user interface component that can be used for selecting one of several options.

RAM (Random-Access Memory)   Electronic circuits in a computer that can store code and data of running programs.

Random access   The ability to access any value directly without having to read the values preceding it.

Reader   In the Java input/output library, a class from which to read characters.

Realizing an interface   Implementing a class that defines all methods specified in the interface.

Recursion   A method for computing a result by decomposing the inputs into simpler values and applying the same method to them.

Recursive method   A method that can call itself with simpler values. It must handle the simplest values without calling itself.

Redirection   Linking the input or output of a program to a file instead of the keyboard or display.

Reference   See **Object reference**

Regression testing   Keeping old test cases and testing every revision of a program against them.

Regular expression   A string that defines a set of matching strings according to their content. Each part of a regular expression can be a specific required character; one of a set of permitted characters such as [abc], which can be a range such as [a-z]; any character not in a set of forbidden characters, such as [^0-9]; a repetition of one or more matches, such as [0-9]+, or zero or more, such as [ACGT]*; one of a set of alternatives, such as and|et|und; or various other possibilities. For example, "[A-Za-z]*[0-9]+" matches "Cloud9" or "007" but not "Jack".

Relational operator   An operator that compares two values, yielding a Boolean result.

Reserved word   A word that has a special meaning in a programming language and therefore cannot be used as a name by the programmer.

Return value   The value returned by a method through a return statement.

Reverse Polish notation   A style of writing expressions in which the operators are written following the operands, such as 2 3 4 * + for 2 + 3 * 4.

Roundoff error   An error introduced by the fact that the computer can store only a finite number of digits of a floating-point number.

Run-time error   See **Logic error**

Run-time stack   The data structure that stores the local variables of all called methods as a program runs.

Scope   The part of a program in which a variable is defined.

Scripting language   A programming language that favors rapid development over execution speed and code maintainability.

Selection sort   A sorting algorithm in which the smallest element is repeatedly found and removed until no elements remain.

Sentinel   A value in input that is not to be used as an actual input value but to signal the end of input.

Sequential access   Accessing values one after another without skipping over any of them.

Sequential search   See **Linear search**

Serialization   The process of saving an object, and all the objects that it references, to a stream.

Server   A computer program or system that receives requests from a client, obtains or computes the requested information, and sends it to the client.

Set   An unordered collection that allows efficient addition, locating, and removal of elements.

Shadowing   Hiding a variable by defining another one with the same name.

Shallow copy   Copying only the reference to an object.

Shell   A part of an operating system in which the user types command lines to execute programs and manipulate files.

Shell script   A file that contains commands for running programs and manipulating files. Typing the name of the shell script file on the command line causes those commands to be executed.

Shell window   A window for interacting with an operating system through textual commands.

Short circuit evaluation   Evaluating only a part of an expression if the remainder cannot change the result.

Side effect   An effect of a method other than returning a value.

Sign bit   The bit of a binary number that indicates whether the number is positive or negative.

Signature   See **Method signature**

Simple statement   A statement consisting only of an expression.

Single-stepping   Executing a program in the debugger one statement at a time.

Software life cycle   All activities related to the creation and maintenance of the software from initial analysis until obsolescence.

Source code   Instructions in a programming language that need to be translated before execution on a computer.

Source file   A file containing instructions in a programming language such as Java.

Spaghetti code   Tangled control flow that is difficult to understand.

Spiral model   An iterative process model of software development in which design and implementation are repeated.

Stack   A data structure with "last in, first out" retrieval. Elements can be added and removed only at one position, called the top of the stack.

Stack trace   A printout of the call stack, listing all currently pending method calls.

State   The current value of an object, which is determined by the cumulative action of all methods that were invoked on it.

State diagram   A diagram that depicts state transitions and their causes.

Statement   A syntactical unit in a program. In Java a statement is either a simple statement, a compound statement, or a block.

Static method   A method with no implicit parameter.

Static field   A variable defined in a class that has only one value for the whole class, which can be accessed and changed by any method of that class.

Stream   An abstraction for a sequence of bytes from which data can be read or to which data can be written.

String   A sequence of characters.

Stub   A method with no or minimal functionality.

Subclass   A class that inherits variables and methods from a superclass but adds instance variables, adds methods, or redefines methods.

Superclass   A general class from which a more specialized class (a subclass) inherits.

Swing   A Java toolkit for implementing graphical user interfaces.

Symmetric bounds   Bounds that include the starting index and the ending index.

Syntax   Rules that define how to form instructions in a particular programming language.

Syntax diagram   A graphical representation of grammar rules.

Syntax error   An instruction that does not follow the programming language rules and is rejected by the compiler.

Tab character   The `'\t'` character, which advances the next character on the line to the next one of a set of fixed positions known as tab stops.

TCP/IP (Transmission Control Protocol/Internet Protocol)   The pair of communication protocols that is used to establish reliable transmission of data between two computers on the Internet.

Ternary operator   An operator with three arguments. Java has one ternary operator, `a ? b : c`.

Test coverage   The instructions of a program that are executed in a set of test cases.

Test harness   A program that calls a function that needs to be tested, supplying parameters and analyzing the function's return value.

Test suite   A set of test cases for a program.

Text field   A user interface component that allows a user to provide text input.

Text file   A file in which values are stored in their text representation.

Throwing an exception   Indicating an abnormal condition by terminating the normal control flow of a program and transferring control to a matching `catch` clause.

throws specifier   Indicates the types of the checked exceptions that a method may throw.

Token   A sequence of consecutive characters from an input source that belongs together for the purpose of analyzing the input. For example, a token can be a sequence of characters other than white space.

Total ordering   An ordering relationship in which all elements can be compared to each other.

Trace message   A message that is printed during a program run for debugging purposes.

Tree A data structure consisting of nodes, each of which has a list of child nodes, and one of which is distinguished as the root node.

try block A block of statements that contains exception processing clauses. A `try` block contains at least one `catch` or `finally` clause.

Turing machine A very simple model of computation that is used in theoretical computer science to explore computability of problems.

Two-dimensional array A tabular arrangement of elements in which an element is specified by a row and a column index.

Type A named set of values and the operations that can be carried out with them.

Type parameter A parameter in a generic class or method that can be replaced with an actual type.

Type variable A variable in the declaration of a generic type that can be instantiated with a type.

Unary operator An operator with one argument.

Unchecked exception An exception that the compiler doesn't check.

Unicode A standard code that assigns code values consisting of two bytes to characters used in scripts around the world. Java stores all characters as their Unicode values.

Unified Modeling Language (UML) A notation for specifying, visualizing, constructing, and documenting the artifacts of software systems.

Uninitialized variable A variable that has not been set to a particular value. In Java, using an uninitialized local variable is a syntax error.

Unit test A test of a method by itself, isolated from the remainder of the program.

URL (Uniform Resource Locator) A pointer to an information resource (such as a web page or an image) on the World Wide Web.

User interface component A building block for a graphical user interface, such as a button or a text field. User interface components are used to present information to the user and allow the user to enter information to the program.

Variable A symbol in a program that identifies a storage location that can hold different values.

Virtual machine A program that simulates a CPU that can be implemented efficiently on a variety of actual machines. A given program in Java bytecode can be executed by any Java virtual machine, regardless of which CPU is used to run the virtual machine itself.

Visual programming Programming by arranging graphical elements on a form, setting program behavior by selecting properties for these elements, and writing only a small amount of "glue" code linking them.

void keyword A keyword indicating no type or an unknown type.

Watch window A window in a debugger that shows the current values of selected variables.

Waterfall model A sequential process model of software development, consisting of analysis, design, implementation, testing, and deployment.

White-box testing   Testing functions taking their implementations into account, in contrast to black-box testing; for example, by selecting boundary test cases and ensuring that all branches of the code are covered by some test case.

White space   Any sequence of only space, tab, and newline characters.

Wrapper class   A class that contains a primitive type value, such as Integer.

Writer   In the Java input/output library, a class to which characters are to be sent.

Index

Page references followed by *t* indicate material in tables. Java library classes are indexed under java, as for example "java.util.Scanner class."

Illustration Credits

Chapter 1

Page 4: Copyright © 2007, Intel Corporation.
Page 5 (top): PhotoDisc, Inc./Getty Images.
Page 5 (bottom): PhotoDisc, Inc./Getty Images.
Page 6: Copyright © 2007, Intel Corporation.
Page 8: Courtesy of Sperry Univac, Division of Sperry Corporation.

Chapter 2

Page 57: Corbis Digital Stock.

Chapter 3

Page 111: David Young-Wolff/PhotoEdit.
Page 112: Bob Daemmrich/The Image Works.
Page 117: Punchstock.
Page 121: Copyright © 2001-2007 Lev Givon. All rights reserved.
Page 122 (top): Keith Kapple/SUPERSTOCK.
Page 122 (bottom): Daniel Biggs/SUPERSTOCK.

Chapter 5

Page 205: © 2007 Sidney Harris.

Chapter 6

Page 275: Naval Surface Weapons Center, Dahlgren, VA.

Chapter 8

Page 371: Visicalc screen capture © IBM Corporation. Used with permission.

Chapter 11

Page 520 (left, center, right): © AP/Wide World Photos.

Chapter 12

Page 533: *Unified Modeling Language Users Guide (AW Object Tech Series)*, © 1999 Pearson Education, Inc. Reprinted by permission of Pearson Education Inc. Publishing as Pearson Addison Wesley.

Chapter 13

Page 609: Science Photo Library/Photo Researchers.

Chapter 14

Page 648: Topham/The Image Works.

Chapter 15

Page 687: Photodisc/Punchstock.

Chapter 16

Page 735: Courtesy of Nigel Tout.